WORLD WAR II
PACIFIC THEATER
EXTRAORDINARY STORIES OF
HEROISM, VICTORY, AND DEFEAT

BENNETT FISHER

Author: Bennett Fisher

Publisher:
Elite Online Publishing
63 E 11400 S #230
Sandy, UT 84070
EliteOnlinePublishing.com

ISBN: 978-1790431380

DEDICATION

This book is dedicated to my wife, Diane. She put up with the time required, recommended topics, did much editing, assisted with the computer stuff including the cover collage, etc.

Diane from researching her ancestors discovered that a kinsman fought in the 1754-1763 French and Indian War, and then the 1775-1783 American Revolution. He was a General when the Revolution ended. He owned land in West Point, New York, that the Continental Army used as a fortification to control Hudson River traffic during the Revolution. He sold the land to the United States in 1790. At the behest of President Thomas Jefferson, the U.S. Military Academy was made on this land (established in 1802).

Diane's maternal grandfather served in World War I, fighting in France. Her father fought in World War II in France and Germany (Purple Heart).

In researching the above, the outcome was that she like me became an amateur military historian as well.

This book is also dedicated to those in my near family who served or are serving in the U.S. military. These include the following:

- Navy   Father 1940-1947 active duty WWII Pacific Theater; separated as Chief Quartermaster
- Army   Uncle (father's half-brother) 1956-1991, 90% active duty; served in Germany and Vietnam; separated as Lieutenant Colonel
- Marines Brother-in-law (older sister's husband) 1968-1970 active duty, half that in Vietnam; separated as Corporal
- Air Force Nephew (Marine's son) 1997- still serving active and reserves; many overseas deployments; rank of Colonel
- Air Force Niece (nephew's spouse) 1997-2004 active duty; Pakistan and Uzbekistan deployments for operations into Afghanistan in War on Terror; separated as Captain

PREFACE

My name is Bennett Fisher. I was never in the military. My father David Fisher was though. He was in the Navy, WWII, Pacific. When I say the Pacific, he was in the Pacific Ocean for 14.5 hours. The occasion was the sinking of his Mahan-class, USS Preston DD-379 destroyer (1936 commissioned new – 11/14/1942 sunk at Ironbottom Sound) in the Naval Battle of Guadalcanal. More than 70% of his shipmates were lost – killed by the exploding shells from Japanese warships and maybe even friendly fire, the resulting fires, drowned, run over in the ocean by other USSs, exploding depth charges, and sharks.

Dad survived World War II, discharged in 1947. He met, courted, and married Marjorie Benson. I was born in 1949, the first of four children, spanning almost ten years.

When I was about five, I asked my father about his experiences during the War -- *Daddy, what did you do in the War?* This was a common question from baby boomer kids in the 1950s. In fact, it was part of the American culture after World War II. You would see these words on billboards, in magazine articles or the newspaper; hear it on the radio; etc. Also, you would hear them in a comedy skit such as on a variety show or in the dialogue of a drama on a new, post-War, home entertainment media device -- called broadcast television.

But my Dad would never really respond. Even as a kid I realized that he could not or would not talk about his World War II experiences; so I stopped asking.

Long after his 1966 death, I still had this interest, and researched his military career. I got copies of his military records, went to the library (this was before the Internet was much) to research, etc. I wrote up a summary (19 pages, in fact) of his 6.3 years Navy service for my mother and three younger siblings. As in my case, this information was all new to them as well – even for Mom.

My father developed dengue fever (break-bone fever) twice during World War II, south of the Equator. He lost much of his hearing in the War from the loud guns – hearing loss changes one's personality. He lost more than two thirds his shipmates, when Preston went down. On a warship under combat conditions, your shipmates are your family.

Dad and his two older sisters had inherited some dryland from his mother, down in the Rio Grande Valley of Texas. He tried his hand at farming the 380 acres. This did not work out. He became an alcoholic. He was not a good husband or father. I finally came to realize that he most likely suffered from posttraumatic stress disorder and survivor's guilt from the War – from losing his sailor buddies, as hearing impaired, as a failure as a farmer, as not being able to be a family man. He died from alcoholism, at the age of 46.

Researching my father's naval career got me interested in military history in general; World War II more so; and the Pacific Theater even more specifically. I soon ran into others, with similar interests. I attended military history meetings at YMCAs, museums, Rice University continuing education, etc. I gave presentations on my Dad's military experiences, and other presentations on military topics. I became the Speaker Coordinator of a veterans group of seniors, at a YMCA in Houston.

I wrote up some accounts of notable World War II, Pacific Theater battles, incidents, episodes, etc. These are this book.

TABLE OF CONTENTS

1- FIRST USS SUNK BY ENEMY AIRCRAFT

The 3,950-mile Yangtze River is the third longest in the world, behind the Nile and Amazon Rivers. It is the sixth largest by discharge volume. The Yangtze's headwaters are more than three miles high on the Tibetan Plateau, in west central China. It runs west to east, emptying into the East China Sea (an extension of the Pacific Ocean) at Shanghai on China's central east coast. Shanghai today is the second most populous city in the world at 24 million, and 34 million in the metropolitan area.

One-third of China's 1.4 billion people live in the Yangtze River (and its tributaries) basin. Many major cities are on the river. These include Wuhan, Fendu, Luzhou, Chongqing (formerly known in the West as Chungking), and Nanjing (formerly known in the West as Nanking).

Chongqing is 1,037 miles west of Shanghai. It was Generalissimo Chiang Kai-shek's (1887 Qing China – 1975 Taiwan, also known as the Republic of China) provisional capital 1937-1946 (Second Sino-Japanese War), or the capital of free China. Chongqing today is the most populous city in the world at 30 million.

Nanjing is 190 miles upriver (to the west again) from Shanghai. Nanjing served as the capital of various Chinese dynasties, kingdoms, and republican governments dating from the third century to 1949, four years after World War II ended.

To sum up, the Yangtze River plays a large role in the history, culture, and economy of China.

In the late 1850s, a terrorist-type warlord (he went by the name of *Yeh*) conducted attacks on Yangtze River (including tributaries) ship and boat traffic. Others (more warlords, bandits, soldier outlaws) joined in. Vessels were hijacked, including some from different countries trading with China. Cargos were stolen. Crewmen and civilian business persons and passengers were injured, sometimes even killed. The latter included foreigners as well as Chinese.

Due to the losses (vessels, cargo, humans), the United States, Great Britain, and several other western countries (the latter to a lesser degree) that traded with and/or had business operations in China decided to intervene on behalf of the somewhat impotent Chinese government, to patrol the river. The goal was to eliminate this piracy, so that lucrative trade and business with China could continue without deaths and injuries to crew and passengers, and loss of cargo and ships.

Regarding the use of the word *lucrative,* China of course benefitted as did the trading nations. Therefore, China was motivated to accept the aid, especially as not having to bear the great costs of acquisition or construction and operation of the river boats. An agreement was made in 1858. A multinational, expeditionary force of riverine gunboats of various sizes and shapes began to patrol the Yangtze River. These efforts were successful in subduing Yeh and other bandits. However, this submission was not total. Gunboat crews usually stayed under cover, as occasional bullets would fly in from shoreside brush cover.

Grateful China authorized the trading countries' peacekeeping boats to continue patrolling. The agreement though allowed defensive actions only.

The commerce ships included oil tankers. These tankers were ocean-going, but small enough with modified hulls to operate on inland waters (rivers, lakes). These included those operated by the American company, Standard Oil Company of New York (North China Division). Standard Oil was selling American petroleum products to China.

The Empire of Japan defeated the Qing Dynasty of China in the six-month 1894-1895 First Sino-Japanese War. This conflict mainly had to do with who controlled Korea. In the surrender agreement, China (Qing Dynasty ruled 1644 to 1912) was forced to cede the following to Japan in perpetuity:

- Formosa (now called Taiwan) is a 13,976 square mile island (5% the size of Texas), 81 miles off the east coast of China; Taiwan was returned to the Republic of China after World War II
- Penghu is an archipelago of 90 islands and islets in the Taiwan Strait between Taiwan and China, comprising a total of 54 square miles; returned to Formosa (again, now called Taiwan) after World War II
- Liadong Peninsula is the southern tail of Manchuria, projecting into the Yellow Sea; it historically has been known in the West as Southeastern Manchuria; China paid 450 million yen to Japan 12/1895 to get the peninsula back
- Its sphere of influence over Korea; Korea is a peninsula off China; it is bordered by China and Russia to the northwest and northeast; Korea is separated from Japan by the Korea Strait, which connects the East China Sea, the Yellow Sea, and the Sea of Japan; the shortest distance between Korea and Japan is 120 miles; Japan's claim on Korea was forfeited at the end of World War II

To sum up, sometimes perpetuity does not work out.

Additionally, the Qing Empire was required to pay Japan war reparations in the form of silver. This amounted to 510 million Japanese yen, which was 6.4 times the annual revenue of the Japanese government at the time. This 510 million yen windfall was on top of the 450 million yen China paid to buy back its stolen Liadong Peninsula.

The Qing government also was forced to sign a commercial treaty permitting Japanese ships to operate on the Yangtze River, and to operate manufacturing factories in Chinese treaty ports.

To sum up, China was an enormous country in size. It was the second largest in the world next to the Soviet Union. It was 25 times larger than Japan. It was the most populous country in the world. However, China's lack of military power left it to the mercy of a small but militaristic, belligerent, imperialistic country.

It goes without saying that the people living in Formosa, the Liadong Peninsula (again, Southeastern Manchuria), the Penghu Archipelago, and Korea had no say as to whether they wanted to be Chinese or Japanese (or Russian, see below) – or even independent states as opposed to being part of some totalitarian Kingdom or Empire.

China at this 1895 juncture after losing to Japan faced the threat of being further partitioned and colonized by imperialist powers such as Britain, France, Germany, Russia, and Japan even more.

The U.S. won the ten-week, 1898 Spanish-American War. In so doing, it bought and annexed the Philippines from Spain for $20 million, to pay for infrastructure that Spain made in the Philippines. This is $579 million in 2019 dollars. This increased the U.S.'s Asian presence.

U.S. State Secretary John Hay (1838 IN – 1905 NH) under President William McKinley (1843 OH – 1901 NY, pistol assassination) knew little of the Far East. He turned to diplomat William Rockhill (1854 Philadelphia – 1914 Honolulu) for guidance. Rockhill worked for the American legation in Peking.

Rockhill had studied several languages, including Chinese. His command of the language was good enough that he translated books written in Chinese to English. He made trips to the Chinese countryside. At Hay's request, Rockhill prepared a memorandum to safeguard the business interests of the U.S. and other countries, that desired trade or investment with China.

From this memorandum, Hay drafted and distributed the anti-imperialistic, fair-trade *Open Door Note* policy on China. He dispatched it 9/1899 to the major European powers of France, Germany, Great Britain, Italy; and to Japan and Russia. The note asked the countries to declare formally that they would uphold Chinese territorial and administrative integrity, and would not interfere with the free use of the treaty ports within their spheres of influence in China. More specifically on the economic side, the Open Door Note policy stated that all nations would enjoy equal access to the Chinese market as follows:

- That all countries could trade with China on an equal basis
- That no country could gain control of China or parts of China in any way
- That no country would interfere with any treaty port or vested interest
- That all countries would allow China to collect tariffs, and said tariffs to be equal with all trading partners
- That all countries would show no favors to their own citizens or companies in China, such as for harbor dues or railroad charges

Trade (money) was not the only issue. Another purpose of the agreement was simply to promote good will between the U.S. and other countries and China. Hopefully, this would lead to long-term, favorable alliances down the road favoring peace with China. As China was such a big country both in land area and people, this would even foster world peace.

As mentioned above, another goal was to protect the thousands of citizens of other countries living and working in China and their families. These were mostly Americans, British, and French at the time.

The Open Door Policy was a principle. It was never formally adopted via treaty or international law, although efforts to do so were made over the years. However, all the imperial nations concurred with Hay and his policy, except for the Russian

Empire. China shares a border with 14 sovereign states. The longest is with Russia, at 2,264 miles.

Hay announced this international concurrence on China to the world 7/1900, again excepting Russia.

For the record, the six nations in concurrence were Great Britain, France, Germany, Italy, Japan, and the United States. The intention and understanding though was that the policy held for all countries.

The 22-month, 1899-1901 Boxer Rebellion in China was a violent, anti-foreign, anti-colonial (anti-West), and anti-Christian uprising. It began 11/1899, two months after Hay dispatched the Open Door Policy. The Chinese Militia United of Righteousness secret society initiated the rebellion. The society was pro-nationalistic and much opposed to Western colonialism, and Christian missionary activity that usually came along with Western contact. The Chinese Boxers killed 32,000 Chinese Christians and 200 Western missionaries in Northern China.

Many of this Militia United of Righteousness were practitioners of Chinese martial arts, especially kung fu. Westerners referred to these martial arts as Chinese boxing. This is where the name Boxer Rebellion came from.

Anyway, the Boxer Rebellion left China in turmoil. Russia took advantage of the turmoil in the year after the Rebellion (1902) and moved into Manchuria. The U.S. protested that this was a violation of the Open Door Policy. Russia would not budge, noting of course that it had never agreed to the Open Door Policy anyway.

Japan won the 1904-1905 Russo-Japanese War, gaining part of Manchuria and Korea. The war was over both countries' imperial ambitions in Manchuria and Korea. The fighting was mostly on the Liaodong Peninsula, at Mukden in Southern Manchuria, and on the seas around Korea and Japan. Russia was like China, enormous but militarily a weakling. As noted above, China is 25 times larger than Japan in area. Russia was 59 times larger than Japan.

Japanese influence extended to include more of Manchuria in the wake of the 1917 Russian Revolution, which in turn was during what later came to be called World War I.

Germany also had possessions in China. The Allied Triple Entente (Russia, France, United Kingdom) in secret treaties during World War I (1914-1918) promised Japan, Germany's China possessions when the War ended. Japan was an ally of the Triple Entente during World War I.

These treaties were revealed as part of the 1919 Versailles Treaty which ended the state of war (again World War I) between the Central Powers (Germany, Austria-Hungary, Bulgaria, and the Ottoman Empire) and the Allied Triple Entente Powers. This of course angered China, with other countries making secret decisions unilaterally on dividing and assigning Chinese territory to imperialistic countries.

The 1922 Nine-Power Treaty (six European countries, U.S., Japan, and China) was negotiated during the 1921-1922 Washington Naval Conference in Washington, D.C. The Treaty expressly reaffirmed the sovereignty and territorial integrity of China, as per the Open Door Policy. The purpose of the treaty was to make the Open Door Policy, international law.

Russia became the Union of Soviet Socialist Republics (the Soviet Union) 12/1922, when the Russian, Ukrainian, Byelorussian, and Transcaucasian Soviet republics (each ruled by local Bolshevik parties) united. The Soviet Union refused to make the Nine-Power Treaty the Ten-Power Treaty. The Soviet Union regained control of part of Manchuria (the northern part) by 1925.

Japan staged a false event (Japanese soldiers detonated dynamite along a rail line near Mukden, Liaoning Province, China) in 1931 as a pretense to invade Manchuria. Japan annexed Manchuria, declaring that Inner Manchuria was now an *independent state*. Japan renamed Manchuria *Manchukuo*. Japan appointed the deposed Qing emperor Puyi (1906 Beijing – 1967 Beijing) as puppet emperor.

Japan now ran Manchuria brutally, conducting systematic campaigns of terror and intimidation against the Russian and Chinese populations including arrests for no reason, military riots against the population, and other forms of subjugation. Japan grabbed natural resources from Manchuria.

The Geneva, Switzerland based League of Nations was formed in 1920 as a result of the Paris Peace Conference after World War I, in an effort to ensure world peace forever (did not happen). Its primary goals were to prevent wars through disarmament and collective security, and to settle international disputes peaceably through arbitration and negotiation.

The League condemned Japan's invasion and annexation. Japan responded, by withdrawing its membership from the League.

Manchuria has been mentioned several times, and needs to be defined. Manchuria is a large area in northeast China. Its boundaries have been differently defined over the centuries by different countries. Korea (now the two Koreas) are attached to its southeast corner. Russia is on its north side. Part of its eastern edge is on the Sea of Japan (Pacific Ocean). It is the part of China closest to Japan. Geographically, Manchuria is part of China. As noted above, both the Soviet Union and Japan said they deserved Manchuria, for some trumped up reason or reasons.

Manchuria is an important region as rich in natural resources such as coal and some minerals, plus it has much fertile farmland.

Japan's 1931 annexation with the gain of Manchuria's natural resources and use of Manchuria as a base to launch attacks, put Japan in a much better position to continue its conquest efforts of Southeast Asian countries and other imperial aggression.

The Empire of Japan conducted fourteen sneak attacks on holdings or possessions of the U.S. and Great Britain in or on the Pacific Ocean, and Thailand; 12/7/1941. Japan used its Manchuria and Formosa and Penghu dependencies and Korean protectorate in World War II in a number of ways, which supported these attacks. Resources (food crops, minerals, etc.) were taken for Japan. Bases were made in the Penghus and Formosa. Chinese and Koreans were conscripted for the Japanese military. Chinese and Korean women including children were forced into sex slavery, for the pleasure of Japanese soldiers.

To sum up, without these resources and facilities, Japan would not have launched the just mentioned sneak attacks on 12/7/1941, or the attacks would have been fewer, or the attacks would have been fewer and later.

The outcome of the sneak attacks was that the U.S. declared war on Japan the day after the sneak attacks. This was Monday, 12/8/1941. The peace period between the World War I Armistice Day and World War II for the U.S. was a little more than 23 years.

From the late 1850s as noted above, the U.S. Navy operated a hodgepodge of boats as its Yangtze River Squadron, as did some other countries. By the 1920s with many more Americans working and living in China and trade increasing and bandits becoming more active and Japan and the Soviet Union still imperialistic, the Navy decided that purpose-built boats were necessary. Accordingly, six similar design river gunboats were made at Shanghai shipyards. Two were 159' long, two were 191' long, and two were 211' long. Their beams ranged from 27 to 31'. Their hulls were gently rounded, to ensure shallow drafts of five to six feet. Therefore, they were suitable only for inland work (river or lake). In fact, the intention when made was that they would serve out their lives on the Yangtze River.

The six river gunboats were commissioned, 1927-1928. They were all named after Pacific Ocean Islands.

The gunboats had crews of 55 to 60 enlisted men and officers. Their speed was about 17 miles per hour from their two steam engines, each rotating a screw.

One of these six was the 474-ton displacement, 191' long and 29' beam and 5' draft, USS Panay PR-5 (1928 – 12/12/1937 aerial bomb sunk, Yangtze River). Panay is the sixth largest Philippine Island.

Panay's armament was as follows:
- 2 × 3"/50 caliber gun, one forward and one aft
- 8 × single .30 caliber (7.62 millimeter) Lewis anti-aircraft machine guns

The eight, gas-operated (long stroke piston with rotating bolt), Lewis anti-aircraft machine guns shot 550 rounds per minute, with a muzzle velocity of 2,440 feet per second. They were mounted four per side, about amidships. Although just noted as anti-aircraft guns, they were mounted so could shoot horizontally. This was so they could defend from shore attack, or attack from river gunboats or even larger warships of other countries (namely Japan).

1884 U.S Military Academy graduate Isaac Lewis (1858 PA – 1931 NJ, heart attack) became an authority on ordinance in the Army. From an earlier design, he improved the gun in 1911 which came to be named after him. Lewis separated from the Army in 1913 as a Colonel, due to disability incurred in the line of duty. The British further improved the design of the Lewis gun, and mass produced it. Allied militaries used the Lewis in both World Wars and also the Korean War.

The Lewis' effective range was only a half-mile. The Yangtze is much wider than a half mile, in many places. To sum up, the Lewis gun was outdated and inadequate.

All eight Lewis guns had splinter shields installed. This turned out to be wise. Potshots at some sections of the river from concealed bandit and outlaw soldier snipers were routine.

The Navy hired Chinese to help run the river patrol boats. Each had about a dozen or more coolies (meaning laborers). The coolies worked in the hot engine room, cooked and served and cleaned the boat, did the laundry, fetched supplies, sanded and painted and polished woodwork, ran boats to shore and back, etc. As assigned the heavy and dirty and unpleasant work, the coolies made the on-duty lives of the American sailors much easier. YangPat (Yangtze River Patrol) duty was considered a plum assignment for a U.S. Navy sailor in the 1920s and 1930s.

The coolies were happy, as the U.S Navy paid and treated them very well, compared to either land-based work or merchant marine work for that matter at the time in China.

As already noted, Japan was one of the signatories of the 1922 Nine-Power Treaty, affirming China's sovereignty. Despite this and despite the presence of the foreign gunboats, Japan fabricated the already mentioned, 9/18/1931 Mukden (Liaoning Province) Incident (Japanese soldiers detonated dynamite along a rail line) as a pretext to invade and annex Manchuria (or more of Manchuria). As already noted, Japan had declared Manchuria to be an *independent state*, and changed the area's name to *Manchukuo*.

Again as already noted, Japan already controlled the southern part of Manchuria as a land grab from the 1904-1905 Russo-Japanese War; and had grabbed even more of Manchuria after the 1917 Russian Revolution.

Japan's goals were to stifle Chinese nationalism, and to continue to take raw materials not available in Japan. Other countries protested that Japan had reneged on its agreement in annexing parts of China, to no avail. China pled openly for assistance.

Of course, there was tension in the air – from lurking bandits, and from the belligerent Japanese who now controlled Manchuria. Japan added its own gunboats to the Yangtze River mix in the 1930s, after grabbing more of Manchuria.

As noted at the beginning of this chapter, the Yangtze River gunboats were first used in the 1850s to subdue bandit types who were menacing river shipping. By the 1920s, the gunboats were used some to buffer disturbances, as China tried to modernize and create a strong central government. As described above, Japanese belligerence toward China (and friends of China) grew in the 1930s, with the result that the gunboats played a role in countering Japanese aggression.

In 1933 in his first year of office, U.S. President Franklin Roosevelt (1882 NY – 4/12/1945 GA, cerebral hemorrhage) reaffirmed American and other countries' trading and business rights; under the above-described 1900 McKinley-era Open Door with China policy. Japan though rejected the China Open Door Policy. Japan announced that countries that did not recognize Manchuria (or again Manchukuo as Japan now called the area) as belonging to Japan, were now banned from trading with all of China.

In 7/1937, Japan used the more of the non-event than event Marco Polo Bridge incident near Peking as an excuse for a full-scale invasion and occupation of China. This started the Second Sino-Japanese War which ran to the end of World War II, 8/1945 -- so more than eight years. By the end of the year (1937), Japan occupied a big portion of China besides Manchuria.

Foreigners had already fled China in droves. Japan's invasion and increase in occupied areas of China stepped up the outward flow of foreigners.

As already described, the U.S. Navy now had six, shallow-draft, river gunboats operating on the Yangtze. As the Japanese moved through south China, the gunboats evacuated most of the American embassy staff from Nanjing, 11/1937. Nanjing was on the lower Yangtze River, 190 miles upriver from Shanghai on the East China Sea coast. Other neutral nations with people and interests in China (including Great Britain) did the same evacuations with their gunboats.

In 1937, Colonel Kingoro Hashimoto (1890 Japan – 1957 Japan) was the senior Army officer in charge of artillery units in China. From the early 1930s, Hashimoto and some other junior Japanese Army officers had become increasingly involved in ultra-nationalist (right wing) politics within the military.

As part of the above, Hashimoto founded or co-founded radical, ultra-nationalist secret societies within the Japanese Army. The most notable was called *Sakurakai,* which translates to *Cherry Blossom Society*. Army Captain Isamu Cho (1895 Japan – 6/22/1945 Okinawa as a Lieutenant General, seppuku) co-founded Sakurakai with Hashimoto, in 1930.

Hashimoto and Cho were both graduates of the Imperial Japanese Army Academy and the Army War College. Both institutions were in Tokyo. The Sakurakai members were mostly under the age of 50. General Sadao Araki (1877 Tokyo – 1966 Japan) and General Kuniaki Koiso (1880 Japan – 1950 Tokyo) were exceptions as older, allying with Sakurakai later. Araki and Koiso were also both graduates of the Imperial Japanese Army Academy and the Army War College. Most of the other members were graduates of the Imperial Japanese Army Academy, and some from both the Academy and War College. To sum up, these highly educated and trained commissioned officers were the elite of the Japanese Army.

Sakurakai's goal was to reorganize the state as a totalitarian, militaristic entity with the Emperor as the dictator; via a military coup d'état if necessary.

The government and cabinet would be replaced, but all the power would be assigned to Emperor Michinomiya Hirohito (1901 Tokyo – 1989 Tokyo). Michinomiya Hirohito died in 1989 at age 87. His 62-year reign ran 1926-1989. The Sakurakai members considered the current civilian government as corrupt in its thought and politics, as westernized.

Hashimoto led two coup efforts with other military men in 1931. He may have been involved in later efforts. For some reason, he and the others involved although found out were not locked up (or if jailed, not for long) or severely punished. In fact, they retained their ranks and were allowed to return to their previous positions, for the most part. This reason probably had to do with their loyalty to the Emperor who after all was the head of the Shinto state religion and considered divine, and their intention to change his role to more of a dictator.

Again, Colonel Hashimoto and other senior officers longed for the dictatorial Japan of old. Hashimoto was a loose cannon in more ways than one. After all, he commanded artillery operations.

On 12/12/1937, Hashimoto ordered his men to fire on any non-Japanese vessels sailing through certain sectors, regardless of nationality or status. His soldiers dutifully fired on Panay, and also two British river gunboats in the area. Panay was anchored at the time, 27 miles above Nanjing. She had been assigned as station ship to guard the remaining Americans as the Japanese advanced through South China, and take them off at the last moment if necessary. She had evacuated the remaining Americans from Nanjing the day before and sailed upriver, to avoid the fighting around the doomed capitol city.

The Navy crew including coolies and evacuees came to seventy-three aboard Panay. The seventy-three included four American embassy staff and civilians from ten countries. Some of the internationals worked for national news organizations.

The artillery shells missed Panay.

The two British river gunboats that the Japanese fired on near Wahu were the Insect-class HMS Ladybird (1916 – 5/12/1941 German dive bombers severely damaged off Libya, scuttled) and also Insect-class HMS Bee (1915 – 1939 scrapped), when escorting a convoy upriver from Nanjing. At 238' long with a 36' beam, the Insects were large for a river gunboat. They were in fact half as long longer than the two smallest of the six USS river gunboats completed 1927 and 1928, and 13% longer than the largest two. However, they only drew 4' of water due to their wide beam which was 24% more than Panay's beam, and close to flat bottom. The Insects anti-aircraft guns, like Panay's Lewis guns, also dated back to World War I.

A dozen shells hit HMS Ladybird killing one sailor and injuring several others, but she was able to continue. The shells missed HMS Bee.

When shot at, Panay was preparing to escort three American merchant river tankers (Standard Oil). The tankers were also ferrying many Chinese employees who worked for Standard Oil, to evacuate them as well. The Japanese senior naval commander in Shanghai was informed both before and after the fact, of this planned movement.

Later the same day, three Japanese Navy, single engine, conventional landing gear, three crew (pilot, navigator, radio operator/gunner), Yokosuka B4Y Type-96 biplane bombers aimed and dropped eighteen, 132-pound bombs at Panay. Two connected.

Nine, Japanese Navy, single engine, conventional landing gear, single crew, Nakajima A4N Type-95 biplane fighters followed up, strafing. Both the bombers and flights were carrier-capable, but were land based for this attack. The top speeds of the bomber and fighter biplanes were 171 and 219 miles per hour. This was much less than World War II planes a few years later. Therefore, they were easy to shoot down with modern anti-aircraft fire. However as noted above, the effective range of Panay's outdated Lewis guns was only a half mile. Panay's gunners did not connect.

Panay's forward 3" gun was damaged. The radio room was destroyed, preventing the transmission of an SOS message. An oil line was cut which put out Panay's engines and emergency pumps.

Panay's pilothouse was hit. Captain (Lieutenant Commander) James Hughes was knocked unconscious. His femur was broken. He later recovered. He served as Captain of the Arcturus-class, 459' long and 63' beam and 20' draft, USS Electra (1942 – 1974 scrapped) attack cargo ship during World War II. After the War though, Hughes took medical retirement related to his injuries on Panay.

1927 U.S. Naval Academy graduate, Executive Officer Lieutenant Arthur Anders (1904 – 2000) was hit in the throat by shrapnel and could not talk. Now in charge with Hughes unconscious, he hand-wrote orders. The attack began at 13:27. Panay sank at 15:54. Anders' last (written) order, was *abandon ship*. He was awarded the Navy Cross as well as the Purple Heart.

Anders by the way was the father of NASA astronaut William Anders (1933 British Hong Kong -). Like his father, William Anders graduated from the U.S. Naval Academy (1955). He retired from the Air Force as a Major General in 1969. He was the lunar module pilot on Apollo 8 December, 1968. This was the first spacecraft to reach the moon, and also the first to orbit the moon.

Panay Storekeeper First Class Charles Ensminger (19?? CA – 12/13/1937 Yangtze River), Panay Coxswain Edgar Hulsebus (1911 MO – 12/19/1937 Yangtze River), and Italian journalist Sandro Sandri (1895 Italy – 12/13/1937 Yangtze River) all later died from shrapnel wounds.

Panay was the first ever USS sunk by enemy aircraft. Of course, this was during peacetime – no country had declared war.

The Japanese aircraft also destroyed the three Standard Oil river tankers that Panay was escorting. These vessels had shallow drafts so as to be able to navigate rivers and lakes, but were also designed to be ocean-going. The Mei An, Mei Hsia, and Mei Ping had displacements of 934, 1,048, and 1,118 tons each. In comparison, Panay's displacement was 474 tons. The Captain of one of the tankers (Carl Carlson) was killed, as were many Chinese civilians and coolies on the tankers.

Survivors abandoned Panay. When rowing to shore in lifeboats, the Nakajimas and also a Japanese river gunboat strafed the survivors wounding many. Besides the three men killed, forty-eight of the seventy-three aboard Panay were wounded. The 48 wounded were 43 and five sailors and civilians. Fourteen were wounded so severely that they were stretcher cases.

Three river gunboats picked up the Panay survivors when hiding out in the brush, on day three. These were the Panay's same size, sister river gunboat USS Oahu (1928 – 5/5/1942 Japanese warship gunfire sank off Corregidor), and the two British, Insect-class gunboats mentioned above.

The survivors were taken to the Northampton-class, 570' long and 66' beam and 16' draft, USS Augusta CA-31 (1931 – 1960 scrapped) heavy cruiser stationed offshore. Augusta's purposes were to stand by if needed for assistance, rescue, medical care, etc. A Japanese destroyer tailed Augusta.

Japan accepted responsibility for sinking and destroying the Panay and the three tankers. However, Japan insisted the attack was unintentional. This was not the case, as follows:

- The U.S. Navy had advised Japan of the location of its gunboats and their planned movements, as they had always done. This notification was both before and after the movement.

- Japan stated that its pilots could not distinguish between Chinese and American flags. Panay was flying and displaying several large American flags, plus the flag was painted on its cabin roof. The attacking planes were flying at low altitude on a clear day in the daytime. Other than the fact that both nation's flags used the same colors, the Chinese and the American flags do not resemble each other at all.

- Japan sank three non-military oil tankers as well as Panay. The tankers were flying large American flags as well.

- Navy cryptographers had intercepted and decrypted communications, which indicated that the attack was ordered from higher up. This was not publicized at the time though, as doing so would inform Japan that their code had been broken.

Several Panay survivors were news services (newspapers, magazines, newsreels) correspondents and cameramen. They were reporting on the turmoil in China. They recorded details of the attack, both in words and by taking video. The video included footage of a Japanese gunboat machine-gunning Panay as she sank, as well as the air attack. As a side note, President Roosevelt blocked release of this footage, to not infuriate American citizens.

To sum up, accidental bombing and strafing did not hold water. It appears that the Japanese plan was to get the USSs and HMSs to fight back so that Japan could sink them, as its land and air and naval fighting capabilities in the area were superior to those of the U.S. and Great Britain. Doing so would either compel the U.S. and Great Britain to abandon China or escalate its military capabilities in the area. Japan reasoned (or hoped) that the U.S. and other countries would opt for the former – withdraw from China.

Imperial Japanese Navy Third Fleet Chief of Staff Vice-Admiral Rokuzo Sugiyama (1890 Tokyo – 1947 Tokyo) formally apologized for his country, for the *accidental* destroying of the four American ships (Panay and the three tankers) and the deaths and injuries. Japan paid the U.S. $2,214,007.36 ($39.9 million in 2019 money) four months later, for losses as itemized – property losses, and death/personal injury indemnification.

Nine surviving Panay crewmen died in World War II. Coxswain Morris Rider was one, killed in the 12/7/1941 Oahu (Pearl Harbor), Territory of Hawaii attack, almost four years later. This of course was another sneak attack, courtesy again of the Empire of Japan.

Kaname Harada (1916 Japan – 2016 Japan) was a pilot of one of the Nakajima fighters that strafed the Panay. Four years later, he flew a Mitsubishi A6M Zero off an aircraft carrier as protective patrol again in the 12/7/1941 sneak attack on the U.S. military bases and harbor at Oahu. He shot down nine to nineteen Allied aircraft through 10/1942. On 10/17/1942, Grumman F4F Wildcat fighters shot him down, when he was escorting torpedo bombers attacking American targets on Guadalcanal. He crash-landed near the Japanese base at Rekata Bay on Santa Isabel Island. Santa Isabel is the third largest of the Solomon Islands. He recovered from his injuries.

Harada worked as a flying instructor for the rest of World War II, including training kamikaze pilots late in the War. He became an anti-war activist in 1991. He was the last surviving Japanese pilot who attacked the Panay. He was also the last surviving Japanese pilot involved in the 12/7/1941 Oahu sneak attack. He died at 99.7 years old.

Fon Huffman (1913 IA – 2008) enlisted in the Navy at age 16, with his father's permission. He was a Panay boilerman. He gave his life jacket to one of the civilians during the attack. Huffman served on destroyers in both the Pacific Ocean and the Atlantic Ocean during World War II. He retired from the Navy as a Chief Petty Officer, 1949. He worked more than 30 years for a railroad before retiring. He was buried at Arlington National Cemetery. He was the last Panay crew survivor.

The USS Panay is shown below. Also, note how difficult it is to tell the Chinese and American flags apart, on a sunny afternoon, from a low altitude.

The Yangtze River patrols continued. However, the Navy sent three of the remaining five riverboats to the Philippines 11/1941. This left two, as Yangtze River station ships.

By early 12/1941, Japan's Army occupied all of Shanghai except the International Settlement and French Concession. The International Settlement was occupied by mostly British and American citizens. The French Concession is where mostly French nationals lived. Supposedly, the Japanese military was hands-off these international zones; at least until the 12/7/1941 sneak attacks. This hands-off policy ended that date. Japanese troops rushed in.

The fate of the last two USS Yangtze River gunboats (not sent to the Philippines) was as follows:

- The 159' long and 27' beam and 5' draft, USS Wake (1927 – 1960s retired) was berthed at Shanghai, functioning as a fixed radio spy ship. She was rigged with scuttling charges. Japanese marines stormed Wake 12/7/1941 at 04:00. This was two hours after the Oahu Pearl Harbor sneak attack. They prevented the Wake crew from fighting, fleeing, or scuttling. Captain Columbus Smith (1891 GA – 1966) was not on board at the time. When he returned, Smith was taken prisoner along with his crew of 14.

- This little river gunboat was the only USS the Japanese captured in World War II. Note though that it was captured in peacetime. The U.S. Congress declared War on Japan the next day 12/8/1941, which was a Monday.

- Japan renamed Wake *Tatara*, and used the gunboat until the end of World War II. The U.S. then took Wake back. The U.S. transferred her to the Republic of China, in 1946. She was renamed *Tai Yuan*. Chinese Communist forces captured her in 1949. She was commissioned into the Reorganized National Government of China, which operated her into the 1960s.

- At Chongqing which is a thousand miles upstream the Yangtze from Shanghai on the coast, the crew of the 159' long and 27' beam and 5'draft, USS Tutuila (1928 – 2/16/1942 transferred to China) were ordered to fly out. Chongqing again was Generalissimo Chiang Kai-shek's provisional capital of China during World War II – so the capital of free China.

- They did fly out, 1/18/1942. The Naval Attaché attached to the American Embassy in Chongqing took Tutuila under his jurisdiction. The Navy transferred her to China under the Lend-Lease program. Her crew scuttled her 5/1949 to avoid capture by the Communists. This was during the Civil War in China, which followed World War II.

At about the same time that Japanese marines boarded the USS Wake in Shanghai Harbor, they also rushed the 177' long and 29' beam and 3' draft, HMS Peterel (1927 – 12/8/1941 sank Shanghai Harbor) river gunboat and demanded her surrender. Peterel like USS Wake was in use as a communications base (spy ship), berthed in Shanghai Harbor. Also like Wake, she had a skeleton crew.

The British Consulate had advised Peterel's Captain, Temporary Lieutenant Stephen Polkinghorn (1879 New Zealand – 19??), of the Oahu attack. He had orders to scuttle, should the Japanese attack. He rigged Peterel with demolition charges. He sent his men to action stations.

To stall for time to light the demolition charges and pass the codebooks down to the boiler for burning, Captain Polkinghorn discussed matters (or tried to) with the Japanese marine officers. They refused to talk. Captain Polkinghorn ordered them off the gunboat. They complied. Within minutes, Peterel was attacked by gunfire from three directions as follows:

- The 434' long and 69' beam and 24' draft, IJN Izumo (1900 – 7/24/1945 sunk by American aircraft off Kure) cruiser; Izumo also illuminated Peterel with her searchlights, making her easier to hit
- The 180' long and 27' beam and 3' draft, IJN Toba (1911 – 9/1945 abandoned to the Republic of China Navy at Shanghai when World War II ended, then to the People's Liberation {free China} Navy 11/29/1949, scrapped 1964) river gunboat; Toba was Izumo's escort
- Japanese shore batteries mounted next to the French Concession, this was almost at point-blank range

Peterel returned fire with her Lewis machine guns and small arms, inflicting several casualties (including deaths) on the Japanese. Most likely, these were the marines on the departing launch. The breechblocks from her 3" guns had been removed though, and taken to the Royal Navy dockyard in Hong Kong. Peterel was hit many times, and quickly capsized.

Peterel's crew was 22. Eighteen of the 22 were aboard when Japan attacked. The crew were mostly radiomen, not gunners. They could fire the machine guns, but lacked the specialist training needed to operate the bigger guns. In fact, the 3" guns had been disabled anyway, as just noted.

Six Peterel crew were killed, some when machine-gunned in the water. Some of the other twelve including Captain Polkinghorn sought refuge on a neutral, Norwegian-officered, Panamanian-registered merchant vessel. This was the SS Marizion. In violation of international law, the Japanese boarded Marizion and took the survivors prisoner. They along with other British prisoners of war were imprisoned at various prisoner of war camps in China. Later some were moved to camps in Japan. Some died during captivity, due to the appalling conditions and treatment.

Captain Polkinghorn survived the War. He was awarded the Distinguished Service Cross. Able Seaman James Mariner also survived. He died in 2009, age 90. He is noted as the first British military man to fire on the Japanese, in World War II.

Several of Peterel's crew on shore at the time of the attack were captured. Another crewman though remained at large in Shanghai for the duration of the

War, working for a Sino-American spy ring. This was Petty Officer Telegraphist James Cuming.

Several of the Chinese coolies on Peterel were also killed in the attack. Again, some of these were shot in the water. The number is not known.

Peterel like Wake had a skeleton crew (normal crew complement when sailing was in the fifties). As noted above, both gunboats were being used as communications stations – spy ships, spying on the Japanese.

As already noted, three of the six USS river gunboats made in Shanghai were sent to the Philippines. This was a treacherous voyage, as these boats were not made for ocean-going travel. Japanese ships sank one by gunfire off Corregidor. The crew scuttled the other two, to prevent capture. However, the Japanese recovered, repaired, and used one of the scuttled gunboats. An American submarine torpedoed this one 3/3/1944, but she did not sink. The Japanese scuttled her to block a channel in Manila Bay, 2/5/1945.

The USS Augusta heavy cruiser is mentioned above as receiving survivors from Panay. Augusta had sailed up the 70 mile, Whangpoo River (Huangpu River in Chinese) to evacuate endangered American citizens and other westerners. The Whangpoo is a tributary of the Yangtze River, and flows through the city of Shanghai.

Augusta Seaman First Class Freddie Falgout (1916 LA – 8/20/1937 off Shanghai) was killed by a shell on the well deck, the day before his 21st birthday. The shrapnel wounded another 18 Augusta sailors. This was a little less than four months before Panay was sunk. The shell was thought to be a one-pound, pom-pom shrapnel shell fired from a 36 millimeter Japanese gun, aimed at low-flying Chinese aircraft. The Japanese did apologize for the casualties and damage; but allowed that if they were responsible, it was an accident. Accidents happen, you see.

Falgout's home town of Raceland (forty-four miles southwest of New Orleans) had a population of 500. However, more than 10,000 attended his memorial service back home. In the 1930s, death of an American military man from any cause was a rarity.

Some historians consider the start of the Second World War to be 7/7/1937, when Japan used the Marco Polo Bridge incident as an excuse to launch a full-scale war against China. If so, Falgout's death six weeks later would be the U.S.'s first military death of World War II. Japan's invasion of China was more than five months before the Panay was sunk and more U.S. military deaths.

Colonel Hashimoto was mentioned above, as firing artillery on Panay and the British river gunboats 12/12/1937; earlier on the same day that Panay was struck and sunk by Japanese aerial bombs. His belligerent actions and militaristic ways stemmed from his radical thoughts. The immediate question at the time was whether he unilaterally decided to fire on the American and British gunboats; or whether his orders to fire on any foreign boats on the Yangtze River above Nanjing came from above. It was later confirmed and as already noted, that the latter was the case.

For the record, Japan did recall Hashimoto from his China duty station for initiating fire; and gave him a minor reprimand as well. The reprimand may have just been for show (see below).

The Empire of Japan conducted sneak attacks against five U.S. military installation and harbor sites on five Pacific Ocean Islands, 12/7, 8/1941. The 1907 Hague Convention addressed the requirement to declare war in its *Convention Relative to the Opening of Hostilities* statements. These clauses describe the international actions a country should perform, before opening hostilities. Article 1 states: *The Contracting Powers recognize that hostilities between themselves must not commence without previous and explicit warning, in the form either of a reasoned declaration of war or of an ultimatum with conditional declaration of war.* Again, Japan took a pass on giving an advance warning to the United States (and also Great Britain and Thailand) attacked the same day. Japan had a history of such invasions (China and other countries) without such warnings. Shame on Japan.

The attacks were on the same day, but the sites were over the International Date Line which explains the two dates. The International Date Line is an imaginary line from the North Pole to the South Pole. It marks the change from one calendar day to the next. It roughly follows the 180° line of longitude, through the middle of the Pacific Ocean.

As noted above, Japan also captured a USS and its crew in Shanghai Harbor the same day. This river gunboat was the only USS Japan captured in World War II. However, note that War had not yet been declared. For the record, a Japanese submarine also gun-sank an Army-chartered, unarmed cargoman off California, at the same time as the Oahu attack. For the record again, Japanese bombers off Kwajalein Atoll (one of the Marshall Islands) dropped on two, U.S. Pacific Ocean island protectorates this same day (Howland Island and Baker Island of the Phoenix Islands).

The five attacked Pacific Ocean islands where the U.S. had military installations were Oahu (Pearl Harbor, etc.), Guam, Wake, Midway, and Philippines. After these attacks, the Japanese Army quickly reinstated Hashimoto. In fact, he was awarded a medal for his initiative in firing on the American and British gunboats on the Yangtze River, four years earlier.

At the end of World War II, Hashimoto was captured. The International Military Tribunal for the Far East indicted him on two charges as follows:

1) For waging wars of aggression in violation of international law, treaties, agreements, and assurances
2) For breaches of laws and customs of war committed as a Commander, in invading Manchuria and in World War II

The trial began 4/1946. The Tribunal recognized Hashimoto as among the most extremist among the accused and described his role in planning to seize the Japanese government and conduct an aggressive policy of territorial expansion. He was found guilty more than 2.5 years later 11/1948 of criminal conspiracy in the commission of crimes against peace, for his participation in the 9/18/1931 Mukden Incident, and his ongoing participation in the following invasion of

Manchuria by Japan. He was acquitted though of the charges of command responsibility in the commission of war crimes during World War II. He was sentenced to life imprisonment. He was released on parole in 1955. He died in 1957, age 67.

So again, the Panay was the first USS sunk in combat, 12/12/1937. This was a Sunday. But as already noted, War had not yet been declared.

The next U.S. Navy ships sunk by enemy aircraft were six (four were battleships), plus another thirteen badly damaged including the other four Pacific Fleet battleships. Instead of two crew lost in the case of the Panay, 2,335 U.S. military personnel were lost, mostly Navy again. This was also on a Sunday, almost four years later at Pearl Harbor, Oahu, U.S. Territory of Hawaii. Again, the aggressor was the Empire of Japan. Again, this was during peacetime. As already noted, Congress as requested by President Roosevelt declared war on Japan the next day which was 12/8/1941, a Monday.

The war ended 45 months later. However, this required use of weapons of mass destruction (two atomic bombs). Nuclear weapons have not been used in anger since.

2- JAPANESE MIDGET SUBMARINES AT PEARL HARBOR

World War I ran 7/28/1914 – 11/11/1918, which was 4.3 years. The United States entered the War 4/6/1917, so was involved only the last 1.6 years. This was 37% of the 4.3 years. Of these 19 months, most of the almost 117,000 American military deaths occurred in the last 14 months of the War. It takes a few months to get into fighting mode. Only 46% of these deaths were in combat. This low percentage is due to the fact that half the 116,700 died from influenza. The other 4% died from other diseases, in captivity, or in accidents.

Another 204,000 American military men were wounded in some way, or made ill (use of chemical warfare occurred in World War I, for one thing). Some had permanent disabilities.

The 1918-1919 influenza A pandemic (subtype H1N1 virus) sickened half a billion people (at a time when the planet's population was 1.8 billion) and killed 40 million (some estimates though state up to 100 million deaths). Six hundred and seventy-five thousand or 1.7% of the 40 million were Americans. Another estimate was that 15% of those infected died. The influenza hit in three waves as follows:

- Spring of 1918 - first wave was mild, symptoms were chills, fever and fatigue; recovery was quick
- Fall of 1918 - second wave symptoms onset were sudden; many developed a virulent strain of pneumonia; lungs filled with fluid; many died within days or even hours after symptoms set in; most of the world deaths were during this period; most who died were in their twenties, thirties, and forties; deaths of adults in their prime years was (and still is) very uncommon for influenza which usually kills the very young and the very old, so this influenza pandemic was way out of the ordinary
- Winter of 1918-1919 - third wave like the first wave was mild

As World War I created so many refugees on the move and with troops transported all over, and these groups in close quarters, more were exposed and became infected. Besides increased viral transmission, the mass movements probably augmented mutations, increasing the lethality of the virus. Due to malnourishment and the stress of combat (living and fighting in muddy trenches, constant bombardment, chemical attacks, etc.), the immune systems of soldiers may have been diminished; increasing susceptibility. Civilian refugees likewise may have had compromised immune systems.

The influenza pandemic deaths were a major contributing factor to warring countries agreeing to an armistice, 11/11/1918.

Because of these casualties and not to mention the financial costs, the U.S. had a majority isolationist attitude in the 1920s (but no significant wars in the 1920s) and into the 1930s, even as some countries armed up and became belligerent and imperialistic.

The Empire of Japan attacked China without provocation and also minus a war declaration, 7/1937. The 1907 Hague Convention addressed the requirement to declare war in its *Convention Relative to the Opening of Hostilities* statements. These clauses describe the international actions a country should perform, before opening hostilities. Article 1 states: *The Contracting Powers recognize that hostilities between themselves must not commence without previous and explicit warning, in the form either of a reasoned declaration of war or of an ultimatum with conditional declaration of war.* Again, Japan took a pass on giving an advance warning to China, of maybe attacking. Japan had a history of such invasions (not just China, but other countries as well) without such warnings. Shame on Japan.

Nazi Germany in 1938 and 1939 seized Austria, parts of Czechoslovakia (Sudetenland, Bohemia, Moravia, Czech Silesia), the Slovak Republic, and Lithuania. Germany invaded (and occupied) Poland 9/1/1939, again with no justification or war declaration. Like Japan, shame on Germany.

This 9/1/1939 date is usually the date stated as the start of World War II. However, some military historians use the 7/7/1937 date when Japan invaded and occupied China without warning. Japan had already invaded and occupied part of China (Manchuria) in 1931, again without warning or provocation.

By the end of 1940, Nazi Germany controlled most of Poland, Lithuania, France, Belgium, Norway, Denmark, North Africa, etc. Great Britain and other countries were much threatened.

The Empire of Japan on one day sneak attacked thirteen sites on or in the Pacific Ocean, again in violation of the international rules of war.

The dates were 12/7 and 8/1941. Again this was the same day, but shown as two dates as the attacked sites were on both sides of the International Date Line. The International Date Line is an imaginary line from the North Pole to the South Pole. It marks the change from one calendar day to the next. It roughly follows the 180° line of longitude, through the middle of the Pacific Ocean.

Nine of the thirteen attacked sites belonged to the United States. Five of these nine were U.S. military bases and airfields and harbors on five Pacific Ocean islands. These were Oahu (Pearl Harbor, etc.), Guam, Wake, Midway, and Philippines. This *date which will live in infamy* as President Franklin Roosevelt (1882 NY – 4/12/1945 GA, cerebral hemorrhage) termed it, led the U.S. to immediately drop its isolation stance left over from World War I and declare war on Japan the next day. This was 12/8/1941, a Monday.

Germany and Italy declared war on the U.S. 12/11/1941. The U.S. reciprocated against both countries the same day. The peace period for the United States between the World War I Armistice Day and World War II was a little more than 23 years.

On 12/5/1941 which was a Friday two days before the sneak attacks, 1927 U.S. Naval Academy graduate Lieutenant Commander William Outerbridge (1906 Hong Kong {father a British merchant sea captain} – 1986 GA) assumed command of the Wickes-class, 314' long and 31' beam and 10' draft, four-piper, 40 miles per hour, USS Ward (1918 – 12/7/1944 kamikaze hit and damaged at

Ormoc Bay, Leyte, Philippines; deliberately sank) destroyer. His new wage after assignment was $356 a month, which is $4,272 a year. This is $73,119 in 2019 money. His crew of 231 men was mostly reservists from the St. Paul, Minnesota area.

For the record, Ward was named in honor of Commander James Ward (1806 CT – 6/27/1861 VA). He was one of the five co-founders of the U.S. Naval Academy in Annapolis, Maryland in 1845. At the 6/27/1861 Mathias Point Battle of the Civil War in King George County, Virginia, Ward as flagship officer sent a landing party ashore to dislodge Southern forces from a battery. The infantry sailors encountered heavy resistance. The Federals gave up the attack. They retreated under heavy sniper and cannon fire to their ships. Ward brought his flotilla in close to the shoreline to provide gunfire support for the retreating landing party. As he was sighting the bow gun on his 143' long and 27' beam, side-wheel paddle USS Thomas Freeborn (made as a tug unknown date, 1861 acquired – 7/20/1865 sold, scrapped 1887) steamer gunboat flagship, a Rebel shot him on the deck. He died. This was 2.5 months after the Civil War began 4/12/1861. Ward was the first U.S. Navy officer killed in the Civil War. He served 1823 to his death.

Ward was one of 111 Wickes destroyers made 1917-1921. They were rush made, as urgently needed for World War I. For example in the case of Ward, keel laying to her 7/24/1918 commissioning was only ten weeks. As World War I fighting ended though with an 11/11/1918 Armistice, most Wickes destroyers including Ward did not fight in World War I.

In the 1930s in anticipation of war or at least needing to have defensive capability, some older and mothballed USSs were prepared and re-commissioned. Ward was one of these. She was ready 1/1941. She was now at the venerable age for a destroyer, of more than 23 years.

Most Wickes did see action in World War II. However as outdated in several ways, most Wickes were modified to be used for other purposes. Some Wickes destroyers were transferred to the British Royal Naval and the Royal Canadian Navy. Great Britain in turn transferred some to the Soviet Navy. All the surviving Wickes were scrapped by 1950. Ward as just noted was one the Navy selected for its battle fleet, in case of War with Japan.

Ward's armament included the following:
- 4 × 4 inch (100 millimeter)/50 caliber guns
- 2 × 3 inch (76 millimeter)/50 caliber anti-aircraft guns
- 12 × 21 inch (533 millimeter) torpedo tubes (4x3)

Ward's homeport was Pearl Harbor. Her assignment under her new commander was to make back and forth laps across the entrance line to Pearl Harbor, in sight of Oahu. Her sentinel duty mission was to challenge any unknown surface or subsea vessel, attack if necessary, and radio the alarm upon any such detections and actions.

The Navy acquired the 86' long and 25' beam and 9' draft, 10 miles per hour, 17 crew, wooden hull New Example (1937 – 1946 transferred) purse seiner 10/28/1940. This is a type of commercial fishing boat that drags a net, weighted down at the bottom to drag along the sea bottom and buoyed at the top with floats so that its top edge is at the surface; to catch fish. The Navy had her converted into a coastal minesweeper. The conversion included installation of two .30 caliber machine guns. Her new name was the USS Condor. The Navy transferred Condor to the Coast Guard for operation. The Coast Guard put Condor into service 4/18/1941. She arrived Oahu 5/1941 for duty in Hawaiian waters.

Condor's Deck Officer and Night Watch Ensign McCloy spotted a white wake with his binoculars at 03:42 on 12/7/1942 which was a Sunday, fifty yards ahead. McCloy assumed that it was the wake of a submarine's periscope. McCloy asked for a second opinion from Quartermaster Uttrick, who concurred. The submarine was motoring westerly at ten miles an hour. Condor Captain (Lieutenant Commander) Monroe Hubbell was notified.

Condor was less than two miles off the entrance to Pearl Harbor. This was near the entrance buoys to the harbor, where USS submarines were not allowed to sail submerged. Captain Hubbell using his binoculars agreed that the wake was from a submarine's periscope.

Condor blinkered signal lights to Ward at 03:57 of the sighting. Ward's Officer of the Deck Lieutenant Junior Grade Oscar Goepner (a reservist) recorded the message. He roused Captain Outerbridge. Outerbridge summoned the above-mentioned reservists to general quarters. Outerbridge searched for the submarine an hour and a half visually and by sonar, to no avail. Outerbridge requested confirmation of the sighting from Condor. When a positive response was received, he renewed the search.

By 6:00, Ward resumed its regular patrol pattern off the entrance to Pearl Harbor. Outerbridge chose to not report his search effort at this time, and nor did Condor. Both Captains suspected that the mystery submarine was American, motoring submerged in error.

The Navy operated the U.S. Army's Hawaiian Department, Antares-class, 401' long and 54' beam and 24' draft, 13 miles per hour, 197 crew, USS Antares (1922 – 1947 scrapped) as an auxiliary transport and general stores ship. Her armament included six guns. These were two 5" and four 3". She did not have anti-aircraft guns. Antares was used as part of the urgent program to develop an air ferry route through the southern Pacific Ocean to the Philippines, which would avoid Japanese mandated islands in the central Pacific Ocean. This route would be used, if war developed between Japan and the United States.

Antares departed Oahu 11/3/1941 for Canton Island with Army sappers and civilians (308 men total aboard), and supplies. Canton is one of the Phoenix Islands, which were (and still are) controlled by the United States. She towed a 510' long, 500-ton barge carrying construction equipment and two smaller barges. The two smaller barges foundered en route to Canton and were dropped.

Antares returned to Oahu by way of Palmyra Atoll, towing the 510' barge. Palmyra is one of the Northern Line Islands. Palmyra was part of the Hawaiian Territory annexed by the United States in 1898. Today, Palmyra remains controlled by the U.S.

Antares arrived at the mouth of the entrance to Pearl Harbor early Sunday morning, 12/7/1941. Antares lay to near the harbor entrance awaiting a pilot, or possibly planning to transfer the barge to a tug. Antares altered course, slowly turning eastward. Her watch at 06:30 spotted a suspicious white wake, 0.85 miles off Antares' starboard side. This most likely was the same submarine (this determined later to be the case) that Condor had espied and reported to Ward. Antares blinkered Ward as had Condor. Lieutenant Junior Grade Goepner recorded the message. He again woke up Captain Outerbridge.

Condor and Antares' speeds were 10 and 13 miles per hour, compared to Ward's 40. Condor and Antares were lightly armed, compared to Ward. Condor and Antares did not have torpedoes or depth charges or sonar, which destroyers had. As slow and under-armed, this is why Condor and Antares when sighting the suspicious wakes, notified Ward to respond and investigate and attack if necessary.

At about the same time, a patrolling Navy PBY Catalina flying boat from Patrol Squadrons VP-14 noted the submarine's location. Pilot Ensign William Tanner had his crew drop smoke markers, on the contact.

The submarine was tailing or trying to tail Antares to enter the harbor, when the anti-submarine nets at the harbor entrance were pulled out of the way. The nets had been opened at 04:58 to allow passage by Condor and Antares, and some smaller ships.

An enormous Imperial Japanese Navy attack fleet had departed a naval port (separately) at Hittokapu Bay (now called Kasatka Bay) on Kasatka Island (now called Iturup Island) in the Kurile Islands 11/26/1941. The ships were headed to a staging point northwest of Hawaii. This departure site was chosen for the base of the attack fleet as its population was all Japanese (no foreigners) and sparse, and as fog was almost constant. Also, the Kuriles are in the direction of Hawaii.

The 56 Kurile Islands are northeast of Japan's major islands. Japan owned these islands. After World War II though, the Soviet Union annexed the Kurile Islands. The Soviet Union expelled the Japanese living there, forcing them to move to another of the Japanese islands.

To avoid detection, the Japanese fleet followed a storm front and maintained radio silence. At the same time, Tokyo broadcast radio signals from other sites to disguise the location of the warships.

The fifty-one ships and boats of the Task Force included six aircraft carriers (two fleet carriers, two light carriers, two converted carriers {one converted from a battleship hull, one converted from a battlecruiser hull}), two battleships, two heavy cruisers, one light cruiser, nine destroyers, eight tankers, and twenty-three fleet submarines. The submarine spotted by Condor and Antares was a mini-submarine, launched from one of five fleet mother submarines. Counting the five piggyback, mini-submarines, the naval fleet was 56 ships and boats.

The purposes of the twenty-three fleet submarines were as follows:

- protect the surface ships (especially the carriers) en route to Hawaii
- in the case of five of the submarines, convey and launch five, top-secret, midget submarines

- loiter outside the entrance/exit channel of Pearl Harbor to torpedo sink USSs fleeing the aerial attack if detected or during the attack, and/or searching for the Japanese fleet; also if these USSs could be sunk in the channel, this would block the exit of other USSs, or damage their hulls if not seen or detected and struck; as it turned out, this action was not needed
- protect the Japanese fleet on its return to Japan

The mother submarines were modified so that the baby submarines could be lashed aft of their conning towers. These toting submarines were Type-C cruiser submarines. They were newly commissioned, 1940 or 1941. They were 359' long with a 30' beam, and pulled 18' of water. For comparison purposes, almost all USS submarines used in World War II were only 312' long, with a 27' beam. The most common German submarine was 220' long with a 20' beam.

To sum up, Japan's World War II submarines were generally the largest. They were fifteen and 63% longer than their American and German counterparts, and eleven and 50% wider. Considering that interior space of submarines is at a premium and the fact that the average American sailor and average German sailor were physically larger than the average Japanese sailor, there is an incongruity.

The Type-Cs were capable of long-range missions, able to cruise more than 16,000 miles surface at 18 miles per hour. Submerged under battery power, the range was 69 miles at 3.5 miles per hour. Their maximum surface and submerged speeds were a swift 27 and nine miles per hour.

Armament wise, the Type-Cs were equipped with a 5.5" inch deck gun as well as an anti-aircraft gun, and up to 20 torpedoes.

As designed to ferry mini-submarines, Type-Cs did not have aviation facilities.

Type-Cs and other Japanese submarines were later in the war modified to convey kaitens (manned, suicide torpedoes).

Type-C submarine crew size was 100 to 110. None of the five Pearl Harbor bound, mother submarines or their crewmen (more than 500 sailors total) survived the War, as follows:

Submarine	Sinking
I-22	12/11/1942: Elco-class, USS PT-122 motor torpedo boat sank off New Britain
I-18	02/11/1943: Fletcher-class, USS Fletcher destroyer depth charge sank southeast of Guadalcanal
I-24	06/11/1943: PC 461-class, USS PC-487 submarine chaser depth charge surfaced off Kiska Island, then rammed twice to sink
I-20	09/03/1943: Buckley-class, USS Ellet destroyer depth charge sank off New Hebrides
I-16	05/19/1944: Benham-class, USS England destroyer hedgehog sank northeast of Buin

This mini-submarine that Ward was hunting was one of five, Ko-hyoteki-class, 78.5' long and 5.9' beam and 9.9' in height (keel to top of the conning tower), 46-ton displacement submerged, two crew, Japanese midget submarines. The midgets had one periscope. A 32", rubber-encased radio antenna was just forward of the conning tower hatch. They were equipped with external, net-cutting shears; operated from inside. Propulsion came from a 600 horsepower, electric motor; driving contra-rotating propellers on the same shaft. They were very fast under and on top at 22 and 26 miles per hour. Their underwater range was 21, 92, and 115 miles at 22.0, 6.9, and 2.3 miles per hour. Surface range at puttering speed was over 200 miles.

They did not have a diesel engine to recharge their batteries. Therefore, necessity required meticulous planning for each mission. The exception would be if recovery or escape was not a concern. This seemed to be the case at Oahu.

The midgets' armament consisted of two 450 millimeter torpedoes, fitted with a half-ton of explosives. The tubes were one above the other on the port side. The torpedo warheads were more than twice that of the warhead of the aerial bombs, now winging their way toward Oahu on Japanese bombers launched from carriers. The midgets did not have guns.

To launch the midgets, the mother submarine surfaced. The two crewmen exited the mother submarine onto her deck, through a hatch. They opened the midget's hatch, climbed in, and closed and dogged the hatch. After systems were checked, sailors unfastened the baby from the deck mounts. The deck hands then climbed back into the mother submarine, and then closed and dogged that hatch. The mother submarine then dived, floating the midget off.

The midgets remained in radio communication with the mother submarine. In fact, the radio operator on the mother submarine was considered part of the midget's crew. He had trained on the operation of the midgets, so as to understand how it operated. A junior officer conned the boat. A petty officer manipulated valves and moved ballast to control trim and diving.

These midgets were completed only several months before the Pearl Harbor attack. Their development and manufacture were top secret of course. In fact, the U.S. Navy did not know that Japan had developed and made these undersea torpedo conveyances. In fact again, no other countries were aware of these mini-submarines.

The timing was such, that the crews had not had much training.

The main advantage of the babies of course was that as smaller; they were harder to see on the surface or detect when under. If spotted or detected, they were harder to hit with guns, hedgehogs, or depth charges. Also, they were able to navigate shallow waters such as lakes, bays, rivers, and harbors.

The five midgets were launched at about 01:00, 12/7/1941. The launch sites varied from five to 13 miles off the entrance to Pearl Harbor. The plan was that they would enter the narrow, net-protected channel into Pearl Harbor by trailing a USS or cargoman. They would then surface and torpedo USSs either:

- during the aerial attack when at anchor
- or when USSs were headed out of the harbor to escape the Japanese attack, and/or trying to find and attack the Japanese armada

The midgets would then dive, escape the harbor, rendezvous with their mother submarines under cover of darkness for recovery, and then sail for home (but see below for likelihood of this happening). In regard to escaping the harbor, the nets would have been open to allow undamaged USSs to exit to flee the aerial attack and/or search for the Japanese warships. The recovery would be the next morning (12/8/1941). If the midget was damaged and could not be attached to the mother submarine or otherwise disabled, the two crewmen would scuttle the midget using an explosive charge to penetrate the hull, and then board the mother submarine.

Captain Outerbridge again called general quarters. Ward sped from six to 29 miles an hour toward the target. Outerbridge ordered gunfire with number one and three cannons. These were 4" (100 millimeter)/50-caliber guns. Number one's projectile was high. Number three though hit the submarine's conning tower, just above its merge point with the hull. As the distance was almost a third of a mile, (another source though states that the distance was only 50 yards) and at such a small target, and as this aiming was before dawn -- this was an amazing shot, whether 50 or 580 yards. The gunners were reservists, as noted above.

Ward charged toward the midget, to ram. The submarine dived, or maybe just sank at this point. Ward rolled four depth charges off its stern, set to go off at 100'. Ward circled back and sighted an oil slick. Sound detection equipment heard nothing. Both submariners died (drowned or suicide). Thus, Ward fired the first in anger American shots of the not yet declared Pacific Theater War; an hour before the first wave of Japanese aircraft arrived.

Outerbridge radioed word of the sighting and attack at 06:51 to the Fourteenth Naval District, as follows:

We have dropped depth charges upon subs operating in the defensive sea area.

Outerbridge thought over his message and feared that his superiors may have construed that he had only responded to underwater noise; when of course the crew had spotted a suspicious submarine on the surface, shot at it, depth charged it, and apparently sank it (per the oil slick). Accordingly, he sent a second much more earnest message two minutes later (06:53), as follows:

We have attacked, fired upon, and dropped depth charges upon submarine operating in the defensive sea area.

Outerbridge's messages were received by two Navy commands, the 14th Naval District and the Pacific Fleet. Due to delay in translating the encrypted messages, skepticism, a busy phone line, the hour of the day and the day of the week which was before 7:00 on a Sunday, etc.; communication of the emergency message up the chain of command was delayed. It was not until 07:40 that the 14th Naval District duty officer received the decrypted message.

Lieutenant Commander Harold Kaminski (1886 – 1953 SC) relayed the message to Admiral Husband Kimmel (1882 KY – 1968 CT). Kimmel was Commander in Chief of the U.S. Pacific Fleet. This was 47 minutes after Outerbridge's second radio report, on attacking a submarine. Eight minutes later, the first wave of Japanese, carrier-launched aircraft struck. The 23 years and 26 days of peace for the United States had ended.

Ward was converted to a fast transport the next year. Three years later to the day of sinking the mini-submarine (so 12/7/1944), Ward was escorting a convoy in

Ormoc Bay, Philippines. Three, twin engine, Mitsubishi G4M kamikaze bombers dived for Ward. Ward diverted two of the bombers into the ocean, with 20 millimeter and 76 millimeter anti-aircraft fire. The third though crashed into Ward at the waterline at 09:56 on the port side. The bomber entered the forward part of the boiler room, and the after part of the lower troop space. One of the bomber's engines passed through Ward, exiting at the waterline on the starboard side. Severely damaged, flooding, and afire with no or low water pressure to extinguish, Ward's Captain (Lieutenant R. E. Parwell, USNR) ordered *abandon ship*. Miraculously, Ward had no deaths, and only one sailor wounded.

The new, Sumner-class, 376' long and 40' beam and 13' draft, 39 miles per hour, 336 crew, USS O'Brien (1944 – 1972 target sunk) destroyer was part of the convoy. She was ordered to finish Ward off with gunfire to sink her, to prevent the Japanese from capturing. Ward's crew was taken off. O'Brien's Captain since 6/1944 ordered the sinking of Ward, with nostalgic regret. His name was William Outerbridge. As ordered, his sailors fired upon and sunk Ward. Even in the enormous expanse of the Pacific Ocean during the chaos of a War, it can be a small world.

The USS Ward is shown below. The next photograph is the 4" gun used to sink the mini-submarine, on display at the Minnesota State Capitol building in St. Paul. The gun was removed when Ward was converted to a fast transport in 1942. The gun monument was installed in 1958, the year of the Minnesota Centennial as a state.

A plaque lists the naval reservists from Saint Paul who served on Ward. It is mounted in the St. Paul City Hall on the third floor, between the council and mayoral offices.

The third image is a propaganda picture made to honor the nine Japanese submariners who died in the attack. By this time, Japan knew that the tenth submariner was a prisoner of war (details below). He had signed on to an apparent suicide mission. A USS destroyer shot at his mini-submarine. He almost drowned when his craft sank, collapsing into unconsciousness when he finally floated to shore. He was unconscious or near it when captured. As he did not die in the effort and had not since committed suicide, he was considered unworthy to be included on the *heavenly* poster.

The Imperial Japanese Navy struck his name from their records. He ceased to exist, as far as the Japanese military was concerned.

Seaman First Class Alan Sanford (1923 – 2015 PA) was the last surviving member of Wards' gun crews. At age 18, he headed the crew that fired the first shot, but missed the submarine. Sanford is buried at Arlington National Cemetery. Outerbridge was awarded the Navy Cross for his actions at Pearl Harbor. The Cross is the Navy's second-highest decoration awarded for valor in combat.

In 1942, Outerbridge was assigned to the Office of the Chief of Naval Transportation, Washington, D.C. He returned to sea 6/1944, to command the already-mentioned USS O'Brien destroyer. The O'Brien was part of the 6/6/1944 D-Day invasion of Normandy, protecting Allied forces landing on the beaches by shelling German positions near the landing zones. O'Brien did similar when Allied forces landed at the French deep-water port of Cherbourg. The Cherbourg Battle ran 6/6/1944 – 6/30/1944, when the remaining German forces surrendered. The Allies desperately needed a deep-water port, to bring in more troops and supplies and equipment directly from the United States, instead of through England.

Outerbridge and O'Brien then sailed to the Pacific Theater to participate in the liberation of the Philippines. In a strange twist of fate already described above, the O'Brien gun-sank the USS Ward 12/7/1944, which had been severely damaged by a kamikaze attack.

After World War II, Outerbridge saw both shore and sea duty. He commanded Destroyer Division 42 1945-1946. He next joined the staff at the Naval War College at Newport, Rhode Island. He returned to sea in 1949 to command Destroyer Squadron Four. He was Chief of Staff and Aide to the Commander of Destroyer Flotilla Four 1950-1951. He joined the staff of the Industrial College of the Armed Forces (Washington, DC) 1951-1952. He was Assistant Chief of Staff for Plans, Operations and Intelligence, Naval Forces, Far East 1952-1953.

Outerbridge returned to sea yet again, to command the Baltimore-class, 674' long and 71'beam and 21' draft, 38 miles per hour, 1,142 crew USS Los Angeles (1945 – 1975 scrapped) cruiser 1953-1955. He was head of the Transportation and Petroleum Branch in the Office of the Chief of Naval Operations (Logistics, Plans) until his 1957 retirement, rank of Rear Admiral. Outerbridge served 30 years.

The 1970 Japanese-American, biographical *Tora, Tora, Tora* movie dramatizes the attack on Oahu and Pearl Harbor. Jerry Fogel (1936 NY -) portrayed Outerbridge. The about the same size as Ward, Edsall-class, 306' long and 37' beam and 10' draft, USS Finch (1943 – 1974 scrapped) destroyer escort portrayed the USS Ward in the movie.

Commander Mitsuo Fuchida (1902 Japan – 1976 Japan, diabetes) led the first aircraft attack group 12/7/1941 on Oahu and Pearl Harbor. He saw no activity of note. Fuchida slid back the canopy of the single engine, three crew (commander, pilot, gunner/radio operator), low wing Nakajima B5N2 torpedo bomber; and fired a single dark blue flare called a *black dragon.* This was the signal to the others to attack.

Fuchida ordered his radio operator at 7:53 to send the coded signal *tora, tora, tora* to his superiors on the 855' IJN Akagi (1927 – 6/5/1942 American aircraft damaged at Midway, Japanese destroyers torpedoed to sink to avoid capture, 267 of 1,630 crew lost {16%}), the flagship for the assault. The word *tora* means *tiger* in Japanese. However, Fuchida was not communicating about jungle cats. *Tora* is an abbreviated radio code word. It is short for *totsugeki raigeki* which translates to *lightning attack.* Fuchida was telling his superiors that the objective of complete surprise had been achieved.

Fuchida admired Adolph Hitler (1889 Austria - 4/30/1945 Berlin, pistol suicide), to the point where he grew a Hitler-style mustache during World War II.

Fuchida served in the Japanese Navy 1924-1945, retiring as a Captain. After the War, he was dumbfounded when he learned of the humane way that the Americans treated Japanese prisoners of war. This was inexplicable to him, as the bushido code mandated revenge as not optional, but a responsibility for an offended party to restore honor. In the fall of 1948, Fuchida read a pamphlet (*I Was a Prisoner of Japan*) about the life of Doolittle Raider Jacob DeShazer (1912 OR – 2008 OR), who was much abused by the Japanese as a prisoner of war. After the War, DeShazer attended a Methodist Church connected college to train to be a missionary. He worked as a Christian missionary in Japan 1948-1978.

DeShazer's story affected Fuchida. He read the Bible. He became a Christian 9/1949. Fuchida and DeShazer met 5/1950, which further impressed and motivated Fuchida. Fuchida traveled throughout the United States and Europe, telling his stories as a Christian evangelist.

The U.S. Navy had several run-ins with German warships in the Atlantic Ocean September and October, 1941. Ward's early morning 12/7/1941 action however was the first naval action by American forces in the Pacific Ocean area, for what became known as World War II.

After launching their torpedoes, the midget submarine crews were to either:

- Scuttle their boats next to other USS warships in the shallow harbor to temporarily block them from leaving the harbor, or hopefully even damage their hulls when rushing to sea and not seeing or detecting the sunken submarine in the scramble to get underway; the two crewmen were then to swim ashore, and try to mingle with the population for who knows how long

- Sail back out of the harbor and beach a distance from Pearl Harbor, swim to shore, and hide out until later rescued; some suspected that safe houses on Oahu had been arranged for the submariners, but no evidence of such has ever emerged

- Sail back out of the harbor and rendezvous with their mother submarines or Japanese surface ships early 12/8/1941 morning, eight miles west of Lanai; this would be coordinated by radio communication

However, the ten crewmen (and everybody else for that matter, enlisted men as well as officers) realized that their batteries would not get them to the recovery point at the designated time. Therefore, the submariners knew that their fate was bleak – they would be killed in combat, drown, be captured, try to hide out in the mountains or brush, or try to fade into the local population.

The latter was unlikely. However, many Japanese lived on the Hawaiian Islands, so blending in was a possibility. These Japanese Hawaiians for the most part were fluent in Hawaiian, or at least able to communicate to get by. The submariners did not speak Hawaiian at all. Also, the submariners had not even brought civilian clothes to change into, from their IJN uniforms. To sum up, it appears that the Japanese Navy expected them to die in one way or another, if they could not be recovered. And as just noted, recovery was very unlikely. And again as noted, mixing in with the locals was a very, very long shot.

The Japanese military code at the time was that the only options were victory or death – certainly not surrender and capture. The Emperor and military leaders much contorted this philosophy from the Bushido, samurai warrior code of conduct. The code developed and evolved in Japan between the 16th and 20th centuries -- but especially during the 1660 to 1868 Shogunate ruling period. Therefore, the submariners probably considered and accepted their mission to be of a suicidal nature.

Again in the Japanese military, it went without saying that death in combat or by suicide if victory not attainable was honorable; and wonderful things would happen to one's spirit. Conversely, defeat with capture was immensely disgraceful and shameful to self, family, community, country, and Emperor. In fact per the brainwashing, capture was much worse than death. To reiterate, defeat was acceptable, well even admirable and desirable, if dying in the process from the enemy or by own hand.

As it turned out and as hard as it is to believe, Japan managed to brainwash its military personnel to this effect. The number of Japanese soldiers, airmen, sailors, and marines who fought to the death even when overwhelmed instead of surrendering (so this basically a route to suicide) or killed themselves, numbered in the tens of thousands for World War II. The prisoner of war (POW) camps in the U.S. were flush with Germans and some Italians, but very few Japanese. Some Japanese POWs were locked up in Australia, as well as the U.S. Wherever, there were not many Japanese POWs.

As a supporting statistic, only one Japanese military man surrendered for every 120 Japanese killed in battle in World War II. The figure for the Allies was one military man surrendering for every three killed in battle.

This brainwashing even extended to Japan's civilians as well, with many buying into it; willing to fight to death or kill selves, than to be part of a defeat. In fact, hundreds of civilians did such on Saipan Island in 1944 and the Ryukyu Islands (especially Okinawa) in 1945. A few even killed their children, to spare them the abuse and torture and then execution they had been told was coming from the non-human, monster, American soldiers. They were also told that the Americans would cook up and eat their children, after torturing them to death. Again, Japanese propaganda that Americans were beyond cruel took as well.

Japanese military men were mostly in the know as were some civilians as to how their side treated Allied POWs, so from this standpoint they also expected the same.

It is astoundingly difficult for normal people to grasp how effective these propaganda campaigns on death is best and great, capture is horrible, and Americans being sadistic torturers and killers were, from the Emperor and the government and the military of all ranks on down to military personnel and even civilians.

By the way, the mini-submarines were equipped with swords and pistols -- and this was not just for some form of symbolism.

To sum up, the midget submariners were expected to die in the effort or by their own hand to avoid capture, if recovery was not possible.

As noted above, the plan was for the midget submarines to follow USSs or merchantmen into the harbor when anti-submarine netting was pulled back, to allow passage of USSs or American civilian ships. Alternatively, some or all of the submarines had net cutting devices mounted on the bow, controlled from the cabin. Of the five submarines, only two made it into the harbor. The circumstances of the midget encountered by and sunk by Ward, were described above. The actions of the other four were as follows:

- One had a broken gyrocompass. It struck a reef thrice just outside the entrance to the harbor. It grounded at 8:00. The Bagley-class, 342' long and 36' beam and 13' draft, 44 miles per hour, 158 crew, USS Helm (1937 – 1947 scrapped) destroyer spotted the stranded submarine and attacked at 08:17. Helm missed, but its fire created waves which ended up freeing the submarine from the reef. However, Ensign Kazuo Sakamaki (1918 Japan – 1999 Japan) was knocked unconscious. Chief Warrant Officer Kiyoshi Inagaki

(1915 Japan – 12/8/1941 drowned near Pearl Harbor) dived the submarine. Inagaki resurfaced at 8:18. Helm fired again and missed again. Inagaki dived the submarine again.

The grounding damaged the vessel, to the point where she could not fire one of her torpedoes. Part of the submarine flooded. The seawater came into contact with the batteries, emitting a toxic gas affecting the two sailors. Sakamaki came to and decided to make another effort to enter the harbor. Again, they hit the reef. They reversed off the reef to make another attempt. The submarine grounded again. They adjusted the ballast and freed the submarine. On their next attempt to enter the harbor, depth charge attacks from Helm disabled her one operating torpedo and damaged the periscope. Sakamaki and Inagaki decided to abort their attack efforts, and return to their mother submarine off Lanai. The battery gases overcame them. The submarine was carried by the currents.

The pair came to. By this time, it was the next morning (12/8/1941, Monday). They decided to beach at Waimanalo (east side of Oahu). The motor broke or the batteries died, and they hit a reef. Sakamaki ordered Inagaki to abandon ship. Sakamaki set the scuttling charge and followed Inagaki out. The charge did not detonate, probably as it had been contaminated by seawater.

Sakamaki swam to shore. He collapsed on the beach near Bellows Field, and lost consciousness. Hawaiian-American Army Corporal David Akui (1920 – 1987 Honolulu) and Lieutenant Paul Plybon when out on patrol the morning after the sneak attacks found the prone and still unconscious Sakamaki on the beach. Sakamaki came to. Akui and Plybon took him into custody. Sakamaki was the only one of the ten mini-submariners who survived.

Inagaki drowned. His body washed ashore the next day and was picked up.

Corporal Akui by the way served in the Army 1940-1945, retiring as a Master Sergeant. He joined Merrill's Marauders, fighting the Japanese in Burma.

When beached, Army planes bombed the submarine but missed. The waves from the explosions though again freed the submarine from the reef. It floated toward shore, near Bellows Field. Cables were attached. An Army tractor pulled her ashore. The submarine was dismantled. The pieces were trucked to the Submarine Naval Base at Pearl Harbor for inspection. Some documents were recovered.

After inspection and analysis, the mini-submarine was reassembled, placed on a barge, and towed to California. She was hauled around the country on a trailer to motivate young men to enlist and sell war bonds.

She was put on outdoor display in 1991 at the National Museum of the Pacific War in Fredericksburg, Texas, where she is today. She was designated a National Historic Landmark.

Sakamaki became the first POW captured by the Americans in World War II. He was known as *Japanese POW #1*. He resided the rest of the War at POW camps in the United States including at Kenedy, Texas. As already noted, Sakamaki as a POW was not joined by many of his brethren. He asked his

American captors to kill him or give him the means to commit suicide, per the contorted Bushido code. His American captors did not oblige.

By the time Sakamaki was repatriated at the end of World War II, he was a strong pacifist. He wed. They had two children. He worked for Toyota as an executive, becoming president of its Brazilian subsidiary in 1969. Many Japanese live in Brazil, and Toyota sold many cars. Sakamaki returned to Japan in 1983. He worked for Toyota until his 1987 retirement at age 68.

Sakamaki published his war memoirs in 1949. However, he refused to speak about the war – too painful. In 1991 fifty years after his capture at the age of 73, he attended a historical conference at the National Museum of the Pacific War in Texas, mentioned above. At that conference, he was reunited with his submarine after a 50-year absence. He cried from the memory, and over the death of Chief Warrant Officer Inagaki and the other Japanese submariners that day. He also finally started to speak on his wartime experiences. He died in 1999, age 81.

- One midget was damaged by a depth charge from either USS Ward or the Farragut-class, 341' long and 34' beam and 9' draft, 42 miles per hour, 100 crew, USS Monaghan (1933 – 1944 typhoon sank east of the Philippines, 94 of 100 crew lost) ready-duty destroyer, before she could fire her torpedoes. She sank. The crew abandoned ship and drowned. Navy divers found her off Keehi Lagoon east of the Pearl Harbor entrance at a depth of 75' in 1960. She was raised. The hatches were un-dogged. No human remains were found. The bow, still armed with the two torpedoes, was removed and dumped at sea. What was left was sent to Japan. Japan fabricated and attached a replacement bow, and otherwise restored it. It was put on display in 1962 at the Imperial Japanese Naval Academy at Etajima Island, Hiroshima Bay, Japan.

- Another midget entered the harbor. From the channel on the northwestern side of Ford Island, she fired her torpedoes at the Curtiss-class, 527' long and 69' beam and 22' draft, 23 miles per hour, 1,195 crew, USS Curtiss (1940 – 1972 scrapped) seaplane tender, and the already mentioned USS Monaghan destroyer. Curtiss had been able to get under way right after the Japanese bombers arrived, without getting hit. The torpedoes from the midgets' missed. However, one came within 50 yards of Monaghan. One torpedo smashed into a dock at Pearl City; the other into the shore of Ford Island.

Pearl City is a community on the north shore of Pearl Harbor. Ford Island is a round island, in the center of Pearl Harbor. The U.S. Navy increased the island's size from 0.52 square miles to 0.69 square miles (32% larger) in the 1930s, with dredge out of Pearl Harbor. The dredging was done to deepen the harbor for deep draft battleships.

Curtiss was firing at the Japanese aircraft. At 08:36, Curtiss spotted the submarine's periscope and began fire. The submarine surfaced at 8:40. Curtiss claimed they hit the conning tower, twice.

The 492' long and 70' beam and 24' draft, 34 miles per hour, 1,075 crew, USS Tangier (1940 – 1962 scrapped) seaplane tender (converted from a cargo ship) responded quickly, as had Curtiss. She also fired on the submarine and may have hit it.

Destroyer Monaghan rammed the submarine. The submarine sank or dived. Monaghan dropped two depth charges at 8:43. The ramming and/or depth charges sank the submarine, which again was probably already damaged from the shelling from Curtiss and/or Tangier.

The submarine was later recovered. The wreck was used as construction fill for a new landside pier at the Pearl Harbor submarine base. The hulk was recovered in 1952 with the intention of restoring it. However, she was so badly corroded from chlorine gas from the batteries, that she was re-buried at the same location. This location today is thought to be under a parking lot near the submarine base.

Per one account, the two crew were buried in a nearby cemetery in 1941. Per another account, the crew's bones remain entombed in the boat.

- The fifth and last submarine (one of two that entered the harbor) fired her torpedoes at the St. Louis-class, 609' long and 61' beam and 20' draft, 37 miles per hour, 868 crew, USS St. Louis (1939 – 1951 sold to Brazil, sank 1980 when under tow to ship-breakers in Taiwan) light cruiser; as she sortied from the harbor. This was 20 minutes after the last air raid had ended. St. Louis veered successfully. Both torpedoes hit a reef near shore and exploded. The midget surfaced, as now so much lighter with her torpedoes launched. St. Louis fired. Her gunners claimed they hit the submarine and sank it. Destroyers also pounded the harbor bottom with depth charges. The submarine escaped to the relative quiet of the West Loch area. The crew scuttled the submarine there. Their fate is unknown – maybe drowned trying to make it to shore, maybe suicide.

  Almost 2.5 years later, the 5/21/1944 West Loch disaster (explosion of munitions) occurred. Six tank-landing ships sank, and two more were damaged. These ships were 328' long with a 50' beam. Death estimates were 163 to more than 400 sailors and marines. The six wrecks were craned up, loaded on barges, and dumped three miles south of Pearl Harbor.

  Although not recognized at the time, this midget submarine was part of the debris collected and moved. In 2009, a research team assembled by PBS Nova identified one of the wrecks as the fifth mini-submarine. Its torpedo tubes were empty.

  The PBS member television station WGBH of Boston has produced the award-winning Nova science series since 1974. It is broadcast in more than 100 countries besides the United States.

Some experts think a torpedo from one of the two submarines that made it into the harbor struck the Colorado-class, 624' long and 97' beam and 31' draft, 24 miles per hour, 1,407 crew, USS West Virginia (1923 – 12/7/1941 sank Pearl Harbor, raised and repaired, 1959 scrapped) battleship; or the Nevada-class, 583' long and 96' beam and 29' draft, 24 miles per hour, 1,398 crew, USS Oklahoma (1916 – 12/7/1941 sank Pearl Harbor, raised but not repaired, scrapped 1946) battleship. West Virginia was hit by seven aerial torpedo bombs (one did not detonate); and two bombs made from 16", armor-piercing naval shells fitted with wooden, aerial fins. Neither of the latter exploded. Oklahoma was hit by up to eight aerial torpedo bombs. Again, one of the mini-submarines may have hit one of the battleships with one of its torpedoes, contributing to its sinking.

A photograph taken from a Japanese plane during the attack bolstered this theory. It appears to show a midget submarine inside the harbor, firing torpedoes at Battleship Row. This suggests that the capsizing of Oklahoma may have been accelerated by a midget submarine torpedo hit. As already noted, the mini-submarine's torpedo had roughly twice the explosive power of those toted by the aircraft from the carriers.

In that photograph where the torpedoes' paths had supposedly started, sprays indicated that a midget submarine was rocking up and down due to the force and great weight loss of a launched torpedo or torpedoes. The forces and sudden decrease in weight caused the back end to rise, to the point where the propellers surfaced and kicked up sprays of seawater.

To sum up, four of the five midgets sank for one reason or another. The fifth beached on the east side of Oahu. Again, this mini-submarine was hauled around the U.S, as a prop in recruiting for the military and selling war bonds.

As already mentioned, nine of the ten midget submarine crewmen died. The tenth was captured. The cause of death for some of the nine is not known – but drowned, killed by shells or depth charges, or suicide some way.

Research submersibles located the midget submarine that Ward sank in 2002. This was in 1,250' of water, 3.5 miles outside the entrance to Pearl Harbor. However, its identity was not confirmed until 2009. The inspection showed that the submarine sank from the damage to the conning tower just above the hull from Ward's gun, as opposed to damage from the depth charges. As already noted, this was a fantastic shot.

The Navy's failure to respond to this warning from Outerbridge and to assume radar showing incoming Japanese aircraft were friendlies (although the friendly aircraft {four engine B-17 bombers} were to fly in from the northeast, and those detected were coming from the northwest), led to the 12/7/1941 debacle at Oahu. Two thousand, three hundred and thirty-five and 1,143 American military men died and were wounded. Another 68 and 35 civilians died and were injured. Nineteen ships were sunk or damaged, including all eight battleships. Hundreds of aircraft were damaged or destroyed, most on the ground.

If Outerbridge's warnings had been heeded, fighters would have been sent up and warships sent out of the harbor. Even though American fighters based at Oahu were second-rate compared to Japan's fighters, the outcome would have been much less. These second-rate American fighters were Curtiss P-36 Hawks and Curtiss P-40 Warhawks, introduced in 1938 and 1939. Of note, several of each did manage to get fueled and armed and up, and downed a few Japanese aircraft;

maybe as many as ten. This was the only combat seen by the Hawks though in World War II, as so deficient to the Zeroes. The Warhawks though saw service throughout World War II; and did well. However, the Army Air Forces got much better fighters than Warhawks by 1942; thank goodness.

Also, damage to USSs would have been much, much, much less if they had steamed out of the harbor, and separated from each other as opposed to one big, immobile, sleeping target. It is much more difficult for an aircraft to drop a bomb on a moving ship compared to one anchored; especially if that ship is firing back at you. It took many minutes for the U.S. to respond; minutes the U.S. did not have.

Lastly, the Japanese Commander probably would have aborted the second air attack wave, if the Americans' response had not been so feeble.

The IJN two crew Ko-hyoteki-class midget submarine on display at the U.S. Navy Submarine Force Library and Museum near Groton, Connecticut; and the contra-rotating stern propellers of that submarine are shown below:

In the run up to World War II, Japan made fifty, two-man, electric powered midget submarines of several different classes; and another 355 during the War. These were all about 78' long with only a 6' beam, and 6' high (not counting the conning tower). Displacement was 47 tons. The fact that Japanese men (sailors in this case) are small, worked in their favor. Many of these submarines never saw service, though.

These midget submarines were marvels for the day, but they were far from perfect. Trim and balance control was difficult, battery life was short, monitoring remaining battery power was only an estimate, etc. As the War progressed, Japanese engineers made improvements.

Besides Pearl Harbor, Japan used the midgets at Guadalcanal, Aleutians, Philippines, Saipan (Mariana Islands), Okinawa, Diego Suarez (Madagascar) Harbor, and Sydney (Australia) Harbor. The contribution of the midgets to Japan's war effort was meager, due to their limited range; and effective defenses by the Allies. A few notable Japanese Navy successes though, included the following:

- On the night of 5/29-30/1942, mother submarines launched two babies near Diego Suarez harbor.

- o One entered the harbor. The Flower-class, 205' long and 33' beam and 12' draft, HMS Genista (1941 – 1947 sold) and also Flower-class HMS Thyme (1941 – 1947 sold) corvettes detected the submarine and tossed depth charges. The depth charges caused no or only minor damage.

  The submarine managed to fire one torpedo into the Revenge-class, 621' long and 101' beam and 34' draft, HMS Ramillies (1913 – 1949 scrapped) battleship. Ramillies was severely damaged, but repaired. The midget then hit and sunk the British Loyalty tanker with its second torpedo. Loyalty was refloated and repaired.

- The two crewmen beached and ran inland (Madagascar). The plan was to be picked up by a Japanese submarine at a designated location. However, both were killed in a firefight with Royal Marines three days later.

  - o The second midget submarine was lost at sea. The body of one crewmember washed ashore a day later, cause of death probably drowning. The fate of the other crewmen is not known.

- On the night of 5/30-31/1942, mother submarines launched three midgets near Sydney (Australia) harbor. The harbor's eight submarine detection loops were inactive, not functioning, unmanned, or detections ignored.

  - o One became entangled in an anti-torpedo net. The HMAS Yarroma channel patrol boat moved in to investigate and unloaded depth charges. The Japanese crew destroyed their submarine with demolition charges and committed suicide.

  - o The second submarine entered the harbor and was detected. The Northampton-class, 600' long and 66' beam and 23' draft, USS Chicago (1931 – 1/30/1943 Japanese aircraft torpedo sank off Rennell Island in the Solomons, 62 of 691 crew lost {9%}) heavy cruiser fired at the submarine. The submarine launched its two torpedoes. One torpedo ran ashore on Garden Island, but failed to explode.

    The other torpedo went under a docked Dutch submarine. This torpedo then hit a breakwater and exploded under the 183' long and 37' beam, steel hull, HMAS Kuttabul (1922 – 1942 torpedo-sank in Sydney Harbor) steamer. The Australian Navy acquired the double-ended harbor ferry Kuttabul 11/1940, and had her converted to a depot ship. She was being used as an accommodation for Allied naval personnel awaiting transfer to their warships. Kuttabul split into two pieces, which both sank. Nineteen and two Australian and British sailors died, and another ten were injured.

    The submarine slipped out of the harbor. Its wreck was found 18 miles north, in 2006. The fate of the two crewmen is unknown.

- o The 211' long and 35' beam and 12' draft, HMAS Yandra (1928 – 1959 ran aground into South Neptune Island, scrapped) coastal patrol ship/anti-submarine/mine sweeper (converted from a cargoman) espied the third submarine at the harbor entrance and tossed depth charges. The submarine fled but returned four hours later. It was depth charge sank this second time around. The two crew were killed by the explosions or committed suicide.

The Australians recovered the bodies of four Japanese mini-submarine crewmen. For the cremation, their coffins were draped with the Japanese flag and full naval honors rendered; and this in a public ceremony. The service presumably was not well attended. However, Australian politicians hoped that the Japanese Government would as a result, improve the conditions Australian POWs were experiencing in Japanese POW camps.

Japanese authorities in fact noted the respectful funeral services, and publicized same in Japan for propaganda purposes. The ploy did not work. The Japanese continued to mutilate, torture, and execute POWs, including Australians. As a result, Australia forbade similar respectful and public funerals for Japanese dead in the future.

Midget submarines are classified as submersible boats, with displacements less than 150 tons. This is the common definition. This would of course include human or manned submersible torpedoes which may be as short as 18', so there is overlap in the definitions between midget submarines and human torpedoes. But generally speaking, the definition to be a mini-submarine or midget submarine includes the following:

1) The crew must be sealed inside the craft to be a mini-submarine. This is stated as for some World War II human torpedoes, the crew externally straddled the torpedo usually behind a fairing, sort of like riding a horse. They wore diving suits, masks, and underwater breathing apparatus.
2) The torpedoes may be external (attached to the hull of the craft) or internal. If internal, the torpedoes must be launched from tubes. If the conveyance is the torpedo itself, this is not a mini-submarine.

Some vessels did not launch torpedoes. They instead were just electric-powered conveyances designed for harbor attacks. The operator attached a timed limpet mine or dropped the timed bomb on the harbor bottom, under the target ship; and then skedaddled away.

Manned torpedoes were electric propelled only, made to bomb enemy ships in harbors. The Italian and British versions were two crew, riding externally. The 24' long Italian SLC had a range of fourteen miles at three miles an hour. The 22' and 31' long British chariots had a range of 11 miles at four miles an hour. Both had successes placing their limpet mines.

The German Neger and the Japanese kaiten were both one crew, with the operator inside. The 25' long Neger's range was 56 miles at five miles an hour. It toted an exterior torpedo. The Neger though was not submersible, so was not a mini-submarine. It was a surface manned torpedo conveyance. Negers sank five warships in 1944 (four British, and one Polish) and damaged others.

The 48' long Japanese kaiten had a range of 49 miles at 14 miles an hour. It blew up upon impact with the target.

None of these manned torpedoes were made as suicide weapons, except for the kaiten. The kaiten did sink three American ships or boats. However, more than a thousand Japanese kaiten pilots died in training or on missions.

From the above discussion and generally speaking, World War II mini-submarines or midget submarines were usually at least 35' long. Crew sizes for these mini-submarines ran two to four during World War II.

Over on the other side of the world during World War II, Great Britain, Germany, and Italy designed, made, and used midget submarines. They were less technically advanced than Japan's boats. For one thing, their speed was less than half as much as Japan's Type A Ko-hyotekis and Japanese successor Type B and Type C models which came out in 1943.

Great Britain made 20 X-Craft mini-submarines, 1942-1943. They were much shorter than the 78' Japanese version described above, at 51'. The beam was 6'. They were designed to be towed underwater to the attack zone, by a mother submarine. These submarine tugs were usually either the 203' long and 24' beam and 11' draft, S-class; or the larger 277' long and 26' beam and 15' draft, T-class submarines. The mother submarine surfaced, and then transferred the mini-submarine crew by dinghy to the X-craft. After the attack, the X-craft rendezvoused with the towing submarine, attached, and was then towed away. The crew were three (commander, pilot, engineer), but sometimes four. The mini-submarines had an airlock to release and recover a diver (frogman). Therefore, one of the crew was usually a diver.

Propulsion came from a four cylinder, 42 horsepower diesel engine, and a thirty horsepower electric motor. Surface and submerged speeds were seven and six miles per hour. The boats were fitted with electromagnets to prevent detection by anti-submarine sensors. Some had hydraulically-powered torpedo net cutters operated from inside.

Armament consisted of two, detachable, 4,400-pound, time-fused, amatol bombs. Amatol is a mixture of trinitrotoluene and ammonium nitrate. The combination explosion is much more powerful than trinitrotoluene alone. These were to be dropped on the seabed beneath the target ship, and detonated after the midget moved off.

The first successful use was not until 9/1943, Operation Source. The mission was to damage or even sink German warships based in Northern Norway. Germany occupied Norway 4/1940 through the end of the European War, 5/1945. Four X-Craft were launched. Two of the four placed charges under the Bismarck-class, 824' long and 118' beam and 31' draft, German battleship Tirpitz (1941 – 11/12/1944 British bombers sank off Norway, 1,000 of 2,065 crew lost {48%}), moored in Kafjord Harbor (northern Norway).

Tirpitz spent much of World War II stationed in several fjords along the coast of Norway, to deter the Allies from invading and freeing Norway. Tirpitz also menaced Allied convoys bound for Russia. The Allies were required to keep a large fleet in northern waters to keep Tirpitz off the offensive.

Besides hiding out in fjords, Tirpitz generated a fog from chlorosulphuric acid for concealment purposes. In 2018, Professor Claudia Hartl determined that the acid prevented the growth of pine and birch trees in the area, apparently by damaging the needles of the trees. To this day, trees in the area show damage from the fog. Hartl is a scientist at Johannes Gutenberg University, located at Mainz, Rhineland Palatinate, Germany.

The X-craft bombs severely damaged Tirpitz. Repairs took seven months. British aircraft sank Tirpitz seven months later.

Tirpitz observed the two X-craft retreating, fired, and sank both. The six British sailors abandoned, but were captured.

One of the midgets and her crew disappeared. Most likely, Tirpitz shot and sank this midget with all three hands lost. The fourth midget returned safely. In all, three midgets were lost; and three and six crew lost and captured. This was Britain's only multiple X-craft attack.

In 4/1944, an X-Craft placed a bomb which sank a German merchant ship at Bergen in southern Norway (on the North Sea coast). A floating dock also at Bergen was damaged as well by a placed bomb from an X-craft. This same mini-submarine returned five months later, and sank the same floating dock with a bomb.

X-Craft were used to prepare for Operation Overlord (6/6/1944 invasion of the Germany-occupied Continent at northwestern France {Normandy} from England), by surveying landing beaches. Crewmen went ashore to take soil samples from Normandy beaches. On D-Day, X-craft served as lightships to direct the invading naval fleet to the specified beaches.

The Royal Navy made six XE-class midget submarines in 1944, as an improved version of the X-class midgets. They were 2' longer than the X-class boats, at 53'. Their surface and submerged speeds were about the same as the predecessor X-Craft. They had a crew of four (commander, deputy commander, engineer, seaman). One of the crew was also a diver. Besides the two, heavy amatol bombs, they carried six 20-pound limpet mines, which the diver attached to the target.

Four XE-class boats saw action before the War ended. One severed two underwater Hong Kong to Saigon telephone cables (Operation Sabre) 7/31/1945, using a powered net/cable cutter. The cutters were operated from inside the boats. This was near Cape St. Jacques in French Indochina. Another XE the same day severed the Hong Kong to Singapore cable. This was near Lamma Island, Hong Kong.

The Japanese Army had attacked Hong Kong 12/8/1941, four hours after the air attack on Oahu (Pearl Harbor). Hong Kong fell 12/25/1941. Japan occupied Hong Kong through the end of the War 8/1945.

Japan bombed strategic sites in Singapore 12/8/1941, about the same time as the sneak attack on Oahu. Japan did not invade Singapore until 2/8/1942. Singapore surrendered one week later. Japan occupied Singapore as in the case of Hong

Kong, until the end of the War. Many, many thousands of citizens of Hong Kong and Singapore either fled or died in one way or another during the occupation.

Japan used these cables for communications and controlled their use. Therefore, severing these cables hindered Japan's occupation of Hong Kong, Singapore, and what use to be called French Indochina (today Vietnam, Cambodia, and Laos).

The Gato-class, 312' long and 27' beam and 17' draft, 60 crew, USS Darter (1943 – 10/24/1944 grounded in Palawan Strait, scuttled, no men lost) submarine hit the Takao-class, 669' long and 67' beam and 21' draft, 773 crew, IJN Takao (1932 – 1946 Royal Navy sunk as target ship) heavy cruiser 10/23/1944 at Singapore Harbor with two torpedoes. As so damaged and not seaworthy, the Japanese moored Takao, and used as a floating anti-aircraft battery for the defense of Seletar Naval Base on the north side of Singapore. On the night of 7/31/1945, two HMS XEs attached limpet mines and dropped their larger mines under Takao. The limpets were attached with rope as Takao's hull was covered with a thick layer of seaweed, to the point where the magnets would not hold. The mines went off, causing much more damage. However, Takao did not sink. Then again, she was never repaired to sail again.

As mentioned above, the two X-craft which attempted to sink the German battleship Tirpitz battleship in a Norwegian Harbor, sank. The Germans recovered and salvaged these for study. German engineers designed a two-man, mini-submarine, based on the inspection of the British boats. Whereas the British midgets had both a diesel engine and an electric motor, the first German versions had electric propulsion only. This was a twelve horsepower torpedo motor. Endurance was 79 miles, at 4.6 miles per hour. The crew was two. Armament was either an underslung mine or torpedo, plus a limpet mine in the nose. The torpedo would allow attacks in coastal waters, if such an opportunity should arise. These 34' long submarines were called Hechts.

As the Germans planned to use for harbor kills, the Hechts had no hydroplanes or fins which could snag on anti-submarine/torpedo nets. Trim for the sleek boats was to be controlled by shifting adjustable weights forward and aft. In tests, the weights could not be moved quickly enough, so hydroplanes and fins were added after all. Despite this, control when submerged was still poor as the boats did not have ballast tanks. The engineer sat up front. The commander behind him. The commander had a clear acrylic dome as well as a periscope, to navigate and aim.

Fifty-three Hechts were made May-August, 1944. As it turned out, none saw action. They were two small, had limited range as no diesel engine to charge their batteries, and did not maneuver well. These instead were used for training purposes for the slightly larger and improved variants, called Seehunds.

The two crew Seehunds were 5' longer than the Hechts, at 39'. The beam was 5'. Propulsion came from a 60 and 25 horsepower diesel engine and electric motor, pushing to 8.1 and 3.5 miles per hour surface and under. Range was 310 and 72 miles, surface and submerged. Armament was two, 24' torpedoes; slung externally in recesses in the lower hull. The Seehund had a small, raised, amidships platform for the air intake mast, magnetic compass, and a 10' fixed periscope. The periscope incorporated lenses for scanning the sky for enemy aircraft, before surfacing. Like the Hechts, the Seehunds also had a clear viewing dome. The hull's weakest point was the viewing dome. However, the design and material were such that dives up to 148' deep were safe.

The German Navy considered the improved Seehund a winner. One thousand were ordered. Due to a shortage of raw material, labor problems, and transport problems, only 285 Seehunds were completed; 8/1944 into 1945.

The first Seehund operation was on the last day of 1944. Eighteen Seehunds in a wolf pack off Netherlands were hit by a storm. Sixteen sunk. As submarines have the advantage of avoiding storms and rough water by simply diving, the storm apparently caught them on the surface.

The first success was 2/1945, when a Seehund torpedo sank a freighter off Great Yarmouth, Norfolk, England. Great Yarmouth is on England's southeast coast.

Due to the small size, quietness, and slow running speed of the Seehunds, the Allied detection methods of ASDIC (a primitive type of radar) and hydrophone were not effective.

One hundred and forty-two Seehund sorties were conducted January-April, 1945, mostly around the German coast and in the English Channel. Nine and three merchantmen were sunk and damaged; totaling 100,000 gross tons. To sum up, the Seehunds were effective. Fortunately for the Allies, their emergence came late in the War. Of the 285 made, only 138 saw action (48%). Thirty-five of the 285 (12%) were lost in battle, bad weather, or due to mechanical problems.

The last Seehund sorties were 4/28/1945 and 5/2/1945, when the midgets re-supplied the besieged German garrison at Dunkirk (northern France) with food rations. Submarines of any size cannot carry much cargo, and these were midgets. Therefore, probably not much food was delivered. The Seehunds on the return carried mail from the German soldiers back home. Adolph Hitler (1889 Austria – 4/30/1945 Berlin, pistol suicide) was now dead. Victory in Europe Day was 5/8/1945.

Germany made hundreds of very small, one-man midgets, in 1944. They carried underslung torpedoes, or mines. The 29' long and 5' beam, diesel engine and electric motor propelled Biber was Germany's smallest midget of World War II. Its surface and submerged speeds were seven and six miles per hour. More than 300 were made.

Germany also made almost 400, electric-only, 34' long and 6' beam, one-man midgets called Molches. Molches toted two torpedoes.

From 1/1945 through 4/1945, Biber and Molch midget boats went out on 102 sorties. Seven small ships (491 tons total) were sunk. Two much larger ships were damaged. Seventy of the midgets were lost. To sum up, these micro-midget Bibers and Molches were not that effective. Again, they were completed too late in the War to be used much.

Germany toward the end of the War designed and made (at least prototypes) other improved mini-submarines. These included the Hai, Delphin, and Schwertal. The War ended before they saw action.

Italy made four, 33' long and 6' beam, diesel and electric propulsion, two crew CA-class midgets 1938-1941. They carried either two torpedoes or two mines. All four were scuttled by 1/1943, with no or little damage done.

Italy followed up its CA-class, with its improved CB-class. These 49' long (so 48% longer than the CAs), diesel and electric propulsion midgets were very wide for their length (for a submarine), with a 10' beam. The crew was up to four men. Twelve and nine were made before and after 9/1943, when part of Italy switched to the Allied side. These ended up being used by several countries on both sides of the War. Whichever, they did little damage.

The Italian Navy planned to use one of its CB midgets in a concerted attack with commando frogmen, to sink ships in New York City harbor. The Marconi-class, 251' long and 22' wide and 16' draft, 57 crew, 21 and 9 miles per hour surface and under, Leonardo da Vinci (1940 – 5/24/1943 British warships depth charge sank 300 miles west of Vigo, Spain; all 57 crew lost) submarine was to be the mother ship. Leonardo was modified for the mission. Trials were conducted to train for the raid. However, Leonardo da Vinci when returning to Bordeaux 5/1943, was sank by the escorts of convoy KMF 15. There were no survivors. The KMF convoys were those from Great Britain to the Mediterranean Sea.

The just mentioned port city of Bordeaux is on the Garonne River where it enters the Atlantic Ocean in southwestern France. Bordeaux was a submarine base for both the German and Italian navies in World War II. Germany made massive, reinforced concrete berthing pens to protect its submarines. These structures were so substantial, that dropped bombs did little damage. They were so large and strong that dismantling is not practical. Therefore, they remain to this day, more than 70 years later. Some of the pens have been renovated, to be used as a cultural center for exhibitions.

Commerce raider Leonardo da Vinci was Italy's most successful submarine in World War II. She sank seventeen ships of nine countries over twenty-two months 1941-1943, totaling 120,243 tons. These were twelve freighters (two were American, both 442' long and 56' beam Liberty ships), two tankers, a collier, a schooner, and a troopship; so no warships. This also made her Captain Italy's leading submarine skipper. This was the young Lieutenant Gianfranco Gazzana-Priaroggia (1912 Milan – 5/23/1943 Atlantic Ocean).

Again, Leonardi da Vinci was one of Italy's six Marconi-class submarines. They were launched 1939-1940. Four were sunk in 1941, and one 5/1943. This last one was Leo. These five were sunk in the Atlantic Ocean.

The sixth Marconi was converted to a cargo submarine, to exchange rare or irreplaceable trade goods with Japan.

When Italy capitulated to the Allies 9/1943, this submarine went to the German Navy (renamed UIT-25). When Germany surrendered 5/1945, she went to Japan (renamed I-504). This tanker submarine shot down a B-25 Mitchell twin engine bomber near the end of the Pacific War, Japan's last naval success. A submarine using a deck gun to shoot down an enemy aircraft is an infrequent occurrence. The U.S. Navy found this submarine at Kobe (Honshu) after Japan's surrender, and scuttled her in Kii Suido (strait separating Shikoku Island from the Kii Peninsula on Honshu Island).

To sum up, Italy had no submarines to serve as a mother ship, to launch a midget submarine to sink ships in New York City harbor. Anyway again, Italy (well, most of the country) switched over to the Allied side, 9/1943.

Back to Japan. Toward what turned out to be the end of the War, the Japanese planned to make 760, 19-ton displacement, 56' long and 4' beam, two crew Kairyu (translates to *sea dragon*) mini-submarines. These were more or less civilian versions of the military kaitens. Their purpose was to protect the homelands (mainly Honshu Island where Tokyo and Osaka are) from the anticipated, upcoming Allied invasions. There were several designs. A diesel engine and electric motor pushed to eight and twelve miles an hour, surface and submerged. Surface and submerged ranges were 518 and 44 miles.

At first, the design was to tote two torpedoes outside the hull, along with a 1,300-pound explosive charge fitted to the prow which would explode upon impact. An ambitious and competent and lucky operator could take out two USSs with torpedoes, and a third USS on the suicide leg. With torpedoes in short supply and defenses diminished, the decision was made to convert the Kairyu to a single-bomb, impact-trigger, solely suicide machine.

Two hundred and ten had been made by the time the War ended; most at the Yokosuka shipyard (Yokosuka is part of the Greater Tokyo area). Most were stored there at Yokosuka to defend the entrance to Tokyo Bay, if the U.S. invaded mainland Japan from that direction. Volunteer operators were lined up, with a waiting list. Again, these were to be used as suicide machines, to sink or try to sink USSs. None saw action, thanks to the two atomic bombs dropped 8/1945 on Hiroshima and Nagasaki, three days apart.

Today, three Kairyu submarines remain. Two are in museums in Japan. The third is at the U.S. Navy Submarine Force Library and Museum in Groton, Connecticut. The first picture shows a restored Kairyu, at the Kure Maritime Museum (Yamato Museum), in Kure, Hiroshima Prefecture, Honshu. The second picture shows 80 of these suicide machines (as variants), awaiting action to sink USSs. Again, operators were lined up, with a waiting list. This picture was taken at a Kure dry dock, 10/19/1945.

Japan also modified one of its torpedoes to carry an enclosed pilot. It was 48' long, but only 3.25' wide – so the pilot was squeezed in. The control planes were enlarged and altered to allow both gyroscope and pilot control. The warhead was 3,420 pounds, much greater than the standard Japanese torpedo. Its cruise and maximum speeds were fourteen and thirty-five miles per hour. They could be launched from submerged submarines. These manned torpedoes were called kaitens. Three hundred and thirty were made. About 105 were sent out on suicide missions. According to the U.S., kaitens sank three Navy craft in World War II, as follows:

- Cimarron-class, 553' long and 75' beam and 32' draft, 21 miles per hour, 299 crew, USS Mississinewa (1944 – 11/20/1944) fleet oiler when anchored at Ulithi, Caroline Islands; 63 of 299 crew lost (21%); tanks were full of aviation fuel, diesel, and fuel oil which was lost, and ocean polluted
- An LCI-600-class, 159' long and 23' beam and 6' draft, infantry landing craft; three men lost
- Buckley-class, 306' long and 37' beam and 14' draft, 26 miles per hour, 213 crew, USS Underhill (1943 – 7/24/1945) destroyer escort 250 miles northeast of Cape Engano (off Luzon, Philippines); 112 of 234 crew lost (48%)

Six days after Underhill, IJN B3-type, I-58 (1944 – 4/1/1946 scuttled off Goto Islands) cruiser submarine torpedo-sank the Portland-class, USS Indianapolis (1932 - 7/30/1945) heavy cruiser in the same area. Indianapolis' Captain was not informed that Japanese submarines were in the area. The 879 Indianapolis sailors and marines aboard who died are the most ever for a USS at sea. I-58 by the way had kaitens ready with eager operators, but they were not needed.

For the record, Japan claimed a much larger number of USSs sunk and damaged with kaitens. More than a thousand kaiten operators died in training or on missions.

As already noted, manned torpedoes even if the pilot is enclosed are not considered to be in the same category as midget submarines.

The mini-submarine wrecks still in the Pearl Harbor area from the 12/7/1941 sneak attack are considered both historic sites and war graves. In agreement with the government of Japan, the U.S. National Oceanic and Atmospheric Administration and the U.S. National Park Service monitor and manage the wrecks.

The 2016 *The Lost Submarines of Pearl Harbor* book by seven researchers and authors published by Texas A&M University Press is the definitive source of information, on the technology of the Japanese mini-submarines and their history of operation on 12/7/1941 in the sneak attack.

Most Word War II midgets were electric only. Therefore, their range was limited, as no engine to recharge their batteries. They had no or little on-board living accommodation. They worked off mother ships, either lashed to their decks or towed behind. The mother ships were usually large submarines, but were surface ships in some cases (craned off and on or towed). After their missions which usually ran only a few hours, the midgets rendezvoused with their mother ships for recovery. The mother ship carried replacement batteries or charged their batteries. The midget submarine crewmen lived on the mother boat or ship, boarding the midget at the time of launch for their mission.

To sum up, these baby submarines put into service by both sides had little effect on the war due to their limited range; and as both the Allies and the Axis had or quickly developed ways to detect and attack them.

The U.S. used submarines with great success in World War II, especially in the Pacific Theater. As Exhibit A, they are credited with sinking 55% of Japan's merchant ships during the War, and also many IJN warships. This was the case, despite the fact that USS submarine torpedoes were often not effective until the fall of 1943.

On the other hand, the U.S. lost 52 submarines in World War II and thousands of men. Fifty were lost in the Pacific, and only two in the Atlantic. The causes were mostly from combat, but included several friendly fire cases. Two of these friendly fire case sinkings were bizarre – the torpedoes that sunk these two submarines were launched by the victims. The torpedoes ran a circular route.

Most of these U.S. World War II submarines were of the Gato, Balao, and Tench classes; introduced in 1943, 1943, and 1944. These were all 312' long, and 27' in the beam. Each successive class had evolutionary improvements.

The United States did not use midget submarines in World War II. One has to wonder that if the U.S. with its engineering expertise and resources had designed and made mini-submarines by 1943, as to how much their success would have shortened the Pacific War.

Paul Allen (1953 Seattle – 2018 Seattle, non-Hodgkin's lymphoma complications) and Bill Gates (1955 Seattle -) formed Microsoft Corporation in 1975. Allen was diagnosed with Hodgkin's lymphoma in 1981. He left Microsoft in 1982, due to his illness. He retained partial ownership of Microsoft. His net worth in 2018 was more than $20 billion.

Allen was treated successfully with radiation therapy and a bone marrow transplant in 1981 and 1982. In 2009, he was diagnosed with non-Hodgkin's lymphoma. He was again treated successfully. However, the cancer returned in 2018 with a vengeance. Allen's billions could not save him.

Allen's 414' long and 69' beam and 19' draft, Octopus mega-yacht was completed in 2003. Besides pleasure use, he made it available for humanitarian work, research, etc. He has also used it to search for shipwrecks.

In 2016, Allen bought a 13-year-old, 251' long and 49' beam and 24' draft, offshore platform service vessel. He had the ship modified and refitted to be a dedicated deep submergence search, research, and equipment test vessel. RV Petrel's autonomous underwater vehicle and remote operated underwater vehicle are able to explore more than 3.7 miles deep. The RV Petrel crew is 21. The project staff is ten.

Petrel has since discovered many World War II shipwrecks in the Pacific Ocean, Atlantic Ocean, and Mediterranean Sea. Archival documents (ship logs, battle reports, etc.) are studied to estimate where the wrecks lie, as a starting point to begin searches.

The Petrel team found USS Ward's wreck 12/1/2017 at the bottom of Ormoc Bay, just off the Philippine Island of Leyte. This was almost 73 years after she was gun-sank by a USS destroyer, to avoid capture by the Japanese. Ward's discovery was a central theme for the 76th anniversary events of the Oahu (Pearl Harbor) attack six days later.

The USS Indianapolis was mentioned above. Allen and Petrel found the Indianapolis wreck 9/8/2017. This was more than 72 years after she sank. She was 18,044' (3.4 miles) down. Allen reported his findings and sent pictures to the Navy. The Indianapolis still belongs to the Navy. Allen did not reveal its location publicly.

3- FIRST U.S. MILITARY KILLED 12/7/1941, OAHU, HAWAII

In the last half of the 1930s, several European countries, particularly Italy and Germany, began training thousands of young people to become pilots. Although these government-sponsored programs were set up as training for civilians, they were more accurately military flight training academies. The leader or leaders of these countries were either contemplating attacking and occupying neighboring countries; and/or anticipating the possibility of being attacked. By now, the military offensive capabilities, even being able to sink anti-aircraft gun armed capital warships with dropped bombs, of aircraft were well recognized and accepted.

For the U.S., this change of thinking in the offensive potency of aircraft came mostly from the internal Army Air Service military recommendations followed by public preaching of Major General (posthumous promotion) Billy Mitchell (1879 France of American parents – 1936 NYC).

Mitchell enlisted in the Army in 1898. He took private flying lessons in 1916 as the law prevented him from military aviation due to his age and rank. He was a 36-year-old Captain. He paid $1,470 for these lessons at the Curtiss Flying School, Newport News, Virginia. This is $35,900 in 2019 money.

Mitchell was promoted to Major and appointed Chief of the Air Service of the First Army 7/1916.

The bilingual (French) Mitchell served in France during World War I. He flew combat. At the end of World War I, he commanded all American combat aviation in France. After World War I, he was appointed Deputy Director of the Army Air Service.

Mitchell much advocated (and later publicly, as already noted) after World War I for the U.S. military to divert funds to building the Army's aviation arm, over increased naval expenditures (ships and boats). He stated that the War Department and the Navy were emphasizing the construction of warships, in lieu of shifting funds to increasing the capabilities of the Air Force. Mitchell added that as aircraft could sink even large ships, that spending money to make large ships (other than aircraft carriers, of course) was stupid. This of course irritated Admirals no end.

The Navy responded that a spindly mosquito of an aircraft could not sink or even much damage a battleship or aircraft carrier – as so large with watertight compartmentalization, and effective anti-aircraft fire. Tests were conducted. Bombers were successful. Mitchell proved right.

Mitchell also advocated that the U.S. military's air power be a separate branch, which he called the Department of Aeronautics. At the time, the air force was part of the Army. This notion of establishing a separate branch for air services agitated Army generals, of course. For the record, the air force did become a separate branch of the U.S. armed forces, in 1947. This was two years after World War II ended.

At one point, Mitchell publicly accused Army and Navy leaders of an almost *treasonable administration of the national defense,* for investing in battleships instead of aircraft carriers and aircraft. Again as noted for the third time, Michell sometimes made his opinions public.

The military and even President Calvin Coolidge (1872 VT – 1933 MA) had enough. Mitchell was court martialed in 1925, mainly because of his public statements. He was convicted (more or less) of insubordination, for going over the heads of his superiors. He was demoted one rank level from Brigadier General (one star) to Colonel and suspended from active duty for five years without pay. President Coolidge though changed this to half pay. Mitchell resigned from the Army shortly after the judgement. He was 45 years old. He served 1898-1926.

British aircraft working in tandem sank a new and modern German battleship 5/1941. This was the 793' long and 36' beam and 31' draft, Bismarck (1940 – 5/2/1941 sank in the North Atlantic Ocean, 2,086 of 2,200 crew lost {95%}) battleship.

British aircraft had also done away with much of the Italian Navy (such as it was) in the Mediterranean Sea.

On 12/7/1941, Japanese aircraft sank four battleships at (Oahu) Pearl Harbor, and severely damaged the other four battleships of the U.S Navy Pacific Fleet. Another two and nine warships were sunk and damaged.

Three days after the Oahu attack, Japanese aircraft sank two British battleships (one was new) off Kuantan, South China Sea.

By this time, the few earlier believers left in the unsinkable battleship by aircraft premise had faded into the woodwork. To sum up, Mitchell was vindicated for his correct and forward thinking, but this was mostly posthumous. President Franklin Roosevelt (1882 NY – 4/12/1945 GA, cerebral hemorrhage) promoted him to Major General in 1942, six years after his death.

As another belated kudo, the twin engine, tricycle landing gear, midwing, twin rudder tail, six crew, 230 and 272 miles per hour cruise and top speed, North American Aviation B-25 Mitchell medium bomber introduced in 1941 five years after his death, was named in his honor. This is the only U.S. military aircraft named after a person. Sixteen of these (modified) bombers conducted the 4/18/1942 Doolittle Raid, taking off on their own power from an aircraft carrier to bomb targets on Honshu. Honshu is Japan's largest island, and the location of its largest cities.

Today, Mitchell is known as the *father of the U.S. Air Force.* That speaks for itself.

By the time of Mitchell's death almost six years before the entry of the U.S. in World War II, just about all countries' military, whether powerhouse or not, recognized and acknowledged the major role that aircraft would play in a future war, and therefore the need for pilots and other airmen. In the case of the upcoming World War II, this recognition turned out to be definitely the case. As already noted, some countries had started training civilian pilots, who could transition to military service.

The United States federal government created the Civil Aeronautics Board in 1938, to regulate aviation services. Its responsibilities included regulating scheduled passenger airline service, investigating severe accidents, etc. The new agency was the predecessor of today's agencies of the Federal Aviation Administration and the National Transportation Safety Board.

The new Civil Aeronautics Board quickly created the Civilian Pilot Training Program (CPTP). The purpose of the CPTP was to enlarge the nation's commercial aviation industry, by teaching college age Americans to fly. As war clouds continued to grow over Europe and as Japan's belligerence and abuses increased in China, the CPTP also became a way for the U.S. to create a pool of trained pilots who could quickly transition to military aviation if necessary. From that standpoint, the CPTP resembled the German and Italian programs.

President Roosevelt unveiled the program 12/27/1938 at a White House press conference. He stated a goal of training 20,000 college students a year to become pilots. Congress passed two laws in 1939 (one in April, one in June), to fund the program. The federal government paid for a 72-hour ground school course, followed by 35 to 50 hours of flight instruction at facilities located near eleven colleges and universities. The first nine schools were selected 5/1939.

Nazi Germany invaded Poland 9/1/1939 without provocation or warning (Germany staged several false flag events on the eve of the invasion), starting what later came to be called World War II. This further emphasized the military value of the CPTP. The U.S. quickly assessed its air personnel capabilities and realized that pilots and instructors were in short supply, if the country should decide to ally with Poland (and later Great Britain, France, Russia, etc., it turned out) and fight. Admission requirements were reduced. The program was quickly and much expanded. Nine more schools were added 8/1940, 11 more 3/1941, and 15 more 10/1941. At its peak in 1942, the program had 1,132 educational institutions for ground school, and 1,460 flight schools for the flying part participating.

Although established as a civilian training program, military personnel could take advantage of the CPTP program -- on their personal time. Their usual goal in learning to fly was to either pursue a civilian aviation career after discharge from the military, or eventually gain their military aviator wings. As Oahu of the Territory of Hawaii had so many U.S. military personnel in all the branches, many of the CPTP slots there went to men stationed there.

Ground school (navigation, aerodynamics, meteorology, etc.) was taught at the University of Hawaii, Honolulu.

Three flying schools in the CPTP program were based at the civilian John Rodgers Airport at Honolulu, Oahu, as follows:

- K-T Flying Service   the name came from owners Robert Knox and Robert Tyce; sales agent for Piper aircraft
- Gambo Flying Service   Robert Tyce taught Marguerite Gambo how to fly; she went into business for herself; sales agent for Aeronca aircraft

- Andrew Flying Service   sales agent for Interstate aircraft

The three schools made most of their income from flying lessons, in lieu of selling aircraft. The training aircraft they used of course were from the manufacturers they represented.

Demand for flight instruction at one point on Oahu was such that students had to schedule flying lessons two weeks in advance. K-T was the largest operation, with ten Piper aircraft trainers.

Several flying clubs formed on Oahu, to reduce flying costs when training or on pleasure flights.

The just mentioned John Rodgers Airport opened in 1927. It was Hawaii's first, full service, civilian airport. The 1,000' runway was soon lengthened, and then again and again. Today, the longest runway is more than 12,000' long.

The location is on the southern tip of Oahu, very near the water (Mamala Bay). In fact, the ocean infringed on the field's edge at high tide. The area was later built up with fill, from making a seaport. The airport has a water runway in the bay, 3,000'. The airport's altitude is 13', so calculations and adjustments to sea level were and are not required.

Rodgers Airport was located several miles south of the Army Air Corps' Hickam Field. The Army Air Corps, Navy, and Marines had several other airfields on Oahu besides Hickman, plus more came later. Strict airspace rules of course were in effect, to separate civilian aircraft from military aircraft.

The airport was named after 1903 U.S. Naval Academy graduate John Rodgers (1881 D.C. – 1926 crashed into the Delaware River near Philadelphia). Rodgers was the great grandson of Commodore John Rodgers (1772 MD – 1838 Philadelphia) who served in the Navy 39 years. He was also the great grandson of Commodore Matthew Perry (1794 RI – 1858 NYC), who served 49 years.

Rodgers was the Navy's second officer to become an aviator. This was 9/1911. 1905 U.S. Naval Academy graduate Theodore Ellyson (1885 VA – 1928 crashed into Chesapeake Bay) was the first, designated 1/1911.

Rodgers had been the Commanding Officer of the Naval Air Station at Pearl Harbor 1923-1925. This was one of the reasons why the airfield was named after him. Another reason to honor him was as he had died on duty. However, Rodgers was best known for making the first attempt of a non-stop flight, from California to Hawaii. This is 2,395 miles, from San Francisco to Honolulu. Due to the risks, the Navy positioned ten guard ships every 200 miles on the route for recovery purposes if needed. The estimate was that the flight would take 26 hours.

The two, 49' long and 73' wingspan and 17' tall, twin engine (525 horsepower per side), five crew, open cockpit, 114 miles an hour top speed, PN-9 flying boat biplanes took off from San Pablo Bay (northern part of San Francisco Bay), California, 8/31/1925. Douglas, Martin, and Keystone made the PN series of flying boats, which set a number of records.

One PN-9 lost an engine several hours later when it lost oil pressure. It landed in the ocean. A USS recovered it.

Rodgers' PN-9 ran out of fuel and landed after a flight of 1,841.2 miles. This occurred as an anticipated tailwind never materialized. The 1,841 miles though did set a new distance record for seaplanes.

Rodgers had no fuel, so no engines and no power. Therefore, he could not send or receive radio signals. Navy aircraft and ships could not find him. The next day, he and his crew fashioned several sails from fabric stripped from the wings. They sailed towards Hawaii. They later used metal floor pieces from the airplane to make leeboards to improve steering of the PN-9. The seas were moderate, which worked in their favor. They sailed 450 miles in nine days. The 187' long and 18' beam and 15' draft, USS R-4 (1919 – 1946 scrapped) coastal and harbor defense submarine found them 15 miles off Kauai, and towed them in.

Despite not meeting their goal, Rodgers and his crew were treated as heroes. He and his crew were praised for their resourcefulness after landing. Their response was we are Navy – therefore, we know how to sail and we know how to navigate. In retrospect and hindsight being 20-20 though, planning was maybe lacking in Rodgers' attempt, especially in the area of rescue (radios that had battery power would have been nice). After all, the Pacific Ocean is quite large.

Rodgers served 1903 until his 1926 death at age 45. His rank was Commander.

U.S. Army Air Corps Lieutenants Lester Maitland (1899 Milwaukee – 1990 AZ) and Albert Hegenberger (1895 Boston – 1983 FL) flew a three-engine, high wing, Atlantic-Fokker C-2 aircraft nonstop (not a seaplane) from Oakland Municipal Airport to Wheeler Army Airfield on Oahu. This was 6/28, 29/1927, twenty-two months after Rodgers' effort. The 2,500 miles took 25.8 hours. They cruised ten miles an hour faster than Roger's flying boat.

Charles Lindbergh (1902 MI – 1974 HA) few the 3,600 miles from NY to Paris 40 days before the Pacific flight, in 33.5 hours. The Army men averaged 97 miles per hour. Lindbergh averaged 103 miles an hour. Lindbergh got fame, fortune, and adulation. He was bigger than the Beatles in the 1960s.

The two Army pilots got pats on the back. They also received the Mackay Trophy. The U.S. Air Force awards the Mackay annually for the *most meritorious flight of the year* by an Air Force person or persons or unit. This is a prestigious award, except nobody has heard of it. And so it goes.

Again, the new civilian airport in Honolulu was named after John Rodgers. It opened 3/1927. This was the year after Rodgers' death in an airplane crash. The name was changed to *Honolulu Airport* in 1947, and *Honolulu International Airport* in 1951.

Today, the airport is called the *Daniel K. Inouye International Airport.* World War II Army hero Japanese Hawaiian Inouye (1924 Honolulu – 2012 MD) earned the Medal of Honor (his actions in Italy, 4/21/1945), Purple Heart (lost half his arm when hit by a rifle grenade that failed to detonate), and many other commendations. He was a long time Democrat Representative and then Senator 1963 to his 2012 death, representing Hawaii. He was President pro tempore of the Senate, from 6/2010 to his death. The President pro tempore is the second highest-ranking official of the Senate behind the Vice-President.

The California 251st National Guard Coast Artillery Regiment deployed to Hawaii in late 1940, anticipating war with Japan. Sergeant Henry Blackwell (1921 – 12/7/1941 shot down off Oahu) and Corporal Clyde Brown (1920 – 12/7/1941 shot down off Oahu) of the 251st learned to fly after hours through the CPTP program. They both took their training at K-T Flying Service. Both earned their licenses 10/1941.

Sergeant Blackwell and Corporal Brown reserved two high wing, tandem seat, conventional landing gear, 765-pound, Piper Cubs at K-T Flying Service for an early morning flight Sunday, 12/7/1941. Cubs are 22' long and 7' tall, with a 35' wingspan. They were mainly designed to be trainers, but as so versatile ended up being used for many other purposes. More than 20,000 were made, 1938-1947. The Piper Cub was the Ford Model T (16.5 million Model Ts produced 1908-1927) for aircraft.

The two guardsmen's Cubs were a model J3C-50 and a more powerful J3C-65. The air-cooled, horizontally opposed, four-cylinder engine of the J3C-65 had 65 horsepower, compared to the 50 horsepower of the J3C-50. The cruise and top speeds of the J3C-65 were 75 and 87 miles per hour, several more than the J3C-50.

This was to be the Guardsmen's last rentals from K-T, as the 251st Artillery Regiment was returning to the mainland the next day after a year of training in Hawaii. Both Cubs were in civilian livery, of course. Sergeant Warren Rasmussen (1920 – 12/7/1941 shot down off Oahu) came along as a sightseeing passenger on one of the Cubs. The Cubs took off at 7:40.

Blackwell and Brown were puttering along 2.5 miles offshore at 500', when seven Japanese fighters swooped down out of nowhere and shot them down. The fighters were single engine, Mitsubishi A6M Zeroes. Just like that, Piper Cubs NC-26950 and NC-35111, and three guardsmen ages 20 and 21 and 21 were history. The three guardsmen were the first three U.S. military men to die in the Oahu (Pearl Harbor) sneak attack, although off duty at the time.

The shoot down site was south of the coastal artillery Fort Weaver (1899 - 1948), located on Keahi Point. This is the west bank of the entrance channel to Pearl Harbor.

As already mentioned, the cruise and maximum speeds of the Piper Cub with the larger engine were 75 and 87 miles per hour. The J3C-50 with a less powerful engine was a little pokier. To sum up, it was a breeze for a military fighter to shoot down the spindly Cubs.

K-T Flying Service co-owner Robert Tyce (1903 – 12/7/1941 Honolulu, strafed) had taught Brown and Blackwell how to fly. He and his wife Edna (1910 – 2000) drove to Rodgers Airport to say good-bye to the two National Guardsmen (who had been good customers), again as they were returning to the mainland the next day. They did so. The guardsmen took off.

The couple was standing on the tarmac when a Zero strafed, at 7:55. Tyce was hit in the back of the head. The 7.7 millimeter bullet (0.3 inches in diameter) exited through the side of his throat, leaving a golf ball size hole. He quickly died. Edna who was standing next to her husband was not hit. Tyce was the first of 68 civilian deaths at Honolulu, in the sneak attack.

Widow Edna Tyce later remarried, a sailor based at Pearl Harbor (Robert Palmer). In 1943, she and Robert Knox who co-owned the flying school with her first (now dead) husband received a check for $2,335.56 from the government's War Damage Corporation, as compensation for the two shot down Cubs. This is $34,300 in 2019 dollars.

A small trainer (Aeronca 65TC) on the ground near Tyce was shredded as well.

A Hawaiian Airlines, twin engine, low wing, conventional landing gear, Douglas DC-3 airliner being prepared for a flight to Maui was hit dozens of times (strafed). The ground crew had hustled the flight crew and passengers off the DC-3 into a hangar, as soon as they realized that Pearl Harbor was under attack. This saved lives and prevented injuries.

A Pan Am Clipper was due to arrive at 8:30, during the attack. Clippers were four engine, Boeing 314 flying boats that cruised at 188 miles an hour. Their maximum load was 85 persons – 11 crew and 74 passengers.

The Clipper was 45 minutes late, which may have prevented it from being shot down. Upon being notified of the attack, the Clipper pilots diverted to Hilo on the island of Hawaii. Hilo is 210 miles southeast of Honolulu, Oahu.

At the same time, three men were airborne taking flying lessons, as follows:

- Age 24   mechanic James Duncan from San Francisco
- Age 28   ironworker Raymond Oderwald from New York City
- Age 31   sheet metal pattern maker Ernest Soumala from Massachusetts

Oderwald and Soumala had met when both worked at the Brooklyn Navy Yard (1806 – 1966), Brooklyn, New York City. All three had been hired on a contract basis and sent to Hawaii to do defense work, as their skills were needed. The three tradesmen all worked at the Pearl Harbor Naval Shipyard. The three were buddies.

Mr. Tyce (now deceased) of K-T Flying Service taught Navy man Tommy Tomberlin how to fly in 1938, under the CPTP program. Tomberlin went on to get his instructor's license, and then his commercial flying license. He retired from the Navy. His main job now was as a copilot for Hawaiian Airlines.

Hawaiian Airlines began 10/1929 as *Inter-Island Airways*, flying sightseers around Oahu. It formalized a schedule the next month of 11/1929, becoming a commercial airline. The operation changed its name to Hawaiian Airlines 10/1941. Hawaiian Airlines is the oldest U.S. airline that has never had a fatal accident or hull loss. This is 90 years. Today, it operates 65 airliners, flies to 28 destinations, and has 6,600 employees. 2017 gross revenues were almost $2.7 billion. It frequently is at the top of the list for being on time, fewest cancellations, least over-selling, fewest lost bags, fewest passenger complaints, etc. It is based in Honolulu.

In his off time, Tomberlin gave flying lessons for Tyce's K-T school, and also for members of the Hui Lele Flying Club in a club plane. Tomberlin was Duncan's instructor this morning. They were 27 miles north of Rodgers Airport in a tandem seat, Aeronca 65TC Defender, owned by the flying club. This was near Oahu's northernmost spot, called Kahuku Point. Heading southwest at 1,000' toward the Mormon Temple at Laie at 7:52, two tracer bullet streams from behind startled Tomberlin and Duncan. Fist-sized holes were punched in the fabric covering the rear fuselage and vertical stabilizer. Two longerons were sheared. Longerons are the thin strips of material to which the skin of an aircraft is fastened along the fuselage, to provide rigidity.

Tomberlin in the rear seat grabbed the controls. He snapped the Aeronca into a descending left bank toward the sea, zigzagging as the plane lost altitude. Several more Japanese fighters from another formation shot at the Aeronca in the next few minutes, but missed. Tomberlin flew just above the waves, threaded his way through Pali Pass to stay low and concealed, and made it back to Rodgers Airport. He landed safely. Tomberlin later counted nine bullet holes. The pair were lucky. Tomberlin by the way later re-enlisted and became a military pilot.

Robert Tyce had also taught Marguerite Gambo to fly, in 1937. She became a commercial pilot. She founded Gambo Flying Service in 1939, based at Rodgers. Her student Oderwald had soloed 12/1/1941, the only one of the three students who had soloed to date. Tomberlin had taught Oderwald how to fly. Today, Gambo was instructing Oderwald on a cross-country trip in an open cockpit, Meyers OTW biplane (another source though says they were in an Aeronca). They were near the Marine Corps Air Station at Kaneohe Bay, another target of the Japanese. She saw the plumes of smoke. The biplane was buffeted by turbulence as the Zeroes pulled up from strafing runs. Gambo turned tail and dodged the attack by taking a seldom-used pass. They landed safely back at Rodgers.

Cornelia Fort (2/5/1919 Nashville – 3/21/1943 TX, midair collision) was the instructor of the third student (Soumala), in an Interstate Cadet. She instructed for Andrew Flying Service. Soumala was practicing touch-and-go's, in preparation for his first solo flight later that day. Just before 8:00, Fort espied a high speed, fighter type aircraft heading straight for their Cadet from the right. She grabbed the stick from Soumala, slammed the throttle forward, and climbed desperately. The Zero went under her, so close that the Cadet's windows rattled. It appears that this Zero and maybe another fired on Fort and Soumala.

The Interstate Cadet is about the same size as the Piper Cub described above, but has a larger engine. Its cruise and maximum speeds are 105 and 114 miles per hour, compared to the Cub's 75 and 87 miles per hour for the larger engine Cub. Nevertheless, it was no match of course for the Zero, which has a top speed of 300 miles per hour, can climb almost like a rocket, and can turn on a dime; so Fort and her student were lucky.

Fort kept the Cadet at full throttle and landed back at Rodgers Airport. She and her student ran for their lives, as a Japanese fighter swooped down on a strafing run. This was the same strafing run that made Edna Tyce a widow. It is thought that Fort and her student were the first shot at in the 12/7/1941 Pearl Harbor attack. The Cadet was riddled with bullet holes. Whether it was hit in the air or on the ground from strafing or both was not determined.

Local attorney Roy Vitousek (1890 CA – 1946) had been a representative in the Hawaii Territorial House of Representatives 22 years, and speaker of that body seven of those 22 years. He and his 17-year-old son Martin (1924 – 1999) were flying in a rented Aeronca (TC-65 Defender) from Gambo Flying Service, sightseeing at 800'. It appears that several Nakajima B5N torpedo bombers shot at them, but they were not hit. Vitousek climbed to 2,000' to be above the fray. He later landed safely at Rodgers.

Restored versions of the Piper Cub, Aeronca Defender, and Interstate Cadet are shown below:

Student pilot M. F. Poston rented a Piper Cub J-3 from K-T Flying Service (or says he did), for a solo flight. A Zero or Zeroes shot him down. He parachuted to safety from 4,000'. Note that many doubt Poston's story. For one thing, it would be very rare that pilots flying a trainer would have a parachute.

To sum up, at least six civilian aircraft were in the air above Oahu at the time of the attack – seven if you believe Poston's account. Three were instructors with their students. Three were rented by sightseers, and two of those three had a passenger aboard. Zeroes attacked five of the six. Two were shot down, with three off-duty military men dying.

Five of the aircraft were tandem seat, fabric-covered, some wood components, high wing, single engine, closed cockpit trainers. The sixth was the same, except an open cockpit biplane.

None had radios. Conflicts in the air were avoided by see and avoid practices. This meant that the aircraft could only fly in the daytime when visibility was good. Of course there were no flying zones, limited to military aircraft.

Four men were killed. These were the three, off-duty military men in the two shot down Piper Cubs, and the flying school owner on the ground. The locations and action are shown on the map below:

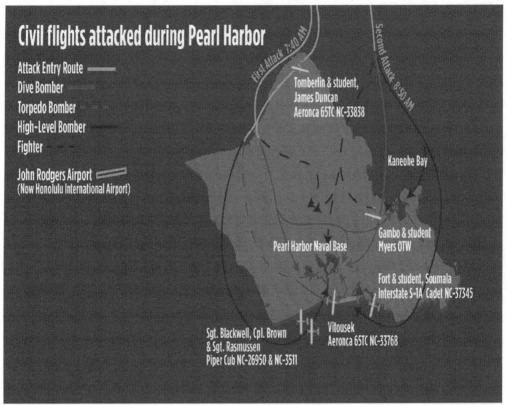

Civil flights attacked during Pearl Harbor

Attack Entry Route ——
Dive Bomber ———
Torpedo Bomber ———
High-Level Bomber ———
Fighter – – –

John Rodgers Airport
(Now Honolulu International Airport)

First Attack 7:40 AM

Second Attack 8:50 AM

Tomberlin & student,
James Duncan
Aeronca 65TC NC-33838

Kaneohe Bay

Gambo & student
Myers OTW

Pearl Harbor Naval Base

Fort & student, Soumala
Interstate S-1A Cadet NC-37345

Sgt. Blackwell, Cpl. Brown
& Sgt. Rasmussen
Piper Cub NC-26950 & NC-3511

Vitousek
Aeronca 65TC NC-33768

The Aeronca Defender piloted by Roy Vitousek is on display at the Pacific Aviation Museum Pearl Harbor (12/7/2007 -), located on the 0.7 square mile Ford Island in Pearl Harbor. The other aircraft at the museum on display include a North American Aviation B-25 Mitchell bomber (B-25s were used in the 4/18/1942 Doolittle Raid), a Mitsubishi A6M Zero fighter, a Grumman F4F Wildcat fighter, and a Curtiss P-40 Warhawk fighter. The Boeing N2S-3 Stearman Kaydet biplane that President George H. W. Bush (1924 MA – 2018 Houston) flew when training (some say he soloed in this very Kaydet) is also on display. The museum's hangars (built in 1939) show actual damage from the 12/7/1941 sneak attack. The museum is a Smithsonian affiliate.

The Interstate Cadet being flown by Cornelia Fort is on display at the Heritage Flight Museum near Burlington, Washington. On the other hand, some say that the Interstate at Heritage was not the one that Fort was flying 12/7/1941. If it is, it was repaired (there are no bullet holes now).

On the other hand again in response to a 10/2018 e-mail query to the Heritage Flight Museum, the response was that the Cadet on display (nicknamed *Pearl*) was the one Fort was flying.

Although early on a Sunday morning, it was common for light aircraft to fly then (and now) at Oahu, as the winds kick up later in the day. High winds make flying a small aircraft rough and difficult. This is especially the case in a gusting crosswind, when landing.

Oahu was one of fourteen sneak attack locations this day, courtesy of the Empire of Japan. The 1907 Hague Convention addressed the requirement to declare war in its *Convention Relative to the Opening of Hostilities* statements. These clauses describe the international actions a country should perform, before opening hostilities. Article 1 states: *The Contracting Powers recognize that hostilities between themselves must not commence without previous and explicit warning, in the form either of a reasoned declaration of war or of an ultimatum with conditional declaration of war.* Japan took a pass on giving an advance warning, of maybe attacking. Shame on Japan, again (Japan had a history of such sneak attacks).

The United States was the target for nine of the fourteen attacked sites. Oahu (Pearl Harbor) of course is the most remembered by Americans, due to the one-sided outcome. Two thousand, three hundred and thirty-five and 1,143 American military men were killed and wounded. Another 68 and 35 civilians died (Robert Tyce was the first of these) and were wounded. In comparison, only 64 Japanese military men died (55 airmen and nine midget submarine sailors) and one (a submariner) captured. This is a ratio of more than 36 American military deaths per one Japanese military death.

Japanese Navy aircraft strafed and bombed Oahu military airfields first thing 12/7/1941. This was to eliminate air-to-air opposition, and to prevent U.S. military aircraft from searching (and attacking) for the location of Japan's carriers and escorts. The three primary airfields attacked were Army Wheeler (Wheeler in fact was the first target hit, four minutes before Pearl Harbor), Army Hickam, and Navy/Marines Ford Island. Navy/Marines Kaonehe, Army Bellows, Navy/Marines Ewa, and Army Haleiwa were secondary airfield targets. High-level bombers and dive bombers aimed for hangars and adjacent barracks. Fighters strafed parked aircraft, with both armor-piercing and incendiary bullets.

To sum up, this worked. For example, Hickam Field suffered extensive damage (aircraft, hangars, etc.) with 189 and 302 killed and wounded. Wheeler Field had 33 and 75 killed and wounded. The U.S. aircraft were tied down wingtip to wingtip, making it easy for the Japanese Navy to maximize damage from bombs or strafing runs. The planes were not fueled or armed in most cases, anyway.

Nineteen USSs sank or were damaged including all eight battleships of the Pacific fleet. Hundreds of aircraft were destroyed (most on the ground). Japan lost only 29 aircraft, nine and 20 in the first and second wave attacks. These were fifteen, nine, and five dive bombers, fighters, and torpedo bombers.

Congress as requested by President Roosevelt declared war on Japan the next day. This was 12/8/1941, a Monday.

General aviation of course ground to a halt in Hawaii this day, until World War II ended. The above-mentioned instructor Cornelia Fort whose trainer was hit, sailed back to the mainland two months later. The delay in getting a berth was because she had to stand in line with others, as so many people were fleeing the islands out of fear of a follow-up attack.

Fort made a short movie, which was used in promoting the sale of war bonds. This led to speaking engagements, again to promote the sale of war bonds.

Back in her Nashville home town, Fort joined the Civil Air Patrol. She gave flying lessons at Berry Field in Nashville, where she had learned to fly.

In 9/1942, Fort was the second woman accepted into government service as part of the Women's Auxiliary Ferrying Service (WAFS). The WAFS went into operation 9/10/1942. It was based at New Castle, Delaware. She had 845 hours of flying time.

The separate but very similar Women's Flying Training Detachment (WFTD) started training several weeks later. It was based in Houston.

The WAFS and WFTD merged 7/1943. The combined entity was called the Women Airforce Service Pilots (WASP). The program trained more than a thousand women, who were already experienced aviators.

The main purpose of the WASP program was to fly military aircraft domestically such as from manufacturing plants to locations of finishing plants such as to add armaments, training fields, or ports for overseas shipment; so as to free up men to fly in combat or transport in the European and Pacific theaters. The program ended 12/1944, as the War wound down.

Fort was stationed at Long Beach, CA. Her job was solo flying new Vultee BT-13 Valiant trainers from the factory in Long Beach, California, to Love Field in Dallas. Love Field was an Army Air Forces training base for both World War I and World War II. Today, Dallas Love Field is a commercial airport. Four airlines fly in and out. Southwest Airlines and Delta Airlines account for most of the flights.

The single engine, tandem seat, low wing Valiant was 29' long and 12' tall, with a 42' wingspan. The fixed landing gear was conventional. Its top speed was 180 miles per hour from its nine-cylinder, air-cooled, 450 horsepower radial engine.

During World War II, the Army Air Forces taught men to fly in the Stearman PT-13 biplane or Boeing-Stearman PT-17 biplane (Boeing-Stearman Model 75 Kaydet) or the Fairchild PT-19 low wing. The Vultee was the next step. It of course was faster, larger, and heavier than the initial trainers. It was more complex, as the cadet had to operate landing flaps (mechanical crank and cable system) and adjust the controllable-pitch propeller. Also, the pilot had to learn to use a two-way communication radio.

The delivery legs were Long Beach to Tucson (Arizona), Tucson to Midland (Texas), and then Midland to Dallas. The stops were made to re-fuel, bathroom, eat, and rest.

Fort and some of the other pilots had practiced formation flying and agreed to practice again on the Midland to Dallas leg. Military pilots do so for mutual defense, concentrating firepower. Formation flying of course has a major negative, of colliding with another aircraft in the formation. Therefore, WASP rules banned formation flying. The pilots were not military pilots, and of course there was no risk of attack from other aircraft or the ground on these domestic flights. The fact that some practiced formation flying was to the dismay of most of the other WASP ferry pilots, who agreed with and respected the no formation flying rule.

Near Merkel, Texas which is 17 miles west of Abilene and 1.5 hours from destination Love Field and flying in formation, she collided with Frank Stamme. Stamme was ferrying another Vultee Valiant. Her wing struck his landing gear. Parts of her wing fell off. She died in the crash, age 24.1 years. Stamme was able to land safely. The date was 3/21/1943, a Sunday.

Fort was the first WAFS aviatrix killed on a delivery mission; and the first female pilot to die on war duty (granted, some do not interpret the domestic ferrying of new aircraft as war duty) in American history. Another thirty-eight WASPs died during World War II – eleven in training accidents, and the other twenty-seven when flying missions. As in the case of Fort, these missions were mostly flying new aircraft, from factories to training bases.

Fort had written an article about her Pearl Harbor Day experience. The *Women's Home Companion* (1873 – 1957) published it posthumously, 7/1943.

Fort was a serious diarist. Two of her diary statements include the following:

> As long as our planes fly overhead, the skies of America are free and that's what all of us everywhere are fighting for. And that we, in a very small way, are being allowed to help keep that sky free is the most beautiful thing I have ever known. I for one, am profoundly grateful that my one talent, my only knowledge, flying, happens to be of use to my country when it is needed. That's all the luck I ever hope to have.
>
> If I die violently, who can say it was before my time? I want no one to grieve for me. I was the happiest in the sky, at dawn when the quietness of the air was like a caress, when the noon sun beat down, and at dusk when the sky was drenched with the fading light. Think of me there and remember me, I hope, as I shall you.

Unfortunately, most of Fort's diaries were lost in her old bedroom when the family home burned to the ground, 12/27/1942. This was a time when much of society (male and female) believed that women should not fly for reasons of propriety, and/or should not fly as women not capable of such abilities. It is assumed that her diaries addressed such issues; so the loss of her writings was the loss of a significant window into the life of a young, female, pioneer aviator.

Cornelia Fort and her three older brothers were raised in Nashville, Tennessee, in a wealthy and prominent family. Her parents were Rufus Fort and Louise Clark Fort. Her physician father went on to co-found a successful, disability insurance company. This was the National Life and Accident Insurance Company of Nashville. Dr. Fort was a vice president and the medical director of the company.

When Cornelia was five years old (1924), her parents took her and her brothers to see a barnstorming pilot demonstrate aviation in a Curtiss JN-4 Jenny. Jennies were a series of tandem seat, conventional landing gear, biplanes made by the Curtiss Aeroplane Company. Its cruise and top speeds were 60 and 75 miles per hour, from its 90-horsepower engine. It was introduced in 1915 as an Army Air Forces training aircraft. The U.S., Canada, and Great Britain used it to train World War I pilots. More than 6,800 of the most common version were made. This was the JN-4, flown by the barnstormer. After World War I, surplus Jennies became the most common civilian aircraft, by far.

Charles Lindbergh (1902 Detroit – 1974 HA) took his first flying lesson 4/9/1922 in a tandem seat, Lincoln Standard Tourabout biplane trainer. He was not allowed to solo, as he did not have the money to put up a damage bond. He spent the next few months barnstorming across Nebraska, Kansas, Colorado, Wyoming, and Montana as a wing walker and parachutist; to earn some money. He worked briefly as an airplane mechanic at Billings, Montana.

Lindbergh bought a war surplus Jenny 5/1923, for $500. He took a half-hour of instruction in it with a pilot who was visiting the field to pick up another surplus Jenny. This was the first time that Lindbergh had touched an airplane in six months. Later that day, Lindbergh soloed in his own Jenny. This was at Americus, Georgia. As to who decided that Lindbergh was ready to solo, he did. Very few pilots then or now solo in an aircraft they own. And of course, pilots today do not solo until a certified instructor gives the go ahead.

Four years later in 1927 (May 20-21) as already mentioned, Lindbergh made another solo flight. This was from Roosevelt Field (1916 – 1951), Long Island, New York, to Le Bourget Aerodrome (1919 – a general aviation airport today), Paris, France. This transatlantic flight was the first for a solo pilot. The flight was also the first from North America to the European continent. Lindbergh became a massive celebrity, as a result.

Anyway, the barnstormer and his flying show in the Jenny at Nashville thrilled Cornelia and her three older brothers.

One day a couple of years after the barnstormer show, Dr. Fort took his three sons into his study, where serious talks occurred. He had his boys promise that they would never learn to fly an airplane, as it was so dangerous. They were nine, eight, and five years older than Cornelia. They agreed.

The beau of a friend of Cornelia owned a flying service at Nashville's Berry Field. Cornelia and her girlfriend had the boyfriend take them up. Cornelia was enraptured by the experience. She started pilot training. Her father heard about the lessons. He called Cornelia into his study, to remind her of the family pact on no aviation. Cornelia's response to her father, was that she had not been invited to the meeting!

Cornelia learned to fly in a Luscombe 50. Like the trainers mentioned above based at Oahu's Rodgers Airport, it was a single engine, high wing, conventional landing gear, tandem seat, aircraft. It had no wood components though, as did the other planes mentioned above. It was also faster from its 90 horsepower engine, with cruise and top speeds of 120 and 128 miles per hour.

Dr. Fort died from health issues, 3/1940. Cornelia soloed five weeks later, 4/27/1940. She was 21.2 years old. She earned her license 6/19/1940, her commercial pilot's license 2/8/1941, and her instructor's rating 3/10/1941.

Cornelia gave flying lessons at Colorado A&M University (now Colorado State University) in Fort Collins. She moved to Oahu and started instructing 9/1941. She was busy training at Oahu. She flew 300 hours in less than three months.

Fort is shown below. The aircraft shown is the Vultee Valiant trainer; her death plane. The inscription on her grave's footstone at Mount Olivet Cemetery in Nashville reads as follows: *KILLED IN THE SERVICE OF HER COUNTRY*

After the sneak attacks and the U.S. entrance into World War II, the CPTP changed forever, including its name. The new War Training Service (WTS) served mainly as the screening program for potential pilot candidates, 1942-1944. Students still attended classes at colleges and universities, and flight training was still conducted by private flight schools. However, all WTS graduates were required to sign a contract agreeing to enter the military if needed, following graduation.

The CPTP/WTS program trained 435,165 people to fly, including hundreds of women and minorities (especially African Americans). Notable program participants included the following:

- Alexander Vraciu, 1918 IN – 2015 CA, World War II super Ace
- Richard Bong, 1920 WI – 8/6/1945 CA, World War II super Ace, died in a jet crash on a test flight
- Robert Rahn, 1920 – 1998, World War II fighter pilot in Europe, Douglas test pilot
- Robert Deiz, 1920 OR – 1992 OH, Tuskegee Airman in World War II
- John Glenn, 1921 OH – 2016 OH, flew fighters Korea, astronaut, U.S. Senator
- Dora Dougherty, 1921 MN – 2013 TX, trained male World War II pilots on flying bombers
- George McGovern, 1922 SD – 2012 SD, World War II super ace

Dora Dougherty above was perhaps the best known of the WASP pilots. She was a four engine, Boeing B-29 Superfortress heavy bomber demonstration pilot. She was one of several WASPs who trained male, military pilots. She earned a doctorate degree in aviation education from New York University, completed in 1955. She worked for Bell Aircraft as a human factors engineer, designing helicopter cockpits. She tested helicopters for Bell, setting records for altitude and distance. She received numerous awards for her pioneer work in aviation. She was inducted into the Military Aviation Hall of Fame.

The CPTP/WTS program was largely phased out in the summer of 1944. By then, the need for military pilots was much less.

The 1970 *Tora, Tora, Tora* drama movie dramatizes the attack on Oahu and Pearl Harbor. Jean Marie Donnell (1921 ME – 1988 Los Angeles) portrayed a flying instructor in the movie named *Cornelia Fort*. Donnell was age 49, heavy-set, and had blond curls in the movie. Fort was 24 years old, dark-haired, and thin. Therefore, it may be that Donnell was portraying Marguerite Gambo, who was closer in age and body shape (but also had dark hair). In the movie, Donnell was flying an open-cockpit Stearman Kaydet biplane. This does resemble the open-cockpit Meyers OTW biplane that Gambo was flying 12/7/1941.

Commander Mitsuo Fuchida (1902 Japan – 1976 Japan, diabetes) led the first aircraft attack group 12/7/1941 on Oahu and Pearl Harbor. He saw no activity of note. Fuchida slid back the canopy of the single engine, three crew (commander, pilot, back-gunner/radio operator), low wing Nakajima B5N2 torpedo bomber; and fired a single dark blue flare called a *black dragon*. This was the signal to the others to attack.

Fuchida ordered his radio operator at 7:53 to send the coded signal *tora, tora, tora* to his superiors on the 855' IJN Akagi (1927 – 6/5/1942 American aircraft damaged at Midway Atoll, Japanese destroyers torpedoed to sink, 267 of 1,630 crew lost {16%}) carrier, the flagship for the assault. The word *tora* means *tiger* in Japanese. However, Fuchida was not communicating about jungle cats. *Tora* is an abbreviated radio code word. It is short for *totsugeki raigeki* which translates to *lightning attack*. Fuchida was telling his superiors that the objective of complete surprise had been achieved.

By the way, the movie was made for $25.5 million, and had a U.S. box office of $29.5 million.

Fuchida admired Adolph Hitler (1889 Austria - 4/30/1945 Berlin, pistol suicide), to the point where he grew a Hitler-style mustache.

Fuchida served in the Japanese Navy 1924-1945, retiring as a Captain. After the War, he was dumbfounded when he learned of the humane way that the Americans treated Japanese prisoners of war. This was inexplicable to him, as the bushido code mandated revenge as not optional, but a responsibility for an offended party to restore honor. In the fall of 1948, Fuchida read a pamphlet (*I Was a Prisoner of Japan*) about the life of 4/18/1942 Doolittle Raider Jacob DeShazer (1912 OR – 2008 OR), who was much abused by the Japanese as a prisoner of war. DeShazer was not repatriated until the War ended 3.3 years later. After the War, DeShazer attended a Methodist-connected college to train to be a missionary. He worked as a Christian missionary in Japan 1948-1978.

DeShazer's story affected Fuchida. He read the Bible. He became a Christian 9/1949. Fuchida and DeShazer met 5/1950, which further impressed and motivated Fuchida. Fuchida traveled throughout the United States and Europe, telling his stories as a Christian evangelist.

The Cornelia Fort Airpark in East Nashville was named in her honor. The Airpark was located five miles east of downtown Nashville. The City of Nashville acquired the airport in 2011 and converted it to parkland (to add to the adjacent Shelby Park).

Rob Simbeck of Nashville wrote a Fort biography. *Daughter of the Air: The Brief Soaring Life of Cornelia Fort* came out in 1999.

Mathilda Burling's (1882 – 1964) stepson Private George Burling (???? – 1918 France, influenza) when overseas fighting in World War I contracted influenza and died. He was eventually buried at the St. Mihiel American Cemetery in Thiaucourt, France. Mrs. Burling was one of the Gold Star Mothers who lobbied Congress and President Herbert Hoover for the U.S. to pay for mothers to fly to France to visit their sons' graves. The legislation passed. Seven thousand mothers made the trip 1930-1933.

When President of the Gold Star Mothers of America, Burling presented the first Gold Star of World War II to the mother of Private Joseph Moser, several days after the Oahu attack. However, there is no way of knowing who was the first of the 2,335 on duty U.S. military person killed 12/7/1941, on Oahu or in the lagoon harbor.

4- NIIHAU EPISODE, INCARCERATION OF JAPANESE

The Tokugawa Shogunate was the last, feudal Japanese military government. It ran 265 years, 1603-1868. Shoguns were hereditary military governors from the Tokugawa clan. They were Japan's rulers. They ruled from Edo Castle which was in Edo, the previous name for Tokyo. Emperor Meiji (see below) changed the name when he took power from the fifteenth and last Shogun in 1868. The Shogunate era therefore was called the Edo period.

Edo was on Honshu, Japan's largest and most populous island. At 88,017 square miles, Honshu is a little less than one-third the size of Texas.

During this time, the Emperor in Kyoto was nominally the country's religious leader, the head of the Shinto state religion. Kyoto is also on Honshu, but distant at 291 miles west-northwest of Edo (Tokyo). The Emperor was considered the titular ruler of Japan. He announced the appointment of Shogun officials and successors. However, this was just a formality. Tokugawa Shoguns selected their own leaders, to be rubber-stamped by the Emperor.

The Shogunate appointed a liaison called the *Kyoto Shoshidai*, to deal with the Emperor and his court and nobility. *Kyoto Shoshidai* translates to the *shoguns' representative in Kyoto*. Again, the Emperor had very little say in domestic rule and state affairs. He was just a figurehead, and generally remained secluded at his Kyoto palace with his family and staff.

The Shoguns controlled Japan, both locally and in affairs of state. This included foreign trade, which was very lucrative. Rice was the main product exported during these centuries.

Tokugawa Iemitsu (1604 Japan – 1651 Japan) was the third of the 15 Shogun rulers. He ruled 1623-1651. Shogun Iemitsu and his Shogunate along with certain other smaller feudal domains enacted and enforced strict regulations on international commerce and foreign relations in the 1630s. The Shoguns expelled all Europeans and Americans, although the latter were few to maybe even none. Foreigners were not allowed to move to Japan, or even visit. Japanese commoners were not allowed to leave. If commoners sailed off somehow, they faced harsh penalties upon return (the edict stated that they would be executed). The ship and cargo were confiscated.

This isolation foreign relations policy was called *sakoku.*

The shoguns also banned Christianity. Bounties were paid to those who discovered Christians on a Japanese island. Bigger bounties were paid in the case of a found Christian priest or minister. These persons were expelled, if they were lucky. They were usually executed.

The sakoku period ran until 1866; although the U.S. forced Japan to open up some in the 1850s through gunboat diplomacy.

The reasons for the establishment and continuation of the sakoku closed society are still debated today. The (generally) consensus explanations though include the following:

- As an effort for Tokugawa Iemitsu to consolidate power, to be held by successor Shoguns
- To block the colonial powers of Spain and Portugal from controlling parts of Japan
- Prevent foreigners from trying to convert Japanese to Christianity, especially Catholicism; for some reason, the Shoguns feared Christianity as a religion

In the eyes of the Shoguns, Spain and Portugal were not able to separate trade from religion, whereas Netherlands and Great Britain could do so; Dutch traders were required to swear to not engage in missionary activities, to continue trade with Japan

Today Japan is 1% Christian, compared to 3, 7, and 29% for China, Vietnam, and South Korea; therefore, sakoku in banning Christians and especially Christian ministers or even laity including missionaries, seems to have worked in this regard; again, as to why the shoguns were anti-Christianity, this is not known

For the record, the traditional and common religion of Japan today is Shinto; Shinto focuses on ritual practices to be carried out diligently, in order to establish a connection between present-day Japan and its ancient past; the religion has many gods; today per surveys, more than three fourths of Japanese participate in Shinto practices or rituals, although less than a fourth identify themselves as *Shintoists*

Japan was not completely isolated under the sakoku policy. The only European influence permitted though was trade with the Dutch, and only at one location. This was the 2.22-acre, fan-shaped Dejima Island in Nagasaki Bay. Dejima was formed by digging a canal in 1634, to separate a peninsula from the main part of the island in Nagasaki Bay. The island was made to constrain Portuguese traders. However, it ended up serving as a Dutch trading post, 1641-1853.

Trade with the Chinese, Koreans, and even indigenous Japanese of the Ryukyu Islands was also limited, to sole gateways of peripheral provinces. Trade with countries of the Americas was banned.

These and other countries or territories though were occasionally allowed to visit the ruling Shogun in Edo at Osaka Castle. Osaka Castle is on Honshu Island as is Edo (Tokyo). It was another base for the Shogun rulers. Osaka was 311 miles southwest of Edo. The castle was completed back in 1583. These visits to the Shoguns were more or less marketing efforts, to establish trade with Japan.

The Japanese Shogun rulers were wise enough though to know that they must learn of Western science, technologies, and methods; to progress and even protect themselves from invaders. Starting in the 1700s, Dejima became a center of study of medicine, military science, navigation, optics, shipbuilding, weaponry, astronomy, etc. These scientific studies became the basis of knowledge and a factor in the *Rangaku* movement. Rangaku translates to *Dutch studies*, and therefore by extension *Western studies*.

Even though the Shoguns were essentially dictators, this 265-year Edo period of the 15 Tokugawa Shogunates was Japan's longest run of peace and stability. To sum up, most of the Shoguns were in the category of *benevolent dictators*.

Fourteenth Shogun Tokugawa Iemochi (1846 Japan – 1866 Japan, beriberi suspected) ruled 1858-1866. He wed 121st Emperor Komei's (1831 Japan – 1867 Japan, probably smallpox) sister Princess Kazu-no-Miya Chikako (1846 Japan – 1877 Japan) in 1862. Emperor Komei reigned almost 21 years, 1846-1867. His reign ended with his death.

This marriage resulted in the Emperor Imperial Court in Kyoto gaining some political influence. Shogun Iemochi occasionally consulted Emperor Komei, now his brother-in-law, on various policies.

Emperor Komei's son Meiji (1852 Japan – 1912 Japan; uremia as a complication from diabetes, nephritis, and gastroenteritis) succeeded his father when he died, as 122nd Emperor. His reign began in 1867, when he was only 14.3 years old. For a number of reasons, Meiji's power was increased greatly. Tokugawa Yoshinobu (1837 Japan – 1913 Japan) was the sitting Shogun. Realizing the futility of his situation, Yoshinobu abdicated political power to the Emperor 11/9/1867. He ruled only fifteen months. Yoshinobu did so with the hope and intention that the Tokugawa house could be preserved, and have a role in the future government.

Several powerful feudal lords allied with the teenager Emperor Meiji and started the 1868-1869 Boshin War. The two sides were forces of the Tokugawa Shogunate and those seeking to return power to the Imperial Court. The latter won, although again Yoshinobu had already abdicated. Terminating the Tokugawa Shogunate left a power void. Again, power had shifted and shifted even more after the civil war to Emperor Meiji, when he was only sixteen years old. He ruled 45.5 years, until his death in 1912 at age 59.

Meiji presided over a time of rapid change in the Empire of Japan. Economically, Japan quickly transitioned from an isolationist feudal state to a capitalist, international power. Industries grew, including design and manufacture of military equipment. His reign was called the *Meiji Restoration* period. He further restored and secured practical imperial rule and power to the Emperor of Japan.

Due to modernization, and to opening the economy to the world from hundreds of years of isolationism, and because of political-cultural-social changes which began with Meiji's reign, Japan's economy went into a recession. As many lacked jobs or other ways to earn a living, many moved to other countries for a better life. The economic diaspora ran mainly from 1869 to 1924. It peaked in the mid-1880s for a number of years.

Several Japanese words related to this diaspora used in this chapter are defined below:

- *Issei* means Japanese who moved to the United States or an American territory (or to other countries for that matter); they were not allowed to apply for American citizenship until 1954
- *Nisei* means the children of Issei; if born in the United States or an American territory, they were automatically citizens per the citizenship

clause of the Fourteenth Amendment (see below), even though their parents were not citizens

- *Sansei* means the grandchildren of Issei and children of Nisei; they like their parents were citizens automatically
- *Kibei* means Japanese Americans whose parents sent them to Japan to live with relatives and to be educated; purposes were to learn and master the Japanese language and Japanese culture; another goal was to be in Japan instead of the U.S. in case war broke out between the two countries, which of course did happen 12/7/1941

There were 10,500 Kibei at the time of the 12/7/1941 sneak attacks; it was very difficult for Kibei to move back to the U.S. after the attacks; most young male Kibei in Japan at the time of the sneak attacks enlisted (and perhaps coerced to do so) in the Japanese military shortly after, or later if not yet of fighting age

- *Nikkei* is the catchall word for all Japanese who moved to other countries and their descendants; such moves were recorded as early as the 1100s to the Philippines; however as noted above, the mass diaspora began in 1885 during the Meiji period; at this time and later, many Japanese moved to the Philippines, to the U.S. Territory of Hawaii, and to the United States (and a few other countries)

Today, there are 3.8 million Nikkei; the five most common countries where they live are Brazil with 1.8 million, the U.S. 1.5 million, the Philippines 265,000, China 127,000 and Canada with 110,000

The states approved the Fourteenth Amendment to the United States Constitution in 1868. It was one of the three Reconstruction Amendments, addressing the status of former slaves after the Civil War. The Fourteenth Amendment includes the Citizenship Clause, in fact as the first sentence of the 435-word Amendment. It states that anyone born in the United States or its territories is a citizen. This is the case regardless of the citizenship, immigration status, length of time living in the U.S. or one of its territories, employment, age, criminal record, etc. of the parents. Therefore, Nisei and Sansei and on were American citizens at birth.

For the record, the Citizenship Clause reads as follows: *All persons born or naturalized in the United States, and subject to the jurisdiction thereof, are citizens of the United States and of the State wherein they reside.*

The amendment was passed to ensure that now free African Americans after the Civil War were citizens. Furthermore, it was to ensure that their children, grandchildren, and on were citizens as well. As worded so broadly (born on American soil the only requirement; if you prefer the Latin words, these are *jus soli* which translates to *right of the soil*) though, many millions of newborns are now U.S. citizens, even though the parents were not citizens.

The freed slaves were U.S. citizens. Some legal scholars state that the Fourteenth Amendment was passed solely to ensure that their children and grandchildren and on were also U.S. citizens, and that the amendment has no relation to granting citizenship to children born in the United States whose parents are non-citizens, whether the mother is in the country legally or not. In recent years, these have numbered about 285,000 births in the U.S. The Canadian figure is about 1,500 a year.

Non-citizen women try to enter the country to deliver their babies in the U.S., so that they will be citizens. In many cases, they are indigent, so the taxpayer pays the medical costs for prenatal care, delivery, and postnatal care. Persons born indigent are very, very much more likely to be non-productive citizens and costly to the taxpayer, compared to those born to non-indigent parents.

Today, about thirty-one countries have such a birthright citizenship clause. All are in the Western Hemisphere. No European or Asian country allows birthright citizenship. Most of the countries that do allow birthright citizenship are not particularly good places to live. In fact, some are horrible places to live. The only two notable exceptions in this group are the adjacent countries of the United States and Canada. The also adjacent country of Mexico also allows birthright citizenship. However, some if not most consider Mexico an undesirable country to live in. Brazil is another country that allows birthright citizenship, but again Brazil has its serious problems.

The United Nations recognizes 193 countries. As only two countries or so that are considered a good place to live have such an automatic citizenship clause upon birth, such a provision is obviously an extreme outlier. Many consider allowing such is radical and destructive for the planet, but that is another story.

Donald Trump (1946 NYC -) when campaigning for President in 2016 and also after taking office 1/2017 stated that birthright citizenship should not be the case, for children born in the U.S. if the parents were not citizens. Some Republicans tend to agree with President Trump, Democrats not so much.

In the Japanese economic diaspora, two hundred thousand Japanese moved to the islands of Hawaii. The men in this group were expected to work on the islands' sugar plantations as laborers, and many did at first. Another 180,000 sailed past Hawaii to the mainland United States. Many moved to the Philippines.

Most of the Japanese who moved to the U.S. settled on the West Coast. Many farmed or ran small businesses.

In 1907, Japan and the U.S. made an informal agreement to curtail immigration of Japanese unskilled workers, but allowing the immigration of businessmen, some family members, and new spouses.

Many Issei men after 1907 arranged marriages with proxy brides, who were often ten to 15 years younger. These women now spouses were allowed in. Despite never meeting before marriage (or at least never courted), most of these arranged marriages worked out.

The 1924 Immigration Act was passed to restrict immigration of Southern Europeans, Eastern Europeans, Arabs, Jews, and persons from countries with Roman Catholic majorities. The law also affirmed the longstanding ban on the immigration of non-white persons, with the exception of black African immigrants. Thus, almost all Asians were banned from immigrating to America.

The ban resulted in unusually well-defined generational groups, within the Japanese American community. Almost all Issei moved to the U.S., before the 1924 ban. Their children (Nisei) were U.S. citizens, as born in the U.S. As noted above, Issei were not allowed to become citizens until nine years after World War II.

As is always the case with first generation immigrants no matter the time or nationality or country, their children were much more attuned to their new country (Americanized, in this case) than their parents. For one thing, they spoke English, whereas their parents mostly never mastered the language. Also as just noted, they were citizens which their parents were not.

The intention of most Issei was to make some money and gain knowledge of American methods and technology, and then move back to Japan someday – to modernize Japan.

Moving back to Japan though had zero appeal to their Nisei children. America was a wonderful place to live for these youths compared to what they heard about Japan, or learned from trips back to visit relatives, or experienced from living in Japan to attend school. To sum up, the generation gap was much more than usual.

As Issei were not naturalized citizens, they were dependent upon their Nisei children in business dealings. These included renting or purchasing land, buying a business, making and owning homes, etc. This was cumbersome, to say the least.

The U.S. annexed the five-year Republic of Hawaii in 1898 with much controversy. The U.S. authorized self-rule for Hawaii, two years later. This move did appease both native Hawaiians and Japanese Hawaiians. Japanese Hawaiians were Hawaii's largest ethnic group next to native Hawaiians, at 37% of the population.

By the 1930s, Japan's military was in charge of the country, with the Emperor again just a showpiece. The military leaders were militant. As Exhibit A, they invaded and occupied China's Manchuria in 1931, by staging a fake event (Japanese soldiers detonated dynamite along a rail line near Mukden, Liaoning Province) as a pretense for the land grab. Manchuria is the northeast part of China, and the closest part of China to Japan. Japan set up a puppet state, renaming Manchuria *Manchukuo*.

Japan made the land grab to quell Chinese nationalism, and as Manchuria had fertile soil and was a source of needed raw materials. Japan banned countries that did not recognize Manchuria (or again *Manchukuo* as Japan called it) as belonging to Japan, from trading with China.

Japan used the 7/1937 Marco Polo Bridge incident (more of a non-event) to initiate a full-blown war against China. Japan's war crime atrocities in China against civilians as well as Chinese military men were countless, and so heinous to be unspeakable.

Some Americans, especially in California, came to resent the Japanese. This wave of anti-Japanese prejudice was as so many Japanese immigrants had moved in -- competing for jobs, setting up businesses, etc. Some bought land and ran small farms, making it difficult for local farmers to compete – the Japanese immigrants were willing to work harder for less money. The same situation existed in the commercial fishing industry, in some coastal areas. Most Americans were suffering financially, as this was during the worldwide, economic Great Depression.

A general anti-Japanese sentiment grew. Reports of the atrocities rendered by the Japanese military in China already mentioned added to the rancor.

A few cities, states, and even Uncle Sam passed laws, which were in effect anti-Japanese. These laws addressed restrictions on citizenship (Issei could not become citizens {until 1954}, although their children and grandchildren were), segregated schools, banned interracial marriage, banned Japanese from voting, banned Japanese from running for public office, banned Japanese from testifying against whites in trials, banned Japanese from owning land, etc.

As already noted, the resentment was not just due to the economic hit or the perceived economic hit. Americans were aware of Japan's belligerence and atrocities in China (the Nanking Massacre and Rape was 12/1937 – 1/1938). Again as already noted, the atrocities were countless and horrible beyond belief. Of course, Japanese in the Hawaiian Territory or the U.S. had no role in Japan's aggressions and imperialism, but just being Japanese established a tenuous link in the minds of some Americans. Furthermore, Japanese American leaders did not speak out about the atrocities, or rarely did. If they did speak out for Japan to reform, their statements were not forceful or demanding.

Japan greatly increased its military power and prowess in the 1930s. Concerned, the Office of Naval Intelligence (ONI) surveilled Japanese-American communities in Hawaii. President Franklin Roosevelt (1882 NY – 4/12/1945 GA, cerebral hemorrhage) emphasized this in 1936, by requesting that the ONI compile a *special list of those who would be the first to be placed in a concentration camp in the event of trouble* between Japan and the U.S.

In 1939 again as ordered by Roosevelt, the ONI and the Military Intelligence Division and the FBI collaborated to compile a larger *Custodial Detention Index.*

In the case of compiling these lists and collecting data, the FBI under Edgar Hoover (1895 D.C. – 1972 D.C.) did so, probably to a much greater degree than Roosevelt probably envisioned. The FBI collected data on German Americans and Italian Americans (again, almost all first generation), as well as on Issei.

Early in 1941, Roosevelt commissioned an investigation on Japanese Americans living on the West Coast and Hawaii. This latter study concluded 11/7/1941 (one month before the sneak attacks) that Japanese Americans would be very loyal to the U.S., if the two countries engaged in War. A later report delivered to Roosevelt 1/1942 also found little evidence to support claims of Japanese-American disloyalty, and argued against mass incarceration if war started between Japan and the U.S.

Congress passed the Alien Registration Act 6/1940. This law required the registration and fingerprinting of all aliens older than 14, the reporting of changes in address, etc. Almost five million foreign nationals registered including Issei, at post offices around the country.

As already noted, Americans had a number of concerns about the attitude and actions of Japan. These they transferred to questioning the loyalty of ethnic

Japanese, in case of war with the U.S. These concerns related to actions even before the 12/7/1941 sneak attacks, and included the following besides those already mentioned:

- 12/1937 Japanese ground artillery fired on, followed by aerial bombing/strafing on the Yangtze River of the 191' long and 29' beam and 5' draft, USS Panay PR-5 (1928 – 12/12/1937 bomb sunk Yangtze River) river gunboat, which sank; three, nearby, anchored Standard Oil river tankers (Standard Oil was an American company) were also air bombed and destroyed on the Yangtze at the same time; two Panay sailors were killed, as was the American Captain of one of the tankers and some civilians; many more were wounded; these attacks were without provocation
- 1/1938   American Embassy Consul John Allison (1905 – 1978) was investigating the case of a woman raped on American property in Nanking (the Nanking Massacre/Rape was 12/1937 - 1/1938), when a Japanese soldier slapped him in the face; Japan's Consul-General in Nanking Katsuo Okazaki (1897 Japan – 1965 Tokyo) apologized four days later, but only after the U.S. demanded such

Also during this same time, Japanese soldiers looted American property in Nanking

Moreover, Americans were aware of Japanese aggressions against China as already noted. Japan invaded and occupied Manchuria 9/1931 with no justification. Japan invaded the Rehe Province 1/21/1933 (Operation Nekka), and then annexed it as part of its Empire of Manchukuo (as already noted, Japan called Manchuria *Manchukuo*). Rehe was on the west side of Manchuria. Japan stated that Rehe was required as a buffer between China and Manchuria. Of course in reality, Rehe and Manchuria were part of China.

Japan initiated again with no reason or war declaration 7/1937, the Sino-Japanese War. Japan occupied much of China through the end of World War II, so this was more than eight years.

Also as noted several times already, Japan's war crimes in China were countless and heinous; directed against civilians as well as soldiers. For example, the Nanking Massacre and Rape was mentioned above. The Japanese Army ran wild over the 12/1937 – 1/1938 six-week period after capturing Nanking. Nanking then was the capital of China. This was looting, arson, mass torture, mass mutilation, mass rape (children and women, many multiple times), and mass murder of Chinese civilians. China's estimate is that more than 300,000 civilians were murdered. Japan stated at the time and over the years that the number was much lower. Furthermore, some vocal Japanese government officials even to this day deny that the Nanking Massacre/Rape happened at all. Others deny pressing women into forced prostitution for the pleasure of Japanese military men. These persons may be compared to the Holocaust deniers.

Using the 300,000 murdered figure and 42 days, this is an average of 7,143 murders a day, or almost 300 an hour, or almost five a minute. How can such atrocities be explained? How could young Japanese men (the soldiers) be convinced that such killings and abuse had justification, was their duty and/or privilege? It belies reason, even despite the fact that their officers approved and even ordered the murders and rapes.

After the War, tribunals on Japanese military atrocities were conducted. Only two high-ranking Japanese Army officers were prosecuted for these war crimes, as follows:

- General Iwane Matsui (1879 Japan – 12/23/1948 Tokyo, hanging execution) was commander of Japan's Expeditionary Forces in China; Matsui contended that the military police of each division were in charge, not Army commanders
- Lieutenant General Hisao Tani (1882 Japan – 4/26/1947 Nanking, firing squad execution) was Commander of Japan's Sixth Army; he reported to General Matsui; Tani contended that it was Korean soldiers that Japan had conscripted, not Japanese soldiers, that looted and mutilated and raped and murdered

Burly Second Lieutenants Toshiaki Mukai and Tsuyoshi Noda were both executed 1/28/1949, for entering a contest to see who could kill a hundred Chinese the quickest using a sword, the end of 1937. When the score was reported to be 106 to 105, the two muscular men *went into extra innings* as there was some debate on the number. The contest may have ended with up to three hundred Chinese slaughtered.

Between 1936 and 1941, Japan rapidly conquered and occupied a large portion of Asia. Well aware of these aggressions and atrocities, the U.S. (and other countries, for that matter) pressured Japan in a number of ways to act right. These methods were not successful. Diplomacy did not work. Economic sanctions did not work.

On 12/7-8/1941, the Empire of Japan attacked without warning thirteen sites in or on the Pacific Ocean. The 1907 Hague Convention addressed the requirement to declare war in its *Convention Relative to the Opening of Hostilities* statements. These clauses describe the international actions a country should perform, before opening hostilities. Article 1 states: *The Contracting Powers recognize that hostilities between themselves must not commence without previous and explicit warning, in the form either of a reasoned declaration of war or of an ultimatum with conditional declaration of war.* Japan took a pass on giving an advance warning, of maybe attacking. Shame on Japan, again (Japan had a history of such unprovoked sneak attacks).

The attacks were on the same day, but targets were over the International Date Line which explains the two dates. The International Date Line is an imaginary line from the North Pole to the South Pole. It marks the change from one calendar day to the next. It roughly follows the 180° line of longitude, through the middle of the Pacific Ocean. The attacked thirteen sites (or ships) were as follows:

- Nine U.S. possessions
  - Storming and capture of a 159' long USS river gunboat and its crew when berthed at Shanghai Harbor; this little Yangtze River gunboat

was the only USS that Japan captured in World War II; for good measure, the Japanese also gun-sank a 177' HMS river gunboat in Shanghai Harbor, at about the same time; if counting this British warship, it is fourteen sneak attacks instead of thirteen

- IJN submarine gun-sank an Army-chartered, 250' long freighter off California
- Howland and Baker Islands of the Phoenix Islands of the U.S. Minor Outlying Islands were bombed, these two islands are 43 miles apart
- Five U.S. military installations (harbors, airfields, bases) on five Pacific Ocean islands; these five islands were Oahu (Pearl Harbor), Guam, Midway, Wake, and Philippines

- Three British Crown colonies – Malaysia, Hong Kong, and Singapore
- Thailand

Japan ended up occupying the three British crown colonies, Thailand, and Wake Island for the duration of World War II. Japan occupied Guam until the U.S. re-captured 8/1944. Japan occupied the major Philippine islands by the spring of 1942. The U.S. wrested the Philippines islands back beginning 10/1944, and into 1945. Douglas MacArthur (1880 AR – 1964 DC) said he would return and he did, but it took 2.6 years.

Some Japanese soldiers held out though on Mindanao Island (second largest of the Philippines) until the end of the War, 8/1945. In fact, 200 well organized and disciplined Japanese infantrymen held out on Mindanao until 1/1948, which was 28 months after the War ended (if you can believe it).

In the next few weeks or months after the sneak attacks, Japan also conquered and occupied Borneo, Burma, New Britain, Gilbert Islands, and the oil-rich and rubber tree plantations Dutch East Indies.

In these thirteen (or fourteen if counting the HMS river gunboat sunk in Shanghai Harbor) attacks on the same day, the Japanese Empire was for the most part stupendously successful in terms of devastation and casualties rendered, versus its own loss of equipment and casualties. Japan's planning and executions were brilliant. Said yet a third way, the outcomes were very one-sided in Japan's favor. To quote President Roosevelt from his next day 12/8/1941 Monday speech to Congress, 12/7/1941 was *a date that will live in infamy* for the United States.

Of the five U.S. military targets on the five Pacific Ocean islands, Americans of course most remember Oahu (Pearl Harbor) of the U.S. Territory of Hawaii, again due to the one-sided outcome. Japan launched two air attacks (bombing and strafing), one hour apart on a Sunday morning. The U.S. military had 2,335 and 1,143 men killed and wounded. Another 68 and 35 Hawaiian civilians were killed and injured. In comparison, only 64 Japanese military men died (55 airmen and nine midget submarine sailors) and one (a submariner) captured. This is a ratio of more than 36 American military deaths per one Japanese military death.

The Japanese Navy sank or damaged nineteen USSs at Oahu (Pearl Harbor) including all eight battleships of the Pacific fleet. Hundreds of aircraft were destroyed, and most of these when on the ground. Japan lost only 29 aircraft, nine and 20 in the first and second wave attacks. These were fifteen, nine, and five dive bombers, fighters, and torpedo bombers. Japan's five mini-submarines were all sunk, which was more or less the (not stated) plan. The other 51 ships of the Japanese Task Force were unseen and undetected, coming and going.

The Navy's aircraft carrier fleet (three flattops) was not in port this day, which was very, very fortunate. The three carriers helped turn the tide of the Pacific War, a half year later off Midway Island.

Japan's surprise attacks without declaring war ended the United States' isolationist attitude, left over from losing 116,700 men in uniform (almost 46% in combat) and another 204,000 wounded or made ill (many with permanent disabilities) in World War I. Congress at President Roosevelt's request declared war on Japan the next day of 12/8/1941, which was a Monday.

In the wake of these attacks and again considering Japan's belligerence as described above, some or many or maybe even most Americans were concerned that some Japanese Americans would be loyal to Japan and the Emperor, to the point where they would join in with invading Japanese forces (should Japan attack the U.S. West Coast), spy for Japan, conduct sabotage activities, etc. These concerns were especially the case on the West Coast as already mentioned, for the following reasons:

- Most Japanese (and definitely more so Issei than Nisei) here lived insular lives – living among other Japanese, and not mixing so much with the natives. Los Angeles, San Francisco, and Seattle had large Japantowns.
- If Japan were to attack the U.S., it would be on the West Coast of course, in lieu of the Atlantic states or a land assault from Mexico or Canada.

As noted already, some native Californians were not in a welcome mood anyway; as they attributed their economic problems to Japanese immigration. This was during the 1929-1941, worldwide, economic Great Depression.

The concerns about loyalty to Japan had some justification, especially for Issei, but probably not at all for Nisei. Nisei were bilingual (many of their parents spoke only a little English), and were overall much Americanized compared to their parents.

These concerns regarding Issei stemmed from a number of events, situations, and stances besides those already mentioned, as follows:

- Most Issei were strong supporters of Japan's militaristic expansions, including annexing parts of China. A few Japanese leaders did speak out that Japan's surprise attacks were uncalled for and unfair. These included some Japanese consulate officials, and officers of the Japanese-Americans Citizens League. However, these were only a few, and they did not direct their statements to the Japanese government, nor did they advise (or demand) Japan to cease its aggressions, expansions, or atrocities. In addition, they had not spoken out before the sneak attacks.
  - Granted, many or most were simply just focused on bettering their lives in the U.S. For almost all, the U.S. was a much better life than the one in Japan they left, or would have if they moved back.

- o Some were in support of Japan's aggressions and colonialism and even proud of same, perceiving it as a way of improving the Japanese economy, so as to be able to move back to Japan; or even to a new country, now controlled by Japan. Some were outspoken, in this regard. These were all Issei.

  Some Issei who had moved back to Japan though from either the U.S. or Hawaii, did publicly laud Japan's aggression.

- Some Japanese living in the Philippines at the time of the 12/8/1941 first attack collaborated with the Japanese invasion troops. These later included sizable populations of Japanese immigrants living in Davao, Mindanao, who aided the invasion forces when Japan attacked 12/13/1942. Mindanao is the southernmost and second largest Philippine island. President Roosevelt and other leaders knew of this fifth column assistance, but the general population did not.

A fifth column is defined as a group of people who undermine (either overtly or clandestinely) a larger group from within, usually in favor of an enemy group or nation.

- There was evidence of espionage from decrypted messages to Japan from agents in North America and Hawaii, before and after the 12/7/1941 sneak attacks. However again, the general public did not know this.

- Following the 12/7, 8/1941 sneak attacks, seven Japanese submarines patrolled the U.S. West Coast. They attacked a number of American freighters and tankers. These included the SS Emidio, SS Samoa, SS Larry Doheny, SS Montebello, SS Agriworld, SS Lahaina, SS Barbara Olson, SS Absaroka, SS L. P. St. Clair, SS Manini, SS Prusa, SS H. M. Storey, and the SS Dorothy Phillips. At least one Canadian freighter was attacked, the Rosebank. At least three ships were sunk and two damaged, with some deaths and more injuries. One sinking was in view from the Pacific Coast Highway. The submarines skirmished at least twice with U.S. Navy air or sea forces.

By the end of 12/1941, the Japanese submarines had returned to friendly waters for replenishment. Some then returned to the hunt, along the U.S. West Coast.

Under much pressure, President Roosevelt reluctantly issued Executive Order 9066 February 19, 1942. The Executive Order authorized the War Secretary to designate certain areas as military zones, from which certain persons could be excluded. Without due process or a declaration of martial law, this cleared the way for relocation and confinement of Japanese Americans, German Americans, and Italian Americans living in these zones.

Regarding the *under much pressure* and *reluctance* wording, historians tend to believe that Roosevelt did not think that internment was necessary from the reports that he had read, and furthermore was not in favor of this. Roosevelt though was apparently in the minority on such thinking; and pressured to incarcerate.

Two incidents less than a week later cemented the plan for incarceration of Japanese Americans, as follows:

- 2/23/1942   The Type B1-class, 357' long and 31' beam and 17' draft, long range, IJN I-17 (1941 – 8/19/1943 Kiwi minesweeper and U.S. floatplanes depth charges sunk off Noumea, 91 of 97 crew lost {94%}) cruiser submarine was part of the Oahu (Pearl Harbor) Task Force. I-17's mission was to reconnoiter and engage any USSs that tried to sortie from Pearl Harbor fleeing the attack and/or searching for the Japanese armada. As it turned out, there was no such need.

I-17 returned to Japan for replenishment. She then with other submarines sailed to the West Coast of the U.S. On 12/20/1942, she gun-sank the 6,912-ton General Petroleum tanker SS Emidio (1921 – 12/20/1941 off Cape Mendocino, five crew lost and others injured) mentioned above, which was sailing from Seattle to San Pedro, California. The submarine connected with five, 14-centimeter shells. As sailing in ballast, a petroleum cargo was not lost and the ocean polluted.

I-17 returned to Japan for replenishment again, and then back to the West Coast. On this date, I-17 surfaced only several hundred yards offshore. Captain Kozo Nishino ordered his men to aim at the Richfield aviation fuel storage tanks of the Ellwood oil field. The Ellwood oil field was 12 miles west of Santa Barbara, and near the ocean. Seventeen, 14-centimeter shells were fired, 19:15 to 19:35. Most landed way off, exploding either miles inland on Tecolote Ranch or splashing in the ocean before making land. However, one shell hit near the Luton-Bell 17 oil well, on the beach just below Fairway 14 of the present-day golf course – several of the Sandpiper Golf Club holes are on the beach. This caused $500 in damage to a pier, catwalk, pump house, etc.

This incident was the first naval bombardment by an enemy power on the U.S. mainland since the German Type U-151, 213' long and 24' beam and 17' draft, SM U-156 (1917 – 9/25/1918 believed sunk by a mine in the Northern Barrage, all 77 crew lost) submarine shelled Orleans, Cape Cod, Massachusetts (no damage), and a 120' long, steel tugboat towing four barges to the Virginia Capes. SM U-156 used its 5.9" deck guns. The Perth Amboy tug was damaged. The four barges were sunk. Some tug crewmen were injured (none killed though). The shells that landed on the Orleans beaches were probably aimed at the tug and barges. This was 7/21/1918, less than four months before the World War I Armistice date.

In the late 1930s, Captain Nishino had been a tanker skipper. He anchored at the Ellwood Oil Field dock in 1938 to take on a load of oil. When walking with his crew to a formal welcoming ceremony onshore, he tripped and fell into a patch of prickly pear cactus. Believe it or not, this patch of cactus is still there, just off fairway 11 of the Sandpiper Golf Club. Cacti does not grow naturally in Japan, so Nishino probably did not know to maintain his distance. The sight of the proud Japanese commander having cactus spines pulled from his rear end, provoked laughter from a group of nearby American oil workers. Therefore, it appears that this 2/23/1942 wild shelling may have been an avenging act, four years later (well, at the least it makes a good story).

- 2/25/1942   The following night after the Ellwood oil field attack shortly after 02:00, Los Angeles military radar detected something 120 miles west of the city, on or above the Pacific Ocean. Air raid sirens sounded. Powerful searchlights were switched on. A blackout was put into effect. Army gunners in Santa Monica unleashed a barrage of anti-aircraft fire to down Japanese fighters and bombers. Other coastal gun locations in other parts of the metropolis opened fire, to come to Santa Monica's aid.

The *all-clear* order came less than an hour later. Los Angeles' artillery batteries pumped 1,440 rounds of 37 millimeter and 76 millimeter anti-aircraft ammunition into the sky over 50 minutes. Ten tons of shrapnel and unexploded ammunition rained down, ripping through buildings and vehicles and shattering windows. No people were killed or injured from the firing. However, five died -- three in automobile crashes, and two from heart attacks.

Twenty Japanese-Americans were arrested, for allegedly trying to signal or direct the non-existing Japanese aircraft and/or warships to targets.

It appears that a meteorological balloon or meteorological balloons sent up on purpose or by mistake that night to determine wind conditions were interpreted as attacking Japanese aircraft. To sum up, there was no enemy, but ample hysteria.

This came to be called the Los Angeles Battle.

These two events 31 hours apart were written up with some to much exaggeration in newspapers. Some radio broadcasts were also misleading. The hysteria part was not too emphasized. As part of that hysteria, some came to believe that the government was covering up the severity of damages and the number of casualties, to avoid terrorizing the populace.

Exaggerated or even false reports of suspected spying and sabotage on the West Coast, later sightings or suspected sightings of Japanese surface warships or submarines or aircraft, or other aggressions by Japanese military by print journalists (newspapers, magazines, etc.) fueled the suspicions and concerns. Again, radio broadcasts skimpy on the facts added to the concerns.

Steven Spielberg (1946 Cincinnati -) directed the 1979, ensemble cast, comedy movie *1941*, which is loosely based on these two, 2/1942 events. The star cast included John Belushi, Dan Aykroyd, John Candy, Slim Pickens, Robert Stack,

Ned Beatty, Christopher Lee, Tim Matheson, Warren Oates, Treat Williams, etc. Its production cost was $35 million, and box office $95 million.

Another confounding issue had to do with the fact that the U.S. had cracked the Imperial Japanese Navy's codes. Japanese communications to Japanese Americans were to spy on the U.S. However, it appears that no Japanese Americans were doing so. If the U.S. had arrested and prosecuted ethnic Japanese thought to be disloyal, this could lead to Japan learning that its code had been broken. The Japanese Navy would change its code, and the U.S. would forfeit a major advantage.

Americans were also aware of the Niihau incident (described below).

The Hawaiian Islands are an archipelago of eight major islands, several atolls, numerous smaller islets, and undersea seamounts in the North Pacific Ocean. An archipelago is an island group. An atoll is a ring-shaped coral reef that completely or partially encircles a lagoon. A seamount is a mountain rising from the ocean seafloor that does not reach to the water's surface, so definitely a navigation hazard. Altogether, Hawaii is 137 islands and islets. The seventy square mile Niihau is the seventh largest (Hawaii is the largest, at 4,028 miles), and the westernmost. Niihau is roughly six miles wide and eighteen miles long.

Scottish homemaker, farmer, and plantation owner Elizabeth Sinclair (1800 Glasgow – 1892 Kauai) moved with her family (husband and six children) to New Zealand. Her husband was a ship's captain, and died at sea in 1846. Sinclair moved to Vancouver Island, Canada. Cutting trees to make farmland was too expensive. Canada was cold. In 1864, Mrs. Sinclair bought Niihau and some land on Kauai for $10,000 in gold. The much larger Kauai at 562 square miles is 19 miles east of Niihau. Kauai is the fourth largest Hawaiian Island.

For the about $9,000 paid for Niihau, this came to $129 a square mile, or 20¢ an acre. In 2019 money, $9,000 is $137,000 – or $1,981 per square mile which is $3.03 an acre. King Kamehameha V (1830 Honolulu – 1872 Honolulu) was the seller.

Twenty cents an acre in 1864 may not have been such a bargain though. Although the weather is nice with an average low and high of 68 and 83° F, the island is arid. Average rainfall is less than 18", and droughts lasting years occur. Ranching and farming were not likely to be profitable.

Sinclair settled there with thirteen kin, bringing Merino sheep to raise in an effort to have income. Merino sheep are known for their high-quality wool. As just mentioned though, raising livestock on Niihau was hit and miss.

As noted above, the U.S. controversially annexed Hawaii in 1898. This acquisition did not include Niihau, as the Robinsons who were descendants of the Sinclairs still privately-owned Niihau. The state of Hawaii and the U.S. government today own 127 and 271 acres of Niihau respectively. The other more than 99% is still owned by the Robinson family.

Japanese planners designated Niihau which was a half hour flying time from Pearl Harbor, as the site for Japanese aviators to fly to for rescue if their aircraft was damaged, low on fuel, etc. After landing or crash landing, the airmen would go to the beach where the rescue submarine would pick them up. That was the plan.

Japan thought that Niihau had no residents. Instead, 136 people lived there. They all or almost all lived in the only community on Niihau, which is Puuwai; on the island's west coast. All were Hawaiian, except for three ethnic Japanese adults. The three Japanese were one Issei and two Nisei. The Issei was married to a Hawaiian woman, and they had children. The two Nisei were husband and wife, and also had children. All were U.S. citizens except for the one Issei.

Petty Officer, Airman First Class Shigenori Nishikaichi (1919 Japan – 12/13/1941 Niihau) was part of the second attack wave, flying a single engine Mitsubishi A6M2 Zero fighter off the 728' long, IJN Hiryu (1939 – 6/5/1942 USS Enterprise dive bombers severely damaged in Midway Battle, scuttled; 389 of 1,100 crew lost {35%}) aircraft carrier. He and seven other fighters escorted a group of bombers off the 845' long, IJN Shokaku (1941 – 6/19/1944 USS submarine torpedo sank, Philippine Sea Battle; 1,272 of 1,842 crew lost {69%}) aircraft carrier. After the bombers dropped,

the fighters strafed targets in southeastern Oahu. These were the U.S. Naval Air Station on Mokapu Peninsula, Bellows Army Airfield ten miles to the south, and other military areas.

Mokapu Peninsula was just mentioned. The 4.6 square miles, windward Peninsula separates Kaneohe Bay and Kailua Bay. President Woodrow Wilson (1856 VA – 1924 D.C.) designated 322 acres (half a square mile) of the Peninsula for military use in 1918. In 1939, the Navy constructed a small seaplane base, called the Naval Air Station Kaneohe Bay. In 1941, Army artillery units were added. The Naval Air Station on Mokapu was attacked 12/7/1941, nine minutes before the anchored ships at Pearl Harbor were bombed. This was done to damage aircraft, so they could not get airborne -- to shoot down Japanese aircraft, and/or locate and attack the Japanese Task Force fleet to the north.

Today, this facility is the Marine Corps Base Hawaii. It occupies the entire Mokapu Peninsula, which is 2,951 acres (4.6 square miles).

After the raids, the eight Zeroes re-assembled for the return to the carriers, 200 miles off. The plan was to rendezvous with returning bombers, just north of Oahu's northern tip. The larger bombers with their more spacious cockpits had more navigation aids than the fighters, so would then lead the fighters to the carriers. Before the Zeroes got to the rendezvous point though, a group of nine, single engine, single crew, lightly armed, Curtiss P-36A Hawk fighters from Wheeler Army Airfield (on Oahu, adjacent to Schofield Barracks) intercepted. Curtiss P-36A Hawks although introduced only in 1938, were already obsolete. Zeroes could out-climb, out-turn, and out-run P-36As. And in fact, that is what they did. All nine Hawks were handily shot down.

Of note, several Curtiss P-40 Warhawks also got aloft. Warhawks were also single engine and single crew. The Warhawks were much larger and faster than Hawks. However although introduced only in 1939, Warhawks were also obsolete compared to Zeros. For one thing, the Zero climbed at 3,100 feet per minute, compared to 2,100 feet per minute for the Warhawk. Despite these deficiencies, the Hawks and Warhawks managed to shoot down four and maybe up to ten Japanese aircraft.

Hawks and/or Warhawks hit Nishikaichi's Mitsubishi A6M2 Zero six times. One of the bullets punctured his fuel tank. Nishikaichi was lucky in that the Zero's aviation fuel did not ignite. The fuel tanks on Zeroes at the time were not self-sealing. However, he was losing fuel. His engine was running rough. He fell behind the other fighters.

Another Zero ominously trailing smoke hooked up with him at the rendezvous area. The pair decided to try and make the 140 miles to Niihau, and then be picked up by a Japanese submarine per the contingency plan. In tandem, the two faltering Zeroes arrived Niihau. They saw buildings and people so realized Japanese intelligence was wrong in stating that Niihau was uninhabited. They flew away from the island.

Nishikaichi knew that finding one of the Japanese carriers without navigational assistance from the bombers would be difficult. He knew that the carriers were probably 200 miles off by now and steaming for home. He decided to return to Niihau. Having just been there and as a large island and as daytime with good visibility, he knew he could find it.

Nishikaichi signaled to the other Zero pilot to make a U-turn and crash land on Niihau. Twenty minutes later, the two pilots passed to the south of Kauai's green slopes. A few minutes later, the pair spotted the lava cliffs of Niihau's east coast. Approaching lower this time, they quickly discovered that island co-owner and manager Alymer Robinson (1888 Kauai – 1967) fearing that war was coming with Japan, had workers (these were Niihauns) plow or place rock piles on smooth areas of the island, to prevent aircraft from landing. The two pilots circled the island in their faltering fighters, looking for a flat space to land. Nishikaichi signaled to the other Zero to go ahead and pick a spot, and land.

Airman Second Class Saburo Ishii (19?? Japan – 12/7/1941 off Niihau) flying the other damaged Zero waved off the suggestion. He radioed back to his carrier that he was returning to Oahu, and crash-diving into a worthy target. Instead, Ishii inexplicably put his Zero into a steep climb, and then vertically dived at high speed into the sea. He assumedly realized that he could not make it back to Oahu or find his carrier, and preferred death to maybe being captured.

Nishikaichi thought differently than Ishii. In other words, he was not ready to die. Almost dry of fuel, he finally found a relatively level, uncluttered stretch of pasture on Niihau near an isolated house. His wheels though struck a wire fence that he had not seen. He nosed in hard. His safety harness tore loose. He slammed against the instrument panel.

The rescue submarine had been in the area at 13:30. However, it was ordered to sail to Oahu to intercept and torpedo sink any immediate, incoming American relief ships (which by the way, never came).

Hawaiian Hawila Kaleohano was born and educated on the big island of Hawaii, Hawaii. Alymer Robinson allowed him to visit his sister on Niihau in 1930. He met a local woman who he courted and wed. He worked as a ranch hand. He was one of the few on Niihau who was bilingual, Hawaiian and English.

The Zero came to a halt, practically in Kaleohano's front yard. Kaleohano was sitting on his front porch this Sunday morning, sipping coffee. To say the least, he was quite startled.

Kaleohano and everyone else on Niihau as the island had no telephones and very few radios, was unaware of the attack at Pearl Harbor. Niihau was 142 miles west-northwest of Oahu. However, he knew that the relationship between the U.S. and Japan was poor due to Japanese belligerence, expansionism, and war atrocities. He rushed to the crashed Zero and pulled the dazed Nishikaichi out of the cockpit. Recognizing Nishikaichi and his plane as Japanese, Kaleohano thought it prudent to relieve the pilot of his sidearm, papers, and maps before the dazed airman could react; which he did do.

Nishikaichi came around. Kaleohano brought him to his house. His wife served the pilot breakfast. Known for their hospitality, the islanders even threw a welcoming party for the pilot later that day, at a neighbor's house.

Nishikaichi's crashed Zero (photograph taken several days after) is shown below. The flying Zero is one maintained by the Commemorative Air Force (CAF). The CAF is a Texas non-profit organization, dedicated to preserving and showing historical aircraft. It was formed in 1953 in Montgomery, Alabama. Today, it is based in Dallas, Texas.

 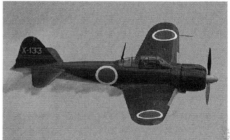

Nishikaichi spoke a little English, but not enough for Kaleohano to understand him. Nishikaichi did not speak Hawaiian. They sent for Issei beekeeper Ishimatsu Shintani (1881 Japan – 1970 Hawaii), who had moved to Hawaii in 1900. He spoke Japanese of course. He had wed a Hawaiian woman. Their children had been born on Hawaii, so were U.S. citizens. Shintani was barred from U.S. citizenship, by the law then applicable to the Territory of Hawaii. Nishikaichi explained the Pearl Harbor attack to Shintani in Japanese. Shintani turned pale, refused to elaborate, and departed quickly.

The puzzled Hawaiians then sent for Nisei Yoshio Harada (1903 Kauai of Issei parents – 12/13/1941 Niihau, shotgun suicide). Island co-owner Robinson had selected Harada as the island's Paymaster -- so he was somewhat official, had some stance. Harada's wife Irene was Nisei as well. Harada had three brothers, living in Japan. Shintani and the Haradas were the only ethnic Japanese adults on Niihau. Again, Shintani was Issei so not an American citizen; and the Haradas were Nisei, so American citizens. As already noted, the Haradas' and Shintanis' children were American citizens.

Shintani and the Haradas were the only bilingual persons (Japanese and Hawaiian) on Niihau.

Nishikaichi informed Harada of the attack on Pearl Harbor, a revelation Harada thought prudent not to share with the Niihauns; thinking the same way as Shintani apparently.

Nishikaichi desperately wanted his papers returned. The pilots and ten mini-submarine sailors had been told that their maps and orders should by no means fall into American hands. However, Kaleohano refused to return them. He turned over the pilot's pistol though, which had been stored in Mr. Robinson's ranch house.

Niihau had neither electricity nor telephones, but later that night the Hawaiians heard about the Pearl Harbor attack on a battery-operated radio. The Niihauns confronted Harada (and the pilot). Harada had no choice now. He told the Niihauns what the pilot had told him about the attack.

Harvard graduate and island co-owner Aylmer Robinson was scheduled to arrive on his regular weekly trip from Kauai the next day, 12/8/1941 Monday. He was fluent in Hawaiian. He lived on Kauai, 17 miles east. He came to Niihau weekly, by powerboat. Robinson limited visitors to Niihau to only friends and relatives of Niihauns.

The natives decided they would send Nishikaichi back with Robinson, for Robinson to turn over to the authorities. This would probably be the American military. Robinson did not arrive, as the U.S. military banned boat traffic in the islands after the attack. In fact, Hawaii had been placed under martial law just several hours after the attacks. The Niihauns did not know of the ban. They were puzzled and uneasy related to Japan's attack, as the well-liked Robinson always showed up on Mondays.

Nishikaichi stayed the night at the house, where the luau welcoming party had been. The Haradas stayed there as well.

The next day, the Haradas brought the pilot to their house. They brought Shintani back into the picture. The pilot re-explained to the three ethnic Japanese that the Oahu sneak attack had gone very well (which was definitely the case), that the U.S. was militarily way behind Japan, and that the U.S. would surely decide to not get involved in the war – if not now, soon. The pilot won the three ethnic Japanese over with his conclusions, that the U.S. would negotiate a quick peace with Japan to avoid a prolonged war.

The natives agreed to Nishikaichi staying at the Haradas' house. However, they did post guards.

On Friday 12/12/1941, Shintani approached Kaleohano in private and offered him $200 in cash ($3,423 in 2019 money) for Nishikaichi's papers. Although $200 was a huge sum for a Niihaun, he refused the offer. Shintani muttered a threat, stating that there would be trouble if the papers were not returned, that it was a matter of life and death to Nishikaichi. Maybe so, but Kaleohano was unimpressed, or fearless, or maybe something else. He threw Shintani out of his house.

Harada as Paymaster had access to Robinson's house on the island. He took a shotgun and pistol from the house.

Harada and Nishikaichi not waiting for Shintani's return from the denied money offer to Kaleohano, attacked and subdued the lone guard posted outside the Harada residence. Irene Harada played loud music on a phonograph to cover up the sounds of the struggle. Three other guards apparently not taking their duties seriously were elsewhere. The overcome guard was locked in a warehouse. The now armed Harada and the pilot then went to Kaleohano's house.

When he saw the armed Harada and Nishikaichi coming along with a 16-year-old girl as a hostage, Kaleohano hid out in his outhouse (bathroom). Realizing that they would soon look for him there, he dashed out. They shot at him with the shotgun but missed. Kaleohano ran to the nearby village and alerted the residents, warning them to evacuate. However, the villagers did not believe that Harada was a confederate of Nishikaichi as island owner Robinson had designated him as an official, and as they knew him well as he had lived among them on Niihau three years. At this time though, the overwhelmed guard had escaped the warehouse and run to the village, screaming. This finally convinced the residents. They fled to caves, thickets, distant beaches, etc.

Kaleohano gave the pilot's papers to his mother-in-law for safekeeping. He borrowed a horse to rush to the north end of the island, intending to make a signal fire. A bonfire had already been burning from the 1,280' Mount Paniau, the island's highest point. In lieu of another fire, Kaleohano and five other men decided to row from Kii Landing near the northern tip of the island to Waimea, Kauai, in a lifeboat. Again, Robinson lived on Kauai. This was a ten-hour pull against the wind. They left at 00:30. Kii Landing is where Robinson docked, on his weekly visits to Niihau.

Upon arrival, the tired men informed the stewing Robinson of the events on Niihau. Robinson by this time knew that there was some trouble on Niihau, as the islanders had flashed signals the 18 miles toward Kauai with kerosene lanterns and reflectors. Also, the bonfire was visible. This was the first time that the Niihauns had signaled these ways. Robinson had tried several times to get permission to go to Niihau, but the authorities would not grant.

Meanwhile, Harada and Nishikaichi went to Nishikaichi's crashed Zero. Nishikaichi unsuccessfully tried to make contact using the aircraft's radio – it was broken in the crash. The two with the help of one of their Hawaiian captives removed at least one of the two 7.7 millimeter machine guns from the Zero, and ammunition. They then torched the Zero, so it could not be salvaged for study. They went to Kaleohano's house and set it ablaze as well.

Nishikaichi and Harada captured the guard they had locked up, who had managed to escape. They forced him to walk through the deserted village, calling on any remaining civilians to come out. Only one man appeared, Kaahakila Kalima. With the two hostages (Kalima and the guard), Nishikaichi and Harada then walked through the village firing their weapons, and demanding that Kaleohano come out and surrender.

During the night, Nishikaichi maybe with Harada's assistance took Niihau resident Kaahakila Kalimahuluhulu captive. They agreed to release him if he would go search for Kaleohano. Instead, Kalimahuluhulu somehow enlisted his friend Benehakaka Kanahele to sneak back in the darkness, to grab the weapons and ammunition. Kanahele was a 6' tall Hawaiian (way above average), noted for his strength as well as his size. He got his physique and muscle from carrying sheep as a shepherd.

However on the morning of 12/13/1941 Saturday (six days after the sneak attacks), Harada and Nishikaichi captured Kanahele and his wife Kealoha Kanahele (1907-1974), holding them at gunpoint. They ordered Kanahele to find Kaleohano, keeping wife Kealoha hostage. Kanahele knew that Kaleohano was rowing toward Kauai, but made a pretense of looking for him. Out of concern for his wife, he returned.

Nishikaichi realized he was being deceived. Harada told Kanahele that the pilot would kill him and his wife and everyone in the village, if Kaleohano was not found.

Kanahele had noticed the fatigue, of his two captors. When the pilot was handing the shotgun to Harada, Kanahele and his wife Kealoha both jumped the pilot as a team. Nishikaichi pulled his pistol out of his boot. Kealoha (the wife) grabbed the arm holding the pistol and pushed it down. Harada pulled her off the pilot. The pilot then shot Ben Kanahele three times; in the groin, stomach, and upper leg. Despite three bullets in his body, Ben Kanahele picked Nishikaichi up and hurled him into a stone wall. His wife quickly picked up a large rock and bashed Nishikaichi in the head, several times in fact. Her wounded husband finished the pilot off, slitting his throat with his hunting knife.

At this point, Harada realized that he had abetted a disastrous turn of events – arson, attempted murder, hostages, a dead Japanese fighter pilot, a thrice-shot Niihaun, etc. This was too much. He shoved the shotgun muzzle into his own belly and pushed the trigger. At age 38, he left a wife and children.

Kealoha Kanahele picked up the shotgun and pistol and ran for help for her thrice-shot husband. She threw the weapons aside. In 1946, a flood washed the shotgun up, where it was found by islanders. Somebody grabbed the pistol and the machine gun from the Zero. They never showed up again.

Ben Kanahele was taken to Waimea Hospital on Kauai for treatment and to recuperate.

Kanahele was awarded the Medal for Merit and the Purple Heart 8/1945. The Medal for Merit at the time was the highest U.S. civilian decoration. President Roosevelt had established it 9/8/1939, for exceptionally meritorious conduct in the performance of outstanding services. The Purple Heart medal at the time could be awarded to civilians (no longer the case, as of 1998).

The just as deserving (it would seem) Kealoha Kanahele (the wife) did not receive any official recognition, or at least not much.

The next afternoon which was Sunday 12/14/1941, First Lieutenant Jack Mizuha headed a group of soldiers who arrived by powerboat. Robinson and the six Niihauns who had rowed to Kauai came along. The grieving, new widow Irene Harada and Ishimatsu Shintani were taken into custody. Shintani was sent to an internment camp for the duration of the War. He rejoined his family on Niihau after the War. He attained U.S. citizenship in 1960.

Widow Harada was charged with being a spy. She was not charged with treason though. She was imprisoned for 31 months for her involvement in abetting Nishikaichi. She was released 6/1944.

By the way, Nishikaichi's family back in Japan had been told that he had died in the 12/7/1941 Oahu attack, shot down. This is what was thought to be the case. His hometown (Hashihama, Imabari, Ehime, Japan) erected a 12' granite cenotaph in his honor. The engraving on the cenotaph is what was believed at the time -- *Having expended every effort, he achieved the greatest honor of all by dying a soldier's death in battle, destroying both he and his beloved plane. His meritorious deed will live forever.*

It was not until more than fourteen years later in 1956 that the circumstances of Nishikaichi's death were revealed to his family, and his ashes delivered to them.

The remains of Nishikaichi's crashed and burned Zero are on permanent display at the Pacific Aviation Museum Pearl Harbor, Ford Island, Oahu. A Japanese American group in Hawaii criticized the museum display as originally designed, and demanded that the museum remove mention of the Hiradas in the display. They were successful in this regard. The Robinson family was very unhappy with this censorship; especially as they had donated the aircraft based on how they were told the display would read (factually, in other words).

These events in the week after Pearl Harbor were well publicized. Kaleohano, Ben Kanahele, and his wife some were much lauded for their actions in resisting Nishikaichi and the three ethnic Japanese on the island who became his collaborators, and bringing the events to an end.

The actions of Nishikaichi's Japanese abettors were compiled in a 1/1942 U.S. Navy report. The report concluded that there was a likelihood that Japanese residents previously believed loyal to the United States, may aid Japan in some way.

These actions also became public. The collusion of the only three ethnic Japanese on Niihau with the downed pilot contributed to the sense in the American military and citizenry that some Japanese, even those who were American citizens or otherwise thought loyal to the U.S., might aid Japan in some way – overtly or covertly. After all, all three ethnic Japanese adults on Niihau turned to the Japanese pilot's side, and much aided him. This was even more surprising considering that they were long-time residents, that two of the three were American citizens, and that the Nisei couple and the Issei who had married the Hawaiian woman all had children who were American citizens.

Along with the uproar over the 12/7, 8/1941 attacks, the Niihau events undoubtedly influenced the Roosevelt administration to decide to incarcerate (at least) West Coast ethnic Japanese, for the duration of World War II.

Just after the sneak attacks, the FBI did arrest 5,500 men of Japanese ancestry living in the United States. They were confined by either the Army or the Justice Department. These were all or almost all Issei. These men were in the category of being community leaders. Another 5,000 men (again all or almost all Issei) were allowed to move to inland states.

When the U.S. entered World War II, 127,000 Japanese and Japanese Americans lived in the continental U.S. (so not counting those living in the U.S. Territories of Hawaii and the Philippines). Sixty-three percent were born in the U.S. (Nisei and Sansei), so citizens. The other 37% were first generation (Issei), so not citizens. About 120,000 (94% of the total) lived in the west coast states of California, Oregon, and Washington; and southern Arizona.

President Roosevelt issued the already-mentioned Order 9066 February 19, 1942, for internment to proceed. The Order authorized Secretary of War Henry Stimson (1867 NYC – 1950 NY) and military commanders to establish areas of exclusion of certain populations, as a wartime exigency. More specifically, the order allowed defining certain areas as military zones to clear the way for the relocation and confinement of residents and their descendants from the Axis nations of Japan, Germany, and Italy; if they happened to reside in these areas. Again, this was to be done if the opinion of the War Department, was that these persons posed a threat to national security.

Roosevelt by Executive Order 9102 created the War Relocation Authority 3/18/1942, as the federal agency to handle the evacuation and confinement of such persons. Military Areas 1 and 2 were created. They encompassed all of California, and much of Oregon and Washington and southern Arizona. The 120,000 Japanese Issei and Nisei who lived in these areas were told to move from these areas, or be interned. Some 10,000 did move to interior states to live, work, go to college, etc.; beginning 4/1942. About half were minors. The about 7,000 living in other states, were not affected.

Some may have moved back to Japan. If so, these were very, very few in number; if any.

Of note, very few German Americans or Italian Americans were incarcerated compared to the Japanese; especially in proportion to their numbers in the U.S. population.

In the case of those Americans who thought the internment unfair, the 2/23/1942 Japanese submarine shelling of the petroleum tank farm near Santa Barbara, plus the hysteria associated with the false Los Angeles Battle the next night (both described above), swayed many to favor internment.

The Philippines were an American territory, where many Japanese had moved. The Japanese had invaded and occupied much of the Philippines. The Philippines now belonged to Japan, so incarceration of the Japanese there could not happen.

Hawaii was also an American territory. Thirty-seven percent of the population was Japanese – 158,000. Japanese were the largest ethnic group on the islands next to Native Hawaiians, by far. About 1%, suspected strong loyalist types were relocated and confined as well. These numbered 1,600, mostly Issei. They were confined in camps on one of the Hawaiian Islands or sent to a mainland camp. Hawaii knew that it would be next to impossible to imprison more than one-third of its population. For one thing, doing so would have wrecked the local economy.

Martial law though had been put into place 12/8/1941 in Hawaii, therefore making the supposed risk of espionage and sabotage work by ethnic Japanese more difficult.

The B1-type (I-15-class), IJN I-25 (1941 – 9/13/1943 USS destroyer depth charge sank off New Hebrides Islands, all 100 crew lost) cruiser submarine was part of the 12/7/1941 Oahu (Pearl Harbor) sneak attack force. I-25 and eight other submarines split from the retreating Task Force and sailed to the West Coast of the U.S., to attack ships. I-25 torpedoed and sank the SS Connecticut tanker 5/6/1942 off Cape Disappointment. Cape Disappointment is in southwestern Washington state.

I-25 shelled Battery Russell on Fort Stevens (1863 – 1947) in Oregon 6/21/1942 with its fourteen-centimeter deck gun. Fort Stevens defended the Oregon side of the Columbia River mouth at the Pacific Ocean. The Columbia River separates Oregon and Washington.

This same IJN-25 submarine launched a seaplane that dropped incendiary bombs on Oregon several times 9/1942, in unsuccessful efforts to start forest fires.

These aggressions resulted in little damage but deaths and injuries did occur. These attacks were terrifying to the populace. They all gave argument to the thinking, that internment of the Japanese should continue for the duration of the War.

Most of the incarcerated Japanese endured their suffering with *gaman*. This Japanese word translates to enduring the seemingly unbearable, with patience and dignity. Its origin is from Zen Buddhism. The Japanese used the term much during World War II such as in regard to the Hiroshima and Nagasaki atomic bombings; as well as the previous, devastating, conventional bombings suffered by the citizenry. The latter (conventional bombing) killed, injured, and made homeless many more Japanese than the nuclear bombs.

The *gaman* term is still used today in Japan, when disasters or tragedies occur. For example, it was used in regard to hundreds of thousands of area residents affected by the 2011 Tohoku earthquake and tsunami which hit the northern part of Honshu (Japan's largest island, where its largest cities are). This caused seven meltdowns at three reactors of the Fukushima Daiichi Nuclear Power Plant complex, located on Honshu. Other examples when the word *gaman* was put forward were the 1982 Nagasaki area floods which killed 300, and the 2018 floods in the Hiroshima area which killed more than 200.

Gaman or not as expected in regard to the internment of Japanese American citizens mentioned above, some Japanese sued. Four legal challenges of FDR's decision for military detention went all the way to the Supreme Court, as follows:

- Hirabayashi v. U.S. University of Washington student Gordon Hirabayashi (1918 WA – 2012 Canada) was arrested and convicted, for curfew violations and failure to report for re-location violations. He was sentenced in 1942 to 90 days in prison. The Supreme Court held 6/21/1943 that the application of curfews against members of a minority group was constitutional, when the nation was at war with the country from which that group originated.

Hirabayashi later spent a year in federal prison for refusing induction into the armed forces, contending that being asked about his loyalty to the United States or Japan was racially discriminatory; as other ethnic groups (namely

German American and Italian American in this case) were not also required to answer such queries on a loyalty questionnaire.

- Yasui v. U.S.   Minoru Yasui (1916 OR – 1986 CO) earned bachelor and JD degrees in 1937 and 1939 at the University of Oregon. At the time, two-year participation in the U.S. Army's Reserve Officer Training Corps was mandatory at the university. He was commissioned a Second Lieutenant in the Army's Infantry Reserve, 12/8/1937.

After law school, he passed the bar. He set up his practice in 1939 in Portland, Oregon. He found little work. Japanese Americans did not need much legal assistance, and non-Japanese would not hire him. For that matter, some Japanese may have been reluctant to hire him anyway, feeling that a Japanese attorney would not be effective in a white profession, especially as at war with Japan. He got a position working for the Japanese government at its Chicago consulate, but mainly doing clerical work. The day after the Pearl Harbor attack, he resigned from the consulate.

Yasui went to an Army facility in Vancouver, Washington: *Second Lieutenant Minoru Yasui, reporting for duty, Sir!* He was told to go home. He tried seven more times at the same base, but denied each effort.

He opened a law practice in Portland, to aid Japanese in putting their affairs in order before internment. He was arrested for violating curfew. The court decided that he was not a citizen of the United States. The Supreme Court overruled this 6/21/1943, stating that Yasui was a U.S. citizen. However, the Supreme Court ruled unanimously that the government did indeed have the authority to restrict the lives of certain persons living in the country, during wartime. Yasui moved to one of the Japanese internment camps. He was released in 1944.

- Korematsu v. U.S. Fred Korematsu (1919 CA – 2005 CA) was drafted. The Navy rejected him, due to stomach ulcers. He trained to be a welder, to contribute to the defense effort. He was fired from several jobs before the U.S. entered World War II, as Japanese. He could not find employment after Pearl Harbor Day.

He underwent plastic surgery on his eyelids to pass himself off as a Caucasian. He changed his name to *Clyde Sarah*. As his Caucasian claim was dubious (and that *Clyde Sarah* name probably did not help), he changed his story to being of Spanish and Hawaiian heritage. That did not work either. He was arrested for refusing to go to an internment center.

The Supreme Court sided 6-3 with the federal government 12/18/1944 -- that the exclusion order was constitutional, that the need to protect against espionage outweighed Korematsu's individual rights and the rights of Americans of Japanese descent. The Court limited its decision to the validity of the orders to leave the West Coast military area, not addressing the issue of incarceration of U.S. citizens.

- Ex parte Endo   Mitsuye Endo (1920 Sacramento – 2006 Chicago) worked as a clerk and stenographer for the California Highway Commission in Sacramento. After the 12/7-8/1941 sneak attacks, she and other Nisei state employees were harassed and eventually fired, because of their Japanese ancestry. She and her family were confined at the Tule Lake (California) internment camp.

The Japanese American Citizens League selected Endo as a test case to file a writ of habeas corpus, as she was an *assimilated* American. She spoke, understood, read, and wrote only English. She was a practicing Christian. She had never been to Japan. Her brother was in the U.S. Army. The Court ruled that the U.S. government could not continue to detain a citizen who was *concededly loyal* to the United States. In this case, the Court did not touch on the constitutionality of the exclusion of people of Japanese ancestry from the West Coast. Instead, the court focused on the actions of the War Relocation Authority. The Endo ruling led to the release of incarcerated Japanese Americans, starting 1/1945.

In the first three cases listed above, the three male defendants purposely got themselves arrested. The Endo case was the only of the four which arose from a habeas corpus petition. A habeas corpus petition is a legal recourse in law whereby a person can report an unlawful detention or imprisonment at trial, usually through a prison official.

Note that all four cases involved Nisei, so Americans.

The American Civil Liberties Union supported all four cases, paying legal costs.

The first two cases were companion cases, decided the same day (6/21/1943). Both had negative results for the interned Japanese, that the incarceration was justified. The second two cases a year and a half later were also companion cases, and also decided the same day in December 1944. One was negative. The other resulted in the release of interned Japanese soon after. For this reason, it is difficult to reconcile Endo with Korematsu; or with the other two cases for that matter. As an explanation, the three negative cases stated that constitutionality of curfews based on Japanese ancestry and military exclusion was legal as at war with Japan; whereas Endo stated that the subsequent incarceration was not legal. It is also realized that these last statements are also contradictory – take it up with the United States Supreme Court!

The Roosevelt administration, having been alerted to the Court's decision on Endo, issued Public Proclamation No. 21 December 16, 1944, the day before the decision was announced. This proclamation rescinded the exclusion orders, and declared that the Japanese internees would be released to live wherever they wanted. The releases began next month, 1/1945. As many had lost most of their assets, some did not leave the camps until 8/1945 when the War ended or even later. Uncle Sam paid for their rail transport and gave each family up to $50 ($699 in 2019 money).

It was later determined that the federal government either submitted false information on the threat of Japanese complicity with Japan, or did not disclose studies during World War II which showed no or little risk. As a result, the convictions of Korematsu, Hirabayashi, and Yasui were overturned 1983, 1986, and 1987; as *coram nobis* cases. Coram nobis writs are legal orders allowing a court to correct its original judgment if a fundamental error is discovered later, which did not appear in the records of the original judgement's proceedings. In these cases, the errors were fraudulent testimony and withholding of known evidence.

For their principled stands against Japanese internment, the Presidential Medal of Freedom was awarded to Fred Korematsu in 1998, and posthumously to Gordon Hirabayashi and Minoru Yasui in 2012 and 2015. This decoration is the United States' highest award for a civilian.

Many Japanese Americans had lost their property, when forced to camps. They either did not have time to sell, or assumed (hoped) that their incarceration would be for only a short time. Otherwise, they hoped that their property would still be theirs, when released. The latter often was not the case though – other non-Japanese Americans somehow got away with claiming and owning it.

To sum up, incarcerated Japanese Americans had little sympathy from other Americans at this time in the War. This thinking was not sound or fair, but again Japan's aggression in Asia and now the sneak attacks, and atrocities (these innumerable and horrible beyond human concept) rubbed off on the Japanese Americans.

Under the 1948 American Japanese Claims Act, Japanese who had been incarcerated applied for compensation. The act required documentation of ownership, which many had lost. The Act excluded lost opportunities, wages, appreciation of value (such as of land and homes), interest earned, etc. Almost 24,000 claims were filed, for $148 million in losses. This was an average of $6,200 per case, which is $64,727 in 2019 money. Only $37 million was approved and paid (25% of what was asked for).

Swept up in the larger movement for civil rights and ethnic pride of the 1960s and 1970s, a group of Nikkei activists pushed for a re-examination of their parents' and grandparents' wartime experiences; seeking apologies and reparations. As defined earlier, Nikkei is the term used for members of the Japanese diaspora (and their descendants) who moved to another country, especially those who moved during the Meiji period. These activists were mostly Sansei (grandchildren). Some of these Sansei had been incarcerated as children, but most were born in the post-war baby boom.

Several Japanese American civil rights groups (some newly formed) formalized proposals, for apologies and compensation.

Congress responded in 1980. The Wartime Relocation and Internment of Civilians Commission was established, to assess whether the incarceration was justified. The commission's *Personal Justice Denied* report condemned the internment, as *unjust and motivated by racism rather than real military necessity.* The report also noted that very few German Americans and Italian Americans were incarcerated.

The Commission found little evidence of Japanese disloyalty during World War II. The Commission in 1983 recommended that redress payments be made to each interned person, or their heirs.

In 1988, President Ronald Reagan (1911 IL – 2004 CA) signed the Civil Liberties Act. The law apologized to Japanese Americans, and paid $20,000

($42,900 in 2019 money) in restitution to those who were incarcerated or their survivors. The legislation publicly acknowledged that government actions were based on race prejudice, war hysteria, and a failure of political leadership.

President George H. W. Bush (1924 MA – 2018 Houston) signed Amendments to the Civil Liberties Act into law in 1992, to pay out an additional $400 million (worth $724 million in 2019), to ensure that all remaining internees (or their heirs) received $20,000 in redress payments.

Of note, Bush fought the Japanese in World War II. His torpedo bomber was shot down. He was injured, and almost captured and consumed (the cannibalism is another story).

Roosevelt's 2/19/1942 Executive Order 9066 to approve incarceration was rescinded in 1976.

Several U.S. Presidents (Ford, Reagan, and Bush Senior in 1976, 1988, and 1991) formally apologized to the internees for the Japanese American confinement program. Ford's wording included that the incarceration was a *setback to fundamental American principles.*

Canada also imprisoned its citizens, of Japanese ancestry. These numbered 22,000, 64% of whom were born in Canada. Like the U.S., Canada apologized, and made reparations -- $21,000 per person.

For the U.S. and Canada both, most Japanese decided to remain in the U.S. after the War. For those who stayed, it was an easy decision – devastated Japan was in shambles after World War II. A very few did choose to move back to Japan though. These were all or almost all Issei.

To sum up, the incarceration of Japanese Americans was wrong – just about all agree to that. On the other hand, it was understandable in the minds of most) at the time, and even now – for the many reasons listed above.

Writer William Hallstead makes this point, that these events of the downed pilot on Niihau had an influence on decisions leading to the internment of ethnic Japanese. Hallstead referred to an official Navy report by Lieutenant C. B. Baldwin, dated 1/26/1942. Baldwin wrote:

> The fact that the two Niihau Japanese who had previously shown no anti-American tendencies went to the aid of the pilot when Japanese domination of the islands seemed possible, indicate likelihood that Japanese residents previously believed loyal to the U.S. may aid Japan, if further Japanese attacks appear successful.

Baldwin does not mention the third Japanese person (Harada's also Nisei wife Irene) who also supported the Japanese pilot.

Although already stated, authorities were even more surprised at the actions of these three ethnic Japanese persons and the Hawaiian spouse of one also, in that their children were Americans.

Regarding the reparations made above by the U.S. and Canada, Japan's reparations to war crime victims did not start until 1955; and none was paid to the U.S. (or Canada, for that matter). Considering the gargantuan costs incurred by the U.S. associated with fighting all over the planet, and losing almost 417,000 persons in uniform (27% in the Pacific Theater) and 12,100 civilians, and millions more injured and diseased, and an American POW death rate of 29% at the hands of the Japanese......

At the time of World War II, the Niihauns made money raising sheep and cattle, gathering honey, and making and selling jewelry made from tiny shells collected from the beaches. Some of this jewelry is made from pupu. These tiny shells wash ashore in the winter months. Shells from several pupu species are used to make leis. Fancy ones can sell for thousands of dollars. These are so popular, that the state of Hawaii passed a 2004 bill to ban the sale of counterfeit pupu leis.

Bruce and Keith Robinson (1941 -) are the current owners. Bruce married a Niihaun woman. The brothers shut down the long-running cattle and sheep ranching operation in 1999, as not profitable. In fact, livestock raising had never been profitable. This put many out of work. Honey cultivation was also shut down; again, as not profitable. Charcoal was once a big export, but cheap charcoal from Mexico ended that.

Mullet as food fish are raised in Niihau ponds and lakes, and sold on other Hawaiian Islands.

Eighty percent of the island's income today comes from a small U.S. Navy installation, atop the island's highest cliffs. Remote-controlled tracking devices are used for testing and training, with Kauai's Pacific Missile Range Facility. The missiles detected are those of the U.S. and its allies. However, the same technology can be used to monitor the missiles from other countries. The installation brings in millions of dollars a year and provides the island with a stable economic base, without the complexity and negatives of mass tourism or industrial development.

Regarding tourism, the Niihau owners do offer half-day helicopter and beach tours of the island (since 1987). However, contact with residents is avoided. There are no accommodations on the island.

Also, the brother owners imported big game herds from stock on Molokai Ranch. Molokai is the fifth largest of the eight major Hawaiian Islands. Eland, aoudad, oryxes, wild boars, and feral sheep roam Niihau's forests and flatlands. Hunters pay big to kill the animals, as another source of income for the Robinsons. The hunters take the meat or give it to the island inhabitants.

Keith Robinson visits Niihau weekly or so. He is credited with saving numerous, endemic, endangered Hawaiian plants from becoming extinct. These include the Cyanea pinnatifida which is extinct in the wild. Another is the Brighamia insignis flowering plant, a Hawaiian lobeliod species.

Niihau serves as a wetland habitat for the Hawaiian coot, the black-winged stilt, and the Hawaiian duck.

The Robinsons have banned radios, televisions, and mobile phones on the island, to preserve the indigenous island culture.

The island is generally off-limits to all but relatives of the island's owners, U.S. Navy personnel, the Ellison family, and some government officials. As a result, its nickname is the *Forbidden Isle.*

The Ellison family was just mentioned. Billionaire Larry Ellison (1944 The Bronx -) is the executive chairperson of the multinational Oracle Corporation computer technology company. 2017 revenues were $38 billion.

Ellison bought 98% of Lanai in 2012 for $300 million. The 141 square mile Lanai is the sixth largest of the eight major Hawaiian Islands. The state of Hawaii owns the other two percent. Lanai is 221 miles southeast of Niihau. The population is 3,100.

Ellison is an acquaintance of the Robinsons. They collaborate on projects. These are usually related to environmentalism.

Despite the helicopter tours and exotic game hunting, the Robinsons lose millions of dollars a year on running the island and supporting its inhabitants.

Niihau's population today is 160, a few more than during World War II. Almost all are descendants of those who were invited to live on Niihau, back when Mrs. Sinclair bought it in 1864.

There are still some Niihau residents who were young during World War II, who remember the six days that the Japanese pilot terrorized the island (or the story, as heard from their relatives).

5- LIEUTENANT COLONEL VIVIAN BULLWINKEL

Vivian Bullwinkel (1915 Australia – 2000 Australia) was born and raised in the little town of Kapunda, South Australia. Kapunda is near the south, central coast of the continent. She trained as a nurse and midwife at the small mining community of Broken Hill, New South Wales. Broken Hill is in the outback, 317 miles north-northeast of Adelaide, South Australia. She began her nursing career at Hamilton, South Australia. Hamilton is 185 miles west of Melbourne, Victoria. She then moved to Jessie McPherson Hospital (1930 established as a women's hospital – still in operation today as the Jessie McPherson Private Hospital, connected to a teaching hospital) in Melbourne. Melbourne is in southeast Australia, on the Southern Ocean (part of the Indian Ocean) coast.

With war clouds forming, Nurse Bullwinkel applied to join the Royal Australian Air Force. The Air Force rejected her, because of her flat feet.

Flat feet are a condition in which the arches of the feet collapse (or could be just one foot). Therefore, the entire sole of the foot comes into complete or near-complete contact with the ground. About one fourth of persons have this condition. They were either born that way, or the arch collapses later in life – this may be as an infant, child, juvenile, or adult. As such a large percentage, the condition is not considered to be a deformity or abnormal.

In the case of the 75% with arches, the arches provide an elastic, springy connection between the forefoot and the hind foot. This allows the dissipation of most of the weight by the foot, before the force reaches the long bones of the leg and thigh. As a result, the incidence of injury in the case of flat footers without arches to leg bones, tendons, ligaments, and muscles was thought to be above average; before and at the time of World War II. Heavy use (marching, long hikes, carrying a load, etc.) would more likely result in injuries. Therefore, the militaries of some countries historically banned those with flat feet from enlisting. Studies of military recruits though have shown no evidence of flat footers having foot problems or increased leg injuries if the person is asymptomatic, or the results of these studies were inconclusive. One study in fact showed that those with flat feet had fewer injuries. To sum up, militaries today generally do not consider flat feet to be an impediment, if the recruit is asymptomatic.

Anyway, the Australian Army was not as picky as the Australian Air Force, as to Bullwinkel's feet. She enlisted 1941. Seemingly, Army recruits march and hike more than Air Force enlistees hike. Whatever.

Bullwinkel was one of 3,400 Australian, female, military nurses who served in World War II.

The Australian Army sent Bullwinkel to Johor on the Malay Peninsula, 9/1941. Johor is the southernmost Malaysian state, with the Straits of Johor to the south. The Straits separated Johor, Malaysia, from the British possession of Singapore. Singapore consists of 63 islands. Only the largest one of Pulau Ujong was inhabited at the time of World War II, which is almost still the case today. Pulau Ujong then was 220 square miles in area (is 270 square miles today, built up with dredge soil). For the record, Singapore today is a sovereign city-island republic (independent country).

Malaysia eventually had 130 Australian Army nurses. All the nurses were over the age of 24, a requirement at the time for females in the Australian military. The work was pretty much routine the first few months. This was caring for soldiers of the British Indian Army and the Australian Army – injured in training or accidents, diseases, etc.

That routine ended 12/7, 8/1941, when the Empire of Japan sneak attacked fourteen locations or targets in or on the Pacific Ocean on the same day. The 1907 Hague Convention addressed the requirement to declare war in its *Convention Relative to the Opening of Hostilities* statements. These clauses describe the international actions a country should perform, before opening hostilities. Article 1 states: *The Contracting Powers recognize that hostilities between themselves must not commence without previous and explicit warning, in the form either of a reasoned declaration of war or of an ultimatum with conditional declaration of war.* Again, Japan took a pass on giving an advance warning, of maybe attacking. Shame on Japan, again (Japan had a history of sneak attacks).

Two days are shown, as the locations were on both sides of the International Date Line. The International Date Line is an imaginary line from the North Pole to the South Pole. It marks the change from one calendar day to the next. It roughly follows the 180° line of longitude, through the middle of the Pacific Ocean. But again, the attacks were all on the same day.

Four of these fourteen sites were British. These were a river gunboat and the three British Crown possessions of Malaysia, Singapore, and Hong Kong, as follows:

- HMS Peterel (1927 – 12/8/1941 sank) Shore artillery and two Japanese warships gun-sank this 177' long and 29' beam and 3' draft river gunboat in Shanghai Harbor, China. The British were using the gunboat as a communications station, spying on the Japanese. Six of eighteen crew aboard were killed. Some crew escaped to a Norwegian ship. In violation of international law, the Japanese stormed the Norwegian ship and removed the Peterel crewmen. The twelve crewmen became prisoners of war (POWs). Thanks to ongoing supply shipments from the British Residents Association and the International Red Cross, all twelve of the surviving crewmen survived the War until 8/1945 repatriation, forty-five months later.

- British Crown Colony of Malaysia Japan launched an amphibious assault on the northern coast at Kota Bharu, and advanced swiftly down Malaysia's eastern coast. Japanese forces also landed at Pattani and Songkhla in Thailand, and then raced south over Thailand's border with Malaysia to attack the western part of Malaysia.

Western Malaysia had many hard-surfaced roads. The Japanese soldiers used bicycles for part of its infantry. This allowed the soldiers to carry more equipment and move faster, even on jungle paths. Japan used the same two wheelers also in Singapore.

The British Indian and Australian Army fled Malaysia across the narrow Johor Strait, which again separates Johor (Malaysia) from Singapore. The two thirds of a mile Johor-Singapore Causeway was completed in 1923 (today, there are two causeways Johor to Singapore). The last crossed 1/31/1942. Retreating British troops blew up two sections of the Causeway that day, to prevent the Japanese from using.

Of note, the British Army had already blown up more than two hundred bridges in Malaysia to slow down the Japanese advance, with little effect. Japanese sappers were good and quick. Also, the bridges were over mostly narrow and shallow creeks, so the Japanese soldiers were able to wade or swim over. They did so, toting their gear and the bicycles.

- British Crown Colony of Singapore Japan launched 65 bombers from airfields in southern Indochina to bomb Singapore. These were twin engine Mitsubishi G3M and twin engine Mitsubishi G4M bombers. The distance is 600 miles. Great Britain (well, everybody) thought that Japan did not have bombers with that range. They were wrong. The bombers flew into bad weather over the South China Sea, separating the formations. Forty-eight bombers were forced to turn back, due to lack of visibility and high winds.

Seventeen, twin engine, Mitsubishi G3M medium bombers did get through though. They dropped at 04:30 on the British naval base and airfields on the northern part of Singapore, Keppel Harbor which is on the south side of Singapore, and the city's center. These seventeen bombers all returned to Indochina safely. The bombs killed and wounded 61 and 700. Damages to the airfield and harbor were minor, as most of the bombs missed their targets. If almost three fourths of the bombers had not turned around due to poor weather, damages and casualties would have been much greater.

Then and later, the Japanese seemed to have much luck in locating British aircraft to bomb and strafe. As it turned out, British Indian Army air liaison officer Captain Patrick Heenan (1910 New Zealand – 2/13/1942 pistol shot execution Keppel Harbor, Singapore) was spying for the Japanese. He used a radio, a Morse code transmitter disguised as a typewriter (it had an alphanumeric keyboard), etc. to transmit information. He was discovered 12/10/1941, court martialed, and executed for treason.

The Japanese forded the Johor Strait to Singapore 2/8/1942 on landing craft. Japanese sappers also made girder bridges to patch the two Johor to Singapore Causeway sections that the retreating British had blown up. The Japanese were able to use the Causeway by 2/12/1942. Surrender or annihilation was near. Eighty thousand British, Indian, and Australian troops surrendered 2/15/1942; ceding the Malaysian Peninsula and Singapore to the Japanese. British and Japanese casualties were 22,500 and 14,700.

The British had referred to Singapore as their *Gibraltar of the East* as they had made a large naval base there and had a garrison there – no more.

- British Crown Colony of Hong Kong   The 426 square mile island of Hong Kong is located on China's south coast. Japan bombed Hong Kong, plus landed troops. This was four hours after the Oahu attack. The British Army supported by Australians and Indians resisted; but ended up surrendering 12/25/1941. Six hundred and seventy-five Japanese were killed. The Japanese killed three times that number. For the record, Hong Kong today is owned by China.

Ten thousand British, Indian, Canadian, and Chinese troops surrendered.

The British Indian Army combined with Australian troops outnumbered the Japanese Army. However, the Japanese were superior in close air support, armor, coordination, tactics, and experience (so in almost all ways).

The British, Indian, and Australian troops on Singapore numbered 85,000. They had 5,000 casualties from defending Singapore. These casualties were mostly Australians. The Japanese had about the same number of casualties. The remaining 80,000 Allied military were 41 and 38 and 21% British and Indian and Australian. They surrendered and became prisoners of war (POWs). They joined another 50,000 who had surrendered in the earlier Malayan campaign, and the other 10,000 who later surrendered on Hong Kong. Of course, the Japanese had no men captured.

By just about any measurement, Singapore was the worst defeat ever for a British or British-led military effort. In fact, Prime Minister Winston Churchill (1874 England – 1965 London) made a statement to this effect. His straightforward words were that Singapore's fall was *the worst disaster and largest capitulation in British military history.* As just noted, Malaysia and Hong Kong added greatly to the total surrendered.

Many of these 140,000 military men (again, 80,000 and 50,000 and 10,000 from Singapore and Malaysia and Hong Kong surrendering) died in Japanese captivity during World War II, in one way or another.

Japan occupied and ruled Malaysia and Singapore and Hong Kong through the end of the War, 8/1945. The number of civilians who were mutilated, tortured, raped, worked to death, and died of other causes including execution during the occupation were many, many thousands. Many thousands were able to flee though.

As noted above, the British Army including the Australian nurses fled Malaysia to Singapore. They transformed a school into a hospital. Their stay would not be long though.

In the days before the Singapore surrender, British and Australian military officers decided to evacuate as many wounded and healthy military personnel and civilians as possible. These were all or almost all British or Australian (no or only a very few natives, no or only a very few Indians). In desperation, 44 vessels were rounded up of various types, sizes, ages, and seaworthiness. They were made ready, as much as time would allow. Most were old, slow, and unarmed. Most sailed unescorted. They departed Singapore 2/12/1942 – 2/15/1942.

Forty of the 44 (this is 91%) ships and boats were air bombed and sunk in the Bangka Straits, from Singapore to Java. Java is the fifth largest of the Dutch East Indies Islands. They were easy pickings, a turkey shoot for Japanese bombers and strafing fighters.

For the record, the Dutch East Indies won independence from Netherlands in 1949. The country today is the Republic of Indonesia.

The 524' long and 70' beam and 43' draft, twin-screw, armed MV Empire Star (1935 – 10/23/1942 German submarine torpedo sank in the North Atlantic, 42 of 84 crew and gunners lost) refrigerated cargo ship was made to transport fresh meat from Australia and New Zealand to Great Britain and other United Kingdom colonies. The Empire Star was the largest of these 44 fleeing vessels. She was one of the few that had anti-aircraft guns installed. In fact, she was heavily armed for a cargo ship. She had a 4" gun, a 12-pounder gun, two 20 millimeter cannons, and five anti-aircraft machine guns.

Empire Star was also one of the few evacuation ships that had escorts, provided as it was the largest of the fleeing vessels. These were the Danae-class, 473' long and 47' beam and 15' draft, HMS Durban (1921 – 6/9/1944 deliberately sank as a Mulberry harbor breakwater in support of the D-Day Normandy invasion) light cruiser, and an anti-submarine HMS frigate.

Sixty of the 130 Australian nurses, wounded military men, healthy military men, and civilians summed up to 2,160 aboard. One hundred and sixty of the 2,160 were civilian women and their children, which is 6.4%.

Empire Star departed Singapore in the early hours of 2/12/1942, along with another cargoman. This second freighter was not carrying evacuees.

Six Japanese, twin engine dive bombers attacked at 9:10, in the Durian Straits. The Durian Straits are south-southwest of Singapore, and to the east of Kundur Island of the Dutch East Indies. The escorts and/or Empire Star shot down one Japanese bomber, and damaged another – good, but not good enough.

Three bombs hit Empire Star, killing and wounding fourteen and seventeen. The pumps still worked, so the crew was able to extinguish the fires. The nurses tended to the wounded. The Japanese attacked repeatedly over the next four hours, dropping bombs from 7,000 to 10,000' – to reduce risk from Empire Star and her two escorts' productive, anti-aircraft fire. Empire Star weaved, to advantage. Near misses were plenty, but Empire Star was not hit again. She reached Australia safely, with no more casualties. The other freighter and the two warship escorts were not hit.

The 241' long and 41' beam and 16' draft, twin-screw, 14 miles per hour, SS Vyner Brooke (1928 – 2/14/1942 bomb sunk off Bangka Island, Dutch East Indies) steamer yacht was another evacuation ship. She was among the last to depart.

For the record, Vyner Brooke (1874 England – 1963 London) was the third and last White Rajah of Sarawak. The Kingdom of Sarawak was a British protectorate since 1888. It was in the northwest part of the island of Borneo. The protectorate ended when Japan attacked 12/16/1941, and occupied the Sarawak Kingdom within two weeks. Rajah Brooke was in Australia at the time (on purpose), so safe.

The Japanese occupied Sarawak until the end of the War. In 1946 the year after the War, Sarawak became a British crown colony. In 1963, Sarawak became part of the Malayan Federation.

Brooke used the yacht for personal pleasure. Later though when the yacht got older, she was used as a merchant ship. As a cargoman, her usual voyages were between Singapore and Kuching (capital of Sarawak).

The Royal Navy requisitioned the Vyner Brooke after the 12/8/1941 sneak attacks, to be used as an armed trader. She was painted gray. A four-inch deck gun was installed forward. Two Lewis anti-aircraft guns were mounted aft. These guns were outdated, but all that was available. Depth charges were stored aft.

The yacht's Australian and British officers were mostly Malay Royal Navy Volunteer Reserves. Upon requisition, they asked to remain aboard the now christened HMS Vyner Brooke. This included peacetime captain Richard Borton. Additional recruited crew were reservists. Some surviving sailors from the sinkings of the recently commissioned new, 745' long and 103' beam and 34' draft, HMS Prince of Wales (1941 – 12/10/1941 Japanese aircraft sank off Kuantan, South China Sea; 327 of 1,521 crew lost {21%}) battleship, and the 750' long and 90' beam and 27' draft, HMS Repulse (1916 – 12/10/1941 Japanese aircraft sank off Kuantan, South China Sea; 508 of 1,181 crew lost {43%}) battlecruiser joined Vyner Brooke as crewmen.

Escorts were not available. The yacht departed Singapore 2/12/1942, the same day as Empire Star. Hundreds of wounded British and Australian soldiers, 65 of the 130 Australian nurses, and civilians (men, women, and children) were packed on.

Two days later on 2/14/1942 at 14:00, Japanese bombers dropped. Vyner Brooke was hit. The converted yacht sunk within a half hour. Some (including two nurses) were killed by the bombs, and some drowned. Japanese aircraft strafed, killing and wounding more. Vyner Brook survivors and survivors from other watercraft fleeing Singapore that the Japanese sank made it to shore of several Dutch East Indies islands in lifeboats, or by hanging on to debris and kicking/floating in, or swimming.

Shore in the case of the Vyner Brooke survivors was the 4,515 square mile Bangka Island. It is the ninth largest of the Dutch East Indies Islands, just east of the 182,812 square mile Sumatra which is the largest. The Japanese had also without warning invaded the larger Dutch East Indies Islands 12/1941. Japan ended up occupying and controlling the Dutch East Indies through the end of World War II, which was 8/1945. Japan took oil, rubber, etc. from the Islands. At the time, the Dutch East Indies were the fourth largest producer of oil worldwide, behind the U.S., Iran, and Romania.

Japan forced four to ten million Indonesians into labor. Some were paid a pittance at least for a while. Most were not paid at all. The estimate is that four million Indonesians died during the Japanese occupation, in one way or another.

Vyner Brooke survivors crawled up on different parts of Bangka Island, as did survivors from at least one other ship fleeing Singapore that Japanese aircraft bomb sank. Some were in the ocean more than two days. About one hundred, bedraggled survivors assembled on Bangka's Radjik Beach, including 22 of the 65 nurses who had been on Vyner Brooke. Bullwinkel was one. Radjik Beach is on Bangka's north side.

They were alive, but their situation was dire – no escape, no rescue, no communication methods, no allies on the island or even in the area, no weapons, no food, no water (fresh water later found though), no clothing, no shelter, no medical supplies, etc. Also, they had no reason to think that rescue was on the way. On these points, these depressing conclusions were all correct.

The group sent several to a village, asking for assistance. The villagers though would not aid, fearing reprisals from the Japanese if they did. This thinking on the part of the locals was correct and wise. The repercussions if caught aiding would have been swift and severe (torture, mutilation, rape, murder).

Once it was discovered that the Japanese held Bangka Island, a Vyner Brooke officer went to surrender the group. Seventeen civilians (women and children) went with him. These civilians became prisoners of the Japanese. The nurses stayed back, to care for the wounded who had made it to shore. They set up a shelter of sort on the beach with a large Red Cross on it, to hopefully deter more bombing. The Vyner Brooke officer returned mid-morning 2/15/1942, with a Japanese Army officer and twenty heavily-armed soldiers.

The Japanese officer ordered his soldiers to immediately march half of the healthy and wounded men who could walk, over a headland. They were therefore out of sight, but not out of hearing range. The Japanese soldiers shot and bayoneted them. This was next repeated for the other half. The group of disabled and wounded men lying on the beach and the nurses could hear the shooting and screams.

The Japanese soldiers returned to the 22 female Australian nurses and one civilian woman and the lying wounded, on the beach. They cleaned their guns and bayonets in the presence of the women and wounded. The Japanese soldiers then raped the 23 women, right there on the beach. The women were then told to put their uniforms and clothing back on. The nurses' uniforms included Red Crosses on their sleeves.

The soldiers then ordered the 23 women to wade out into the surf. When they were waist deep, the Japanese soldiers machine-gunned them in the back from the beach. All were killed, except Bullwinkel. A bullet went through her left side, just above her hip. Her diaphragm was penetrated, but the bullet missed her vital organs. The diaphragm is the thin muscle that separates the thorax from the abdomen. It facilitates respiration.

The Japanese soldiers then shot and/or bayoneted the wounded soldiers who had not been able to walk who were lying on the beach – either on the sand, or on stretchers. These men had heard the rifle fire killing their comrades not to mention their screams from being bayoneted, had observed the raping of the women, and then witnessed the mowing down of the nurses in the surf.

Bullwinkel feigned death in the surf. She raised her head a little off and on, to steal a breath of air. When she saw that the Japanese had left the beach, she made it to shore. She stumbled through the dead men on the beach – her fellow nurses' bodies had not yet washed ashore. She found a fresh water spring in the jungle. She drank. She then became unconscious and/or slept from loss of blood, fatigue, and trauma; for more than 24 hours.

British Army Private Patrick Kingsley found her. He was one of the wounded (shrapnel wounds), who had somehow survived the bayonet piercings and also being shot. He had also crawled into the jungle. She nursed him (and herself) for twelve days, the best she could with no supplies or medicine. They started to hobble to a village. The Japanese picked them up, and they became prisoners of war. Private Kingsley died several days later from his wounds and as no medical care provided, age 29.

Bullwinkel kept the fact that she had been part of the massacre/rape group secret from her captors. She knew that if she asked for medical help for her wound, they would know that she was a witness to the rapes and massacre as well as a victim; so would have killed her. She healed up on her own. The Japanese assumed that she was a survivor from one of the other vessels fleeing Singapore that had been aerial bomb sunk, but not part of the massacre/rape group. After all, the commanding officer who ordered the killings and rapes, reported to his superiors that all had been done away with.

In all, the Japanese shot and/or bayoneted 60 Australian and British soldiers and Vyner crew, 22 Australian nurses, and the one civilian woman. All died except for Nurse Bullwinkel, and two soldiers. This atrocity is known as the Bangka Island Massacre.

Of the 65 Vyner Brooke Australian nurses, two died from the bombs, ten died at the time of the sinking (drowned or strafed), 21 were executed in the surf as just described, and eight died in captivity. The remaining 24 nurses made it back to Australia, when the War ended 3.5 years later. This comes to a 63% death rate for the 65 Australian nurses fleeing Singapore on the yacht.

Thirty-one other Australian nurses survived. They had landed on other beaches, and the Japanese did not execute them. Eight died in captivity though. Captivity was hard labor. They were told they would be paid 80¢ a day which is $12.35 in 2019 money, which did not happen. They were fed, clothed, and housed poorly. The only medical care they got was what they were able to provide themselves, and this of course with no supplies or medicine. They were beaten.

Bullwinkel was a POW until the end of the War. This was 3.5 years, at several camps. She went barefoot during this time, flat feet and all.

Bullwinkel testified on Japanese war crimes in 1946, at the 1946-1948 Tokyo War Crimes Tribunal. She did not include the rapes, as the Australian government ordered her to not disclose. She was still in the Australian Army at the time, and again her orders were to not include the rapes in her testimony.

The Japanese commander accused of ordering the executions and rapes committed suicide in his cell.

Bullwinkel retired from the Army in 1947, with the rank of Lieutenant Colonel. She was highly decorated.

The International Committee of the Red Cross awarded her the International Nightingale Medal. It is the highest international distinction a nurse can achieve. It is awarded to nurses or nursing aides for *exceptional courage and devotion to the wounded or sick or disabled, or to civilian victims of a conflict or disaster,* or *exemplary services of a creative and pioneering spirit in the areas of public health or nursing education.*

Bullwinkel continued her nursing career in Australia. She was instrumental in changing the methods of educating and training nurses, and increasing wages for nurses in Australia.

Bullwinkel wed late in life in 1977 at age 62.

Bullwinkel worked to honor those murdered on Bangka Island. She and others raised funds for memorials to Australian nurses, erected in Australia and on Bangka Island.

Bullwinkel returned with others to Bangka to tour in 1992, 50 years later. She found the fresh water springs where she and the British Army Private got water. She visited one of the prisoner of war camps that she survived.

Bullwinkel died of a heart attack, at age 84.

For the record, the Japanese Army Regulations manual in place at the time of World War II included this statement:

> *Prisoners of war shall be treated with a spirit of good will, and shall never be subjected to cruelties or humiliation.*

6- USS HOUSTON HEAVY CRUISER CA-30

Franz Joseph I (1830 Vienna – 11/21/1916 Vienna) was Emperor of Austria, King of Hungary, and monarch of other states in the Austro-Hungarian Empire 1848 to his 1916 death. He was also President of the German Confederation 1848 to 1866. At almost 68 years, he was the longest-reigning Emperor of Austria and King of Hungary, as well as the third-longest-reigning monarch of any country in European history. He presided over an odd collection of fifty million Poles, Czechs, Austrians, Magyars, Croats, Serbs, Slovaks, Turks, Transylvanians, Slovenes, Gypsies, etc.

Franz Joseph had three daughters and a son. His married son Rudolph (1858 Austrian Empire – 1889 Austria-Hungary) killed his thirteen-year younger mistress and then himself in an apparent suicide-pact agreement in 1889, at age 30.

Franz Joseph's nephew Archduke Franz Ferdinand (1863 Austria – 6/28/1914 Sarajevo) was heir apparent. Franz Ferdinand was the son of Franz Joseph's brother.

Young Bosnia was a revolutionary movement active in Bosnia and Herzegovina, formed in 1911. The group of mostly college students was seeking an end to Austro-Hungarian rule in Bosnia and Herzegovina. They or most of them could be described as Yugoslav nationals. With assistance from other groups, Young Bosnia recruited and trained seven, young men to assassinate Austrian Archduke and heir presumptive Franz Ferdinand. The goal of such an assassination was to separate Austria-Hungary from its South Slav provinces, so they could be combined into a larger and independent Yugoslavian nation.

The main assisting other group mentioned above was the secret military society Black Hand, formed in 1911 by Serbia Kingdom Army officers. Black Hand in turn originated from the conspiracy group that assassinated the Serbian royal couple, Prime Minister, and Army Minister in 1903; in a successful coup effort.

Ferdinand and his morganatic wife Sophie Ferdinand (1868 Germany – 6/28/1914 Sarajevo) of fourteen years traveled to Sarajevo (capital and largest city of Bosnia and Herzegovina today), to grand open a new state museum. A morganatic marriage is one between a man and a woman of unequal social or royalty rank, which prevents the passage of the upper spouse's titles and privileges to the other spouse (and children) upon death. In other words, neither Sophie nor their children in this case were in line to assume Ferdinand's titles, privileges, and authorities (such as a ruler) should Ferdinand die before Sophie. In other words again, Sophie was a commoner, or something close to it.

Ferdinand and Sophie were scheduled for a public motorcade to tour the Bosnian capital. The seven separatist assassins took their positions along the route – much redundancy was built in. The first two assassins lost their nerve. Nedeljko Cabrinovic (1895 Sarajevo – 1916 Bohemia, in prison from tuberculosis) was number three. He tossed a hand grenade. The grenade bounced off the back of Ferdinand's car into the street. It exploded under the following car. The explosion disabled that car and wounded two people in the car. A dozen bystanders were injured by shrapnel. No one was killed, though. Cabrinovic swallowed a cyanide capsule and then jumped into the Miljacka River to end his life. The cyanide pill had expired. It made him sick, but he did not die. The river was only four inches deep here, so he did not drown either. The police captured him. Because of this grenade incident, the other four assassins down the route lost their opportunities.

Ferdinand decided later that day as a good will gesture to visit the injured persons in the hospital. Riding in a phaeton (open touring car, like a convertible), another of the assassins ran up to the phaeton when it was stalled in traffic, and shot Ferdinand and Sophie 6/28/1914 from only five feet away. Both died on the way to the hospital. The couple left three children, ages ten and eleven and thirteen. Gavrilo Princip (1894 in what is today Bosnia and Herzegovina – 1918 Bohemia, in prison from tuberculosis) was the successful assassin.

For the record, Franz Ferdinand's nephew Charles took the throne when his grand uncle Franz Joseph died in 1916.

Austria-Hungary delivered an ultimatum to the Serbian Kingdom on certain demands relating to the assassination and its investigation. These bordered on threatening war. The Serbian government, although contrite, felt that these requests were overly harsh. The stalemate resulted in a diplomatic crisis. Russia sided with Serbia. France sided with Russia, which again sided with Serbia. Germany sided with Austria-Hungary.

Entangled international alliances and disagreements had formed over the previous years, which in turn resulted in arms races, rising nationalism, border squabbles, etc. Many of these tensions related to blood and marriage connections of rulers of adjoining countries over the previous decades. For example, the leaders of the British Empire, German Empire, and Russian Empire were all descendants of Queen Victoria (1819 London – 1901 England). As a result, militarism (arms buildups) and alliances and imperialism and ethnic nationalism had European countries in a tinderbox situation, as it was.

On 7/28/1914 which was a month after the assassinations, Austria-Hungary declared war on Serbia with the backing of Germany. Germany declared war on Russia 8/1/1914. German troops invaded Luxembourg 8/2/1914, which was not able to resist. Germany occupied Luxembourg through the end of what later came to be called World War I. The landlocked, 999 square mile Luxembourg borders Germany, Belgium, and France.

On the same day of 8/2/1914, a German cavalry unit crossed the border into France and exchanged fire with French infantry. The Germans had one and three killed and injured. France had one and one killed and wounded. This skirmish was the first shooting of World War I.

The next day of 8/3/1914, Germany declared war on France. German infantry marched on France 8/4/1914, taking a route through Belgium. As Great Britain had agreed to maintain the neutrality of Belgium, Great Britain declared war on Germany 8/4/1914 and sent troops to Belgium. British and Germany forces fought at the Battle of Mons in Belgium 8/23/1914. This was the first significant battle of World War I. The Mons Battle had over 4,000 combined casualties.

World War I ran 4.3 years, ending with an 11/11/1918 armistice. An armistice is an agreement to cease fighting with neither side surrendering, followed by negotiating a peace settlement.

There were several such settlements. The main one though between the Allied Powers (the good side) and Germany was the Treaty of Versailles, signed more than seven months after the armistice on 6/28/1919. This was the five-year anniversary date of the assassination of Mr. and Mrs. Ferdinand. A Treaty key provision was that Germany was required to permanently disarm and limit military personnel, to a level where offensive moves were not possible. Instead, Germany manufactured much war equipment starting in the 1920s, and built up its army, navy, and air force to boot. European countries and the United States for that matter did not nip this in the bud, which would have been easy to do. After all, Germany was in shambles after World War I. Adolph Hitler (1889 Austria – 4/30/1945 Berlin, pistol suicide), the Nazi regime, and World War II was the result.

As credited to philosopher, essayist, poet, and novelist George Santayana (1863 Madrid – 1952 Rome), *Those who cannot remember the past are condemned to repeat it* (history repeats itself).

At the beginning of World War I, Great Britain was a naval powerhouse. It threw up a blockade around Germany.

A number of German freighters and ocean liners (non-warships all) were moored in U.S. ports at the start of World War I, plus others arrived in the next few weeks and even months. As of 1/1917, there were 54 such vessels in mainland U.S. ports, and one in San Juan, Puerto Rico. Puerto Rico was then (and still is) an unincorporated territory of the U.S.

All or maybe most all owners of these German ships directed their Captains to stay in port, as the U.S. was neutral. Sailing back to Europe would risk being either turned around or seized or sunk by the formidable Royal Navy mentioned above that was successfully blockading Germany, or same by even the smaller but still potent French Navy.

Germany's State Secretary for Foreign Affairs Arthur Zimmermann (1864 Prussia – 1940 Germany) sent a coded telegram 1/19/1917 to Germany's ambassador to revolution-torn Mexico (the internal Mexican Revolution ran 1910-1920). The telegram advised the ambassador that Germany planned to resume unrestricted submarine warfare 2/1/1917 in the North Atlantic, sinking ships of neutral countries.

On 2/1/1917, Germany did just that. German submarines quickly sank seven American freighters. Despite that, President Woodrow Wilson (1856 VA – 1924 DC) tried to maintain neutrality. Guns were installed on American merchant ships. These guns were powerful enough to sink German submarines on the surface, but useless when the torpedo-armed submarines submerged (which is what submarines were designed to do).

The telegram also advised the ambassador to approach Mexico about secretly allying with Germany against the United States. In return for the Mexicans attacking the U.S. from the south, Germany would assist Mexico in reclaiming some of the tens of thousands of square miles it had ceded to the U.S. for $18.25 million in payment for the property and for assuming debt owed to American citizens. This is half a billion dollars in 2019 money. This settlement was negotiated after Mexico lost the 1846-1848 Mexican-American War (Treaty of Guadalupe Hidalgo). For the record, the U.S. had offered Mexico up to $58 million in 1845 before the war so as to avoid war, which is $1.583 billion in 2019 money.

This offered land was California, Nevada, Utah, Arizona, Colorado, New Mexico, Texas, Oklahoma, Kansas, and Wyoming; or parts of these states or territories.

British intelligence intercepted and decrypted the telegram and relayed it to the U.S. government. President Woodrow Wilson (1856 VA – 1924 D.C.) released the telegram to the public, 2/28/1917.

The sinking of the American freighters by German submarines, the disclosure of the secret incentive German offer to neighbor Mexico to attack the U.S., and the (latent) desire of many Americans to come to the aid of (mainly) Great Britain and France; led Congress to declare war on Germany, 4/6/1917. This was 2.7 years after World War I started. Armistice came 1.6 years later.

For the record, Wilson's campaign slogan for his 1916 re-election was *he kept us out of the war*. Congress declared war as Wilson requested, one month after his inauguration.

With the declaration of war, 1,800 merchant sailors on German freighters and passenger liners in U.S. ports became prisoners of war (POWs). During World War I, over 2,000 German merchant mariners (including ship officers) were interned at the resort town of Hot Springs, North Carolina, on the grounds of the luxurious Mountain Park Hotel. Hot Springs is 36 miles north-northeast of Asheville, North Carolina. Hot Springs has been a resort destination since the early 1800's, known for its *healing* mineral springs and scenic mountain setting.

The merchant sailors were not allowed to leave (so were prisoners), but were otherwise well cared for. The mariners were happy with their status, although they of course would not say as much. If sailing, their ships would be subject to sinking; and they subject to death or injury or capture. Or worse, they may have been conscripted in the German Navy or Army, again facing hardship and injury or death in battle or from disease. They were released when the War ended 11/1918, none the worse for wear. Some had been interned up to 19 months, so maybe homesick. Of course, after the War Germany was a devastated mess economically; so not a particularly good country to return to.

The German-flagged, 392' long and 51' beam, coal-fired, 13 miles per hour, SS Liebenfels (1903 – 1958 scrapped) freighter sailed between Europe and North America. She arrived Charleston (South Carolina) 8/1914, the month of the first fighting of World War I. Her owners told her Captain to stay put, again to avoid the risk of being sunk or captured.

Liebenfels' Captain scuttled her there in Charleston Harbor 2/1917, which was 2.5 years later. U.S. Customs took ownership, raised her, and sent her to the Charleston Navy Yard for repairs.

As noted above, the U.S. entered World War I 4/6/1917, which was two months after Leibenfels' Captain deliberately sank his cargoman. As the U.S. needed more ships to transport supplies to France for the war effort, the Navy requisitioned Liebenfels.

Liebenfels is unique as to its acquisition as she had been scuttled, compared to the other ships in U.S. ports which were requisitioned when still afloat, when the U.S. declared War on Germany. Of note, the German Captains though of many of these ships sabotaged their freighters and liners. For example, some damaged their engines. Again, Liebenfels' Captain scuttled, which of course required much money and effort to raise and restore.

Liebenfels was commissioned as *USS Houston*, 7/1917. Her installed armament was 4 × 3 inch (76 millimeter)/23 caliber guns. Her crew complement was 145.

The War Shipping Administration operated her under charter to the United States Lines. She made four round trips between New York and France during World War I; carrying coal, oil, radio equipment, trucks, aircraft, etc.

World War I fighting ended 11/1918. Liebenfels was assigned to the Naval Overseas Transportation Service, and made four more voyages between the U.S. coasts, 12/1918 to 4/1921. She carried coal, lumber, ordnance, etc. between coasts, transiting the Panama Canal (completed in 1914) in support of the Navy's two-ocean operations. Houston was next assigned to trans-Pacific duty. She sailed from New York 5/1921 stopping at Philadelphia and Norfolk to take on cargo, and then to San Francisco, Oahu (Territory of Hawaii), and the Philippines. She returned to San Francisco, arriving 1/1922. The Navy decommissioned her 3/1922, in favor of newer and more modern (especially faster) ships. For one thing, oil as a fuel had many advantages over coal.

The Navy sold Liebenfels to Frank Warren of Portland, Oregon, 9/1922. Warren renamed her *SS North King*. She supported the Alaska salmon trade until 1940. Warren sold her to a Panama company.

When the U.S. entered World War II, the War Shipping Administration chartered her from the Panama company and named her *Houston* again. She operated as an auxiliary Navy vessel (USNS Houston), so that the USS Houston name could be used for a new cruiser (see below). United States Lines again operated, delivering freight for the World War II effort. She made 57 convoy trips. Receiving ports were in Russia, Iceland, France, etc. She delivered supplies for the Normandy invasion, 6/6/1944 (D-Day).

World War II ended 8/1945. The Navy returned Houston to her Panama company owner 2/1946 at New York City, 43 years after she was commissioned new. She was scrapped in Japan in 1958, after 55 years of shipping.

The Navy used this first USS Houston as a freighter in both World War I and World War II. To use the same coal-fired freighter operated by the same contractor in both World Wars which were 23 years apart, was definitely odd. This was especially odd, as she was somewhat outdated even at the time of World War I. However, the need for cargo ships was urgent, for both World Wars.

Liebenfels was the first of four Navy ships, named for the City of Houston. Her name for World War I was USS Houston, even though not a warship. Her guns were installed for defensive purposes only. For World War II, she was re-christened as Houston, but as an auxiliary ship (USNS). She is shown below in a 1918 photograph, a year after she was re-commissioned for U.S. Navy use the first period:

William Bernrieder (1900 Houston – 1993) served in the Navy 26 years, 1926-1952. Five of the 26 years were on active duty, spanning World War II. He worked as an assistant to Houston Mayor Oscar Holcombe (1888 Mobile – 1968 Houston) 1923-1926. Holcombe was Houston's mayor twenty-two (non-consecutive) years.

Bernrieder spearheaded a campaign for the Navy to name a cruiser after the city. Houston was one of 30 cities so lobbying. Thousands of telegrams and letters including many from Houston schoolchildren were sent to Washington D.C., supporting this effort. The campaign was successful. The Navy announced 9/1927 that a new cruiser would be so named.

She was the third of six Northampton-class cruisers, commissioned 1930-1931. The Northamptons were designed as light cruisers, due to their thin armor. They were re-designated as heavy cruisers 7/1931; as provisions of the 1930 London Naval Treaty rated warships with 8" main guns as heavy cruisers. Houston had nine 8" guns, in three turrets. The guns of two of the triple turrets pointed toward the front of the ship. The third triple turret was aft, with the guns pointing that way.

The 570' long and 66' beam and 23' draft, Northampton cruisers including Houston cruised at 37 miles per hour, pushed by four screws. Power came from eight boilers feeding four Parsons reduction steam engines, generating 107,000 shaft horsepower total. Range was 12,000 miles, if loping along at a sedate seventeen miles per hour.

The Northamptons carried seaplanes, usually four. The two catapults were amidships. They were explosive-powered. The charge was similar to that used for 5" guns. The seaplanes were catapult launched, to avoid buffeting from ocean waves. When landing, they would light on the relatively smooth ocean surface created on the lee side of the vessel as it made a wide starboard turn -- it was a matter of timing and coordination of the warship and aircraft with the ocean. They then taxied up to the awaiting cruiser. A deck crane hoisted the seaplane back aboard. They were then serviced and stowed.

The U.S. seaplanes at the beginning of World War II were usually two crew (pilot and observer/gunner) sitting tandem, single engine, folding-wing, Curtiss SOC Seagull biplanes. The *SOC* stands for *Scout Observation Curtiss*. Seagulls were introduced in 1935.

Seagulls found duty on USS battleships and cruisers. The wings folded back against the fuselage for compact storage ashore or aboard ship. When based ashore, the middle float was replaced by fixed wheeled landing gear. However, the Seagull did not have amphibian capability – it was one or the other. The Seagull's length, wingspan, and height were 31, 36, and 15'.

The Seagull's cruise and maximum speeds were 133 and 165 miles per hour from its air-cooled, nine cylinder radial, 550 horsepower engine. Its range was 675 miles.

For armament, the Seagull had one fixed, forward firing and one flexible-mounted rear-firing Browning M2 AN machine guns; both 7.62 millimeters. The Seagull could also tote a 650-pound bomb.

The Seagull was replaced with the single engine, two crew Vought OS2U Kingfisher midwing later in the War. Its size and speed were about the same as the Seagull, but its range was 805 miles compared to the Seagull's 675 miles. The Kingfisher's armament was the same as the Seagull's. The Kingfisher in turn was replaced with the Curtiss SC Seahawk low wing, toward the end of the War. After World War II, helicopters on warships replaced catapult-launched seaplanes.

Like any aircraft hauling three heavy, bulbous hulls through the air, Seagulls and Kingfishers and Seahawks were slow in speed and maneuverability – easy to shoot down. Therefore, missions were not considered unless there was no risk or little risk of attack – from either fighters, or anti-aircraft fire from land or ship. In practice therefore, the Seagulls were used mostly for limited range scouting and gunfire observation to aid surface warship gun crews in distant aiming; in lieu of offensive bombing or strafing.

The Northampton's crew complement was 785. The Northamptons were designed to be flagships, so had accommodations for an Admiral and his staff. This could add more than 100 aboard, easy.

The Japanese sank three of the six Northamptons with aircraft or warship launched torpedoes – one 3/1942, one 11/1942, and the third 1/1943. The other three survived World War II and the Korean War. They were sold for scrap in 1959.

The USS Houston CA-30 timeline of production and commissioning was as follows:

- 5/1/1928   Keel laid down, at Newport News Shipbuilding and Dry Dock Company (Virginia)
- 9/7/1929   Houston Mayor Oscar Holcombe's daughter Elizabeth (1915 TX – 2001 Houston) sponsored the launching; the Champagne bottle Elizabeth dashed against the bow pushing Houston down the James River contained Houston Ship Channel water, as alcohol could not be used during Prohibition; more than 2,000 Texans showed up for the launch

- 6/17/1930   Commissioned

The armament varied some on the Northamptons. Houston's armament at completion included the following:

- 9 × 8 inch (203 millimeter)/55 caliber guns (3x3), in three turrets
- 8 × 5 inch (127 millimeter)/25 caliber anti-aircraft guns as secondary battery
- 2 × 3-pounder 1.9 inch (47 millimeter) saluting guns; these fire blanks designed to be loud and create smoke for ceremonial purposes
- 6 × 21 inch (533 millimeter) torpedo tub, this later removed though

Houston's pre-War voyages carried President Franklin Roosevelt (1882 NY – 4/12/1945 GA, cerebral hemorrhage) four times 1934-1939. These voyages and activities included the following:

- 1930   Shakedown cruise in the Atlantic; sailed to England, France, Netherlands
- 1930   Visited Houston, Texas, Navy Day (October 27); 250,000 toured over a week, when Houston's population was 292,352

The Navy League of the United States is a national association with a membership of 50,000; it is an advocacy group for the U.S. Navy, U.S. Marines Corps, and U.S. Merchant Marine; it was founded in 1902, at the suggestion of Theodore Roosevelt (1858 NYC – 1919 NY, blood clot in lungs); T. Roosevelt was a promoter of U.S. sea power; he was Assistant Secretary of the Navy under President William McKinley (1843 OH – 1901 NY, pistol assassination) thirteen months 1897-1898, which overlapped the first nineteen days of the Spanish-American War; anyway, the Navy League organized the first Navy Day in 1922; it was conducted 10/27/1922, as October 27 was T. Roosevelt's birthday; annual celebrations continue to this day

- 1930   Joined the fleet at Hampton Roads (harbor off Virginia)
- 1930   Became the Asiatic Fleet flagship; the Asiatic Fleet mainly patrolled Philippine Islands before World War II; the Asiatic Fleet was mostly destroyed by 2/1942; what was left became part of the Southwest Pacific Area Command naval component; the Southwest Pacific Area fleet in turn later became the Seventh Fleet
- 1931   Sailed to Hawaii, then Manila; sailed for Shanghai to protect American interests, after Japan invaded China; landed Marine and Navy gun platoons to help stabilize the China situation; remained in the area
- 1933   Sailed to Philippines for good will tour
- 1933   Sailed to Japan for good will tour; relieved by the one year newer, also Northampton-class USS Augusta (1931 – 1959 scrapped), as flagship of the Asiatic Fleet
- 1933-1941   Participated in fleet problems maneuvers in the Pacific, as a unit of the Scouting Force; the Scouting Force consisted of destroyers and cruisers, and a training squadron of three old battleships and eight destroyers; Admiral Frank Brumby (1874 GA – 1950 VA) commanded the Scouting Force 1933-1934

- 1934   Carried President Roosevelt 13,700 miles from Annapolis to Virgin Islands, Haiti, Hawaii, and then Portland, Oregon; Roosevelt was the first sitting president to transit the Panama Canal, and the first to visit the Territory of Hawaii
- 1935   Carried Navy Assistant Secretary Henry Roosevelt (1879 NJ – 1936 MD) who was a distant relative to Franklin Roosevelt on Hawaiian Islands tour; returned to San Diego
- 1935   Cruised Alaskan waters
- 1935   Carried President Roosevelt on a vacation cruise from Seattle to Cedros Island, Magdalena Bay, Cocos Islands, and Charleston (South Carolina)
- 1936   Visited Houston, Texas, a second time
- 1937   Present at the grand opening of the Golden Gate Bridge at San Francisco
- 1938   Carried President Roosevelt for a one-day Fleet Review of San Francisco and from there on a 24-day cruise to Pensacola, where the President disembarked
- 1939   Became flagship of the U.S. fleet 9/19/1939 until 12/28/1939, under command of Admiral Claude Bloch (1878 KY – 1967 DC); returned to the Scouting Force end of the year, now commanded by Vice Admiral Adolphus Andrews (1879 Galveston – 1948)
- 1939   Fleet Problem XX training exercise in the Caribbean and Atlantic; XX simulated the defense of the East Coasts of the U.S. and Latin America from an invasion; 134 ships, 600 planes, and 52,000 men participated in the maneuvers; President Roosevelt (his fourth and last excursion on Houston) and Naval Operations Chief Admiral William Leahy (1875 IA – 1959 MD) were on board to observe
- 1939   Visited Houston, Texas a third time
- 1939   Arrived Pearl Harbor as flagship of the Hawaiian Detachment
- 1940   Arrived Mare Island (peninsula at Vallejo, California) for repairs
- 1940   Sailed to Hawaii, and then on to Manila; became flagship of the Asiatic Fleet, relieving USS Augusta
- 1940   Sailed to Manila; Admiral Thomas Hart (1877 MI – 1971 CT) came on board as flag officer
- 1941   Four quad-mount, 1.1 caliber anti-aircraft cannons installed at Cavite Naval Yard, Manila Bay, Philippines, for additional air defense; additional searchlights installed

Pre-War, Houston got the nickname of *Rambler,* for her many voyages in the Atlantic and Pacific Oceans. The ship's baseball team was called the *Houston Ramblers.* Besides baseball, Houston teams competed against the crews of other ships in basketball, small boat sailing, rowing, wrestling, and shooting.

The Empire of Japan on the same day of 12/7, 8/1942 sneak attacked thirteen locations, in or on the Pacific Ocean. The 1907 Hague Convention addressed the requirement to declare war in its *Convention Relative to the Opening of Hostilities* statements. These clauses describe the international actions a country should perform, before opening hostilities. Article 1 states: *The Contracting Powers recognize that hostilities between themselves must not commence without previous and explicit warning, in the form either of a reasoned declaration of war or of an ultimatum with conditional declaration of war.* Again, Japan took a pass on giving an advance warning, of maybe attacking. Shame on Japan, again (Japan had a history of sneak attacks).

The locations were on both sides of the International Date Line which explains the two dates, all in or on the Pacific Ocean. The International Date Line is an imaginary line from the North Pole to the South Pole. It marks the change from one calendar day to the next. It roughly follows the 180° line of longitude, through the middle of the Pacific Ocean. But again, the attacks were all within hours of each other.

The thirteen attacked sites (or ships) were as follows:

- Nine U.S. possessions
  - Storming and capture of a 159' long USS river gunboat and its crew when berthed at Shanghai Harbor; this little Yangtze River gunboat was the only USS that Japan captured in World War II; for good measure, the Japanese also gun-sank a 177' HMS river gunboat in Shanghai Harbor, at about the same time; if counting this British warship, it is fourteen sneak attacks instead of thirteen
  - IJN submarine gun-sank an Army-chartered, 250' long freighter off California
  - Howland and Baker Islands of the Phoenix Islands of the U.S. Minor Outlying Islands were bombed, these two islands are 43 miles apart
  - Five U.S. military installations (harbors, airfields, bases) on five Pacific Ocean islands; these five islands were Oahu (Pearl Harbor), Guam, Midway, Wake, and Philippines
- Three British Crown colonies – Malaysia, Hong Kong, and Singapore
- Thailand

Japan ended up occupying the three British crown colonies, Thailand, and Wake Island for the duration of World War II. Japan occupied Guam until the U.S. re-captured 8/1944. Japan occupied the major Philippine islands by the spring of 1942. The U.S. wrested the Philippine islands back beginning 10/1944, and into 1945. General Douglas MacArthur (1880 AR – 1964 DC) said he would return and he did, but it took 2.6 years.

Some Japanese soldiers held out though on Mindanao Island (second largest of the Philippines) until the end of the War. Actually, the last holdouts on Mindanao were 200 well organized and disciplined soldiers, who surrendered 1/1948. This was 29 months after the War ended (if you can believe it).

In the next few weeks or months after the sneak attacks, Japan also conquered and occupied Borneo, Burma, New Britain, Gilbert Islands, and the oil-rich and rubber tree plantations Dutch East Indies.

In these thirteen sneak attacks on the same day, the Japanese Empire was for the most part stupendously successful in terms of devastation and casualties rendered, versus its own loss of equipment and casualties. Japan's planning and executions were brilliant. Said yet a third way, the outcomes were very one-sided in Japan's favor. To quote President Roosevelt from his 12/8/1941 Monday speech to Congress, 12/7/1941 was *a date that will live in infamy* for the United States.

Nine of the thirteen (or fourteen if counting the HMS sunk in Shanghai Harbor) targets were possessions of the United States. Americans of course most remember Oahu (Pearl Harbor) of the U.S. Territory of Hawaii, again due to the one-sided outcome. Japan launched two air attacks (bombing and strafing), one hour apart on a Sunday morning. The U.S. military had 2,335 and 1,143 men killed and wounded. Another 68 and 35 Hawaiian civilians were killed and injured. In comparison, only 64 Japanese military men died (55 airmen and nine midget submarine sailors) and one (a submariner) captured. This is a ratio of more than 36 American military deaths per one Japanese military death.

The Japanese Navy sank or damaged nineteen USSs including all eight battleships of the Pacific fleet. Hundreds of aircraft were destroyed, and most of these when on the ground. Japan lost only 29 aircraft, nine and 20 in the first and second wave attacks. These were fifteen, nine, and five dive bombers, fighters, and torpedo bombers. Japan's five mini-submarines were all sunk, which was more or less the unstated plan. The other 51 ships of the Japanese Task Force were undetected and unseen, coming and going.

Japan's surprise attacks without declaring war ended the United States' isolationist attitude, left over from losing 116,700 men in uniform (almost 46% in combat) and another 204,000 wounded or made ill (many with permanent disabilities) in World War I. Congress at President Roosevelt's request declared war on Japan the next day, which was a Monday. The peace between the World War I Armistice Day and World War II was a little more than 23 years.

USS Houston had departed Cavite Navy Yard (Manila Bay, Luzon, Philippines) 12/1/1941. She sailed to Iloilo City, Panay Island, on 12/7/1941. Iloilo City is a port city on Panay's southeast coast. Panay is one of the central Philippine islands. She went to general quarters and cleared the harbor, avoiding Japanese air strikes which devastated ships and the port of Iloilo. The Japanese occupied Iloilo City until the U.S. liberated 3/25/1945. The Japanese left the city's infrastructure in ruins. As with all the Philippine Islands that the Japanese occupied, the citizens much suffered during the War.

To sum up, Houston was not attacked and did not fight on the day of the thirteen sneak attacks.

Houston steamed south through the South China Sea and then the Java Sea to Manila Bay (Philippines). A constant watch was maintained. Her scout planes were up 24/7. The ship was at general quarters, most of the time.

Houston got underway along with the Clemson-class, 314' long and 32' beam and 9' draft, USS Peary (1920 – 2/19/1942 Japanese aircraft bomb sank at Darwin Harbor, 88 of 101 crew lost {87%}) destroyer and other warships, bound for Port Darwin on Australia's north central coast. The Task Force arrived Darwin

12/28/1941 after many engagements with the Japanese, by way of Balikpapan (Borneo) and Surabaya (East Java). The goal was to shore up the defenses of Australia and the Dutch East Indies (today, the Republic of Indonesia). She joined the American-British-Dutch-Australian (ABDA) naval force at Surabaya.

Houston continued escort duty for supply ships between Port Darwin and Surabaya into 1/1942. She splashed four enemy aircraft 2/4/1942 off Balikpapan but was damaged (see below).

Japan had invaded the Dutch East Indies, beginning several weeks after the 12/7 and 8/1941 sneak attacks. The Dutch East Indies are the world's largest archipelagic country with 17,504 islands on both sides of the Equator. Six thousand of the 17,504 islands (34%) are inhabited today. The islands span 3,181 miles east to west and 1,094 miles north to south.

The main islands of the Dutch East Indies were occupied by 3/9/1942. These islands had oil fields, rubber plantations, and other resources; not available in Japan internally. At the time, the Dutch East Indies were the fourth largest oil producer worldwide, behind the U.S. and Iran and Romania.

Another major resource which Japan had in mind was the Indonesian people, to use as forced laborers and sex slaves for its soldiers and sailors. This they did, with many thousands abused and dying as a result. In all, several million Indonesians (usual estimate is four million) died prematurely in one way or another, during the Japanese occupation.

Japan advanced from their Palau Islands colony, and captured bases at Sarawak and the southern Philippines. Sarawak was a British-controlled part of Borneo at the time. From there, they seized bases in eastern Borneo and northern Celebes (another island of the Dutch East Indies, east of Borneo). Japan captured a key oil port on Sumatra (another of the Dutch East Indies islands, on the west side). During this time, Japanese troop convoys steamed southward through Makassar Strait (strait between the islands of Borneo and Sulawesi in the Dutch East Indies); into the Molucca Sea. The Molucca Sea is between the Indonesia islands of Celebes to the west, Halmahera to the east, and the Sula Islands to the south. The Japanese soldiers were headed for Java (also one of the Dutch East Indies islands), where more airfields would be made. The Japanese transports were well protected, screened by cruisers and destroyers with air support from swarms of fighters. The Japanese aircraft were operating off both captured land bases, and aircraft carriers.

Japan's only opposition now was the small, naval ABDA naval force. As already mentioned, Houston had joined the ABDA Task Force at the port of Surabaya, Java. The Task Force had no aircraft carriers or submarines.

Components of the ABDA Task Force tangled with Japanese warships several times in January and February, 1942. These included naval battles at Makassar Strait 1/23/1942, off Palembang (large city on Sumatra, site of several oil refineries) 2/13/1942, and at Badung Strait 2/19, 20/1942. Badung Strait is between the islands of Bali and Nusa Penida, in the Dutch East Indies. However, Houston was not involved in these three fights. Houston's actions during this period included the following:

- 2/4/1942: several ABDA warships were en route to intercept a (reported) Japanese Task Force in Makassar Strait; 36 Mitsubishi G4M1 and 24 Mitsubishi G3M2, twin engine, land-based medium bombers attacked when the convoy was steaming in the Madura Strait north of Bali, which forced the ABDA fleet to retreat; damages included the following:
    - a bomb connected and destroyed Houston's aft turret (three 8" guns), killing and injuring 48 and 20 Houston sailors; Houston's gunners though shot down four Japanese planes, even though only a fourth of her anti-aircraft shells detonated; much of the ammunition was defective, as old; this came to be called the Makassar Straits Battle (also known as the Bali Sea Battle)
    - the Omaha-class, 556' long and 55' beam and 14' draft, USS Marblehead (1924 – 1946 scrapped) light cruiser was also hit by two bombs and severely damaged, including her rudder; Marblehead had 15 and 84 crew killed and wounded
- 2/5/1942: arrived Tjilatjap (Java); repair facilities at Tjilatjap were inadequate to fix Houston's gun turret; nevertheless, Houston was ordered for more escort duty (in desperation)
- 2/10/1942: sailed to Darwin (Australia) to escort a convoy of four transports carrying troops to reinforce forces already defending Timor Island (Timor is at the eastern end of the Lesser Sunda Islands; at the time part of Timor belonged to Portugal and part belonged to the Dutch East Indies)

Japanese planes showed up, but Houston was successful in defending herself and the convoy; the convoy was ordered back to Darwin

- 2/15/1942: sailed with the USS Peary destroyer and two Australian corvettes to transport American and Australian troops to Koepang (Timor); Japanese flying boat dropped bombs, which missed; convoy attacked by 36 land-based bombers and ten flying boats in two waves; the U.S. War department chartered, 423' long and 55' beam and 24' draft, single screw, 12 miles an hour, SS Mauna Loa (1919 – 2/19/1942 Japanese aircraft sank at Darwin) cargoman was hit, with some damage and two (one crew, one passenger) killed; Houston splashed seven of 44 planes in the second wave; launched scout plane seeking enemy; the Task Force though was able to protect the transports
- 2/17/1942 left Darwin for Surabaya, Java, to join the ABDA fleet mentioned above; the fleet came to fourteen warships, and had no submarines or aircraft carriers as already noted; goal was to counter two Japanese naval groups converging on Java from two directions; one group was coming from the north through the South China Sea; the other group was sailing through Makassar Strait east of Borneo
- 2/18/1942: returned to Darwin; engaged in anti-submarine operation off Darwin, thus escaping the Japanese air attack on Darwin 2/19/1942 (see below); Houston under almost constant air attack 2/18-20/1942

- 2/26/1942: Houston and other Allied ships put to sea looking for an enemy convoy which was found (unfortunately); a Dutch destroyer and a British destroyer were sunk; a British cruiser was damaged

The Japanese reported that they sank Houston several times in the first few two months of 1942. For this reason, she got another nickname besides *Rambler*. This was the *Galloping Ghost of the Java Coast*.

Also as mentioned above on 2/19/1942, the Japanese conducted two air raids on Darwin, Australia, a little more than two hours apart. The aircraft on the first raid flew off four aircraft carriers. For the second raid, the aircraft took off from captured airfields in the Dutch East Indies. Eleven, three, and twenty-five 25 vessels were sunk, grounded, and damaged. Some of these were USSs. One was the USS Peary which had departed Philippines with Houston. Peary lost 88 sailors, including 1905 U.S. Naval Academy graduate Captain John Bermingham (1905 NYC – 2/19/1943 Darwin Harbor). Port infrastructure and airfields were damaged. Thirty aircraft were destroyed. Two hundred and forty and 350 were killed and wounded. This attack was very similar to the one at Oahu (Pearl Harbor) 2.5 months back.

The destruction at Darwin eliminated Darwin as a supply and naval base, for the ABDA defensive effort to support operations in the Dutch East Indies. Japan accomplished this lopsided victory (like Pearl Harbor 2.5 months back) with few losses. Only four Japanese aircraft did not return. Two airmen died when their dive bomber crashed (believed hit by ground fire). A Zero pilot was captured when he crash-landed after striking a tree from flying so low.

The ABDA group was desperate to protect the Dutch East Indies from occupation. Many of the citizens were Dutch. As noted above, the islands were rich in resources. Japan desperately needed these resources and slave labor. The Allies desperately needed Japan not to have these resources and slave labor.

The ABDA fleet at this time consisted of fourteen warships from the four countries. As noted for the third time, none were submarines or aircraft carriers. The purpose of the fleet was to delay the Japanese advance, to allow Australia to build up its defenses. The ABDA as a fighting force though had deficiencies to the Imperial Japanese Navy (IJN), as follows:

1) Fewer ships than Japan
2) Older ships than Japan (many were of World War I vintage); for one thing, the ships were slower than those of the opposition
3) Ships needed repair work
4) Weapons, both torpedoes and guns, were less modern so less deadly; Japan had twenty 8" guns, compared to twelve for ABDA
5) Munitions were in short supply
6) Japan's gunners were more skilled
7) Japanese ships launched reconnaissance floatplanes, which added the advantage of the accuracy of fire from IJN ships; the ABDA ships did not have aviation capabilities except for the cruisers Houston and Perth (and Perth had only one seaplane)

8) The ABDA did not have air cover (combat air patrol)
9) The ships were from four countries; they had not worked together much; cohesion and coordination for battle were lacking
10) Air support was not always available
11) Task Force commanders were whoever was highest ranked from the four countries; this changed from battle to battle and even during battle
12) There was a language barrier (English and Dutch); some of the Dutch ships had no English-speaking interpreters, and vice versa

The morale of the ABDA crew was poor, made worse by the lack of support due to the one-sided whipping received by the Allies 2/19/1942 at Darwin. Crewmen were on almost constant alert, as air strikes were frequent and naval strikes on the horizon. The mindset that the Japanese were unbeatable due to their more and better warships and weapons and as more experienced in fighting, was pervasive. These suppositions by both the officers and enlisted men of the USS Houston about the enemy were correct at the time. Another way of saying that morale was poor was to say that the fatigued ABDA sailors were in a state of terror, for good reason. The ABDA was outgunned and isolated with no support on the way.

Three disastrous (for the Allies) naval battles over three days occurred, as follows:

1942 Date	Naval Battle	ABDA Strength	Japanese Strength	ABDA Casualties	Japanese Casualties	Comments
2/27	First Java Sea	2, 3, 9 heavy cruisers, light cruisers, destroyers; 5, 4, 4, 1 USS, HMS, HNLMS, HMAS	2, 2, 14, 10 heavy cruisers, light cruisers, destroyers, transports	2, 3 light cruisers, destroyers sunk; 1 heavy cruiser damaged; 2,300 dead; Houston hit twice by 8" shells, neither exploded	1 destroyer damaged; 36 dead	First surface warship to surface warship action in Pacific theater; ABDA Task Force sailed northeast from Surabaya to intercept Japanese Eastern Invasion Force Convoy, approaching from Makassar Strait to advance on Eastern Java; IJN Task Force engaged ABDA ships north of Surabaya in Java Sea; remaining ABDA ships retreated as destroyers sent back for torpedoes; Japan much superior in number of ships,

						communications between ships, air cover, fighting savvy; to sum up, 6 ABDA ships out, and others dispersed in the eight hour battle; Task Force Admiral Karel Doorman (1889 Netherlands – 2/28/1942 Java Sea) one of the dead
2/28 3/1	Sunda Strait	1, 1, 1 heavy cruiser, light cruiser, destroyer; 1 each USS, HNLMS, HMAS	58, 12, 5, 1, 1, 1 transports, destroyers, cruisers, minelayer, light carrier, seaplane carrier	All 3 sunk; 1,071 and 675 dead and captured; dead included captains of both cruisers	1, 4, 1 minelayer sunk, transports sunk or grounded, cruiser damaged; some by friendly fire; 10, 37 dead, wounded; unknown number of troops lost	Doorman's replacement Perth Captain Hector Waller (1900 Australia – 3/1/1942 Sunda Strait) ordered Houston and Perth to disengage and feint to southeast; replenished at Tanjong Priok (Jakarta), but fuel and ammunition short; departed 19:00 Perth leading for Sunda Strait (passage between Java and Sumatra) to Tjilatjap on Java's north coast, for safer Indian Ocean and then even safer Australia; Sunda Strait clear that night per Dutch air reconnaissance reports; cruisers charged Japanese Army's 16th Western Java Invasion Convoy of 56 transports in Bantam Bay, as

						only escorted by a destroyer; destroyer fired 9 torpedoes, all missed; Japanese Task Force though of 2 heavy cruisers, 1 light cruiser, 9 destroyers, 2 carriers showed up, and launched unprecedented number of torpedoes (87); Houston and Perth torpedo and gunfire sank 00:25 and 00:45 Bantam Bay, on Java's northwestern tip; tailing Dutch destroyer Evertsen gunfire sank; Japan's many torpedoes also sunk its own minesweeper and a transport, plus damaged 3 other transports which were unloading supplies and troops
3/1	Secon d Java Sea	1, 2 heavy cruiser, destroye rs; 1 each USS, HNLMS, HMS	4, 5 heavy cruisers, destroyers	All 3 sunk; 800 captured	1 destroyer damaged	ABDA warships tried to evade Japanese ships by making smoke, heading for rain squall, and fleeing; Japanese caught up with aid from reconnaissance aircraft and sank; Japanese forces attacked and conquered Dutch East Indies, occupying for rest of War

In these three battles, the ABDA had 11 ships sunk, and one damaged. The Japanese had three ships sunk, and five damaged or grounded.

The ABDA had 3,371 dead, and another 1,475 captured (at the time of the sinkings). The Japanese had only 46 and 37 sailors dead and wounded. However, this does not include an unknown number of Japanese soldier casualties on the transports who died and were injured.

The Japanese were making a major landing of troops on the northwestern tip of Java. The Japanese Task Force sank the three Allied ships in the 2/28 and 3/1/1942 Sunda Strait battle with torpedoes and gunfire. Details of the three are as follows:

Ship Class Length X Beam X Draft Speed Life	Aboard	Died When Sunk Captured Ashore Died in Captivity #/% Survived War	Captain Rank Allegiance Service Life
USS Houston heavy cruiser Northampton 600' X 66' X 23' 38 miles per hour 1930 - 3/1/1942	1,068 crew, Marines, airmen	696 included 50 Marines 372 81 291/27.2%	Albert Rooks Captain United States 1914 – 3/1/1942 gunfire 1891 WA – 3/1/1942 Sunda Strait
HMAS Perth light cruiser Leander 562' X 57' X 20' 37 miles per hour 1936 - 3/1/1942	686 crew, airmen, civilians	362 329 108 216/31.5%	Hector Waller Captain Australia 1913 – 3/1/1942 drowned 1900 Australia – 3/1/1942 Sunda Strait
HNLMS Evertsen destroyer Admiralen 322' X 31' X 10' 41 miles per hour 1926 - 3/1/1942	149 crew (estimate)	9 ? ? ?/?%	W. M. DeVries, Lieutenant Commander Netherlands ? - ? ? Netherlands – ? died in captivity

To sum up, most of the ABDA naval force was now underwater. The twenty-year-old, USS Marblehead light cruiser was the only USS larger than a destroyer to survive from the ABDA naval force. Marblehead was severely damaged 2/4/1942 in the Battle of Makassar Strait. She was patched up some at Tjilatjap, and then more at Simonstown, South Africa. Marblehead finally arrived New York City 5/4/1942 for extensive dry dock repairs at the Brooklyn Navy Yard. She did not put to sea until more than five months later. As it turned out, the Japanese most likely would have sunk Marblehead within a few weeks, if she had not been damaged and sent for repairs.

After repairs, Marblehead fought in the safer waters of the North Atlantic, South Atlantic, and Mediterranean Sea for the rest of World War II. She was not damaged again. She was scrapped in 1946.

To sum up, the ABDA Naval Command was dissolved by 01:00 on March 1, less than two months after its inception. The reason was simple – all ships underwater. 1914 U.S. Naval Academy graduate Captain Albert Rooks (1891 WA – 3/1/1942 Sunda Strait) commanded four submarines and a destroyer, before being named Houston's Captain in 1941. He was killed by enemy gunfire on the bridge (age 50). As Houston went under shortly after, he was more or less buried at sea, Rooks was posthumously awarded the Medal of Honor for his actions over several weeks in February, 1942. The citation reads as follows:

> *For extraordinary heroism, outstanding courage, gallantry in action and distinguished service in the line of his profession, as commanding officer of the USS. Houston during the 2/4-27/1942 period, while in action with superior Japanese enemy aerial and surface forces. While proceeding to attack an enemy amphibious expedition as a unit in a mixed force, Houston was heavily attacked by bombers; after evading four attacks, she was heavily hit in a fifth attack, lost 60 killed and had one turret wholly disabled. Captain Rooks made his ship again seaworthy and sailed within three days to escort an important reinforcing convoy from Darwin to Koepang, Timor, Dutch East Indies. While so engaged, another powerful air attack developed which by Houston's marked efficiency was fought off, without much damage to the convoy. The commanding general of all forces in the area thereupon canceled the movement, and Captain Rooks escorted the convoy back to Darwin. Later, while in a considerable American-British-Dutch force engaged with an overwhelming force of Japanese surface ships, Houston with HMS Exeter carried the brunt of the battle, and her fire alone heavily damaged one and possibly two heavy cruisers. Although heavily damaged in the actions, Captain Rooks succeeded in disengaging his ship when the flag officer commanding broke off the action and got her safely away from the vicinity, whereas one-half of the cruisers were lost.*

The Fletcher-class, 376' long and 40' beam and 18' draft, USS Rooks (1944 – 1962 transferred to Chile, scrapped 1983) destroyer was named in his honor. Rooks' widow Edith sponsored.

Houston's Chaplain (Commander) George Rentz (1882 PA – 3/1/1942 Sunda Strait) and other crew members attained a measure of safety, by hanging on to a destroyed airplane's float. When the float took on water, Rentz relinquished his space and life jacket to wounded survivors nearby. He stated *You men are young, I have lived the major part of my life, and I am willing to go.* However, the other survivors would not hear of it. When Rentz pushed off, they grabbed him and pulled him back. Rentz gave his life jacket to Seaman First Class Walter Beeson (1911 – 1968). He told Beeson that his heart was failing him, and that he could not last much longer. He said a prayer and pushed off. Beeson refused the life preserver. Rentz was gone for good, age 59. Beeson donned the preserver. For these actions, Rentz was posthumously awarded the Navy Cross, the only World War II Navy chaplain so honored. Rentz's citation reads as follows:

> *The President of the United States takes pride in presenting the Navy Cross posthumously to George S. Rentz, Commander (Chaplain), U.S. Navy, for extraordinary heroism and distinguished service in the line of his profession as a Navy Chaplain, serving on board the Heavy Cruiser USS Houston (CA-30), in action against the enemy 2/28/1942, in the South Pacific War Area. On that date Chaplain Rentz survived the sinking of the Houston, but gave his place on a spare seaplane float and his life jacket to others of the crew, as they awaited their fate in the Java Sea at night. His conduct throughout was in keeping with the highest traditions, of the Navy of the United States. He gallantly gave his life for his country.*

The Oliver Hazard Perry-class, 453' long and 45' beam and 22' draft, USS Rentz (1984 – 2016 target ship sunk) guided missile frigate was named in his honor. Rentz's daughter Jean Lansing sponsored 7/1983, and also attended the commissioning ceremony 6/1984. Others in attendance were survivors of USS Houston, who managed to also survive Japanese imprisonment.

The Houston is shown below:

So less than three months into the War, Cruiser Houston and her Captain and Chaplain and 694 other men were history. In all, Houston sank seven Japanese warships and downed many aircraft in her short World War II career. She was awarded two battle stars.

As noted above in the three days of 2/27/1942 to 3/1/1942, eleven Allied ABDA ships were sunk or damaged, and thousands of Allied sailors killed or wounded or captured; in three naval battles. These battles over three days were the end of Allied ships operating in the waters around Java.

In addition, the land forces on the Dutch East Indies islands were quickly overwhelmed, and surrendered within two months of the initial assaults. The Allies and Japan had 2,384 and 671 killed from the land battles. More than 100,000 Allied troops were captured. To sum up, Japan occupied the Dutch East Indies, pretty much unhindered for the rest of the War except for the following:

- The 11,883 square mile Timor was partly controlled by Portugal, and partly controlled by the Dutch as one of the Dutch East Indies Islands; it took the Japanese a year to shove all the Australian soldiers off the island, 2/1942 – 2/1943; some Timorese civilians resisted, but paid the price; the estimates of the number of civilians dying at the hands of the Japanese on Timor before the War ended 9/1945 are up to 70,000
- The U.S. recaptured most of the 690 square mile Morotai Island at the north end of the Dutch East Indies 9/1944; Japan and the Allies uncomfortably co-occupied parts of Morotai until the War ended; Allied sappers made harbors and airstrips, stored fuel, etc. on Morotai; the Allies were able to use Morotai as a base in liberating the Philippines

As already noted, Japan milked the islands to the maximum for pretty much free resources and forced labor. Japan's acquisition of the Dutch East Indies definitely extended the War.

For the record, the Dutch East Indies won their independence from Netherlands in 1949. This is the Republic of Indonesia today.

These battles resulted in not only Japan securing the vast resources of the Southwest Pacific, but also firmly establishing a defensive perimeter along the arc of large islands stretching from Singapore east through Sumatra and Java across the north shore of New Guinea, and then on to Rabaul in New Britain. Again, this was less than three months after the 12/7/1941 sneak attacks.

The Houston, Perth, and Evertsen crew members and others aboard who survived the shelling and fires and sinking, and who were not shot in the water by Japanese with machine guns, and who did not drown (no mention of sharks though) kicked to Java and ran inland. Villagers grabbed them, locked them up, and turned them over to the Japanese the next day. These villagers were not necessarily pro-Japanese, as the Japanese had already abused the natives much. They just feared severe reprisals (for good reason), if they aided the American or Australian or British or Dutch sailors in any way.

The POWs were marched over a hot asphalt road to the town of Serang, Java. As the horses intended to pull supply carts had been lost on one of the Japanese transports, the Japanese hitched POWs to the carts to pull supplies and ammunition over four days. Some were barefoot and developed severe blisters from the hot asphalt. They were allowed to stop, only to rip the blisters off their feet. They were held at Serang in a place the POWs called the Bicycle Camp (as the Indonesian troops used bicycles) until 4/1942. Most were then sent to another camp at Batavia (now Jakarta).

Five hundred and thirty-four captured troops from the 2nd Battalion, 131st Field Artillery joined the POWs from the ABDA ships. This was a National Guard unit from Texas, now U.S. Army. The Battalion of originally 558 men (21 were transferred, three killed in combat) sailed from San Francisco 11/21/1941, for the Philippines. When the U.S. entered the War after the 12/7/1941 sneak attacks, the battalion was rerouted to Brisbane, Australia. The battalion was then transported on a Dutch freighter to Java, arriving 1/11/1942. The battalion's mission was to deter Japan from attacking the Dutch East Indies, or assist the Dutch in repelling such an attack. The 2nd Battalion was the only American ground force sent to the Dutch East Indies in World War II.

Japan had invaded and occupied some of the Dutch East Indies islands 1/1942. To avoid annihilation, the Allies in the Dutch East Indies surrendered, 3/8/1942. The 534 Americans of the Second Battalion were among the 32,500 soldiers, taken prisoner. The others were Dutch, British, Australian, and New Zealanders.

The Americans were referred to as the *Lost Battalion*. It was not known if they were alive or not until 9/1944 or later. At this time, USS submarines rescued large numbers of Allied survivors from sunk, unmarked, Japanese hell ships. USSs or U.S aircraft sank these hell ships purposely as follows:

- Assumed that they were cargomen or transports
- In some cases though, it was suspected that these were hell ships transporting Allied POWs, or this was even known to be the case, as the U.S had broken the IJN's codes; despite that, the hell ships were attacked killing Allied POWS; avoiding attacking these ships would lead Japan to realize that its codes were broken; Japan would then change its codes, and the U.S. would lose a major disadvantage, extending the War; hard decisions such as this one of having to kill Allied POWs including own Americans, have to be made in War; some POWs were rescued though

Four Perth sailors were survivors and provided details on the sinkings of Perth and Houston. They also provided information on the horrific abuses rendered as prisoners, including to members of the Lost Battalion. This was the first information received on the fate of the surviving and then captured ABDA fleet sailors and Lost Battalion members, and others captured (British, Dutch, Australian, as well as American).

In 10/1942, most of the POWs were taken to Moulmein, Burma, while the rest were sent to work in various camps throughout Asia (other camps in Burma, Thailand, and Vietnam). Most POWs in Burma slaved on the 262-mile Burma Railway between Ban Pong, Thailand, and Thanbyuzayat, Burma. The purpose of the railway was to deliver supplies to Japan's forces fighting in Burma. This slave labor is portrayed (much made up though) in the 1957 epic film, *The Bridge on the River Kwai*. The film starred the following:

- Alec Guinness (1914 London – 2000 England) played the senior officer of the POWs as a British Army Lieutenant Colonel
  Guinness served in the Royal Navy 1941-1943 including seeing combat; he separated as a Lieutenant
- William Holden (1918 IL – 1981 CA, bled to death when fell down and cut head when drunk) played a U.S. Navy sailor who escapes the POW camp; he

makes it back to a British base; he poses as a commissioned officer until found out; as he knows the territory from the escape, the British Army recruits him to be part of a commando team to place a bomb on a just completed major bridge on the railway

Holden was in the Army Air Forces during World War II 1942-1945, acting in propaganda films

▪ Sessue Hayakawa (1889 Japan – 1973 Tokyo) played the commandant of the prison camp

Hayakawa was rejected by the Japanese Navy due to an injury as a youth (broken eardrum)

▪ James Donald (1917 Scotland – 1993 England) played a British medical officer trying to care for the POWs without medical supplies or medicines; Donald played the Senior British Officer in another epic World War II movie, the 1963 *The Great Escape*

Donald was in the British Army in World War II (Intelligence Corps) 1944-1945

River Kwai was made for $2.8 million. Its initial box office take was $30.6 million.

The building of the Burma Railway is also portrayed in the 2013 *Railway Man* drama film, which starred Colin Firth (1960 England -) and Nicole Kidman (1967 Honolulu -). This movie was made for $18.0 million. Its box office was $22.3 million.

Of note, the abuse rendered by the Japanese to the POWs in both war movies was much toned down to avoid a high violence rating – and also as more than moviegoers can handle.

Sixty-one thousand Allied POWs and more than 200,000 Asian natives worked on the Burma Railway which stretched between mountains, across rivers, and through jungles. The men were fed starvation rations, beaten frequently, had only shorts (actually sort of a diaper type garment) for clothing, and had little or no medical care. In fact, medical care was provided by other POWs; and this without benefit of medications or medical supplies. The prisoners developed tropical illnesses such as beriberi, pellagra, malaria, dengue fever, typhus, dysentery, and tropical ulcers.

Almost 13,000 Allied POWs and 100,000 romusha and kinrohoshi died (these are rough estimates) building the *Death Railway*, as it came to be called.

Romusha is the term used to describe Indonesian laborers who were paid a pittance, early on at least. Kinrohoshi were forced laborers who were not paid at all. The estimate is that Japan forced up to ten million Indonesians to work during World War II. Another common estimate is that four million Indonesians died during the War when under Japanese control – from forced labor, exposure, famine, lack of medical care (mostly from preventable and treatable tropical diseases), forced sex, executions, etc.

For the record, the below statement is from Japanese Army Regulations, in place at the time of World War II:

Prisoners of war shall be treated with a spirit of good will, and shall never be subjected to cruelties or humiliation.

These American deaths on the railway project included 79 sailors and marines from the USS Houston, and 84 soldiers from the Lost Battalion.

The railway was completed 10/1943. However, the Japanese were never able to use the railway much, as the Allies were successful in air bombing its bridges almost as soon as they were repaired.

The surviving POWs were then sent to various forced labor work camps in Singapore, Burma, Indochina (including Vietnam), and Japan; until the War ended. More died at these camps, as well. Repatriation did not come, until the War ended 8/1945.

The full accounting of the demise of Cruiser Houston and the imprisonment of crew was not known, until these men were released to tell their horrific stories.

The American POW survivors from Houston and the Lost Battalion were scattered by the end of the War, as were British and Dutch and Australian captives. Some were still in Java, some on the Malay Peninsula, some in the jungles of Burma and Thailand, and a few on various islands of Japan; at the time of repatriation.

The location of the sunken Houston has been suspected since at least 1994. Sports divers looted her illegally. They removed rivets and a steel plate from the hull, and artifacts. Illegal salvaging occurred also in the case of Perth and Evertsen.

In a Cooperation Afloat Readiness and Training (CARAT) exercise in 2014, U.S. Navy divers assisted by personnel from the Indonesian Navy confirmed that the wrecks were Houston and Perth. The divers documented the condition of the wrecks. This data was presented at a conference in Jakarta on the preservation of wartime shipwrecks in the Java Sea, and also on preventing the illegal salvage of said wrecks.

The Houston and Perth wrecks lay at depths of 98 and 115' of water in Bantam Bay, off the northwest tip of Java. This is at the approaches to Sunda Strait.

For the record, the CARAT is a series of annual bilateral military exercises conducted by the U.S. Pacific Fleet with ASEAN member nations, in Southeast Asia. CARAT's objectives include enhancing regional cooperation, building friendships, and strengthening professional skills. ASEAN is the Association of Southeast Asian Nations. It was formed in 1967 from a predecessor organization. Today, ASEAN is an organization of ten Southeast Asia countries; which promotes and facilitates economic, political, security, military, educational, and sociocultural integration cooperation among its members and other countries in Asia.

Due to the disappearance of the USS Houston, a drive began 5/1942 in Houston for volunteers to replace the men lost and imprisoned – although their fate was not known at the time. Of course, the worse was feared. One thousand, six hundred and fifty Houston area young men stepped forward. The Navy though set a limit of one thousand, as all that were needed at the time. These men became known as the *Houston Volunteers.*

As part of this recruitment during this period, $85 million in war bonds were sold to pay for a replacement ship named for the city of Houston. The money came from many sources, including coins from children. There was enough money left over to make a light aircraft carrier as well.

On Memorial Day (5/30/1942) accompanied by a crowd of more than 150,000, the volunteers paraded in downtown Houston with several hundred Navy officers and sailors. Four bands played. Forty-eight bombers, one for each state, from Ellington Field overflew the festivities, which included induction.

Ellington Field opened in 1917 as a training facility for Army pilots. It was used during World War II to train bomber pilots, bombardiers, navigators, etc. Ellington is 18 miles southwest of downtown Houston. Today, Ellington Field Joint Reserve Base is a joint installation shared by various active component and reserve component military units, as well as aircraft flight operations of the National Aeronautics and Space Administration (NASA) under the aegis of the nearby Johnson Space Center.

Rear Admiral William Glassford (1886 San Francisco – 1958 San Diego) administered the Navy Oath. Age sixteen, volunteer Robert Bradley was too young to enlist. Despite that, he was allowed to participate, as his brother Leonard was lost when Houston went down. However again, it was not known at the time if Leonard was alive or dead. Lieutenant Commander Simon Shade swore Bradley into the Navy three days later when he turned 17. Shade had sworn in Bradley's brother, two years before.

Admiral Glassford then described Houston's last battle, at Sunda Strait. At this time, some details were known. However again, the fate of the crews of the three ABDA warships sunk 3/1/1942 at Sunda Strait and the Lost Battalion was still a mystery. Death and or imprisonment of course were known. However, the percentages in each category were not known.

Houston Mayor Neal Pickett (1902 Houston – 1990) read a message from President Roosevelt at the ceremony. As already noted, Roosevelt had taken four pre-war cruises on Houston. The statement was as follows:

> Not one of us doubts that the thousand naval recruits sworn in today will carry on with the same spirit shown by the gallant men, who have gone before them. Not one of us doubts that every true Texan and every true American will back up these new fighting men, with all our hearts and all our efforts.

A 10% to scale, 60' model of the new Houston was unveiled and dedicated.

The one thousand inductees immediately marched to Union Station and boarded five arranged trains for San Diego for initial training.

A pink granite marker as a memorial to the men killed and imprisoned and to denote the $85 million raised to make the replacement USS Houston and also the Independence-class, 623' long, USS San Jacinto (1943 – 1971 scrapped) light aircraft carrier was placed at 1000 Main Street in downtown Houston, between Lamar and McKinney Streets. This is near the site where the one thousand volunteers were inducted. The plaque read as follows:

On this site on May 30, 1942, one thousand Houston Volunteers took the Oath of Service in the United States Navy, and dedicated their lives to avenging the Cruiser USS Houston and her valiant crew, lost in the Battle of the Java Sea.

In 10/1942, the Cleveland-class, 610' long and 66' beam and 23' draft, 37 miles per hour, 1,255 crew complement, light cruiser USS Vicksburg (1943 – 1960 scrapped) then under construction at Newport News, Virginia, was renamed Houston. This was the same shipyard where the sunk USS Houston had been made. President Roosevelt declared:

Our enemies have given us the chance to prove that there will be another USS Houston, and yet another USS Houston if that becomes necessary, and still another USS Houston, as long as American ideals are in jeopardy.

The good citizens of Vicksburg, Mississippi were appeased though, as the also Cleveland-class USS Cheyenne cruiser under construction also at Newport News was quickly renamed the USS Vicksburg (1943 – 1961 scrapped). It was in fact commissioned six months before the replacement USS Houston.

And as far as the good and presumably very patient folks of Cheyenne, Wyoming are concerned, their next Navy namesake warship was not commissioned until more than fifty years later in 1996. This was the Los Angeles-class, nuclear attack submarine USS Cheyenne, now in service.

From the swearing in 5/1942 to the 12/1943 commissioning of the new Houston cruiser was nineteen months.

For the record, only one of the one thousand Houston volunteer sailors ended up serving on the replacement Houston.

This third USS Houston CL-81 (1943 – 1959 scrapped) was commissioned the end of 1943. In World War II, she primarily operated as a screen to protect aircraft carriers from air attacks. She escorted carriers during invasions of the Mariana Islands including Saipan, Palau, and Okinawa. She operated off Formosa (Taiwan today). She shot down four aircraft 10/12/1944, and another three two days later.

Houston was hit by an aerial torpedo bomb in the 10/14/1944 Formosa Battle, resulting in a loss of propulsion and 55 men. When under tow to Ulithi (Caroline Islands) for repairs, she was hit by another aerial torpedo which flooded her scout planes hangar. Houston evacuated surplus sailors to escorting ships. She underwent temporary repairs at Ulithi (Caroline Islands). As west coast shipyards were swamped, she arrived New York Navy Yard 3/24/1945 under her own power for permanent repairs. These were not completed until after the War ended. She earned three battle stars. After the war, she engaged in training exercises, readiness tests, and good will tours. She was decommissioned 12/15/1947, laid up in reserve, and finally scrapped in 1959.

By the way, the USS San Jacinto (1943 – 1971 scrapped) aircraft carrier made with the raised extra money is also known, as the Navy's youngest aviator of World War II flew off her. His name was George H.W. Bush (1924 MA – 2018 Houston). Ensign Bush made one more carrier takeoff from San Jacinto than landings as he was shot down 9/2/1944 and narrowly escaped death (and cannibalism, but that is another story). His two crewmen died though. Actually, young Bush had ditched earlier. In this case, he developed engine trouble immediately after catapult launch in the 6/19, 20/1944 Philippine Sea Battle, maybe as hit by shrapnel from a Japanese dive bomber. He was able to circle around to land. However, the carrier waved him off. He and his two were not injured, and rescued. Therefore, his San Jacinto carrier landings were two less than his takeoffs. Bush went on to be the 41st President of the U.S., presiding 1989-1993.

Indonesian divers recovered the bell from the USS Houston wreck at the bottom of Bantam Bay, in 1973. Indonesia delivered the bell to Francis Galbraith (1913 SD – 1986), 8/24/1973. At the time, Galbraith was Ambassador to Singapore. He was an Army veteran.

The bell was stored on the New York-class, 573' long and 95' beam and 29' draft, USS Texas (1914 – 1949, floating ship museum today on the Houston Ship Channel) battleship at the San Jacinto Battleground State Historic Site, on the east edge of Houston. When Navy veteran Captain Carl Ragsdale (1925 MO – 2003 TX) learned that the bell was stored in a crate on the USS Texas, he conceived of the idea of making a monument to display the bell. Ragsdale served in the Navy 43 years, 1942-1985.

A committee was formed as follows:

- Lieutenant Commander Clarke Coldren, retired Navy
- Commander William Kendall, retired Navy
- Commander James Sterling, retired Navy
- Captain Carter Conlin, retired Navy
- Captain Arthur Gralia, retired Navy
- Captain Cal Hill, retired Navy
- Captain George Holyfield, retired Navy
- Captain Rodney Koenig, retired Navy
- Raymond Nelson

Former Houston Mayor Bob Lanier (1925 TX – 2014 Houston) was Honorary Chairman. Lanier was mayor 1992-1998, and then term limited. He is known as being Houston's oldest mayor, age 72.

President George Bush (retired Navy) was Honorary Wardroom President. Again, Bush was President 1989-1993, which was during the fundraising period. In the Navy (also Marines and Coast Guard), the wardroom is the mess cabin or compartment for commissioned naval officers above the rank of midshipman.

Fundraising started in 1991. Hundreds of individuals (many were veterans) including children, businesses, corporations, civic associations, etc. paid for the construction of the monument. The major donors were the Battle Mountain Gold Company, Gallery Furniture (Jim and Linda McIngvale), Shell Oil, Tenneco, Mr. and Mrs. Paul Howell, Bob Whorton, the Strake Foundation, the Houston Independent School District, and the USS Stout (DDG 55) Committee. The USS Stout is an Arleigh Burke-class guided missile destroyer, commissioned new in 1994 and still in service.

Jeff Ryan designed the 20' monument. The names of the crew are engraved on the pedestal.

On 1995 Veterans Day (11/11/1995), the Texas Commandery of the Naval Order of the United States dedicated the monument to the memory of the crew of the USS Houston. The site is Sam Houston Park, downtown Houston.

Many Houston cruiser survivors attended the event. This was more than 53 years after the sinking, so these men were mostly in their seventies and eighties.

The pictures below show the granite pedestal monument. It is topped by Houston's 500-pound bell.

The annual commemoration of the sailors who died in the sinking or later as captives is conducted at the monument.

Of note as part of Navy Week 10/2012, Seabees under the direction of Lieutenant E. R. Weatherall from Naval Mobile Construction Battalion 28 renovated and restored the monument. The Seabees' work included remodeling the plaza behind the Heritage Society Museum building, which abuts Sam Houston Park. The Seabees also made sidewalks to connect the monument to the existing walkway in front of the Nichols-Rice-Cherry House, Heritage Park. Heritage Park is a group of restored, historical homes on display.

USS Houston survivor Seaman Second Class Otto Schwarz (1923 NJ – 2006) had enlisted 1/1941. His battle station was the powder magazine, which put him at the bottom of the cruiser, placing powder bags on hoists to the gun turrets. He and twelve others barely made it up in the dark through fire and smoke when Executive Officer Commander David Roberts (as Captain Rooks dead) issued the abandon ship order. In fact, Houston was hit by a shell or torpedo when the thirteen were half way up. Schwarz lost consciousness. He came to, and continued to climb. On top, Schwarz found a life jacket, but it was on fire. He ran into another sailor who had two good life jackets, who gave one to Schwarz. He jumped. He heard screams of Houston sailors being shot in the water with machine guns. He swam and kicked fourteen hours, until a Japanese ship picked him up. He never saw those twelve men of his battery again.

Schwarz was put to work as a slave laborer on the Burma-Siam death railway. He was working on a railroad in Vietnam when the War ended. He weighed 103 pounds when repatriated. He received no rehabilitation (counseling, etc.) related to his almost 3.5 years as a POW of the Japanese. Schwarz was discharged in 1946, as a Chief Boatswain's Mate. He worked for the U.S. Post Office in various jobs for 32 years. He then retired in New Jersey.

Schwarz suffered from posttraumatic stress disorder from the naval battles, the sinking and loss of his fellow sailors, and abuse during imprisonment. To cope, he with assistance from his wife Trudy (1924 -) formed the USS Houston CA-30 Survivors Association in 1946.

Schwarz started a quarterly newsletter named *Blue Bonnet* for the ship's survivors and families. This was the same name as the ship's original newsletter, before and during World War II. With so many men aboard and to spread the news; newsletters printed on board and distributed were common for cruisers, battleships, and carriers during World War II.

Annual reunions were conducted to commemorate the service of USS Houston, HMAS Perth, HMNLS Evertsen, ABDA Command fleet, and Lost Battalion survivors. Survivors and their relatives from all of the above have attended over the years. The event date is March 1 or around March 1, which was the date that the three ships were sunk.

In 1981, the Association donated a collection of archival materials and memorabilia to the University of Houston. Today, the University's Special Collections Department houses the Cruiser Houston Collection and related archival collections, which document the ship's history and crew. The University also made a Cruiser Houston Memorial Room to display the items.

In 1991, the Survivors Association formed a complementary group called the *USS Houston Survivors/Next Generation.* This group consists of younger relatives (children, nieces and nephews, grandchildren) of Houston crewmen – both those who died in the War and those who survived. Otto Schwarz's son John today, helps run the USS Houston Survivors/Next Generations group. These relatives now run the activities and events, as very few Cruiser Houston survivors remain.

The group runs the annual memorial service at the downtown Houston monument. They put out the *Blue Bonnet* quarterly newspaper. They raise money for these efforts. They award scholarships. Some scholarships are awarded to relatives of survivors or victims of Houston. Other scholarships are awarded to pay for preparatory military school education for students who plan to apply to attend the U.S. Naval Academy in Annapolis, Maryland.

The annual activities include educational events, as well as a memorial event.

At the 3/2016 annual event, Houston Maritime Museum (HMM) Associate Curator & Archivist Erica Peaslee presented an update on the Museum's plans for a permanent exhibit about the vessel, at its new museum on the Houston Ship Channel to be completed in 2021. HMM has a strong bond with the Association, and serves as one of the stewards of the Houston's artifacts and documentary history. The Museum has a display on the USS Houston and HMAS Perth, at its current facility.

At the annual event 3/2017 which was the 75th anniversary of the sinking, none of the three living Houston survivors still living were able to attend, due to age and health. Widow Trudy Schwarz at age 93, did attend though. On this date, Perth had only three living survivors (and also unable to attend).

The exhibit *Guardians of Sunda Strait: The Wartime Loss of HMAS Perth and USS Houston* was shown three months at the city-owned Julia Ideson Building in downtown Houston, in 2017. The Ideson building opened new in 1926, as the city's library. Today, the city still owns and operates. It houses mostly historical archives, manuscripts, etc. Again, this display was part of the 75th anniversary of the sinkings. The Australian National Maritime Museum based in Sydney was the organizer. The USA Bicentennial Gift Fund and the City of Houston funded, along with the Australian National Maritime Museum.

The crew of Houston are honored alongside the crew of Perth at the Shrine of Remembrance in Melbourne, Victoria; and also at St. John's Anglican Church, Freemantle, Western Australia. These are both Australian port cities.

The Los Angeles-class, 362' long and 33' beam and 32' draft, 110 crew complement, nuclear-powered, 23 miles per hour both surface and submerged (reported though that capable of 38 miles per hour submerged), USS Houston attack submarine (1982 – 2016 decommissioned) was the fourth USS Houston. Barbara Bush (1925 NYC – 2018 Houston) sponsored. Some USS Houston survivors attended the sponsor ceremony, and later the commissioning ceremony.

This submarine was used to make the 1989 *The Hunt for Red October* movie. The movie was based on espionage and military science, bestselling author Tom Clancy's (1947 Baltimore – 2013 Baltimore) debut novel of the same name. During the shoot, the Houston submarine snagged a tow cable sinking a tugboat near Santa Catalina Island. A tug crewman drowned. This submarine was known for many mechanical problems and accidents.

Todd Houston Shipyard made the *SS Houston Volunteers* Liberty Ship, which was commissioned 10/1942. She served in the Mediterranean Sea, during World War II.

At this time, there are no plans for a fifth USS Houston.

7- DOOLITTLE RAID, INSTRUMENT FLYING

The Empire of Japan sneak attacked thirteen locations in or on the Pacific Ocean 12/7, 8/1941. Japan as usual did not bother to warn the victims, by declaring war. This was in violation of the international rules of war. The 1907 Hague Convention addressed the requirement to declare war in its *Convention Relative to the Opening of Hostilities* statements. These clauses describe the international actions a country should perform, before opening hostilities. Article 1 states: *The Contracting Powers recognize that hostilities between themselves must not commence without previous and explicit warning, in the form either of a reasoned declaration of war or of an ultimatum with conditional declaration of war.* Japan took a pass on giving an advance warning, of maybe attacking. Shame on Japan, again (Japan had a history of sneak attacks).

The attacks were all on the same day, within nine hours of each other. Two days are shown, as the locations were on both sides of the International Date Line. The International Date Line is an imaginary line from the North Pole to the South Pole. It marks the change from one calendar day to the next. It roughly follows the 180° line of longitude, through the middle of the Pacific Ocean. But again, the attacks were all on the same day.

The attacked thirteen sites (or ships) were as follows:

- Nine U.S. possessions
  - Storming and capture of a 159' long USS river gunboat and its crew when berthed at Shanghai Harbor; this little Yangtze River gunboat was the only USS that Japan captured in World War II; for good measure, the Japanese also gun-sank a 177' HMS river gunboat in Shanghai Harbor, at about the same time; if counting this British warship, it is fourteen sneak attacks instead of thirteen
  - IJN submarine gun-sank an Army-chartered, 250' long freighter off California
  - Howland and Baker Islands of the Phoenix Islands of the U.S. Minor Outlying Islands were bombed, these two islands are 43 miles apart

- Five U.S. military installations (harbors, airfields, bases) on five Pacific Ocean islands; these five islands were Oahu (Pearl Harbor), Guam, Midway, Wake, and Philippines
- Three British Crown colonies – Malaysia, Hong Kong, and Singapore
- Thailand

Japan ended up occupying the three British crown colonies, Thailand, and Wake Island for the duration of World War II. Japan occupied Guam until the U.S. re-captured 8/1944. Japan occupied the major Philippine islands by the spring of 1942. The U.S. wrested the Philippines islands back beginning 10/1944, and into 1945. General Douglas MacArthur (1880 AR – 1964 DC) said he would return and he did, but it took 2.6 years.

Some Japanese soldiers held out though on Mindanao Island (second largest of the Philippines) until the end of the War. Actually, the last holdouts on Mindanao were 200 well organized and disciplined soldiers, who surrendered 1/1948. This was 29 months after the War ended (if you can believe it).

In the next few weeks or months after the sneak attacks, Japan also conquered and occupied Borneo, Burma, New Britain, Gilbert Islands, and the resource-rich Dutch East Indies (oil reservoirs, rubber tree plantations, etc.). The locals had no say in this grab of territory and resources.

In these thirteen (or fourteen if counting the HMS river gunboat sunk in Shanghai Harbor) attacks on the same day, the Japanese Empire was for the most part stupendously successful in terms of devastation and casualties rendered, versus its own loss of equipment and casualties. Japan's planning and executions were brilliant. Said yet a third way, the outcomes were very one-sided in Japan's favor. To quote President Franklin Roosevelt (1882 NY – 4/12/1945 GA, cerebral hemorrhage) from his 12/8/1941 speech to Congress, 12/7/1941 was *a date that will live in infamy* for the United States.

Of the five U.S. military targets on the five Pacific Ocean islands, Americans of course most remember Oahu (Pearl Harbor) of the U.S. Territory of Hawaii, again due to the one-sided outcome. Japan launched two air attacks (bombing and strafing), one hour apart on a Sunday morning. The U.S. military had 2,335 and 1,143 men killed and wounded. Another 68 and 35 Hawaiian civilians were killed and injured. In comparison, only 64 Japanese military men died (55 airmen and nine midget submarine sailors) and one (a submariner) captured. This is a ratio of more than 36 American military deaths per one Japanese military death.

The Japanese Navy sank or damaged nineteen USSs including all eight battleships of the Pacific fleet. Hundreds of aircraft were destroyed, and most of these when on the ground. Japan lost only 29 aircraft, nine and 20 in the first and second wave attacks. These were fifteen, nine, and five dive bombers, fighters, and torpedo bombers. Japan's five mini-submarines were all sunk, which was more or less the unstated plan. The other 51 ships of the Japanese Task Force were unseen and undetected, coming and going.

Japan's surprise attacks without declaring war ended the United States' isolationist attitude, left over from losing 116,700 men in uniform (almost 46% in combat) and another 204,000 wounded or made ill (many with permanent disabilities) in World War I. Congress at President Roosevelt's request declared war on Japan the next day, which was a Monday. The peace between the World War I Armistice Day and World War II was a little more than 23 years.

Japan's aim with the devastating sneak attack at Oahu was to eliminate much of the U.S. Pacific naval fleet and its port infrastructure, so that the U.S. could not interfere with Japan's planned continued military actions in Southeast Asia. These of course included conquests of overseas territories of the U.K., the Netherlands, and the U.S. Japan's thinking (or maybe hopeful thinking), was that the U.S. in turn would reason as follows:

- In only one day, we have lost a large part of our military prowess including all eight Pacific naval fleet battleships sunk or damaged and thousands of military men killed and wounded – who needs another overseas war; after all, what did we gain, from having so many of our boys die in World War I, which ended only 23 years ago
- That what goes on in Southeast Asia, is of little concern to the U.S.
- That entering a war would worsen the country's financial condition, already bad as this during the 1929-1941, worldwide, economic Great Depression, which originated in the U.S.; in actuality, gearing up for a war economy ended or much reduced the Great Depression in many countries, including the U.S.

Japanese leaders or at least some of them also thought that the U.S. would accept its ruthlessness of the citizens and military of other countries, as an ongoing heritage. After all, the European colonists who had settled North America went on to murder or shove aside and otherwise conquer the *inferiors* (Native Americans), to dominate a large part of the world. These battles lasted until the 1920s (southwestern United States) and even into the 1930s in Mexico.

Therefore, Japan assumed (or again maybe hoped) that the U.S. would not want any part of an Asian war thousands of miles from home – so would negotiate a peace agreement. As it turned out, that is not how the U.S. reacted – what was Japan thinking (or hoping)?

Furthermore, Japan reasoned that if the U.S. did get involved in the war, they would lean toward the European Theater, instead of the just created Pacific Theater. Japan was somewhat right on this second supposition. This was the case despite the fact that Japan had just very successfully sneak attacked five U.S. military locations on five Pacific Ocean islands, bombed two U.S. controlled Phoenix islands, captured a USS river gunboat and its crew berthed in Shanghai's Harbor (the only USS that Japan captured in World War II), and sank an Army-chartered freighter 300 miles off California. Again, these attacks were all on the same day. Japan's military accomplishments this one day were stellar.

Nevertheless, the U.S. first concentrated on coming to the aid of Great Britain, occupied European countries, and Russia. In fact, the U.S. was already aiding much here supplying these countries (and also China) with military equipment, munitions, supplies, etc. through the Cash and Carry program and then the Lend-Lease program.

The War in Europe did in fact end more than three months before the war in the Pacific – and this only as the U.S. developed and used weapons of mass destruction (atomic bombs) against Japan.

The devastating Pearl Harbor attack (and the other attacks as well) was a profound shock to Americans. Strong, domestic support for isolationism immediately disappeared. Muted (or at least not touted) support of Britain and France and other countries was replaced by active alliance.

The U.S. declared war on Japan the next day, 12/8/1941. This was a Monday. Germany and Italy declared war on the U.S. 12/11/1941, Thursday. The U.S. in turn declared war on Germany and Italy, also 12/11/1941.

Americans were very demoralized, at the one-sided nature of the Oahu and other military installation attacks. This was for good reason as walloped as caught off guard and so unprepared despite numerous warnings. Furthermore, Japan in the next few weeks and months also rolled over other countries, territories, and protectorates. These included Borneo, Philippines, Thailand, Malaysia, Singapore, Hong Kong, Burma, Wake Island, Gilbert Islands, New Britain, New Guinea, Guam, and the oil-rich and rubber tree plantations Dutch East Indies. The thinking here was that it will take years and great costs (in lives and money) to unravel Japan's successes – and this turned out to be the case.

President Roosevelt told the Joint Chiefs of Staff at a 12/21/1944 White House meeting two weeks after the sneak attacks, that the military must do something offensively against Japan to boost public morale. Roosevelt's thinking was to bomb Japan, somehow. Besides boosting morale of Americans, such bombings would show the Japanese that the U.S. was capable of striking back; and that Japan was vulnerable to attack, and that therefore Japan should shift its war resources to protect the homeland. Such would reduce Japan's ability to make more conquests and hold recently occupied territories. President Roosevelt also realized that such an attack would further engage Americans, in supporting the War effort. Roosevelt asked his military advisors to come up with a plan.

1915 U.S. Naval Academy graduate, Anti-Submarine Warfare Officer, Vice-Admiral Francis Low (1894 NY – 1964 CA) assessed the capability of the Navy's newest aircraft carrier at the naval base at Norfolk, Virginia. This was 1/1942. The $32 million, Yorktown-class, 827' long, USS Hornet (1941 – 10/26/1942 Japanese aircraft sank at Santa Cruz Battle, 140 sailors lost of 2,919 crew {4.8%}) fleet aircraft carrier was commissioned 10/1941.

The Norfolk airfield had the outline of an aircraft carrier painted on it, to help naval aviators remain proficient in their launch and landing techniques. Low observed twin engine B-25 Mitchell bombers making passes at that outline in a mock attack. He knew that the wings of twin engine bombers would fit on the deck of a carrier. He wondered if land-based B-25 bombers could be modified to take off from a carrier.

Low discussed this idea with Naval Operations Chief Admiral Ernest King (1878 OH – 1956 MN). King thought it had merit. Navy Air Operations Officer Captain Donald Duncan (1896 – 1975 FL) was brought in. Duncan consulted his staff, per these considerations and discussions. The outcome was that Duncan recommended a bombing attack on Tokyo, using twin engine bombers launched from an aircraft carrier.

To sum up, per Roosevelt's request for a morale-building attack against Japan, the plan of bombers taking off from an aircraft carrier, bombing Japan, and then landing on neutral territory; rose to the top. The planned action was called *Special Aviation Project Number One*. Duncan's team got specific, proposing that B-25s be used and that Hornet be the carrier. This would be the first combat test for the carrier and the bombers. As it turned out though, B-25s did make several bomb runs just before the planned raid.

The 53' long, 67' wingspan, 16' tall, twin engine, twin-tail, retractable tricycle landing gear, six crew, North American Aviation, B-25B Mitchell medium bomber was selected, as Captain Duncan had recommended. The B-25's fourteen cylinder, air-cooled, radial engines were rated at 1,700 horsepower per side. Cruise and maximum speeds were 230 and 272 miles per hour at 13,000'. Its range was 1,350 miles, as built.

The B-25 was known for having the most forward-firing guns of any Allied aircraft of World War II; so was formidable when strafing, or if air attacked head-on by an enemy aircraft. It had up to eighteen, .50 caliber (12.7 millimeter), Browning machine guns. It could also tote a 75 millimeter cannon and rockets, as well as bombs.

B-25s were introduced in 1941. Their first bombing mission (six B-25s) was 4/6/1942; bombing Gasmata, New Britain, Papua New Guinea. The second and third missions were 4/12/1942 and 413/1942 against Cebu City and Davao respectively, both in the Philippines. This Raid over Japan would be their fourth combat mission, and quite a bit different. Of course, B-25s had never launched from an aircraft carrier on a mission. Twin engine bombers were not designed and made for such.

1933 U.S. Naval Academy graduate Lieutenant Commander Steve Jurika (1910 Los Angeles -1993) was a consultant to Captain Duncan, on the medium bombers launched from an aircraft carrier to bomb Japan proposal. His father owned plantations in the Philippines. Jurika went to school in the Philippines, China, and Japan. He was a naval pilot.

Jurika was the last Air Naval Attaché at the American Embassy in Tokyo, 6/1939 – 8/1941, before the Pacific War started. Because of his position and especially as fluent in Japanese, he was able to collect significant information about Japanese military and industrial capabilities, so as to be able to prioritize targets. He even photographed many sensitive sites. He collected specific information about the new, Mitsubishi A6M Zero high performance fighter. Jurika was assigned as Hornet's Flight Deck and Intelligence Officer.

The plan was presented to Army Air Forces head General Henry Arnold (1886 PA – 1950 CA). Arnold approved the plan. Whether Arnold and other Generals and Admirals (and maybe even Roosevelt) considered it a suicide plan or not – statements were never made. However, many military historians believe that Arnold thought he was sending these men to their doom.

Anyway, this project was historic, as it was the first joint action between the Army Air Forces and Navy.

Arnold selected Lieutenant Colonel (promoted to Lieutenant Colonel 1/1942) James Harold Doolittle (1896 CA – 1993 CA) as the Army's project manager officer. At the time, Doolittle was a famous military test pilot and civilian aviator from before the war, and an aeronautical engineer with a doctorate degree. Duncan remained in charge on the Navy side.

When Doolittle was 14 years old, his school attended the Los Angeles International Air Meet at Dominguez Field (where Dominguez Field was then is today in Carson, California; Carson is thirteen miles south of downtown Los Angeles). This was the first time that Doolittle saw an airplane. He attended college, but took a leave of absence 10/1917 to enlist in the Army Signal Corps Reserve as a flying cadet. He learned to fly. He was commissioned as a First Lieutenant in the Army Signal Officers Reserve Corps, 3/11/1918. The U.S. military's first aeronautical operations was first assigned to the Army Signal Corps, in 1907. This was less than four years after the first heavier-than-air aircraft flight.

During World War I, Doolittle served as a flight instructor at Army air bases in Texas and Ohio. World War I fighting ended 11/11/1918. He had a number of flying duties in the 1920s. He earned master's and doctorate degrees in aeronautics from the Massachusetts Institute of Technology in 1924 and 1925. The latter was the first awarded in the United States.

Doolittle continued to fly, setting records. He performed an outside loop in 1927 - - thought to be impossible and thought to be fatal as well.

Doolittle won the three big air-racing trophies of the time: Schneider, Bendix, and Thompson. After this trio of wins, he retired from air racing. He made the statement: *I have yet to hear anyone engaged in this line of work, dying of old age.*

Doolittle set a world speed record of 246 miles an hour, 10/1925. His aircraft was a wooden, single engine, single crew, biplane, Curtiss R3C-2 floatplane racer; introduced earlier that year. Doolittle had won the Schneider Trophy the day before, in the same aircraft. This R3C-2 has been preserved. It is on display at the National Air and Space Museum's Steven F. Udvar-Hazy Centre at Washington Dulles Airport, Virginia.

Eight pilots broke Doolittle's record. One was Amelia Earhart (1897 KS – 7/2/1937 crashed into Pacific Ocean on an around the world flight attempt). Doolittle though reclaimed the record. For this second time, he was flying an all metal, single engine, low wing, Gee Bee R-1; introduced in 1932. His speed was 296 miles per hour. This was in the 1932 Thompson race, which he won.

Doolittle transferred to the Reserves. He returned to active duty 7/1940 as a Major. He worked in the area of procurement, assisting large automobile manufacturers on how to convert their plants to produce aircraft, which would be needed if the U.S. entered World War II.

Again, General Arnold appointed Doolittle as Raid planner. Doolittle calculated that much modified B-25s could take off on their own engines from a carrier 575 miles from Tokyo with a 2,000-pound bomb load, drop on key industrial and military targets on Honshu Island (Tokyo and other large cities are on Honshu), fly over the China Sea, and land at the port city of Vladivostok, Russia – with much fuel to spare. Upon landing, the Raiders would turn the B-25s over to their Russian ally, through the Lend-Lease program.

However, the Russians refused the arrivals of the B-25s. Russia had signed a neutrality agreement with Japan, 4/1941. Considering that Germany who was allied with Japan had invaded and attacked Russia 6/22/1941, that Japan's horrendous abuse of civilians and prisoners of war (POWs) was already well known, and that the U.S. was much aiding Russia -- Russia logically should have foregone its treaty agreement (either announced or not announced) and made airfields available to the U.S. Shame on Joseph Stalin (1878 Russia – 1953 Soviet Union, cerebral hemorrhage).

Doolittle's plan B then was to land at the friendly airfield in Chuchow, China. This was 690 more miles though than the Soviet airfield, leaving only 20 minutes of fuel per his calculations. The B-25s would then join the U.S. Army Air Forces in China, and continue bombing missions in the China-Burma-India Theater.

The bombers returning to Hornet to land was not considered. Such was not feasible. Modifications to add tail hooks would have to be extensive. The additional weight to strengthen the B-25 frames and that of the tail hook would have reduced range and bomb load.

As insurance, the carburetors of the B-25s were adjusted for maximum fuel efficiency in low-level flight. Without Doolittle's knowledge and also in violation of his orders, the carburetors of one of the B-25s were replaced and not adjusted (see below).

The usual B-25 take-off roll was a minimum of 1,200'. The pilots trained extensively to lift the much-modified B-25s off in little more than a third of the usual distance, although they did not practice from carriers at all. The training was at Eglin Field and Wagner Field, both in northwest Florida. The training included cross-country flying, skimming, night flying, navigating without radio references or landmarks, low-level bombing, aerial gunnery, etc.

Modifications included adding fuel tanks and cells to expand fuel capacity from 646 to 1,141 gallons (77% increase) to increase range. The radio set, some armor, lower gun turret, and tail gun turret were removed to reduce weight; and further increase range. Guns in the upper turret and nose remained. Broomsticks painted dark were installed in the tail, as fake guns. It was hoped that the fakes would fool Japanese fighter pilots. Broomsticks of course are much lighter than machine guns and ammunition.

As well as the B-25s lacking a full complement of guns, they also would not be escorted by fighters. Fighters were not able to fly that distance and get back fuel-wise, especially considering that Hornet and her escorts would make a 180 after the B-25s took off.

The advanced Norden bombsight was ineffective at low altitudes. Also, it was heavy at 50 pounds, and even more if connected to an autopilot system. For these reasons, it was also removed. Mission pilot Captain Ross Greening (1914 IA –

1957 MD) was also armament officer. Greening designed a replacement bombsight. It was connected to the cockpit through the pilot direction indicator, allowing the bombardier to give the pilot maneuvering directions without having to use voice communication. The materials cost $3.20, or 20¢ per bomber. This is $51 in 2019 money, which is a little more than $3 per B-25. The metal working shop at Eglin Field made the devices.

Two of the modified B-25s fully fueled, were craned onto the six-month-old Hornet at Norfolk. They took off without difficulty. The second takeoff required only 275' of carrier runway. This is 76% of a football field (counting the end zones). Lieutenant John Fitzgerald and Lieutenant James McCarthy were the Army pilots. Neither Fitzgerald or McCarthy though were assigned to the upcoming mission. This was off the Virginia Capes, 2/2/1942.

On 3/4/1942, Hornet rendezvoused with the Brooklyn-class, 608' long and 62' beam and 24' draft, USS Nashville (1938 – 1951 sold to Chilean Navy, 1985 scrapped) light cruiser off the Virginia Capes. Nashville accompanied Hornet through the Panama Canal to San Diego, arriving 3/20/1942. The carrier and cruiser then steamed to San Francisco. The sixteen B-25s were craned onto Hornet 4/1/1942 at Naval Air Station Alameda (on San Francisco Bay). The two warships departed Alameda 4/2/1942, to conduct maneuvers.

On 4/4/1942, the Navy, L-class, twin engine, 180' long, 46 and 61 miles per hour cruise and maximum speeds, helium L-8 blimp lowered a 300-pound bundle of B-25 parts to the deck of Hornet on a cable with its power winch. These were needed to complete the modifications of the B-25s, and to deliver spare parts needed by aboard maintainers.

L-8 had been a commercial (used for advertising) helium blimp, acquired from Goodyear. The Navy used L-8 and other similar blimps mainly for coastal patrol on both the west and east coasts. As blimps could hover and did not use much fuel, they were ideal for this purpose. They carried depth charges on external racks in case a German or Japanese submarine was detected or sighted. They also toted a .30 caliber machine gun and 300 rounds of ammunition. Again as able to hover, accuracy of dropped depth charges and when strafing was maximized. On the negative side, shooting down blimps was easy due to lack of speed and agility, and as so large.

On 8/16/1942, L-8 floated off Treasure Island in the middle of San Francisco Bay for anti-submarine patrol. People on the beach five hours later sighted L-8, incoming. The blimp scraped along the ground several miles and came to rest in Daly City. Daly City is eight miles southwest of San Francisco. The gondola door was open. The two crew were nowhere to be seen. Their bodies were never found. Their disappearance remains a mystery to this day.

L-8 was repaired. It was returned to Goodyear after the War, and retired from commercial duty in 1982.

On 4/13/1942, Hornet and Nashville rendezvoused with Task Force 16 north of Midway Atoll. The Task Force set course toward Japan.

Vice Admiral William Halsey (1882 NJ – 1959 NY) commanded Task Force 16. Besides Hornet and Nashville, the Task Force included one other fleet aircraft carrier, three heavy cruisers, eight destroyers, and two oilers. The carrier was the Yorktown-class, 827' long, USS Enterprise (1938 – 1960 scrapped). Enterprise's fighters and scout planes went up to provide reconnaissance and protection (combat air patrol) for the Task Force in case of aerial, surface ship, or submarine attack. Hornet's fighters and scouts were below decks. These aircraft could not be brought up, as the sixteen large B-25s took up so much deck space.

The convoy proceeded in radio silence toward the intended launch point. En route, Jurika and Doolittle spent many hours briefing the aircrews on air routes, locations of high value targets, evasion, escape, etc. Jurika advised the crews on Japanese culture. This was in case airmen had to bail out over Japan or crash-landed on one of the Japanese islands. Of course, the airmen realized that Japanese authorities would beat and torture them before killing them; or turn them loose on the street to allow brainwashed citizens to do the same. The crews were also taught a little Chinese, to be able to verbally identify themselves to peasants if necessary depending upon where they landed or bailed out in China.

The Japanese had given several medals to Jurika, when he served at the U.S. embassy in Japan. Doolittle tied them and some other Japanese medals received by American servicemen before the war to the tail of the bombs, for *special delivery*. In fact, one of the medals was one that the Japanese had awarded to Doolittle.

When 1,000 miles from Japan 4/17/1942, the oilers underway refueled Nashville, the other cruisers, and the two carriers. The destroyers detached as not enough fuel available. The cruisers and carriers then accelerated into a high-speed dash towards the planned launching point -- 500 miles from Japan.

The next day (4/18/1942) at 6:05, Lieutenant Osborne Wiseman (1915 OH – 6/4/1942 his Douglas SBD Dauntless scout plane and dive bomber shot down by Zeroes in Midway Battle; his gunner/radioman killed also) flew low and slow over Enterprise's deck. His radioman dropped a weighted message. The message stated that a Japanese picket boat had been spotted 42 miles ahead; and furthermore, it was likely that she had spotted his aircraft. This form of low-tech communication (dropped, hand-written message) was necessary to maintain radio silence.

Per the orders of Admiral Isoroku Yamamoto (1884 Japan – 4/18/1943 shot and killed in a twin engine, Mitsubishi G4M bomber over Bougainville on a morale-boosting trip), the Japanese Navy set up a defensive surveillance system around Japan with 116 small ships. These were mostly fishing and whaling boats, that the Japanese Navy requisitioned and converted into picket boats. The conversion included installation of sensitive radar, powerful radios, and usually at least one anti-aircraft gun. Again, the purpose of the picket boats was to monitor activity around the Japanese islands. Oddly, Yamamoto died on the same day of the Raid, one year later.

Later, the American ships intercepted broadcasts from another Japanese picket boat that the American Task Force had been sighted. Scout planes from Enterprise sank the picket boat, but again the surprise advantage was lost.

When still 750 miles away at 07:39 (4/18/1942), Hornet spotted another picket ship. This was the 98' long, Nitto Maru (1935 – 4/18/1942 USS Nashville gun-sank). Again, the American ships intercepted broadcasts from Nitto, reporting the sighting of the American Task Force. Due to heavy seas, Nashville required more than 900 shells to sink Nitto, at 8:20. Nashville's gunners got a lot of practice. Nitto had 11 crew. Five died from the gunfire or drowned. Nitto's Captain chose suicide in lieu of being rescued by Nashville. Nashville picked up the other five who became prisoners of war (POWs), repatriated 3.4 years later.

Enterprise aircraft in all sank four, small surveillance vessels (Nagato Maru and Iwata Maru were two others), and damaged eight others. No Enterprise aircraft were shot down.

At this point, Hornet was 196 miles and ten hours from the planned launch point and time. Admiral Halsey issued an order: *Launch Planes. To Lieutenant Colonel Doolittle and Gallant Crew: Good Luck and God Bless You.* Doolittle and Hornet skipper Captain Marc Mitscher (1887 WI – 1947 VA, myocardial infarction) were in agreement with Halsey's order and immediately complied. Mitscher was a graduate of the U.S. Naval Academy, 1910. He was the Navy's 33rd aviator, earning his wings 6/2/1916.

As mentioned above, two B-25s in 2/1942 had taken off from the Hornet's deck in tests. The sixteen Raid pilots had never taken off from a carrier, in any type of aircraft. They were Army pilots, not Navy. They took off though this day though with ease, over 59 minutes – 8:20 to 9:19. The reasons included the following:

- Captain Mitscher steaming Hornet at 25 miles per hour into a strong wind certainly helped.
- Hornet's launching officer timed the start of each B-25's take-off roll so that it would reach the forward end of the flight deck just as Hornet pitched up in the heavy seas, giving a few extra yards from the ocean to accelerate and climb out.

At 467', Doolittle had the least runway, as the other 15 Mitchells were parked behind him. Twin engine, medium bombers with non-folding wings are too big to store below. As 53' long with a 67' wingspan, they were much larger than a typical World War II carrier-based fighter, or even a fighter/bomber. For example, the single engine, Grumman F8F Bearcat fighter was only 28' long with a 35' wingspan. Even the twin engine Lockheed P-38 Lightning fighter was only 38' long, with a 52' wingspan. Obviously, fighters and bombers have different purposes. Bombers to tote heavy bombs must have big wings.

Again, the fifteen aircraft behind him pushed Doolittle further than the deck than optimal. As it turned out, deck length was not an issue. Again, steaming at high speed into the wind and coming off the carrier when the bow was pitched up, gave more insurance than was needed.

This was the first time that Army Air Forces bombers launched from an aircraft carrier on a combat mission.

Immediately after launching the Mitchells, Mitscher reversed course and increased speed from 25 miles per hour to 29 miles per hour. Mitscher also brought up and launched fighters, for combat air patrol. The Task Force encountered no enemy, arriving at Oahu (Pearl Harbor) 4/25/1942.

Doolittle as first off was 702 miles from Tokyo. The last off of the 16 was 690 miles away from Tokyo.

As already noted, these were not catapult launches. The sixteen, very heavy (much fuel, one ton of bombs, ammunition, five airmen) B-25s took off on their own engines. For the record though, a B-25 was modified later during World War II for catapult launching and carrier landing tests. This of course required structural work. The tail hook was modified from the assembly of a single engine, Douglas SBD Dauntless scout and dive bomber aircraft. The first carrier landing was made 11/15/1944. The B-25 was inspected. It then taxied to the catapult position and was steam launched for the flight back to Norfolk (Virginia). Although successful, American occupations of Pacific Ocean islands this late closer to Japan in the Pacific War negated the necessity for carrier-based, twin engine, medium bombers.

Of note, all 80 Raider crewmen were volunteers. This should be clarified though, in that the men did not know what they were volunteering for. They were only told that airmen volunteers were needed, for a dangerous mission.

Each B-25 toted four, 500-pound bombs. Three were high explosive. The fourth was a bundle of incendiaries in an effort to start fires. The incendiaries were long tubes, designed to separate and scatter over a wide area after release.

The 16 B-25s after takeoff and climb out grouped two to four together, for a short distance. They then dived to wave-top level and flew separately to avoid detection. They navigated to Honshu Island by dead reckoning. Dead reckoning is the process of navigation by starting from a known fixed location, and then advancing position based upon known (preferred) or estimated speed and direction over a period of time.

Enemy fighters and ground anti-aircraft fire were encountered. Anti-aircraft fire hit one B-25, but it was able to continue. Another had to jettison its bombs over Tokyo Bay to gain speed, when attacked by fighters and a gun turret malfunctioned. However, no B-25s were lost to the enemy. Two of the B-25s in fact, shot down three Japanese fighters.

They arrived at noon, six hours after launch. This was a Saturday. They climbed to 1,500'. The fifteen B-25s bombed ten military and industrial sites in Tokyo, two in Yokohama, and one each in Yokosuka, Kanagawa, Kobe, Osaka, and Nagoya. These are all cities on Honshu Island, which is Japan's largest island. They also strafed some military targets. The targets included an army hospital, oil tank farm, a shipyard, a steel mill, other factories, and several power plants.

In Yokosuka, at least one bomb hit the almost converted from a submarine tender, 707' light aircraft carrier IJN Ryuho (1934 – 3/19/1945 damaged beyond repair by bombs and torpedoes from USS carrier launched aircraft near Kure), delaying her completion until 11/1942. Although all targets were military or industrial, Japanese dwellings and schools were so close that some were damaged as well.

The bombs destroyed and damaged 112 and 53 buildings. Per the Japanese report after the War, about 87, 151, and 311 Japanese were killed, seriously injured, and had minor injuries. Most of these were civilians, including some children.

In actuality, the bombing damages were minor, both in number of casualties and property destroyed. Also, the damages were reversed quickly, except in the case of the Ryuho aircraft carrier conversion which took another seven months to repair and complete.

The fact that rather large, twin engine, (made as) land-based bombers were used definitely confused Japan's high command about the source of the attack. When it was realized that the bombers had taken off from an aircraft carrier, the Imperial Japanese Navy took much berating, for allowing an American aircraft carrier force to approach the Japanese home islands. Even more berating followed, in that fighters had not diverted or taken out the B-25 bombers before arriving Honshu – after all, picket boats had sounded the alarm.

At first, the U.S. also did not disclose much about the Raid to the American people, concealing details for purposes of military secrecy. When the press asked President Roosevelt where the bombers launched from that dropped on Tokyo, his coy response was *Shangri-La*. Shangri-La was the Himalayan paradise in James Hilton's (1900 England – 1954 CA, liver cancer) 1933 *Lost Horizon* novel. Roosevelt soon after changed the name of the presidential retreat in Maryland from *Camp Hi-Catoctin* which opened in 1938 to *Shangri-La*. President Dwight Eisenhower (1890 TX – 1969 DC, congestive heart failure) when President changed the name to *Camp David*, naming it after his grandson. Camp David is the name used today.

Somebody (probably Roosevelt, again) liked the name *Shangri-La*. The Essex-class, 888' long USS Shangri-La (1944 – 1988 scrapped) aircraft was a departure from the usual practice at the time of naming aircraft carriers after battles, or using previous names for USSs.

Anyway, this attack was in a manner very similar to that of Japan's much larger naval fleet (this was 51 ships and boats, plus another five piggyback mini-submarines) getting close to Oahu undetected on 12/7/1941; and a similar Japanese sneak attack against Darwin, Australia 2/19/1942 (2.4 months later). The Darwin attack fleet was only 17 IJN warships. However, some of the attacking aircraft at Darwin were land-based. These two, Japanese surprise aerial assaults both involved two attack waves, one to two hours apart.

Although damage was not great as mentioned above, this mission four and a third months after Oahu (Pearl Harbor) and the other twelve sneak attacks that day had several, very positive outcomes for the U.S. and its Allies, as follows:

- The bombings gave a much-needed lift in spirits to Americans, still reeling from being slapped so hard and suddenly at five Pacific Ocean island military sites, having two Phoenix Islands bombed, having a USS and its crew captured in Shanghai Harbor (this little river gunboat was the only USS that Japan captured in World War II), and having an Army-chartered freighter sunk off California – all on the same day

Also in the four months since, Japan's military was like a steam roller, with many successes

The previous month had been more than depressing, as General Douglas MacArthur (1880 Little Rock – 1964 DC) had been forced to flee the Philippines 3/12/1942, and Bataan (Philippines) fell 4/9/1942 just nine days before the Raid with 10,000 killed, 20,000 wounded, and 75,000 taken as prisoners; the Japanese Philippines campaign casualty numbers were a fraction of these, and no prisoners were taken

The Raid showed that the U.S. could retaliate, even though was almost 4.5 months after the 12/7/1941 devastating, sneak attacks

- The bombings of course had a reverse effect on the Japanese, de-moralizing Japanese civilians and military alike; Japan's military leaders had repeatedly assured the citizenry that defenses were such that the homeland islands were safe from Allied attack, either by sea or air; as a result, the Japanese people now doubted their army generals and navy admirals (and even the Emperor), although they knew enough to not say as much

- The bombings forced the Japanese to use resources for home defense for the remainder of the war; these included from its army, navy, and air corps; most notably, Japan withdrew its powerful aircraft carrier force from the Indian Ocean to protect the home islands; these changes to increase homelands defense, probably ended up bringing the end of the war closer

- The bombings contributed to Isoroku Yamamoto's hasty decision to attack Midway Island in the Central Pacific; this 6/3-7/1942 battle did not go well for Japan; Japan lost four fleet aircraft carriers, a cruiser, and 248 aircraft; this was equipment it was never able to replace; the U.S. lost one aircraft carrier, a destroyer, and 150 aircraft; Japan and the U.S. lost 3,057 and 307 men; the men Japan lost included highly trained airmen, which Japan was not able to replace quickly

The Midway Battle was the beginning of the end of the Japanese Navy's control of the Pacific Ocean

Japan capitalized on the Doolittle attack. The government told the newspapers to write up as a cruel, indiscriminate attack against women and children. Of course with China as Exhibit A (and Japan had much abused other countries as more Exhibits), one has to ask how hypocritical can a country be. Parents of killed and injured children were asked to share their opinions on how the captured Raiders should be treated. These responses were also published.

After Japan attacked China in 1937, mock air raids were conducted in all Japanese cities. This was done despite the fact that the Chinese Air Force was almost nonexistent. The purpose was to keep warlike emotions at a peak in Japan. This training though (citizens knowing to take shelter and where) probably reduced the number of casualties, when the Raiders dropped their bombs.

After dropping their bombs, fifteen of the sixteen B-25s flew southwest off Japan's southeastern coast, then across the East China Sea, headed toward Zhejiang province in eastern China. This area was a base for the anti-communist Kuomintang. The Kuomintang were the allied U.S. and China forces, which had kept the Japanese Army out of this part of China. The main such base was at Zhuzhou, which the fifteen B-25s navigated toward.

Ten days before the Doolittle Raid (so 4/8/1942), Colonel William Old (1901 – 1965) and another pilot flew requisitioned Pan American Airways, twin engine, Douglas DC-3s from the Royal Air Force jungle airfield at Dinjan, Assam, India (far northeast India) over 14,000' Himalayan peaks to China. They were the first U.S. Army Air Forces pilots to do so. In fact, they were the first pilots period to do so. The cargo of the two DC-3s was 8,000 gallons of 100-octane gasoline in barrels and lubricants to replenish the sixteen Doolittle B-25 Mitchells after they landed in China, so they could fly out from there. As it turned out, the gasoline and lubricants were not used; at least not for these B-25s.

Old's treacherous flight over the *high hump* (later called F*lying the Hump*) showed that long-range resupply from northeast India over the Eastern Himalayan Uplift to China, was workable – inefficient and costly, but workable.

Zhuzhou and other air bases in the area supposedly had several airfields outfitted with electronic homing beacons, to guide the B-25s in. However, the navigation aids were not activated, perhaps because of a perceived threat to the carrier Task Force. The navigation aid anyway was a moot point, as the bombers did not have enough fuel to reach the designated airfields. Again, this was as they had launched almost 200 miles further out than planned, when the carrier Task Force scout plane was spotted by the Japanese picket vessels. They got lucky though, as a tailwind increased their ground speed by 29 miles per hour on the seven-hour flight to inland, recovery landing fields in China. Conversely, the favorable winds came with a storm. The storm and as night coming led to zero visibility conditions.

The wind boost helped, but not enough. The crews realized that they probably would not be able to reach the designated bases in China. This left the option of either bailing out along the Chinese coast, ditching near shore if visibility adequate, or crash landing on the China mainland. The fate of the 16 B-25s and their crews was as follows:

- 11   Crews bailed out over China (in one case, the pilot stayed aboard and crash landed, but survived)
- 1   Belly landed in a rice paddy
- 3   Ditched in the China Sea
- 1   As low on fuel, the pilot headed for much closer Russia, as his only other option was to ditch in the middle of the East China Sea; he
    landed at an air base at Vozdvizhenka, which was 40 miles past Vladivostok, Siberia; the Soviets kept the bomber

The carburetors on the two engines of the B-25s had been modified to use less fuel, when flying at low altitudes. However, Sacramento depot workers replaced the carburetors on this last B-25 without Doolittle's knowledge and also in violation of his orders. The change was noticed at sea before launch, but the expertise to modify the carburetors was not on-board Hornet. As a result, this B-25 was a gas burner compared to the others, so had to fly to Russia instead of China

To say the least, these were the longest flights ever made by B-25 Mitchells. The average distance flown was 2,588 miles, over 13 hours.

B-25 crews are usually six -- pilot, co-pilot, navigator/bombardier, turret gunner/engineer, radio operator/waist gunner, and a tail gunner. Doolittle's planes had five each though – this saved weight. The sixth crewman would have been a gunner, but the tail gun was removed to save weight.

Of the 80 crewmen, 69 survived their historic mission and eventually made it back to American lines, most with the help of Chinese civilians and guerillas, and also Western missionaries. Of the other eleven, their fate was as follows:

- 3   died (killed in action)
  - 1 when he bailed out over China
  - 2 when they ditched off the coast of China (either from the impact of the crash or drowned)
- 8   became POWs; as common with the Japanese, they were tortured, beaten, starved, received no medical treatment for injuries or diseases, etc.
  - 3 Japanese officers convicted in an 8/28/1942 mock show trial of killing civilians, and firing squad executed 10/14/1942 at Shanghai; the Japanese instructed the three to write letters to their loved ones, which they did; however, the Japanese never mailed them; the letters were found though after the War and forwarded
  - 1 died of torture, starvation, and mistreatment 12/1/1943 while captive
  - 4 repatriated 8/1945 at the end of the War; one was bombardier Jacob DeShazer (1912 OR – 2008 OR) who became a Christian when imprisoned; after repatriation, he attended missionary school and worked as a missionary in Japan 1948-1978

In addition to being tortured, the eight American Doolittle Raider POWs contracted dysentery and beriberi from their deplorable confinement conditions, which was not treated. At the end of the war, four Japanese officers were tried for mistreatment and war crimes against the eight POWs. The four were all found guilty. One was sentenced to nine years. The other three were sentenced to three to five years of hard labor.

For the record, the below statement is from Japanese Army Regulations in place at the time of World War II:

> *Prisoners of war shall be treated with a spirit of good will, and shall never be subjected to cruelties or humiliation.*

Doolittle himself and his four crew bailed out safely over China, when their bomber ran out of fuel. Age 45 Doolittle was on the old side to parachute. He had a bad ankle, from a previous injury. However, he landed in a heap of soft dung, which worked in his favor. The five linked up after the bailout. Chinese guerrillas, Chinese civilians, and Western missionaries guided them through Japanese lines. American Baptist missionary John Birch (1918 India of American missionary parents – 8/25/1945 shot in China in a confrontation with Communist Party supporters) also aided the airmen. When Doolittle arrived in Chungking (capital of Free China, now called Chongqing), he told Flying Tigers leader Colonel Claire Chennault (1893 TX – 1958 New Orleans) about Birch's help. Chennault, knowing the immense value of a Chinese-speaking American who knew the country well, commissioned Birch as a Second Lieutenant 7/4/1942.

Chennault asked Birch to serve as a field intelligence officer, although Birch had expected to work as a chaplain. Birch served with the China Air Task Force which became the 14th U.S. Air Force 3/5/1943. He was later seconded to the U.S. Office of Strategic Services (OSS), working as an effective spy. The OSS was the predecessor agency to today's Central Intelligence Agency.

Birch was promoted to Captain. He led a party of eleven Americans, Chinese Nationalists, and Koreans on a mission to gather intelligence in Xuzhou. This was 8/25/1945, eleven days after Japan surrendered. A People's Liberation Army unit (these were Communists) stopped Birch's group. They demanded that Birch hand over his revolver. Birch refused. Words and insults were exchanged. Birch was shot dead, age 27. One of his party was shot and wounded but survived. Birch's party was taken prisoner but released two months later.

As noted above, one B-25 landed in Russia as running out of fuel. The Russians interned the five but treated them well. The U.S. made diplomatic efforts for their return which were not successful. Russia moved the five to Ashgabat which was 20 miles from the border with Iran. The pilot somehow bribed a smuggler who aided the five to escape into Iran. They reached the British consulate and freedom, 5/11/1943. This was more than a year after the Raid.

From declassified NKVD (Russia's secret police organization 1934-1946) documents after the War, it was determined that the Russians had facilitated their repatriation, while managing to portray it as an escape. The Soviet Union was allied with the U.S. Despite that, the Soviet Union wanted to conceal from Japan that it aided the U.S. in any way. Joe Stalin was a taker, not a giver. Whatever.

The Chinese paid dearly for the fact that a few Chinese citizens sheltered and helped the downed Americans. Japan's leaders were enraged and instructed its army to extract vengeance. A massive search for the American airmen was conducted. In the case of towns that the Japanese suspected of harboring the Americans, the Japanese looted and then burned these villages down.

Irrigation systems, bridges, roads, and airfields were destroyed. Crops were burned.

Females ages 10-65 were raped, repeatedly. Venereal diseases resulted. Babies resulted nine months later.

Twenty thousand square miles were left a blackened pyre. For months, the countryside reeked of rotting carcasses, human and animal. These contaminated the water supply as well.

Japan followed these atrocities with germ warfare against the Chinese. Cholera, malaria, dysentery, typhoid, plague, anthrax, and syphilis pathogens were released. The pathogens were spread in the air, water, food, and by releasing infected fleas as transmitters. As already noted, diseases were also spread by forced sex.

Some of the reports of the atrocities came from Western missionaries in the area. One of these was Bishop Patrick Cleary (1886 Ireland – 1970 Ireland), who headed a Roman Catholic Diocese based in Nancheng. Nancheng, a city of 50,000, was the capital of the Jiangxi Province in southeastern China. Bishop Cleary was known for aiding anyone who needed assistance during World War II. These included Japanese as well as Chinese. Bishop Cleary aided some of the Doolittle Raiders. When the Japanese learned of this, they looted and demolished Nancheng and severely beat Father Cleary.

The nature and quantity of the executions, mutilations, rapes, etc. is so horrible, that it cannot be printed. If printed and read, it is beyond human comprehension (vomiting occurs).

These mammoth Japanese atrocities are called the *Zhejiang-Jiangxi Campaign* (per Japan's Army, this was Operation Sei-go), from the names of the two Chinese provinces where the Americans bailed out. The Chinese estimate is that 250,000 civilians were killed over four months. Japan quotes a much smaller number.

Japan publicized these atrocities against civilians as a military operation. The pronouncements fooled nobody.

Besides revenge, Japan assumed that these atrocities would prevent the Chinese from ever again aiding the U.S. or another Allied country, in any manner. To be sure though, the Japanese also moved some troops in to occupy these provinces; to prevent the U.S. Army from establishing and using air bases in China within flying distance of Japan. For Japan, troops were scarce. So posting more soldiers in China reduced its fighting capability elsewhere.

The crews were honored as follows:

- Lieutenant Colonel Doolittle feared that he would be court-martialed for losing 16 new B-25s and some airmen, and also due to the atrocities that Japan rendered relating to assistance received from Chinese civilians and guerillas, and from Western missionaries. In fact though, one of the sixteen was intact and turned over to Russia, an ally. Instead, he was promoted two ranks (skipped Colonel) to Brigadier General (one star). He was awarded the Medal of Honor, and later the Presidential Medal of Freedom. He is the only person to receive both. The first award is the military's highest valor medal. The second is the nation's highest civilian honor, presented to individuals who have made especially meritorious contributions to the security or national interests of the U.S. and /or world peace.

- A gunner/flight engineer and a surgeon/flight engineer were each awarded the Silver Star, for their efforts in helping wounded crewmembers evade Japanese troops in China.
- All 80 Raiders received the Distinguished Flying Cross.
- The Raiders who died or were injured received the Purple Heart, of course.
- The Chinese government gave a decoration to all 80 Raiders.

Many of the surviving crewmen continued to fly as follows:

- 28   Remained in the China-Burma-India Theater flying missions, most for more than a year; five were killed in action
- 19   Flew North Africa combat missions; four of these 19 were killed in action and another four became POWs
- 9   Flew in the European theater, with one killed in action

Altogether, twelve of the survivors died in air crashes within fifteen months of the Doolittle Raid. Two more Raid survivors were mustered out of the military in 1944, due to the severity of their injuries from bailing out or crash landing after the Raid.

Doolittle served the rest of World War II, commanding Allied bomber units of B-17s and B-24s based in England, Italy, and North Africa. These included the 8th Air Force, the 12th Air Force, and the 15th Air Force. He was promoted to Major General (two star) 11/1942.

On 6/10/1944, Doolittle flew as co-pilot on a twin engine, Martin B-26 Marauder medium bomber with pilot Jack Sims (1919 MI – 2007 FL). Sims had been one of the B-25 co-pilots on the 4/1942 Raid. Doolittle continued to fly.

Doolittle's major influence on European Theater bombing occurred early in 1945, when he changed the policy requiring fighters to escort bombers at all times. The twin engine, Lockheed P-38 Lightning and single engine, Republic P-47 Thunderbolt fighters flew far ahead of the bombers' box formations, on bomber defense missions. In this role, they cleared the skies of any Luftwaffe fighters. This strategy crippled the twin engine Zerstorergeschwader heavy fighter wings; and crippled again their replacement of single engine Sturmgruppen of also heavily armed Fw 190As. As part of this game-changing strategy especially after the bombers had hit their targets, the fighters were then free to strafe German airfields when returning to base. This was effective, reducing the threat of confrontations even more by disabling tied down fighters.

These changes contributed significantly to the achievement of air superiority by Allied air forces over Europe. Another game changer was the fact that the Lightning and Thunderbolt fighters were also steadily being replaced with the single engine North American P-51 Mustang. Mustangs had been put into European service the winter of 1943-1944. The Mustangs had a greater range than other Allied fighters.

When the War ended in Europe 5/1945, Doolittle commanded the 8th Air Force. The 8th was transferred to the Pacific, but trading out B-17s and B-24s for B-29s (all four engine bombers). However, the Pacific War ended 8/1945, before the 8th was ready to fly and fight.

Ted Lawson (1917 CA – 1992) was one of the 16 B-25 Raider pilots. He ditched off Nantien Island. All five crew survived. However, four of the five had severe injuries. Lawson had a severe gash on his leg. Friendly Chinese transported Lawson a great distance. His leg became infected.

Lieutenant Thomas White (1909 Maui - 1992) was the mission's flight surgeon. Dr. White had managed to get himself included on the Raid as a gunner. His B-25 ditched in the sea. The crew swam safely to shore. Upon arrival, they noted that Dr. White was absent. He had stayed behind to dive to the sunken bomber and retrieve his medicine box and surgical instruments box. He only found his instruments box. Later, he heard from the Chinese about Lawson's injury. The Chinese directed him to where Lawson was laid up. Dr. White amputated in the field. How he accomplished this single-handedly and without a fatal infection setting in – he was skilled, and Lawson lucky. Dr. White later stated that if he had found his medicines, he maybe could have saved Lawson's leg. Lawson lived almost 50 years longer, to the age of 75. He had no complaints.

Lawson and newspaper columnist Bob Considine (1906 – 1975) wrote a 1943 book about the mission, titled *Thirty Seconds over Tokyo*. The 1944 same name movie starred Van Johnson as Lawson, Spencer Tracy as Doolittle, and Robert Mitchum as one of the pilots. In both the book and movie, Lawson with his one leg gives an eyewitness account of the training, the mission, and the aftermath.

The book and the film are noted for their historical accuracy. The film used actual wartime footage of the bombers in some flying scenes. An aircraft carrier was not available due to wartime needs. Hornet for one was not available, as it had been sunk six months after the Raid in the 10/1942 Santa Cruz Islands Battle.

For the movie, filming was done on made sets, plus again original newsreel footage was used. Movie production costs were $2,924,000. The box office was $6,247,000.

In the year after the War (1946), Doolittle headed a commission which addressed the relationship between officers and enlisted men in the Army. Many of Doolittle's recommendations were implemented. He transferred to the Army reserves in 1947. He served 1917-1959. In 1985, 26 years after his retirement and eight years before his death, Congress promoted him to General (four star).

Doolittle probably got ribbing all his life with people poking fun at his surname when he did not get something done, or somebody's serious or joking perception of such. In this case, he got the impossible done – using bombers that had barely seen combat (and not by these airmen), taking off from a carrier deck one-third as long as the recommended minimum takeoff distance, all sixteen pilots making their first carrier takeoffs, attacking a heavily defended Japan who knew they were coming, crash-landing or bailing out at night in a country (China) partially occupied by Japanese troops, etc.

One has to wonder and be in awe of a man like Doolittle – imagine an aviator with a wife and two sons and a Ph.D. in aeronautical science (again, the first such degree in the U.S.), volunteering to lead such a dangerous raid at the age of 45.

His superiors appointed him as project manager. There was no expectation that he do more than plan and coordinate the Raid. Instead, he chose to lead it. Doolittle loved to fly. He was an expert aviator. There is no doubt about that – but still.

The Raiders got together 12/1946 on the occasion of Doolittle's 50th birth anniversary, to commemorate those Raiders now dead. They decided to meet every year for a toast, and did in fact do so (a few years were skipped). The high point of each reunion was a solemn, private ceremony in which the surviving Raiders conducted a roll call, then toasted (cognac) their fellow Raiders who died during the previous year. Eighty engraved silver goblets, one for each of the 80 Raiders, were used. The goblets are engraved with the airmen's names, both right side up and upside down. When a Raider died, his goblet was inverted.

In 12/1956 on his 60th birth anniversary, Hennessy presented Doolittle with a vintage 1896 (his birth year) bottle of cognac. Cognac distiller Hennessy was founded in 1765 in Cognac, France, and still operates from there. Doolittle decreed that the bottle not be opened until there were only two Raiders left, and that the pair should then open and share it with a toast. In 2012, the four surviving Raiders decided that the bottle would be opened and shared by all living Raiders at the 2013 annual meeting – this because 90-year-old men could all die before the next occasion, or not be capable of opening a bottle and toasting.

At the 2013 meeting, three of the four survivors were able to attend, and shared the cognac. This meeting was at the National U.S. Air Force Museum at Wright-Patterson Air Force Base near Dayton, Ohio. The four men decided that this meeting would be their last, due to their ages. These four were as follows:

- Age 98: Lieutenant Colonel Dick Cole, number 1 co-pilot (Doolittle was the pilot) (born 9/7/1915)
- Age 93: Lieutenant Colonel Robert Hite, number 16 co-pilot
- Age 93 Lieutenant Colonel Edward Saylor, number 15 engineer/gunner
- Age 92 Staff Sergeant David Thatcher, number 7 engineer/gunner

Hite was not able to attend due to age and health issues, but he viewed and participated (he appeared on screen at the ceremony) via a live Internet broadcast. This was the first time that the meeting had been broadcast. The 2013 meeting included a wreath-laying ceremony, a B-25 Mitchell flyover, and the final toast ceremony to their fallen comrades.

Saylor, Hite, and Thatcher died 1/2015, 3/2015, and 6/2016 at the ages of 95, 95, and 94. Hite is the blindfolded POW shown on the first page. He was a POW for 40 months.

As of 2019, only Cole remains – age 103. He is also the only Raider to live longer than Doolittle, who died at 96.8 years. Cole was Doolittle's co-pilot, on the Raid.

The Raid was 4/18/1942, again on a Saturday. On 4/18/1992 which was also a Saturday to commemorate the 50th anniversary of the Raid, two B-25s launched from the 1,046' long, USS Ranger (1957 – 2017 scrapped) fleet aircraft carrier. The pair maneuvered into a missing man formation with five other Mitchells, for that ceremony. Note that Ranger was 174' longer than the 1942 Hornet.

The 2001 *Pearl Harbor* movie depicts the Doolittle Raid at the end. It is historically inaccurate as portrayed. No matter. It was a dramatic and uplifting ending. The movie made $449 million, versus its $140 million production cost. Alec Baldwin played Doolittle.

In 2014, Congress awarded the Congressional Gold Medal to the Raiders, *for outstanding heroism, valor, skill, and service to the U.S. in conducting the bombings of Tokyo.* Lieutenant Colonel Richard Cole accepted the medal on behalf of the Raiders. The medal is on display at the National USAF Museum, mentioned above.

As noted above, Hornet was sunk 10/26/1942 (six months later) at the Santa Cruz Islands battle; with the loss of 140 sailors of a crew of about 2,900 (4.8%). Japanese dive and torpedo bombers in coordination connected. These bomb hits were followed by two, single engine, two crew Aichi D3A Type 99 carrier bombers crashing into Hornet, apparently deliberately. These two bombers had been damaged by anti-aircraft fire from Hornet. With her engines knocked out, Hornet was unable to launch or land aircraft; forcing its aviators to either land on Enterprise or ditch in the ocean. This was another battle in which the surface warships had no visual contact with the enemy.

In the Santa Cruz fight though, Hornet's planes had success, as follows:

- Severely damaged the Shokaku-class, 844' long, IJN Shokaku (1941 – 6/19/1944 USS submarine torpedo sank, Philippine Sea Battle, 1,272 of 1,842 crew lost {69%}) aircraft carrier
- Severely damaged the Tone-class, 620' long and 64' beam and 20' draft, IJN Chikuma (1939 – 10/25/1944 U.S. torpedo bombers sunk, at the Samar Battle which in turn was part of the Leyte Gulf Battle; Japanese destroyer picked up some survivors of 874 crew; USSs gun-sank this rescue destroyer, with only one Chikuma sailor surviving overall) heavy cruiser
- Some damage to two more cruisers

Rear Admiral George Murray (1889 Boston – 1956 San Francisco) ordered the Northampton-class, 600' long and 66' beam and 20' draft, USS Northampton (1929 – 11/30/1942 IJN destroyer torpedo-sank at Tassafaronga Battle) heavy cruiser to tow Hornet clear of the action. However, nine more torpedo planes attacked. One connected. As Japanese surface warships were approaching, Vice Admiral Halsey ordered Hornet sunk. Hornet Captain Charles Mason (1891 PA – 1971 FL) was the last off. USS destroyers picked up all the survivors.

The two, Sims-class, 348' long and 36' beam and 13' draft, USS Mustin (1939 – 1948 target sunk off Kwajalein) and USS Anderson (1939 – 1946 target sunk off Bikini Atoll) destroyers hit Hornet with nine torpedoes, (some did not explode though) and more than 400 five-inch rounds from their deck guns. As this was less than a year into World War II, the destroyers' torpedomen and gunners needed practice, and they got it.

U.S. submarine and destroyer torpedoes which did not explode was a major problem. For the first eighteen months of World War II, the Mark 14 torpedo failure rate was about 75%. The torpedoes ran too deep, exploded prematurely, failed to explode, ran circular, etc. In running circular, at least two World War II submarines (both had been commissioned only the year before) were sunk by their own torpedoes as follows:

1) Gato-class, 313' long and 27' beam USS Tullibee (1943 – 3/26/1944 sunk north of Palau); all 60 crew died except for one, which is 98%; this lone survivor was a Gunner's Mate who was on the bridge at the time of the strike; he was knocked unconscious and thrown into the ocean; his life jacket saved him; he came to; the next day a Japanese destroyer picked him up; he was a POW until repatriated after V-J Day

2) Balao-class, 313' long and 27' beam USS Tang (1943 – 10/24/1944 sunk off China in Taiwan Strait); 78 of 87 (90%) crew lost; some of the survivors used a Momsen lung (primitive underwater rebreathing device) to reach the surface; the nine were picked up by a Japanese frigate, and became POWs; they were repatriated after V-J Day; despite her short career, Tang set the record for a World War II USS submarine in both number of ships sunk (thirty-three) and tonnage (116,454 tons); she accomplished this over a period of only eight months and one week

Submarine skippers reported this high torpedo failure rate. At first, they were told that their crews had not prepared the torpedoes correctly or aimed incorrectly. But after tests, defects were found. Finding these defects led to finding other defects. Finally, the torpedoes were fixed, but this was not until the fall of 1943. Theodore Roscoe (1909 NY – 1992 FL, blood clot in lungs) who wrote the Navy's official history of World War II submarine operations (the 1949 *United States Submarine Operations in World War II*) stated that *the only reliable feature of the torpedo was its unreliability.*

As another quote, military historian Clay Blair (1925 VA – 1998 WI) stated that the scandal was *the worst in the history of any kind of warfare.* Blair wrote extensively on the use of submarines in World War II. He wrote the bestselling, 1975 *Silent Victory: The U.S. Submarine War Against Japan.* Blair served on a Gato-class submarine in World War II.

The Pacific War was no doubt lengthened, as so many U.S. torpedoes were duds for the first 1.75 years of the War. Conversely, Japanese Navy torpedoes were better than U.S. Navy torpedoes, in just about all ways. This was the case, even at the end of World War II.

USS destroyers steamed away from Hornet when a Japanese surface force hove into view. Upon finding the carrier that had launched the Doolittle Raid six months earlier, the Japanese considered capturing her as a war trophy, but quickly decided she was too damaged to mess with. The two, Kagero-class, 389' long and 35' beam and 13' draft, IJN Akigumo (1941 – 4/1/1944 USS submarine torpedo sank, all 240 hands lost) and IJN Makiguma (1942 – 2/1/1943 hit a mine, scuttled, all crew saved) destroyers buried two torpedoes each into the Hornet, sinking her. As already noted, Hornet lost 140 men from the earlier bombs dropped by Japanese aircraft.

Hornet was the last American fleet carrier sunk by enemy fire in World War II (and since). Several smaller carriers were sunk after Hornet though, in World War II.

Attu is the westernmost of the U.S. Aleutian Islands. Japan occupied Attu 5/1942. The U.S. re-captured 7/1943. The Army Air Forces built a larger airfield on Attu. From the new airfield, an air attack was launched 7/10/1943 on the Japanese-held Kuril Islands, now part of Russia. This was the first air attack on Japanese soil since the 4/1942 Doolittle Raid – almost 15 months later.

The first attack after the Doolittle Raid though on Japanese home islands was not until 6/1944, 26 months after the Doolittle Raid. In this case, 68 B-29s took off from Chengtu (Southwest China) to bomb the Imperial Iron and Steel Works at Yawata on the north end of Kyushu Island, more than 1,500 miles distant. Like the Doolittle attack, it achieved little physical destruction. Only 47 of the 68 B-29s (69%) hit the target area – four aborted with mechanical problems, four crashed, six jettisoned their bombs because of mechanical difficulties, and others bombed secondary targets or other targets of opportunity. Only one B-29 was shot down though.

This was the first bombing raid of the unsuccessful *Operation Matterhorn.* Matterhorn was the B-29 strategic bombing campaign of Japanese forces in China and India, and also some targets in Japan.

This mission marked the beginning of the strategic bombardment campaign against Japan. These raids continued from Southwest China. However, the logistics of getting fuel, equipment, bombs, etc. from India over the Himalayas to the B-29s in China were overwhelming. It took six B-29s flying cargo over the Hump, for every B-29 that attempted a bombing run to Japan. Overall, nine raids from Southwest China were made as part of Operation Matterhorn. Matterhorn was not successful, as only Kyushu Island could be reached. Kyushu is the most southwesterly of Japan's four main islands, and the third largest. Only one small aircraft factory was destroyed.

The solution was much shorter flying distance. This finally came in late 1944 when the Allies captured the Mariana Islands between June and August, 1944, and set up six air bases there – mainly on Saipan and Tinian. Besides the much shorter distance, the air bases could be supplied by armed and usually escorted cargo ships, in lieu of having to fly in fuel, bombs, parts, etc. over the Himalayas.

As mentioned already, President Roosevelt awarded the Medal of Honor to Doolittle for conducting and leading the Raid. The citation reads as follows:

For conspicuous leadership above and beyond the call of duty, involving personal valor and intrepidity at an extreme hazard to life. With the apparent certainty of being forced to land in enemy territory or to perish at sea, Lt. Col. Doolittle personally led a squadron of Army bombers, manned by volunteer crews, in a highly destructive raid on the Japanese mainland.

His other commendations from his Army career include two Army Distinguished Service medal citations, three Distinguished Flying Cross citations, a Silver Star, and many others. He also received numerous awards from other countries.

The most extensive display of Doolittle Raid memorabilia is at the USAF National Museum, Wright-Patterson Air Force Base, Dayton, Ohio. The display includes a re-built B-25 Mitchell tied down on a reproduction of Hornet's flight deck. Doolittle and Mitscher mannequins in authentic dress are on the deck. Other mannequins are handling bombs and ammunition. The silver goblets used by the Raiders at the annual reunions are displayed. Medals are displayed.

As soon as the 1920s, pilots' ability to control powerful aircraft exceeded their capability, in sensing the amount and direction of motion. This was especially the case when there were no visual cues outside the cockpit -- such as when flying in clouds, rain, or at night. Flying of course is movement in three dimensions so operation much more difficult, as compared to operating a vehicle on the ground or ship on the ocean (two dimensions). To sum up, the physiological abilities (sometimes called seat of the pants flying) of human beings (pilots) was not up to the task.

Doolittle was among the first to recognize these limitations of the human senses. He knew that true operational freedom in the air could not be achieved unless pilots had the ability to control and navigate aircraft in flight from takeoff run to landing rollout, regardless of the range of vision from the cockpit. He grasped that pilots must be trained to use instruments to fly blind – smoke, clouds, precipitation of all forms, at night, etc.; in lieu of the pilot's own possibly confused motion sense inputs. Doolittle started studies of the connections between visual cues and motion senses (forces and accelerations). The research resulted in the development of instruments and methods that trained pilots to read, understand, and use navigational instruments.

Doolittle's research and development into flying solely on instruments took money. That came from the Daniel Guggenheim Foundation for the Promotion of Aeronautics. The Foundation paid for the aircraft used, and also the development of new instrumentation.

Meyer Guggenheim (1828 Switzerland – 1905 FL) moved to the U.S from Switzerland in 1847. He and his heirs made a fortune in mining and mineral investments and smelting (application of heat to ore to extract a base metal). Meyer's son Daniel Guggenheim (1856 Philadelphia – 1930) was the most involved in the family business. Daniel and his son Henry Guggenheim (1890 NJ – 1971 NYC) had an interest in aviation – the father because he saw its business potential; and the son who was a pilot, as he enjoyed flying. Both father and son also felt that aviation could help bring the world's peoples together.

Yale College of New Haven, Connecticut, founded the Sheffield Scientific School (1847 – 1956 folded into Yale University) for instruction in science and engineering in 1847. The Sheffield helped establish the model for the transition of U.S. higher education from a classical model, to one which incorporated both the sciences and the liberal arts. Henry Guggenheim (Daniel's son) attended Sheffield.

Yale Sheffield sophomore Frederick Davison (1896 - 1974) recruited eleven other Yale students and alumni to form the First Yale Unit in 1916, as an aviation group. He and the others felt that the U.S. would soon be dragged into World War I. They were concerned that the U.S. military was unprepared for war, especially in the field of military aviation. They acquired a Curtiss Model F flying boat and took flying lessons. When the group grew to 29 pilots and student pilots, they enlisted in the Navy. This was 3/1917. This First Yale Unit of civilian airmen volunteers is considered the first U. S. Navy air reserve unit.

When taking his test flight to be enlisted in the Navy 7/28/1917, Davison suffered a panic attack and crashed into the ocean. His injured his back. He was hospitalized for six weeks. He never saw combat, but was involved in managing the Yale unit. After the War, Davison was Assistant Secretary of War, Personnel Director for the Central Intelligence Agency, and President of the American Museum of Natural History.

Henry Guggenheim (again, grandson and son of Meyer and Daniel) was aware of this program, from attending Yale. He joined this group 9/1917, at age 17. Again, it was now part of the U.S. Navy Reserves. Guggenheim served overseas (as a pilot) in France, England, and Italy during World War I. His rank was Lieutenant Commander at the end of World War I. The Navy called him up for active duty for World War II, and he reached Captain rank.

The research effort involved the Army Air Corps, the Navy, General Electric, MIT, AT&T, Sperry Corporation (gyroscopes), and the Bureau of Standards. The outcome was the development of an accurate altimeter, attitude indicator (artificial horizon), and directional gyrocompass.

Army Air Corps Chief Major General James Fechet (1877 TX – 1948 D.C.) authorized the use of Long Island's Mitchel Field, and detailed two pilots for the tests. One of these was Doolittle, as noted above. Doolittle was just 31. He was an expert pilot, plus also had earned a Ph.D. from MIT in aeronautical engineering.

Benjamin Kelsey (1906 CT – 1981 VA) was the other pilot. He had a bachelor's degree in aeronautical engineering, also from MIT. After graduating, Kelsey stayed at MIT a while to teach and conduct research in the aeronautics department. He was nine years younger than Doolittle.

The program's nickname was the *Guggenheim Fog Flying Laboratory*. It all came together 9/24/1929, more than 12 years from the start of World War II for the United States. Doolittle was in the back seat, his cockpit covered and sealed with a canvas hood so he could not see. Safety pilot Kelsey was in the front seat, holding his hands up in the air. For the 15-minute blind flight, Doolittle became the first pilot to take off, fly, and land an airplane using instruments alone without a view outside the cockpit. His instruments were a stopwatch, compass, a rudimentary radio beam receiver, and the newly developed cockpit instruments. The aircraft was a single engine, conventional landing gear (non-retractable), open tandem cockpit, Consolidated NY-2 Husky biplane trainer.

The description below is excerpts (with some minor editing) from the 4/30/1930 issue of *Astounding Stories of Super-Science:*

> On 9/24/1929, U.S. Army Air Corps Lieutenant James Doolittle made the *first completely blind airplane takeoff, flight, and landing, solely by reference to instruments on board his aircraft. Flying from the rear cockpit of a civil-registered two-place Consolidated NY-2 Husky training biplane, NX7918, Doolittle had his visual reference to earth and sky completely cut off by a hood enclosure over his cockpit. Safety pilot Lieutenant Benjamin Kelsey rode in the forward cockpit, but the entire*

flight was conducted by Doolittle. He took off from Mitchel Field, climbed out, flew a 15-mile set course and returned to Mitchel Field and landed.

The experimental gyroscopic compass, artificial horizon and a precision altimeter were developed by Elmer Sperry and Paul Kollsman. Funding for the Full Flight Laboratory at Mitchel Field was provided by the Daniel Guggenheim Fund for the Promotion of Aeronautics. The blind flight led Daniel Guggenheim Fund President Harry Guggenheim, to announce that the problem of fog-flying, one of aviation's greatest bugbears, had been solved at last.

Blind flying has been done in the past, but never in the past has a pilot taken off, circled, crossed, re-crossed the field, and then landed only a short distance away from his starting point, while flying under conditions resembling the densest fog. It was something uncanny to contemplate.

The dense fog was produced artificially by the simple device of making the cabin of the plane entirely light-proof. Lieutenant Benjamin Kelsey was the safety pilot in the forward seat. Doolittle relied on three new flying instruments, developed during the past year in experiments conducted over the full-flight laboratory established by the Fund.

The chief factors contributing to the solution of the problem of blind flying consist of a new application of the visual radio beacon, the development of an improved instrument for indicating the longitudinal and lateral position of an airplane, a new directional gyroscope, and a sensitive barometric altimeter. The latter is so delicate, as to measure the altitude of an airplane within a few feet of the ground.

Thus, instead of relying on the natural horizon for stability, Lieutenant Doolittle used an artificial horizon on the small instrument which indicates longitudinal and lateral position, in relation to the ground at all time. He was able to locate the landing field by means of the direction-finding, long-distance radio beacon. In addition, another smaller radio beacon was used, which casts a beam 15-20 miles in either direction. This beam governs the immediate approach to the field.

To locate the landing field the pilot watches two vibrating reeds, tuned to the radio beacon, on a virtual radio receiver on his instrument board. If he turns to the right or left of his course the right or left reed, respectively, begins doing a sort of St. Vitus dance. If the reeds are in equilibrium the pilot knows it is clear sailing straight to his field.

The sensitive altimeter showed Lieutenant Doolittle his altitude and made it possible for him to calculate his landing to a distance of within a few feet from the ground.

Although Doolittle of course is most remembered for leading the 4/18/1942 bombing rain on Honshu, he is most recognized in the aeronautical technology field for these advances in the development of instrument flying.

Doolittle retired from the Air Force in 1959 as a Lieutenant General (three star). He served 42 years (1917-1959) active and reserves. As mentioned above, he was promoted to General (four star) on the retired list, in 1985.

Doolittle married Josephine Daniels (1895 IL – 1988 CA) 12/24/1917. She died in 1988. Doolittle outlived her five years. At a dinner celebration after Doolittle's 1929 all-instrument flight, Josephine asked her guests to sign her white damask tablecloth. Later, she embroidered the names in black. She continued this tradition, collecting hundreds of signatures from the aviation world. She donated the tablecloth to the Smithsonian Institution.

The Doolittles had two sons, James II (1920 San Antonio – 1958 Austin, suicide) and John (1922 – 2015 CA). Both became military officers and pilots. James II joined the Army Air Forces in 1941. He flew the midwing, tricycle landing gear, twin engine (18-cylinder radial engine, 2,805 cubic inches each, 2,100 horsepower each), three crew, Douglas A-26 Invader ground attack and light bomber aircraft in World War II, 50 missions. The A-26 first saw action 6/1944 in the Pacific Theater during World War II, bombing Japanese-held islands near Manokwari, New Guinea. It was also used in the European Theater, starting 9/1944.

James II transferred to the Air Force in 1947, when it was established as a separate branch of American armed forces. He later flew the twin-jet engine, two crew, midwing, retractable tricycle landing gear, supersonic McDonnell F-101 Voodoo fighter. Major Doolittle was Commander of the 524th Fighter-Bomber Squadron based at Bergstrom Air Force Base in Austin, Texas, at the time of his suicide death at age 38. He left a wife and two teenage sons.

John Doolittle retired from the Air Force as a Colonel.

Doolittle's grandson James Doolittle III was the vice commander of the Air Force Flight Test Center at Edwards Air Force Base, California.

8- MITSUBISHI AKUTAN A6M ZERO

In the few years before what came to be called World War II and even into World War II, the Allies knew little about Japanese military air power for several reasons:

- In the case of the U.S., the citizenry generally had an isolationist and/or appeasement attitude; this sentiment came about mainly as 116,516 Americans in uniform died in World War I (50% to influenza, 46% in combat, 4% to other diseases and in captivity and in accidents) and another 204,000 wounded or made ill (many with permanent disabilities), which ended only a generation ago (turned out to be 23.07 years, from the World War I Armistice Day to the 12/7/1941 sneak attacks)

In fact, Congress passed and President Franklin Roosevelt (1882 NY – 4/12/1945 GA, cerebral hemorrhage) reluctantly signed into law four so-called Neutrality Acts 1935-1939, to ensure that the U.S. would not get involved in foreign conflicts; these were in response to the growing turmoil in Europe and Asia that eventually led to World War II; the laws banned selling or loaning or transporting war materials to belligerent nations, and banned Americans from traveling in war zones; the latter was to avoid situations where American civilians were captured or injured or killed by or in a belligerent country, which would require the U.S. to take some type of action (rescue, demand for recompense, exchange of prisoners, etc.)

The 1936 Neutrality laws were more or less replaced with the 10/1939 Cash and Carry program; this allowed the sale of non-war materials to countries, as long as they paid up front in cash, and used their own ships to transport the goods; Congress again was not in favor of this program, but Nazi Germany attacking and invading Poland 9/1/1939 the month before gave the impetus for it to be passed; this program much supported Great Britain and France to a lesser extent; Roosevelt promoted the program from the standpoint that bolstering Great Britain and France would help the two countries tamp down the Fascists (Italy) and Nazis (Germany), so that the U.S. would not have to come to their rescue

Cash and Carry in turn paved the way for the Lend-Lease program, enacted 3/1941; the U.S. supplied the U.K., Free France, Republic of China, and later the Soviet Union and other countries with food, oil, and materiel through the end of the War; the supplies and equipment included war goods such as ships, planes, munitions, etc.; all was free; in return, the U.S. got leases on army and naval bases controlled by these countries in Allied territory during the war; but note that the U.S. did not enter the War until 12/1941

The Cash and Carry policy to some degree and then the Lend-Lease law to a major degree effectively ended America's pretense to neutrality

Historians are sure that Roosevelt and other leaders of both political parties were not in favor of the Neutrality Laws; Roosevelt went along to get re-elected in 1936, and even had to take this stance somewhat to win the 1940 election, which was 14 months after Germany invaded Poland, and seven months after Germany invaded Denmark and Norway and France and Belgium and Luxembourg; Roosevelt knew that it was very likely that the U.S. would have to enter World War II (militarily) soon to bail out European countries

For the record, Roosevelt got 60.8 and 54.7% of the 1936 and 1940 popular vote

Roosevelt though was successful in putting into motion a more than massive build-up in military equipment before the country's entry into World War II; for example, note the following:

- o 544 major ships made in 1941   compared to zero in 1940
- o 26,100 aircraft made in 1941   compared to 12,000 in 1940
- o 4,052 tanks made in 1941   compared to 400 in 1940
- o 29,100 artillery pieces made in 1941   compared to 1,800 in 1940

This mammoth increase in manufacturing helped ease the U.S. out of the Great Depression, so even isolationists did not complain much here

As another indicator, the country's first peacetime draft became effective 9/1940, fifteen months before the U.S. entered World War II; the Army increased from 130,000 men in 1939 to 1.4 million in 1941 (more than tenfold)

Anyway because of this non-intervention stance, American intelligence was not much monitoring Japan's military build-up closely

- As already noted, Germany started World War II by invading Poland without a declaration of war 9/1/1939; (future) European Allies and the U.S. (the U.S. even though not yet in the War) were then preoccupied with the Germans (and Italians) in Europe, not so much the Japanese
- This was during the worldwide, financial Great depression (especially severe in the U.S.), so budgets were tight, which limited intelligence gathering and military spending; the priority of course was to end the Depression; ironically, gearing up for war was a major factor in ending the Depression in the U.S., and other countries for that matter
- The Allies including the U.S. generally dismissed Japan's ability to make superior aircraft (or tanks, ships, munitions, rifles, etc. for that matter); after all, Japan was just a small and distant island country in the middle of an enormous ocean; it is 6,852 islands, but altogether the land area was only little more than half that of Texas; most Americans in fact could not find Japan on a map

This attitude prevailed, despite the fact that Claire Chennault (1893 TX – 1958 New Orleans) who was the leader of the Republic of China Air Force had sent reports to the U.S. military of Japan's superior military capabilities; the Republic of China Air Force by the way was more American than Chinese

Some U.S. military men in Japan operating such as through the American embassy in Tokyo also tried to raise the alarm; these concerns also went unheeded

American military recognition manuals did not even include pictures or descriptions of much of Japan's military equipment (ships including submarines, aircraft, artillery pieces, etc.)

These attitudes and lack of actions led to the same-day, 12/7, 8/1941 debacle, when the Empire of Japan very successfully sneak attacked thirteen locations on the other side of the world on the same day, with devastating results. Japan as usual did not bother to warn the victims, by declaring war. For the record, Germany also gave no warning on some of its land acquisitions. This was in violation of the international rules of war. The 1907 Hague Convention addressed the requirement to declare war in its *Convention Relative to the Opening of Hostilities* statements. These clauses describe the international actions a country should perform, before opening hostilities. Article 1 states: *The Contracting Powers recognize that hostilities between themselves must not commence without previous and explicit warning, in the form either of a reasoned declaration of war or of an ultimatum with conditional declaration of war.* Again, Japan took a pass on giving an advance warning, of maybe attacking. Shame on Japan (and Germany).

The attacks were all on the same day, within nine hours of each other. Two days are shown, as the locations were on both sides of the International Date Line. The International Date Line is an imaginary line from the North Pole to the South Pole. It marks the change from one calendar day to the next. It roughly follows the 180° line of longitude, through the middle of the Pacific Ocean. But again, the attacks were all on the same day. The attacked thirteen sites (or ships) were as follows:

- Nine U.S. possessions
  - Storming and capture of a 159' long USS river gunboat and its crew when berthed at Shanghai Harbor; this little Yangtze River gunboat was the only USS that Japan captured in World War II; for good measure, the Japanese also gun-sank a 177' HMS river gunboat in Shanghai Harbor, at about the same time; if counting this British warship, it is fourteen sneak attacks instead of thirteen
  - IJN submarine gun-sank an Army-chartered, 250' long freighter off California
  - Howland and Baker Islands of the Phoenix Islands of the U.S. Minor Outlying Islands were bombed, these two islands are 43 miles apart
  - Five U.S. military installations (harbors, airfields, bases) on five Pacific Ocean islands; these five islands were Oahu (Pearl Harbor), Guam, Midway, Wake, and Philippines
- Three British Crown colonies – Malaysia, Hong Kong, and Singapore
- Thailand

Japan ended up occupying the three British crown colonies, Thailand, and Wake Island for the duration of World War II. Japan occupied Guam until the U.S. re-captured, 8/1944. Japan occupied the major Philippine islands by the spring of 1942. The U.S. wrested the Philippines islands back beginning 10/1944, and into 1945. General Douglas MacArthur (1880 AR – 1964 DC) said he would return and he did, but it took 2.6 years.

Some Japanese soldiers held out though on Mindanao Island (second largest of the Philippines) until the end of the War. Actually, the last holdouts on Mindanao were 200 well organized and disciplined soldiers, who surrendered 1/1948. This was 29 months after the War ended. This is hard to believe, but was the case.

In the next few weeks or months after the sneak attacks, Japan also conquered and occupied Borneo, Burma, New Britain, Gilbert Islands, and the resources rich (oil, rubber, etc.) Dutch East Indies (today, this is the Republic of Indonesia).

In these thirteen (or fourteen if counting the HMS river gunboat sunk in Shanghai Harbor) attacks on the same day, the Japanese Empire was for the most part stupendously successful in terms of devastation and casualties rendered, versus its own loss of equipment and casualties. Japan's planning and executions were brilliant. Said yet a third way, the outcomes were very one-sided in Japan's favor. To quote President Roosevelt from his 12/8/1941 (Monday) speech to Congress, 12/7/1941 was *a date that will live in infamy* for the United States.

Of the five U.S. military targets on the five Pacific Ocean islands, Americans of course most remember Oahu (Pearl Harbor) of the U.S. Territory of Hawaii, again due to the one-sided outcome. Japan launched two air attacks (bombing and strafing), one hour apart on a Sunday morning. The U.S. military had 2,335 and 1,143 men killed and wounded. Another 68 and 35 Hawaiian civilians were killed and injured. In comparison, only 64 Japanese military men died (55 airmen and nine midget submarine sailors) and one (a submariner) captured. This is a ratio of more than 36 American military deaths per one Japanese military death.

The Japanese Navy sank or damaged nineteen USSs, including all eight battleships of the Pacific fleet. Hundreds of aircraft were destroyed, and most of these when on the ground. Japan lost only 29 aircraft, nine and 20 in the first and second wave attacks. These were fifteen, nine, and five dive bombers, fighters, and torpedo bombers. Japan's five mini-submarines were all sunk, which was more or less the (unstated) plan. The other 51 ships of the Japanese Task Force were undetected and unseen, coming and going.

Japan's surprise attacks without declaring war ended the United States' isolationist attitude, left over from losing the already mentioned 116,516 men in uniform and another 204,000 wounded or made ill in World War I. Congress at President Roosevelt's request declared war on Japan, the next day. This was Monday, 12/8/1941.

Dr. Jiro Horikoshi (1903 Japan – 1982 Tokyo, pneumonia) was the chief designer and engineer of Japanese World War II fighters. He worked for Mitsubishi Aircraft Company. The Mitsubishi Corporation today is based in Tokyo. It is one of the largest corporations in the world, employing more than 60,000 people. It traces its roots to the 1860s. Mitsubishi subsidiary Mitsubishi Heavy Industries was launched in 1934, and produced war goods for Japan's war effort. Mitsubishi Aircraft Company in turn was a unit of Mitsubishi Heavy Industries. Mitsubishi today is developing a twin jet engine, 80-passenger airliner, so is still in the aircraft manufacturing business.

Mitsubishi in 1929 sent Horikoshi to Europe and the U.S. to observe and work at aircraft factories. He worked several months at a Curtiss Aeroplane and Motor Company plant in New York, as an acceptance inspector for a batch of single engine, single crew, conventional landing gear, P-6 Hawk pursuit fighter biplanes that the Japanese Army had ordered. The P-6 was introduced in 1927.

Horikoshi is best known for designing the 30' long, 39' wingspan, 10' tall, low wing, all-metal, single engine, one crew, conventional landing gear with retractable mains, carrier-capable, Mitsubishi A6M Zero fighter, for the Japanese Navy. The Zero was introduced in 1940, which in the Japanese imperial calendar system was the year 2600. As 2600 ends with a zero, the fighter somehow assumed that nickname. The Allied reporting name was *Zeke*. However, Americans commonly referred to it as the *Zero*, as did the Japanese.

The Zero was introduced 7/1940. Ten thousand, nine hundred and thirty-nine Zeroes were made 1940-1945. It was the most made of any Japanese aircraft for World War II.

For the record, claims have been made that Horikoshi and Mitsubishi were influenced by American and British, low wing monoplane fighters or fighter prototypes, and their components. These include the American Chance Vought V-143, which was never developed past a prototype. The V-143 prototype first flew in 1936. The U.S. Army Air Corps rejected it though. Chance Vought sold the prototype to the Japanese Army in 1937. The Zero also resembled the 1937 British Gloster F.5/34. The Gloster first flew in 1937. Only two were made and used only for tests. Some though discredit such allegations that the Zero was a copy of these or other designs. However, the Zero did have some commonalities with the Chance Vought and the Gloster.

In retrospect though, allowing Japan detailed access to prototypes developed by other nations such as the U.S. and Great Britain in the 1930s was probably not wise.

The Zero had empty and loaded weights of 3,704 and 5,313 pounds. Its 940 horsepower, 14-cylinder radial engine (second engine for the Zero) gave it a maximum speed of 331 miles per hour. Its never exceed speed in a dive was 410 miles per hour. It climbed at 3,100 feet per minute. Its service ceiling was 33,000'. This data is for the A6M2 Type 0 Model 21, the most common made early in the War. Later, engine power was increased; with a concomitant increase in speed and climbing ability.

Of note, the Zero was also the first aircraft designed from inception to carry an external fuel tank, which could be jettisoned. The light Zero's range with the detachable tank was enormous. In fact early in World War II, the Allies often assumed that Japan had carriers in the area that had gone undetected when Zeroes appeared. In actuality, they had flown from land bases several hours distant. Also, this long-range capability gave Allied Commanders the impression that Japan had several times more Zeroes than it did.

In a conservative test, one Zero flew 12 hours before running out of fuel. That cocky pilot dead-sticked the Zero in. Presumably, he brought sandwiches and strapped on a motorman's friend.

Zeroes carried four machine guns. The two firing from the engine cowling through the propeller arc were 7.7 millimeters -- 500 rounds per minute. The 20 millimeter wing cannons fired at 60 rounds per minute. The latter were later increased to 100 rounds per minute.

The Zero could tote two bombs, weighing 132 pounds each. Later, when converted for kamikaze use (stripped to greatly reduce weight), the single bomb weighed 551 pounds.

The first prototype was completed 3/1939. Its 780-horsepower engine spun a two-blade propeller. The propeller was changed to a triple blade to solve a vibration problem. The Japanese Navy was pleased with the Zero in tests, but asked for more power. A 940-horsepower engine from a different manufacturer (Nakajima Sakae) was substituted. The engine was modified to include a two-speed supercharger for better altitude performance. This increased power to 1,130 horses. Later models had engines up to 1,560 horsepower.

Variants included models with folding wingtips, so as to fit on some carrier elevators. Larger wing tanks and drop tanks were added to some models. The tail assembly was modified on some. A tandem crew trainer was made. A night fighter version was made.

Even a floatplane was developed from the Zero. The Nakajima A6M2-N (Navy Type 2 interceptor/fighter-bomber) was deployed in 1942 for defensive actions in the Aleutian and Solomon Islands, to support amphibious operations and defend remote bases. In the Solomons, they harassed American patrol torpedo boats, including dropping flares to signal their location to Japanese destroyers. The large float and wing pontoons reduced performance only 20%. Three hundred and twenty-eight were made.

The wing shape was modified, which gave the Zero better roll and less drag. This upped the never exceed speed to 420 miles per hour, but maneuverability and range and ceiling (due to less lift) were reduced.

The later Model 52 Zero was considered the most effective variant. It was introduced in the fall of 1943. The modifications were made to contend with the Vought F4U Corsair introduced the end of 1942, and the American Grumman F6F Hellcat introduced in 1943. The changes included shortening the wings to increase speed; and revisions to the ailerons, aileron trim tab, and flaps. The wing skin was thickened to allow faster diving speeds. The engine was more powerful. The engine exhaust system was improved, by using four ejector exhaust stacks. This added an increment of thrust, as less back pressure on the engine. Armament was improved.

Late in the game, the windscreen was made of armored glass. Also, armor plate was installed behind the seat to protect the pilot. A fuel tank fire extinguisher system was installed. This protection was much needed. Of course though, flight capabilities were reduced, due to the extra weight.

Despite Horikoshi's close ties to the Japanese military establishment and his direct participation in the nation's military buildup in the 1930s, he was strongly opposed to war. He especially considered war with the U.S. futile. In other words, he was a realist. His personal diary excerpts during the final year of the war were published in 1956, and included these statements:

When we woke 12/8/1941 morning, we found ourselves - without any foreknowledge - to be embroiled in war...Since then, the majority of us who had truly understood the awesome U.S. industrial strength never really believed that Japan would win this war. We were convinced that surely our government had in mind some diplomatic measures which would bring the conflict to a halt, before the situation became catastrophic for Japan. But now, bereft of any strong government move to seek a diplomatic way out, we are being driven to doom. Japan is being destroyed. I cannot do anything other but to blame the military hierarchy and the blind politicians in power, for dragging Japan into this hellish cauldron of defeat.

Horikoshi's statement above remarks on America's industrial might. Japanese researchers and planners had in fact evaluated this in the late 1930s. Their conclusion was that America's industrial capacity was 74 times greater than that of Japan.

Horikoshi was an engineer. His grasp of Japan's strategic and political position during World War II was accurate. Of course, this was obvious to anybody by 1944 or 1945 when he wrote this, if not by late 1942.

The aircraft carrier-capable Zero was Japan's ablest fighter at the beginning of the war, due to its excellent maneuverability and great range. Its agility and distance came from the fact that it was so light. At 3,704 pounds, it was only half as heavy as U.S. Navy fighters. The lightness came from using a new lightweight aluminum alloy (see below), its unibody construction (see below), and from not installing armor (some armor came later) or self-sealing fuel tanks (and this came later as well). Weight was also shed by cutting holes out through every internal airframe part, but obviously not to the point of over-stressing that component.

The single heaviest component of an airplane is the main wing spar. Horikoshi reduced the Zero's wing spar weight 30% by using a new zinc-aluminum alloy, called Super Ultra Duralumin. German metallurgist Alfred Wilm (1869 – 1937) at Durener Metallwerke developed the original aluminum alloy which led to duralumin, in 1903. The company was located at Duren, Nordrhein-Westfalen; which is in western Germany. Improvements led to the introduction of duralumin in 1909. However, duralumin was corrosion-prone. This was certainly a concern for naval aircraft (salt water). This was countered by applying an anti-corrosion coating after fabrication. The coating added very little weight.

Construction was high quality, compared to U.S. fighters at the time. The rivets were flush. Even the guns were flush with the wings.

Most impressive, the fuselage and wings were made as one piece, compared to the U.S. method of making the parts separately and then connecting the right and left wings to the fuselage. The unibody method was slow and expensive, but resulted in a very light (no spar brackets and fasteners required) but strong structure. It was the fastest turning fighter, until the U.S. caught up in 1943. The designers made the control forces required light up to 200 miles per hour, but heavier above that speed to safeguard against wing failure.

The Zero's speed and maneuverability were even more impressive, considering that it was a Navy, carrier-capable aircraft. Airplanes are compromises. Those that have the capability to be steam catapult-launched and jerked to a sudden and abrupt stop on floating sea-bases must have very beefy and strong frames and landing gear, not to mention the heavy tail-hook assembly. The Zero though was so light, that catapult-launching usually was not required when the carrier was steaming (even if no wind). It took off on its own power.

On the other hand, due to the non-sealing fuel tanks and lack of armor, the Zero was easy to shoot down with anti-aircraft guns from the ground, ships, or other aircraft. Bullets often set the Zeroes afire. Bullets also were more likely to connect with the pilot, due to lack of armor around the cockpit. It should be said though that self-sealing tanks and armor for military aircraft in the late 1930s were none, or at least not common.

Later, the windscreen was made of armored glass. Also, armor plate was installed behind the seat to protect the pilot. A fuel tank fire extinguisher system was installed. This protection was much needed. Of course though as already noted, these enhancements reduced flight capabilities due to the extra weight.

The Zero first engaged in combat over China 8/1940, flying off aircraft carriers and from land bases. On the first such mission 8/19/1940, twelve Zeroes accompanied 32 Japanese Navy bombers from Hankow in Eastern China, on an attack on the temporary (free) Chinese capital of Chungking (now Chongqing).

The Chinese did not send up any opposition on these early escort missions, until 9/13/1940. That day, China sent up 30 interceptors to confront 13 Zeroes. The aircraft were Soviet made, open cockpit Polikarpov I-15 biplanes and open cockpit Polikarpov I-16 monoplane fighters, flown by Chinese pilots. The latter's cantilever low wing, retractable landing gear, and enclosed cockpit were revolutionary at the time of its 1934 introduction.

The I-15 biplane's maximum speed and rate of climb were two thirds and less than half that of the Zero, so it was mincemeat. The I-16 monoplane approached the Zero in performance, but not close enough. The Japanese aviators shot down 27 of the 30 Chinese interceptors, and this in three minutes, without losing a Zero. It should be said also, that the not much trained Chinese pilots were inexperienced, as this was their first combat.

Through 9/1941, Zeroes shot down or destroyed on the ground 99 Chinese military aircraft losing only two Zeroes, and those two to ground fire in lieu of in dogfights.

To sum up, the Zero was unsurpassed in maneuverability and firepower at the start of World War II. Its performance even exceeded the British Supermarine Spitfire (introduced in 1938), in most ways. As a dogfighter, the Zero's kill ratio was twelve to one, until the U.S. designed and made better fighters. By 1944,

American fighters exceeded the Zero's speed, armor, and firepower; but not its agility necessarily.

On 12/7/1941 off Oahu (Pearl Harbor), Territory of Hawaii, 78 Zeroes were among the 360 (22%) aircraft launched from carriers in two waves one hour apart on a Sunday morning surprise attack. Another 39 Zeroes were used or available for use, for combat air patrol. The purpose of the Zeroes was to protect the bombers, so they could maintain their flight tracks and drop their bombs and torpedoes without having to dodge anti-aircraft fire from land, ship, or another aircraft – messing up their aim. As it turned out, fighter protection was not needed for the first wave, and not much needed either for the second attack wave an hour later.

Warnings in the form of radar detection of incoming aircraft and sighting of midget submarines (one of which was sunk, and the sinking reported no less) were considered false or friendlies, or delayed in interpretation. The Zeroes were for the most part free to strafe, instead of having to protect their bombers.

The Zero pilots shot at a number of small civilian aircraft, just to have something to do. These were instructors with students or sightseers. Two such small aircraft were downed, with three off-duty National Guardsmen killed. One civilian on the ground at Honolulu's civilian airport was killed, when strafed. Several non-military aircraft were destroyed by strafing also at the airport.

The U.S. did get a few fighters up, to attack second wave aircraft. These Curtiss P-36 Hawks and Curtiss P-40 Warhawks were introduced in 1938 and 1939, but already obsolete. Despite lesser performers, the Hawks and Warhawks managed to shoot down at least five and maybe up to ten Japanese aircraft. One American pilot was wounded, and another shot down and killed.

To sum up, when the U.S. was shoved into World War II, the Zero was the best fighter in the Pacific; plus was carrier-capable. It was superior in range and maneuverability to its U.S. counterparts, the just mentioned P-40 Warhawks, and also the Grumman F4F Wildcat (introduced the end of 1940). However, the U.S. and its Allies did not realize this. In fact, they debunked the reports on the Zero's prowess, feeling (maybe hoping) that Japan was not capable of making such a superb fighter. The attack on Pearl Harbor changed that thinking.

The British did not fare much better against the Zero in Japanese air attacks against two British Ceylon port cities, than did the Chinese mentioned above in 1940. The two attacks were as follows:

- 4/5/1942   36 Zeroes escorting 53 torpedo bombers and 38 dive bombers (all carrier launched) to attack Columbo engaged 60 British aircraft flown by well-trained pilots; 21 Hawker Hurricanes, six Fairey Swordfish, and four Fairey Fulmars were shot down; the RAF shot down one Zero and six dive bombers, and damaged another fifteen Japanese aircraft; the Japanese bombers sank a cruiser and a destroyer and damaged five more HMSs, with 756 British and Commonwealth sailors killed; port city Columbo was Ceylon's largest city, located on Ceylon's west coast

- 4/9/1942   41 Zeroes escorting 91 torpedo bombers (all carrier launched again) to attack Trincomalee (port city on Ceylon's east coast) engaged sixteen Hawker Hurricanes; eight and three Hurricanes were shot down and damaged; the RAF shot down three Zeroes and two bombers, and another ten bombers damaged; the Japanese sank a light aircraft carrier, a destroyer, a corvette, and damaged a cargoman, with hundreds of sailors lost

For the record, Ceylon was a British Crown colony 1815-1948. It was an independent country in the (British) Commonwealth of Nations 1948-1972. Ceylon changed its name to Sri Lanka in 1972, when it became a republic within the Commonwealth that year.

The Midway Battle ran 6/4-7/1942, six months after Pearl Harbor Day. On the day before which was 6/3/1942, Japan launched aircraft carrier air strikes against the U.S. Navy Base at Dutch Harbor in the Aleutian Islands, plus occupied several of the Aleutian Islands. For the record, the Aleutian Islands are a chain of 71 islands, which extend southwestward from Southern Alaska toward Russia. The 54 closest to Alaska belong to the U.S., bought as part of the 1867, $7.2 million ($117.3 million in 2019 dollars) purchase of Alaska from Russia. The seventeen islands closest to Russia belong to Russia (then the Soviet Union).

Dutch Harbor is located on the 3.3 square mile Amaknak Island. Unalaska is the name of the town.

Military historians at first considered the Aleutians activity a feint, to divert part of the U.S. Pacific fleet away from the Midway battle. Over time though, it was realized that the Northern Pacific Aleutians campaign was distinct. It was probably triggered by the 4/18/1942 Doolittle Raid on Tokyo. Japan needed to strike American territory closer than Hawaii, as the U.S. had struck Japanese homeland soil. Japan knew that such a strike would have a major negative effect on American morale, just as had the Doolittle Raid on Japan. Japan even probably hoped that such a strike would lead to negotiating a peace settlement with the U.S. Also anxious to protect their northern flank, the Japanese decided that grabbing parts of the Aleutian chain would discourage U.S. attacks on its home islands, while extending the Empire's security perimeter.

Rear Admiral Kakuji Kakuta (1890 Japan – 8/2/1944 Tinian Island, suicide in a cave to avoid capture when Americans approaching) led the seven ship Task Force 900 miles past the Kurile Islands, which were Japan's northernmost islands. His fleet included the 590' long, IJN Ryujo (1933 – 8/24/1942 U.S. aircraft bomb sank in Eastern Solomons Battle, 120 of 600 crew lost {20%}) and 720' long, IJN Junyo (1942 – 1947 scrapped) light aircraft carriers. The ships also carried 2,500 ground troops. To elude Consolidated PBY Catalina scout floatplanes, Kakuta hid his ships in a storm front. On 6/3/1942 at dawn when 180 miles south of the U.S. base at Dutch Harbor, the two carriers launched 46 aircraft – fighters, high level bombers, and dive bombers.

Flight leader Lieutenant Masayuki Yamaguchi led a group of bombers off Junyo. Yamaguchi by the way was one of the pilots who bombed and sank the USS Panay river gunboat and three Standard Oil tankers on the Yangtze River,

12/12/1937. Panay was the first ever USS ship sunk by enemy aircraft (but note that this was not during a declared war).

Yamaguchi abandoned the usual tight formation, due to adverse flying conditions – low ceiling, mist, and turbulence. In fact, weather forced back most of the Junyo carrier aircraft. These pilots felt lucky, that they were even able to locate Junyo to land. The remaining aircraft, most from Ryujo, reached Dutch Harbor at 5:45. They found an infrequent 10,000' ceiling, so had plenty of room to work. Zeroes strafed the base. The first victim was a PBY Catalina floatplane when taking off on the daily mail run to Kodiak, Kodiak Island.

The Catalina was hit with more than 100 rounds. It skidded off the runway on to a beach and caught fire. Two crew were killed. Another Zero hit another Catalina, taxiing in the bay. The pilot managed to take off though, and successfully fled into a misty draw.

Twenty-five and 25 Americans were killed and wounded in the raid. However, property and material damage besides the totaled and damaged Catalinas were not much – some damage to the radio station and oil storage tanks.

For the record, the PBY Catalina was a twin engine, high wing of course, ten crew (included four gunners) floatplane. It was 64' and 21' long and tall, with a 104' wingspan. Its cruise and maximum speeds were 125 and 196 miles per hour.

Yamaguchi rallied his force. He led the bombers into a rain squall to evade single engine, Curtiss P-40 Warhawk fighters responding from Fort Randall Army Airfield at Cold Bay, Alaska. Cold Bay is 261 miles northeast of Dutch Harbor. Fog, rain, and turbulence forced Yamaguchi to skim the ocean. Sea spray ice formed on the aircraft's windshields. Ditching would mean quick death, in the frigid water. All made it back to the carriers though.

After the Dutch Harbor raid, the Americans searched for the enemy, but rain and fog obscured Kakuta's seven ship armada.

On the afternoon of the same day (6/3/1942), the weather had cleared. Admiral Kakuta launched a second raid. Some grounded aircraft, a hangar, oil storage tanks, barracks, the hospital, and several merchant ships in the port were damaged, but the damage was not significant. However, 43 Americans were killed.

Petty Officer Tadayoshi Koga (1920 Japan – 6/3/1942 Akutan Island, crash landing) piloted a Zero on the second raid (he may have been on the first raid as well). Koga and one or both of his two wingmen shot a PBY Catalina down near Egg Island, at the far end of the Aleutians chain. The Catalina survivors got into a life raft. The Zeroes returned to strafe them. They then headed for Dutch Harbor.

At some point over Dutch Harbor, an anti-aircraft round from either the ground (probably) or a PBY Catalina struck the oil return line of Koga's engine. Realizing that his engine would soon be history, Koga reduced speed to keep the propeller spinning as long as possible. With his two compatriots flying guard, Koga nursed his Zero 25 miles to the northeast of Dutch Harbor to land on Akutan Island.

Akutan Island was one of the Aleutian Islands which belonged to Alaska. The Japanese Navy had designated the unoccupied, 129 square mile Akutan as the emergency landing site, for crippled (or mechanical problems, or out of fuel) if any carrier planes. A rescue submarine would pick up the aviators on the beach. That was the plan.

Koga made a full flaps down approach, to reduce his landing speed as much as possible for the forced landing. At this point, his engine was probably dead. He assumed he was landing on a level stretch of clear, firm turf; what looked like a flat, grassy field. This was not the case though. He set down on muskeg. Muskeg is an acidic soil common in boreal areas. It consists of dead plants in various states of decomposition. It often has a water table, near the surface. In fact, these dead plants can hold up to 30 times their weight in water.

The wheels of Koga's Zero instantly dug in deep in the water-mud mire, and anchored. The Zero flipped violently over onto its back. Koga died probably very quickly, from a snapped neck due to the impact. Koga should have landed on the beach.

Japanese pilots had standing orders to strafe and destroy any aircraft that landed on land. This was to prevent the enemy from reverse engineering the aircraft, to determine its characteristics. Koga's wingmen circled the wreck, looking for activity. They saw none. However, they did not shoot the Zero. They hoped Koga was still alive inside and capable. If so, Koga would destroy the Zero himself, and then make his way to the beach to be picked up by the rescue submarine.

The Japanese submarine on station off Akutan did search for Koga. However, the Clemson-class, 314' long and 31' beam and 9' draft, USS Williamson (1920 – 1948 scrapped) light seaplane tender (converted from a destroyer) detected and attacked the submarine, so it quickly departed the area. The two other Zeroes as low on fuel returned to Ryujo, again choosing to not strafe Koga's Zero.

Koga is shown below in 1942. The Zero trailing oil is Koga's.

The crash site was out of sight of standard flight lanes, and not visible by ship.

Five weeks later on 7/10/1942, a Consolidated PBY Catalina patrolling by dead reckoning got lost. On spotting the Shumagin Islands (part of the Aleutian Islands), pilot William Thies realized where he was at and reoriented his plane to return to Dutch Harbor by the most direct course. This was over Akutan Island. A crewman spotted the crashed Zero. The Catalina circled the crash site for several minutes noting its position, and then returned to Dutch Harbor.

The same Catalina and crew returned the next day, landed off Akutan, taxied to shore, and anchored. With sidearms at the ready, they cautiously hiked to the crash site to inspect the wreck. They searched the Zero for anything of intelligence value and found none. They pulled Koga out of the cockpit and buried him in a shallow grave near the crash site.

The map below shows the location of Akutan Island (large dot halfway down the island chain). Akutan is definitely a forsaken place. The big land mass to the upper left is Russia.

The pilot on the left in the other picture is William Thies, shown next to the PBY Catalina he was flying when the Zero was accidentally discovered. The man next to Thies is Captain Leslie Gehres (1898 – 1975), commander of the PBY Catalina amphibious wing defending the Aleutians.

Thies successfully pushed for its recovery and salvage with Dutch Harbor base commander Paul Foley (1909 – 1990).

Thies successfully pushed for its recovery and salvage with Dutch Harbor base commander Paul Foley (1909 – 1990).

The next day (7/12/1942), a salvage team arrived. They moved Koga's body to a nearby knoll and gave him a Christian burial and service, whether he or his family wanted it or not. The average low and high in this area at this time of the year is the mid-40s and the mid-50s, so some deterioration in the body had already occurred.

In 1947, Koga's body was exhumed and re-buried on Adak Island with other Japanese military men's bodies. Adak is another of the Aleutian Islands. Like Akutan, it belongs to Alaska.

Adak cemetery was excavated in 1953, and 236 bodies including Koga's sent to Japan. Most (including Koga) were re-interred in Chidorigafuchi National Cemetery in Japan. Chidorigafuchi is Japan's national cemetery for 352,297 (mostly) unidentified, World War II war dead. It is located near the Imperial Palace and Yasukuni Shrine in Tokyo. Japan had 2.2 million military men die in World War II. Sixteen percent are buried at Chidorigafuchi.

For comparison purposes, the U.S. lost almost 417,000 men in World War II, which is 19% of 2.2 million.

On 7/15/1942, more U.S. military arrived with heavy equipment. They unstuck the Zero from the mud, hoisted it, and hauled it overland to a nearby barge. The Zero was taken to Dutch Harbor and cleaned up. From Dutch Harbor, the Zero was loaded onto the 448' long and 58' beam and 28' draft, USS St. Mihiel (1922

– 1957 scrapped) troopship, and shipped to Seattle. From there, it was transported by barge to Naval Air Station North Island near San Diego, where it was repaired. The repairs included straightening the vertical stabilizer, rudder, wing tips, flaps, and canopy. The sheared off landing struts of course needed extensive repair. The three-blade propeller was dressed and re-used. The engine was overhauled. The Zero was painted in U.S. Navy colors. This was the first flyable Zero that fell into U.S. hands. At least 12 other Zeroes had been recovered by the Allies before the Akutan Zero. However, these were for the most part too damaged to recover and learn from, as follows:

- 12/7/1941   Nine at Pearl Harbor, all nine pilots died; these nine Zeroes were heavily damaged, way past fixable, so information on their flight characteristics was not learned; however, the Allies did learn from these wrecks that the Zeroes were not armored and did not have self-sealing fuel tanks (as mentioned above); this saved the Japanese much weight, making for a fast and agile aircraft, and one with great range as already mentioned; on the other hand, they were easy to shoot down, and easier to hit the pilot (as already stated)

- 2/19/1942   Hajime Toyoshima (1920 Japan – 8/15/1944 Australia, killed in an escape attempt as a POW) crashed 2/19/1942 on Melville Island in Australia (this was the Darwin bombing); the Zero was heavily damaged though; Melville Island is in the Eastern Timor Sea, several miles from Darwin; it belongs to Australia

Toyoshima survived, and became Australia's first Japanese prisoner of war (POW); more than 1,100 Japanese POWs including Toyoshima (now using a false name though) tried to escape the camp near Cowra (New South Wales) 8/5/1944, simply by climbing over the barbed-wire fences using blankets for protection; 359 POWs did escape; some of the escapees committed suicide or were killed by other escapees at their request; the remainder were all recaptured within ten days of the breakout; four Australian soldiers and 231 Japanese were killed in the round-up; this was the largest POW escape of World War II, and the bloodiest; Italian and German POWs kept at Cowra did not try to escape

- 4/28/1942   Yoshimitsu Maeda (1918 – 4/28/1942) crashed near Cape Rodney, New Guinea; the team sent to recover the Zero chopped off the wings in error, severing the wing spars and rendering the hulk un-flyable

- 11/26/1941   A group of Zeroes took off from Tainan air base on Taiwan for Saigon, 11 days before the Pearl Harbor surprise attack; two separated from the formation, got lost; when low on fuel, they landed on the Luichow Peninsula (Southern China) beach; the pair asked for assistance; they were escorted somewhere, and never seen again; it is assumed that the Chinese killed the pilots

One Zero was badly damaged; Chinese farmers cut it up, and carted the parts off so as not be visible from the air; the undamaged Zero was dismantled, the parts placed in carts, and transported to the inland city of Liuchow; Chinese mechanics re-assembled and repaired the Zero

Aviation engineer Gerhard Neumann (1917 Germany – 1997) was in China, working for the already mentioned Colonel Claire Chennault who set up the Chinese Air Force (known as the *1st American Volunteer Group*, and even better known as the *Flying Tigers*) with Madame Chiang Kai-shek (1898 China – 2003 NYC); Neumann took possession of the Zero; he made further repairs, including replacing parts from other downed Zeroes; some American pilots flew it in tests; it was sent to the U.S. for more testing; it underwent flight tests at Wright Field, Ohio, and the Army Proving Grounds at Eglin Field, Florida; by this time though, the Akutan Zero had already been studied In 1945, this Zero from China was photographed in California on a War Bond tour; it then disappeared, and no one has seen it since

On 9/20/1942, Lieutenant Commander Eddie Sanders took the Akutan Zero up for its first test flight. He made 20 test flights through 10/15/1942. His observations included the following:

> *These flights covered performance tests such as we do on planes undergoing Navy tests. The very first flight exposed weaknesses of the Zero which our pilots could exploit with proper tactics... immediately apparent was the fact that the ailerons froze up at speeds above 200 knots, so that rolling maneuvers at those speeds were slow and required much force on the control stick. It rolled to the left much easier than to the right. Also, its engine cut out under negative acceleration due to its float-type carburetor. We now had the answer for our pilots who were being outmaneuvered and unable to escape a pursuing Zero: go into a vertical power dive, using negative acceleration if possible to open the range while the Zero's engine was stopped by the acceleration. At about 200 knots, roll hard right before the Zero pilot could get his sights lined up.*

In later test flights, Anacostia Naval Air Station (this was at Washington, D.C.) flight testing director Frederick Trapnell (1902 NJ – 1975 San Diego) flew the Akutan Zero in performance. Sanders simultaneously flew American fighters performing identical maneuvers, simulating aerial combat. Following these, U.S. Navy test pilot Lieutenant Melvin Hoffman flew the Akutan Zero in dog-fighting tests, against recently commissioned Navy pilots flying newer Navy fighters. These included Wildcats, Lightnings, Mustangs, Corsairs, and Hellcats. The last three were introduced in 1942 and 1943.

The Zero was later used as a training plane for U.S rookie pilots being sent to the Pacific.

A Model 52 Zero (this a later and improved variant) was captured 8/1944 during the liberation of Guam, and was studied as well.

In 2/1945 when the Akutan Zero was taxiing at the San Diego Naval Air Station, a single engine, carrier-capable, Curtiss SB2C Helldiver dive bomber overran it, chopping it into pieces with its propeller. Neither pilot was hurt though. Parts of the Akutan Zero ended up in several museums.

Anyway, much was learned from reverse-engineering and flying the Akutan Zero. This knowledge aided Grumman engineers in designing and making the superior F6F Hellcat, which was introduced in 1943. The Hellcat was faster, a quicker climber at 3,500' a minute, nimbler at high altitudes, better at diving, armored, and had more and better guns (six machine guns, firing 120 bullets per minute each). The Hellcat had a superior gun-sight, which facilitated deflection shooting at an angle.

The Hellcat was heavier than the Zero. The Army Air Forces chose to not reduce its weight, by forgoing armor and self-sealing fuel tanks. Instead, it went with more power – 2,200 horsepower. The Grumman Hellcat again due to its weight and gas-sucking engine, had a shorter range than the Zero. Overall though, the Hellcat was a superior weapon.

Learned details of the Zero's flight characteristics were relayed to U.S. pilots in the Pacific. This knowledge gave F6F Hellcat and other fighter pilots an edge against the Zero, in dogfights.

To sum up, the Zero was at the top of the heap worldwide in 1940, whether the U.S. Army Air Forces and U.S. Navy believed it or not. It was designed almost solely for the attack role, emphasizing long range, maneuverability, and firepower; at the expense of protection of its pilot. It quickly gained a legendary reputation as a dogfighter, achieving the outstanding kill ratio of 12 to 1. Japan tweaked and improved the Zero over its five-year manufacturing period, but it never caught up to the later U.S. fighters (note that Japan did make a much-improved fighter though, introduced in 1943; see below). These later American fighters could out-maneuver the light Zero, even at high speeds. Also, the Zero's low never-exceed speed, made it vulnerable in a dive.

From what the Allies learned from the Akutan Zero, new tactics were developed to engage the Zero on more equal terms; plus new fighters were designed to take advantage of the Zero's weak points, as noted above in the case of the Grumman Hellcat. By 1943, the new fighters with more power, more firepower, and armor gave the Allies the upper hand – even though the Zero was nimbler in some cases. The Zero was definitely outdated by 1944.

For sure, finding the Akutan Zero was lucky. However, the Allies did set up joint military intelligence units during World War II to recover Japanese aircraft, to obtain data regarding their technical and tactical capabilities. Also, armament (cannons, guns, bombs), bombsights, equipment, etc. were recovered and studied. The investigation sites were based in the U.S., England, and Australia.

Crashed and captured aircraft were located, identified, transported, and studied. If not too badly damaged, they were salvaged, repaired to be airworthy, and tested. In many cases, those that ended up flying in tests consisted of pieces from several crashed or captured aircraft. These rebuilt aircraft provided valuable information, as did the Akutan Zero. This information included speed capability, rate of climb, maximum altitude, diving capability, maneuverability, pilot protection, fuel consumption, range, power, capability of guns, etc.

Japan did design and make better fighters than the Zero, as the war progressed. For example, the single engine, single crew, low wing, conventional landing gear with retractable mains, Army (the Zero was a Navy, carrier-capable plane) Nakajima Ki-43 Hayabusa (Allied reporting name *Oscar*) shot down more Allied aircraft than any Japanese aircraft in World War II. It was introduced in 1941. Like the Zero, it was light and agile; and could out-maneuver any Allied aircraft, but not for long.

Like the Zero again, the Hayabusa was not armored or only lightly armored, and did not have self-sealing fuel tanks. It was about the same size as the Zero but had a larger engine – 1,150 horsepower compared to the Zero's 950 horsepower (later Zeroes got more power though). They both had about the same maximum speed though, of 330 miles per hour. However, the Hayabusa could climb 3,500' higher than the Zero. It also climbed at 3,900' per minute, compared to 3,100' feet per minute for the Zero. These climbing capabilities were quite useful in downing American bombers. The Hayabusa was the second most common Japanese fighter made for World War II. Five thousand nine hundred and nineteen were made 1939-1945, behind the Zero with more than 10,000 produced. As the War waned, the Hayabusa was used as a kamikaze bomb plane against USSs – again, like the Zero.

Japan's fighters as the war progressed generally had problems, as their design and re-designs were rushed. Likewise, manufacturing was rushed, so quality lagged. On top of this, Japan lacked experienced pilots and other airmen (gunners, bombardiers, navigators, etc.) as the War progressed; faced with flying outdated and sometimes defective aircraft.

When the war for Japan continued to deteriorate, the next step was to convert fighters into kamikazes, which was done by the hundreds. These aircraft were stripped of many components, which allowed them to fly further and carry a much larger bomb. These *precision-guided weapons* resulted in many damaged and sunk USSs, accompanied by many Allied (mostly American) casualties.

9- SIGNALMAN FIRST CLASS DOUGLAS ALBERT MUNRO

Douglas Munro was born in Vancouver, British Columbia, Canada, two years behind a sister. Although Canadian-born, he was a U.S. citizen as both parents were Americans. The family moved 300 miles south to Vancouver, Washington in 1922. Apparently, Mom and Dad preferred cities named Vancouver.

Munro attended college one year. He decided college was not for him. He enlisted in the United States Coast Guard, 1939. He was promoted rapidly through the ratings to Signalman, First Class.

The Empire of Japan sneak attacked thirteen locations in or on the Pacific Ocean 12/7, 8/1941. Japan as usual did not bother to warn the victims, by declaring war. This was in violation of the international rules of war. The 1907 Hague Convention addressed the requirement to declare war in its *Convention Relative to the Opening of Hostilities* statements. These clauses describe the international actions a country should perform, before opening hostilities. Article 1 states: *The Contracting Powers recognize that hostilities between themselves must not commence without previous and explicit warning, in the form either of a reasoned declaration of war or of an ultimatum with conditional declaration of war*. Again, Japan took a pass on giving an advance warning, of maybe attacking. Shame on Japan, again.

The attacks were all on the same day, within nine hours of each other. Two days are shown, as the locations were on both sides of the International Date Line. The International Date Line is an imaginary line from the North Pole to the South Pole. It marks the change from one calendar day to the next. It roughly follows the 180° line of longitude, through the middle of the Pacific Ocean. But again, the attacks were all on the same day. The attacked thirteen sites (or ships) were as follows:

- Nine U.S. possessions
  - Storming and capture of a 159' long USS river gunboat and its crew when berthed at Shanghai Harbor; this little Yangtze River gunboat was the only USS that Japan captured in World War II; for good measure, the Japanese also gun-sank a 177' HMS river gunboat in Shanghai Harbor, at about the same time; if counting this British warship, it is fourteen sneak attacks instead of thirteen
  - IJN submarine gun-sank an Army-chartered, 250' long freighter off California
  - Howland and Baker Islands of the Phoenix Islands of the U.S. Minor Outlying Islands were bombed, these two islands are 43 miles apart
  - Five U.S. military installations (harbors, airfields, bases) on five Pacific Ocean islands; these five islands were Oahu (Pearl Harbor), Guam, Midway, Wake, and Philippines
- Three British Crown colonies – Malaysia, Hong Kong, and Singapore
- Thailand

Japan ended up occupying the three British crown colonies, Thailand, and Wake Island for the duration of World War II. Japan occupied Guam until the U.S. recaptured, 8/1944. Japan occupied the major Philippine islands by the spring of 1942. The U.S. wrested the Philippine Islands back beginning in 1944, and into 1945. General Douglas MacArthur (1880 AR – 1964 DC) said he would return and he did, but it took 2.6 years.

Some Japanese soldiers held out though on Mindanao Island (second largest of the Philippines) until the end of the War. Actually, the last holdouts on Mindanao were 200 well organized and disciplined soldiers, who surrendered 1/1948. This was 29 months after the War ended (hard to believe).

In the next few weeks or months after the sneak attacks, Japan also conquered and occupied Borneo, Burma, New Britain, Gilbert Islands, and the oil-rich and rubber tree plantations Dutch East Indies. So by the spring of 1942, most of Southeast Asia was controlled by Japan.

In these thirteen (or fourteen if counting the HMS river gunboat sunk in Shanghai Harbor) attacks on the same day, the Japanese Empire was for the most part stupendously successful in terms of devastation and casualties rendered, versus its own loss of equipment and casualties. Japan's planning and executions were brilliant. Said yet a third way, the outcomes were very one-sided in Japan's favor. To quote President Franklin Roosevelt (1882 NY – 4/12/1945 GA, cerebral hemorrhage) from his 12/8/1941 Monday speech to Congress, 12/7/1941 was *a date that will live in infamy* for the United States.

Of the five U.S. military targets on the five Pacific Ocean islands, Americans of course most remember Oahu (Pearl Harbor) of the U.S. Territory of Hawaii, again due to the one-sided outcome. Japan launched two air attacks (bombing and strafing), one hour apart. The U.S. military had 2,335 and 1,143 men killed and wounded. Another 68 and 35 Hawaiian civilians were killed and injured. In comparison, only 64 Japanese military men died (55 airmen and nine midget submarine sailors) and one (a submariner) captured. This is a ratio of more than 36 American military deaths per one Japanese military death.

The Japanese Navy sank or damaged nineteen USSs including all eight battleships of the Pacific fleet. Hundreds of aircraft were destroyed, and most of these when on the ground. Japan lost only 29 aircraft, nine and 20 in the first and second wave attacks. These were fifteen, nine, and five dive bombers, fighters, and torpedo bombers. Japan's five mini-submarines were all sunk, which was more or less the plan. The other 51 ships of the Japanese Task Force were undetected and unseen, coming and going.

Japan's surprise attacks without declaring war ended the United States' isolationist attitude, left over from losing 116,700 men in uniform (almost 46% in combat) in World War I, and another 204,000 men injured or made ill (some with permanent disabilities). Congress as requested by President Roosevelt declared war on Japan, the next day. This was 12/8/1941, a Monday.

The predecessor to the United States Coast Guard dates back to 1790. Congress then created the Revenue Cutter Service (Revenue-Marine) at the request of Treasury Secretary Alexander Hamilton (1756 Nevis Island, West Indies – 1804

NYC). The express purpose was to collect tariffs on imports to finance the new government after the Revolution, as smuggling was rampant. The armed sea guard has gained additional missions since then, including fighting in international wars. The name Coast Guard came in 1915, when the Revenue Cutter Service and the Life-Saving Service were combined.

The President has the authority to transfer control of the entire or a portion of the Coast Guard to the Department of the Navy, in case of war or anticipation of war. The President has done so twice. These were total transfers for both World War I and II. In the latter case, President Roosevelt did so 11/1/1941 by Executive Order 8929. This was five weeks before the 12/7/1941 sneak attacks. President Harry Truman (1884 MO – 1972 MO) returned the Coast Guard to the Treasury Department 1/1/1947, by Executive Order 9666.

Of note, Congress is also authorized to make such a transfer of the Coast Guard to the Navy, but only after it has declared war.

For the record, the Coast Guard was transferred from the Treasury Department to the Transportation Department in 1967, and then to the new Homeland Security Department in 2003. Homeland Security was created as a result of the 9/11/2001 terrorist attacks, to more effectively and efficiently protect the country. However, these changes in organization did not negate the President's or Congress' authority to transfer the Coast Guard or a portion of it to Navy authority and control.

It of course took the U.S. several months to gear up to fight after the sneak attacks. Also, the U.S. made the European Theater a priority despite Japan's direct, sneak attacks on the five U.S. military sites on five Pacific Ocean islands, the capture of a USS river gunboat and crew in Shanghai Harbor, the bombing of two U.S. controlled Phoenix Islands, and the sinking of the Army-chartered cargo ship off California.

The U.S. (and Allies) had some offensive successes in the Pacific Theater during these early months as follows:

- 4/18/1942   Doolittle Air Raid   Fifteen   of   sixteen   North American Aviation, twin engine B-25 bombers which took off from an aircraft carrier dropped on targets on Honshu; Honshu is Japan's largest island; casualties were few and damages minor, but the offensive attack was a great morale booster for U.S. citizens; for Japanese citizens who had been told over and over that the home islands were well protected, just the opposite on that morale thing

- 5/4-8/1942   Coral Sea Battle   The Coral Sea is located in the South Pacific between New Guinea and the Solomon Islands, 500 miles northeast of Australia; the U.S. had three and one ships sunk and damaged, 69 aircraft destroyed, and 656 dead; Japan had five and five ships sunk and damaged, 92 aircraft destroyed, and 966 dead; also noted as first naval battle where the warships never fired upon another, or even saw each other for that matter; the sinkings and damages both sides and casualties were from aircraft launched from carriers; this was the first time that the Allies (Australia played a minor role, with two cruisers) checked a major Japanese advance

- 6/3-7/1942   Midway Sea Battle   The 2.4 square mile Midway Atoll in the North Pacific Ocean is about equidistant between North America and Asia, hence its name; the U.S. (no Allies involved) sank four aircraft carriers and a cruiser and damaged another cruiser and downed 248 aircraft, at a cost of an aircraft carrier and a destroyer and 150 aircraft; U.S. and Japan lost 307 and 3,057 men; this battle marked the beginning of the end of the Japanese Navy's control of the Pacific Ocean

The 54 Nggela Islands are part of the 910 Solomon Islands chain. Japan occupied Nggela Island Nggela Sule 4/1942, ending Great Britain's protectorate claim to the Solomons since 1893. Japan occupied the less than one square mile Nggela Island Tulagi (Operation Mo) 5/3/1942. Tulagi is swimming distance from Nggela Sule. Tulagi at the time was the capital of the British Solomon Islands Protectorate. The British and the few Australian troops on Tulagi had fled earlier – some Australian military getting out only hours before superior Japanese forces invaded.

The next day of 5/4/1942, a USS carrier launched aircraft which destroyed or damaged several of the Japanese ships and aircraft of the occupation effort. Despite this, Japanese troops successfully occupied Tulagi and started construction of a small naval base. Over the next few months, Japan made a port, seaplane reconnaissance base, refueling facility, communications facility, etc. on Tulagi and the neighboring islets of Gavutu and Tanambogo. Japan placed 900 men on these four islands. Japan's goals of these occupations were as follows:

- Provide reconnaissance support for Japanese forces which were advancing on Port Moresby, New Guinea; and then act as a base to cover the flank for the attack
- Provide greater defensive depth for the major Japanese base at Rabaul, New Britain, Papua New Guinea
- Serve as a base for its forces to threaten and then prevent the supply and communication routes between the U.S., and allies Australia and New Zealand
- Establish a staging area for possible future offensives, such as against Fiji, New Caledonia, and Samoa (Operation FS)

The day after the Midway Sea Battle, Japan also occupied Guadalcanal, which is 22 miles south of Tulagi. This was 6/8/1942. At 2,047 square miles (less than 0.8% the size of Texas), it is the largest of the Solomon Islands. The natives leaned toward the Allies, but were not able to offer any resistance.

There are no islands between Guadalcanal and Australia. Guadalcanal and other nearby Solomon Islands were so situated to serve as communication, supply, and war bases to attack or defend Australia and New Zealand. Cargomen in this area (such as from the U.S. to Australia) would be in great peril, as well. The Japanese installed artillery positions, and other fortifications. However, the Allies were not too concerned about these fortifications – ships would just steer wide, and later the Allies could try to throw a blockade up (island hopping strategy) and air bomb and shell from USSs.

This lack of concern changed though, when Japan began construction of an airfield. This was at Lunga Point, a flat area on the central, northern coast of Guadalcanal. A land airfield (compared to carrier-based planes and seaplanes) to send off fighters and long-range bombers from this strategic location would have been disastrous for the Allies, for several reasons:

- As mentioned above, the supply routes from the West Coast of the U.S. to the populous East Coast of Australia and to New Zealand (southeast of Australia) would be susceptible to air attack, from Japanese fighters and bombers flying off Guadalcanal.

- The Allies needed to secure the Solomons as the first step in capturing the major Japanese base at Rabaul, New Britain, Papua New Guinea. New Guinea was a mandated territory of Australia, now occupied by the Japanese. This was necessary to begin the advance towards the Japanese Home islands. Japan had invaded and occupied Rabaul 1/1942, and had 110,000 men there a year later.

As it turned out, the Allies instead just bypassed Rabaul, by setting up a ring of naval bases and airfields around it. Deprived of re-supply and as air attacks were frequent, the stranded Rabaul resources became next to useless. In fact, using resources to try to supply Rabaul almost made it more of a liability than an asset.

Japan never abandoned Rabaul though, until the War ended. But again, Japanese forces based there were not able to contribute much.

- Control of the Solomons was needed to support other (later) campaigns in the area.

Accordingly, 11,000 U.S. Marines waded in to Guadalcanal 8/7/1942 (Operation Watchtower). The 550 and 50 Japanese soldiers and sappers and 2,200 Korean forced laborers had already fled into the jungle, from advance aerial bombing and naval shelling. They left behind construction equipment, supplies, and thirteen dead. Bad weather also concealed the landings from Japanese reconnaissance aircraft, flying off Tulagi. Therefore, the Marines encountered no resistance on Guadalcanal. The Marines took over the not yet completed airfield, and continued construction. They even used some of the abandoned Japanese equipment to do this work. Navy Seabees arrived early September, to add refinements and infrastructure.

Another 3,000 marines landed on Tulagi, Gavutu, and Tanambogo this same day. Resistance was encountered here. The marines lost 122 men. Japan lost 863 men and had another 20 captured. Most of the captured were South Korean forced laborers. Eighty Japanese escaped these three islets by swimming to Nggela Sule Island. The marines killed or captured them over the next few months.

Regarding these ocean-to-beach landings on these Solomons islands, these were the first ever made by U.S. Marines. The landings did not go well. Information was lacking on weather, terrain, tide, layout (maps were inaccurate), where the enemy was, etc. As just noted though in the case of Guadalcanal, there was no immediate resistance thanks to the earlier naval and aerial bombardments and the cloud cover hiding movements from air reconnaissance. But also as noted, there was resistance on the Nggela Island assaults with resulting casualties.

This began a six-month long land, sea, and air attrition battle, for control of strategically located Guadalcanal. Both sides were desperately trying to reinforce their beleaguered troops with more men, food, supplies, ammunition, etc., while trying to prevent the other from doing the same. The fighting was naval, air, and ground; with the Japanese and Americans both fighting to kill the other off, and/or push off Guadalcanal.

In the ground Second Matanikau Battle 9/27/1942 (the Matanikau River is in the northwest part of Guadalcanal), Munro led a detachment of ten landing craft. After landing the Marines, Munro directed the boats to an offshore rally position. Observing that the Marines were facing annihilation by an unexpected large and well-armed Japanese force from both infantry and artillery fire, he directed the landing craft fleet back to shore for the extraction, under heavy enemy fire. When most of the Marines had re-boarded, he maneuvered his boat into harm's way to provide cover for the last few Marines boarding. Enemy small arms or machine gun fire hit Munro and two of his crewmen. The two crewmen survived. Munro did not. He was not quite 23 years old.

Of note, very highly decorated Lieutenant Colonel Lewis *Chesty* Puller (1898 VA – 1971 VA) was one of the Marines that Munro rescued. This allowed Puller to fight in a later war, the 1950-1953 Korean War. Puller turned age 52, the day after that war started. Puller served 37 years, 1918-1955. He retired as a Lieutenant General.

Puller by the way is considered the most decorated Marine in American history. He is one of only two military persons awarded five Navy Crosses and one Army Distinguished Service Cross. His six Crosses are next in number to the eight Crosses earned by World War I flying ace Eddie Rickenbacker (1890 OH – 1973 Switzerland).

Coast Guardsmen receive the Navy version of the Medal of Honor, for actions in wartime. President Roosevelt awarded the Medal of Honor to Munro's parents at the White House. He is the only U.S. Coast Guardsman to receive the Medal of Honor. The medal is on display at the USCG Training Center in Cape May, NJ. The citation reads as follows:

> *For extraordinary heroism and conspicuous gallantry in action above and beyond the call of duty as Officer-in-Charge of a group of Higgins boats, engaged in the evacuation of a Marines Battalion trapped by enemy Japanese forces at Point Cruz, Guadalcanal, 9/27/1942. After making preliminary plans for the evacuation of nearly 500 beleaguered Marines, Munro, under constant risk of his life, daringly led five of his small craft toward shore. As he closed the beach, he signaled the others to land, and then in order to draw the enemy's fire and protect the heavily loaded boats, he valiantly placed his craft with its two small guns as a shield between the beachhead and the Japanese. When the perilous task of*

evacuation was nearly completed, Munro was killed by enemy fire, but his crew, two of whom were wounded, carried on until the last boat had loaded and cleared the beach. By his outstanding leadership, expert planning, and dauntless devotion to duty, he and his courageous comrades undoubtedly saved the lives of many who otherwise would have perished. He gallantly gave up his life in defense of his country.

Munro's other medals include the Purple Heart, American Defense Service, American Campaign, Asiatic-Pacific Campaign Medal with one battle star, and World War II Victory Medal, as shown. The medal is the Navy version of the Medal of Honor.

Munro's mother Edith (1895 England – 1983) enlisted in the USCG Women's Reserves (SPARS) after his death. She was commissioned as a Junior Grade Lieutenant, 5/27/1943. She served two years as an active duty officer. Her duty stations included Seattle, Long Beach, Philadelphia, and Houston. She was promoted to Lieutenant 7/1/1944. She retired 11/1/1945.

Three warships were named for Munro, as follows:

- 55th of 83 John C. Butler-class, 306' long and 37' beam and 13' draft, 28 miles per hour, destroyer escorts; the USS Douglas A. Munro was commissioned in 1944 four months after launching, hastened to aid in ending the War; served in both World War II and the Korean War; sunk for target practice in 1966
- Tenth of 12 Hamilton-class, 378' long and 43' beam and 15' draft, 31 miles per hour, high endurance cutters; the USCGC Munro cutter was commissioned in 1971, and still active; first USCG cutter named after a Coast Guardsman
- Sixth of eleven planned Legend-class, 418' long and 54' beam and 23' draft, 32 miles per hour, high endurance cutters to replace the Hamilton-class cutters; the USCGC Munro cutter was commissioned in 2017; these are the largest ever Coast Guard cutters; they have stern launch-recovery ramps; they have two diesel engines for cruising, and a gas turbine engine

for high speed; top speed is 32 miles per hour; they are capable of 13,800 mile voyages lasting up to two months

Munro's mother Edith Munro sponsored in the first two cases above.

USCG facilities named in honor of Munro include the following:

- USCG Training Center in Cape May, NJ
- A building at the USCG Academy in New London, CT
- The USCG's headquarters building in the D.C.

10- SULLIVAN BROTHERS, KIN SERVING TOGETHER

Tom Sullivan (1883 IA – 1965 IA) and Alleta Abel (1895 IA – 1972 IA) were the children of Irish immigrants, who had moved to Iowa. They met, courted, and wed in 1914. As did many Irish Catholic families of the time, they had a large family. The seven children were five boys and two girls. The boys were born 1914, 1916, 1918, 1919, and 1922 – 7.6 years apart.

Father Tom was a railroad freight conductor for the Illinois Central Railroad. Mother Alleta – well obviously with all these babies, she was a stay at home housewife and child raiser.

All five boys worked for major employer Rath Packing Company (1881 – 1985), at one time or another in their hometown of Waterloo, Iowa. The meatpacking plant first slaughtered, processed, and packaged pork, but later added beef and lamb. By the end of World War II, it was the nation's fifth largest meat packing company. Due to high labor costs and outdated equipment, the company was liquidated in 1985.

Waterloo by the way is located 110 miles northeast of Des Moines, and 265 miles west of Chicago.

Several of the brothers dropped out of high school, to help support the family. This was during the 1929-1941, worldwide, economic Great Depression, so they were lucky to be employed much of the time.

All the brothers were single except for the youngest, who married at 17. Their son was born 5/1940.

The two oldest boys served four-year Navy tours and were discharged. This was before the Empire of Japan conducted thirteen sneak attacks, 12/7/1941. The 1907 Hague Convention addressed the requirement to declare war in its *Convention Relative to the Opening of Hostilities* statements. These clauses describe the international actions a country should perform, before opening hostilities. Article 1 states: *The Contracting Powers recognize that hostilities between themselves must not commence without previous and explicit warning, in the form either of a reasoned declaration of war or of an ultimatum with conditional declaration of war.* Again, Japan took a pass on giving an advance warning (made up stories as to why did not). Japan had a history of such invasions without such warnings. Shame on Japan.

Five of the attacked sites were U.S. military installations (harbors, airfields, bases) on five Pacific Ocean islands. Of these five locations, the most remembered by Americans of course was the attack at Oahu (Pearl Harbor), Territory of Hawaii. This was due to the very one-sided outcome. Japan launched two air attacks (bombing and strafing), one hour apart on a Sunday morning. The U.S. military had 2,335 and 1,143 men killed and wounded. Another 68 and 35 Hawaiian civilians were killed and injured. In comparison, only 64 Japanese military men died (55 airmen and nine midget submarine sailors) and one (a submariner) captured. This is a ratio of more than 36 American military deaths per one Japanese military death.

The Japanese Navy sank or damaged nineteen USSs including all eight battleships of the Pacific fleet. Hundreds of aircraft were destroyed, and most of these when on the ground. Japan lost only 29 aircraft, nine and 20 in the first and second wave attacks. These were fifteen, nine, and five dive bombers, fighters, and torpedo bombers. Japan's five mini-submarines were all sunk, which was more or less the (unstated) plan. The other 51 ships of the Japanese Task Force were unseen and undetected, coming and going.

To quote President Franklin Roosevelt (1882 NY – 4/12/1945 GA, cerebral hemorrhage), 12/7/1941 was *a date that will live in infamy.*

The surprise attacks without declaring war ended the United States' isolationist attitude, left over from losing 116,700 men in uniform (almost 46% in combat) and another 204,000 wounded or made ill (many with permanent disabilities) in World War I. Congress as requested by President Roosevelt declared war on Japan the next day 12/8/1941, which was a Monday. The peace between the World War I Armistice Day and when the United States entered World War II was a little more than 23 years.

The Sullivans of Waterloo knew the Balls of Fredericksburg, Iowa. Fredericksburg is 42 miles north-northeast of Waterloo. Two Ball sons joined the Navy. Chief Petty Officer Fireman First Class Masten Ball (1919 IA – 1985 CT) and his younger brother Seaman First Class William Ball (1920 IA – 12/7/1941 Pearl Harbor, Oahu, Territory of Hawaii), both served on the Pennsylvania-class, 608' long and 97' beam and 29' draft, USS Arizona (1916 – 12/7/1941 Pearl Harbor, sunk by aerial bombs) battleship.

Japanese aircraft carriers launched bombers which bombed and sunk Arizona in the 12/7/1941 sneak attack. One thousand one hundred and seventy-seven of the 1,512 crewmen on board (77.8%) died; from the explosions, fires, or drowning. This was more than half the military lives lost in the entire attack. The Arizona's crew complement was 2,290. Many of the sailors were on shore (this was a Saturday night), so there was some luck here.

Masten Ball was on Arizona's deck when hit. He was thrown in the water but survived. Brother Bill Ball went below to help crewmates get out. He was never seen again. Bill Ball had signed a contract with the minor league baseball Seattle Cubs, to try out after his Navy hitch. He was sweet on the brothers' sister, Genevieve. They had dated. Bill was well liked by the Sullivan family.

Upon hearing that their buddies Masten Ball and Bill Ball were injured and killed, and another three sailors that they also knew killed at Oahu, the five Sullivan brothers along with two other men from their motorcycle group joined the Navy 1/3/1942. This was less than a month after the sneak attack. As noted above, the youngest brother was married and had a son, so could have gotten a deferment as a husband and father. However, he chose to enlist with his brothers. Also as noted above, the two oldest brothers had already served a four-year hitch in the Navy.

The joint enlistment was written up in the 1/4/1942 *Des Moines Register* newspaper:

> *Five husky Waterloo brothers who lost a pal at Pearl Harbor were accepted as Navy recruits, yesterday at Des Moines. All passed their*

physical exams "with flying colors," and left by train last night for the Great Lakes (Illinois) naval training station. "You see," explained George Sullivan, "a buddy of ours was killed in the Pearl Harbor attack, Bill Ball of Fredericksburg, Iowa." "That's where we want to go now, to Pearl Harbor," put in Francis, and the others nodded.

George and Francis quoted in the newspaper article were the two oldest brothers, who again were Navy veterans.

The quintet insisted that they remain together. The Navy had a policy that relatives (fathers, sons, brothers, etc.) were not allowed to serve on the same ship, but obliged – in this case and many others in fact during World War II. One such case in fact was mentioned above (Ball brothers if Iowa), on the USS Arizona. It was obviously a loose policy. Oldest brother and Navy veteran George wrote a letter to the Navy Secretary, which included the statement: *We will make a team together, that can't be beat.*

The five were assigned to the new, Atlanta-class, 542' long and 52' beam and 23' draft, lightly-armored, USS Juneau (2/14/1942 commissioned – 11/13/1942 torpedo sank off Guadalcanal Island) light cruiser. Juneau was known as the first USS, commissioned in camouflage livery.

Japan was on a roll after the 12/7/1941 sneak attacks. Within a few months, Japan invaded and occupied Borneo, Malaysia, Singapore, Hong Kong, Thailand, Wake Island, Philippines, Burma, New Britain, Gilbert Islands, and the oil-rich (fourth leading producer in the world at the time) and rubber tree plantations Dutch East Indies. Japan several years back had attacked and invaded China, and occupied large parts of that country.

As just noted by the spring of 1942, Southeast Asia was in Japanese hands. However, the U.S. (and Allies) had some offensive successes during this time, as follows:

- 4/18/1942   Doolittle Air Raid   Fifteen of sixteen North American Aviation, twin engine B-25 bombers which took off from an aircraft carrier dropped on targets on Honshu; Honshu is Japan's largest island; casualties were few and damages minor, but the offensive attack was a great morale booster for U.S. citizens; for Japanese citizens who had been told over and over that the home islands were well protected, just the opposite on that morale thing

- 5/4-8/1942   Coral Sea Battle   The Coral Sea is located in the South Pacific between New Guinea and the Solomon Islands, 500 miles northeast of Australia; the U.S. had three and one ships sunk and damaged, 69 aircraft destroyed, and 656 dead; Japan had five and five ships sunk and damaged, 92 aircraft destroyed, and 966 dead; also noted as first naval battle where the warships never fired upon another, or even saw each other for that matter; the sinkings and damages both sides and casualties were from aircraft launched from carriers; this was the first time that the Allies (Australia played a minor role, with two cruisers) checked a major Japanese advance

- 6/3-7/1942 Midway Sea Battle The 2.4 square mile of land Midway Atoll in the North Pacific Ocean is about equidistant between North America and Asia, hence its name; U.S. (no Allies involved) sank four aircraft carriers and a cruiser and damaged another cruiser and downed 248 aircraft, at a cost of an aircraft carrier and a destroyer and 150 aircraft; U.S. and Japan lost 307 and 3,057 men; this battle marked the beginning of the end of the Japanese Navy's control of the Pacific Ocean

The 54 Nggela Islands are part of the 910 Solomon Islands chain. Japan occupied Nggela Island Nggela Sule 4/1942, ending Great Britain's protectorate claim to the Solomons since 1893. Japan occupied the less than one square mile Nggela Island Tulagi (Operation Mo) 5/3/1942. Tulagi is swimming distance from Nggela Sule. Tulagi at the time was the capital of the British Solomon Islands Protectorate. The British and the few Australian troops on Tulagi had fled earlier – some Australian military getting out only hours before superior Japanese forces invaded.

The next day of 5/4/1942, a USS carrier launched aircraft which destroyed or damaged several of the Japanese ships and aircraft of the occupation effort. Despite this, Japanese troops successfully occupied Tulagi and started construction of a small naval base. Over the next few months, Japan made a port, seaplane reconnaissance base, refueling facility, communications facility, etc. on Tulagi and the neighboring islets of Gavutu and Tanambogo. Japan placed 900 men on these four islands. Japan's goals of these occupations were as follows:

- Provide reconnaissance support for Japanese forces which were advancing on Port Moresby, New Guinea; and then act as a base to cover the flank for the attack
- Provide greater defensive depth for the major Japanese base at Rabaul, New Britain, Papua New Guinea
- Serve as a base for its forces to threaten and then prevent the supply and communication routes between the U.S. and allies Australia and New Zealand
- Establish a staging area for possible future offensives, such as against Fiji, New Caledonia, and Samoa (Operation FS)

The day after the Midway Sea Battle, Japan also occupied Guadalcanal, which is 22 miles south of Tulagi. This was 6/8/1942. At 2,047 square miles (less than 0.8% the size of Texas), it is the largest of the Solomon Islands. The natives leaned toward the Allies, but were not able to offer any resistance.

There are no islands between Guadalcanal and Australia. Guadalcanal and other nearby Solomon Islands were so situated to serve as communication, supply, and war bases to attack or defend Australia and New Zealand. Cargomen in this area (such as from the U.S. to Australia) would be in great peril, as well. The Japanese installed artillery positions, and other fortifications. However, the Allies were not too concerned about these fortifications – ships would just steer wide, and later the Allies could try to throw a blockade up (island hopping strategy) and air bomb and shell from USSs.

This lack of concern changed though, when Japan began construction of an airfield. This was at Lunga Point, a flat area on the central, northern coast of Guadalcanal. A land airfield (compared to carrier-based planes and seaplanes) to send off fighters and long-range bombers from this strategic location would have been disastrous for the Allies, for several reasons:

- As mentioned above, the supply routes from the West Coast of the U.S. to the populous East Coast of Australia and to New Zealand (southeast of Australia) would be susceptible to air attack, from Japanese fighters and bombers flying off Guadalcanal.

- The Allies needed to secure the Solomons as the first step in capturing the major Japanese base at Rabaul, New Britain, Papua New Guinea. New Guinea was a mandated territory of Australia, now occupied by the Japanese. This was necessary to begin the advance towards the Japanese Home islands. Japan had invaded and occupied Rabaul 1/1942, and had 110,000 men there a year later.

As it turned out, the Allies instead just bypassed Rabaul, by setting up a ring of naval bases and airfields around it. Deprived of re-supply and as air attacks were frequent, the stranded Rabaul resources became next to useless. In fact, using resources to try to supply Rabaul almost made it more of a liability than an asset.

Japan never abandoned Rabaul though, until the War ended. But again, Japanese forces based there were not able to contribute much.

- Control of the Solomons was needed to support other (later) campaigns in the area.

Accordingly, 11,000 U.S. Marines waded in to Guadalcanal 8/7/1942 (Operation Watchtower). The 550 and 50 Japanese soldiers and sappers and 2,200 Korean forced laborers had already fled into the jungle, from advance aerial bombing and naval shelling. They left behind construction equipment, supplies, and thirteen dead. Bad weather also concealed the landings from Japanese reconnaissance aircraft, flying off Tulagi. Therefore, the Marines encountered no resistance on Guadalcanal. The Marines took over the not yet completed airfield, and continued construction. They even used some of the abandoned Japanese equipment to do this work. Navy Seabees arrived early September, to add refinements and infrastructure.

Another 3,000 marines landed on Tulagi, Gavutu, and Tanambogo this same day. Resistance was encountered here. The marines lost 122 men. Japan lost 863 men and had another 20 captured. Most of the captured were South Korean forced laborers. Eighty Japanese escaped these three islets by swimming to Nggela Sule Island. The marines killed or captured them over the next few months.

Regarding these ocean-to-beach landings on these Solomons islands, these were the first ever made by U.S. Marines. The landings did not go well. Information was lacking on weather, terrain, tide, layout (maps were inaccurate), where the enemy was, etc. As just noted though in the case of Guadalcanal, there was no immediate resistance thanks to the earlier naval and aerial bombardments and the cloud cover hiding movements from air reconnaissance. But also as noted, there was resistance on the Nggela Island assaults with resulting casualties.

This began a six-month long land, sea, and air attrition battle, for control of strategically located Guadalcanal. Both sides were desperately trying to reinforce their beleaguered troops with more men, food, supplies, ammunition, etc., while trying to prevent the other from doing the same. The fighting was naval, air, and ground; again with the Japanese and Americans fighting to kill the other and/or push them off the island.

Juneau's Task Force of five cruisers and eight destroyers arrived Guadalcanal Island in the wee hours of the morning of 11/11/1942. The purpose of the Task Force was to escort and protect transports delivering reinforcements and supplies to the island. The site was between Guadalcanal and Nggela Sule Island. This is Sago Strait, but later given the nickname of *Ironbottom Sound,* owing to the many ships and aircraft littering the sea floor from naval and air battles. It needs to be said that most of the ships, sailors, aircraft, and airmen in this watery grave were American.

Thirty Japanese planes showed up at 14:05. Juneau splashed six herself with anti-aircraft fire. American fighters arrived. To sum up, only one Japanese plane got away.

The approaching Japanese Task Force consisted of two battleships, a light cruiser, and eleven destroyers. At 01:45 on 11/12/1942, they engaged. Both sides had warships gunfire or torpedo sank or heavily damaged, but the U.S. more so than the Japanese.

Just a few minutes into the battle, the Kagero-class, 389' long and 35' beam and 13' draft, IJN Amatsukaze (1949 – 4/6/1945 U.S. B-25s severely damaged off Amoy, scuttled) destroyer sent two torpedoes into the new, Benson-class, 348' long and 36' beam and 17' draft, USS Barton (1942 – 11/13/1942 sunk off Guadalcanal, 164 of 206 crew lost {80%}) destroyer, splitting her into two pieces. She sank within minutes.

Shortly after, Amatsukaze launched another torpedo into Juneau's port side, near the forward fire room – so much for that new camouflage. The shock wave from the explosion buckled the deck and the keel, shattered the fire control computers (so no guns), removed steering ability, jammed one of the propellers, and knocked out most power. Nineteen men in the forward engine room were killed.

The cruiser limped away from the battle, 12' down by the bow and listing to port. Although much crippled, Juneau was able to maintain 15 miles per hour on her one working screw – her normal speed was 37 miles per hour. She kept station 800 yards off the starboard quarter of the New Orleans-class, 588' long and 62' beam and 23' draft, USS San Francisco (1934 – 1959 scrapped) heavy cruiser. San Francisco had been hit and was also crippled (San Francisco lost 81 men and had 105 captured). The two cruisers joined four other USSs from the Task Force at dawn (11/13/1942). The group retreated, toward the Allied harbor at Espiritu Santo.

The 1,527 square mile Espiritu Santo is the largest island in the nation of Vanuatu of the New Hebrides archipelago, and off the northeast coast of Australia. The

Allied forces used Espirtu Santo in World War II as a military supply and support base, naval harbor, and airfield.

As a side note, Espiritu Santo in highly fictionalized form was the locale of James Michener's (1907 PA – 1997 TX) 1947 *Tales of the South Pacific* novel. The book won the 1948 Pulitzer Prize for Fiction. The book was made into the big hit, composer Richard Rodgers (1902 NYC – 1979 NYC) and lyricist-dramatist Oscar Hammerstein (1895 NYC – 1960 PA) 1949 *South Pacific* live musical. In addition, movies were released in 1959 and 2001 (this last one made for TV).

Michener had enlisted as an apprentice seaman in the Naval Reserve in 1942. He was called to active duty in 1943. He was a historian in the Navy, chronicling the Navy's campaigns in the South Pacific. He traveled to many islands. He was discharged at the end of the War, as a Lieutenant Commander. The book is based on observations and anecdotes he collected during his naval career. However, much of the plot is made up.

Back to the War. At 11:01, the Type B1-class, 357' long and 31' beam and 17' draft, IJN I-26 (1941 – 10/26/1944 USS destroyer escorts sunk in Leyte Gulf Battle, all 105 crew lost) submarine launched three torpedoes at the crippled USS San Francisco. None hit San Francisco, but one struck Juneau at her ammunition magazine on the port side near her previous wound. One minute later Juneau exploded, breaking the cruiser in two. She sank in less than a minute.

IJN I-26 already had a record, including the following:

- 12/7/1941   She gun-sank the U.S. Army chartered lumber freighter Cynthia Olson 345 miles off California, during the same time of the sneak attack at Oahu (Pearl Harbor). Olson was carrying lumber to be used by the Army on Oahu. Olson's 35 crewmen plus two Army soldier attendants all died. This was the first U.S. merchant ship that Japan sunk in World War II.

- 6/7/1942   She torpedo-sank the 324' long, American Coast Trader freighter in the Strait of Juan de Fuca, with one crewmen dying. Coast Trader was carrying newsprint.

- 6/20/1942   She surfaced and shelled the lighthouse and radio-direction-finding installation at Estevan Point, on the west coast of Vancouver Island, Canada. Damages were minor. However as a result of the attack, lighthouses along the North American West Coast were extinguished, which slowed coastal shipping.

- 8/31/1942   She crippled the USS Saratoga (1927 – 1946 sunk in atomic bomb test) aircraft carrier when one of six torpedoes launched, connected.

The Juneau is shown below:

Fearing more attacks from I-26, and wrongly assuming from the massive explosion that there were no survivors, the American warships withdrew. About 570 Juneau crew were killed in the explosions or drowned quickly or died in the ocean from fuel oil poisoning. More than 100 sailors survived though. A four engine, Boeing B-17 Flying Fortress heavy bomber a half hour later spotted these sailors in the water, clinging to three oval rafts and debris. The B-17 circled around to drop supplies; and reported their location. However for some reason, the Navy did not return to rescue until six days later. All but ten more than exhausted sailors died, before being fished out 11/19, 20/1942.

The death causes were from injuries from the explosions, exhaustion, exposure, lack of water and food, from drinking salt water, drownings, shark attacks, despair – or some combination of these. Juneau Captain Lyman Swenson (1892 UT – 11/15/1942 off Guadalcanal) was one of those who survived the sinking, but died later in the water. The final death count was 687, of a crew complement of 697 (98.6%).

Three Sullivans were killed in the magazine explosion. A fourth Sullivan died the next day in the ocean. Oldest and last brother George was one of the survivors. He did not know what his brothers' outcomes were. Several nights later, he took his clothes off, dived in the ocean, and was never seen again. It is thought that a shark got to him, or maybe hypernatremia, or maybe suicide due to despair, or maybe he had just lost his mind.

The ten survivors told investigators that George hollered out his brothers' names, into the nighttime darkness. As the oldest brother and already a Navy veteran, he had made a promise to Mom and Dad that he would look out for his four younger brothers.

The U.S. did not release news of the Juneau sinking for security reasons. However, Tom and Alleta feared the worst as not receiving any mail from their sons. The *Waterloo Daily Courier* newspaper quoted Aletta Sullivan as saying that she hoped that they may *Show up somewhere someday soon, but if they are gone it will be some comfort to know that they went together as they wanted, and gave their lives for their country's victory.*

On the morning of 1/12/1943 which was two months after Juneau was torpedoed to a watery grave, a lieutenant commander, a chief petty officer, and a physician approached the parents' front door in Waterloo. Father Tom was walking out of the house headed for work. The dialogue was about as follows:

- Naval officer: *I have some news for you about your boys.*
- Father Tom: *Which one?*
- Naval officer: *I'm sorry. The Navy Department deeply regrets to inform you that your sons George Sullivan, Francis Sullivan, Joseph Sullivan, Madison Sullivan, and Albert Sullivan are missing in action in the South Pacific.*

The five brothers (and two sisters) were as follows:

Name	Life	Death Age	Cause of Death	Rank at Death	Comments
George	12/14/1914-11/17/1942	27.9	Hypernatremia, grief, wounds, shark, exhaustion, etc.	Gunner's Mate 2nd Class	Navy vet already, served 5/1937-5/1941; discharged as Gunner's Mate 3rd Class
Francis	02/18/1916-11/13/1942	26.7	Explosion, died instantly	Coxswain	Navy vet already, served 5/1937-5/1941, discharged as Seaman 1st Class
Joseph	08/28/1918-11/13/1942	24.2	Explosion, died instantly	Seaman 2nd Class	
Madison	11/08/1919-11/13/1942	23.0	Explosion, died instantly	Seaman 2nd Class	
Albert	07/08/1922-11/14/1942	20.4	Drowning	Seaman 2nd Class	Only brother married, left wife and 22-month-old son
Genevieve	1917-1975	58	Unknown		Joined WAVES, also Bill Ball's girlfriend
Kathleen	1931-1931	0.4	Pneumonia		Seventh and last child

The loss of the five Sullivan brothers ages 20 to 27 (average 24.4), was the greatest in number to any American family during World War II, or before or since for that matter.

President Roosevelt sent Mr. and Mrs. Sullivan a personal letter dated 2/1/1943, as follows:

Dear Mr. and Mrs. Sullivan:
The knowledge that your five gallant sons are missing in action against the enemy inspires me to write you this personal message. I realize full well there is little I can say to assuage your grief. As Commander-in-Chief of the Army and Navy, I want you to know that the entire nation shares in your sorrow.

I offer you the condolence and gratitude of our country. We who remain to carry on the fight will maintain a courageous spirit, in the knowledge that such sacrifice is not in vain.

The Navy Department has informed me of the expressed desire of your sons, George Thomas, Francis Henry, Joseph Eugene, Madison Abel, and Albert Leo, to serve in the same ship. I am sure that we all take heart in the knowledge that they fought side by side. As one of your sons wrote, "We will make a team together that can't be beat." It is this spirit which in the end, must triumph.

I send you my deepest sympathy in your hour of trial, and pray that in Almighty God you will find the comfort and help, that only He can bring.

Very sincerely yours,

Franklin D. Roosevelt

In spite of their great loss, parents Tom and Alleta went on tour at plants, shipyards, etc. on behalf of the war effort – encouraging recruitment, hard work, buying war bonds, etc. Their daughter Genevieve did similar.

Genevieve joined the WAVES 6/1943, five months after her brothers died. The WAVES was the World War II, female auxiliary unit of the U.S. Naval Reserve. The acronym stood for *Women Accepted for Volunteer Emergency Service*.

Mrs. Sullivan christened a new Navy fleet tug 2/22/1943 at Portland, Oregon. This was the Cherokee-class, 205' long and 39' beam and 15' draft, USS Tawasa (1943 – 1976 scrapped).

When touring for the War effort, the Sullivans carried and showed a Gold Star Banner, as part of their presentation. As far as is known, the Sullivans are the only family known to have displayed one with five gold stars (for any U.S. war to date). Blue stars signify a family member in the military. Gold stars signify a family member died while serving or when a prisoner of war. The Sullivans' unique Gold Star Banner is shown below, along with a memorial made in Juneau, Alaska:

Two destroyers were named *USS The Sullivans* after the brothers to honor them, as follows:
- 377' long and 40' beam and 18' draft, Fletcher-class destroyer (1943 – 1965 decommissioned, 1978 museum ship)
  - o Alleta Sullivan sponsored (4/1943), mother of the brothers
  - o First USS named after more than one person
  - o Youngest brother Albert Sullivan's son James served on her
  - o Served for the rest of World War II and the Korean War

- One of four Fletcher Class destroyer museum ships today (Buffalo, NY) – other three are *Cassin Young* at Boston, *Kidd* at Baton Rouge, and *Charrette* at Athens (Greece)
- 505' long and 66' beam and 31' draft, Arleigh Burke-class guided missile destroyer (1991 – 2019 in service)
  - Brother Albert Sullivan's granddaughter Kelly Sullivan Loughren sponsored
  - Al-Qaeda terrorists tried to blow up 1/3/2000 as part of the 2000 millennium attack plots; this was to bomb four tourist sites in Jordan and the Los Angeles Airport and the USS The Sullivans, and to hijack an Indian Airlines airliner, all on or about 1/1/2000; the terrorists loaded a small powerboat with explosives, and motored toward the destroyer when docked for a fueling stop in Aden, Yemen; however, the boat was so overloaded with heavy bombs that it sank en route
    Whatever the U.S. Navy learned from this failure was not enough; ten months later (10/2000) at the same Yemen port, al-Qaeda repeated the same effort in the same manner but this time successfully, when another Arleigh Burke-class guided missile destroyer was refueling; 17 and 39 sailors of the USS Cole (1996 – in service) were killed and injured; Cole was repaired and put back in service in 2003

The motto of both of the USS The Sullivans was and is *We Stick Together*. This was the motto adopted by the brothers during World War II.

The 1944 movie *The Sullivans* told their story. The film's name was later changed to *The Fighting Sullivans*. The movie was nominated for the Best Story Academy Award.

The population of Waterloo, Iowa today is 68,000. Waterloo's convention center is named *The Five Sullivan Brothers Convention Center*. The town has a street and public park named after them. The park is at the location of their childhood home.

The Sullivan Brothers Iowa Veterans Museum opened in 2008 in Waterloo. It was partly funded by citizens. Besides telling the story of the Sullivan Brothers, the museum also addresses the history and service of all Iowa military personnel.

There were nine to thirty brother pairs on Juneau (different sources quote different numbers) during at least part of her short life – from the date of commissioning to her sinking was only nine months. None of the brothers were among the ten survivors.

Juneau sibling numbers though were not impressive, compared to the Pennsylvania-class, 608' long and 97' beam and 29' draft, USS Arizona (1916 – 12/7/1941 aerial bombs sank at Pearl Harbor, Oahu) battleship. It had 37 brother pairs or trios, totaling 77 young men. Sixty-two of the 77 brothers died, including 23 sets. These 62 were part of the 1,177 enlisted men and officers who died when Arizona exploded and sank.

Of note, Arizona also had a father-son pair. Thomas Free (1891 AL – 12/7/1942 Pearl Harbor, Oahu) and Thomas Free, Jr. (1923 VA – 12/7/1942 Pearl Harbor, Oahu) went down together.

Similar circumstances in World War II involved other branches of the armed forces, including the following:

- Alben and Gunda Borgstrom of Thatcher, Utah had ten children. Seven were sons. One son died of appendicitis before World War II started. Five sons (including one set of twins) were drafted or enlisted. Four were killed over a 23-week period in 1944 – one Army, one Marine, and two (these were the twins) in the Army Air Forces. Three were killed in combat, and one in an accident (tree fell on him).

The Borgstrom family, with help from neighbors and the Utah congressional delegation successfully petitioned for their surviving Marine son to be released from service. He was sent back to the U.S. and discharged. The sixth son who was not yet of enlistment age, was exempted from future military service.

- The three Butehorn brothers were from Bethpage, New York. One Army brother was killed in action in France in 1944. One Marine brother was a gunner on a torpedo bomber and died when shot down in 1945. The War Department ordered the third brother (Army Air Forces, serving in Italy) home.

- The four Niland brothers from Tonawanda, New York, all enlisted in the Army. Two enlisted before the U.S. entered the War. The other two enlisted 11/1942. They were assigned to separate units. One was a pilot and shot down over Burma, 5/1944. He was presumed dead. Two died in the Normandy (D-Day) invasion, one 6/6/1944 (first day) and the other the day after. The fourth and youngest brother had parachuted into Normandy also as part of the D-Day invasion and had separated from his unit. When the Army heard of the deaths June 6 and 7, 1944, the fourth brother when found was sent back to England and then to the U.S. He served out the rest of the War stateside as a military policeman. Later, it was determined that the brother in Burma was alive and in a POW camp. He was repatriated before World War II ended. The four brothers were as follows:

  o Technical Sergeant Edward Niland's (1912 NY – 1984 NY) B-25 Mitchell twin engine bomber was shot down over Burma. He parachuted out. He hid out in the jungle but was captured 5/16/1944. He was imprisoned in a Japanese POW camp in Burma. He was assumed dead though. He was liberated 5/4/1945, a year later.

  o Second Lieutenant Preston Niland (1915 NY – 6/7/1944 Normandy, near Utah Beach) was killed in action.

  o Technical Sergeant Robert Niland (1919 NY – 6/6/1944 Normandy) parachuted in. He volunteered to stay behind with two other soldiers, to hold off a German advance while his company retreated from

Neuville-au-Plain. He was killed when manning a machine gun. The other two soldiers survived.

o Frederick Niland (1920 NY – 1983) was the baby brother who had parachuted in, and the one sent back to England and then home.

Preston and Robert rest in peace in side-by-side graves at the American cemetery near Colleville-sur-Mer, Normandy, France.

Stephen Ambrose (1936 IL – 2002 MO) mentioned the Nilands' story in his 1992 *Band of Brothers* book.

The plot of Steven Spielberg's (1946 Cincinnati -) 1998 movie *Saving Private Ryan* has to do with a squad of Army Rangers searching for a D-Day (6/6/1944) paratrooper, who was the last-surviving brother of four servicemen. Tom Hanks (1956 CA -) starred. The movie is very loosely based on the story of the Niland brothers. The Sullivan brothers' deaths from 19 months back in the War were mentioned in the dialogue of the movie. The movie was made for $70 million and had a box office of $482 million.

- Twin brothers Henry Pieper (1925 NE – 6/19/1944) and Louie Pieper (1925 NE – 6/19/1944) were crossing the English Channel in the 328' long and 50' beam, Landing Ship Tank LST-523 (1944 – 6/19/1944) headed for Utah Beach 6/19/1944. This was thirteen days after D-Day. They were delivering equipment and supplies, and picking up wounded to return to England. LST-523 hit an enemy mine just off the Normandy beachhead and sunk. One hundred and thirty-five men died. These were 94 men of the 300th Combat Engineers and 41 LST-523 crew.

Both Piepers died. Louie's body was found immediately and buried at the Normandy American Cemetery, Colleville-sur-Mer, Normandy, France. French divers in 1961 retrieved a body's bones from the radio room of LST-523. The bones were buried at Ardennes Cemetery in Belgium, as *Unknown X-9352.*

In 2015, high school sophomore Vanessa Taylor of Ainsworth, Nebraska and her teacher Nicole Flynn were looking for a silent hero from Nebraska as a National History Day project. They came across the names of Henry and Louis. As they had the same last name and as *Pieper* is not a common name, they did research which determined that they were twin brothers who died together in action. They notified the Defense Department POW/MIA Accounting Agency. The Agency exhumed the unknown remains and conducted dental and X-ray comparisons. From these studies, it was determined that the remains were Henry Pieper.

On 6/19/2018 seventy-four years after their deaths to the day, the two brothers were buried side by side in new graves at Normandy American Cemetery.

Of course, there were many cases in World War II where relatives (usually brothers) were on the same ship or in the same unit and survived, or at least one survived. One such case was Francis Fenton (1892 – 1978), who enlisted in the

Marines 8/1917. He became an engineering officer. He was awarded Bronze Stars for his World War II duties and actions at Peleliu and Okinawa. He was a Colonel when World War II started. His two sons Francis, Jr. (1922 CA – 1998) and Michael (11/30/1925 CA – 5/7/1945) enlisted in the Marines also, for World War II. Michael trained as a scout-sniper.

Both father and son Michael were in the Okinawa campaign, assigned to different units. The two by great coincidence met on Okinawa.

Private First Class Michael was later shot dead. He was 19.5 years old. Colonel Fenton was notified. He was able to get to his son's area on Okinawa. He conducted his son's funeral service. Father and son were ages 52 and 19.

After the service, Colonel Fenton surveyed the area which was spotted with dead marines from recent fighting. His statement was *Those poor souls. They didn't have their fathers here.*

Colonel Fenton (kneeling) and Private First Class Fenton (under the flag) are shown below.

Fenton and his older son Francis survived the War. Fenton the father separated from the Marines as a Brigadier General. His son Francis separated from the Marines as a Colonel.

Due to these World War II multiple casualty occurrences (and similar had occurred in previous wars such as the Civil War and World War I), the Armed forces has generally strongly discouraged siblings serving together (same ship, same aircraft, same unit, etc.), at least in combat situations. But again, the military relented much for World War II.

The Defense Department created its Sole Survivor Policy, which was enacted as law in 1948. It has been revised several times since. The policy protects members of a family from the draft (1973 was the last year of conscription though in the U.S.) or from combat duty if already in the military, if that family has already lost a family member or members in military service. The policy came about because of the multiple family death occurrences mentioned above in World War II, but mostly motivated by the Sullivan Brothers. Because of the number (five brothers) and as all died, the press was enormous. The public demanded change.

Of note, the Sole Survivor Policy is voluntary. This means that an overseas military person who has lost a family member in the military who wishes to be sent back to the U.S. to avoid combat, must make a formal request. Of note though, the military does advise and suggest in these cases, to make the request. The policy includes all U.S. military branches, and all ranks.

Two cases of the policy in action were as follows:

- Brothers Jason and Nathan Hubbard joined the army after their brother Jared died in Iraq in 2004. In 2007, Nathan died in a helicopter crash. Military officials ordered Jason home.

- Brothers Jeremy, Beau, and Ben Wise served in active combat roles in the Afghan War. Former Navy Seal Jeremy became a military contractor. He died in a suicide bomber attack at a CIA base in Afghanistan. Later in 2011, Ben was shot eight times in Afghanistan, and later died. Beau was taken out of active military service.

Thirty-nine brother pairs were killed in action in Vietnam. However, none were in the same unit. Brothers Army Staff Sergeant Samuel Nixon (8/15/1942 AR – 3/21/1968 South Vietnam, multiple fragmentation wounds) and Army Captain William Nixon (10/15/1939 AR – 5/8/1968 South Vietnam, small arms fire) died over the narrowest span, 48 days apart in 1968. They were ages 25.6 and 28.6 years at the time of their deaths. They served six and ten years.

Brothers Army Private First Class Lane Hargrove (1/31/1948 NC – 4/21/1968 South Vietnam, land mine explosion) and Marine Lance Corporal Joseph Hargrove (5/15/1951 NC – 5/15/1975 Koh Tang Island, Cambodia; presumed shot in battle) were on the opposite end for Vietnam, killed 7.1 years apart, 1968 and 1975. Joseph was killed in battle, or maybe captured by the Khmer Rouge {Cambodian Communist Party members} and then executed. He died in the American container ship Mayaguez (1944 – 1979 scrapped) incident. The official date for the end of the Vietnam War was 4/30/1975. Lane and Joseph were ages 20.2 and 24.0 (in fact, Joseph died on his birthday) at the time of their deaths.

Charles Hagel (1946 NE -) was Defense Secretary two years (2/2013 – 2/2015) during the Obama administration. He served in the Army 1968-1969, retiring as a Sergeant. He and his brother Tom fought in the same unit in Vietnam. They both saved each other's life, and this more than once. They are thought to be the only brothers who served in the same unit in Vietnam.

The Majestic-class, 702' long and 80' beam and 25' draft, HMAS Melbourne (1955 – 1985 scrapped) light aircraft carrier collided with the Sumner-class, 377' long and 41' beam and 15' draft, USS Frank E. Evans (1945 – 6/3/1969 sank in collision, South China Sea) destroyer, during 1969 sea trials. The smaller Evans was cut in half. Seventy-four of a crew of 336 (22%) Evans' sailors died. Melbourne had no deaths. Only one body from Evans was recovered. The dead Evans crew included Nebraska brothers Gary, Gregory, and Kelly Sage. They had requested to serve together. They were the first siblings assigned to the same ship since World War II. The Navy (apparently) went along, as Evans was not involved in combat.

To sum up, multiple relatives (usually brothers) have died when serving together in the U.S. Armed Forces numerous times, at least up to 1969.

The Seventh Coalition (Great Britain and Prussia) Army defeated Napoleon Bonaparte's (1769 France – 1821 Saint Helena Island) French Army 6/18/1815 near Waterloo, in present-day Belgium. This ended the 1803-1815 Napoleonic Wars, and also ended Napoleon's ten-year rule as French Emperor. He abdicated four days later. Coalition forces occupied Paris 7/7/1815. Since then, the word *Waterloo* has come to mean *final defeat or demise.* In telling the story of the Sullivan brothers from Waterloo, Iowa, and the USS Juneau; this is often pointed out, as fitting the outcome.

Waterloo, Iowa, was originally known as Prairie Rapids Crossing, settled in 1845. One of the early settlers petitioned for a post office in town. He was asked to come up with a name for the post office. He picked Waterloo in 1851, just on a whim. The town over time assumed the name of the post office. As already noted, Waterloo's population today is 68,000.

Paul Allen (1953 Seattle – 2018 Seattle, non-Hodgkin's lymphoma complications) and Bill Gates (1955 Seattle -) formed Microsoft Corporation in 1975. Allen was diagnosed with Hodgkin's lymphoma in 1981. He left Microsoft in 1982, due to his illness. He retained partial ownership of Microsoft. His net worth in 2018 was more than $20 billion.

Allen was treated successfully with radiation therapy and a bone marrow transplant in 1981 and 1982. In 2009, he was diagnosed with non-Hodgkin's lymphoma. He was again treated successfully. However, the cancer returned in 2018 with a vengeance. Allen's billions could not save him.

Allen's 414' long and 69' beam and 19' draft, Octopus mega-yacht was completed in 2003. Besides pleasure use, he made it available for humanitarian work, research, etc. He has also used it to search for shipwrecks.

In 2016, Allen bought a 13-year-old, 251' long and 49' beam and 24' draft, offshore platform service vessel. He had the ship modified and refitted to be a dedicated deep submergence search, research, and equipment test vessel. RV Petrel's autonomous underwater vehicle and remote operated underwater vehicle are able to explore more than 3.7 miles deep. The RV Petrel crew is 21. The project staff is ten.

Petrel has since discovered many World War II shipwrecks in the Pacific Ocean, Atlantic Ocean, and Mediterranean Sea. Archival documents (ship logs, battle reports, etc.) are studied to estimate where the wrecks lie, as a starting point to begin searches.

Petrel's autonomous underwater vehicle identified the Juneau 3/17/2018, with its side-scan sonar. This was St. Patrick's Day. Saint Patrick (385 Roman Britain – 461) of course is the foremost patron saint of Ireland. The Sullivan brothers were Irish Americans.

Petrel's remotely operated underwater vehicle confirmed the finding through its live video feed, the next day. This was more than 75 years after Juneau sank. She rests 13,800' down, in several large pieces.

This paragraph is saved for the end, as maybe a downer. In actuality, the Sullivan family was apparently not as all-American (hot dogs, baseball, apple pie, voluntary enlistment, and Mom) as some think. Accounts are that father Tom drank too much too often, that Mother Alleta was good at having babies but did not put much effort into raising her children, and that the Sullivan brothers (at least some of them) ran wild – drinking and brawling in a motorcycle gang. So, so much for that. If so though, it may be that the five brothers were moving toward maturity, enlisting in the Navy after Pearl Harbor Day, as part of a self-reform movement.

11- ONLY NAVAL BATTLE, U.S. LOST TWO ADMIRALS

The Nggela Islands are a group of 54 small islands, which in turn are part of the Solomon Islands. They are also known as the Florida Islands. They include Tulagi, Gavutu, Tanambogo, and Nggela Sule. Nggela Sule Island, also known as Florida Island, is the largest of these four islands. The other three are very small, more islets than islands.

Japan occupied these four Nggela Islands the first week of 5/1942, which was six months into the Pacific War. A garrison, seaplane reconnaissance base, naval and aircraft fuel storage battery, communication facility, etc. were quickly made on the islands.

The Solomons are more than 900 islands. The largest Solomon Island is Guadalcanal, at 2,047 miles. This is three fourths of one percent the size of Texas. All 900 plus Solomons together sum to 11,000 square miles, which is 4.1% the size of Texas. The Nggela Islands group is north of Guadalcanal Island. The distance from Guadalcanal to Tulagi is 33 miles.

The Solomon Islands were a British protectorate at the time of World War II. Tulagi was the capital island of the Solomons, at the time of World War II.

Japan dispatched engineers to Guadalcanal to survey the island for construction of an airfield. Guadalcanal is mostly jungle, cliffs, and slopes. However, Japanese engineers found a flat area for an airfield. This was a promontory site on Guadalcanal's north, central coast called Lunga Point. Construction began early 7/1942.

A Guadalcanal land airfield would allow the launching of much more capable fighters and bombers from this strategic location – compared to seaplanes. This would have been disastrous for the Allies, for several reasons:

- The supply routes from the West Coast of the U.S. to the populous East Coast of Australia and to New Zealand (southeast of Australia) would be susceptible to air attack, from Japanese fighters and bombers flying off Guadalcanal.
- The Allies needed to secure the Solomons as the first step in capturing the major Japanese base at Rabaul, New Britain, Papua New Guinea. New Guinea was a mandated territory of Australia, now occupied by the Japanese. This was necessary, to begin the advance towards the Japanese home islands. Japan had invaded and occupied Rabaul 1/1942, and had 110,000 men there a year later.

As it turned out, the Allies instead just bypassed Rabaul, by setting up a ring of naval bases and airfields around it. Deprived of ship re-supply and as U.S. air attacks were frequent, the stranded Rabaul resources became next to useless. In fact, using resources to try to supply its forces made Rabaul more of a liability than an asset. Japan never abandoned Rabaul though. But then again, the Japanese forces based there were not able to contribute much.

- Control of the Solomons was needed to support other (later) campaigns in the area.

Accordingly, the U.S. planned an attack. Early on 8/7/1942, Allied warships bombarded the planned landing beaches on Guadalcanal, Tulagi, Gavutu, Tanambogo, and Nggela Sule. U.S. carrier aircraft also bombed Japanese positions on the target islands. On Guadalcanal, the 2,800 enemy (550 and 50 Japanese soldiers and sappers, 2,200 Korean forced laborers and trustees) at the airfield construction site at Lunga point did not hesitate, for good reason. They fled into the jungle, three miles west to the Matanikau River and Point Cruz area. They left behind food, supplies, intact construction equipment and vehicles, and thirteen dead.

Eleven thousand marines landed on Guadalcanal this day. Due to storms and heavy cloud cover, Japanese reconnaissance seaplanes off Tulagi did not spot the landing force. Also as just noted, the enemy had retreated from the naval and aerial shelling and bombing. The Marines encountered no resistance. They took control of the not yet completed airfield.

Three thousand U.S. Marines landed on the four smaller islands also 8/7/1942, and eliminated the Japanese in several days with some casualties.

Regarding these ocean-to-beach landings on these Solomons Islands, these were the first ever made by U.S. Marines. The landings did not go well. Information was lacking on weather, terrain, tide, layout (maps were inaccurate), where the enemy was, etc. As just noted, there was no immediate resistance at Guadalcanal; thanks to the earlier naval and aerial bombardments and the cloud cover hiding movements from air reconnaissance. Some of the other 8/7/1942 Solomon Islands landing locations had resistance though, and the Marines had casualties.

The Marines named the Guadalcanal airfield and base *Henderson Field.* 1926 U.S. Naval Academy graduate and Marine aviator Major Lofton Henderson (1903 OH – 6/4/1942 shot down off Midway) was leading 16 Douglas, single engine, SBD Dauntless dive bombers on a glide bombing attack on the 746' IJN Hiryu (1939 – 6/5/1942 scuttled due to aerial bomb damage in Midway Battle, 389 of 1,100 {35%} crew lost) aircraft carrier. An intercepting Mitsubishi Zero or Zeroes shot him down. His gunner Private First Class Lee Reininger (1922 – 6/4/1942 off Midway Island) died as well.

The Marines used some of the Japanese equipment as well as their own equipment, to complete the airfield 8/18/1942. Seabees arrived the next month to add infrastructure and make improvements.

With both the U.S. and Japan now occupying parts of Guadalcanal, both sides were desperately trying to reinforce their beleaguered troops with more men, food, supplies, ammunition, etc., while trying to prevent the other from doing the same. This began a six-month long land, sea, and air attrition battle, for control of strategically located Guadalcanal.

The 11/12-15/1942 Naval Battle of Guadalcanal (Solomon Islands) was the largest at sea fight, during this six-month period. Two Admirals were killed. Information on the two men includes the following:

- Their ages were less than a year apart

- Both were 1911 U.S. Naval Academy graduates, so good buddies
- Both fought in World War I
- Both were killed on the same day (11/13/1942) several hours apart in the same naval battle
- Both were killed by gunfire on the bridge of their ships which killed others as well
- One was apparently killed by friendly fire, from the other's ship
- One was second in command to the other
- Both were Rear Admirals at the time of their death
- Both were awarded the Medal of Honor
- Both were buried at sea sharing space with thousands of sailors and airmen, and dozens of ships and aircraft of Ironbottom Sound
- Both later had two ships named after them
  - First two were both Fletcher-class, 378' long and 40' beam and 18' draft, destroyers, both commissioned 11/1943
    - USS Callaghan (1943 – 7/28/1945 kamikaze sank off Okinawa, 47 crew lost, last USS sank by kamikazes in World War II)
    - USS Norman Scott (1943 – 1973 scrapped)
  - Second two were both Kidd-class, 563' long and 55' beam and 32' draft, guided missile destroyers, both commissioned in 1981
    - USS Callaghan (1981 – 2003 sold to Taiwan, still in service)
    - USS Scott (1981 – 2003 sold to Taiwan, still in service)

The two were as follows:

- Rear Admiral Norman Scott (1889 Indianapolis – 11/13/1942 gunfire off Guadalcanal) was second in command of the Task Force. He reported to Admiral Callaghan (see below). Scott was aboard the Atlanta-class, 542' long and 53' beam and 27' draft, USS Atlanta (l941 – 11/13/1942 sunk off Guadalcanal, 204 lost of 673 crew {30%}) light cruiser as his flagship. Atlanta was hit by gunfire from the enemy and the USS San Francisco (1934 – 1959 scrapped) heavy cruiser. The estimate is that she was hit 19 times with 8" shells from San Francisco *in the urgency of battle, darkness, and confused intermingling of friend or foe*. San Francisco's shells included a green dye, which confirmed the friendly fire. Atlanta's Captain Samuel Jenkins (1893 IN – 1975 CA) prepared to return fire. However, the gun flashes from San Francisco distinctly disclosed a non-Japanese hull profile, so he realized that he had been hit by friendly fire.

Atlanta was also badly damaged by an enemy torpedo and enemy gunfire. Efforts were made to tow her to Lunga Point, but she was taking on water too fast. Captain Jenkins had the remaining crew and himself offloaded onto Higgins boats, sent out from Guadalcanal. He then had Atlanta sunk with a demolition charge. More than 200 Atlanta sailors died.

- Rear Admiral, Task Force Commander Daniel Callaghan (1890 San Francisco – 11/13/1942 gunfire off Guadalcanal) was aboard the New Orleans-class, 588' long and 62' beam and 24' draft, USS San Francisco (1934 – 1959 scrapped) heavy cruiser as his flagship, as mentioned above. He and others were killed by an enemy shell. Callaghan was born in San Francisco, California; and died on the USS San Francisco. What are the odds?

Seventy-six others on San Francisco were killed in the battle. San Francisco Captain (rank of Commander) and 1916 U.S. Naval Academy graduate Cassin Young (1894 DC – 11/13/1942 off Guadalcanal) was one. Young was a Medal of Honor recipient at Oahu (Pearl Harbor) 12/7/1941, for his fighting and rescue efforts as Captain of the USS Vestal (1909 – 1950 scrapped) repair vessel.

San Francisco was much damaged. She was repaired and upgraded, returning to the Pacific War 2/1943.

As just mentioned, it appears that shells from USS San Francisco killed Scott and others on the USS Atlanta cruiser.

As noted above, Callaghan (also Scott) was awarded the Medal of Honor. Lieutenant Commander Herbert Schonland (1900 ME – 1984 CT), Lieutenant Commander Bruce McCandless (1911 DC – 1968 DC), and Boatswain's Mate 1st Class Reinhardt Keppler (1918 WA – 11/15/1942 off Guadalcanal) of San Francisco's crew were also so honored. Schonland and McCandless were both Naval Academy graduates, classes of 1925 and 1932 respectively. Both retired from the Navy as Rear Admirals. Anyway, four Medal of Honor recipients for one day of fighting on a USS was the most, for World War II.

Five naval flag officers (all Rear Admirals {two star}) were killed in action in World War II. All were U.S. Naval Academy graduates. Besides Scott and Callaghan above, the other three were as follows:

▪ Rear Admiral Isaac Kidd (1884 Cleveland – 12/7/1941 Pearl Harbor, Oahu, Territory of Hawaii) died aboard the Pennsylvania-class, 608' long and 97' beam and 29' draft, USS Arizona (1915 – 12/7/1941 Pearl Harbor sunk by aerial bombs) battleship. Like Scott and Callaghan mentioned above, Kidd was awarded the Medal of Honor. He was the first of the five World War II Rear Admirals killed. In his case, he died on the first day of the War for the United States (although Congress did not declare war until the next day which was a Monday); during the 12/7/1941 Pearl Harbor attack. He was the highest-ranking casualty at Pearl Harbor. He was also the first U.S. Navy flag officer, ever killed in action against any foreign enemy.

As mentioned above, Scott and Callaghan were buried at sea. Kidd was also buried at sea; but in a different matter. His body was never recovered, as in a million particles. His Naval Academy ring was found, heat fused to a bulkhead on the Arizona's bridge – if you can believe it. His trunk of gear was recovered and is on display at the USS Arizona Memorial Museum at Pearl Harbor.

The Navy named three destroyers in Kidd's honor. The first was a Fletcher-class destroyer which fought the last two years of World War II. It is now a museum ship on the Mississippi River at Baton Rouge. The depth of the Mississippi River varies as much as 40' a year. The Kidd floats half the year, and is in dry dock the other half. This USS Kidd was never modernized. She is the only destroyer museum ship to retain its World War II appearance.

The second two Kidd-named destroyers were a Kidd-class guided missile destroyer (1981 – 1998 sold to the Taiwanese Navy and still active), and an Arleigh Burke-class guided missile destroyer. The last was commissioned in 2007 and is now in service.

Kidd's son was also a U.S. Naval Academy graduate. He reached Admiral rank. Kidd's grandson served in the Navy, retiring as a Captain.

- Rear Admiral Henry Mullinnix (1892 IN – 11/24/1943 off Butaritari Island) earned an aeronautical engineering degree at the Massachusetts Institute of Technology in 1923. He became a naval aviator, 1924. He played a key role in developing the air-cooled engine for naval aircraft. He commanded a Task Force. The new, Casablanca-class, 512' long USS Liscome Bay (1943 – 11/24/1943 torpedo sank off Butaritari Island) escort carrier was his flagship. The Kaidai-type (KD6B sub-class) IJN I-175 (1938 – 2/4/1944, USS destroyer hedgehog sank, all 70-crew lost) cruiser submarine launched a torpedo into the carrier's stern, which detonated the aircraft bomb stockpile. The explosion engulfed the ship and sent shrapnel flying 2.8 miles. Liscome Bay went under twenty-three minutes later.

  Casualties were 644 of 916 crewmen and Mullinnix's flag staff (70%). Deaths included Liscome Bay Captain Harold Wiltsie (1898 Hartford – 11/24/1943 off Butaritari Island), and Third Class Messman Doris Miller (1919 Waco – 11/24/1943 off Butaritari Island). African American Miller was famous for his heroic exploits aboard USS West Virginia (1923 – 12/7/1941 sunk at Pearl Harbor, raised and repaired and modernized, 1959 scrapped) battleship, at Pearl Harbor 12/7/1941.

  Mullinnix was awarded the Legion of Merit.

  A Forrest Sherman-class destroyer was named after Mullinnix and served more than 30 years (1958-1992 scrapped).

- Rear Admiral Theodore Chandler (1894 Annapolis – 1/7/1945 off Manila Bay) was born in Annapolis, Maryland; which is the home of the U.S. Naval Academy. As far as is known, he and Lieutenant Ernest Cody (1914 Annapolis – 8/16/1942 disappeared) are the only two Academy graduates who were born in Annapolis. Cody was commander of the L-class, L-8 helium blimp on anti-submarine patrol off San Francisco. The blimp landed several hours after launch in Daly City, eight miles southwest of San Francisco. The gondola door was open. Neither Cody nor his crewman were in the gondola. Their bodies were never discovered. Their disappearance remains a mystery.

  When commanding the Northampton-class, 600' long and 66' beam and 23' draft, USS Louisville (1931 – 1959 scrapped) heavy cruiser, she was struck by a kamikaze but was able to continue. The next day, another kamikaze struck near the bridge. Chandler helped deploy fire hoses alongside enlisted men to put out fires. He waited his turn for first aid, with those same ratings. He died the next day from scorched lungs.

Chandler was awarded the Legion of Merit and the Silver Star.

A Gearing-class destroyer and a Kidd-Class guided missile destroyer were named after Chandler. Both ships sailed many years.

Again, all five were Naval Academy graduates, and Rear Admirals (one star).

Battleship Arizona's surviving superstructure was scrapped in 1942. Both forward turrets were left in place. The second turret guns were salvaged, straightened, relined; and then installed on the Nevada-class, 583' long and 95' beam and 29' draft, USS Nevada (1916 – 1948 target sunk Bikini Atoll) battleship, in the fall of 1944. Nevada was much damaged in the Pearl Harbor raid. Repairs took until 10/1942. Nevada used these Arizona guns later in the War, including at Iwo Jima and Okinawa.

Legislation during the administrations of Presidents Dwight Eisenhower (1890 TX – 1969 D.C., congestive heart failure) and John Kennedy (1917 MA - 1963 Dallas, rifle assassination) resulted in the designation of the Arizona wreck as a national shrine in 1962. A memorial structure was made over the ship's sunken remains. The structure and the ship though do not touch. A shrine room lists the names of the dead crewmen on a marble wall. The national memorial was listed on the National Register of Historic Places in 1966. The ship herself was designated a National Historic Landmark in 1989.

The USS Arizona Memorial visitor center opened in 1980. It is operated by the National Park Service. The Arizona gets a million visitors a year. Access is by boat. The Memorial marks the resting place of the 1,102 sailors and Marines killed on the battleship.

As already mentioned, there was some luck here. More than a thousand Arizona sailors and marines were on shore leave at the time of the strike, which was early on a Sunday morning.

Many Navy, Coast Guard, and Merchant Marine vessels entering Pearl Harbor participate in the manning the rails tradition. Ship personnel stand at attention at their ship's guard rails and salute the Arizona Memorial in solemn fashion, as their ship slowly glides into port. In some cases, the sailors of foreign warships do similar when participating with the U.S. in naval war games.

USS Arizona is an active U.S. military cemetery. The flagpole is attached to the severed mainmast of the sunken battleship.

Crewmembers assigned to the USS Arizona who survived the sneak attack have the option of having their ashes placed aboard. Chief Petty Officer Stanley Teslow (1917 IA – 1982 CA),was the first who chose to return to his ship and shipmates, in 1982. As of 2019, more than 30 cremains of Arizona survivors have been placed inside the barbette of gun turret four. The Fleet Reserve Association conducts the two-bell ceremonies. The Navy or the Marines provide a rifle salute. A benediction is delivered. Taps are played. The divers swim out with the urn, and then dive to place it.

Sailors who served on the Arizona before she was sunk have the option of having their ashes scattered over her, and some have.

The USS Arizona Memorial has come to commemorate all U.S. military personnel killed in the Oahu (Pearl Harbor) attack. This sum is 2,335. These were 86 % Navy, 9% Army including Army Air Forces, and 5% Marines.

1905 U.S. Naval Academy graduate Rear Admiral John Wilcox (1882 GA – 3/27/1942 off Sable Island) was appointed Task Force 39 Commander 3/1942. The Task Force consisted of the North Carolina-class, 729' long and 108' beam and 38' draft, USS Washington (1941 – 1961 sold for scrap) battleship as his flagship, one aircraft carrier, two heavy cruisers, and eight destroyers. He went overboard off Sable Island (off Canada) two days later. His body was spotted, but efforts to recover were not successful due to rough seas. The investigation was not able to determine why he went overboard.

To sum up, six U.S. Navy Admirals (all Rear Admirals) died in World War II; five in action and one who went overboard for unknown reasons. Admiral Kidd on Pearl Harbor Day was the first of the six. As already noted, he was also the first U.S. Navy Admiral to die in action.

Only one U.S. Navy flag officer has died during duty, since World War II. Rear Admiral Rembrandt Robinson (1924 PA - 5/8/1972 Gulf of Tonkin). Robinson commanded Cruiser Destroyer Flotilla 11 and Seventh Fleet Cruiser Destroyer Group Vietnam. His flagship was the Cleveland-class, 610' long and 66' beam and 26' draft, USS Providence (1945 – 1980 scrapped) light cruiser. Robinson and three others on his command staff flew by helicopter from Providence to the Midway-class, 968' long, USS Coral Sea (1947 – 1980 scrapped) aircraft carrier. The purpose of the meeting was to address air and surface attack coordination for the upcoming Operation Pocket Money (aerial mining campaign to halt or slow down the enemy's transport of supplies and materials). The twin engine helicopter on the night return flight to Providence lost an engine on approach and crashed into the Gulf of Tonkin. Robinson and two of his command staff died (a Captain and a Commander) in the crash. One of his command staffers survived, as did the helicopter crew.

To sum up again, seven Admirals (flag officers) have died on duty, in the history of the United States Navy. All seven were Rear Admirals. Six of the seven were graduates of the U.S. Naval Academy, Annapolis, Maryland (all except the last, Rear Admiral Rembrandt). As noted above, six died during World War II – five in battle in the Pacific Theater and one went overboard for unknown reasons off Canada. The seventh was killed in a non-combat helicopter crash during the Vietnam War.

12- MESSMAN THIRD CLASS DORIS MILLER - RACISM IN THE NAVY

African American Doris Miller was the third of four sons, raised by farm sharecroppers near Waco, Texas. One of his brothers served in the Army during World War II.

Besides a big man at 75" tall and more than 200 pounds, he was very strong and athletic. He played high school football one year, as a star fullback. At age 17, he was put back in the eighth grade with 14-year olds for academic reasons. For this reason and as the family farm made little money (this was during the 1929-1941, worldwide, economic Great Depression), he dropped out of school. He worked on the family farm. He also worked as a cook at a small Waco restaurant.

When he was almost 20 years old, Miller enlisted in the Navy. At the time, African Americans were denied most ratings in the Navy. They worked all or mostly all in supply, food service, housekeeping, and laundry; on shore or at sea. On USSs, these were referred to as *messman* or *steward* duties.

Other minorities and whites also worked in these messman positions. However, whites and other minorities had no limitations as to ratings and opportunities.

After initial training, Miller was assigned to the 482' long and 60' beam and 20' draft, USS Pyro (1920 – 1946 scrapped) ammunition ship briefly, as a Mess Attendant. In 1/1940, he transferred to the Colorado-class, 624' long and 97' beam and 31' draft, USS West Virginia (1920 – 12/7/1941 aerial bombs sunk Pearl Harbor, raised and repaired and modernized, 1959 scrapped) battleship. He was the main cook, which was considerable work and responsibility with the ship's crew of 1,407 men. He also was the battleship's heavyweight boxing champion.

In 7/1941, he transferred to the Nevada-class, 583' long and 95' beam and 29' draft, USS Nevada (1916 – 1948 target sunk) battleship, where he received gunnery training. After several months, he was transferred back to USS West Virginia.

West Virginia was in port at Pearl Harbor, Oahu, Territory of Hawaii; the morning of 12/7/1941. Miller got up at 6:00. He prepared and served breakfast. At 7:57 when he was collecting soiled laundry, the first of nine Japanese aerial torpedoes and/or armor-piercing bombs sliced into West Virginia. Miller ran to his battle station. This was an anti-aircraft, battery magazine, amidships. A Japanese aerial torpedo though had just destroyed this station.

Miller carried some wounded sailors to places of greater safety. An officer, well aware of Miller's youth and size and strength, ordered Miller to follow him to the bridge to help carry the battleship's severely wounded Captain Mervyn Bennion (1887 UT – 12/7/1941 Pearl Harbor) below. A shrapnel shard had hit Bennion in the gut. Miller and another sailor moved Bennion to a more protected area on the bridge, behind the conning tower. He was too grievously wounded to move down below. Bennion was still aware though. He refused to leave his command post anyway. He questioned his officers on the condition of his ship and issued orders.

Another officer ordered Miller to assist in loading and firing two, unmanned Browning .50 caliber anti-aircraft machine guns; aft of the conning tower. Although African Americans at the time were only allowed to be messmen or stewards, they were still required to race to battle stations when General Quarters was called, and to also respond when damage control was necessary. Miller had received some training, but not much. Minimal training in the areas of battle and ship emergencies (fires, flooding) was the rule, in the case of African Americans.

As it turned out, Miller had not been trained on the Browning .50 caliber anti-aircraft machine gun. From instructions provided by other sailors and from observation, he learned fast. He ran out of ammunition.

Another officer ordered Miller back up to the bridge to move Bennion to the navigation section of the bridge, as the Captain was now engulfed in thick oily smoke from the many fires on and around the West Virginia. They toted the semi-unconscious Captain up. Bennion died shortly thereafter. He was a U.S. Naval Academy graduate, third in his 1910 class. He was awarded the Medal of Honor posthumously.

When there was a lull in the attack, Miller helped move injured sailors through oil and water to the quarterdeck, saving lives.

West Virginia was severely listing. Her crew prevented her capsizing, by counter-flooding several compartments. The battleship sank in the shallow harbor but remained level.

This put out some fires. Part of the superstructure though remained above water (the harbor was shallow here), requiring sailors to fight these fires. One hundred and six West Virginia sailors died in the attack. Sixty-six of these were found during repairs. At least one or maybe three of these 66 lasted at least 16 days. Rescuers did not realize they were trapped in a storeroom compartment. These three survived these days on emergency rations and fresh water from a battle station. They apparently died of suffocation, replacing the oxygen in the sealed compartment with their exhaled carbon dioxide.

West Virginia was raised, repaired, and modernized. However, she did not return to fighting status (after sea trials) until 9/1944. She fought in the Leyte Gulf, Philippines, Iwo Jima, and Okinawa campaigns. After Japan surrendered 8/1945, West Virginia ferried American military home. She remained inactive until scrapped in 1959.

Miller was recognized as one of the first U.S. heroes of World War II. After such a one-sided shellacking, the U.S. needed heroes. Navy Secretary Frank Knox (1874 Boston – 1944 D.C.) commended him in a 4/1/1942 letter.

On 4/2/1942, CBS radio dramatized his actions on its *They Live Forever* series.

Miller was the first African American to be awarded the Navy Cross, the Navy's third highest valor medal at the time. However, there was some foot dragging because of Miller's race. President Franklin Roosevelt (1882 NY – 4/12/1945 GA, cerebral hemorrhage) finally approved, 5/11/1942. This was more than five months after his actions.

Pacific Fleet Commander in Chief Admiral Chester Nimitz (1885 TX – 1966 CA) personally recognized Miller 5/27/1942 aboard the 827' long, USS Enterprise

(1938 – 1960 scrapped) aircraft carrier. Nimitz said of Miller's commendation: *This marks the first time in this conflict that such high tribute has been made in the Pacific Fleet to a member of his race, and I'm sure that the future will see others similarly honored for brave acts.*

Miller's citation reads as follows:

> *For distinguished devotion to duty, extraordinary courage, and disregard for his own personal safety during the attack on the Pearl Harbor Fleet, Hawaii Territory, by Japanese forces 12/7/1941. While at the side of his Captain on the bridge, despite enemy strafing and bombing and in the face of a serious fire, assisted in moving his Captain, who had been mortally wounded, to a place of greater safety, and later manned and operated a machine gun directed at enemy Japanese attacking aircraft, until ordered to leave the bridge.*

Miller is shown below. The second picture is Admiral Nimitz pinning the medal.

Miller's valor was heavily publicized in the black press. This made him an iconic emblem of the war for blacks. Up to this time, many African Americans were not so much anti-Japanese as one would think, even considering the Empire of Japan's fourteen sneak attacks 12/7, 8/1941. Nine of the 14 targets belonged to the U.S., as follows:

- Storming and capture of a 159' long USS river gunboat and its crew when berthed at Shanghai Harbor; this little gunboat was the only USS that Japan captured in World War II
- Gun sinking of an Army-chartered, 250' long freighter off California; all aboard died
- Bombing of Howland and Baker Islands of the Phoenix Islands of the U.S. Minor Outlying Islands, these two islands are 43 miles apart
- Attack of five U.S. military installations (harbors, airfields, bases) on five Pacific Ocean islands; these five islands were Oahu (Pearl Harbor), Guam, Midway, Wake, and Philippines

This lack of patriotism in the case of some African Americans stemmed from the fact that some African Americans favored Japanese as after all persons of color;

and also of course because of the racial discrimination existing in the U.S., especially in the South. In regard to the persons of color statement, this is based upon the usual American definition that anyone who is not white, is a person of color. For the record, others define differently.

Miller was transferred to the Portland-class, 610' long and 66' beam and 24' draft, USS Indianapolis (1932 – 7/30/1945 Japanese submarine torpedo sank between Guam and Leyte, loss of 879 of 1,196 sailors and marines{74%}) heavy cruiser, 12/1941. He was promoted to Mess Attendant First Class 6/1/1942.

Miller returned to the U.S. 12/1942 to participate in a war bond tour. He gave talks in Oakland, California; Dallas; his Waco, Texas hometown; and to the first graduating class of black sailors from Great Lakes Naval Training Station, Chicago.

Miller was promoted to Petty Officer, Ship's Cook Third Class, 6/1/1943. He was assigned to the new, Casablanca-class, 542' long, USS Liscome Bay (1943 – 11/24/1943 IJN submarine torpedo sank) escort aircraft carrier. The Kaidai-type (KD6B sub-class), 345' long and 27' beam and 15' draft, IJN I-175 (1938 – 2/4/1944 American destroyers hedgehog-sank off Kwajalein Atoll of the Marshall Islands, all 70 crew lost) cruiser submarine torpedoed Liscome Bay in the stern, in the Makin Atoll Battle off the Gilbert Islands. This was during Operation Galvanic, which was the effort to seize Makin and Tarawa Atolls in the Gilbert Islands. This detonated the aircraft bomb magazine. The carrier sank in minutes.

Six hundred and thirty-two of 904 crew (69.9%) died, including Miller. Liscome Bay Captain Irving Wiltsie (1898 CT – 11/24/1943 off Gilbert Islands) also died. He was a 1921 graduate of the U.S. Naval Academy.

Liscome Bay was Rear Admiral Henry Mullinnix's (1892 IN – 11/24/1943 off Gilbert Islands) flagship. He also died. He was one of five Navy flag officers killed in action in World War II. All five were Rear Admirals (one star). All five were U.S. Naval Academy graduates. All five died in the Pacific Theater. These five were also the U.S. Navy's first admirals ever, to die in battle. A sixth Rear Admiral who was also a Naval Academy graduate died during World War II. The cause of his death is not certain, but probably suicide by jumping overboard off Canada.

Besides the Navy Cross and the Purple Heart, Miller was awarded the Combat Action Ribbon, Good Conduct Medal, American Defense Service Medal, American Campaign Medal, Asiatic-Pacific Campaign Medal, and the World War II Victory Medal.

Miller's picture wearing his Navy Cross medal was used for a 1943 recruiting poster, created by David Stone (1913 Chicago – 1992 CT).

The USPS issued a stamp to honor Miller, in 2010.

Dozens of entities (schools, community centers, housing projects, military installations, etc.) were named in his honor after his death. The Veterans Administration Medical Center in Waco carries his name.

The Knox-class, 438' long and 47' beam and 25' draft, USS Miller (1973 – 1999 sold to Turkey) destroyer escort was named in honor of Miller. She was the third USS named after an African American. The first two were as follows:

- Buckley-class, USS Harmon (1943 – 1967 scrapped) destroyer escort; Mess Attendant First Class Leonard Harmon (1917 TX – 11/13/1942 Ironbottom Sound, struck by enemy gunfire on the New Orleans-class, USS San Francisco cruiser in Guadalcanal Naval Battle) was awarded the Navy Cross for valor; he was assisting a Pharmacist's Mate caring for wounded by deliberately positioning self between the Pharmacist's Mate and enemy gunfire, to protect him; 77 San Francisco sailors were killed, including San Francisco's Captain and the Rear Admiral using San Francisco as his flagship
- Benjamin Franklin-class, nuclear-powered USS George Washington Carver (1966 – 1994 scrapped) ballistic-missile submarine; Carver (1864 MO – 1943 AL) was a botanist and environmentalist (was never in the military)

As of 2019, four more USSs have been named in honor of African Americans. Furthermore, two more are under construction.

As noted above at the time of World War II, African Americans in the Navy were limited to messman type ratings only. There was at least one exception. A letter to the editor printed in the January/February 2017 *World War II* magazine (page 9) from George Rumble of Moon Township, Pennsylvania, stated that he met an African American sailor in 1943 at the Casco Bay, Maine recruiting station. His last name was Cobb. Chief Petty Officer Cobb told Mr. Rumble that he had enlisted in the Navy and was assigned as a stoker on an old coal-burning ship. He was promoted several times, to eventually Watertender First Class. Watertenders tended to the fires and boilers on external-combustion, steam-powered ships. Watertenders were a petty officer rating, which ran 1884-1948. So per Mr. Rumble's report, there was at least one exception of an African American in the Navy with a rating other than messman (was a non-commissioned officer).

The Navy enlisted African Americans for general service from its second formation in 1794 after the Revolution until 1893, which was 28 years after the Civil War ended. In that year and on, African Americans were only allowed to join the messman's and steward's branches. This segregated African Americans from others in the Navy. It also prevented African Americans from becoming non-commissioned or commissioned officers. From the end of World War I (1918) to 1932, African Americans were barred from joining the Navy for any position – but there were a few exceptions.

Some African Americans were in the U.S. military when World War II started; but only in segregated units. The officers of these units were all or almost all white men.

In 6/1941, President Roosevelt issued Executive Order 8802, which banned racial discrimination by any government agency. This included the U.S. military. Included or not, the military branches made no changes in regard to integration -- or if any, very minor. This was six months before the U.S. entered World War II.

On 12/9/1941 which was two days after the Empire of Japan sneak attacked five U.S. military sites (bases, airfields, harbors) on five Pacific Ocean islands, the

National Association for the Advancement of Colored People (NAACP) sent a telegram to Navy Secretary Frank Knox (1874 MA – 1944 D.C.), asking that African Americans be accepted into the Navy in other than the messman branch. The Navy replied, *thank you but no thank you.*

A 12/17/1941 NAACP follow-up letter to Roosevelt resulted in the President turning the matter over to the Chairman of the Fair Employment Practices Committee. The Committee told the Navy to meet the request. The Navy again replied negatively. Roosevelt then sent a note to the Navy Secretary stating: *I think that with all the Navy activities, BuNav might find something that colored enlistees could do, in addition to the rating of messman.*

BuNav was the Bureau of Navigation. BuNav was established in 1862 to provide nautical charts and instruments and to oversee navigation research. In 1889, BuNav was given responsibilities for personnel management, and this eventually became its primary function. The name BuNav of course was now misleading. The name was changed to the Bureau of Naval Personnel (BuPers) in 1942, This name is still used today.

The Navy's General Board, the body charged with the formulation of changes in Navy policy, countered with a disingenuous and/or misleading suggestion that African Americans either be enlisted as messmen only (as in the past), or for general service if limited to messmen ratings was not feasible. The Navy (or the Navy decision makers here) believed that integrated units would disrupt discipline aboard ships. This was despite the fact that the Navy had no known issues of note as noted above during the 100-year, 1794-1893 period (which included the War of 1812 and the Civil War) when the Navy was integrated, and African Americans were eligible for all ratings.

President Roosevelt responded in compromise mode, agreeing that *...to go the whole way in one fell swoop would seriously impair the general average efficiency of the Navy.* However, Roosevelt knew the following:

- that blocking African Americans from ratings other than messmen/steward had no basis
- that the Navy (and all the military branches, for that matter) needed good men, so blocking African Americans from duty of any type slowed and hindered the War effort

Therefore, Roosevelt kept pushing. Roosevelt was also being pushed as well, from the NAACP, labor groups, Assistant Navy Secretary Adlai Stevenson (1900 Los Angeles – 1965 London), his wife Eleanor Roosevelt (1884 NYC – 1962 NYC), etc.

Roosevelt was definitely pro-integration. Most historians credit him as masterful in getting integration of the military to occur, sooner than later.

On 3/27/1942, the Navy Board replied, *The General Board fully recognizes, and appreciates the social and economic problems involved, and has striven to reconcile these requirements with what it feels must be paramount at any consideration, namely the maintenance at the highest level of the fighting efficiency of the Navy...,* adding that *...if so ordered... Negro units could be used*

...with least disadvantage... in shore establishments, local defense vessels, construction units, and selected Coast Guard cutters.

Roosevelt accepted this half-hearted response as a *yes*. He ordered the Navy on 4/7/1942 to move forward. The Navy announced that Negroes could enlist for the general service, beginning 6/1/1942.

Also, the Navy began an accelerated two-month officer training course for 16 African American enlisted men at Camp Robert Smalls, Recruit Training Center Great Lakes (now Naval Training Great Lakes) near Chicago, Illinois.

For the record, enslaved African American Robert Smalls (1839 SC – 1915) was the pilot on the 140' long and 30' beam and 4' draft, CSS Planter (1861 – 1876 sprang a leak, beached, damaged beyond repair) side-wheel steamer, transport ship. The South used Planter as an armed dispatch and transport ship.

On 5/13/1862, Planter's captain and her two junior officers were ashore for the night at Charleston Harbor. All white officers ashore was against standing orders, in the case of a slave crew. Smalls at age 22 donned a Captain's hat, hoisted the flag, and ascended to the bridge. In other words, he took command. This was before dawn. He had been planning such an escapade for more than a year. He had the crew build steam up. First Smalls backtracked up the Cooper River to pick up his wife and children (four-year-old daughter, infant son), and families of other slaves who were crew on Planter. The family members were ready, as this had been pre-arranged.

Smalls sailed past four Confederate checkpoints on or in the harbor. These were Castle Pinckney, Fort Ripley, Fort Johnson, and Fort Sumter. This he accomplished by flying the South Carolina and Confederate flags, and greeting with the correct signals of the Confederate Navy. Smalls had learned these signals from his officer masters. As soon as he was out of range of successive Confederate forts, he hauled down the two flags and hoisted a white (surrender) flag (this was a bedsheet) – so as to not engage USSs blockading Charleston Harbor.

Smalls turned Planter and its cargo of artillery and explosives over to the three-mast, 175' long and 35' beam and 21' draft, USS Onward (1852 – 1884 sold) clipper ship of the South Atlantic Blockading Squadron. As Union officers boarded Planter, Smalls came to attention, saluted, and stated: *I am delivering this war materiel including these cannons, and I think Uncle Abraham Lincoln can put them to good use.*

Besides the ship and its armament and its cargo, Smalls also brought South Atlantic Blockading Squadron Commander Rear Admiral Samuel Du Pont (1803 NY – 1865 Philadelphia) valuable intelligence, including word that the Confederates had abandoned defensive positions on the Stono River. The tidal channel Stono River is located southwest of Charleston. This was 13 months into the Civil War.

To say the least, this was a gutsy thing to do. Smalls and fifteen slaves (seven crewmen, five women, three children) gained their freedom. If Smalls had been caught, he would have been imprisoned or sold or even executed – or maybe not, the Confederate Navy had a great need for skilled pilots. Most likely, the other crew slaves aboard (and maybe their families, as well), would have fared harshly as collaborators.

In 12/1863, the Union Navy appointed Smalls captain of Planter, now a USS gunship. He was the first black man to command a USS. However, he was a civilian, not in the Union Navy. He served as Planter's captain or as a Union warship pilot, until 1866.

Smalls' actions helped convince President Abraham Lincoln (1809 KY – 4/15/1865, pistol assassination in the DC) to accept African American soldiers into the Union Army and Navy.

After the Civil War, Smalls opened a general store in South Carolina which served freedmen. He bought his deceased master's mansion in Beaufort, which had been foreclosed on due to failure to pay taxes. He edited the *Beaufort Southern Standard* newspaper. He became a politician, a Republican of course.

In 1868, Smalls was a delegate to the South Carolina convention charged with writing a new state constitution, which guaranteed voting rights to freedmen and free public education for their children. Over the next three decades, he was elected to both houses of the South Carolina legislature, and then to the U.S. House of Representatives where he served five terms. He worked closely with Andrew Johnson (1808 NC – 1875 TN) and social reformer, abolitionist, orator, writer, and statesman Frederick Douglass (1818 MD – 1895 DC) on plans for Reconstruction.

In 2007, the U.S. Army commissioned a new Kuroda-class, 314' long, logistics support vessel named in Smalls' honor. The USAV Major General Robert Smalls was the first Army ship named in honor of an African American. The Army uses ships of this type to transport general and vehicular cargo. The vessel has huge bow and stern loading ramps. The ship has a 10,500 square foot central cargo deck, big enough to hold 24 M-1 Abrams battle tanks. Many of Smalls' relatives were on hand for the commissioning ceremony. USAV stands for U.S. Army Vessel.

Twelve of the sixteen graduates from the training program at Great Lakes mentioned above were commissioned as ensigns, 3/1944. One was appointed as a Warrant Officer. The *Golden Thirteen* (as they came to be called) were the first African Americans commissioned and warrant officers in the Navy (with the at least one exception of Warrant Officer Cobb, mentioned above). At the time, the Navy had 100,000 African American men, serving in the enlisted ranks.

At the time again, Navy policy prevented combat ship assignment for African American officers. These thirteen black officers ended up running labor gangs ashore. What a waste of talent and training.

As part of the program to integrate though, two new World War II warships were staffed with partial African American crews, as follows:

- The PC-461-class, 174' long and 23' beam and 6' draft, 22 miles per hour, 65 crew, USS PC-1264 (1944 – 2008 sold for scrap, still floating though in 2019) patrol and submarine chaser was made to intercept and destroy German submarines prowling off U.S. coasts, and to provide convoy protection. She served 4/1944 – 2/1946, almost 22 months. Her commanders were as follows:

o White Lieutenant Eric Purdon (1913 Philippines – 1989 MD) from her 1944 commissioning to 9/17/1945 (after World War II ended)
o White Lieutenant Junior Grade Ernest Hardman to 10/31/1945
o White Lieutenant Junior Grade Jack Sutherland was next to 2/7/1946, when de-commissioned
o African American Ensign Samuel Gravely (1922 VA – 2004 MD) was in charge after the decommissioning; he reported aboard 5/2/1945, and was serving as Executive Officer when assigned command after the ship's decommission; Gravely was commissioned as an Ensign eight months after the Golden Thirteen mentioned above; his training and then commission track was driven by the demand for Naval and Marine officers, because of World War II; Gravely's path was as follows:

- Attended Virginia Union University, a historically black university in his home town of Richmond, Virginia; did not graduate
- Joined the Naval Reserve in 1942
- Received basic training at Naval Station Great Lakes, Illinois
- Entered the V-12 Navy College Training Program at the University of California Los Angeles (UCLA)I; the V-12 program was set up to train men to be Navy and Marine commissioned officers, as needed greatly to meet World War II staffing requirements; the U.S. Naval Academy in Annapolis as just one university, was not able to meet the demand; between 7/1943 and 6/1946, more than 125,000 men enrolled in 131 U.S. colleges and universities in this program
- Upon graduation from UCLA, completed the U.S. Navy Reserve Midshipmen's School at Columbia University, Upper Manhattan, New York City; Midshipmen's School was an expedited (four-month program) auxiliary naval officer training program which began in 1940; its mission was to train 36,000 Naval Reserve officers for commands in the greatly-expanding Navy, which was being built up, as U.S. entry into World War II seemed likely; several of these new Naval Reserve Midshipmen's Schools were established, mostly on college campuses; many who attended Midshipmen's School were graduates of the V-12 training mentioned above, which was the case with Gravely; most program graduates went on to active duty in the Pacific Theater

Gravely was commissioned as an Ensign 11/14/1944; as just noted, this was eight months after the Golden Thirteen described above became the first African American officers in the U.S. Navy (except for warrant officer Cobb, mentioned above); he was released from active duty in 1946; he remained in the Reserves though; Gravely wed (three children); the couple moved to his hometown of Richmond; he returned to Virginia Union University, and graduated in 1948 with a degree in history; he got a job as a postal clerk

Gravely was recalled to active duty in 1949 and worked as a recruiter in the D.C.; he held both shore and sea assignments during the Korean War; during the Korean War, he served on the Iowa-class, 887' long and 108' beam and 37' draft, USS Iowa (1943 – 1990 Los Angeles museum ship) battleship as a communications officer; he transferred from the Reserves to the regular Navy in 1955; he specialized in naval communications; he served during the Vietnam War; Gravely's career achievements included many firsts for an African American Navy officer:

- To command a USS combat ship, 1961; this was the Gearing-class, 391' long and 40' beam and 14' draft, USS Theodore E. Chandler (1947 – 1975 scrapped) destroyer
- To command a second USS combat ship, 1962; this was the Edsall-class, 306' long and 37' beam and 10' draft, USS Falgout (1943 – 1977 target sunk) destroyer escort
- To lead a USS into combat, 1966; this was the Sumner-class, 377' long and 37' beam and 16' draft, USS Taussig (1944 – 1974 transferred to Taiwan) destroyer; performed airplane guard duty and gunfire support off the coast of Vietnam
- To reach the rank of Captain, 1967
- To reach the rank of Admiral (Rear Admiral), 1971

    At the time of his promotion to Rear Admiral, Gravely commanded the Somers-class, 547' long and 55' beam and 11' draft, USS Jouett (1939 – 1946 scrapped) destroyer

    Gravely later commanded Cruiser-Destroyer Group 2; next named the Naval Communications Director; commanded the Hawaii-based Third Fleet (more than one hundred ships) 1976-1978; transferred to Virginia to direct the Defense Communications Agency, until his 1980 retirement as a (three star) Vice Admiral; he was buried at Arlington National Cemetery; the Arleigh Burke-class, 510' long and 66' beam and 33' draft, USS Gravely (2010 – in service) guided missile destroyer was named in his honor

The job of eight white petty officers, one in each specialty required for a submarine chaser, was to train the African American crew, until these officers and Lieutenant Purdon considered black men expert enough in their specialty, to rate promotion to petty officer. Several months later, eight African American crewmen were promoted in their specialties. At this time (9/1944), the eight white petty officers were transferred. This made PC-1264 the only Navy ship with an all-black crew (but with a white Captain). Again however, the crew including the Captain (Samuel Gravely) were all black men, after the decommissioning.

The crew experienced various degrees of racial intolerance, especially in the South. For example, crew members were not allowed to qualify in swimming off a pier at the municipal public beach at Miami Beach; as the city of Miami Beach refused the use of its public beach for the training of Negroes.

PC-1264 operated in the Atlantic, along the East Coast of the U.S. and south to the Caribbean Sea area. She trained and drilled, did anti-submarine patrol, and escorted convoys. When the Atlantic Battle of World War II ended 5/1945, she was ordered to report to the Commander-in-Chief, Pacific Fleet. Anti-aircraft guns were installed and gunners trained, to protect from kamikazes. She got as far as Key West, when V-J Day came. This is the furthest west that PC-1264 ever sailed.

PC-1264 was decommissioned. She was transferred to the Maritime Commission for final disposition. She floats (just barely) today at the former Donjon Marine Yard in New York.

Purdon entered the Naval Reserve. He worked as an intelligence analyst for the Central Intelligence Group until 1948. He was called back to active duty. He retired from the Navy as a Commander in 1963. He held civilian jobs with the Commerce Department, Office of Economic Opportunity, and the Job Corps.

Purdon kept in touch with many of the black crew members from PC-1264. They submitted recollections for his 1972 book, *Black Company*. Sam Gravely was one who provided memories and thoughts.

- The Evarts-class, 289' long and 35' beam and 8' draft, 24 miles per hour, 156 crew, USS Mason (1944 – 1947 scrapped) destroyer escort sailed in the Atlantic as a submarine chaser and convoy escort. She never had any black officers.

On 10/18/1944, Mason supported Convoy NY-119 in a severe North Atlantic storm. She suffered critical structural damage, but still was able to rescue ships in the convoy. Mason's crew was issued a letter of commendation for meritorious service during this action, but not until 50 years later in 1994.

The Arleigh Burke-class, 510' long and 66' beam and 32' draft, USS Mason (2003 – in service) guided missile destroyer, was named in honor of the African Americans who crewed on the World War II Mason.

In 1987, the U.S. Navy reunited the seven living members of the Golden Thirteen to dedicate a building in their honor at Great Lakes Naval Recruit Training Command, Illinois. This is Building 1405 at RTC Great Lakes, where recruits first arrive for basic training.

Darion Ivy III was the last of the thirteen. He died in 2015.

Racism problems did occur in the Navy after integration was mandated. Significant examples included the following:

- 7/1944 The Port Chicago, California munitions disaster reeked of racism
- 12/1944 Racial violence between white and black marines base at a naval base in Agana, Guam; related to black sailors socializing with the local women

- 3/1945 A Seabee battalion of 1,000 African American men staged a hunger strike at their Port Hueneme, California base as blacks were only assigned manual labor, and were not allowed to lead labor details

Other such cases occurred. After the War, Fleet Admiral Ernest King (1878 OH – 1966 MN) and Navy Secretary James Forrestal (1892 NY – 1949 MD) worked with a civilian expert, on further integrating the Navy.

President Harry Truman (1884 MO – 1972 MO) desegregated the entire U.S. military in 1948, by Executive Order 9981. The order abolished discrimination *on the basis of race, color, religion or national origin* for all the U.S. Armed Forces. The executive order eventually led to the end of segregation in the services.

To sum up for the United States Navy, in regard to African American men:

- 1775 – 1785   The Continental Navy for the Revolution ran these years; many sailors were black patriots; others were British black Loyalists, who had been captured from Royal Navy ships; the new Navy disbanded in 1785, due to lack of money, and as thought was that the new country did not need a Navy anyway
- 1794 – 1893   The U.S. created the new Navy to deal with the Barbary Pirates who were preying on American merchant ships in the Mediterranean Sea; the new Navy was mostly integrated

  At the beginning of the 1812 War, Navy policy forbade recruitment of black sailors; due to lack of sailors though, the Navy changed its policy and accepted black sailors who made up at least 15% of the Navy; the British promised Negroes their freedom if they defected and joined the Royal Navy, and many did so

  In the 1840s, Navy regulations limited black sailors to 5% of the enlisted force; this increased to 20% during the Civil War
- 1893 – 1919   Ratings limited to messmen, stewards, coal passers, firemen; some African Americans promoted to petty officers during World War I
- 1919 – 1932   Banned from enlisting
- 1932 – 1942   Ratings limited to messman and steward or a few other ratings, but the latter only in segregated units; Navy was 2.3% African American 6/1940; these numbered 4,007; all were enlisted men; all were steward's mates, except for six regular-rated seamen
- 1944 – to date   Navy fully integrated race-wise, for all ratings

Today, the proportion of the U.S. military that is African America is greater than in the civilian workforce, except for the Marine Corps.

Women were first allowed officially in the Navy in 1908, as nurses. They were allowed to enlist in 1917 for other positions. Navy women in recent years have been eligible for all ratings and assignments as well, except for submarine duty. This changed though in 2011, when female submarine officers were introduced, with enlisted female submariners assigned a few years later.

All Navy combat jobs were made available to women, beginning in 2016.

13- CAPTAIN LOUIS SILVIE ZAMPERINI

Twelve thousand, seven hundred and thirty-one, 74' long and 104' wingspan and 19' tall, low wing, conventional landing gear (retractable), 182 and 287 miles per hour cruise and maximum speeds, 2,000 mile range, four-engine, Boeing B-17 Flying Fortress heavy bombers (including variants) were made 1936-1945 and used in World War II. However, it almost was not accepted by the Army Air Forces, as policy was to not approve purchase of any aircraft prototype if it crashed during test flights.

The prototype took off 10/30/1935 from Wright Field, Dayton, Ohio, on its second evaluation test flight. The crew failed to remove the gust locks. These hold the aircraft's movable control surfaces in place when on the ground, so that they do not flap in the wind when parked and tied down. The plane entered a steep climb, stalled, nosed over, and crashed. The Army Air Corps test pilot and a Boeing observer died. Others aboard survived with injuries. The Army Air Corps was so impressed though with the B-17 that it ordered it through some legal loophole – or maybe just ignored its own requirement.

As a result of the crash, one suggestion adopted was the use of a written pre-flight checklist to avoid accidents, such as the above on not removing the gust lock devices. This is the first known use of such a checklist in aviation. Use of such today is the rule in aviation, no matter the type or size of the aircraft.

Surgeon, author, and public health researcher Dr. Atul Gawande (1965 Brooklyn -) described the B-17 crash and the resultant creation and use of a checklist in his 2009 bestseller book, *The Checklist Manifesto*. The book describes how the medical profession now uses checklists, especially in the case of operative procedures as modern medicine and surgery is so complicated -- as is aviation.

Early on to boost production, the U.S. Army Air Corps in 1938 asked Consolidated Aircraft of San Diego to make B-17s, under license. Consolidated executives including President Reuben Fleet (1887 WA – 1975 CA) visited the Boeing factory in Seattle to evaluate the request.

Consolidated decided instead to submit a more modern design of its own for a heavy bomber, using the newly designed Davis wing. The thick but short chord Davis yielded less drag, and provided much lift at low speeds. The chord is the straight-line distance from the leading to the trailing edges of an airfoil.

The result was the 68' long and 110' wingspan and 18' tall, high wing, twin rudder tail, tricycle landing gear (retractable), two bomb bay, 215 and 290 miles per hour cruise and maximum speeds, 2,100 mile range, four-engine Consolidated B-24 Liberator heavy bomber. Its cruising speed and range at 215 miles per hour and 2,100 miles were more than that of the B-17, although its service ceiling of 28,000' was much less than that of the B-17's 35,600'. It could tote a slightly heavier bomb load. Nineteen thousand and two hundred and fifty-six were made, 1940-1945. The B-24 holds the worldwide record for the most made, of any military aircraft.

The below shows the B-17 Flying Fortress and the B-24 Liberator (restored planes, flying today):

To counter the advantages over the B-17, the B-24 though had some disadvantages. These included the following:

- More difficult to fly, with heavy control forces; so a challenge to fly in formation
- Poor performance at low speeds
- Its greater speed and range came from being light and placing fuel tanks in the upper part of the fuselage, so more vulnerable to flight damage
- Had an irritating tendency to catch fire, again as its fuel tanks were in the upper part of the fuselage
- High fuselage-mounted Davis wing increased likelihood of fuselage breaking apart, if ditching in the ocean or making a belly landing
- The wing when hit a certain way folded or broke off
- Only one exit, at the rear; narrow 9" catwalk from flight deck to rear (if needed to bail out), made passage for flight deck crewmen and nose gunner very difficult, and in fact close to impossible when wearing a parachute; bigger airmen fared the worst here

From the above, it should be mentioned that another B-24 nickname besides *Liberator,* was *Flying Coffin.* This can hinder recruiting, or assignment after fight training.

Louis Zamperini's family moved to Torrance, California from New York State when he was two years old. His parents were both from Italy. They and the children (older brother, two younger sisters) did not speak English (only Italian) at the time of the move, making him a target for bullies. His father taught him how to box, in self-defense. He learned well and became sort of a bully himself. He started smoking and drinking, got into trouble (caught stealing some beer, for one), etc.

Louis' older brother Pete Zamperini (1915 NY – 2008 CA) was a star on the Torrance High School track team, and got Louis involved as well. Being on a team and competition turned Louis around, especially as he turned out to be an excellent mid-distance runner. In 1934 in high school, he ran the mile in 4:21.2. He got a scholarship to the University of Southern California. He qualified for the 1936 Olympics in Berlin. At age 19, he finished eighth in the 5,000 meters. Adolf

Hitler (1889 Austria – 1945 Berlin, pistol suicide) when attending the Olympics asked to meet Zamperini, and they had a few words.

Back at the University of Southern California, Zamperini ran a 4:08 mile in 1938. He graduated in 1940.

Zamperini made the U.S. team for the next Olympics, scheduled to begin 9/1940 in Tokyo. These games of course did not happen, as Hitler started World War II 9/1/1939. Also, Japan was doing horrible things to the Chinese (for several years already, in fact).

Zamperini enlisted in the Army Air Corps 9/1941, commissioned as a Second Lieutenant. He became a B-24 bombardier. After training, he was based at Funafuti Atoll, one of the three Tuvalu Islands. Funafuti is about halfway between Hawaii and Australia.

In a 4/1943 bombing mission on the Japanese-held island of Nauru (Micronesia), his bomber was hit and badly damaged. As his B-24 was no longer flightworthy and some of his crew members injured, Zamperini was transferred to Oahu, Territory of Hawaii, to await reassignment.

Zamperini was sent on a mission 5/27/1943 to conduct a search for another B-24 that had not returned. The search B-24 was called *Green Hornet*. Green Hornet was notorious among the pilots as a lemon. It had one mechanical problem after another. The crew though was reassured, that Green Hornet had recently undergone thorough maintenance checks. The maintenance work turned out to not be that thorough. Green Hornet developed yet another mechanical problem. Pilot Lieutenant Allen Phillips (1916 IN – 1998) was forced to ditch. It did not go well. Eight of the 11-man crew died in the crash water landing, 850 miles south of Oahu.

Besides Zamperini, the other two survivors were pilot Phillips and Staff Sergeant Frank McNamara (19?? – 6/30/1943). They got into a life raft. They subsisted on captured rainwater, and small raw fish they managed to catch. They caught two albatrosses which fed them for a few days, plus they used the bird meat as bait to catch fish. Albatrosses are big birds, over 20 pounds; so provided a lot of (raw) meat. They apparently also are not wary, of humans – at least of humans floating in the middle of the ocean.

They fended off many shark attacks. They were strafed multiple times by a Japanese bomber. They were not hit, but their life raft was punctured. They almost capsized, many times.

On day 33, Sergeant McNamara died of starvation. Zamperini and Phillips said a few words and tossed him into the ocean (buried him at sea).

The Marshall Islands consist of 1,156 islands and islets, summing up to seventy square miles. They are part of the larger island group of Micronesia, which adds up to about 2,100 islands. The Marshalls are located near the equator in the Pacific Ocean, just west of the International Date Line. Spain claimed the Marshalls in 1874. Germany bought the islands from Spain in 1898. When World War I started in 1914, Japan grabbed control of the Marshalls.

Zamperini and Phillips floated 2,000 miles and landed on one of the Marshall Islands on day 47. This was 7/14/1943. The Japanese Navy quickly captured the pair. They were held on Kwajalein Atoll (one of the Marshall Islands) 42 days. They were then transferred to POW camps in Japan. For Zamperini, these were Ofuna outside Yokohama, then Omori in Tokyo, and then Naoetsu in northern Japan. Zamperini was at Naoetsu when repatriated upon Japan's surrender 8/1945. For the record, American forces landed on Marshall Island Kwajalein Atoll 1/31/1944 and then Marshall Island Enewetak Atoll a few days later. The Americans defeated the Japanese. The U.S. controlled the Marshalls as a trust until 1979, when the Marshalls became an independent Republic.

Although abused horribly (especially Zamperini, as he had been an Olympian) for more than two years at prisoner of war (POW) camps on several islands and the Japanese mainland, he and Phillips both survived imprisonment and were repatriated when Japan finally surrendered, 8/1945.

The two men remained in contact. Both wed, Zamperini in 1946. Both had two children. Zamperini and Cynthia Applewhite's (1926 MO – 2001 CA) children were son Luke and daughter Cynthia.

Zamperini's war experiences and time as a much-abused prisoner of war resulted in posttraumatic stress disorder. He became an alcoholic. He had fits of rage and nightmares. He obsessively dreamed of taking revenge on his Japanese tormentors.

Wife Cynthia had gone to Christian evangelist Billy Graham's (1918 Charlotte – 2018 NC) crusade session in Los Angeles. She became a born-again Christian. In a last-ditch effort to save their marriage and him, she and her also born-again friends convinced Louis to attend as well. It worked. He was saved at Graham's 1949 tent revival in downtown Los Angeles.

Zamperini said that Graham's preaching reminded him of his continual prayers on the life raft and in the POW camp, when he made repeated promises to seek and serve God. He said as soon as he made his decision for Christ, he forgave his captors, and never had another nightmare. He stopped drinking and smoking.

Later Graham helped Zamperini launch a new career as a Christian inspirational speaker, focusing on forgiveness and reconciliation.

Also later, Zamperini founded an Outward Bound style program called Victory Boys Camp.

Zamperini forgave his captors, including the notorious, sadistic Corporal Mutshiro Watanabe (1918 Japan – 2003) who beat and tortured him and others over and over and over.

Watanabe was born into a very wealthy family (owned and operated mines, hotels, etc.). After graduating university, he joined the Army. His abuses of POWs are too many and horrible to list (read one of Zamperini's books mentioned below, if you have the stomach for it).

After the War, General Douglas MacArthur (1880 AR – 1964 DC) was military governor of Japan. He and his staff compiled a list of the worst Japanese war criminals.

Watanabe was number 23 on the list. He hid out for seven years. He emerged in 1952 after war crimes prosecutions stopped, and as the U.S occupation of Japan was ending. He sold life insurance and ended up a millionaire. He owned a $1.5

million apartment in Tokyo, and a vacation condominium on the Gold Coast of Australia.

Prior to the 1998 Winter Olympics in Nagano, Japan, CBS's *60 Minutes* interviewed Watanabe in Tokyo as part of a feature on Zamperini, who was carrying the Olympic flame part of the route. In the interview, Watanabe did not apologize. He did acknowledge beating and kicking prisoners. He admitted that he was not ordered to do so; but did so because of his own personal feelings. This was something along the lines, of treating the prisoners as enemies of Japan. This was the best he could come up with. To sum up, he never showed a repentant attitude.

Watanabe was also reported to be a pedophile or pederast. He was accused repeatedly of molesting boys, including relatives.

Zamperini forgave Watanabe and wanted to meet with him, but Watanabe declined the meeting. He was probably fearful of repercussions after some accusatory questions in earlier press interviews, regarding his many abuses of American POWs.

The Worldwide Forgiveness Alliance named Zamperini the Hero of Forgiveness, in 1999.

Zamperini's wife died in 2001.

Zamperini wrote three memoirs (with professional writers) about his experiences, as follows:

- 1956 *Devil at My Heels: The Story of Louis Zamperini* with Helen Itria
- 2003 *Devil at My Heels: A World War II Hero's Epic Saga of Torment, Survival and Forgiveness* with David Rensin
- 2014 *Don't Give Up, Don't Give In: Lessons from an Extraordinary Life* with David Rensin

Zamperini carried the Olympic torch for the 1984 and 1996 Summer Games in Los Angeles and Atlanta, and the 1998 Winter Games in Nagano (Japan). For the latter, he ran past a POW camp where he had been imprisoned. At the time, he was four days shy of age 81.

Zamperini sold his story rights to Universal Pictures, 1957. Tony Curtis (1925 Manhattan – 2010 NV) was receptive to portraying Zamperini. However, he made the 1960 blockbuster *Spartacus* instead with other big-name stars (Kirk Douglas, Charles Laughton, Peter Ustinov, John Gavin, Laurence Olivier). Other efforts were made to make the movie, but again it did not happen.

Author Laura Hillenbrand (1967 VA -) wrote the 2001 bestseller *Seabiscuit: An American Legend,* about the racehorse Seabiscuit (1933 – 1947). The 2003 movie starring Jeff Bridges (1949 CA -) was a moneymaker. Its box office was $148 million versus its $87 million production costs.

When researching Seabiscuit's career, Hillenbrand bought old newspapers to get a sense of context. On the back of one page on the thoroughbred was a story about this running phenomenon, named Louis Zamperini. From this, she later tracked Zamperini down, and interviewed him. She ended up writing the 2010 biography entitled *Unbroken: A World War II Story of Survival, Resilience, and Redemption.*

It became a bestseller. More than four million books sold. It was translated into 29 languages.

Finally, Angelina Jolie (1975 Los Angeles -) directed the 2014 movie (her second movie to direct) titled *Unbroken,* taking the name from Hillenbrand's book. Jack O'Connell (1990 England -) played Zamperini. The film was made for $65 million. Its box office was $163 million.

Oddly, Jolie and Zamperini were neighbors in Hollywood. They could see each other's houses from their own residences.

Zamperini died in 2014, at 97.4 years old. He did not get to see the movie. On the other hand, Jolie went to see him at the hospital before he died. She showed him the movie in 20-minute segments on her laptop computer. However, she did not show him the parts where Watanabe was beating him and other abuses delivered.

14- LIEUTENANT COMMANDER EDWARD HENRY O'HARE

Alphonse Capone (1899 Brooklyn – 1947 FL) had seven siblings. The family lived in a typical Brooklyn tenement building. He joined gangs. In succession, these were the Junior Forty Thieves, the Bowery Boys, the Brooklyn Rippers, and the Five Points Gang. During this time, he worked as a bouncer in organized crime premises such as brothels, among other jobs.

Johnny Torrio (1882 Italy – 1957 Brooklyn, heart attack) headed a crime syndicate in New York City which ran illegal activities such as gambling, loan sharking, prostitution, and opium trafficking. Torrio's aunt Victoria Moresco was the wife and business partner of crime boss Vincenzo Colosimo (1878 Italy – 1920 Chicago, shot). Colosimo owned and operated 100 brothels in Chicago. The Colosimos were also engaged in gambling and racketeering. Their operations were concentrated on Chicago's south side.

For the record, organized crime racketeering means the collection of assets through extortion or coercion, using intimidation or force. These assets are usually in the form of money, but can be property of some sort.

Colosimo continued to expand his operations. Other gangs tried to move in on his territory or extort money from him. Colosimo summoned his nephew Torrio to move to Chicago, to deal with these other gangs. Torrio did so move. He and his henchmen eliminated the competition. He stayed on to continue to aid Colosimo in dealing with threats to his operations, and to assist in running the various illegal businesses.

Torrio knew Capone from his New York City operations. He invited him to move to Chicago as a bodyguard, club manager, and trusted assistant. Capone accepted. This was 1919. Colosimo's and Torrio's operations became known as the *Chicago Outfit.*

Colosimo was murdered. It is suspected that Torrio ordered the wipeout so as to take over the illicit operations, and that Capone was the gunman (we will never know). Torrio though did take over the Chicago Outfit.

The prohibition of alcoholic beverages (Volstead Act) ran 1919 to 1933. Torrio moved into bootlegging, as well as prostitution and gambling and racketeering.

The North Side Gang severely injured Torrio in a 1/24/1925 assassination attempt. He was shot multiple times and beaten; but survived. Torrio was rich. He desired a long life. He chose to retire. He left the Chicago Outfit to Capone. Remnants of the Chicago Outfit are still thought to be operating today.

Capone's main business was bootlegging liquor, plus he also continued with prostitution, gambling, loan sharking, money laundering, extortion, etc. The liquor sales were mostly to brothels. So the two rackets of prostitution and booze complemented each other. Some of the newspapers estimated Capone's income some years during Prohibition to be $100 million. This is $1.49 billion in 2019 money.

Capone gained much fame as well. He became increasingly violent in the case of other gangsters moving on to his turf, or if he thought they were trying to do such. He was implicated for ordering the death of at least 34 men. For what it is worth, these men like Capone were all criminals in some way or another.

Capone threatened and/or bribed (or tried to) city officials including mayors, police chiefs, etc. Numerous police officers were paid off. To sum up, he was not much pursued or encroached on by either other criminals due to his propensity to order killings which were done; or by politicians and the law due to threats and or as bought off.

When it came to prosecution, Capone intimidated witnesses, bought off or tried to buy off jurors and even judges, etc.

Capone made donations to various charities, so many looked favorably on him. This is the Robin Hood effect, of stealing from the rich and giving some to the poor. However, the 1929 Saint Valentine's Day Massacre of the shooting of six rival gang members (North Side Irish gang) and a mechanic in a Lincoln Park (Chicago) garage damaged Capone's reputation. This in fact led influential citizens to demand his arrest and prosecution. Note though that the police were never able to gather enough evidence to charge Capone with ordering the wipeouts.

Edward O'Hare (1893 St. Louis – 1939 Chicago, shot) passed the Missouri bar exam in 1923. He joined a law firm in St. Louis. Starting in 1925, he operated greyhound dog tracks in Chicago, Boston, and Miami. He represented inventor Owen Smith, who was also high commissioner of the International Greyhound Racing Association. Smith patented the mechanical running rabbit that the greyhounds pursue, which creates the race.

Smith payed O'Hare very well. O'Hare and his wife drove deluxe cars. The couple bought a fancy new house, with a swimming pool and a skating rink. He and his family (wife, two daughters, and a son) took long vacations in the summer. O'Hare divorced though in 1927. He moved to Chicago from St. Louis.

Aviation fascinated O'Hare. He somehow once managed to hitch a ride with Charles Lindbergh (1901 Detroit – 1974 HA, lymphoma). He learned to fly himself. He even flew U.S. airmail for a short period of time. He provided opportunities for his teenage son (also) Edward to take the controls. Edward Junior went by the nickname of *Butch*. Butch was a natural aviator.

O'Hare Senior decided that Butch was lazy and lacked direction. For this reason, he enrolled Butch at the Western Military Academy (1879 – 1971) in Alton, Illinois. Alton is 22 miles north of St. Louis. This was a boarding school.

In Chicago, O'Hare Senior met Capone in 1928. Capone hired O'Hare to defend him from various charges. These included contempt of court, for carrying a pistol, for violations of prohibition laws, for vagrancy, for perjury, for bribe attempts, for ordering executions, etc. The authorities were not able to get enough evidence on him for his severe crimes, including having rivals killed. O'Hare was generally successful in getting such charges dropped or reduced against Capone on some technicality, or at least delayed. When tried, O'Hare was similarly successful in getting Capone acquitted, or at least a light sentence.

Owen Smith of the greyhound dog tracks mentioned above, paid O'Hare very, very well. Capone paid O'Hare very, very, very, very well. Also, O'Hare went in on deals with Capone. The result though was that lawyer O'Hare was in Capone's pocket, not able to divest himself.

In 1927, the U.S. Supreme Court ruled that illegally earned income was subject to federal income taxes. In this decision, Justice Oliver Holmes (1841 Boston – 1935 DC) rejected the argument that the Fifth Amendment protected criminals from reporting illegal income. The 1791 Fifth Amendment protects individuals from being compelled to be witnesses against themselves, in criminal cases.

The IRS investigated and determined that Capone must have an enormous income, based upon his prodigious spending. However, Capone paid very little in income taxes, as he could not report his illegal income. As further evidence, Capone had even offered in the past to pay income taxes. Capone did this in an effort to keep the Feds off his back.

Attorney O'Hare came to have regrets in defending such a scoundrel; and getting Capone off to commit more mayhem including murder. He provided evidence in 1930 which greatly contributed to Capone's prosecution and conviction for income tax evasion.

In 1931, Capone was charged with various Volstead Act violations (again, this was the law banning alcoholic beverages) as well as income tax evasion. Later, O'Hare even tipped the government that Capone had fixed or tried to fix the jury.

Capone was convicted and sentenced to 11 years, beginning 5/1932. He appealed unsuccessfully. He was imprisoned 7.7 years. He was released early due to terminal illness (syphilitic dementia).

When driving home from work 11/8/1939, two men in another car pulled up alongside O'Hare Senior. They were armed with shotguns loaded with big game slugs. O'Hare died instantly. No one was ever arrested. This was one week before Capone was released from Alcatraz Federal Penitentiary, California. Presumably though, Capone ordered the killing.

O'Hare was carrying a .32-caliber, semi-automatic pistol when he was killed, but he did not have the opportunity to defend himself.

Some say that O'Hare turned against Capone to improve the chances of his son Butch getting into the U.S. Naval Academy, and to just improve his reputation with his son – Butch knowing that his dad was protecting with legal gyrations and technicalities, a bootlegging, pimping, and murdering gangster.

Butch did in fact matriculate at the Naval Academy. He graduated 1937. He served two years on the New Mexico-class, 624' long and 97' beam and 30' draft, USS New Mexico (1918 – 1947 scrapped) battleship.

Butch took flight training. After flight training, he was assigned to the Lexington-class, 888' long, USS Saratoga (1927 – 1946 atomic bomb sunk test off Bikini Atoll) aircraft carrier; then to the Yorktown-class, 827' long, USS Enterprise (1938 – 1960 scrapped) carrier when Saratoga went in for repairs; and then to the Lexington-class, 888' long, USS Lexington (1927 – 5/8/1942 Japanese air torpedo sank at Coral Sea Battle, 216 of 2,951 crew {7.3%} lost) carrier.

Lexington had been assigned the dangerous task of penetrating enemy held waters, north of New Ireland. The 2,859 square mile New Ireland Island is part of Papua New Guinea. Their offensive mission was to air strike Japanese shipping at Rabaul Harbor. Rabaul is a town on the island of New Britain, Papua New Guinea. An aircraft carrier's first defense of course is its aircraft, fending off enemy ships and aircraft before they can shoot or bomb the carrier.

On 2/20/1942 when still 400 miles from Rabaul harbor, Lexington's radar picked up unknown aircraft 35 miles out. She launched six aircraft. Two fighters intercepted and shot down a four-engine Kawanishi H6K4 Type 97 flying boat, 43 miles out at 11:12. Two other American fighters shot down a second H6K4 at two minutes past noon, 35 miles out. Kawanishis carried four machine guns and a cannon and bombs, so formidable. As flying boats though, they were slow and not maneuverable; so fairly easy for a fighter to shoot down.

A third contact was noted 80 miles out. That aircraft though, turned back.

Lexington aircraft then shot down five of nine approaching Mitsubishi, twin engine, G4M bombers.

Lexington radar detected more unknown aircraft at 16:25, 47 miles west and approaching fast. Lexington launched several aircraft to investigate, including O'Hare in a single engine, Grumman F4F Wildcat. At 16:49, Lexington's radar picked up yet another incoming formation of G4M bombers, only 12 miles out. Lexington's Captain Frederick Sherman (1888 MI – 1957 CA) ordered O'Hare and his wingman Marion Dufilho (1916 LA – 8/24/1942 shot down in aerial combat off Eastern Solomons) to divert, to intercept this closer group of Japanese bombers. The pair headed east and spotted eight G4M bombers at 1,500', nine miles out from Lexington.

Dufilho's guns jammed, leaving O'Hare as Lexington's sole protector. O'Hare had no choice but to take the solo offensive. The Wildcat had four .50 caliber guns, 450 rounds per gun. This came to only 34 seconds of firepower. O'Hare shot down three G4Ms, and damaged two more. Noel Gayler (1914 AL – 2011 VA) shot one of the damaged G4Ms down. The other damaged G4M made it back to base. The two, not hit, Japanese bombers turned tail.

Gayler became an ace in World War II. He was the first person to receive three Navy Crosses. He retired from the Navy in 1976 as a four star Admiral.

O'Hare's marksmanship output was more than impressive, hitting five enemy bombers with so little ammunition. His actions may have saved Lexington from severe damage or even being sunk. However, this lease on life for Lexington did not last long. Japanese torpedo bombers sank Lexington eleven weeks later 5/8/1942 in the Coral Sea Battle. As already noted, two hundred and sixteen of 2,951 crew were lost (7.3%).

When O'Hare returned to land, a Lexington gunner fired on him in error with a .50 caliber anti-aircraft machine gun. After landing, the not yet 28-year old Butch approached that gunner and told him: *Son, if you don't stop shooting at me when I've got my wheels down, I'm going to have to report you to the gunnery officer.* O'Hare's Wildcat had only one bullet hole. This was in the port wing, and disabled his airspeed indicator. Whether it was from the enemy or his own gunner is not known.

Butch was awarded the Medal of Honor for the above, the first naval aviator of World War II to receive. His citation read as follows:

> *For conspicuous gallantry and intrepidity in aerial combat, at grave risk of his life above and beyond the call of duty, as section leader and pilot of Fighting Squadron 3 on 2/20/1942. Having lost the assistance of his teammates, Lieutenant O'Hare interposed his fighter between his ship and an advancing enemy formation of nine attacking twin engine heavy bombers. Without hesitation, alone and unaided, he repeatedly attacked this enemy formation, at close range in the face of intense combined machine gun and cannon fire. Despite this concentrated opposition, Lieutenant O'Hare, by his gallant and courageous action, his extremely skillful marksmanship in making the most of every shot of his limited amount of ammunition, shot down five enemy bombers and severely damaged a sixth before they reached the bomb release point. As a result of his gallant action -- one of the most daring, if not the most daring, single action in the history of combat aviation -- he undoubtedly saved his carrier from serious damage.*

Back in the U.S., Butch flew publicity footage, was awarded the Medal of Honor by President Franklin Roosevelt (1882 NY – 4/12/1945 GA, cerebral hemorrhage) in a ceremony attended by dignitaries, rode in a welcome parade in his hometown of St. Louis, participated in several war bond tours, etc. He earned his Medal of Honor in only the third month of the War. The nation needed a live war hero (the Doolittle Raid came two months later), and he played the role well.

Butch transferred to Maui 6/1942 to train fighter pilots. He returned to combat 8/1943, assigned to USS Enterprise. He was awarded more medals, for his combat actions off Marcus Island and Wake Island 8/1943 and 10/1943 respectively. These are both coral atolls, only 0.5 and 2.7 square miles in land area. Marcus and Wake are located 1,148 and 1,991 miles southeast of Tokyo. Japan occupied Marcus before the War. Wake in turn was occupied by the U.S. Japan sneak attacked Wake 12/8/1941, and killed or captured all American military and civilians by 12/23/1941.

The arrival of the Grumman F6F-3 Hellcat fighters with their powerful engines coupled with the deployment of the Essex-class and Independence-class carriers, immediately gave the U.S. air superiority in areas where operating. The U.S. ruled the skies, at least in daytime. The Japanese quickly developed tactics to send G4M bombers on night missions from their bases in the Marianas, against U.S. Navy Task Groups. In late 11/1943, the Japanese launched these low-altitude strikes almost nightly at USSs, including Enterprise.

O'Hare and his superiors collaborated to develop counter tactics. O'Hare's plan was that the carrier's Fighter Director Officer would spot incoming enemy formations at a distance using the carrier's superior radar, then radio the information to a trio of aircraft launched to intercept. These three planes were two Hellcat fighters, and a single engine, three crew, Grumman TBF Avenger torpedo bomber. The other two Avenger crew besides the pilot were the turret gunner and radioman/bombardier/ventral gunner. They sat one behind the other.

U.S. radar systems for aircraft at the time (1943) were primitive. The radar equipment was also large; so big in fact that the vacuum tube, radar units would not fit in fighter cockpits. The three cockpits of the Avenger as a larger plane were more spacious. The Avenger was 40' long with a 54' wingspan, versus 34' and 42' for the Hellcat. Therefore, the better, radar-equipped Avengers would lead the fighters to the incoming Japanese, torpedo-toting bombers. At this point, the American fighters would be close enough to see the blue exhaust flames of the Japanese bombers. The pilots would aim for these flames, to shoot the incoming bombers down.

The night of 11/26/1943 was selected to put the experiment to the test. O'Hare volunteered to lead the sortie, flying one of the Hellcats behind the Avenger. The trio took off at dusk. Problems arose. The Hellcats took a while to locate the Avenger and get lined up.

As expected, Mitsubishi G4M bombers approached. Enterprise's Flight Director Officer radar-detected, but had difficulty guiding the formation to the incoming bombers. O'Hare was shot down. Most likely, he was shot down by the nose gunner of one of the incoming Japanese bombers. However, some suspect he was shot down by friendly fire when caught in a crossfire.

Three planes were sent out the next morning (11/27/1943) to search. A PBY Catalina flying boat made another search 11/29/1943. Neither O'Hare nor his Hellcat were ever found. He left a wife (Rita) and nine-month-old daughter (Kathi).

This was the Navy's first ever nighttime fighter attack from an aircraft carrier, to intercept a large force of enemy torpedo bombers. Much was learned. The methods were refined.

Butch was awarded the Navy Cross posthumously, for his efforts in developing these night-time fighting methods. The citation reads as follows:

> The President of the United States of America takes pride in presenting the Navy Cross (posthumously) to Lieutenant Commander Edward Henry "Butch" O'Hare (NSN: 0-78672), United States Navy, for extraordinary heroism in operations against the enemy while serving as Pilot of a carrier-based Navy Fighter Plane in Fighting Squadron TWO (VF-2), attached to the U.S.S. Enterprise (CV-6), and deployed over Tarawa in the Gilbert Islands, in action against enemy Japanese forces on 11/26/1943. When warnings were received of the approach of a large force of Japanese torpedo bombers, Lieutenant Commander O'Hare volunteered to lead a fighter section of aircraft from his carrier, the first time such a mission had been attempted at night, in order to intercept the attackers. He fearlessly led his three-plane group into combat against a large formation of hostile aircraft and assisted in shooting down two Japanese airplanes and dispersed the remainder. Lieutenant Commander O'Hare's outstanding courage, daring airmanship and devotion to duty were in keeping with the highest traditions of the United States Naval Service. He gallantly gave his life for his country.

The Gearing-class, 391' long and 41' beam and 19' draft, USS O'Hare (1945 – 1973 transferred to Spain, 1992 scrapped) destroyer was named in his honor. His mother Selma sponsored.

Chicago changed the name of its Orchard Depot Airport to *O'Hare International Airport* in 1949. The name remains today. The airport has a Grumman F4F-3 Wildcat on display, the fighter he flew for his Medal of Honor flight. This aircraft was recovered virtually intact from the bottom of Lake Michigan, where it sank in a 1943 accident off the 500' long, USS Wolverine (1912 - 1947 scrapped) training aircraft carrier. The Air Classics Museum (located today in Aurora, Illinois) renovated it. It was installed in 2001, in the west end of Terminal 2.

Butch O'Hare is shown below. The aircraft are restored versions of the Grumman Wildcat, that O'Hare flew in World War II.

15- CANNIBALISM ON CHICHIJIMA ISLAND

An archipelago is an island group. Stratovolcanic refers to a land mass formed over time from volcanic emissions. These are layers of hardened lava, pumice, tephra, and volcanic ash. Japan is a stratovolcanic archipelago, of 6,852 islands. The four largest are Honshu, Hokkaido, Kyushu, and Shikoku, at 87,200 and 32,200 and 14,200 and 7,300 square miles. These four islands comprise 97% of Japan's total land area, of 145,936 square miles. For comparison purposes, these four islands combined are 52% the size of Texas. All of Japan is 54% of Texas.

Japan's four largest metropolitan areas in terms of population today are all on the largest island, again which is Honshu. These cities and metropolitan areas from most to least in population today are Tokyo, Yokohama, Osaka, and Nagoya. The population of the Tokyo metropolitan area is more than 38 million, the most worldwide.

The Nanpo Islands is a collective term for the tropical and sub-tropical island groups located south of the Japanese archipelago. These number 48 islands and islets. They extend from the Izu Peninsula west of Tokyo Bay, 750 miles south to within 310 miles of the Mariana Islands. The Nanpos belong to Japan.

The Nanpo Islands consist of three sub-groups, as follows:
- 32   Ogasawara Islands (also known as the Bonin Islands), two are inhabited today
- 13   Izu Islands, nine are inhabited today
- 3   Volcanic Islands, none are inhabited today

Chichijima of the Ogasawara group is the largest of the 48 Nanpo Islands, at 9.1 square miles. Chichijima is 640 miles south of Tokyo, and 145 miles north of Iwo Jima. Iwo Jima in the Volcanic group is the second largest, at 8.1 square miles. Hahajima in the Ogasawara group is the third largest, at 7.7 square miles.

Only Chichijima and Hahajima of the Ogasawara Islands are inhabited today, with 2,000 and 440 persons each.

Second largest of the Nanpo Islands Iwo Jima was mentioned above. The uninhabited, active volcano (minor activity several times a year {fumaroles}) Iwo Jima Island of course is the best known of all the Nanpo Islands. This is so because of the 36-day, February-March, 1945 World War II battle; and the iconic, Joe Rosenthal (1911 DC – 2006 CA) photograph taken on Iwo Jima's highest point. This was atop the 554' Mount Suribachi at the southern tip of the island. This is the highest point on Iwo Jima. Mount Suribachi and the whole island for that matter was formed from volcanic activity.

This photograph of course was the six American marines planting the American flag atop Mount Suribachi. Rosenthal took the picture on 2/23/1945, the third day after the marines landed on Iwo Jima. The photograph became the first photograph to win the Pulitzer Prize in Photography in the same year of its publication. This in fact has not been repeated.

Chichijima is a lush island, with plenty of fresh water. Again, it is the largest of the Nanpo Islands. It is hilly. Its two highest points are both a little over 1,000' high. These are Mount Yoake and Mount Asahi. It has a natural harbor.

The first map below shows the location of the Nanpo Islands, relative to Japan. As already noted, another name for the Ogasawara Islands is the Bonin Islands (labeled on the map below as Bonin Islands). The middle map shows the Ogasawara Islands again – these include the Nishino Shima, Mukojima, Chichijima, and Hahajima Island sub-groups. The third map shows the odd-shaped Chichijima Island.

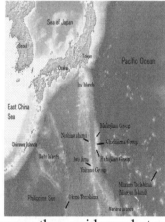

The Nanpos are a little more than midway between Japan and the Mariana Islands.

As already noted, the Nanpo Islands belonged to Japan at the time of World War II, which is still the case today.

The 15 islands of the Marianas include Guam, Saipan, Tinian, etc. Portuguese explorer Ferdinand Magellan (1480 Portugal – 1521 Philippines, killed by natives) sailing under the Spanish flag was the first European to visit the Marianas. He claimed them for Spain. Guam became a U.S. possession as a result of the 1898 Spanish-American War. Spain sold the other Mariana Islands to Germany, in 1899.

Japan though seized the Marianas from Germany during World War I. The 6/1919 Versailles Treaty after World War I granted control of the Mariana Islands (excepting Guam, still under U.S. control) to the League of Nations. The League in turn authorized Japan continuing oversight of the Marianas. This should have been reversed when Japan invaded Manchuria 9/1931 with no justification, but this was not done. Even ten years before the fourteen, 12/7/1941 sneak attacks by the Empire of Japan, Japan knew that the Marianas were key to building a perimeter defense. Therefore, Japan would not have given up the Marianas anyway.

Japan also without provocation started the second Sino-Japanese War 7/1937. Again, an effort should have been made at this time to remove the Marianas from Japan's control.

As just noted, Japan attacked fourteen locations 12/7/1941. These were all on or in the Pacific Ocean. The Marianas Island of Guam, and Guam already noted as an American possession, was one target. Japan occupied Guam until the U.S. wrested the island back, 8/1944. This was 2.7 years later. The U.S. eliminated the Japanese from the other Marianas June-November, 1944. The U.S. quickly made airfields, harbors, and other infrastructure on the Mariana Islands of Saipan and Tinian. The flight distance to bomb the Japanese home islands was now much less than before. Japan was right, in knowing that losing the Marianas would be a disaster. Japan should have surrendered at this point, as its air and naval defenses were not much. Japan did not do so, though.

The Marianas remain today, as jurisdictions (a Commonwealth) of the United States.

The Tokugawa Shogunate was the last, feudal Japanese military government. Fifteen Shoguns ruled 1603-1868, which is 265 years. Shoguns were hereditary military governors from the Tokugawa clan. They were Japan's rulers. They ruled from Edo Castle which was in Edo, the previous name for Tokyo (name changed in 1868). The era therefore was called the Edo period.

Edo (Tokyo) is on Honshu, Japan's largest and most populous island as already noted. At 87,200 square miles, Honshu is 32% the size of Texas.

Japan had an Emperor during this time. However, he was a figurehead and had little power. He was allowed to announce the new rulers over time, but the shoguns made the selections. Again, the Tokugawa Shoguns ruled.

Despite the fact that the Shoguns were essentially dictators, this 265-year Edo period of the 15 Tokugawa Shogunates was Japan's longest run of peace and stability. To sum up, the Shoguns were in the category of benevolent dictators.

Tokugawa Iemitsu (1604 Japan – 1651 Japan) was the third of the fifteen Shogun rulers. He ruled 1623-1651. He enacted isolation policies in the 1630s. The Shogunate along with certain other smaller feudal domains, enforced strict regulations to commerce and foreign relations. This foreign relations policy was called *sakoku*.

The Shoguns expelled all Europeans (no Americans or only a very few lived in Japan at the time). Foreigners were not allowed to move to Japan, or even visit.

Japanese commoners were not allowed to leave. If commoners sailed off, they faced harsh penalties upon return. The ship and cargo were confiscated. The ship owner, captain, and crew were imprisoned, or even executed.

Also, Christianity was banned. Bounties were paid to those who discovered Christians on a Japanese island. Bigger bounties were paid in the case of a found Christian priest or minister or missionary. These persons were expelled, if they were lucky. They were usually executed.

The sakoku period ran until 1866; although the U.S. forced Japan to open up some in the 1850s per the efforts of U.S. Navy Commodore Matthew Perry (see below). The reasons for the establishment and continuation of the sakoku closed society are still debated today. The (generally) consensus explanations though include the following:

- As an effort for Tokugawa Iemitsu and successor Shoguns to consolidate power

- To block the colonial powers of Spain and Portugal from controlling parts of Japan
- Prevent foreigners from trying to convert Japanese to Christianity, especially Catholicism

In the eyes of the Shoguns, Spain and Portugal were not able to separate trade from religion, whereas Netherlands and Great Britain could do so; Dutch traders were required to swear to not engage in missionary activities, to continue trade with Japan

Today Japan is 1% Christian, compared to 3, 7, and 29% for China, Vietnam, and South Korea; therefore, sakoku in banning Christians and especially Christian ministers or even laity including missionaries, seems to have worked in this regard

For the record, the traditional and common religion of Japan today is Shinto; Shinto focuses on ritual practices to be carried out diligently, in order to establish a connection between present-day Japan and its ancient past; the religion has many gods; today per surveys, more than three fourths of Japanese participate in Shinto practices or rituals, although less than a fourth identify themselves as *Shintoists*

Japan was not completely isolated under the sakoku policy. The only European influence permitted though was trade with the Dutch, and only at one location. This was the 2.22-acre, fan-shaped Dejima Island in Nagasaki Bay. Dejima was formed by digging a canal in 1634, to separate a peninsula from the main part of the island in Nagasaki Bay. The island was made to constrain Portuguese traders. However, it ended up serving as a Dutch trading post, 1641-1853. Trade with the Chinese, Koreans, Ryukyu Islands (Okinawa, etc.), and indigenous Japanese on other islands was also limited, to sole gateways of peripheral provinces. Trade with countries of the Americas was banned.

These and other countries or territories though were occasionally allowed to visit the ruling Shogun in Edo at Osaka Castle. Osaka Castle is on Honshu Island as is Edo (Tokyo). It was another base for the Shogun rulers. Osaka was 311 miles southwest of Edo. The castle was completed back in 1583.

These meetings with the Shoguns were more or less marketing efforts, to establish trade with Japan.

The Japanese Shogun rulers were wise enough though to know that they must learn of Western science, technologies, and methods; to progress, and even protect themselves from invaders. Starting in the 1700s, Dejima became a center of study of medicine, military science, navigation, optics, shipbuilding, weaponry, astronomy, etc. These scientific studies became the basis of knowledge and a factor in the *Rangaku* movement. Rangaku translates to *Dutch studies*, and therefore by extension *Western studies*.

The Shoguns sent samurai to Dejima, to study. Samurai were the military nobility and officer caste for the Shogun leaders. As the Shogun period was one of peace, the samurai over time lost their military needs. They transitioned to being administrators, managers of civic programs, scholars, and courtiers. A courtier is a person in attendance in the court of a monarch or other leader.

Expanding Western powers made a number of efforts to end Japan's seclusion. These included arriving warships or trading ships from Portugal, Russia, France, Great Britain, and the U.S. Their motivations (and of other groups) during this insular period included the following:

- Protestant and Catholic missionary societies, to try and convert Japanese to Christianity
- Family members who wanted their kin back; these were usually whaler crewmen who ended up on the islands when their ships or boats sank in the area; Japan would not allow these men to leave; in fact, they were imprisoned
- Countries and companies plying the sea lanes to trade with China needed to set up coaling stations on the route to China
- Countries and merchants who simply wanted commercial trade with Japan

These efforts were not successful. The ships were turned back, or the crews were captured and imprisoned. Again, this was per the Shoguns' sakoku policy.

American Nathaniel Savory (1794 MA – 1874 Chichijima) went to sea at age 20. He lost a finger in an accident on Oahu Island of the Kingdom of Hawaii, and had to have surgery. As a result, he missed his outgoing boat. Instead, he became part of an adventure-economic expedition, led by the Italian-British Matteo Mazzaro. The group of 30 included Americans, British, and Hawaiians. They eventually settled in Ogiura, Chichijima, of the already described Ogasawara Islands. Leader Mazzaro died. Savory become governor of the group.

The group consisted of seventeen men and thirteen women. The women were all Hawaiians. The group hoped for success fishing, hunting seals, harvesting sandalwood, etc. The economic part did not work out too well, though. Conditions were difficult. Typhoons struck. Pirates and other unruly seamen showed up. Conflicts over the women were many and even resulted in violence – the men fighting over the women. A few seamen stayed, but the colony did not grow by much. Chichijima was not Shangri-La.

They raised farm animals (hogs, goats, cattle), planted some seeds, etc. They made a living mainly by selling food (meat, vegetables, tropical fruit) to passing whalers.

Savory's descendants still live there today. American settler and leader Savory is introduced here, as addressed several times below.

Between 1790 and 1853, American ships intruded on Japan on at least 27 occasions. Three of the cases were USS warships. All were turned away though. Several notable of the later voyages and excursions over these 63 years were as follows:

- 1837 American businessman Charles King lived in Canton, China. He tried to return Japanese sailor castaways (shipwrecked, and washed up on Oregon) to Japan, to thaw relations with Japan. He sailed to Japan in the unarmed merchant ship Morrison. The Japanese fired on Morrison with shore cannon, plus sent out hundreds of small gunboats. He sailed on to another Japanese port. He was able to land several of the Japanese sailors. The Japanese lit their cannons again, so he sailed back to China. Several of the Japanese sailors who wanted to go home, were not landed.

Due to internal criticism for attacking King's ship on what was a humanitarian mission and also as related somewhat to Great Britain's defeat of China in the First Opium War (1839-1842), Japan in 1842 agreed to not execute foreigners, and to sell provisions to foreign ships needing replenishment. Therefore, progress was made.

- 1845 The American whaling ship Manhattan rescued 22 Japanese shipwrecked sailors in the Ogasawara (Bonin) Islands, 3/1845. The first eleven were found on an island. The second half were rescued from a foundering boat. Manhattan's Captain Mercator Cooper (1803 NY – 1872) set sail for Tokyo to repatriate the sailors.

It is thought that Cooper was named after cartographer, geographer, and cosmographer Gerardus Mercator (1512 Netherlands – 1594 Holy Roman Empire). Mercator is known for creating the 1569 world map, which represented sailing courses of constant bearing as straight lines. This innovation is still used in nautical charts today. If so on his given name, his parents were prescient as he became a ship captain.

Cooper set anchor outside of Tokyo Bay. He released four of the Japanese in a small boat with a message that he wanted to sail the Manhattan into Tokyo Harbor, to release the other 18 Japanese sailors.

On 4/18/1845, the Emperor sent out three hundred boats with fifteen men in each. Some of the boats hitched to the Manhattan, and towed her closer to shore. Several emissaries of the Emperor including the Governor of Edo (Tokyo) boarded. The Japanese examined the ship. They took their countrymen (the shipwrecked men). They also took all the weapons on Manhattan.

In (apparent) gratitude for the rescue and delivery of the shipwrecked sailors, they gave Captain Cooper water in barrels, twenty sacks of rice, two sacks of wheat, a box of flour, eleven sacks of sweet potatoes, fifty live fowl, two cords of wood, radishes, and ten pounds of tea.

On 4/21/1845, the three hundred boats and 4,500 men rowed out again, attached lines, and towed the Manhattan sixteen miles out to sea. They thanked Cooper and his crew for returning the shipwrecked sailors, and told them to never return. Cooper never did.

- 1846 President John Tyler (1790 VA – 1862 VA) signed the Wanghia Treaty between Qing-Dynasty China and the United States. Navy Commodore James Biddle (1783 Philadelphia – 1848 Philadelphia) arrived China 12/1845 to exchange ratifications of the Treaty. This was the first treaty between China and the U.S. The treaty addressed extra-territoriality, tariffs on trade, right to buy land in China, right to learn to speak Chinese, and for the U.S. to be named a favored nation.

Biddle sailed on to Japan in 1846 on two warships, in an effort to negotiate a similar treaty with Japan. As with the Wanghia Treaty, this was an official mission under now President James Polk (1795 NC – 1849 Nashville). The Japanese Shogunate responded that Japan forbade all commerce and communication with foreign nations except Netherlands. Biddle was told to leave immediately and never come back. He did as he was told.

- 1849 Navy Commodore David Geisinger (1790 MD – 1860 Philadelphia) ordered Captain James Glynn (1800 – 1871) to sail to Japan on the 117' long and 32' beam, 16-gun USS Preble (1840 – 1863 Pensacola Bay, destroyed in an accidental fire when a Civil War guard ship) sloop-of-war to collect fifteen American whaling crewmen. Their whaler wrecked off a Japanese island 6/7/1848. The Japanese were holding the men in deplorable conditions, as prisoners.

  The Japanese tried to block Preble's entrance. However, Glynn forced his way through a row of boats and anchored in Nagasaki Bay. He demanded the release of the fifteen sailors. The Japanese refused. He responded that the U.S. would attack Japan.

  With negotiating help from the Dutch in the area, Japan finally turned over the prisoners. This was nine days after Glynn's arrival. However, several of the prisoners had died during imprisonment from abuse and lack of care. The Preble brought the men back to the U.S. Back home, the stories of the repatriated whalers (their capture and harsh treatment) was big news.

For the U.S., Captain Glynn's 1849 success in the release of shipwrecked, civilian crewmen was the first successful, official negotiation with Japan. This success led President Millard Fillmore (1800 NY – 1874 NY) to make another official effort. Fillmore and State Secretary Daniel Webster (1782 NH – 1852 MA) selected Navy Commodore John Aulick (1790 VA – 1873 DC) who was then commander of the East India Squadron, to return seventeen shipwrecked Japanese men then in San Francisco; as an opportunity to open commercial relations with Japan.

Webster sent a letter 5/1851 to the Japanese Emperor, assuring him that the expedition had no religious purpose; that the goal was to request *friendship and commerce*, and replenishment services (coal, food, water) for U.S. ships en route to China. The letter boasted of American expansion across the North American continent, and the country's technical prowess. President Fillmore signed the letter.

In the meantime though, Aulick became involved in a diplomatic row with a Brazilian diplomat, and also publicly quarreled with the Captain of his flagship. As a result, he was relieved of his command before he could undertake the Japan expedition. Webster and Fillmore replaced Aulick with Navy Commodore Matthew Perry (1794 RI – 1858 NYC). Perry's commendable naval career included extensive diplomatic experience.

Perry served in the War of 1812 against Great Britain. He had a number of command assignments in the 1846-1848 Mexican-American War.

Perry felt that the education of seamen was deficient. He supported an apprentice system to improve this training. He played a key role in developing the curriculum of the U.S. Naval Academy in Annapolis, which was founded in 1845. Perry was a vocal proponent to modernize the U. S. Navy. In fact, he became known as the *father of the U.S. Steam Navy* – conversion from sails to coal-fired, external combustion engines for propulsion. He oversaw the construction of the Navy's second steam frigate. This was the 180' long and 35' beam and 13' draft, sidewheel steamer, USS Fulton (1837 – 1861 Confederacy captured Pensacola 1/1861, Confederacy destroyed 5/1862 at Pensacola to prevent re-capture when evacuating Pensacola) gunboat. Perry commanded USS Fulton after commissioning.

Perry as noted above also had experience in diplomacy, negotiating agreements with other countries. To sum up, Perry had gravitas for such a mission.

The President's goals were to open Japan to U.S. trade, obtain protection for American seamen, and set up coaling stations in Japan. Contributing factors for the U.S. were as follows:

- The growing commerce between America and China, Japan was a close neighbor of China
- As American whalers operated offshore Japan
  - Japan could provision the whaling ships
  - If Americans washed up on Japanese shores if their ships or boats sank, the U.S. expected Japan to rescue and care for them, and then allow them to return to the U.S. (instead of imprisoning and abusing them)
- As the British and French were in Asia, and moving toward monopolization of potential coaling stations in the region

Fillmore's directive to Perry was to be forceful if necessary. In other words, Perry was authorized to use *gunboat diplomacy* if needed to force Japan into a treaty; and furthermore a favorable treaty. In international politics, gunboat diplomacy means the pursuit of foreign policy goals by displaying conspicuous naval power. The implication is that attack will occur, unless favorable agreements are made. President Theodore Roosevelt's (1858 NYC – 1919 NY, blood clot in lungs) *big stick diplomacy* is similar in definition. For the record, Roosevelt's words were *speak softly and carry a big stick, you will go far*.

The U.S. was also driven by concepts of manifest destiny, and the desire to impose the benefits of western civilization on what (at least some) perceived as backward Asian nations. The Dutch warned Japan that Perry was coming. However, Japan remained steadfast in not changing their 220-year sakoku policy of national seclusion. There was considerable internal debate in Japan on how best to meet this potential threat to its political sovereignty, and how it may affect Japan's economy.

On his way to Tokyo Bay with a fleet of eight warships, Captain Perry sailed into Chichijima's harbor 6/15/1853. He claimed the island for the U.S. as a coaling station for steamships. On behalf of the U.S., Perry purchased fifty acres bordering the harbor from Nathaniel Savory (mentioned above) for $50. Perry stocked it with cattle. Perry formed a governing council, naming Savory as the leader.

Perry was acting boldly. President Franklin Pierce (1804 NH – 1869 NH) who succeeded Fillmore later repudiated Perry's declaration, that Chichijima was now a U.S. possession.

Perry landed and drilled troops on the Ryukyu Islands (the closest of Japan's islands to the home islands), knowing that this would be reported to the Japanese leaders at Edo. He arrived Edo Bay 7/8/1853, with four warships. He turned his guns toward the town of Uraga, Yokosuka Kanagawa Prefecture; which is at the entrance to Tokyo Bay. The Japanese told him to sail to Nagasaki, the only Japanese port open to foreigners. Perry's actions instead were as follows:

- Presented a white flag and a letter; the letter stated that if the Japanese chose to fight, that his ships would destroy them
- Fired blank shots from the 73 cannons on his ships (he said it was a late celebration of the Fourth of July) to demonstrate the power of his modern, accurate, long-range Paixhans cannons; Japan had nothing near the Paixhans as to killing power, on ship or shore

   French Army General Henri-Joseph Paixhans (1783 France – 1854 France) developed these cannons in 1822 as the first naval guns to fire explosive shells; these weapons led to the practice of cladding wood ships with iron to keep the hull from igniting, and then later making ship hulls from steel instead of wood
- Launched boats, to survey the coastline and surrounding waters

Finally, Japanese leaders allowed Perry to land, 7/14/1853. He did so in fifteen ship's boats accompanied by 250 marines, a thirteen-gun salute from one of the frigates, and a band playing *Hail Columbia*. Perry presented a letter from President Fillmore to attending delegates (of note though, Fillmore was now out of office). He also delivered (obsolete) small arms as gifts. These were rifles, muskets, pistols, and also swords and sabers. He told the Japanese that he would return a year later, giving them a year to stew on their response. He sailed off 7/17/1853.

The Tokugawa Shogunate had assigned Shogun official Egawa Hidetatsu (1801 Japan – 1855 Japan) the task of protecting Edo from outsiders, motivated by businessman Charles King's unwelcome arrival in 1837 on Morrison (described above). Starting in 1839, Hidetatsu made defenses on islands in Edo Bay to attack any arriving foreign ship with cannon fire. With the increased urgency from Perry's promise to return, Hidetatsu in 1853 made six additional island fortresses in Edo Bay. Perry was aware of these batteries on these islands in Edo Bay, and steered wide.

One of these defensive islands was man-made. It was and is called Odaiba. Today, it is a commercial, residential, and entertainment place. It is connected to the mainland by the 2,618' Rainbow Bridge (1993 -). The Rainbow Bridge is a two decker – one level for cars, and the other for light rail.

Hidetatsu also made a furnace, to cast cannons. However, these cannons were low in quality and marginal in performance. The casting technology was lacking.

The Shogunate tried to make warships, from studying Dutch textbooks.

Perry returned though a half year early, on 2/13/1854. He arrived early as the Russians had attempted to get Japan to sign a treaty; and as France and the U.K. both had announced that they planned to accompany Perry, to ensure that the U.S. was not treated special. This time, his fleet was ten ships, carrying 1,600 men. Also, three bands were playing the *Star-Spangled Banner*. Again, the Japanese rebuffed him. Eventually, he was allowed to land. He negotiated with the Japanese almost a month.

The result was the 3/31/1854 Kanagawa Convention Peace and Amity Treaty. Kanagawa Prefecture is a section of Edo (Tokyo), and was where the Treaty was signed.

The Treaty included care of American shipwreck victims who washed up on Japanese Islands, establishment of a consulate office in Shimoda (Shimoda is on the main island of Honshu, 110 miles southwest of Tokyo), and establishment of most favored nation status (including coaling rights). The Treaty opened two ports to American whaling ships seeking coal and other provisions. However, general trade was still banned.

The Russians followed suit in 1855, with the similar Shimoda Treaty.

When Japan finally agreed to the treaty, Perry presented Japanese officials with gifts again – a miniature steam locomotive, a telegraph apparatus, various agricultural tools, small arms, one hundred gallons of whiskey, clocks, stoves, and books about the U.S. The Japanese responded with gifts as well – gold-lacquered furniture and boxes, bronze ornaments, porcelain goblets, and a collection of seashells (collecting shells was Perry's hobby).

Perry's arrival in 1853 began the bakumatsu period, which was the final years of the Edo sakoku (isolation) period when the Tokugawa feudal Shogunate ended. The Meiji period of much change (especially an economic diaspora) when the Emperor gained power followed the bakumatsu period, beginning in 1868.

The later 1858 Treaty of Amity and Commerce addressed trading rights, import and export duties, right to make churches for Americans to attend in Japan, etc. American envoy Townsend Harris (1804 NY – 1878 NYC) negotiated. This took more than two years, before the Tokugawa Shogunate capitulated. The treaty was signed on the deck of the 254' long and 45' beam and 19' draft, thirteen miles per hour, USS Powhatan (1852 – 1887 scrapped) sidewheel steam frigate in Edo Bay (now Tokyo Bay). Powhatan was the Navy's largest paddle frigate.

The treaty opened the ports of Kanagawa and four other Japanese cities to trade, granted extraterritoriality to foreigners, etc. The Tokugawa Shogunate rulers finally gave in, maybe as the British were also demanding similar terms.

In 1862, Japan sailed a ship into Chichijima's harbor, and officially annexed the thirty-two Ogasawara Islands without opposition. Japan made up some lies, as to why they owned the Ogasawara Islands. Both the U.K. and U.S. had some claims on the islands as well. In the case of the U.S., American Savory mentioned above had co-founded the settlement there in 1830 and now managed it. Neither the U.K. nor the U.S. contested though. It goes without saying that the Chichijima residents were not asked for their opinions.

Most of the settlers were Hawaiians. At the time, Hawaii was a Kingdom. However, it became a U.S. territory in 1898.

Japan moved in Japanese immigrants, who became neighbors of the Savory colony. They fished and mined sulfur. After eighteen months, Japan moved the Japanese settlers off Chichijima as suffering economically. More Japanese settlers though moved to Chichijima later.

Japan did allow the 1830 Savory colony on Chichijima to stay. In 1875 though, Japan made these colonists renounce their citizenship and become Japanese citizens. They were required to drop their western names for Japanese names. However, they were not necessarily allowed to move to the Japanese home islands. Also, Japan barred future non-Japanese from moving to Chichijima. Due to immigration of Japanese people and then births, the population on the Ogasawaras grew to 6,000 by 1923.

When the United States fought and reclaimed the Marianas (Guam, Saipan, Tinian, etc.) from the Japanese in 1944 in World War II, Japan began to heavily fortify Iwo Jima and Chichijima to serve as bases and to protect the homeland, as follows:

- Chichijima was a major communications spot, and also served as a staging point for supplies and soldiers; in regard to communications, Japan used Chichijima to both send and receive military messages and to also intercept U.S. military radio transmissions, to prepare offensively and defensively early on, and then just defensively later in the war; this was effective, as Japan was able to shoot down many U.S. airplanes (especially four engine, B-29 heavy bombers) when detected by equipment on Chichijima; the two main island communication points were concrete-hardened radio facilities on Chichijima's two, 1,000'-plus mounts, Yoake and Asahi

- Regarding Chichijima's role in communications, one of the many (not respected, obviously) Japanese messages about the fourteen, 12/7/1941 planned sneak attacks intercepted by the Americans came from Chichijima; these attacks included Oahu (Pearl Harbor, bases and airfields)

- Chichijima served as the staging area for supplies intended for Iwo Jima; freighters and troop transport ships sailed the 600 miles from Japan to Chichijima, and berthed for unloading in the island's natural harbor; supplies were transferred to smaller boats, and ferried the 150 miles to Iwo Jima; Iwo Jima had no harbor (natural or manmade) so the small boats had to ride the waves onto the beach at low tide, or were lightered with even smaller boats

- Japan installed concealed defensive cannon and anti-aircraft guns in Chichijima's hills, shielded by thick concrete; some of the anti-aircraft gunners were transferred in from the guns protecting Akasaka Palace in Tokyo, the residence of Emperor Michinomiya Hirohito (1901 Tokyo – 1989 Tokyo), as they were so expert
- Iwo Jima's main contribution was as an airfield – Japanese fighters took off from three air strips to shoot down many American B-29 bombers; kamikaze planes later took off from Iwo Jima
- Chichijima and Iwo Jima both served as rendezvous points

To sum up, these two islands were critical for Japan to run the war and protect its homelands. Twenty-two thousand and 25,000 soldiers defended Iwo Jima and Chichijima.

Japan evacuated its citizens from both islands in 1944 – 1,000 from Iwo Jima, and 6,900 from Chichijima.

In support of the on and off campaigns to take the Marianas, Iwo Jima, and Okinawa, Navy and Army aircraft bombed Chichijima 7/1944 to 7/1945. The goal was to take out Chichijima's communication outposts, atop the islands two highest points.

More than one hundred airmen were shot down over and around Chichijima. Most died when their aircraft crashed, or drowned, or died of hypothermia or other exposure. Rescue submarines were only able to save three. The Japanese captured twenty-two airmen. Three of these twenty-two were sent to Japan. The rest were tortured and killed.

One of these shot down was one fourth of a sortie group of Grumman, single engine, three crew, TBM Avenger torpedo bombers, on a 9/2/1944 glide bombing drop. George Bush (1924 MA -) piloted this one. His two crew were a turret gunner and radioman/bombardier/ventral gunner.

Bush graduated high school from the private, boys only, Phillips Academy Andover (1778 -) boarding high school 5/1942. Phillips is in Andover, Massachusetts, 25 miles north of Boston. At his graduation ceremony, War Secretary and Phillips alumnus Henry Stimson (1867 NYC – 1950 NY) advised the graduating seniors to go on to college. Bush indeed had been accepted to Yale University in Connecticut. However, he had decided that he was going to enlist in the military. He selected the Navy, as the Navy had lost so many men in the Japanese 12/7/1941 sneak attacks. Years later, he wrote *My dad...with whom it was not easy to disagree, hoped I would listen to Secretary Stimson and go on to Yale. After the ceremony, he asked if I had changed my mind. I told him no, that I was joining up. Dad simply nodded his okay.* His dad was banker and then politician Prescott Bush (1895 OH – 1972 NYC). Prescott was a Senator to Congress from Connecticut, 1952-1963.

Bush trained for ten months. He was commissioned as an ensign in the U.S. Naval Reserve at Naval Air Station Corpus Christi 6/9/1943, which was three days before his nineteenth birth anniversary. This made him the youngest naval aviator, to date.

Bush developed engine trouble immediately after catapult launch in the 6/19, 20/1944 Philippine Sea Battle, maybe as hit by shrapnel from a Japanese dive bomber. He was able to circle around to land. However, the new, Independence-class, 623' long, USS San Jacinto (1943 – 1971 scrapped) light aircraft carrier waved him off. He and his two crewmen ditched without injury and were rescued. The U.S. in the Philippine Sea Battle lost 123 aircraft and 109 men, and a battleship was damaged. The Japanese lost five ships (three carriers, two oilers), 600 aircraft and 2,987 men; plus another six ships were damaged. This battle eliminated the Imperial Japanese Navy's ability to conduct large-scale carrier actions.

Bush trained in aerial photography. His pictures were used to advantage in developing strategy in the Pacific Theater, mainly in determining where marines should be landed. He was promoted to Junior Grade Lieutenant 8/1/1944.

As just noted, Bush was the third in line of four bombers 9/2/1944, again off the USS San Jacinto. On his 190 mile per hour gliding dive, a Japanese shell hit his bomber. Instantly, smoke came out of the engine into the cockpit, to the point where he could not see the controls or gauges. Flames ran along the wings, toward the fuel tanks. Despite the fact that he could barely see and the explosion threat, Bush chose to continue his glide. He dropped all four 500-pound bombs; scoring damaging hits. He then hollered to his two crewmen to bail out. He put the bomber into a slip to facilitate their exit. These were Radioman Second Class John Delaney and Lieutenant Junior Grade William White. Both men died. Their bodies were never found. There is uncertainty as to the cause of their death – died in the flames, shot in the aircraft, parachute failed to open, drowned, etc. It is certain though that neither survived the strike to be captured, and then died in captivity.

Bush opened the cockpit, climbed out, and jumped. He pulled his ripcord too soon, so struck his head on the tail of the Avenger, cutting his forehead. His parachute hooked on the tail and was damaged. As a result, he fell faster than normal to the ocean. If he had landed on land instead of water, he probably would have been severely injured, or even died. His afire bomber exploded mid-air before it hit the ocean and also before Bush himself splashed – so Bush was a spectator for that, dangling from his parachute.

Bush landed four miles northeast of Chichijima. A U.S. aircraft dropped a collapsible, yellow, one-man raft. Bush inflated it, and got in. The wind was blowing him toward Chichijima. The Japanese launched several small boats to capture him. He had no paddles, so paddled with his hands. He feared for the fate of his two crewmen. A Portuguese man-of-war jellyfish stung him. He had swallowed seawater and was vomiting. His head was bleeding. He was crying.

Bush knew what the Japanese did to war prisoners. He had heard the stories and seen the pictures (especially an infamous one of the Japanese beheading an Australian prisoner of war). He was 20.2 years old.

American fighter planes strafed the Japanese pick-up boats coming for Bush, so they retreated for the moment. He floated 193 minutes in the life raft, protected by the circling fighters. The Gato-class, 312' long and 27' beam and 17' draft, USS Finback (1941 – 1959 scrapped) lifeguard submarine picked him up. The exhausted and terrified Bush could only say four words: *Happy to be aboard.* Although Finback was there for rescue purposes if needed, Bush was very lucky that the Japanese did not get to him first – shot or captured.

Bush later wrote *I know what it is like to be a 20-year-old kid out there in the middle of the Pacific Ocean, disoriented, nauseous, agonizing over the death of my closest friends, and terrorized by the thought of imminent capture.*

Bush and four other rescued airmen (two were pilots) remained on board the rest of Finback's eleventh patrol, another thirty days. Although ecstatic that they had been rescued, the voyage was not overly pleasant. Finback endured attacks by bombs and depth charges during this period. Finback torpedo-sank two small Japanese freighters, September 9 and 10, 1944. These were the 866-ton and 536-ton Hakuun Maru No.2 and the Hassho Maru. This was accomplished, despite having to fend off an armed escort. To sum up, the rescued pilots probably did not feel much safer on Finback than they did in the air.

Finback's captain put the pilots to work. This mainly was standing watch, searching for enemy planes and vessels. Young pilots have excellent eyesight. Finback disembarked the five aviators at Midway. Bush flew to Hawaii for a period of rest and relaxation. He flew from there to Guam, and then back to the USS San Jacinto.

By the way, this was Bush's first parachute jump, unplanned of course. Considering his injury and the damage to his chute from opening it too soon, he definitely should have had more training – even an actual jump; or better yet, jumps.

Bush made seven tandem skydives as a civilian, after the Navy. The last four were on the occasion of his 75th, 80th, 85th, and 90th birth anniversaries. On his last jump when he turned 90 in 2014, partner Master Jumper Mike Elliot was on his 10,227[th] jump. This jump was from a helicopter, at 6,500'. It was a hard landing. Bush was OK though. His family picked him up and put him back in his wheelchair. His wife Barbara Bush (1925 NY - 2018 Houston) discouraged these jumps, unsuccessfully.

Bush returned to the USS San Jacinto, 11/1944. He participated in operations in the Philippines, until his squadron was replaced and sent home. Through 1944, he flew 58 combat missions. In all, he made 126 carrier landings (versus 128 carrier takeoffs!), and logged 1,228 hours. He received the Distinguished Flying Cross and three Air Medals. The Presidential Unit Citation was awarded to USS San Jacinto. The Presidential Unit Citation is awarded to units of the Armed Forces for extraordinary heroism in action against an armed enemy.

Because of his valuable combat experience, Bush was assigned to Norfolk Navy Base in Virginia, and put in a training wing for new torpedo airplane pilots. He was later assigned as a naval aviator in a new torpedo air squadron. Japan surrendered 8/1945. Bush mustered out of the Navy 9/1945, with the rank of Junior Grade Lieutenant. He served more than three years.

Bush's acceptance to Yale was still good. He matriculated. Bush graduated 2.5 years later on an accelerated program, with a degree in economics.

For the record, Bush was not the only President to be or sitting President to land on an aircraft carrier. His son George W. Bush (1946 CT -) served 1968-1974 in the Texas Air National Guard, the Alabama Air National Guard, and the U.S. Air Force; separating as a First Lieutenant. Bush Junior when President landed on the Nimitz-class, 1,092' long, nuclear-powered, USS Abraham Lincoln (1989 -) aircraft carrier 5/1/2003, to give his *Mission Accomplished* speech regarding the war on Iraq. In its deployment for Operation Iraqi Freedom, this carrier launched 16,500 sorties. The carrier was just off San Diego, having returned from combat operations in the Persian Gulf.

Bush Junior's flying experience was way back, almost 30 years. Accordingly, he was just a passenger in this case. He sat in the co-pilot's seat. Bush is the only sitting President (or President to be for that matter) to make an arrested landing in a fixed-wing aircraft on a carrier. The aircraft was a four seat, twin engine turbofan, high wing, 405 and 450 miles per hour cruise and maximum, Lockheed S-3 Viking. The S-3 Viking was introduced in 1974. The Navy used it mostly for anti-submarine warfare, but later for surface warfare and aerial refueling. The carrier was just off San Diego, having returned from combat operations in the Persian Gulf.

Bush Senior was one of several American aircraft shot down by Chichijima Island gunners, 8/1944 through 3/1945. Twenty-two airmen survived their bailouts or crashes but were captured. Bush would have been one of these, if he had been captured 9/2/1944. The Japanese tortured and executed these men. The execution methods included penetration by sharpened bamboo stake, bayonet spearing, beheading, and bludgeoning with a heavy club. In regard to the stabbings, the ordered executioner soldiers were advised to miss the heart, to prolong the pain and agony and suffering of the death process.

Several senior officers including the commanding Japanese Army officer of the island then had a surgeon remove meat (thigh muscle) and organs (the liver mostly, gall bladder some) from some of the killed Americans, and had their chefs cook it up for dinner.

Senior Japanese Army officers hosted a sake (this is a rice wine) party for their Navy counterparts, and served roasted American liver as the appetizer. The Japanese Navy officers subsequently reciprocated by hosting a party, where they butchered and served their own American prisoners of war (POWs). Again, the Japanese preferred American livers and thigh muscle.

At the time, there was no food shortage on Chichijima. The Japanese were motivated by thinking that eating their enemies would make them stronger (or this is what they later said), or maybe just because they were sick in the head.

For the record, the below statement quote is from Japanese Army Regulations, in place at the time of World War II:

Prisoners of war shall be treated with a spirit of good will, and shall never be subjected to cruelties or humiliation.

In regard to Japanese war atrocities, some were not discovered until after the War. These included the above as described, uncovered in late 1945. Secret war-crimes trials for the Pacific Theatre were conducted in 1946 in Guam. Besides some Japanese soldiers who chose to talk, other witnesses were Korean forced laborers (more like slaves) that the Japanese had moved to Chichijima to cater to their Japanese masters.

Of the 144 charged military and civilian war criminals, 136 were found guilty (94.4%). Of these 136, 111 (81.6%) were convicted of murder, in addition to other offenses. Five were found guilty of permitting subordinates to commit atrocities against POWs; fourteen were convicted of torture, cruelty or maltreatment of prisoners; two were convicted of cannibalism; and several others for the mutilation of dead bodies.

Of the Japanese military serving on Chichijima, 30 were tried for Class B war crimes. These included torture, extrajudicial execution, and prevention of honorable burial. The last charge came about, as *non-survival cannibalism* (also known as *homicidal cannibalism*) was not covered under international law at the time as a crime – sometimes one just does not think of these things in advance. The Chichijima Army Commander and Navy Commander were both tried, convicted, and hung, as follows:

- 1913   Imperial Japanese Army Academy graduate Lieutenant General Yoshio Tachibana (1890 Japan – 9/24/1947 Guam, hung)
- 1917   Imperial Japanese Navy Academy graduate Vice Admiral Mori Kunizo (1890 Japan – 4/22/1949 hung); known for lecturing his colleagues on the medicinal value of human liver; sentenced to life imprisonment for cannibalism on Rabaul (New Britain, Papua New Guinea; Papua New Guinea was a mandated territory of Australia) as well as Chichijima; also under his command, POWs were murdered (some beheaded); Dutch later tried, convicted, and hung him for atrocities committed in the Dutch East Indies

Others were sentenced to imprisonment. These included Probationary Medical Officer Tadashi Teraki and some enlisted men. All were released within eight years.

In total, only thirteen, Japanese World War II officers were executed for war crimes. Others would have been convicted and executed but were dead – a few killed in the War, and others committed suicide. Many others simply were just not pursued. This was because there were so many, as evidence lacking, and due to expensive costs (finding, arresting, incarcerating, trying in court, etc.).

The Japanese government did cooperate with the Allies in compiling lists of (suspected) war criminals.

By the way, Emperor Hirohito was never charged with any war crimes, although certainly guilty. Many historians believe he was directly responsible for the atrocities committed by Japan's armed forces in the Second Sino-Japanese War and Word War II. These same historians reason that Hirohito's relatives (brother, two cousins, and three uncles) should have also been tried.

The U.S. granted authority to General Douglas MacArthur (1880 AR – 1964 DC) to control Japan, after the surrender. Knowing that the Japanese considered the Emperor to be a living god, MacArthur chose to leave him on the throne to give continuity and cohesion to the Japanese people – and so it was. Before the war crime trials began, Allied authorities and Japanese officials worked behind the scenes not only to prevent the Imperial family from being indicted, but also to influence the testimony of the defendants to ensure that the Emperor was not implicated.

Of course, the Emperor was much guilty. Again though as noted above, historians disagree on how much sway he had with military leaders. For the record though, Hirohito was considered the military leader of the country. When his Grandfather Emperor Meiji (1852 Japan – 1912 Japan) died in 1912, Hirohito's father Yoshihito (1879 Japan – 1926 Japan) assumed the throne. At the same time as his father becoming Emperor, Hirohito at the age of eleven was commissioned into the Imperial Japanese Army as a Second Lieutenant and the Imperial Japanese Navy as an Ensign. He was promoted 1914, 1916, 1920, and 1923. He attained Army Colonel and Navy Captain rank in 1924. Hirohito's father died 12/25/1926 at age 47. Hirohito assumed the throne then, at age 25. Simultaneously, he was promoted (skipped several ranks) to Grand Marshall and Supreme Commander-in-Chief of the Empire of Japan.

Hirohito was 25 years old at the time. He ruled 62 years (1926 – 1989), until his 1989 death at age 87. He was 44 years old when he surrendered his country in 1945. For the rest of his long life, he never spoke about the War (not publicly at least) or wrote about it, or his role in it.

Hirohito's son Akihito (1933 Tokyo -) ascended to the Chrysanthemum throne upon his father's 1989 death. Akihito announced in 2017 that he will abdicate the Chrysanthemum Throne 4/30/2019, in favor of his son Naruhito (1960 Tokyo -).

The U.S. military told the families that their service men were missing in action, to protect them from the horror of the facts. However, *Time* magazine, *Life* magazine (note that *Time* and *Life* magazines were owned by the same company, and still are today, except *Life* now only puts out special issues), and some newspapers somehow got wind of some of the atrocities and published. The articles addressed the executions and cannibalism. At least one of these news sources mentioned that livers were extracted immediately and served as sukiyaki (this is a meat and vegetable soup).

However, it was not until decades later in 1997 that this information (from the war crimes trials) was declassified, and so therefore verified or re-verified. James Bradley (1954 -) researched this information for his 2003 book on these eight airmen captured while bombing or attempting to bomb Chichijima. The book is entitled *Flyboys: A True Story of Courage.*

Bradley by the way was the same historian who wrote the 2000 *Flags of Our Fathers* about the six marines in the iconic Iwo Jima flag-raising photograph. At the time, one of those six men was thought to be Bradley's father, a Navy corpsman. This was determined in 2016 to not be the case though. The sixth man was another Marine.

Besides the classified material, Bradley received secret transcripts of the war crime trials. A former officer and lawyer who had a role in the trials gave him the transcripts.

Bush and Bradley after the book came out went to Chichijima, to make a CNN documentary. Bush even at the age of eighty in 2004 ventured out into the water on a life raft, to recreate the experience.

Bradley contacted the relatives of six of the eight Chichijima victims. One was unknown at the time, and he could not find relatives of one. Bradley assumed that all their parents were dead. The two mystery men were solved though after publication of the book as follows:

- Three weeks after the book came out, John Luke gave Bradley a sheaf of papers at a Barnes and Noble bookstore book signing in Westport, Connecticut. The information showed that the missing man was Ensign Warren Hindenlang (1920 – 8/6/1944). Hindenlang's mother had hired the five-year older Luke (then a sophomore at Yale) for the summer to be a buddy and overseer for her son, as her older son (who later became a Marine pilot) had left home to work. Luke went back to college at summer's end, but he and Hindenlang stayed in touch. Luke enlisted in the Navy after he graduated from Yale.

- Six months after the book came out, relatives of one of the eight contacted Bradley and told him that his mother was still living. Bradley sent age 97 Dorothy his book in 2004. They talked by telephone, and she told Bradley that knowing how her son had died gave her closure, despite the horrific details.

The Japanese engaged in cannibalism in numerous cases during World War II. They would kill POWs, excise tissue, cook, and dine. They also killed civilians for this purpose.

In some cases, they would hack off an arm or leg or cut muscle (usually six to eight pounds from the thigh) without bothering with anesthesia or analgesia, for supper. Then they would allow the pitiful victim to survive (threw him in a ditch) to keep the human meat fresh and healthy for the next meal (muscle meat from another limb). They would save the liver and other internal organs (gall bladder was favored by some Japanese officers) for last, as their extraction resulted in death.

In some cases, the Japanese killed and ate POWs, when food was scarce. This was particularly the case in New Guinea, as the Japanese were not able to supply their troops with food, and as foraging was not effective (as it was in China). However, this was not the case on Chichijima, as food was available. In defending themselves for cannibalism from anecdotal statements, the Japanese military officers offered several justifications as follows:

- That consumption of the enemy made them better warriors, showed spirit, etc.
- That human tissue (especially the liver) had medicinal value

- To increase the morale of their troops
- To terrorize the prisoners (although already terrorized) to increase the ordeal of captivity

For the record, there was cannibalism in Russia during World War II as well, as follows:

- The 872-day (this is 2.4 years) Leningrad Siege (Leningrad today is Saint Petersburg) ran 9/1941 to 1/1944. The German Army controlled the south side of the city, and the Finnish Army the north side. Some 2.8 million Soviets died in Nazi custody in less than eight months. This was 1941-1942. The causes of death were mostly starvation and disease. The trapped civilians first ate all the available pets, birds, and rodents they could catch. They then turned to cannibalism some – Russians eating Russians. This cannibalism included both types, as follows:
  - o Homicidal cannibalism whereby a person is killed, and then eaten raw or body parts cooked up
  - o Necro-cannibalism whereby a person dies (usually from lack of nutrition and/or disease) and then eaten raw, or muscle or organs cooked up and then consumed
- Following the Soviet victory after more than five months of fighting at Stalingrad (now Volgograd) 2/1943, German soldiers there in the besieged city were cut off from supplies. Some resorted to cannibalism, German soldiers eating German soldiers.
- When Germany surrendered to Russia in 1945, 100,000 German soldiers became POWs. Stalin sent them to camps in Central Asia or Siberia. As starved, these German soldiers also started eating their dead. Less than 5,000 of the 100,000 prisoners survived captivity.

Chichijima has few if any sloping beaches, as does Iwo Jima. Therefore, the U.S. did not try to land troops to capture Chichijima. The marines would have been sitting ducks (as they were on some of the Iwo Jima beaches).

The 25,000 Japanese troops on the island surrendered at the end of the war. The U.S. loaded them on American ships and ferried them back to the main islands.

Japanese casualties on Chichijima from American bombs were few, as the Japanese had bomb shelters (caves more or less).

The eight executed and consumed airmen were three gunners, two pilots, two radiomen, and a navigator. Their average age was less than 21 years old. They were as follows:

Date Shot Down	Details	Airman/Home State Branch Rank	Death	Life

7/4/1944	Curtiss SB2C Helldiver dive bomber hit and exploded, gunner was able to yank his chute open	Richard Woelloff/KS Navy Radioman 2nd Class	Bayonet penetrated	1925-8/6/1944
?	Consolidated PB4Y-1 heavy bomber, details not known	Warren Hindenlang, MA Navy Ensign (pilot)	Bayonet penetrated, decapitated	1920-8/6/1944
2/18/1945	Grumman TBF Avenger torpedo bomber made safe water landing, all three swam to shore, all three captured, first combat mission for all three	Floyd Hall, MO Navy Ensign (pilot)	Sword beheaded	1921-3/24/1945
		Glenn Frazier, KS Navy Gunner's Mate 3rd Class	Drunk officer beat to death with a club	1926-2/23/1945
		Marvelle Mershon, CA Navy Radioman 3rd Class	Sword beheaded	1926-2/23/1945
2/18/1945	Anti-aircraft fire knocked wing off Grumman Avenger TBF which slammed into this Avenger, chewing 4' off a wing; went into spin; pilot ordered York and Dye out; the two swam to shore, captured; pilot recovered despite shortened wing and flew to safety; first combat mission for both captured men	Grady York, FL Navy Gunner's Mate 3rd Class	Bamboo spears stabbed	1926-2/261945
		Jimmy Dye, NJ Navy Radioman 3rd Class	Sword beheaded at the edge of his freshly-dug grave	1925-2/28/1945
2/23/1945	Chance Vought F4U Corsair pilot bailed out, swam to shore, captured; his first combat flight	Warren Vaughn, TX Marines Second Lieutenant (pilot)	Sword beheaded in front of 150 Japanese soldiers and sailors	1922-3/17/1945

Japanese Hawaiian Nobuaki Iwatake (1923 HA -) was the oldest son of six children. He was and is an American citizen. His store clerk father drowned on a fishing trip off Maui. With the loss of her husband and the family source of income, Iwatake's mother and five of his siblings moved to Hiroshima 11/1940 to live with an uncle. Iwatake stayed on Maui to graduate high school, 5/1941. He then moved to Hiroshima to live with his family and attend college.

The Imperial Japanese Army drafted Iwatake in 1943. He was of much value, as he was bilingual – English and Japanese. He was trained as a radio operator and communications interceptor. He boarded a transport at Yokohama bound for Chichijima. A USS submarine torpedo sank the transport. Iwatake survived. A Japanese oiler picked him up and delivered him to Chichijima. He was put to work listening in on U.S. military communications, and interrogating prisoners. He oversaw some prisoners, who were charged with also listening to U.S. military communications.

Iwatake was at Chichijima when Bush was shot down 9/1944. He in fact observed Bush being rescued by the American submarine. He was also present when Warren Vaughn, the last airman in the chart above, was captured.

Iwatake developed a friendship with Vaughn. One evening when they were walking back from a bath, Iwatake fell into a bomb pit and could not get out. Vaughn pulled him out. After Vaughn was beheaded, Iwatake adopted and went by the name of *Warren*, to honor Vaughn. Iwatake's story is included in the above-mentioned, 2003 James Bradley book, *Flyboys: A True Story of Courage*.

One of Iwatake's brothers was vaporized in the 8/6/1945 Hiroshima atomic bomb attack.

After the war, Iwatake worked at the American embassy in Tokyo for 35 years as a translator.

Iwatake and Bush met on Chichijima in 2002 when they were ages 79 and 78, in a symbolic reunion of veterans from Japan and the U.S.

Information on the four shot down aircraft above is as follows:

- The Grumman TBF Avenger torpedo bomber was introduced in 1942. Its first action was the 6/1942 Midway Battle. Its length, wingspan, and height were 41', 54' and 15'. Its 1,900-horsepower radial engine pulled it up to 275 miles per hour. The three crewmen were the pilot, turret gunner, and radioman/bombardier/ventral gunner (sitting one behind the other). Four or five machine guns were installed. It carried bombs or torpedoes, weighing up to one ton. Bush Senior flew this plane.

- The one-crew, Chance Vought F4U Corsair fighter was also used as a bomber. It was introduced in 1942. Its length, wingspan, and height were 33', 41' and 16'. Its 2,250-horsepower radial engine pulled it up to 425 miles per hour. It had four machine guns, four rockets, and could carry bombs weighing up to one ton. It was a winner – its kill ratio was 11:1 in World War II.

- The Curtiss SB2C Helldiver dive bomber was introduced in 1943. Its length, wingspan, and height were 37', 50', and 15'. The two-man crew were the pilot and the radioman/gunner, sitting tandem. Its 1,900-horsepower radial engine pulled it up to 294 miles per hour. Two cannon and two machine guns were installed. It carried a bomb load up to one ton.

- The Consolidated PB4Y-1 was the Navy variant of the Consolidated B-24 Liberator heavy bomber, introduced in 1941. The B-24 still holds the distinction of the most produced American military aircraft at over 18,000 made 1940-1945, thanks to the Ford Motor Company. Its length, wingspan, and height were 68', 110', and 18'. Its crew was seven to ten men. Its four, 1,200 horsepower engines gave it a top speed of 290 miles per hour. Its armament included ten machine guns. It could carry bombs weighing up to 8,000 pounds.

The eight survivors who became supper were shot down in five planes – three in one, two in another, and three solo. Crewmates did not survive in most cases.

Regarding Chichijima, the U.S. allowed only 129 Western original locals to go back to the island after World War II, and destroyed the rest of the houses.

The U.S. stored nuclear arms on several Japanese islands in the 1950s, including Chichijima.

In 1960, Chichijima's harbor facilities were devastated by tsunamis from the Great Chilean Earthquake.

The U.S. returned the island to Japanese control in 1968. Today, Japan uses Chichijima for several purposes, as follows:

Japan's National Institute of Natural Sciences maintains and operates a radio astronomy facility to conduct deep space studies

- The Japan Aerospace Exploration Agency operates radar equipment to check the flight trajectories, status, and safety of Japanese rockets
- The Maritime Self-Defense Force (Japanese Navy) has a facility (port, seaport, and airfield)
- A green turtle conservation facility, established as these turtles became endangered when served as turtle soup and sashimi in dishes; sashimi is a Japanese delicacy consisting of very fresh raw meat or fish sliced into thin pieces, and usually served with soy sauce

Today, Chichijima's population is about two thousand. Most are Japanese who moved from Yamato Province (on Honshu) after the U.S. returned Chichijima to Japan in 1968. However, some are descendants of American Mr. Savory (again, he moved to Chichijima from Hawaii with others to form a colony in 1830).

16- SEDGLEY .38 GLOVE GUN

During World War II, the U.S. military operated from hundreds of isolated airfields located on atolls (ring-shaped coral reefs), islets, and islands in the Pacific Ocean. Navy construction forces carved these fields with excavators and tractors, often on the edges of dense jungles. They also made support infrastructure such as fuel storage tanks with piping, hangars and other buildings, water wells, roadways, etc. These construction forces were commonly called *Construction Battalions*. The nickname of *Seabees* for these airfield, building, and infrastructure builders comes from the *C* and *B* in *Construction Battalion*.

This infrastructure and the buildings were used by the Army, Army Air Forces, Navy, and Marines.

In some cases when the Japanese hurriedly withdrew, they left a few soldiers behind by mistake, or maybe purposely (who knows?). These infantrymen had a rifle, but were maybe out of ammunition. Of course, they had knives and bayonets. In some cases, they emerged from cover, to kill.

In response as a defense method, 1918 U.S. Naval Academy graduate Captain Stanley Haight (1896 NE – 1975 WY) designed a plunger trigger, single-shot, break-action, smooth-bore, .38 caliber pistol; affixed to the back of a work glove with six brass rivets. The purpose was to serve as a last line of defense against a close-range attacker. The 2.9" long pistol's plunger trigger projected past the wearer's knuckles, when he made a fist. The pistol fired, when the plunger was depressed against the attacker with the safety off. In theory, this occurred when the Seabee struck the attacker with his clenched and gloved fist. These were made for the left or right hand. However, it was not the intention that the wearer would wear two armed gloves.

The glove was to be worn in the case of operating in an area with no perimeter sentries or defense. This would include when working or off duty, including even when asleep.

The Haight Fist Gun patent was granted to Haight and the Navy, 2/29/1944. The Navy hired R. F. Sedgley Company of Philadelphia to manufacture. Philadelphia gunsmith Reginald Sedgley (1876 England – 1938 Philadelphia) started in the firearms business in 1897, as manager of the Henry M. Kolb gun-making firm. He became the owner in 1916, and renamed the company R.F. Sedgley, Inc. He died in 1938. Sedgley went out of business, just after World War II.

Sedgley made up to 200 glove guns including prototypes, for use by the Navy and Marines. The Navy's designation for the weapon was *Hand Firing Mechanism, Mk 2*.

Haight was the Group Beachmaster 10/29/1944 for the assault on Japanese-occupied Leyte (Philippines). His leadership and actions in reorganizing and directing landing parties in the area while under constant enemy fire and frequent air bombing and strafing attacks, resulted in the awarding of a Silver Star. The Silver Star is the Navy's third highest valor medal.

This was the United States' first step in liberating the Philippines. Haight stepped up when the assigned Beachmaster became incapacitated. Haight served many years past World War II, retiring from the Navy as a Rear Admiral.

Gunsmith Henry Deringer (1786 PA – 1868 Philadelphia) is best known for inventing and giving his name to small, non-revolver pistols. The purpose was to have a weapon which would fit in a pocket, purse, boot, etc. These small pistols are called derringers (these different spellings are correct). The Sedgley glove gun is in this category of being a derringer.

John Booth (1838 MD – 4/26/1865 VA) used a derringer made by Deringer's company to assassinate Abraham Lincoln (1809 KY – 4/15/1865 DC). That derringer is now on display at the Ford Theater Museum in Washington D.C., where Lincoln was shot.

Typically, derringers are single shot weapons. However, Remington did make a model with over and under barrels, so two shots. Remington made more than 150,000 of these Model 95 double-shot derringers, 1866-1935. It was 4.875" long and weighed 11 ounces. It fired the 0.41 caliber short rimfire cartridge. Only a few changes were made in the weapon over this 69-year period. As so many were made over such a long period, this double derringer entered popular culture in some cases. Three of these cases were television westerns, as follows:

- The main character in *Have Gun, Will Travel* (1957 - 1963) carried one behind his gun belt buckle. This CBS series ran 1957-1963.
- The CBS *Wild Wild West* series ran 1965-1969. One of the main characters carried up to three. One was carried in a vest pocket or an inside pocket of his jacket. Another was carried under his shirt sleeve. The third was broken into two parts with the barrel-chamber assembly hidden in the hollowed-out heel of one boot and the frame hidden in the heel of the other.
- A nickel-plated Remington derringer is given as a Christmas present in a 1965 episode of *The Big Valley*. This ABC series ran 1965-1969.

The Sedgley derringer weapon is frequently identified as an Office of Strategic Services (OSS) assassination weapon. The OSS intelligence agency OSS was formed in 1942 during World War II. It was the predecessor to today's Central Intelligence Agency, created in 1947. However, there is no substantive documentation that it was assigned to OSS operatives. Use by the Seabees is documented though.

The only known use of the weapon was in fact by a Seabee on some Pacific Ocean island. John Blocker used it to dispatch a lone, knife-wielding Japanese soldier who ambushed him. The Japanese soldier climbed on the back of his road grader, wielding a knife.

Some Beach Jumper Unit 7 officers were also issued the Sedgley. The Beach Jumper units were Navy tactical cover and deception units. The commandos (these were specially trained sailors) faked amphibious landings to divert enemy troops from the real invasion beaches. The commandos were instructed to use it if the enemy boarded or tried to board their boats, or if the enemy rushed them on the beach.

In one scenario, the American commando would raise his hands over his head in surrender with his palms facing forward, so that the enemy could not see the weapon on the back of the glove. If the enemy got close, the sailor would punch him in the head or body with his fist, triggering the weapon. At this point, the American would then physically attack the wounded enemy – as a .38 caliber slug would not necessarily slow the enemy down much, depending upon which part of his body was hit and the size of the enemy soldier.

Movie actor Douglas Fairbanks, Jr. (1909 NYC – 2009 NYC) was commissioned as a Navy reserve officer after the 12/7/1941 sneak attacks. He was assigned to Lord Louis Mountbatten's (1900 England – 1977 offshore Ireland, Irish Republican Army placed a radio-triggered bomb in his 30' wooden pleasure boat, killing him and three others and injuring others) Combined Operations. Combined Operations was Great Britain's commando warfare unit. Combined Operations used methods to deceive and misdirect the enemy. These included visual and audio methods. Later in the War (1943 – 1946), Mountbatten was Supreme Allied Commander of the South East Command. His base was Kandy, British Ceylon.

Fairbanks participated in several nighttime, cross the English Channel, Combined Operations hit and run assaults on German outposts in France. He observed and learned. He attained a depth of understanding and appreciation of military deception, then unheard of in the U.S. Navy. Fairbanks returned to the American Navy 11/1942. He convinced the Navy to adopt some of these techniques.

Fairbanks established and headed the Navy Beach Jumper units. These units again specialized in deception and psychological warfare. The unit simulated gun flashes; and sounds such as of ship engines, bos'n whistles, tank engines, and anchors scraping over decks. Balloons 25' tall covered with metal strips misled enemy radar. Smoke was generated. The Beach Jumpers had success in the European and Mediterranean Theaters.

The vast distances and tiny island objectives blocked effective use in the Pacific Theater. However, Beach Jumpers did stage successful diversions to the south and east of the Tayabas Bay Region, allowing the main assaults on the Zambales and Batangas coasts of Luzon (Philippines) 1/1945 to face less opposition.

The Navy Beach Jumper units were active 1943-1946 and 1951-1972. This was for the European and Pacific Theaters of World War II, the Korean War, and the Vietnam War. Again, their missions were to simulate amphibious landings, with a very limited force. This along with other deception fooled the enemy many times, as to the actual landing site.

Later in the War, Fairbanks commanded a mixed division of American Patrol Torpedo boats and British Insect-class gunboats and other assorted small craft in the Mediterranean Sea. His flagship was the 238' long and 36' beam and 4' draft, Insect-class HMS Aphis (1915 – 1947 scrapped) gunboat. The Task Force gun-sank the Gabbiano-class, 193' long and 29' beam and 8' draft, German UJ-6083 (1943 – 6/1944 sank) corvette. This corvette was made for the Italian navy, and delivered to Germany when Italy switched sides. The Task Force also sank a German armed yacht.

Fairbanks was awarded the Silver Star and the Legion of Merit (valor) for actions during World War II. Four countries (Great Britain, France, Italy, and Brazil) awarded him medals. He served in the Navy 1941-1954, retiring as a Captain.

The Beach Jumpers trained on Ocracoke Island off North Carolina in 1943 and on. A polished granite marker was dedicated there in 2009. Beach Jumpers including a few from World War II attended the event. One side of the marker has the image of the amphibious unit training base building. The other side has the image of a patrol ship and Fairbanks.

The National World War II Museum in New Orleans has a Sedgley in its collection, as do several other museums. Some in private ownership sell for up to $7,000, depending upon condition.

The weapon looks like something that Ian Fleming (1908 London – 1964 England) would have Quartermaster Q fashion for Commander James Bond 007 of her Majesty's Secret Service, but not the case.

The pistol made an appearance in Quentin Tarantino's (1953 Knoxville -) 2009 *Inglourious Basterds*. It also appears in the Keith Melton, 1996 *Ultimate Spy* novel.

The weapon is shown below.

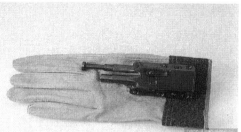

Today, there are six, mobile, active duty Construction Battalions (Seabees) in the Navy, split between the Pacific Fleet based at Port Hueneme, California, and the Atlantic Fleet based at Gulfport, Mississippi.

17- JAPAN GETS DESPERATE - SUPER SUBMARINES

A very, very long time ago, somebody invented or devised or lucked into the first watercraft. This was probably something like a raft, or maybe a canoe. Who knows?

Of course, human power was necessary for propulsion. On day one, this was probably just using a hand and arm as a paddle. On day two if not sooner, a wooden paddle or oar or pole was probably fashioned. Of course in the case of a river, the current would take downstream. In the case of that creek or river though, getting back to the starting point took a lot of energy paddling or poling upstream, depending upon the speed of the current. The poor options were to abandon the boat and hike back, or portage.

The vessel's utility was obvious – not getting wet or wet and cold for one, fishing a distance from shore or wading depth, getting to the other side of the river, moving people and/or heavy stuff around, etc.

Soon, it was realized that the mobility from such a watercraft allowed a person or group of people to project power; as now able to move weapons and provisions as well as selves up or down a river, to the other side of the lake or bay, or even the ocean when the design of the craft was refined – and propulsion methods other than human power came along.

The progression of these propulsion methods of course was wind, wood or coal fuel external combustion steam engines, petroleum fuel internal combustion engines, and finally nuclear for some ships and boats. For the record, the first nuclear propulsion water craft in the world came in the mid-1950s, for USS submarines. Today, most if not all navy submarines and aircraft carriers of at least the larger countries are nuclear powered.

For the record, the 320' long and 28' beam and 26' draft, USS Nautilus (1954 – 1986 museum ship at the U.S. Navy Submarine Force Library and Museum in Groton, Connecticut) submarine was the first nuclear powered vessel worldwide, of any type. As Nautilus' fuel supply was unlimited, the boat set many records. For one notable one, it was the first submarine to complete a submerged transit of the North Pole (1958).

Back to the old days. Eventually, sailing continent to continent occurred. The first known intercontinental voyages were several by Viking/Scandinavian types over 25 years from 986 to 1011, to what is Canada today. These Europe to North America voyages were not repeated until 481 years later, when a Genoan captain and explorer sailing under the Spanish flag from Spain reached one of the Bahama Islands. These of course were sailing (wind) ships.

Much later, manned aircraft came. The first were balloons. At first, the lift came from rising hot air. Later, the balloon envelope was filled with a lighter than air gas for lift. Hydrogen was the lightest gas, so gave the most lift. However, hydrogen was dangerous as flammable. Helium is eight per cent heavier than hydrogen, so required a larger envelope for the same lift. It was not flammable though. The U.S. converted to helium in 1910. Other countries continued with hydrogen, mainly as the U.S. was the only country that had cheap helium at the time. The U.S. would not sell helium to these countries, as they were belligerent.

Before long, again it was realized that power could be much projected in a war situation if the aircraft (again, balloons as the first) carried a sharp-eyed observer. In the 1794 Fleurus Battle, the French used a hot air observation balloon in this manner to monitor Austrian troop movements. Fleurus is in central Belgium. This was during the Flanders Campaign in the Low Countries, during the French Revolutionary Wars. France's enemy here was the Coalition Army of Great Britain, Hanover, the Dutch Republic, and the Habsburg Monarchy. This reconnaissance was the first use of an aircraft, for military purposes.

Even better than just reconnaissance, the balloonist could take an offensive measure by tossing a brick or a rock over the edge of the gondola onto the enemy (factories, bridges, military installations, ships, people {military or civilians}, etc.); or even better yet a bomb.

The first known instance of such was in 1849, when the Austrian naval ship Vulcano released manned, hot air balloons. Besides collecting information on the enemy (number of troops, amount and type of equipment, number and type of ships, location, etc.) and terrain from the aerial platform, the observer on at least one of these balloons dropped a bomb on Venice. So this particular excursion included both reconnaissance and offensive attack. This was the first known aerial attack, in history. Whether there was much damage and/or injury caused by the bomb tossed off the side was not recorded (so probably not).

Again back to projecting power, it was of course soon realized that launching aircraft from a naval ship as described in the Vulcano case above, negated the need to have aircraft and facilities on land near the enemy. This concept of a portable, water-going, air base became reality several years later in the United States. The Union Army in the Civil War converted a coal barge into an aerostat carrier. At the time, *aerostat* was the name for a hydrogen balloon. The barge was towed up and down the Potomac River during the Peninsula campaign, to desired launching points. The launching points of course were determined by the location or suspected location of the Confederacy troops, and the wind direction. The latter of course amounted to a go or not go decision.

This watercraft (a barge in this case) had advantages as could move toward suspected enemy positions, and/or take advantage of favorable winds (speed and direction). Another advantage was that barges draw very little water so could operate in rivers or lakes, depending upon the draft of the tug.

On 9/24/1861 which was five months after the start of the Civil War, an operator ascended and sent messages by telegraph to a concealed Union battery as to the accuracy of their gunfire toward Confederate encampments at Falls Church, Virginia. The messages were to aim more toward the right or left, lower or higher. This worked, enabling the artillerists to hit the target. This was an early use of the artillery forward observer method.

As just noted, the Union Army had some success with its use of aerostats; but halted these efforts 8/1/1863. The Confederacy made some similar efforts, but their use of aerostats was not successful. In several cases, the Union Army captured the South's balloons and pilots.

Aerostats were used much both sides during World War I in Europe (but not by the U.S.), to detect enemy troop movements and to direct artillery fire. Observers phoned their sightings to others on the ground, to make adjustments. Aircraft of both sides shot at balloons. These aircraft used incendiary bullets, to ignite the hydrogen in the balloons.

Observation balloons were used in the Russo-Finnish Wars, the 1939-1949 Winter War, and the 1941-1945 Continuation War. The U.S. used helium aerostats in a few cases in World War II.

The first heavier than air aircraft flight was 12/17/1903 in North Carolina. By 1910, pontoons had been added to make seaplanes. A little later, aircraft with both pontoons and wheels were used, as amphibians.

Also in 1910, aviation pioneer and civilian test pilot Eugene Ely (1886 IA – 1911 GA, crashed demonstrating a too low dive at an exhibition) took off from a 423' long USS cruiser anchored off Norfolk (Virginia) Naval Base. Two months later in 1911, he landed on the deck of another USS cruiser (504' long) anchored in San Francisco Bay. These two USSs of course had been modified to have flat decks with no or few obstacles. The aircraft was a Curtiss pusher biplane. No aids (catapult, arresting cables) for takeoff or landing were used.

The first take-off from an underway ship was in 1912, again from a USS.

The French Navy converted a ship to a seaplane tender, craning seaplanes off and on deck.

Imperial German Naval Air Service Lieutenant Junior Grade Friedrich von Arnauld de la Periere (1888 Germany – 1973 Germany) commanded a unit of two single engine, two seat, Friedrichshafen FF.29 reconnaissance biplane seaplanes during World War I. The seaplanes were based at Zeebrugge, Belgium. Zeebrugge is on Belgium's northwest coast, on the North Sea. Germany occupied Belgium 8/1914 through the 11/11/1918 Armistice Day; so for the entirety of World War I.

The single engine, two seat FF.29 was 34' long with a 53' wingspan. Its top speed was 73 miles per hour. Periere had the FF.29s modified to carry and be able to drop two 26.5-pound bombs.

On 12/25/1914 less than five months into World War I, an FF.29 took off from Zeebrugge, flew across the English Channel and up the River Thames, and dropped its bombs on the outskirts of London. The flight distance was 184 miles. These were the first bombs the Germans dropped on England in World War I. Damage was minor (craters, broken windows). British fighters pursued but did not catch the FF.29. On this first seaplane bombing mission, Periere knew and recognized that the FF.29 lacked adequate range for such missions. In this case, the FF.29 did not have enough fuel for the return leg, if it bombed London proper. Captain Walther Forstmann (1883 Germany – 1973 Germany) commanded the 188' long and 20' beam and 10' draft, SM U-12 (1911 – 3/10/1915 HMS destroyers sank off Scotland, 19 of 29 crew lost {66%}) coastal submarine. SM

U-12 was one of the first German submarines to arrive at Periere's Zeebrugge base.

Periere and Forstmann collaborated on an experiment to have SM U-12 ferry an FF.29 way out to sea for a head start before the seaplane took off, to ensure that it had enough fuel for a bombing run over London's city center, and then back to Zeebrugge. The FF.29 was strapped to the submarine's deck, sideways. However, as soon as SM U-12 sailed out of the harbor 1/15/1915, heavy swells threatened to damage the seaplane. The FF.29 was unhitched. The submarine dived. The FF.29 seaplane floated off. Periere took off successfully. He flew along the British coast, but did not drop his bombs. His intention was to land near the submarine to be recovered. Instead though, he decided to fly back to his base at Zeebrugge. He landed safely.

Periere could have used a surface warship. However, no German warships at the time were equipped with catapults for launching or suitable deck cranes. Likewise, the aircraft's frame would have to be modified to sustain being craned off and on or catapult launched.

Periere and Forstmann proposed further experiments and tests to the Kriegsmarine (German Navy), but the German Naval Command vetoed the project as considered impractical – and as was also of course much involved in fighting World War I with known methods and technologies. The concept though was re-investigated in 1917 to increase the striking power of new German submarines, which had greater range. In this case, the seaplanes would be stored in sealed, on-deck, storage compartments. However, the fighting ended 11/1918 with an armistice before more tests were conducted.

The British conducted similar experiments. The Royal Navy, 181' long and 15' beam, E-class HMS E22 (1915 – 4/25/1916 German submarine torpedo sank when on the surface off Great Yarmouth in the North Sea, 28 of 30 crew lost {93%}) submarine was modified to carry not one, but two seaplanes. These were strapped to her deck. At 23' long with a 20' wingspan, the Sopwith Schneider biplanes were much smaller than the FF.29. The Sopwiths were loosened and floated off when E22 dived. After takeoff, they landed on shore. Only a few experiments were conducted. The intended purpose was to intercept and shoot down German zeppelins as they crossed the North Sea, to bomb England.

As amphibians, the FF.29s and Schneiders could land on land or water. They therefore also could be recovered by a submarine. In this case, the submarine would simply surface near the seaplane, or the seaplane would land near the submarine. Then the boat and seaplane would maneuver so that the seaplane could be attached at the designated spot on the boat's deck. Deck hands would then attach and secure. Aviation fuel, machine gun bullets, aerial bombs, etc. would be carried on the submarine – as would be the airplane crew. As far as known though, the Germans or British never made a recovery by this method. Anyway, these cases in World War I were the first use of submarines, as aircraft carriers.

As noted above, a German submarine torpedo sank the HMS E22 submarine. It is rare for a submarine to sink another submarine with a torpedo or gun, but has occurred several times. In all cases but one or two, the sunk submarine was on the surface. The German submarine in this case was the 119' long and 14' beam and 12' draft, Type UB II, SM UB-18 (1915 – 12/9/1917 trawler rammed in English Channel, all 23 crew lost).

The Royal Navy requisitioned the 106' long and 21' beam and 12' draft, Scottish trawler Ben Lawers (1900 – 1930 sank in North Sea from collision with another trawler in the fog, all crew rescued), and converted her to a minesweeper. Ben Lawers when escorting a coal convoy rammed and sank SM UB-18 in the English Channel.

Ben Lawers was much damaged because of the strike, and barely made it to port for repairs. SM UB-18 sank 126 ships of eleven countries (none American) in less than twenty-two months, so the damage to Ben Lawers was worth it. Fifty-five, twenty-five, and twenty-two of SM UB-18's victims belonged to the United Kingdom, Norway, and France. Only one was a warship, the HMS E22 submarine just mentioned. As successful as SM UB-18 was in World War I, twelve other German submarines were credited with more tonnage sank (for both World Wars).

In these early cases with the aircraft strapped to the deck, the submarine could only cruise on the surface. Once the aircraft floated off though, the submarine could act like a submarine and dive.

As the purpose of submarines is to sail underwater for concealment and to avoid attack from enemy ships or aircraft, some do not consider these German and British boats as legitimate submarine aircraft carriers. But as noted above, the Kriegsmarine during World War I did consider adding sealed hangars to submarine decks.

After World War I several countries considered and/or even developed submarines which had water-tight hangars on deck, for storage of aircraft. The hangers were usually just in front or to the rear, of the conning tower. In some cases, the hangar/conning tower was an integrated unit – shaped to be better streamlined when cruising under water.

To fit in the hangar, the seaplane aircraft's wings and tails either folded, or were dissembled for storage. For a mission, the seaplane or amphibian would be pulled out of the hanger onto the deck of the floating submarine. Then it would be assembled, or the wings and tail unfolded and secured.

The U.S. Navy conducted experiments. The first full cycle occurred 7/28/1926 on the Thames River, New London, Connecticut; as follows:

- Aircraft was loaded and sealed in the on-deck hangar of the submarine
- Submarine dived, sailed a ways underwater, and then surfaced
- Aircraft was moved out of hanger and assembled
- Submarine dived allowing aircraft to float off, and sailed off underwater
- Aircraft took off, flew somewhere, and landed on the river
- Submarine surfaced
- Aircraft and submarine maneuvered, so that aircraft was on the submarine's deck
- Aircraft dismantled or folded

- Aircraft placed back in storage in the hangar, and door shut and sealed
- Submarine dived and continued test voyage

The seaplane was a single engine, pilot only, experimental, Cox-Klemin XS-2 scout biplane. It was 18 and 8' long and tall, with an 18' wingspan. Its maximum speed from its five-cylinder, air-cooled, 85 horsepower radial engine was 115 miles per hour. Its service ceiling was 11,300'.

The technology from the 1920s continued to develop in the 1930s. Japan, Great Britain, Italy, Germany, France, and the United States all researched and pursued. Craning the aircraft off and on from a surface warship was addressed, instead of floating the aircraft off and on the deck of a submarine. Catapult launchings from both surface warships and submarines were considered to avoid seaplanes having to take off in rough seas.

Only Japan though used the concept in World War II (except for one submarine aircraft carrier and effort developed by the French Navy, this described later). The United States, although the first country to conduct the full cycle test mentioned above in Connecticut in 1926, did not use at all in World War II, and not since either.

Japan made 41 such submarine carriers of various classes before and during World War II, which could carry seaplanes or amphibians in sealed compartments. Some could carry two aircraft. Two were made to carry three aircraft.

Japan also did not limit their use to scouting, as a few of these aircraft launched from submarines dropped small bombs. Some also had mounted machine guns for either defense against enemy aircraft or offense (strafing).

On 12/7, 8/1941, the Empire of Japan very successfully sneak attacked five, Pacific Ocean island, U.S. military installations – harbors, bases, yards, airfields, etc. This was in violation of the international rules of war. The 1907 Hague Convention addressed the requirement to declare war in its Convention Relative to the Opening of Hostilities statements. These clauses describe the international actions a country should perform, before opening hostilities. Article 1 states: *The Contracting Powers recognize that hostilities between themselves must not commence without previous and explicit warning, in the form either of a reasoned declaration of war or of an ultimatum with conditional declaration of war.* Japan took a pass on giving an advance warning, of maybe attacking. Shame on Japan again, as Japan had a history of attacking without declaring war.

These attacks were over a nine-hour period. The two dates are shown, as the attacked locations were on both sides of the International Date Line. The International Date Line is an imaginary line from the North Pole to the South Pole. It marks the change from one calendar day to the next. It roughly follows the 180° line of longitude, through the middle of the Pacific Ocean.

These five Pacific Ocean islands were Oahu (Pearl Harbor), Guam, Midway, Wake, and Philippines. Also at about the same time, Japanese marines stormed and captured a USS river gunboat and its crew in port in Shanghai. Also at the same time as the Oahu attack, a Japanese submarine gun-sank an Army chartered cargoman off the coast of California. And again, the Japanese this day bombed two Pacific Ocean islands which were U.S. protectorates (Howland Island and Baker Island). This sums up to nine attacks on the United States. For good measure, Japan also attacked four British sites, and Thailand. This adds up to fourteen successful sneak attacks in one day, an unbelievable military accomplishment.

Up to this point, the U.S. had an isolationist attitude, avoiding entry into World War II as World War I only ended a generation back (twenty-three years). Japan of course was very aware of the U.S.'s isolationist sentiments, due to the fact that 116,700 (almost 46% in combat) American men in uniform had died in the country's only 17 months involvement. Also another 204,000 military men had been wounded or made ill, many with permanent disabilities, in World War I.

Considering this, along with being walloped at these five Pacific Ocean island sites (especially Pearl Harbor and military installations on Oahu), Japan's leaders assumed (or hoped) that the U.S. would quickly negotiate peace to avoid involvement in another World War. At the least, destroying much of the Pacific Fleet at Pearl Harbor would give Japan time to fortify its newly conquered territories.

Many of Japan's military (the power was here) and civic leaders were so wrapped up in the concept of Japanese superiority genetically and the Emperor's infallibility (as after all, he was divine), that they assumed the Pacific War would be won soon, and that Japan would control much of the Asian sphere. What was Japan thinking (or hoping)? Congress declared War on Japan the next day. This was 12/8/1941, a Monday. As noted above, the peace period for America was a little more than twenty-three years, from the World War I Armistice Day to the day of the sneak attacks.

Japan's more realistic (but unfortunately weaker) leaders though knew that Japan had no chance to defeat the U.S. in a protracted conflict, because of the U.S.'s massive manufacturing capability (plants, factories). The U.S. also was flush with internal resources. These included raw materials (mineral ores, timber, etc.), fuel (petroleum), farms and ranches (food, clothing), labor (thanks to women coming into the work force, the Bracero program), etc.

And this was the case. When the U.S. sank a Japanese ship or shot down one of its aircraft, Japan was not able to replace the hardware quickly. For that matter, Japan was also not able to replace the software quickly – meaning sailors, maintainers, and airmen (especially airmen).

By late 1943, this equipment replacement capability was not much; and next to none into 1945. This was because the U.S. had bombed some of Japan's factories, as petroleum was scarce in Japan, and as Japan lacked raw materials to make war equipment. Japan's Axis allies were either not willing nor able (already taxed to the max) to help.

On the other hand, the U.S. geared up and made thousands of ships and planes during the war, and could do so amazingly quick. The U.S. was even able at the same time to amply supply its Allies with food, clothing, medical supplies including medications, equipment (including trucks, tanks, ships, aircraft, etc.), armament, munitions, etc. as well.

Furthermore, the ships, planes, tanks, trucks, guns, munitions, etc. made by the U.S. over the course of the war included improvements; to the point where they were superior to all or at least almost everything Japan (or Germany for that matter) had.

Japan and Germany both did make improvements during the war, but to a much lesser degree. Also as the War dragged on, the quality of war products made by both Japan and Germany suffered.

As already mentioned, these more realistic Japanese warlords hoped that the half-year advantage gained by the walloping of the U.S. Navy and Army and Army Air Corps and Marines at Oahu and the other islands, would allow Japan to consolidate their gains in Asia and the Western Pacific, establish a defensive perimeter, and then demoralize Americans to the point of not entering the war – this from the standpoint of losing our boys' lives and spending all this money to right Japan's wrongs, was just not worth it. In other words, these more realistic Japanese admirals and generals crossed their fingers in hopes of a quick and favorable negotiated settlement with the Allies – which would allow Japan free rein in Asia. Again, their wishful thinking did not pan out.

However, Japan did run wild for almost the next six months, rolling over countries and territories. These included Borneo, Philippines, Thailand, Malaya, Singapore, Hong Kong, Burma, Wake Island, Gilbert Islands, New Britain, New Guinea, Guam, and the resources-rich (oil, rubber, etc.) Dutch East Indies (now the Republic of Indonesia). At the time, the Dutch East Indies was the fourth largest producer of oil worldwide behind the U.S, Iran, and Romania.

As the U.S. did not quickly capitulate, Japan developed a number of grandiose plans after the surprise attacks to continue to demoralize and persuade the U.S., to turn away from the War. Most had to do with attacking the U.S. on its own mainland soil. Another had to do with destroying the Panama Canal locks or dams. The U.S. competed the Canal in 1914 during World War I, and operated it.

Commander-in-Chief of the Japanese Combined Fleet Admiral Isoroku Yamamoto (1884 Japan – 4/18/1943 Lockheed P-38 Lightning machine gun shot him over Bougainville) was the architect of the 12/7/1941 Oahu attack (Pearl Harbor and bases). Yamamoto conceived of the most notable plan just after the Oahu Pearl Harbor attack, which would allow Japan to strike distant U.S. targets. His scheme was to build a large fleet of massive, endurance, submarine aircraft carriers. The launched aircraft from the submarines would bomb cities, factories, military bases, ammunition depots, petroleum refineries, etc.; located on the east and west coasts of the United States. Panama Canal locks and dams and the Canal's hydroelectric plant could be targeted. The plan was approved. The submarines were called the I-400-class.

The Doolittle Bombing Raid on Honshu (Japan's main island) was 4/18/1942. This was 4.3 months after the sneak attacks. Casualties were few and damages minor. However, the raid much decreased the morale of the Japanese citizenry who had been assured repeatedly by the Japanese military that home island reconnaissance and defenses would prevent such. As a result of the Raid, Japan was desperate to strike American mainland soil. It had done so only once since the 12/7/1941 sneak attacks. In this case on 2/23/1942, an IJN submarine lobbed shells at an oil field in California near Santa Barbara. Damages were minor, and there were no casualties.

For the record, Japan attacked American soil four more times after the Doolittle Raid in World War II as follows:

- 6/3/1942   Japan occupied two uninhabited Aleutian Islands. The Aleutians Campaign ended 8/15/1943 when the U.S. landed troops on the 107 square mile Kiska Island, after three weeks of bombing to expel the Japanese. As it turned out, the Japanese had abandoned 2.5 weeks earlier, 7/28/1943. The Allies (U.S. and Canada) had 313 casualties including 32 deaths (28 American and four Canadian) on Kiska Island, from friendly fire, booby traps, frostbite, mines, and disease.

For some reason, the U.S. bombed the three weeks and landed troops, even though it was apparently known that the Japanese had departed (as the U.S. had broken Japan's naval codes). With so many casualties including deaths and no enemy, this was not the U.S. military's finest moment.

In the Aleutians Campaign which ran off and on more than fourteen months, the U.S. lost almost 2,000 men, compared to 4,350 for the Japanese. The U.S. Navy had three and four warships sunk and heavily damaged. USSs sank seven and nine Japanese warships and freighters.

- 6/21/1942   An IJN submarine lobbed shells at an Army fort in Oregon. Damages were minor and there were no casualties.
- 9/9/1942   An IJN submarine launched a single engine, two crew seaplane that dropped incendiary bombs in an effort to catch an Oregon forest on fire. The fire was quickly detected, contained, and put out.
- 9/29/1942   An IJN submarine launched a single engine, two crew seaplane that dropped incendiary bombs in an effort to catch an Oregon forest on fire. The fire did not catch or fizzled out quickly.

For the record, the last three efforts above involved the same submarine. The last two efforts involved the same aircraft and air crew.

As discussed above, submarine aircraft carriers were not a new concept. However, the size and capabilities of the Yamamoto proposed submarines were almost beyond belief. They were in fact the largest submarines made, until nuclear-powered, ballistic missile, submarines were commissioned in the 1960s. Yamamoto's submarines would be able to tote three bomber aircraft. The super submarines would surface; prepare the aircraft; launch them by catapult; submerge to avoid detection; and then surface again to retrieve the aircrews. Two methods of recovery were addressed, as follows:

- The bombers would be equipped with pontoons; after dropping their bombs, they would land on a calm ocean, or an ocean made calmer by a large ship's wake; this would probably be the same I-400-class submarine that had launched the bomber, but could be a surface warship or another submarine; the bomber would be craned (collapsible, hydraulic crane) onto the submarine's deck or deck of a surface warship, replenished, dismantled, and then stowed, ready for its next mission

- The bomber would simply ditch, sacrificing it; the crew would toss a life raft out and jump in, to be picked up by the submarine

Again, Admiral Yamamoto and Japan hoped that stupefied and already numb Americans from the attacks on U.S. military facilities on the five Pacific Ocean islands 12/7/1941, would lose heart due to Japan's prowess, innovation, and extended power from these mammoth boats.

The I-400-class super submarines were called *Sentokus*, which translates to *special type submarine.*

The submarine's dive bombers were called *Seirans*, which translates to *Storm from the Clear Sky* -- as the American military would not know where they came from, or where they went after unloosing their bombs. Again, this is because they would be launched and recovered by submarines, with short surface time required to launch and recover – and then the submarine would disappear (dive).

Characteristics of the submarines and aircraft include the following:

I-400-Class Sentokus Submarines	Aichi M6A Seiran Dive Bomber Seaplanes
▪ 400' long, 39' beam, 23' draft; 5,900 tons displacement	▪ 38' long, 15' tall, 40' wingspan (low wing)
▪ 144 crew	▪ Two crew
▪ Dive to 330'	▪ 1,410 horsepower, liquid-cooled, direct fuel injected, inverted V-12 Aichi Atsuta engine (licensed version of the Daimler-Benz DB 601A aircraft engine)
▪ Range 43,000 miles; translates to a voyage 1.5 times around the world, lasting up to 4 months; could reach even the East Coast of U.S. without Panama Canal passage from Japan without re-fueling	
▪ State of the art radar, sensitive to detecting enemy aircraft 49 miles distant	▪ 184 and 295 miles per hour cruise and maximum speeds
▪ Cylindrical deck hangar amidships, forward of conning tower; 3 dive bombers capacity	▪ Time to climb to 9,850' = 5.8 minutes
o Hangar 115' long, 11.5' diameter	▪ 739 miles range
o Offset 2' to starboard; submarine conning tower offset 7' to port, to balance	▪ 32,500' service ceiling
	▪ 7,277 and 8,907 empty and loaded weights
o Cone-shaped, sealing hangar door hydraulically operated from either inside or outside; rack and spur gear; door seal was 51 millimeter rubber gasket	▪ Wings hydraulically folded 90° against fuselage; horizontal and vertical stabilizers folded; collapsing made aircraft less wide than triple-bladed propeller diameter;
▪ Start point of the 85', compressed air catapult near hangar door	
▪ Collapsible, hydraulic crane stowed in recessed compartment on forward port side, just below	

top deck; motor inside submarine raised crane end to a height of 26'; boom extended out 39'; electrically operated hoist had capacity of 9,000 pounds
- Four 2,250 horsepower engines each
- Surface and under speeds of 21.5 and 7.5 miles per hour
- Armament:
  o 8 × 533 millimeter forward torpedo tubes; 4 above, 4 below; toted up to 20 torpedoes
  o 1 × 14 centimeter/40 11th Year Type naval gun (rear-facing). 9.3-mile range
  o 3 × 25 millimeter, triple-mounted Type 96 autocannon (9 barrels total), mounted atop the hangar; one forward and two aft of conning tower
  o 1 single-mounted 25 millimeter Type 96 autocannon, on bridge

three could fit in hangar
- Armament:
  o 1 × 13 millimeter, flexible mount behind rear cabin, machine gun; folded up, and then locked into place
  o 1 Type 91, 1,870-pound torpedo or bombs, the latter usually two 551-pound bombs or one 1,874-pound bomb

A well-trained crew of four could prepare and launch all three Seirans in 45 minutes. The pontoons were stored in watertight compartments, located just below the main deck on either side of the catapult track. From there they could be quickly slid forward on ramps and attached to the plane's wings. The pontoons could be jettisoned in the air, to fly faster and further.

Later, these plans involving pontoons, deck cranes, ditching and rafts, etc. for recovery of Seirans and crew were dropped, in favor of suicide missions. After all, all three Seirans could be launched in only 15 minutes, if not having to attach pontoons. This reduced the Sentukos exposed surface time by two thirds.

Also, the Seirans without pontoons could fly much higher, further, and faster – making it that much harder to shoot down from the ground, a ship, or by an aircraft. Also again without pontoons and ditching equipment (rafts, life jackets, water and food supply, etc.), the bombers could carry a heavier fuel and/or bomb load.

Twenty-eight production Seirans were made, 1944-1945.

As noted above, the original plan 6/1942 was to make 18 super submarines. Construction began 1/1943. As its wartime fortunes waned, the Japanese reduced the planned number to five. As it turned out, Japan managed to make only three. Only two though made it undersea as aircraft carriers. The third was converted into a tanker submarine.

As already noted, the Sentoku I-400s were the largest submarines ever made. For comparison purposes, the largest submarine at the time was the 358' long (so the IJN I-400 was more than 11% longer) and 38' beam and 16' draft, USS Argonaut

(1928 – 1/10/1943 Japanese destroyers sank off Rabaul with depth charges and guns; all 102 crew lost, most for a USS submarine combat sank in World War II). In fact, Argonaut and her sister boats (these were not boats in the same class, but similar in design) were the largest U.S. made, non-nuclear submarines ever. Argonaut had surface and under speeds of 16 and nine miles an hour. This made her a slowpoke on the surface, compared to the 22 miles an hour for the Sentokus. These Sentoku speeds were very impressive, considering the on-deck hanger, guns, crane, and catapult machinery; not to mention the gargantuan size of the boat itself.

For comparison purposes again, the U.S. commissioned the Triton-class, 448' long and 37' beam and 24' draft, nuclear-powered USS Triton (1959 – 1969 decommissioned, 2009 recycled) boat in 1959; which still holds the record as the longest USS submarine made. It was 11% longer than the World War II, Japanese Sentokus completed 15 years before. However, the Triton's beam was almost 2.5' less than that of the Sentoku.

The largest submarines ever though were Russia's, Typhoon-class, nuclear-powered, ballistic missile, super quiet monster, at 574' long with a 76' beam and 39' draft. It was 28% longer and its beam more than double the U.S.'s biggest. With that enormous width (for a submarine), these mammoth boats had ample space for the crew to get comfortable – close to spacious for a submarine. Six were made and deployed in the 1980s. These have been scrapped or are awaiting scrapping.

Russia's current submarine is the nuclear-fueled Borei-class, with the first put into service in 2013. This also enormous boat is 558' long, but with only a 44' beam. Its draft is 33'.

For the record, the current USS fast attack submarine class is the nuclear-powered Virginia-class. It is 377' long with a 34' beam. The first (USS Virginia) was commissioned in 2004.

Germany and Japan did not collaborate much in World War II. They were half a world apart for one thing; and very busy to say the least. Also in some ways the two countries did not trust each other. This was the case despite the 9/1940 Tripartite Pact between Japan and Germany and Italy, against the U.S. However, there was some equipment and technical cooperation and exchange, including in the case of the Sentuko submarine and its aircraft. This included the following:

- The two, 40' periscopes (one for night and one for day) were made in Germany
- An anechoic coating developed in Germany made from a mixture of gum, asbestos, and adhesives was applied to the hull from the waterline to the bilge keel; the coating's purpose was to absorb or diffuse enemy sonar pulses and dampen reverberations from internal machinery, making detection while submerged more difficult
- A German-made, hydraulically-raised device (a snorkel, more or less) allowed the submarine to run its diesel engines and recharge its batteries, while sailing at periscope depth; this snorkel allowed the diesel engines to suck in air, and eject engine exhaust; the Germans developed this

technology during World War II which the Allies did not realize until later in the War; when they observed German submarines using the snorkel device, they assumed it was a periscope

- The power plant of the Seiran dive bombers was a modified some, liquid-cooled, direct fuel injected, inverted V-12 aircraft engine licensed from Daimler-Benz; this engine powered the Messerschmitt Bf 109E fighter and some other Luftwaffe aircraft; Kawasaki of Japan and Alfa Romeo of Italy also licensed for war equipment; the V-angle was only 60° (90° is common for V-engines), which resulted in a narrow engine only 28" wide (was 85" and 42" long and tall); dry weight was 1,576 pounds; bore and stroke were 5.91 and 6.30"; displacement was 2,071 cubic inches, or 33.9 liters

Sea level takeoff power was 1,410 horsepower

The centrifugal type, single speed supercharger was gear driven

The first plan was to bomb American west coast cities or east coast cities. This was changed though, to bomb the Gatun locks on the Atlantic side of the Panama Canal. The plan was for up to 10 Seirans (three each from the two super submarines, and two more each from two smaller submarine carriers) to attack. Destroying or damaging the locks, dam, and/or hydroelectric plant would prevent the U.S. from transferring ships and troops from the European Theater to the Pacific Theatre, especially as the war in Europe was winding down.

Japan made a wooden replica of the locks off one of its islands, for Seiran pilots to practice dive bombing runs.

For the record, the U.S. banned Germany from Canal use after Germany invaded Poland 9/1/1939. Japan was banned 7/22/1941, 4.5 months before the sneak attacks.

Germany also had a plan to bomb and cripple Canal locks. This was Operation Pelikan. In the fall of 1943, the plan was to ferry two single engine, low wing, Junkers Ju-87 Stuka dive bombers modified to have folding wings and pontoons on submarines with sealed deck hangars to a Columbian island near the coast of Panama. The now seaplane Stukas would then be re-assembled, floated off the submarine when it dived, and take-off to bomb the Gatun Dam. This large earthen dam across the Chagres River impounds the 21 miles across Gatun Lake. A hydroelectric plant generates electricity used to operate the Canal locks and other equipment.

After dropping their bombs, the Stukas would fly to a neutral country and seek asylum, or internment until the end of the War if asylum did not work. It did not happen.

Other Nazi plans included sabotage by agents in place in Panama or Columbia, or commandos landed by submarine. Again, these plans never came to fruition.

The U.S. put up more than significant defenses around the Canal. These included coastal artillery, which at the time was considered the most powerful and effective worldwide. These included eleven 16" guns. Range on the Caribbean Sea side from Fort Sherman (1913 – closed after World War II) was 17 miles. Of course, this was before electronics, so hitting a distant target such as a warship at that distance was not likely. The sole purpose of Fort Sherman and its outposts was to defend the Canal, but specifically the Gatun Locks and the Atlantic port of Cristobal.

Land fortifications were made at the Gatun and Pedro Miguel and Miraflores lock areas. Anti-aircraft guns were scattered around. Naval mines were placed. Anti-torpedo nets were installed. Barrage balloons were up. Chemical smoke generators were installed to conceal locks, land fortifications, etc. if necessary. Long-range radar stations were installed on each coast. Six hundred and thirty-four search lights were placed, as were 30 aircraft warning stations. Troops were stationed at Toro Point (Fort Sherman), Colon, and Margarita Island. At the height of World War II, the U.S. had 65,000 soldiers stationed in Panama, plus thousands of other military and civilian personnel.

For World War II, bombs very often did not land where wanted. The Japanese developed precision guided bombs in the last few years of the War. They were called *kamikazes*. In 4/1945 as mentioned earlier, the plan was changed that the pilot or pilots would simply fly their stripped down and bomb-laden Seirans into the locks, instead of dropping bombs.

Although the U.S. put up defenses around the canal as just mentioned, the sudden appearance (as had approached underwater and undetected) of as many as ten bombers in USAAF livery (see below) aiming for locks and dams, may have caught inexperienced and probably bored anti-aircraft gunners off guard.

In fact, security had become lax. Defensive combat air patrols had stopped. In other words, these kamikazes may have been successful; in putting the Canal out of commission. Repair and reversal would take at least months.

Blocking Allied warships and cargomen passage across the Panama Isthmus would not have lost the war. But the War would have been extended – depending upon whether or not the damage delayed or was a factor in delaying the use of the atomic bombs.

Panama never came under attack by the Axis countries in World War II. However, hostile submarines did visit the area during World War II.

The Japanese painted the Seirans in USAF livery. This of course was in violation of the rules of war. By the way, Japan also painted American insignia on some of its submarines as well. These changes in plans and actions indicated Japan's desperation by this time, and unfairness. Warring nations that cannot stomach defeat and surrender tend to break the rules much, when the losses pile up.

Okinawa fell 6/1945. By this time, the U.S. had amassed an armada at Ulithi, a Carolina Island atoll with a huge harbor. The U.S. staged ships (including 15 aircraft carriers) and troops here for the final assault on the Japanese home islands, to force Japan's surrender.

Japan concluded that damaging the Canal at this point would have little effect on the outcome of the War. This was because the U.S. already had so many ships in the Pacific Theater, and as the supply routes started on the West Coast (Canal not needed).

With its larger cities incinerated by firebombing, its surface warships and submarines mostly sunk, Japan's last (and desperate) hope was a Seiran suicide attack not against the Panama Canal, but at Ulithi (Operations Hikari and Arashi). Their attack was to be coordinated with strikes from kaitens, which were suicide torpedoes. The kaitens would be launched from mother submarines. The desperate goal was to sink a bunch of U.S. Navy warships (aircraft carriers preferred), to hopefully gain a bargaining chip in surrender talks.

The two massive submarines sailed separately for Ulithi. Before they got close enough though to launch a Seiran, Hiroshima was nuclear bombed 8/6/1945, a Monday. The U.S. and its allies and the whole world for that matter were sure that Japan would surrender after the atomic bomb. This was not the case.

Two days later on Wednesday 8/8/1945 the U.S. dropped conventional bombs. The targets were Yawata (Kyoto Prefecture) and Fukuyama (Hiroshima Prefecture). Twenty-one and 73% of these cities' urban areas were destroyed respectively, with many casualties of course. The U.S. and its allies and the whole world for that matter were sure that Japan would surrender after the massive damage to these two cities, two days after the atomic bomb was dropped on Hiroshima. This was not the case.

The second atomic bomb was dropped the next day on Nagasaki, which was Thursday 8/9/1945. The U.S. and its allies and the whole world for that matter were sure that Japan would now surrender. Japan did surrender, but not until five days later on 8/14/1945.

Submarine crews were ordered to destroy their documentation (codes, logs, charts, manuals, etc.) and weapons. The Sentokus fired their torpedoes without arming them. They catapult-shot their Seirans into the ocean without unfolding their wings and stabilizers, or simply pushed them off the side. Both Sentoku carriers surrendered to U.S. warships. This was the first that the Allies knew of their existence – and boy were they surprised.

The U.S. examined the Sentokus and then sank them (Operation Road's End). This was to prevent Soviet engineers from examining them. The deliberate sinking of the Japanese submarines was done in violation of the treaty that ended the Pacific War, which stated that military technology acquired from Japan was to be made available to other Allied powers. The Soviet Union still under tyrant and mass murderer Premier Joseph Stalin (1878 Russia – 1953 Soviet Union, cerebral hemorrhage) was not the type of country a democratic nation could continue to ally with, after the War.

Only one Seiran aircraft survived World War II. It was found at the Aichi Kokuki Aircraft Factory at the end of the War. It was displayed outdoors at the Naval Air Station Alameda (California) until 1962. It was then stored. After an eleven year restoration project, it was put on display in 2000 at the Udvar-Hazy Center of the Smithsonian's National Air and Space Museum. The Udvar-Hazy Center is located at Washington Dulles International Airport (Chantilly, Virginia).

The fate of the I-400s was as follows:

Boat	Laid Down Launched Completed Decommissioned Target Sank	Fate
I-400	01/18/1943 01/18/1944 12/30/1944 09/15/1945 06/04/1946	Surrendered to Bagley-class, USS Blue (1937 – 1977 target sank) destroyer 8/19/1945; decommissioned 9/15/1945; Navy engineers inspected and evaluated; Balao-class, USS Trumpetfish submarine (1946 – 1973 transferred to Brazil) torpedo sank as a target off Hawaii 6/4/1946, to avoid inspection by the Soviets (Operation Road's End); Pisces deep-sea submarines of Hawaii Undersea Research Laboratory discovered wreck in 2013 at a depth of 2,300', off southwest coast of Oahu; the wreck was relocated 2015
I-401	04/26/1943 03/11/1944 01/08/1945 09/15/1945 05/31/1946	Surrendered to Balao-class, USS Segundo (1944 – 1970 target sank) submarine 8/29/1945; decommissioned 9/15/1945; Navy engineers inspected and evaluated; Balao-class USS Trumpetfish submarine (1946 – 1973 transferred to Brazil) torpedo sank off Hawaii as a target 5/31/1946, to avoid inspection by the Soviets (Operation Road's End); Pisces deep-sea submarines of Hawaii Undersea Research Laboratory discovered wreck in 2005 at a depth of 2,690'; the wreck was relocated 2015
I-402	10/23/1944 09/05/1944 07/24/1945 11/15/1945 04/01/1946	Converted to a tanker submarine and completed 7/24/1945, but never made it to sea; decommissioned 11/15/1945; U.S. evaluated at Sasebo Bay, Japan; U.S. sank with another 20 Japanese submarines 22 miles southeast of Fukue Island (largest and southernmost of the Goto Islands) with C-2 explosives 4/1/1946 to avoid inspection by the Soviets (Operation Road's End); the wreck was discovered in 2015, 660' down
I-403 I-406 I-407 I-408 I-409 I-410 I-417		Cancelled 7/1943 or 10/1943
I-404	11/08/1943 07/07/1944	Construction stopped 6/4/1945, when 95% complete; U.S. heavily damaged in 7/28/1945 air raid at Kure Naval Arsenal, Kure, Hiroshima, Hiroshima Province; later scuttled; salvaged; scrapped in 1952
I-405	09/27/1943	Construction stopped at Kawasaki Shipbuilding Corporation, Izumi Province

To sum up, neither of the two submarines launched aircraft or fought in any way.

There is no doubt though. These enormous, long-range submarines with their capability to catapult-launch three bombers were engineering and method marvels. If Japan had a fleet sailing before the sneak attacks or shortly after and had been successful in shutting down the Panama Canal and had bombed American cities – who knows, maybe the U.S. would have negotiated a peace, and Asia today (and maybe even the U.S.) would be a much different place.

At the very least, the Pacific War would have run much longer; from the standpoint that the U.S. would be so involved in protecting its homeland. This would have delayed its involvement in fighting elsewhere. This last statement is based on the assumption that in having to pour money and resources into defending the homeland, that development of the atomic weapons would not have occurred, or development and use would have been much delayed. Again, who knows?

One of the super submarines is shown below, as is one of the toted aircraft.

 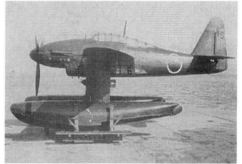

The two I-400, super submarines described above though, were not Japan's first submarine aircraft carriers. Japan made another forty-one, used in World War II. The most were twenty of the twin screw, Type B1-class, long-range submarines. These were commissioned 1940-1942. In fact, the B1s were the IJN's most common submarines, for World War II. They were 357' long, with a 31' beam, and pulled 17' of water. They were fast, at speeds of twenty-seven and nine miles per hour surface and under. Range was up to 16,000 miles, at eighteen miles per hour surface. The crew was ninety-four. They carried one, compressed-air, catapult-launched Yokosuka E14Y seaplane. The watertight hangar was located in front of the conning tower.

Often though, they used the on deck, sealed hanger to carry extra fuel for the submarine instead of a seaplane. Late in the War, the hangar was removed on some of the Type B1s to tote kaitens (manned suicide torpedoes).

The two crew, low wing Yokosuka E14Y seaplane was 28' long and 13' tall, with a 28' wingspan. The wings and tail were made to disassemble, to fit in the hangar. Its air-cooled, radial nine-cylinder, 340 horsepower engine gave it cruise and maximum speeds of 104 and 153 miles per hour. Its armament included a machine gun in the rear, and two bombs at 168 pounds each. The crew were the pilot and an observer/gunner. One hundred and twenty-six were made 1940-1942.

Chief Warrant Flying Officer Nobuo Fujita (1911 Japan – 1997 Japan) was enrolled as part of the Pearl Harbor attack. However, he did not fly as his Yokosuka had a malfunction. His submarine then patrolled the Western Coast of the U.S., with eight other submarines. He flew reconnaissance missions over Australian, New Zealand, and Fijian harbors February and March, 1942. He flew a 5/1942 reconnaissance mission over Kodiak, Alaska, in preparation for Japan's invasion of the Aleutian Islands next month.

The Yokosuka was used mainly for reconnaissance. However, Fujita proposed the idea of submarine-based aircraft dropping bombs on ships or land targets, as mentioned above. The Yokosukas did have this capability, to carry and drop small bombs.

Fujita was older than most Japanese Navy pilots, at age 31 in 1942. Due to his flying experience and age, he had the respect of his superiors as well as his peers. As a result, his idea to drop bombs from a submarine-launched aircraft was approved, and in fact assigned to his submarine carrier. His two efforts described below in starting forest fires were mentioned earlier.

Fujita's submarine was IJN I-25 (1941 – 9/3/1943 USS destroyer depth charges sank off New Hebrides Island, all 100 hands lost), of the above described Type B1-class. As mentioned already, this submarine had been part of the armada which sneak attacked Oahu (Pearl Harbor) 12/7/1941.

When patrolling off the West Coast of the United States along the California and Oregon border, I-25 launched Fujita 9/9/1942. He and Petty Officer Okuda Shoji dropped two, 168-pound, incendiary bombs in the woods. The goal was to start massive forest fires in the Pacific Northwest, to draw military resources away from the Pacific Theater to fight the fires. One bomb started several fires on Wheeler Ridge on the 2,985' Mount Emily in the Siskiyou National Forest, 9.9 miles east of Brookings, Oregon. Forest Service employees quickly spotted the fires. They were put out by the next day.

Brookings is on the Pacific Ocean coast, six miles north of the border with California.

The other incendiary did not catch the forest on fire. There had been a recent rain, and the trees were still green at this time of the year. Under these conditions, fires would not start easily. If they did start, they were slow to spread.

Fujita gave it another try, 9/29/1942. He saw flames, but apparently they died out quickly. These two attacks were called the Lookout Air Raids. Fujita's four, dropped incendiary bombs on these two occasions were the only aerial bombing of the continental United States, in World War II.

This is not counting a few of the 9,340, Imperial Japanese Navy, jet stream carried hydrogen balloon bombs of the 11/1944 through 3/1945 Operation Fu-go, that connected with U.S. soil. They were launched from the east coast of the main Japanese island of Honshu. These balloons were the planet's first intercontinental weapons. Damages in the U.S. were next to none. However, six civilians and a fetus were killed when one went off, when they tampered with one that landed in the Mitchell Recreation Area in south-central Oregon. The mother to be was age 26. The five other dead were all children.

Fujita continued to fly, mostly scout missions. In 1944, he was transferred to train kamikaze pilots. He retired at the end of the War, age 34. He served in the Japanese Navy 13 years. A younger brother was killed in the War.

Fujita opened a hardware store in Ibaraki Prefecture, Honshu. He later worked for a wire manufacturing company.

The town of Brookings in 1962 invited Fujita to visit. He accepted, once the U.S. advised him and Japan that he would not be arrested and tried as a war criminal. Fujita served as Grand Marshal for the local Azalea Festival. He gave the town of Brookings his family's 400-year-old samurai sword as a symbol of World War II regret, but also friendship and peace.

It was later learned that Fujita was ashamed of some of his actions during the War such as training kamikaze suicide jockeys, and had contemplated using the family sword to perform seppuku (ritual suicide, the Samurai warrior bushido code dies hard). In fact, he stated that if Brookings gave him a hostile reception, he would use the sword then (and this at the age of only 51).

As it turned out though, Brookings treated him with respect and affection, realizing that he was just a foot soldier following orders. This was not quite the case though, as he is credited with the forest bombings idea as well as its execution. Nevertheless, he became Japan's informal ambassador of peace and friendship to Brookings. There was some controversy on this visit (and his later visits) to the U.S. though, over Brookings' invitation and welcoming stance.

Fujita in turn invited three Brookings high school students to Japan, in 1985. During that visit, the White House Office sent a thank you letter to Fujita. Ronald Reagan (1911 IL – 2014 CA) was President at the time.

Fujita returned to Brookings in 1990, 1992, and 1995. At the 1992 visit, he planted a tree at one of the bombsites as a peace gesture. During his last visit in 1995 when he was age 84, he moved the samurai sword from City Hall to a display case at the new library in a formal ceremony. The town made him an honorary citizen.

Fujita died in 1997, age 85. The next year his daughter buried some of his ashes at his first bomb site on Mount Emily in Oregon. One would think that the ashes would be buried or scattered at a site symbolizing peace instead of destruction, but whatever.

Fujita's submarine carrier I-25 besides launching him as the only manned aerial bombing of the continental U.S. of World War II, also was responsible for the only enemy shelling of a military installation in the continental U.S. I-25 followed fishing boats to avoid minefields. Near the mouth of the Columbia River, she fired seventeen, 140 millimeter, explosive shells the night of 6/21-22/1942 at Battery Russell on Fort Stevens (1864 – 1947 closed), Oregon.

Fort Stevens defended the Oregon side, of the mouth of the Columbia River. The Columbia River forms the boundary between Oregon and Washington. The Fort's commander had all the lights turned off, so the submarine crew could not see its target. Most of the shells caused no damage. One though severed several large telephone cables.

The Fort's commander chose to not fire back, as the muzzle flashes would have revealed their position. Also, the Fort's obsolete Endicott era guns (1885 - 1905) lacked the range of the submarine's guns, which the Commander did not wish to advertise.

Army Air Forces planes on a training mission spotted I-25, and radioed her location to a twin engine, Lockheed Hudson A-29 bomber. The bomber found IJN I-25, but its bombs missed. I-25 submerged and escaped.

As noted above, Japan made 41 submarine carriers before and during World War II. Two were the enormous, I-400-class boats described above. Twenty were the Type B1s also described above. The other 19 were in eight classes, commissioned from 1932 to 1945.

Japan's first submarine carrier of the forty-plus was the 320' long and 29' beam, Type J1M-class, I-5 scouting submarine, completed in 1932. Only one was made. It was the first functional submarine to carry an aircraft in a sealed compartment – other than just for tests. It actually had two hangars (compartments). I-5 did not have a catapult. Its seaplane was assembled on deck, and then lowered with a crane into the water for takeoff on pontoons. After the flight, the seaplane landed on the ocean, and then taxied up to the submarine. The submarine crane then plucked it up out of the ocean.

Japan's successor boats to the I-5's all had catapults though for launching. The hangar and catapult were usually on the forward deck, so the submarine carrier could sail into the wind to aid takeoff. This avoided the potential of damage from having to take off in the ocean, especially if the seas were heavy. Seaplanes generally do not even attempt to take off (or land) in heavy seas.

As mentioned above, France was the only other country to experiment with a submarine carrier during World War II. The 361' long and 30' beam and 24' draft, 21 and 12 miles per hour surface and under, twin-screw, long-range (11,500 miles surfaced), 130 crew, Surcouf (1934 – 2/18/1942 sank off Panama, cause not determined, all 130 crew lost) cruiser submarine was the longest submarine ever made when commissioned.

Besides the longest, she was different in other ways. She had two, 8" guns, the same size found on a heavy cruiser of the time. These guns' range was 26 miles. She was designed to sneak around underwater, surface, and use her guns to sink enemy ships. With that range, she could also bomb shore positions or even inland targets. She toted 24 torpedoes, also some kind of record. Some were 16" and some 22".

Surcouf carried a 27' long and 39' wingspan and 9' tall, 118 miles per hour maximum speed, Besson BM.411 observation floatplane. The hanger was behind the conning tower. The Besson was used for reconnaissance and gun calibration purposes. A crane lowered and retrieved the Besson.

Surcouf is also known as the only French Navy vessel in British and Canadian ports that the British were not able to commandeer successfully – to avoid French ships going to Germany in World War II. Three British (two officers and a seaman) and one Frenchman (warrant officer mechanic) were killed in the takeover effort. This was 7/3/1940 in the English port of Plymouth, on England's south coast.

After World War II to date, no countries' navies operate submarine aircraft carriers (at least none known). Many countries though of course use unmanned aircraft (drones), launched from land or warships (including submarines).

18- BOY SCOUT JAMBOREE, KARAFUTO ISLAND

Eugene Fluckey (1913 DC – 2007 Annapolis) graduated from the U.S. Naval Academy in Annapolis, Maryland, 1935. His initial assignments were on a battleship, then a destroyer. He attended Navy submarine school in 1938. He served on submarines through 6/1942. This included five patrols on the Barracuda-class USS Bonita (1926 – 1946 scrapped). Bonita was an older submarine, with some current technology lacking. She patrolled some in the Pacific Theater, but was converted to a cargo submarine the end of 1942. She was then used as a training submarine until decommissioned 3/1945.

Fluckey returned to Annapolis for graduate instruction in naval engineering. He attended the Prospective Commanding Officer's School at the New London (Connecticut) Submarine Base, 12/1943 – 1/1944.

Fluckey was transferred to the Gato-class, 312' long and 27' beam and 17' draft, twin screw, 10 and 24 miles per hour under and surface, 60 crew, USS Barb (1942 – 1972 scrapped) submarine. He became Barb Commander 4/28/1944. He held that position through the end of the Pacific War (8/1945). Barb's armament included the following:

- 24 toted, 21" (733 millimeters) torpedoes; six and four forward and aft tubes
- 1 × 3" (76 millimeters) / 50 caliber deck gun
- 1 Bofors 40 millimeter cannon
- 1 Oerlikon 20 millimeter cannon

At the time, many submarine captains considered their role as reconnaissance, and then reporting to surface warships. Fluckey was not in this category. He was in the stalk and kill category. He also preferred to operate mostly on the surface, again not common for submarines of any country in World War II. With these tactics, he set attack precedents and established himself as a great submarine skipper.

Barb made 13 patrols. The first five were in European waters. The last eight were in the Pacific Theater. The Pacific patrols ran 3/1944 to the end of the War (8/1945). Fluckey was on Barb for all eight Pacific patrols, and Captain for the last six. Barb sank seventeen ships (warships, freighters, and tankers), all on her Pacific Ocean patrols. These totaled 96,628 tons. This was the fourth most for a USS submarine in World War II.

The Balao-class, USS Tang (1943 – 10/24/1944 sank by own torpedo on circular route in Taiwan Strait, 78 of 97 crew lost {80%}) was number one for a USS submarine in World War II in tonnage sent to the bottom. Tang sank 33 ships totaling 116,454 tons, over eight months and one week. Her sum would have been much larger, if her own launched torpedo had not circled back, and struck and sank her.

Barb started out big in the Pacific Theater. On her first outing in the Pacific which was her sixth patrol, she sank five Japanese merchantmen with torpedoes over two weeks. She also sank two trawlers with her guns this patrol.

One of Barb's torpedo victims was the Taiyo-class, 591' long, IJN Unyo (1940 – 9/17/1944 off Singapore, death estimates of 250 to 900 crew and passengers) escort carrier. Barb also sank three other Japanese warships. These were a frigate, a destroyer, and a cruiser.

The Japanese were after Fluckey and Barb. For his exploits and as the Japanese were not able to catch him, the Japanese gave Fluckey the nickname, *Galloping Ghost.*

Most of Fluckey's raids were at night, and along the east coast of China. His bold forays were complicated by continual barrages from Japanese airplanes and boats, and by shallow waters that often forced him to the surface. He sometimes sent crewmen to launch sabotage missions on land. One of these is described below.

On the night of January 23 and 24, 1945 of Barb's eleventh patrol, Fluckey found more than thirty Japanese vessels (navy and cargomen) lurking in a concealed harbor off the coast of China. The Japanese ships were protected by mines and rocky shoals. This was Namkwan Harbor, opposite the 36 Matsu Islands archipelago in the East China Sea. The East China Sea is part of the Pacific Ocean. Evading a cordon of armed escort boats, Barb slipped into the harbor on a moonless, cloudy night. She scored eight torpedo hits on six large ships. One was an ammunition vessel, which exploded. The resulting flying shells caused much damage to other nearby Japanese ships.

Barb then fled through uncharted rocky waters thick with fishing junks, pursued by two Japanese gunboats. As the water was shallow, Fluckey was forced to stay topside dodging obstacles such as mines and rocky reefs, not to mention steady fire from Japanese warships. This went on for a full hour before reaching the safer depths of the open ocean, where Barb could dive. Barb's under and surface speeds were ten and 24 miles per hour, so remaining on the surface did allow a much faster retreat. In fleeing, Fluckey went to 150% overload, setting a speed record for a submerged submarine at 27 miles per hour.

The outcome of this attack was that the entire Japanese shipping system was disrupted, for months. This exploit was recognized with the awarding of the Medal of Honor to Fluckey, and the Presidential Unit Citation to Barb. The Medal of Honor citation reads as follows:

> For conspicuous gallantry and intrepidity at the risk of his life above and beyond the call of duty as commanding officer of the USS Barb during her 11th war patrol along the east coast of China from 12/19/1944 to 2/15/1945. After sinking a large enemy ammunition ship and damaging additional tonnage during a running two-hour night battle on 1/8/1945, Commander Fluckey, in an exceptional feat of brilliant deduction and bold tracking on 1/25/1945, located a concentration of more than 30 enemy ships in the lower reaches of Nankuan Chiang (Mamkwan Harbor). Fully aware that a safe retirement would necessitate an hour's run at full speed through the uncharted, mined, and rock-obstructed waters, he bravely ordered, "Battle station — torpedoes!" In a daring penetration of the heavy enemy screen, and riding in five fathoms (nine meters) of water, he launched the Barb's last forward torpedoes at 3,000-yard range.

Quickly bringing the ship's stern tubes to bear, he turned loose four more torpedoes into the enemy, obtaining eight direct hits on six of the main targets to explode a large ammunition ship and cause inestimable damage by the resultant flying shells and other pyrotechnics. Clearing the treacherous area at high speed, he brought the Barb through to safety and four days later sank a large Japanese freighter to complete a record of heroic combat achievement, reflecting the highest credit upon Commander Fluckey, his gallant officers and men, and the U.S. Naval Service.

At Fluckey's request, a Mark 51 rocket launcher was installed at overhaul on the foredeck, after Barb's eleventh patrol. This required that the 4" gun be removed. A 5" gun was installed on the afterdeck.

The Mark 51 fired a 5", ten-pound, spin-stabilized round. The trajectory angle could be set at 30, 35, 40, or 45°. The adjustment was made by removing a setting pin, manually leaning the barrel, and then re-inserting the pin. The barrel would not swivel. To sum up, aiming required the following:

- Distance from the target was a function of the angle set for the barrel
- The submarine had to be aligned with the desired rocket round path

This required flexibility, and constant adjusting, but the Barb crew made it work.

Barb fired rockets at a Japanese air station and some factories 6/1945, causing damage. She fired rockets at the coastal towns of Shari, Hokkaido; Shikuka, Kashiho; Shiritoru, Karafuto; and Kaihyo To, Karafuto. The latter town was 60% destroyed. These bombardments caused damages to factories, shipyards, ships, a lumber mill, an air base, etc. The destroyed or damaged factories included a paper factory, and a leather-tanning factory that made airmen uniforms.

Firing rockets was a first for a submarine. No other World War II submarine (Allied or Axis) had rockets.

Barb sank Japanese supply transports off the northern coast of Japan, in the Sea of Okhotsk. This was in June and July, 1945.

Using Barb's periscope, Fluckey had observed trains bringing supplies and materials to enemy ships on the northern Japanese island of Karafuto. USS submarines including Barb were already successful in stopping most supplies getting to Japanese outposts by transport ships. Fluckey pondered on how to prevent supplies from even getting to the transport ships. He proposed a land raid, to blow up train tracks.

The first plan was to simply damage the rails on a coastal line. If not discovered, the next train would derail. If discovered, Japan would at least have to use its limited resources (at this stage in the War) to repair. The next plan though was to conceal a sailor or sailors who would detonate an explosive as a train passed, destroying the train and its cargo as well as the tracks. That plan was also dropped, in favor of using a microswitch which would be activated when the train passed. This would avoid having to wait for a train (train schedules were not known, or varied); and reduce risk of injury, death, or capture to the saboteurs as well. Fluckey asked for volunteers. He got many. He established some limiting criteria as follows, to form the commando team:

- Only unmarried men; electrician Billy Hatfield (1921 – 1999) was the exception though, as married; Hatfield recalled how when he was a kid, he and his buddies would position walnuts so that the weight of a passing train caused the ties and rails to sag, breaking the carefully placed walnuts open; from this, he conceived the idea of using a microswitch, which would be triggered by the weight of the passing train

Do realize that Third Class Mate Hatfield was an electrician; it was not just his prior, train nut-cracking experience that got him on the team, but also his knowledge and expertise with microswitches

Then again, Hatfield's wife for sure would have voted for him to stay on Barb, in lieu of this commando mission; after all, that was Captain Fluckey's requirement, that the commandos be single; Fluckey approved the exception

- The party would include members from each department; those selected included (as their primary rating) a gunner, a torpedo man, an electrician (this was Hatfield), a signalman, a mate, two motor machinists, a cook, and an officer to lead the group
- The team would consist of both regular Navy and Navy Reserve sailors; as it turned out, it was four and four
- At least half the group had to have been Boy Scouts; Fluckey had been a Boy Scout, making Eagle in fact; he knew that Boy Scouts had skills such as finding their way in unfamiliar territory, first aid, and just overall an ability to improvise as necessary

For the record though, the argument may be made that soldiers and marines tend to have or need to have such land coping skills, more than airmen and sailors; then again, these sailors were on a land mission

- The volunteers had to be American; this is mentioned, as a Japanese prisoner of war that Barb had aboard and not yet deposited also volunteered; the prisoner offered that speaking the language could be a major plus; Fluckey considered, but decided against
- Finally, Fluckey would lead the saboteurs himself; however, the selected crewmen told him no way, that as Barb commander he must stay with Barb; Fluckey protested and pulled rank; however, his crew threatened to report the planned raid to his superiors, who would have ordered Fluckey to stay aboard Barb (and for that matter, probably put the kibosh on the whole, preposterous, scheme; after all, submariners are not commandos), as Commanders were to stay in place of their command (in this case, the submarine), and were not allowed to take such risks; also, Fluckey was married, so by his own criterion, he was disqualified

Lieutenant William Walker was in charge. On the night of 7/22-23/1945, cloud cover darkened the moon. As the crew lowered two, rubber dinghies from Barb into the water 950 yards off shore, Captain Fluckey gave one last piece of advice: *Boys, if you get stuck, head for Siberia, 130 miles north.* As the raid was on an island, this about Siberia was somewhat fanciful advice for a dinghy voyage. The target site was on the southeastern coast of Karafuto (Patience Bay).

The cargo on one of the dinghies included one of the submarine's scuttle charges. The 14" X 14" X 16" and 55-pound explosive package was Torpex. The British developed Torpex, as a secondary explosive. Torpex is 50% more powerful than trinitrotoluene, pound per pound. The explosive was wired to three dry cell batteries, and placed in a pickle can for transport.

Their other cargo included digging tools, a compass, red-lens flashlights, watches, knives, food rations, inflatable life jackets, cigarette lighters, a signal gun, binoculars, electrical wire, carbines, Thompson machine guns, pistols, and hand grenades.

The eight saboteurs took 25 minutes, to paddle to the beach. They found the nearby rail line, only 0.23 miles inland. Three men were posted as guards. They saw a structure. This was a tower or a shed. One of the team climbed or looked in and saw a Japanese guard (probably a civilian) on coastal watch. The sentry, obviously not so dutiful, was asleep. The sailor took care to not wake him. An express train went by, so they hid in the bushes.

Fifteen minutes were required to dig the holes. Barb's engineers had fashioned a pick and a shovel from steel plates, bent and then welded – submarines do not normally tote gardening tools. The explosives, batteries, and microswitch were set in another five minutes.

In the meantime, Captain Fluckey had carefully moved up, so only 600 yards from shore. Here, Barb's clearance was only 6' above the sea bottom.

The 15-car train arrived, as the men were paddling back to Barb. The train's weight bowed the tracks which triggered the microswitch. The charge blew. The engine, twelve freight cars, two passenger cars, and a mail car were destroyed from the explosion and derailment. There were casualties, of course.

The awaiting sailors on the Barb saw the fireworks from the crashed train. The raiders in the dinghies rushed back to the submarine. Barb departed with the Japanese not knowing until the end of the War, who or how the explosive was placed.

This was the only time in World War II, that Allied military personnel set foot on a Japanese home island. The island was Karafuto, which is the southern half of Sakhalin Island. The northern half belonged to the Soviet Union at the time.

The Soviet Union invaded Karafuto 8/11/1945, overwhelming the Japanese Army. This was two days after the second atomic bomb had been dropped. A ceasefire went into effect 8/25/1945. At the time of the invasion, 400,000 Japanese and Koreans lived on Karafuto. One fourth fled to Hokkaido, by the time of the ceasefire. Hokkaido is Japan's second largest island. It is north of Honshu Island, which is the largest. Karafuto/Sakhalin is 27 miles north of Hokkaido. Over the next year, the Russians forced the rest to move to Hokkaido. The whole island today belongs to Russia.

Fluckey wrote his memoirs, *Thunder Below* (1992). He used proceeds from the book to reimburse his World War II crew and their wives' travel costs to attend Barb reunions. By this time, most of the men were in their 70s, at least.

Chief Gunner's Mate Paul Saunders (1918 VA – 2003 FL) was one of the train raiders. He served in the Navy 1936-1962, retiring as a Chief Petty Officer. He crewed on destroyers and a cruiser before qualifying for submarines. Saunders was on all of Barb's war patrols; five and eight in the Atlantic and Pacific Oceans. He was Chief of the Boat for the last four Barb patrols. After World War II, he was Chief of the Boat on three more submarines. Saunders was awarded the Silver Star twice (third highest U.S. military valor medal) for World War II actions. He was one of the most decorated enlisted men in the Submarine Service. He was featured in Fluckey's *Thunder Below* book, mentioned above.

For the record, the Chief of the Boat is the term for an enlisted sailor on board a U.S. Navy submarine. He serves as the senior enlisted advisor to the commanding officer and executive officer. In Navy speak, the executive officer is the second in command of that warship.

The Chief of the Boat assists with matters regarding the good order and discipline of the crew. The commanding officer makes the selection. Usually, he (or could be a woman today, of course) is the most senior enlisted person aboard.

Fluckey's USS Barb was much aimed at – 400 shells, bombs, and depth charges. However, none of his crew received the Purple Heart.

Barb herself was also highly decorated, including the Presidential Unit Citation as mentioned above. This award was created in 1942 to recognize extraordinary heroism in action against an armed enemy. More specifically, the honoree must display gallantry, determination, and esprit de corps in accomplishing its mission under extremely difficult and hazardous conditions, to set it apart from similar units or entities participating in the same campaign.

Barb received eight Battle Stars for her World War II fighting. She was in and out of Navy commission, until 1954. At the end of that year, she was loaned to Italy under the Mutual Defense Assistance Program. The Italian Navy renamed her Enrico Tazzoli. Patriot and priest Tazzoli (1812 Italy – 1852 Italy, execution hanging) was the best known of the Belfiore martyrs. The Belfiore martyrs were a group of pro-independence fighters caught and executed (hanged) in 1852 and 1853, during the Italian Unification.

Barb was sold for scrap in 1972, for $100,000 ($601,800 in 2019 money). Admiral Fluckey stated later that if he and his crew had known of the sale for scrap, that they would have raised the money and made Barb into a museum ship.

Fluckey revolutionized submarine warfare inventing the night convoy attack from astern, by joining the flank escort line. He was much decorated of course, receiving the Medal of Honor as described above, four Navy Crosses, Navy Unit Commendation, and others. In fact, some consider him the most decorated Navy man of World War II.

Just after the War, Fluckey oversaw the fitting out of the new Balao-class, 312' long and 27' beam and 17' draft, single screw, 10 and 23 miles per hour under and surface, 80 crew, USS Dogfish (1946 – 1972 sold to Brazil) submarine.

Fluckey transferred 11/1945 to the Office of the Secretary of the Navy, where he worked for Navy Secretary James Forrestal (1892 NY – 1949 MD, suicide jump) on plans for the unification of the Armed Forces.

Fluckey next worked in the War Plans Division. He then worked for Fleet Admiral Chester Nimitz (1885 TX – 1966 CA), the incoming Naval Operations

Chief. He returned to submarines 6/1947, commanding the Balao-class, USS Halfbeak (1946 – 1972 scrapped). In 5/1948, he transferred to set up the Submarine Naval Reserve Force. In 8/1950, he became the flag secretary to Admiral James Fife (1897 NV – 1975 CT). From 8/1950 to 7/1953, he served as the U.S. Naval Attaché and Naval Attaché for Air to Portugal. He led Submarine Division Fifty-Two of Submarine Squadron Five 8/1953 to 6/1954. He then went back to sea, commanding the Fulton-class, USS Sperry (1942 – 2017 scrapped) submarine tender. He commanded Submarine Flotilla Seven 10/1955 to 1/1956.

Fluckey then returned to the Naval Academy and chaired the Electrical Engineering Department. He became Commander of Amphibious Group 4. In 11/1961, he became the Naval Board of Inspection and Survey President. He was the Pacific Fleet Submarine Force Commander 6/1964 to 6/1966. In 7/1966, he became the Naval Intelligence Director. In 1968, he became Chief of the Military Assistance Advisory Group, for Portugal. Military Assistance Advisory Group is the designation used by the U.S. for military advisers sent to other countries to assist in training of that country's armed forces, and directing strategy as well.

Fluckey retired in 1972, as a Rear Admiral. He served 37 years. He chose to move back to alma mater town of Annapolis for his retirement years. He was buried at the Naval Academy cemetery.

Fluckey's first wife of 42 years died in 1979. He remarried. He had one child with his first wife, a daughter.

Fluckey and the USS Barb's damage blanket are shown below. Although not too clear, note the picture of the train at center bottom. Barb was the first submarine to be involved in destroying a train; and probably the last. The damage flag is on display at the U.S. Navy Submarine Force Library and Museum in Groton, Connecticut.

19- TECHNICAL SERGEANT BEN KUROKI, JAPANESE AMERICANS SERVING

The Hawaiian Islands are a volcanic-formed archipelago (archipelago simply means a collection of islands in an area) of eight major islands, several atolls, numerous smaller islets, and seamounts. A seamount is a usually conical-shaped mountain rising from the ocean seafloor, that does not reach to the water's surface. Seamounts are obviously navigation hazards.

Added up, they are 137 islands. They comprise 6,423 square miles total. For comparison purposes, this is 2.4% the size of Texas. The four largest islands in order are Hawaii, Maui, Oahu, and Kauai at 4,028, 727, 592, and 562 square miles. These four together account for 92% of Hawaii's total area. Hawaii's largest city is Honolulu, on Oahu.

The islands run 1,500 miles from the most southeastern and largest island of Hawaii to the most northwestern Kure Atoll. An atoll is a ring-shaped coral reef, that encircles a lagoon. The uninhabited Kure Atoll is 5.8 miles by 4.8 miles. These dimensions include the lagoon. The land area though of the several islets of Kure Atoll is less than one third of a square mile. Kure Atoll is noted as the northernmost atoll in the world, at 28° latitude above the equator.

Hawaii, Maui, Oahu, Molokai, and Lanai are the first, second, third, fifth, and sixth largest of the eight major Hawaiian Islands. These six united in 1795 to form the Kingdom of Hawaii. The fourth and seventh largest islands of Kauai and Niihau joined the Kingdom fifteen years later in 1810.

For the record, the smallest of the eight major Hawaiian Islands is Kahoolawe, at 45 square miles. Today, Kahoolawe is a nature reserve, and has no permanent population.

Kalakaua (1836 Hawaii – 1891 San Francisco) was the last king of Hawaii. He ruled from 1874 to his 1891 death. During his reign, social and political and/or economic conditions in Japan were such (this during the Meiji period), that a diaspora occurred. A diaspora is an involuntary mass dispersion of a population from its traditional home, and can be for a number of reasons. In this case, the reason was economic. Japan lacked jobs, or other ways to make a living. Hawaii needed laborers, for its sugar industry. The match was made. Many thousands of Japanese moved to the Kingdom of Hawaii, beginning in 1869. And in fact, many of the early immigrant men did work in the sugar industry.

Soon after, many thousands of Japanese sailed past Hawaii, to move to the United States. Most moved to the west coast states; and many of these to California.

King Kalakaua and his wife had no children. Kalakaua's sister Liliuokalani (1838 Honolulu – 1917 Honolulu) succeeded her brother. She was overthrown 1/1893 in a U.S. supported coup d'état, two years after her brother's death. She was Hawaii's first female monarch, and also Hawaii's last monarch. Hawaii was a republic (independent country), until the U.S. annexed Hawaii 5.5 years later in 1898 as a territory.

Most native Hawaiians were opposed to the annexation. For this reason and others, the U.S. quickly transitioned Hawaii to self-rule, in 1900.

The U.S. made improvements to the harbor at Honolulu (Oahu) in 1899, to allow deeper draft ships. This is Pearl Harbor. Since then, other military facilities were added. By the 1930s, the Navy, Army, Army Air Forces, and Marines all had facilities on Oahu (and still do).

So to sum up, Hawaii was a self-governing U.S. territory 12/7/1941 on the day of the sneak attacks (see below paragraph), courtesy of the Empire of Japan. At the time, 150,000 of the 400,000 Hawaiian population (three eighths) were of Japanese descent. Japanese Hawaiians were Hawaii's second largest minority ethnic group, next to native Polynesian Hawaiians.

Japan sneak attacked thirteen locations in or on the Pacific Ocean 12/7, 8/1941. Japan as usual (Japan had a history of sneak attacks) did not bother to warn the victims, by declaring war. This was in violation of the international rules of war. The 1907 Hague Convention addressed the requirement to declare war in its *Convention Relative to the Opening of Hostilities* statements. These clauses describe the international actions a country should perform, before opening hostilities. Article 1 states: *The Contracting Powers recognize that hostilities between themselves must not commence without previous and explicit warning, in the form either of a reasoned declaration of war or of an ultimatum with conditional declaration of war.* Japan took a pass on giving an advance warning, of maybe attacking. Shame on Japan, again.

The attacks were all on the same day, within nine hours of each other. Two days are shown, as the locations were on both sides of the International Date Line. The International Date Line is an imaginary line from the North Pole to the South Pole. It marks the change from one calendar day to the next. It roughly follows the 180° line of longitude, through the middle of the Pacific Ocean. But again, the attacks were all on the same day.

The attacked thirteen sites (or ships) were as follows:

- Nine U.S. possessions
  - Storming and capture of a 159' long USS river gunboat and its crew when berthed at Shanghai Harbor; this little Yangtze River gunboat was the only USS that Japan captured in World War II; for good measure, the Japanese also gun-sank a 177' HMS river gunboat in Shanghai Harbor, at about the same time; if counting this British warship, it is fourteen sneak attacks instead of thirteen
  - IJN submarine gun-sank an Army-chartered, 250' long freighter off California
  - Howland and Baker Islands of the Phoenix Islands of the U.S. Minor Outlying Islands were bombed, these two islands are 43 miles apart
  - Five U.S. military installations (harbors, airfields, bases) on five Pacific Ocean islands; these five islands were Oahu (Pearl Harbor), Guam, Midway, Wake, and Philippines
- Three British Crown colonies – Malaya, Hong Kong, and Singapore

- Thailand

Japan ended up occupying the three British crown colonies, Thailand, and Wake Island for the duration of World War II (which ended 8/1945). Japan occupied Guam until the U.S. re-captured 8/1944. Japan occupied the major Philippine islands by the spring of 1942. The U.S. wrested the Philippine islands back beginning 10/1944, and into 1945. General Douglas MacArthur (1880 AR – 1964 DC) said he would return and he did, but it took 2.6 years.

Some Japanese soldiers held out though on Mindanao Island (second largest of the Philippines) until the end of the War, 8/1945. In fact, a group of 200 well-organized and disciplined Japanese troops also on Mindanao did not surrender until 1/1948, which was almost 2.5 years after the War ended – if you can believe it.

In the next few weeks or months after the sneak attacks, Japan also conquered and occupied Borneo, Burma, New Britain, Gilbert Islands, and the resources-rich (oil, rubber, etc.) Dutch East Indies (today, the Republic of Indonesia).

In these thirteen (or fourteen) attacks on the same day, the Japanese Empire was for the most part stupendously successful in terms of devastation and casualties rendered, versus its own loss of equipment and casualties. Japan's planning and executions were brilliant. Said yet a third way, the outcomes were very one-sided in Japan's favor. To quote President Franklin Roosevelt (1882 NY – 4/12/1945 Georgia, cerebral hemorrhage) from his 12/8/1941, Monday speech to Congress, 12/7/1941 was *a date that will live in infamy* for the United States. Congress declared war on Japan, that day.

Of the five U.S. military targets on the five Pacific Ocean islands, Americans of course most remember Oahu of the U.S. Territory of Hawaii, again due to the one-sided outcome. Japan launched two air attacks (bombing and strafing), one hour apart on a Sunday morning. The U.S. military had 2,335 and 1,143 men killed and wounded. Another 68 and 35 Hawaiian civilians were killed and injured. In comparison, only 64 Japanese military men died (55 airmen and nine submarine sailors) and one (a submariner) captured. This is a ratio of more than 36 American military deaths per one Japanese military death.

The Japanese Navy sank or damaged nineteen USSs, including all eight battleships of the Pacific fleet. Hundreds of aircraft were destroyed, and most of these when on the ground. Japan lost only 29 aircraft, nine and 20 in the first and second wave attacks. These were fifteen, nine, and five dive bombers, fighters, and torpedo bombers. Japan's five mini-submarines all sank, which was more or less the (unstated) plan. The other 51 ships and boats of the Japanese Task Force were undetected and unseen, coming and going.

Japan's surprise attacks without declaring war ended the United States' isolationist attitude, left over from losing 116,700 men in uniform (almost 46% in combat) and another 204,000 wounded or made ill (many with permanent disabilities) in World War I. As already noted, Congress declared war on Japan the next day, which was a Monday. The peace period was a little more than 23 years for America, from the World War I Armistice Day to the day of the sneak attacks.

The two air attacks on Oahu were over in an hour and a half, with all the Japanese aircraft on the way back to their carriers by 9:30. Army Lieutenant General Walter Short (1880 NY – 1949 GA of heart problems) was in charge of the defense of Hawaii. In the immediate aftermath of the attack, Short contacted Hawaiian Governor Joseph Poindexter (1869 OR – 1951 HA) and convinced him that martial law was essential. Short feared further attacks from the Japanese, and/or internal sabotage by Japanese Hawaiians.

Poindexter telephoned President Roosevelt on this issue. Roosevelt immediately authorized martial law. Poindexter did so, at 15:30. General Short simultaneously assumed the title of Military Governor of Hawaii.

Army Chief of Staff George Marshall (1880 PA – 1959 DC) relieved Short of all duties ten days later which was 12/17/1941, for not detecting the Japanese attack and for responding so poorly. In disgrace, Short was ordered back to Washington D.C. He was reduced in rank from his temporary rank of Lieutenant General (three stars) to his permanent rank of Major General (two stars), since his temporary rank was contingent on his command. Short retired from the Army 2/1942, age 61.

Major General (two star) Frederick Martin (1882 IN – 1954 Los Angeles) was Army Air Forces Commander at Hawaii. He was also removed from authority 12/17/1941, for similar reasons as General Short. He was sent to a command at a base in Washington. Martin separated from the Army 8/1944.

For the record, the fate of the head Navy Commander based at Hawaii was more of the same. 1904 U.S. Naval Academy graduate Admiral Husband Kimmel (1882 KY – 1968 CT) was Commander in chief of both the U.S. Fleet and the U.S. Pacific Fleet. The U.S. Fleet was the combined U.S. Pacific Fleet and the U.S. Atlantic Fleet. At the time of the sneak attacks, the U.S. Pacific Fleet was the Battle Fleet (newer battleships and the aircraft carriers), and the U.S. Atlantic Fleet was a Scouting Fleet (older battleships). The Asiatic Fleet, the Naval Forces in Europe, the Special Service Squadron (Caribbean), and all submarines were independent of the U.S. Fleet. Anyway, Kimmel was removed from authority the same day as Army General Short and Army Air Forces General Martin, or 12/17/1941. He was reduced in rank from Admiral (four stars) to Rear Admiral (two stars). This is two steps down. Like General Short, he separated from the military in early 1942. He was 59 years old.

Kimmel's son Manning Kimmel (1913 DC – 1944 Palawan Island, Philippines) was a 1935 graduate of the U.S. Naval Academy, his father's alma mater. He commanded the Gato-class, USS Rabalo (1943 – 7/2/1944 disappeared off Palawan, probably mine sunk) submarine. It is thought that all 60 crew died except for four to seven when the submarine struck a mine. These four to seven survivors which included Manning Kimmel, made it the two miles to shore. This was Palawan which is the fifth largest and most western of the major Philippine Islands. Before they could locate Filipino guerillas, the Japanese captured them. Later, the Japanese pushed Lieutenant Commander Kimmel and other American prisoners of war into a ditch and burned them alive with gasoline. This atrocity is as reported by Clay Blair (1925 VA – 1998 WI), a World War II submariner.

Blair wrote the definitive work, *Silent Victory: The U.S. Submarine War Against Japan* (see volume 2, pages 660-662 for Manning Kimmel's story and demise). The book came out in 1975.

Manning's brother Thomas Kimmel who was also in the military was pulled from combat, when it was learned that Manning was probably dead.

As already noted, General Short and Admiral Kimmel were the Army and Navy heads of the Hawaiian Department. President Roosevelt appointed a commission to investigate why the Japanese were able to surprise the Army, Army Air Forces, Navy, and Marines; and also why the U.S. military's response was so delayed and weak. After all, Pearl Harbor was known as the *Gibraltar of the Pacific.* The warnings of an upcoming attack were plentiful.

U.S. Supreme Court Associate Justice Owen Roberts (1875 Philadelphia – 1955 PA) headed the Commission. The other four members were two retired Navy admirals, a retired Army general, and an active duty Army Air Forces general. The Roberts Commission released its findings to Congress 1/28/1942. These were that both Short and Kimmel were guilty of errors of judgment and dereliction of duty. As already noted, they both separated from the military shortly after the Roberts Commission released its conclusions.

Many feel that Douglas MacArthur should have been removed from duty as well. Although he had been made aware of the attack on Oahu, he reacted poorly. As a result, the Japanese struck a decisive blow nine hours after the attack on Oahu (so time to react was ample), which led to the loss of the Philippines in the next few months. However, unlike Short and Kimmel, MacArthur was actively fighting the Japanese in the Philippines. Roosevelt decided to leave him in place.

To sum up, both Kimmel and Short were drummed out of the military. Roosevelt set up the Roberts Commission to avoid a Congressional investigation. Also, somebody decided that court-martial was not the best approach. Although not recorded in history, conventional wisdom was that this somebody was Roosevelt. Some think Short and Kimmel deserved this treatment or worse, some do not – you be the judge.

Army Short, Navy Kimmel, and Army Air Forces Martin were ages 61, 59, and 59 at the time of the sneak attack on Oahu. Again, Short and Kimmel separated shortly after the Roberts Commission released its conclusions.

For the record, the Roberts Commission also concluded that both Japanese diplomats and persons of Japanese ancestry had engaged in widespread espionage leading up to the attack. This turned out to be a major factor in the decision to intern Japanese Americans.

Lieutenant General (three star) Delos Emmons (1889 WV – 1965) was named Commanding General of the Hawaiian Department effective 12/17/1941, replacing General Short. This meant that he was also the Military Governor of Hawaii. General Emmons named Lieutenant Colonel Thomas Green (1889 MA – 1971) to enforce the provisions of martial law on Hawaii. These included curfews, blackouts, censorship, closing of schools, cessation of radio broadcasts, cessation of communications by telephone and telegraph, control of the mail, control of hospitals and emergency services, control of food and liquor sales, control of employment, control of travel on the islands, control of prostitution, etc.

Additional restrictions were put on Japanese Hawaiians. Some Japanese Hawaiians who were suspect for one reason or another were quickly rounded up by the FBI, and incarcerated. As to suspect Japanese in this emergency situation, this was obviously guesswork due to lack of time to investigate, although some lists had already been prepared.

Those collected included ethnic Japanese in the following (almost humorous in some cases) categories:

- Those who were thought to be sympathizers or partisans of Japan
- Administrators and teachers who taught English as a second language (being bilingual would facilitate spying)
- Leaders – consular, business, civic, religion (Buddhist and Shinto priests for example)
- Fishermen (after all, they had boats)
- Martial art instructors (after all, they were elite fighters)

Almost 2,000 Japanese Hawaiians were incarcerated. About two thirds and one third were Issei (moved to Hawaii from Japan) and Nisei (born on the islands). None were ever found guilty of overt acts (espionage or sabotage).

The martial law status ran 2.9 years until 10/24/1944, although some restrictions were eased before that date.

As already noted, the U.S. declared war on Japan the day after the sneak attacks. This was 12/8/1941, a Monday. Right off, some Americans were concerned that Japanese Americans on the continent as well as Hawaii, would be loyal to Japan. This was especially the case for Issei. Americans generally did not have this concern in the case of Nisei.

For the record, Issei were not citizens of the U.S. (until 1954), but Nisei were automatically citizens by law as born in the American Territory of Hawaii or the United States. This is called birthright citizenship. The Citizenship Clause is the first sentence of the 435-word, 1868 Fourteenth Amendment to the U.S. Constitution. The Fourteenth Amendment is one of the three Reconstruction Amendments, addressing the status of former slaves after the Civil War. The amendment was passed to ensure that now free African Americans after the Civil War were citizens. Furthermore, it was to ensure that their children and grandchildren and on yet to be born were citizens as well. As worded so broadly though (again, the only requirement is that born on American soil), tens of millions of newborns are now U.S. citizens, even though their parents were not citizens.

This is the case regardless of the citizenship, immigration status, length of time living in the U.S. or one of its territories, employment, age, criminal record, etc. of the parents. In recent years, these have numbered about 285,000 births a year for the U.S., whose parents were not citizens of the U.S. The Canadian figure is about 1,500 a year.

Some legal scholars state that the Fourteenth Amendment was passed to ensure that the freed slaves and their descendants were citizens, and that the amendment has no relation to granting citizenship to children born in the United States whose parents are legal or illegal immigrants.

For the record, the Citizenship Clause reads as follows: *All persons born or naturalized in the United States, and subject to the jurisdiction thereof, are citizens of the United States and of the State wherein they reside.* The Latin legal term is *jus soli,* which translates to *right of the soil.*

This birthright citizenship provision is the case today in about thirty-one countries, all in the Western Hemisphere. No European or Asian country allows birthright citizenship. Most of the countries that do allow birthright citizenship are not particularly good places to live. In fact, some are horrible places to live.

The only two notable exceptions in this group are the adjacent countries of the United States and Canada. Mexico is also adjacent and allows birthright citizenship. However, some if not most consider Mexico an undesirable country to live in. Brazil also allows, but again Brazil has its problems.

Donald Trump (1946 NYC -) when campaigning for President in 2016 and also after taking office 1/2017 stated that birthright citizenship should not be the case, for children born in the U.S. if the parents were not citizens. Republicans tend to agree with President Trump, Democrats not so much.

The United Nations recognizes 193 countries. As only two countries considered a good place to live have such an automatic citizenship clause and due to the many adverse outcomes which result, many consider such an outlier provision as radical and destructive (but that is another story).

This concern about the loyalty of Japanese Americans related to a number of reasons, including the following:

- Between 1936 and 1941, Japan rapidly conquered without provocation a large portion of Asia, committing countless heinous acts against civilians as well as military men in the process – especially in China. Well aware of these aggressions and atrocities, the U.S. (and other countries for that matter) pressured Japan in a number of diplomatic and (mostly) economic ways to act right. These methods were not successful.

- Most Issei were strong supporters of Japan's militaristic expansions, including annexing parts of China. A few Japanese leaders did speak out that Japan's 12/7/1941 surprise attacks were uncalled for and unfair. These included some consulate officials, and officers of the Japanese American Citizens League. These were only a few in number. However, note the following:
  - They did not direct their statements to the Japanese government.
  - They did not advise or even demand that Japan cease its aggressions, expansions, or atrocities.
  - They did not advise or even demand that Japan return ceased territories.
  - They did not demand that Japan compensate those wronged.

o They had not spoken out before the sneak attacks.

Some Issei who had moved back to Japan though from either Hawaii or the U.S., did laud Japan's belligerence. They supported Japan's aggressions and colonialism, perceiving it as a way of improving the Japanese economy so as to be able to move back to Japan; or even to a new country now part of and controlled by the Japanese Empire.

On the other hand, most Issei and all or almost all Nisei living in Hawaii and mainland states were simply just focused on bettering their lives. For sure, their lives in the U.S. or Hawaii were much, much better than those living in Japan; or that they would have if they moved back to Japan. Very few Issei (if any) moved back to Japan after 12/7/1941 from Hawaii or the U.S. No Nisei moved back.

- There was evidence of espionage from decrypted messages to Japan from agents in North America and Hawaii, before and after the 12/7/1941 sneak attacks. However, only the federal government knew this.

- Some Japanese living in the Philippines at the time of the attack collaborated with the Japanese invasion troops. Roosevelt and other leaders knew this, but the general public did not.

- Americans became aware of the Niihau Incident, connected with the 12/7/1941 sneak attack at Oahu. The only three ethnic adult Japanese on the Hawaiian Island of Niihau (one Issei, two Nisei), much abetted a downed Japanese Mitsubishi A6M Zero fighter pilot. The one Issei had married a Hawaiian woman, and they had children. The two Nisei were a married couple, also with children. The children as well as the Niseis were American citizens.

- After the 12/7/1941 sneak attacks, seven Japanese submarines patrolled the U.S. West Coast. They torpedo or gun-sank and/or damaged several American merchant vessels, killing and injuring some crew. They skirmished twice with U.S. Navy air or sea forces. By the end of 12/1941, the submarines had returned to friendly waters for replenishment. Some then returned to the U.S. West Coast to attack more cargomen and maybe USSs.

Again, many citizens had concerns that Japanese Americans would turn to espionage or sabotage or even join up with Japanese troops, if Japan attacked the west coast. Under much pressure, President Roosevelt 2/19/1942 reluctantly issued Executive Order 9066; which authorized the War Secretary to designate certain areas as military zones. Without due process or a declaration of martial law, this cleared the way for relocation and confinement of Japanese Americans, German Americans, and Italian Americans living in these zones.

Less than one week later, two alarming events happened, as follows:

- 2/23/1942   The Type B1-class, 357' long and 31' beam and 17' draft, long-range IJN I-17 (1941 – 8/19/1943 Kiwi minesweeper and U.S. floatplanes depth charges sunk off Noumea, 91 of 97 crew lost {94%}) cruiser submarine was part of the 12/7/1941 Oahu (Pearl Harbor) Task Force. I-17's mission was to reconnoiter and engage any USSs that tried to sortie from Pearl Harbor fleeing the attack and/or searching for the Japanese armada. As it turned out, there was no such need.

I-17 returned to Japan for replenishment. She then with other submarines sailed to the West Coast of the U.S. On 12/20/1942, she gun-sank the 6,912-ton General Petroleum tanker SS Emidio (1921 – 12/20/1941 off Cape Mendocino, five crew lost and other crew wounded), which was sailing from Seattle to San Pedro, California. The submarine connected with five, 14-centimeter shells. As sailing in ballast, a petroleum cargo was not lost and the ocean polluted.

I-17 returned to Japan for replenishment again, and then back to the West Coast. On this date, I-17 surfaced only several hundred yards offshore. Captain Kozo Nishino ordered his men to aim at the Richfield aviation fuel storage tanks of the Ellwood oil field. The Ellwood oil field was 12 miles west of Santa Barbara, and near the ocean. Seventeen, 14-centimeter shells were fired, 19:15 to 19:35. Most landed way off, exploding either miles inland on Tecolote Ranch or splashing in the ocean before making land. However, one shell hit near the Luton-Bell 17 oil well, on the beach just below Fairway 14 of the present-day golf course – several of the Sandpiper Golf Club holes are on the beach. This caused $500 in damage to a pier, catwalk, pump house, etc.

This incident was the first naval bombardment by an enemy power on the U.S. mainland since the German Type U-151, 213' long and 24' beam and 17' draft, SM U-156 (1917 – 9/25/1918 believed sunk by a mine in the Northern Barrage, all 77 crew lost) submarine shelled Orleans, Cape Cod, Massachusetts, and a 120' long, steel tugboat towing four barges to the Virginia Capes. SM U-156 used its 5.9" deck guns. The Perth Amboy tug was damaged. The four barges were sunk. Some tug crewmen were injured (none killed though). The shells that landed on the Orleans beaches (no damage) were probably aimed at the tug and barges. This was 7/21/1918, less than four months before the World War I Armistice date.

In the late 1930s, Captain Nishino had been a tanker skipper. He anchored at the Ellwood Oil Field dock in 1938 to take on a load of oil. When walking with his crew to a formal welcoming ceremony onshore, he tripped and fell into a patch of prickly pear cactus. Believe it or not, this patch of cactus is still there, just off fairway 11 of the Sandpiper Golf Club. Being Japanese where cacti if any is only grown for ornamental purposes, he did not know to maintain his distance.

The sight of the proud Japanese commander having cactus spines pulled from his rear end, provoked laughter from a group of nearby American oil workers. Therefore, it appears that this 2/23/1942 wild shelling may have been an avenging act, four years later (well, at the least it makes a good story).

- 2/25/1942   The following night after the Ellwood oil field shelling, Los Angeles military radar detected something 120 miles west of the city on or above the Pacific Ocean. The time was a little past 02:00. Air raid sirens sounded. Powerful searchlights were switched on. A blackout was put into effect. Army gunners in Santa Monica unleashed a barrage of anti-aircraft fire to down Japanese fighters and bombers. Other coastal gun locations in other parts of the metropolis opened fire, to come to Santa Monica's aid.

The *all-clear* order came less than an hour later. Los Angeles' artillery batteries pumped 1,440 rounds of 37 millimeter and 76 millimeter anti-aircraft ammunition into the sky over 50 minutes. Ten tons of shrapnel and unexploded ammunition rained down, ripping through buildings and vehicles and shattering windows. No people were killed or injured from the firing. However, five died -- three in automobile crashes, and two from heart attacks.

Twenty Japanese-Americans were arrested, for allegedly trying to signal or direct the non-existing Japanese aircraft and/or warships to targets.

It appears that a meteorological balloon or meteorological balloons sent up on purpose or by mistake that night to determine wind conditions were interpreted as attacking Japanese aircraft. To sum up, there was no enemy, but ample hysteria.

This came to be called the Los Angeles Battle.

Steven Spielberg (1946 Cincinnati -) directed the 1979, ensemble cast, comedy movie *1941,* which is loosely based on these two, 2/1942 events. The star cast included John Belushi, Dan Aykroyd, John Candy, Slim Pickens, Robert Stack, Ned Beatty, Christopher Lee, Tim Matheson, Warren Oates, Treat Williams, etc. Its production cost was $35 million, and box office $95 million.

These two events 31 hours apart were written up with some to much exaggeration in newspapers. Some radio broadcasts were also misleading. The hysteria part was not too emphasized. As part of that hysteria, some came to believe that the government was covering up the severity of damages and the number of casualties, to avoid terrorizing the populace.

Exaggerated or even false reports of suspected spying and sabotage on the West Coast, later sightings or suspected sightings of Japanese surface warships or submarines or aircraft, or other aggressions by Japanese military by print journalists (newspapers, magazines, etc.) fueled the suspicions and concerns. Again, radio broadcasts skimpy on the facts added to the concerns.

Regarding any naysayers on the 2/19/1942 Executive Order 9066 to confine Japanese living on the West Coast, these doubters (or at least most of them) changed their minds after the just mentioned California submarine shelling four days later of the industrial oil site, and the fake scare the next night in Los Angeles.

Army Major Karl Bendetsen (1907 WA – 1989 WA) of the War Department authored what became Public Law 503, which provided for enforcement of Roosevelt's Executive Order. Congress quickly approved, and Roosevelt signed it into law 3/9/1942. The law made violations of military orders a misdemeanor, punishable by fines up to $5,000 and a year in prison.

Bendetsen also defined Japanese to include persons who were only partially Japanese. Even if the percentage was less than one sixteenth, they were to be interned. Of course, such small percentage Japanese blood persons claimed Asian (or other) ancestry other than Japanese, if they could pull it off. A few even went so far as to have plastic surgery, to change facial features.

Bendetsen developed a plan by which all persons of Japanese ancestry, both Issei and Nisei, were forced to leave the West Coast. Bendetsen pressured Lieutenant General John DeWitt (1880 NE – 1962 DC) to accept his plan, rather than the less-restrictive one which DeWitt had developed. General DeWitt headed the Army's Ninth Core Area which included eight western states and Alaska.

Initially, only southern Arizona and the western parts of California, Oregon, and Washington were designated. Many Japanese simply moved to the eastern portions of the three west coast states. Per Bendetsen's plan, the exclusion zone was expanded to include all of California.

One hundred and twenty thousand Japanese from the three west coast states and Arizona were notified that they must move elsewhere or be interned. Ten thousand (8%) chose to and were able to move (or had already moved) to inland states to live and work or study (attend college). The other 110,000 (92%) were collected at staging points. These were mostly fairgrounds, horse tracks, and migrant camps. From there, most were sent to (mainly) ten, hastily erected internment camps. These were two each in California (and inland California, of course), Arizona, and Arkansas; and one each in Colorado, Utah, Wyoming, and Idaho. The 110,000 Japanese Americans were about 62 and 38% U.S. citizens (Nisei) and non-citizens (Issei). These 110,000 simply did not have the resources to move inland, and/or thought (hoped) that their incarceration would last only a few months.

The obvious rationale was that if Japan attacked the U.S., it would be from the West Coast of course; and that some Japanese living in these states would join their countrymen soldiers in the invasion, or become spies and saboteurs. Later disclosed reports by the FBI, the Office of Naval Intelligence, and the Military Intelligence Division concluded that the vast majority of Issei and Nisei would be loyal to the U.S., over Japan.

No Japanese American citizen or Japanese national residing in the United States was ever found guilty of sabotage or espionage – before, during, or after World War II. Of course it must be said, that 110,000 incarcerated Japanese during World War II did not have the opportunity for such, if so inclined. The conventional wisdom today includes the following:

- In the case of Japan not invading the west coast, ethnic Japanese spying or sabotaging would not have occurred
- In the case of Japan invading the west coast:
  - Some Issei may have abetted, as was the case in the Philippines and on Niihau, Hawaii
  - Nisei would not have abetted; they would have tried to remain neutral, or maybe even resisted one way or another; one way they could resist in the case of young men was to enlist in the U.S. Armed Forces; in the case of young Japanese women, they could enlist in one of the military branch, female auxiliaries; however, Japanese men were banned from enlistment until early 1943, and Japanese women not allowed to enlist in the Women's Army Corps until 11/1943

In regard to the enlistment of German American or Italian American men, the thinking was that if captured by the enemy in Europe, that they would not be treated differently, and this was the case. The thinking though was that if Japanese Americans were captured by the Japanese in the Pacific Theater, the Japanese would torture and execute them. Nobody disagreed with this latter conclusion.

Some Japanese were allowed to leave the camps to work in harvesting crops or factories. They were paid, but not paid well.

The U.S. did not have the same policy of mass imprisonment for citizens of German or Italian ancestry, fighting against the Axis powers in Europe. These ethnic groups were much larger in number than Japanese Americans. The U.S. needed them in uniform to fight.

A few German Americans and Italian Americans were imprisoned though, as suspect for their loyalty. However, the numbers and especially the percentages versus population in America were small.

All Nisei men of draft age were reclassified as 4-C after the 12/71941 sneak attacks, which is enemy aliens. Accordingly they were not allowed to enlist (and many tried) nor were they drafted, after 2/1942. This was done on the grounds that Japanese were not acceptable to the Armed Forces, simply because of their nationality and/or ancestry. The enlistment ban was removed a year later.

The words *Japs* or *Nips* as ethnic slurs were rarely used before the sneak attacks. Their use (especially *Jap*) became more common though during World War II; appearing on signs, posters, in the newspaper, heard on the radio, etc.

Some Niseis who were in the Army before the U.S. entered the War protested the fact that their families were interned, or the validity of the loyalty oath, or the fact that they were being discriminated against. These resisters refused combat training. Some tried to renounce their U.S. citizenship.

Commanders of current Japanese American military men on the mainland were given the option of discharging them from the military or assigning them harmless duties, shortly after the 12/7/1941 attacks. Some 600 Nisei were honorably discharged. Some were given less than honorable discharges. Most were sent to Camp Joseph T. Robinson (1917 – still in use) in North Little Rock, Arkansas. At Robinson, their weapons were taken away. They were assigned menial tasks.

Other Japanese American soldiers ended up as laborers in the 1800th Engineer Service Battalion. The 1800th was made up of soldiers of Japanese, German, and Italian descent, that the U.S. wanted to keep under surveillance. In the case of Japanese Americans, these were ones who had questioned the validity of the so-called loyalty questionnaire, protested the imprisonment of their families, complained of racial discrimination in the Army, etc. Some were sent to the 1800th as they had lived in Japan before the War, or had associated with groups that the U.S. considered subversive. These may have been martial arts clubs or the Buddhist Church.

The 1800th had three companies. These were A, B, and C – German Americans, Japanese Americans, and Italian Americans. Most were demoted to Private. Some were given blue discharges or even dishonorable discharges. This meant they were not eligible for veteran's benefits. However, these discharges later could be changed into honorable discharges.

For the record, blue discharges were a form of administrative military discharge, which were neither honorable nor dishonorable. The U.S. military created the blue discharge in 1916, for commanders to rid their units of homosexual men. They were also issued disproportionately to African Americans, for racial discrimination reasons. These men were not eligible for veterans' benefits. They had difficulty as civilians finding employment, due to the blue discharge. The name came as they were printed on blue paper. The blue discharge was discontinued in 1947.

Some Japanese American soldiers were imprisoned.

A military board convened 6/1942 to address the issue of Japanese Americans enlisting. Their report opposed allowing enlistment, citing the universal distrust in which Japanese Americans were held. Furthermore, the formation of an all Nisei unit was not recommended.

The Empire of Japan used the confinement of the Japanese for propaganda purposes, describing the U.S. as a racist country as locking up Japanese Americans but not German Americans or Italian Americans. To respond to this, and as also under pressure from Japanese American societies and civil rights organizations, the War Department in early 1943 lifted the ban on Nisei joining the armed forces.

Those of Japanese heritage who served for the U.S. in World War II were members of the Military Intelligence Service, the Army including the Army Air Forces, and the Office of Strategic Services. The Army included the 442nd Regimental Combat Unit, the 100th Infantry Battalion, and at least two spies. These are explained below:

1) **Military Intelligence Service**   Before the thirteen 12/7/1941 sneak attacks in or on the Pacific Ocean, the War Department knew that war with Japan was very likely. The Department in 1941 secretly recruited Japanese Americans living on the West Coast for use as Japanese-language interpreters and translators. By 11/1941 which was the month before the sneak attacks, 60 (58 were Nisei) Japanese Americans started training in military communications and intelligence and terminology and order of

battle, organization of Japan's military branches, language skills including Japanese dialects, interrogation, etc. The teachers were four Nisei. This group was called the *Military Intelligence Service.*

The Military Intelligence Service by the way also had a German arm. For both German Americans and Japanese Americans in the Military Intelligence Service -- some were already in the Army, some enlisted in the Army, and some were civilians.

Again, Nisei were the instructors, training other Nisei. The training was at the Presidio Army Fort, San Francisco. New Spain formed the Presidio fort in 1776. New Spain was the term for Spain's territories in North America, Central America, Asia, and Oceania, from 1535 to 1821. The Presidio passed to Mexico, and then to the U.S. in 1848. It ceased operations as an Army fort in 1989.

The school was transferred to Camp Savage, Minnesota 6/1942. Camp Savage was 15 miles south-southwest of Minneapolis. Camp Savage was made for the express purpose as a base for this training. It was not a military installation. It was established in the interest of national security (to be away from the West Coast), and also as technically Japanese Americans were not allowed to live in California. Also, there was less anti-Japanese prejudice in Minnesota, plus the camp was isolated anyway.

The Japanese language was taught to (non-Japanese) American military personnel at this location, as well.

In 8/1944, the school was transferred again, to Fort Snelling (1819 – 1994), Minnesota. Fort Snelling is 12 miles southeast of Minneapolis. It was an Army Fort.

Prominent, Brown University (economics degree) and Harvard Law School educated Nisei attorney John Aiso (1909 Los Angeles – 1987 Los Angeles, killed in a mugging) was drafted and reported for active duty 4/1941. Several months after boot camp, he was selected to be a student of the Military Intelligence Service. His fluency in Japanese resulted in his quick promotion as an assistant instructor and then head instructor. He recruited and trained a staff of over 150, developed course materials, etc. Aiso reached the rank of Lieutenant Colonel, the highest ranked Japanese American in the Army during World War II. He was later promoted to Colonel in the Army Reserve. He retired in 1965.

President Lyndon Johnson (1908 TX – 1973 TX) presented the Legion of Merit to Aiso in 1965. The Legion of Merit medal is awarded for exceptionally meritorious conduct in the performance of outstanding services and achievements.

Aiso constantly reminded the instructors and students that their cooperation and performance would have a direct impact on the future of Japanese Americans in the U.S., after World War II.

A mugger knocked Aiso to the ground, as he was filling his car with gasoline at a gasoline station in Burbank. He hit his head on the concrete. He died two weeks later from the injury.

By the spring of 1942, the first 35 graduates were transferred to duty in the Pacific, serving on Guadalcanal and for the 67-day, 1942-1943 Buna-Gona (New Guinea) campaign. Some served in Burma, including with Merrill's Marauders.

A similar group was trained in Hawaii. Thousands more Nisei were recruited, many from the internment camps. As already noted, some recruited were already in the Army. Those recruited were mostly of course proficient in Japanese as well as English. Some Nisei though did not know Japanese that well, so had to be trained.

A few were sent to Alaska, to help monitor Japanese radio traffic in the Aleutian Islands.

They worked mainly as translators of captured documents, translators of broken Japanese radio transmissions, translators from English to Japanese on pamphlets dropped over Japan or countries occupied by the Japanese, interpreters, interrogators of captured Japanese in the field or later in U.S. or Australian POW camps, etc.

However, there were not many Japanese prisoners to interrogate. The Emperor and military leaders had successfully brainwashed Japanese soldiers, sailors, marines, and airmen to fight to the death; or commit suicide if not managing to get themselves killed in battle. And about this suicide, doing so in a matter which took out the enemy or enemy property was even better, such as the kamikaze and other methods developed to sink or damage USSs. These other methods included kaitens, shinyos, and fukuryus. This was a much-convoluted version of the samurai bushido code. Remarkably, Japanese leaders successfully expanded this brainwashing even to many civilians.

Japanese battlefield instructions were written up in a pocket-sized military code called the *Senjinkun*, issued 1/1941. The Senjinkun in turn was a supplement to the much lengthier *Imperial Rescript to Soldiers and Sailors,* required reading for Japanese military men. In fact, military men were required to memorize part of the Imperial Rescript.

The Senjinkun listed requirements regarding military regulations, combat readiness, esprit de corps (meaning morale of the military unit), filial piety (meaning respect for one's parents, elders, and ancestors), veneration of Shinto kami (the dominant religion of Japan then and now), and Japan's kokutai (system of government including sovereignty). The code specifically forbade retreat or surrender. The wording included the following statements:

- *Never live to experience shame as a prisoner.*
- *...it is essential that each man, high and low, dutifully observing his place, should be determined always to sacrifice himself for the whole, in accordance with the intentions of the commander, by reposing every confidence in his comrades, and without giving even the slightest thought to personal interest and to life or death.*
- *The destiny of the Empire rests upon victory or defeat in battle. Do not give up under any circumstances, keeping in mind your responsibility not*

> *to tarnish the glorious history of the Imperial Army with its tradition of invincibility.*

Acceptance of this along with Japan's also successful brainwashing as to Americans being inhuman and therefore inhumane to the point after capture where they would mutilate, torture, and rape before executing, and even cooking up and eating their children led to numerous suicides; committed by Japanese civilians as well as military men.

Towards the end of the war, Senjinkun copies were also distributed to Japanese civilians, in anticipation of the Allied Forces invasion (Operation Downfall).

The Military Intelligence Service had many de-coding and translation successes. Two notable cases were as follows:

- On Combined Fleet Commander-in-Chief Isoroku Yamamoto's (1884 Japan – 4/18/1943 shot over Bougainville) travel plans on a morale-building trip of the South Pacific, after the defeat and withdrawal at Guadalcanal; the decrypted information included time and location details of his itinerary, as well as the number and types of planes that would transport and escort; these were two, seven crew, twin engine, Mitsubishi G4M bombers and six Mitsubishi, single engine, one-crew A6M fighters; the bombers of course were not carrying bombs so as to fly faster and maneuver quicker, relying on the fighters for protection as well as their own gunners

The U.S. sent a squadron of 16, twin engine, single crew, Lockheed P-38 Lightnings to intercept (Operation Vengeance); a dogfight ensued with Yamamoto's escorting Zero fighters; either mission head Captain Thomas Lanphier (1915 Panama – 1987 CA) or his wingman Lieutenant Rex Barber (1917 OR – 2001 OR) killed Yamamoto midair; he was hit twice, shoulder and head; the two Japanese bombers were shot down with 19 Japanese dying (three from one bomber survived); Yamamoto died from the 0.50 caliber bullet to his head; one Lightning and its pilot were lost (shot down by an escorting Zero)

To hide the fact that the Allies had busted Japanese naval code, the U.S. released information to the press that coastwatchers in the Solomons observed Yamamoto boarding a bomber, and relayed that information by radio to the U.S. Navy; this conveyed to Japan that it was only through a stroke of bad luck, that Yamamoto was killed; the code was not changed, so this ploy worked

- On the Operation Z planned for 3/1944 which was Japan's plan to counter-attack Allied forces in 1944 in the Marianas (especially Saipan); this knowledge led to the Allies gaining victory in the Marianas and Philippines

Over the course of the War, more than 6,000 Japanese Americans served in the Military Intelligence Service. Almost all were Nisei, recruited as already in the Army (a few) or from the internment camps (most).

One third of the 6,000 worked in the Pacific Theater, in combat zones. Some of these Nisei even convinced Japanese soldiers to surrender, using loudspeakers (bizarre) on the battlefield, but such successes were only a very, very few. They also reasoned with civilians, who were terrified as Japan had brainwashed them to expect horrible atrocities from the arriving and then conquering Americans.

General Douglas MacArthur's (1880 AR – 1964 DC) chief intelligence officer Major General Charles Willoughby (1892 Germany – 1962 FL) stated that these trained Nisei *shortened the Pacific War by two years and saved possibly a million American lives and saved probably billions of dollars.*

The Military Intelligence Service was honored with a Presidential Unit Citation, in 2000. The Presidential Unit Citation was created in 1942. This commendation is awarded to units of the uniformed services of the U.S. and those of allied countries, for extraordinary heroism in action against an armed enemy on or after 12/7/1941. The collective degree of valor (combat heroism) against an armed enemy by the unit nominated for the Presidential Unit Citation is comparable to that which would warrant the individual award of the Army Distinguished Service Cross, Air Force Cross, or Navy Cross. The Cross medals are the second highest valor medal of the branches, next to the Medal of Honor.

For the record, the unit with the most Presidential Unit Citations happens to be a submarine. The nuclear-powered, Sturgeon-class, 302' long and 32' beam and 24' draft, USS Parche (1974 – 2006 scrapped) received nine such Citations, ten Navy Unit Commendations, and thirteen Navy Expeditionary Medals. She was much involved in clandestine work in the Cold War. She was lengthened almost a third to 401' in 1991, and then used for research and development work. The USS Parche is the most highly decorated USS vessel in U.S. Navy history.

2) **100th Infantry Battalion**   Hawaii's National Guard (298th, 299th) was federalized 12/7/1941 into the U.S. Army. These were all or most all Nisei. They went on full alert. They aided in clearing the rubble, made or repaired infrastructure, donated blood, helped with the wounded, guarded critical locations, etc. On 12/10/1941 three days after the sneak attacks, they were stripped of their rifles as some members were Japanese Hawaiians. Later though, their rifles were returned.

General Emmons, worried about the loyalty of Japanese-Hawaiians in the case of another invasion from Japan, recommended to the War Department that the 298th and 299th regiments be organized into a Hawaiian Provisional Battalion, and sent to the mainland for training. The move was approved. The expectation at the time was that the new territory guard would defend Hawaii, along with the U.S. military already on Oahu. This did not turn out to be the case though.

Another concern of Emmons was that Japanese soldiers wearing American Army uniforms would infiltrate or invade Hawaii, posing as American Army;

to spy or attack. Considering this concern, no Japanese Americans in the Army in uniform of course should be based in Hawaii.

On 6/4/1942, the weapons of these National Guardsmen (all or mostly all Nisei) were again taken away. On the next day, 1,432 National Guardsmen (now Army) boarded the 501' long by 58' beam by 30' draft, USAT Maui (1918 – 1948 scrapped) transport, and zigzagged to Oakland, California. They arrived 6/10/1942. Two days later, they were sent by train to (Army) Camp McCoy (1909 – still in operation today as Fort McCoy) in Wisconsin 177 miles northwest of Milwaukee, for combat training.

The Army called for additional volunteers – 1,500 from Hawaii and 3,000 from the mainland to expand the battalion. The result was that 10,000 Japanese from Hawaii volunteered, but only several hundred from the mainland. This was not surprising, as most draft-age Japanese on the mainland were held in internment camps. This obviously gave these young men a different perspective, on fighting for the country which had imprisoned them and their families.

The Army revised its quota, to requesting 2,900 from Hawaii and 1,500 from the mainland. As it turned out, 3,000 men from Hawaii and 800 from the mainland were inducted into the new unit.

On 6/15/1943, the battalion was designated the 100th Infantry Battalion. After six months of training at Fort McCoy, the 100th was shipped to (Army) Camp Shelby (1915 – still in operation) in Mississippi for more training. Camp Shelby is fourteen miles south-southeast of Hattiesburg. From there, they went to (Army) Camp Clairborne (1930 – 1948 closed) in Louisiana, for field exercises and war games. Camp Clairborne was twenty-five miles south of Alexandria, Louisiana.

On 7/20/1943, the 100th received its battalion colors and motto. The latter was *Remember Pearl Harbor,* as requested by the unit members.

The 100th arrived in Oran, Algeria (North Africa) 9/2/1943. They took more training. They guarded facilities.

The 100th sailed for Italy 9/19/1943, as part of a division. Their first combat was near Salerno in Southern Italy (Italian Campaign), 9/29/1943.

The 100th was highly decorated. It earned three Presidential Unit Citations. Its 3,147 members received 4,340 individual medals and awards, including 1,703 Purple Hearts. In fact, it was known as the *Purple Heart Battalion.* Most casualties came at the 1/1944 – 5/1944 Anzio and 1/1944 – 4/1944 Monte Cassino campaigns, in Italy. Anzio is a city (and commune) on Italy's western coast, of the administrative region of Lazio. Anzio is on the Tyrrhenian Sea, an extension of the Mediterranean Sea. Monte Cassino is inland, 85 miles to the east of Anzio.

The success of the 100th battalion in training, coupled with the dedication and patriotic activities of the Varsity Victory Volunteers (see below) in 1942, led the U.S. to continue enlisting Nisei in the Armed Forces (almost all Army, a very few Army Air Forces).

On 6/11/1944, the 100th was attached to the newly arrived Japanese 442nd Regimental Combat Team (see below). Because of its distinguished fighting record and as it was the first established Japanese American Army unit, the 100th was allowed to keep its original designation. The 100th/442nd Regimental Combat Team was part of the 34th Division. The officers of both the 100th and 442nd were white. Both units fought until V-E Day.

3) **442nd Regimental Combat Team**   At the time of the Japanese attack on Pearl Harbor and USS facilities on Oahu, Hawaii's National Guard of course was immediately federalized into the U.S. Army. It became the 100th Infantry Battalion as noted above. Also as noted above, the 100th fought in Europe until V-E Day. This left the Territory no military defensive body, controlled by the Territory. At 10:00 during or just after the attack ended, Hawaii's civilian governor Joseph Poindexter ordered the mobilization of the Hawaiian Territorial Guard, to protect Hawaii. Trouble was as just noted, Hawaii had no such thing. Poindexter created and recruited quickly, as follows:

- The University of Hawaii Reserve Officer's Training Corps was activated and assembled, at the University of Hawaii campus. These students were instantly drafted into the new Territorial Guard.
- Some Junior Reserve Officer's Training Corps members were recruited. These were older high school students.
- All American Legion members were called to duty, by radio. This added another 350 (older) men right away.

By the end of 12/1941, the Territorial Guard had a strength of 1,343 men – 1,254 enlisted men and 89 officers. The Territorial Guard served as Hawaii's armed defense component throughout World War II.

As already noted, Lieutenant General Emmons replaced General Short as Military Governor of Hawaii, effective 12/17/1941. He was the Territorial Guard's Commander. He ordinarily would act on the direction and policy set by the civilian head of Hawaii, who again was Joseph Poindexter. However, as Hawaii was now under martial law, all authority rested with Emmons. Accordingly, Emmons made all the decisions.

The martial law status ran with some modifications, until 10/24/1944. This was 2.9 years. The military governor (Emmons) assumed comprehensive control of all executive, legislative, and judicial powers. Never or since have so many Americans (more than 400,000) been under martial law for so long. As a Territorial Guard, the new unit was not subject to federalization.

The Territorial Guard soldiers were armed with five-round, magazine-fed, bolt-action, Springfield M1903 repeating rifles. They had only the five bullets, in the Springfield. The design of their rifles was from 40 years back. Their immediate charge was to patrol, in case of a Japanese assault by sea (landing craft) or air (paratroopers, gliders). When such did not occur, their assignment was to guard vital installations and infrastructure such as armories, bridges, wells, reservoirs, pumping stations, water tanks, high schools, hospitals, radio stations, etc.

Nine other grass roots, civilian militias in Hawaii were formed as well, soon after the attack on Oahu. One of these was the Varsity Victory Volunteers, described below. Several were based on other Hawaiian Islands. One was an all-female group. The U.S. government provided these groups with limited recognition, limited training, limited pay, and limited resources.

These groups disbanded when World War II ended, if not before. The Hawaii Territorial Guard disbanded in 1947. Hawaii has not created a territory or state guard since (Hawaii became the 50th state, 1959), although the states are authorized legally to do so. As of 2019, 22 states (also Puerto Rico) have active state defensive units.

In January 1942, all ethnic Japanese in the Hawaiian Territorial Guard described above were classified as enemy aliens (4-C). Accordingly, they were dismissed. These were mostly college students. The now much smaller, hastily formed Territorial Guard, immediately began recruiting replacements.

Most of the dismissed Japanese men signed and circulated a petition, and sent it to Military Governor General Emmons. The petition read as follows:

We, the undersigned, were members of the Hawaii Territorial Guard until recent removal. We joined the Guard voluntarily with the hope that this was one way to serve our country in her time of need. Needless to say, we were deeply disappointed when we were told that our services in the Guard were no longer needed. Hawaii is our home; the United States, our country. We know but one loyalty, and that is to the Stars and Stripes. We wish to do our part as loyal Americans in every way possible and we hereby offer ourselves for whatever service you may see fit to use us.

The 169 student signatories got their wish. The Varsity Victory Volunteers (VVV) was formed 2/1942 as a civilian, sapper, labor battalion. Organization-wise, the VVV unit was assigned to the U.S. Army Corps of Engineers, attached to the 34th Combat Engineers Regiment. They lived at Schofield Barracks. This Army installation in Honolulu was established in 1908, and is still in operation.

The twelve, VVV work gangs made roads, made and repaired equipment and buildings at military installations, strung up fences, worked in a quarry, etc. They got room and board and medical care and maybe some clothing, but very little pay.

Assistant War Secretary John McCloy (1895 Philadelphia – 1989 CT) visited Hawaii 12/1942. McCloy observed the enthusiasm and patriotic ardor of the men of the VVV. He recommended that an all Nisei Regiment be formed. The Department of War (name changed to the Department of Defense in 1949) was in favor. The War Relocation Authority created 3/1942 to handle the internment of Japanese Americans was against this proposal though.

President Roosevelt considered all the opinions. He announced 2/1/1943 that a segregated Army Nisei battalion would be formed, commanded by white officers. Another factor that motivated Roosevelt already mentioned, was that Japan was publicly criticizing the American military of racism – for the mass incarceration of Japanese Americans, and not doing the same in the case of German Americans and Italian Americans.

The new unit was named the 442nd Regimental Combat Team. Volunteers were called for. The VVV asked to be disbanded, to join the new unit. Their request was granted 1/31/1943. So after eleven months of operation in Hawaii, the civilian VVV unit mobilized to form the base of the new, 442nd Regimental Combat Team. The 442nd was a full-fledged Army unit.

In his announcement on the formation of the 442nd, President Roosevelt stated *Americanism is not, and never was a matter of race or ancestry.* Of course, this smacked of hypocrisy with 110,000 ethnic Japanese in confinement.

To be fair to Roosevelt, by most reports he was not keen on sending ethnic Japanese to internment camps. He did not feel that such was necessary, based upon the reports he had reviewed. Roosevelt just felt that he had to go along with strong recommendations from the military and the general opinion of some or much of the citizenry to proceed with incarceration.

The 442nd volunteers were sent to Camp Shelby in Mississippi for combat training. The 100th Infantry Battalion had trained here as well.

The 442nd departed Hampton Roads, Virginia 5/1/1944, and arrived Anzio, Italy 5/28/1944. It first fought in the Tuscany area of Italy, 7/1944. This was ten months after the 100th first fought, also in Italy. Tuscany is on Italy's central western coast, bordering on the Ligurian Sea and the Tyrrhenian Sea. These two seas are extensions of the Mediterranean Sea.

The 442nd (as noted above, the 100th and the 442nd combined 6/1944) fought the rest of the European war in Italy and France.

Eventually, 14,000 men served in the 442nd during World War II. The Regiment's casualty rate of killed, wounded, missing, and removed from action for other reasons of the 14,000 total was 93%.

Many 442nd sub-units were formed – to train new (Japanese) enlistees, an engineering company, anti-tank company, cannon company, service company, medical detachment, headquarters companies, and even an Army Band.

The 522nd Field Artillery Battalion was a sub-unit of the 442nd. Toward the end of the War though, the 522nd became a roving battalion, sent to wherever Command needed artillery fire. The 522nd liberated three thousand mostly Jewish captives at a Dachau sub-camp 4/29/1945. Dachau is located 10 miles northwest of Munich, Bavaria, Germany. The 522nd was the only Nisei unit to fight in Germany.

The 442nd was (and still is) the most decorated unit for its size and length of service, in the history of American warfare. Eighteen thousand, one hundred and forty-three commendations were awarded. These included 21 Medals of Honor, 52 Distinguished Service Crosses, 560 Silver Stars, 22 Legions of Merit, 4,000 Bronze Stars, and 9,486 Purple Hearts. The unit itself as a whole was awarded eight Presidential Unit Citations.

Only one of the 21 Medals of Honor was awarded during World War II. Private First Class Sadao Munemori (1922 Los Angeles – 4/5/1945 Italy) was the posthumous recipient. He was an automobile mechanic after high school. He volunteered 11/1941, and enlisted 2/1942. His parents and siblings were incarcerated. He knocked out two machine guns with grenades. He dived onto a grenade to save his fellow soldiers.

In the 1990s, it was determined that racial discrimination was a factor in downgrading Japanese American Medal of Honor candidates, to receive Distinguished Service Crosses. This was reversed in 20 cases.

4) **Office of Strategic Services**   Fourteen Nisei men worked for the Office of Strategic Services (OSS), beginning in 1944. The OSS was formed in 1942. The OSS was the U.S.'s wartime intelligence agency, and the predecessor of today's Central Intelligence Agency, created in 1947.

The Nisei operatives studied Japanese language, geography, military protocols, communication methods, etc. They were trained on how to handle a rifle, hand-to-hand combat, use of explosives, survival skills, etc.

An initial plan was to infiltrate Japan and operate as spies. This approach was considered too dangerous though, and dropped.

They operated in the China-Burma-India Theater, beginning 11/1944. White Americans as bodyguards always accompanied, so as to not be mistaken as the enemy. They interrogated captured Japanese, translated documents, monitored enemy radio communications, and conducted covert operations. Their efforts were successful in rescuing downed American pilots, attacking Japanese-held villages, cutting off Japanese supply routes, collecting intelligence, etc. They participated in a series of missions in 1945 to rescue POWs in China, Manchuria, and Korea.

Imagine the incongruity when these Japanese soldiers from the 100th or 442nd on leave during training in uniform passed through a barbed wire gate of a high fence in the shadow of guard towers manned by armed sentries, to visit their families in the internment camps.

The 442nd and its now sub-unit the 100th were de-activated after World War II. Both units have since been reactivated. Today, the 100th/442nd Infantry is the only ground combat unit of the U.S. Army Reserve. The battalion headquarters is at Fort Shafter (1907 – today, headquarters of the U.S. Army Pacific), Honolulu, Hawaii. Subordinate units are based in Hilo (Hawaii), American Samoa, Saipan, and Guam.

Japanese American women could enlist in the Women's Army Corps, beginning 11/1943. This was ten months after Japanese men were allowed to enlist. One hundred forty-two such women joined up. They were not segregated. Most worked in clerical positions. None served overseas.

Nisei soldiers were forbidden to fight (combat roles) in the Pacific and China-Burma-India Theaters, for three reasons as follows:

- Japanese Americans of course, looked like the enemy. The War Department feared that the Japanese Army would put American uniforms on their soldiers to masquerade as Americans, and then infiltrate and kill. This was against the accepted rules of war, but that was not an issue with Japan.

Japan in fact toward the end of World War II did paint some of their submarines and aircraft in U.S. livery, so this scenario of Japanese soldiers in American Army uniforms was a concern. Painting ships or aircraft in the enemy's colors and symbols is also of course against the rules of war.

- The U.S. requirement that its Japanese units be all Nisei (but note that the officers were white), would have made this deception easier.

Japanese Americans looked like the enemy, as just noted. Despite the differences in uniform, friendly fire was a concern.

- It was known that the Japanese would torture and execute any Japanese American soldier they captured, as they considered them traitors. Japan's more than heinous actions regarding abuse of captured soldiers and even (hundreds of thousands) civilians in China and Korea and the Dutch East Indies (and other countries) were well-known. These executions would be preceded by torture. Nobody contested this thinking including Issei and Nisei, including relatives back in Japan, including non-relatives in Japan, etc. Again, everybody knew as much. Once again, there was no doubt here in the case of captured Japanese Americans, on the torture followed by execution issue.

However, it was also expected that the Japanese if they captured these Japanese Americans probably would have tried to convert to being counterspies, or to promote propaganda such as on the radio (especially as these personnel were bilingual). The Japanese would have beat and tortured to force these POWs to do so.

To sum up, 33,000 Japanese Americans who enlisted or were drafted served in World War II in the Military Intelligence Service, the Army, and the Office of Strategic Services. No Japanese men were known to enlist in the Navy or Marines or Coast Guard. Five of the Army men served in the Army Air Forces.

Ben Kuroki (1917 NE – 2015 CA) was one of the five who served in the Army Air Forces. He was one of ten children born to Japanese American immigrant farmers in Hershey, Nebraska. He and his family were not sent to a detention camp, as they did not live on the West Coast or Southern Arizona. After Pearl Harbor, Ben's Issei father encouraged him and his fighting-age brothers Fred, Bill, and Henry to enlist.

The Grand Island, Nebraska (158 miles east of Hershey) recruiting office rejected the brothers, as they were *Japs*. Two months later, their enlistment at another recruiting office (North Platte, Nebraska is 15 miles east of Hershey) was accepted, without any questions asked. One humorous theory was that the recruiters thought that the brothers were Polish Americans, because of their Kuroki surname. This was not the case, as they definitely looked Japanese (both parents were Issei). Ben later stated that the recruiter told him that he was paid $2 per recruit ($31.80 in 2019 money). If this recruiter had an ethnic bias, $2 per enlistee was enough to overcome it.

Ben and Fred enlisted in the Army, two of the very first Nisei to do so. This was just before the U.S. military ban on Japanese enlistees went into effect. In 1/1942, they were sent to basic training at Sheppard Field, Wichita Falls, Texas. Ben wanted to be a pilot. Fred wanted to be a navigator. However, the brothers were assigned menial duties in camp. Fellow trainees ostracized them. Fred was transferred to the engineering corps. Ben worked as a clerk in England.

Ben volunteered for aerial gunner school. He became a four engine, eleven crew, Consolidated B-24 Liberator heavy bomber gunner.

Ben Kuroki's B-24 crash-landed in Spanish Morocco. Spanish Morocco was a Spanish protectorate (zone of influence) in Morocco, established in 1912 by a treaty between France and Spain. The protectorate ended in 1956 when Morocco gained its independence. Anyway, Spanish authorities captured the crew.

Spain did not join the Axis powers in World War II, so officially neutral. However, General Francisco Franco's (1892 Spain – 1975 Madrid) regime supplied materiel and military support to the Axis powers; so not so neutral after all. Franco did so, as payback to Germany and Italy for assistance in fighting the 1936-1939 Spanish Civil War. Franco's anti-democracy side won. He ruled Spain as a military dictator until his 1975 death.

Kuroki and his crewmates survived the crash landing with minor injuries. The Spanish held them for three months, before releasing. They returned to their squadron in England.

Kuroki flew thirty combat missions in the European theater (only twenty-five were required). One was the disastrous 8/1/1943 bombing mission known as *Operation Tidal Wave* over the oil fields and refinery at Ploiesti, Romania.

Ploiesti is in Southern Romania. Romania at the time was the world's third largest petroleum producer, and much fueled the Nazi Germany war effort, until the Soviets captured 8/1944.

Of 177 B-24 heavy bombers that took off from Southern Italy and Libya, 162 reached the target, which is 92%. Fifty-three and fifty-five were destroyed and damaged. This is a two-thirds casualty rate, of the 162 bombers. The U.S. lost 440 men, and another 220 captured or missing. The opposition lost only four aircraft and sixteen killed, and another fifty wounded. On top of everything else, damage was minimal. Petroleum production was back to 100% within days.

On his thirtieth and last mission in Europe, Kuroki was slightly injured, when his gun turret was hit by flak.

During rest and recovery home, the Army had Kuroki visit a number of Japanese American internment camps, encouraging soldier age men to enlist. The U.S. military had started allowing Japanese men to enlist 11/1942. Kuroki gave patriotic speeches. He was the subject of several news articles, including one in *Time* magazine.

Kuroki drew a prolonged ovation from the Commonwealth Club of California in San Francisco 2/1944, when he said: *When you live with men under combat conditions for 15 months, you begin to understand what brotherhood is all about.* The Commonwealth Club is a non-profit, non-partisan educational organization based in Northern California. Founded in 1903, it is the oldest and largest public affairs forum in the U.S. Membership is open to all.

Kuroki requested but was denied the opportunity to participate in the Pacific Theater. He appealed to one of the Nebraska Senators who relayed the request to War Department Secretary Henry Stimson (1867 NYC – 1950 NY). Secretary Stimson made it happen. Kuroki completed another twenty-eight bombing missions in the Pacific Theater, including bombing runs over Japan.

Kuroki is the only (full-blooded) Japanese American who fought in any way in the Pacific Theater. As noted already, Japanese Americans did serve in the Pacific Theater and the China-Burma-India Theater as always escorted Military Intelligence Service personnel and Office of Strategic Services personnel. Two were Army spies (see below) in the Philippines.

Kuroki was heavily decorated for his fifty-eight missions. These included three Distinguished Service Crosses, and the Distinguished Service Medal. The latter medal though was not awarded until 2005, when it was much later decided that Japanese Americans had been discriminated against because of their race in the awarding of commendations. Kuroki served 1942-1946. He was discharged as a Technical Sergeant.

After the war, Kuroki made a series of speaking tours discussing racial issues involving minorities. He funded this travel with his own money or donated money. He got some money from the 1946 Ralph Martin biography, titled *Boy from Nebraska: The Story of Ben Kuroki.*

When asked about his battle to overcome prejudice which almost prevented him from being allowed to enlist and then later fight in the Pacific Theater, Kuroki stated: *I had to fight like hell, for the right to fight for my own country.*

Kuroki later attended the University of Nebraska on the GI bill, earning a bachelor's degree in journalism in 1950. He worked as a reporter and editor for a number of newspapers in several states. He retired in 1984.

PBS aired a 2005 documentary on him when he was age 88, titled *Most Honorable Son: Ben Kuroki's Amazing War Story*. *Most Honorable Son* was the nickname that his crewmates gave him.

Kuroki is shown below. The other picture shows Kuroki's workstation for 58 missions. The B-24 tail guns picture was taken at the National Museum of the U.S. Air Force, Dayton, Ohio.

Kenje Ogata (1919 IN – 2012) was another of the five who ended up in the Army Air Corps in lieu of the Army. He enlisted the day after the 12/7/1941 sneak attacks. Ogata had learned to fly as a civilian. As Japanese, he assumed that he would not be considered for pilot training. He assumed right. In fact, he was told to just go home. He went to another recruiting station, and enlisted in the Army. He became a medical corpsman, working stateside.

Ogata waged a letter writing campaign, to become an airman of some sort. He got letters of recommendation from the mayor, police chief, and the city attorney of his hometown (Sterling, Illinois); and from district judges. This worked, although it took two years. He became a Consolidated B-24 bomber gunner, the same as Kuroki. He flew fifty-five missions, including two that did not go so well, as follows:

- 1944 Shot down over Hungary; last of ten crew to bail out; got separated from his crewmates; walked 20 hours, with assistance from a friendly farmer who guided him to his crewmates; the crew walked to Bucharest, Romania, which took 30 days, before linking back up with the U.S. Army

In 1985, Ogata and his wife visited Magyarkeszi, Hungary, and met with residents who remembered the event; they gave him a fragment from the crashed B-24, which he shared with his still alive and attending crewmates at a 1988 reunion for European Theater airmen

- 1945 Forced down in Yugoslavia; the crew scrambled out, just before the plane caught fire

Ogata was awarded numerous medals. He became a dentist after the War, retiring in 1997 at age 78.

The three others of the five Japanese American Army airmen were Texas radioman Yukio Kishi, Hawaii gunner Herbert Ginoza, and California gunner

John Matsumoto. Again, Kuroki was the only one of the five to fight in the Pacific Theater.

The Army recruited Japanese Hawaiian Niseis Arthur Komori (1915 HA – 2000) and Richard Sakakida (1920 HA – 1996 CA, lung cancer) 3/1941 to be trained and placed as spies in the Philippines. This was nine months before the sneak attacks. Sergeants Komori and Sakakida were operatives of the Counter Intelligence Corps, which was the Army's intelligence/spy unit during World War II.

The two Army spies arrived Manila (Philippines) 4/7/1941 on the 599' long and 68' beam and 34' draft, USS Republic (1903 – 1952 scrapped) troop transport. They posed as civilians working as hired deck hands on the Republic to conceal their identity, even from the Navy sailors aboard. They were assigned to spy on the Japanese community in the city. They now posed as merchant sailors who had jumped ship.

Japan attacked the Philippines 12/8/1941, as one of the thirteen sneak attacks. The two followed the American retreat, first to Bataan and then to Corregidor off the tip of Bataan. Here, Sakakida and Komori both worked as MacArthur's personal interpreters and translators, plus they were sent near the front lines to do the same. They went on patrols, interrogated POWs, interned collaborators, collected and translated enemy documents, transcribed radio messages, etc.

They used loudspeakers on battlegrounds to broadcast in Japanese to the enemy that they should surrender. Other Military Intelligence Service personnel did the same in other campaigns. Success here was next to none.

The Japanese controlled the Philippines Constabulary. The Constabulary picked up Sergeant Sakakida. He was jailed in Bilibid Prison at Muntinlupa, which is just south of Manila. He maintained his cover, that he was a civilian. Fortunately, his story of being a civilian was accepted. He was released. He slipped back to a U.S. Army unit. His duties then involved translating documents, and interrogating Japanese POWs.

As the situation on Corregidor was bleak and as they were Japanese, he and Komori were ordered to fly out (to Australia). As Japanese American POWs, the Japanese would treat them harshly, for sure. Sakakida persuaded his superiors to let civilian Japanese attorney Clarence Yamagata (born in Hawaii) take his evacuating airplane seat. Yamagata had worked for the Japanese, but had secretly gone over to the American side. Also, Yamagata had a wife and children living in Japan. The Japanese would likely harm his wife and children in some way, if they learned that he had allied with the Americans.

Sakakida did not have a family. General MacArthur and General Jonathan Wainwright (1883 WA – 1953 San Antonio) told Sakakida that he was military so had priority; but that it was Sakakida's call. Sakakida forfeited his seat to Yamagata. Yamagata and Komori escaped to Australia on the last flight out – via Panay, and then Mindanao. This was 4/13/1942. The seventeen-hour flight from Mindanao to Australia was the longest that a twin engine B-25 Mitchell had ever made. This B-25 was a much patched up one.

Komori continued to work for the rest of the Pacific War, in Australia. He mainly interrogated Japanese POWs. He transcribed documents. He translated radio messages. After V-J Day, he was sent to Japan to aid in the transfer to peace. He separated from the Army as a Colonel.

Sakakida accompanied General Wainwright as his interpreter, during the surrender negotiations. In the process, Sakakida of course was also captured. He was the only Japanese American captured by Japanese forces in the Philippines. Of course, no Japanese American military were in or fought in the Pacific Theater except those who were behind enemy lines or constantly supervised. B-24 gunner Ben Kuroki was the one exception.

Per Japanese law, Sakakida was considered a Japanese citizen, because of his ancestry. He was charged with treason. The Kempeitai (military police) interrogated and tortured him for two months. Sakakida claimed again that he was a civilian, forced to work for the U.S. Army.

After almost a year in prison, Japanese Fourteenth Army Headquarters Chief Judge Advocate Colonel Nishiharu concluded 2/1943 that Sakakida was most likely innocent. The treason charge was dropped. He was released. Colonel Nishiharu hired him 3/1943, as a staff translator (very few Japanese spoke English) and personal houseboy. Sakakida though faced ongoing devious attempts, to trick him into betraying himself.

Security was lax, as again Colonel Nishiharu considered him loyal to Japan. Sakakida was often left alone with sensitive military documents, which he read or even stole.

Filipino guerilla leader Ernest Tupas was serving a fifteen-year sentence for anti-Japanese activities. Mrs. Tupas showed up to obtain a pass to visit her husband. Sakakida risked revealing his identity to her. Mrs. Tupas put him in touch with the Philippine resistance, to whom he passed information.

Sakakida devised a plan for a mass escape for Tupas and other Filipino prisoners. He obtained Japanese officer's uniforms. He and four guerillas posed as Japanese officers on a 10/1943 night. They marched to the gate of Muntinlupa Prison. They knocked the unsuspecting guards out. Then twenty-five more guerillas joined them and freed almost 500 inmates. Sakakida returned to his quarters, with no one the wiser.

Sakakida has described this commando mission in detail. Per the 1996 Associated Press Sakakida obituary, three former guerrillas including one who is now a Roman Catholic priest claimed that Sakakida *fabricated his role in the escape.* Hawaiian Senator (1990 – 2013) Daniel Akaka (1924 Honolulu – 2018 Honolulu) responded that *Sakakida's story has been confirmed time and time again.*

Tupas organized some of the escaped guerillas. He established radio communications with MacArthur's Australian headquarters. He caused much grief for the Japanese occupiers.

Sakakida continued to spy and pass information. He knew he was pressing his luck. In 12/1944, he fled into the jungle. He lived on grass and wild berries. He developed malaria, beriberi, and dysentery. He was wounded by shrapnel. As isolated, he had no source for news. American soldiers 9/1945 caught up to him, and told him the War was over. To say the least, it took quite a while for the bedraggled and sick Sakakida to convince the American soldiers that he was an American in the U.S. Army.

Sakakida was promoted to master sergeant.

Sakakida testified at the war crimes trial of General Tomoyuki Yamashita (1885 Japan – 2/23/1946 Philippines, execution hanging for war crimes), as he had been an interpreter in the office of the general's Judge Advocate. Yamashita was head of the Japanese Fourteenth Army, defending the occupied Philippines. He was also Japan's Military Governor of the Philippines. His trial spanned almost six weeks. He was tried for the many atrocities in the Philippines and Singapore (he conquered and brutally occupied Malaya and Singapore in ten weeks, 1941-1942) against civilians and POWs. Yamashita's defense was that he was not able to stop the atrocities due to breakdowns in communications, and chaotic battle conditions. The court did not buy it. He was convicted and sentenced to death. He was hung six months after the War ended.

Sakakida stayed in Manila another eighteen months, working on war crime investigations. He met some of his former torturers and forgave them.

Sakakida received a commission, 1947. He transferred from the Army to the Air Force. He retired in 1975 as a Lieutenant Colonel. He married. His wife outlived him.

Sakakida's commendations include the Legion of Merit, Bronze Star, two Commendation Medals, and the Distinguished Service Medal. The latter was awarded posthumously, in 1999. He was inducted into the Military Intelligence Hall of Fame, created in 1988.

Frank Fujita's (1921 OK – 1996) Japanese father was born near Nagasaki. He moved to the U.S. 6/1914, to study American agriculture methods. He married a white American woman in 1919. Frank was born two years later, so half Japanese and half white American. He joined the National Guard. His unit was shipped overseas in 1941. Sergeant Fujita and the other 533 men of his unit were captured on Java 3/8/1942, when the Allies (mainly Dutch here) surrendered to the Japanese. He was one of only two American military with some Japanese blood, captured in the Pacific Theater.

Fujita's unit became known as the *Lost Battalion*, as their fate was not known until 9/1944. He was held prisoner until the end of the War, 8/1945. As part Japanese, he was separated from the other POWs. He was forced to produce propaganda broadcasts. Fujita wrote a memoir, titled *Foo: A Japanese American Prisoner of the Rising Sun.*

The record of the Japanese Americans serving in the 442nd, the 100th, other military units, and the Military Intelligence Service in the Pacific Theater (see next paragraph) helped sway opinions of Americans in regard to Japanese Americans, including the need to incarcerate them. More importantly, a 12/1944 U.S. Supreme Court ruling mandated release of the 110,000 Japanese, which began the next month.

Van Johnson (1916 RI – 2008 NY) played the commanding officer of the 442nd Regimental Combat Team in the 1951 *Go for Broke* movie. *Go for Broke* was the

100th Infantry Battalion's motto. After the 100th merged with the 442nd Regimental Combat Team, the motto followed. The phrase has since been adopted as a motto for all of the Japanese-American units formed during World War II.

The movie starts in 1943 at Camp Shelby, Mississippi, where the Johnson character as a Lieutenant reports for duty to train the 442nd. He is bigoted toward the Japanese soldiers.

The 442nd is sent to Italy and joins up with the 100th Battalion, again the Nisei unit formed in Hawaii before the 442nd. The 442nd and 100th fight in Italy. Johnson observes their fighting spirit and heroism, and replaces his bigotry with respect. He even gets into a fistfight with an Army buddy from his previous unit, who makes disparaging remarks about the Japanese troops. Several Nisei veterans played supporting roles.

The movie includes a brief discussion of the internment camps set up to contain Japanese Issei and Nisei, as some of the soldiers came from these camps.

This movie was a Hollywood rarity for its era, in that it features Asian Americans in a positive light. And rightfully so. The Niseis were fighting, while some had families still locked up.

The 2006 independent film *Only the Brave* (noted that several movies have this title) is also about the 100th Infantry Battalion/442nd Regimental Combat Team. The movie addresses the campaign to rescue the Lost Battalion in the Dutch East Indies, and one soldier's effort to cope years later with his posttraumatic stress. Japanese units never fought in the Pacific Theater, so the movie is pretty much made up.

In 2010, President Barack Obama (1961 HA -) signed a bill into law awarding the Congressional Gold Medal to the 100th Infantry Battalion, the 442nd Regimental Combat Team, and the Military Intelligence Service. The award ceremony was in 2011. The Congressional Gold Medal dates back to 1776. It is awarded in the name of Congress. It is the highest military or civilian award in the United States.

20- CAPTAIN JACK LUCAS, UNDERAGE IN WWII

Jack Lucas' (1928 NC – 2008 MS) North Carolina tobacco farmer father died when he was 10 years old. He was a wild kid, and loss of his father when so young did not help. The next school year when he was 11, his mother enrolled him at the Edwards Military Institute (1874 – 1973), Salemburg, North Carolina. She thought and hoped this would give his life discipline and direction.

Salemburg is 140 miles southwest of his hometown of Plymouth, North Carolina. Edwards was a boarding school. At Edwards, Lucas played many sports. These included basketball, boxing, wrestling, horseback riding, baseball, and softball. He also was on the trap and skeet shooting team, a marksman. He was a leader, named as cadet captain and captain of the football team.

In classes, Lucas was bored and antsy. He was not academics-oriented. He was eager to get in the World War II fight. Such was the case with many young men (and boys) after the thirteen sneak attacks on the same day by the Empire of Japan on 12/7, 8/1941. Japan as usual did not bother to warn the victims, by declaring war. This was (and still the case today) in violation of the international rules of war. The 1907 Hague Convention addressed the requirement to declare war in its *Convention Relative to the Opening of Hostilities* statements. These clauses describe the international actions a country should perform, before opening hostilities. Article 1 states: *The Contracting Powers recognize that hostilities between themselves must not commence without previous and explicit warning, in the form either of a reasoned declaration of war or of an ultimatum with conditional declaration of war.* Japan took a pass on this formality. Shame on Japan again, as had done such several times already in the 20th century.

The thirteen locations were all in or on the Pacific Ocean. The attacks were all on the same day, within nine hours of each other. Two days are shown, as the locations were on both sides of the International Date Line. The International Date Line is an imaginary line from the North Pole to the South Pole. It marks the change from one calendar day to the next. It roughly follows the 180° line of longitude, through the middle of the Pacific Ocean. Again, the attacks were all on the same day. The attacked thirteen sites (or ships) were as follows:

- Nine U.S. possessions
- Storming and capture of a 159' long USS river gunboat and its crew when berthed at Shanghai Harbor; this little Yangtze River gunboat was the only USS that Japan captured in World War II; for good measure, the Japanese also gun-sank a 177' HMS river gunboat in Shanghai Harbor, at about the same time; if counting this British warship, it is fourteen sneak attacks instead of thirteen
- IJN submarine gun-sank an Army-chartered, 250' long freighter off California
- Howland and Baker Islands of the Phoenix Islands of the U.S. Minor Outlying Islands were bombed, these two islands are 43 miles apart
- Five U.S. military installations (harbors, airfields, bases) on five Pacific Ocean islands; these five islands were Oahu (Pearl Harbor), Guam, Midway, Wake, and Philippines
- Three British Crown colonies – Malaya, Hong Kong, and Singapore
- Thailand

Japan ended up occupying the three British crown colonies, Thailand, and Wake Island for the duration of World War II (ended 8/1945). Japan occupied Guam until the U.S. re-captured 8/1944. Japan occupied the major Philippine Islands by the spring of 1942. The U.S. wrested the Philippine Islands back beginning 10/1944, and into 1945. General Douglas MacArthur (1880 AR – 1964 DC) said he would return and he did, but it took 2.6 years.

Some Japanese soldiers hid out though on Mindanao Island (second largest of the Philippines) until the end of the War. For that matter, another 200 well-organized and disciplined Japanese troops hid out also on Mindanao, and did not surrender until almost 2.5 half years after the War ended (if you can believe it).

In the next few weeks and months after the sneak attacks, Japan also conquered and occupied Borneo, Burma, New Britain, Gilbert Islands, and the resources-rich (oil, rubber, etc.) Dutch East Indies (today, the Republic of Indonesia).

In these thirteen (or fourteen if you count the HMS gunboat sunk in Shanghai Harbor) attacks on the same day, the Japanese Empire was for the most part stupendously successful in terms of devastation and casualties rendered, versus its own loss of equipment and casualties. Japan's planning and executions were brilliant. Said yet a third way, the outcomes were very one-sided in Japan's favor. To quote President Franklin Roosevelt (1882 NY – 4/12/1945 Georgia, cerebral hemorrhage) from his 12/8/1942 speech to Congress, 12/7/1941 was *a date that will live in infamy* for the United States. Roosevelt asked Congress to declare war on Japan. Congress did so that day 12/8/1941, a Monday.

Of the five U.S. military targets on the five Pacific Ocean islands, Americans of course most remember Oahu of the U.S. Territory of Hawaii, again due to the one-sided outcome. Japan launched two air attacks (bombing and strafing) from aircraft carriers, one hour apart on a Sunday morning. The U.S. military had 2,335 and 1,143 men killed and wounded. Another 68 and 35 Hawaiian civilians were killed and injured. In comparison, only 64 Japanese military men died (55 airmen and nine midget submarine sailors) and one captured (a submariner). This is a ratio of more than 36 American military deaths per one Japanese military death, at Oahu.

At Oahu, the Japanese Navy sank or damaged nineteen USSs, including all eight battleships of the Pacific fleet. Hundreds of aircraft were destroyed, and most of these when on the ground. Japan lost only 29 aircraft, nine and 20 in the first and second wave attacks. These were fifteen, nine, and five dive bombers, fighters, and torpedo bombers. Japan's five mini-submarines were all sunk, which was more or less the (unstated) plan. The other 51 ships and boats of the Japanese Task Force were unseen and undetected, coming and going.

Japan's surprise attacks without declaring war ended the United States' isolationist attitude, left over from losing 116,700 men in uniform (almost 46% in combat) and another 204,000 wounded or made ill (many with permanent disabilities) in World War I. As noted above, Congress at Roosevelt's request declared war on Japan the next day, which was a Monday. The peace period for America was a little more than 23 years, from the World War I Armistice Day to the day of the sneak attacks.

This change in opinion on the isolationism issue was certainly the case with Lucas. He presented Marine recruiters a notarized, signed document from his mother, that she gave permission for her 17-year-old son to enlist in the Marines. He had forged her signature and somehow got it notary stamped. Lucas was only five feet and eight inches tall but husky at 180 pounds, which helped the lie. He enlisted in the Marine Corps Reserves 8/8/1942, a few days less than 14.5 years in age.

He trained at Marine bases in South Carolina, Florida, and North Carolina. His designation was machine gun crewman. He sailed from San Diego to Oahu, arriving 12/1943. This was two years into the Pacific War.

Lucas was assigned to the 6th Base Depot of the V Amphibious Corps at Camp Catlin. Camp Catlin was located in the Salt Lake suburb of Honolulu. Catlin was set up during World War II, to train Marines for fighting in the Pacific Theater. It was the first home of the Fleet Marine Force, Pacific.

Camp Catlin was closed after World War II.

Lucas was promoted to Private First Class 1/29/1944, two weeks shy of his 16th birthday.

Lucas was sweet on a girl who lived in Swan Corner, North Carolina. Swan Corner is 75 miles south of his hometown of Plymouth, North Carolina. He wrote her a letter, mentioning his upcoming 16th birthday. After all, Lucas was born on Valentine's Day.

The Censorship Office caught this and notified the Marines. The Marines decided to discharge him and send him home. He begged that he not be discharged. He also stated that if was discharged, he would forge papers again and enlist in the Army. The compromise was that he could stay in the Marines at his current rank, but would be kept out of combat – until he was age 18.

His new job for the Marines was driving a truck on the island transporting marines around for training, to the infirmary, to town (Honolulu), etc. Lucas wanted combat. Frustrated, he lashed out. He got into fights with other marines, a Sergeant, and the military police. He got drunk. He was thrown in the brig off and on. He was made to work hard labor some.

On 1/10/1945, he walked out of camp with just a backpack. He stowed away on the new, Haskell-class, 455' long and 62' beam and 24' draft, 20 miles per hour, 536 crew, USS Deuel (1944 – 1974 scrapped) attack transport. His cousin was also on Deuel. Deuel was transporting marines to a Japanese Army occupied island 500 miles south of Tokyo, called Iwo Jima. Iwo Jima belonged to Japan.

Lucas' main hiding place on Deuel for almost a month was inside one of the landing craft, but he also mingled some. With a crew of more than 600 sailors and carrying more than 1,500 marines and everybody in uniform, fading in was not difficult. On the ship at one day less than a month (2/8/1945) to avoid desertion charges, Lucas sort of confessed his situation to Marine Captain Robert Dunlap (1920 IL – 2000 IL). Lucas made up a story – something about the fact that he boarded due to some type of clerical (paper work) error.

Captain Dunlap reported the situation to the battalion's commanding officer, Lieutenant Colonel Daniel Pollock. Dunlap and Pollock assumed that Lucas was over the age of 20 – after all, he had been in the Marines 2.5 years. Lucas had earned sharpshooter designation in boot camp and had the insignia. Pollock advised Lucas that he was now a rifleman, assigned to Dunlap's rifle company – just like that. Dunlap's unit was part of the 5th Division, C Company, 1st Battalion, 26th Marines. Lucas could not have been happier.

It appears that the Marine officers did not suspect that Lucas was underage. However, he was demoted back to Private. The demotion suggests that the officers did not believe Lucas' story, and realized he was a stowaway.

On the other hand, his new superiors probably were pleased to have another gung-ho Marine. In fact, Lieutenant Colonel Pollock is quoted as stating: *I'd like to have a whole shipload of marines that want to fight as bad as you!*

The U.S. wiped out the Japanese at Truk Atoll of the Carolines. The Americans captured the Marshall Islands by 2/1944. Japan knew that the U.S. most likely would drive toward the Mariana Islands and more of the Caroline Islands, to get closer to Japan for much shorter bombing raids on the home islands. To counter such an offensive, the Japanese Army and Navy established an inner line of defenses extending generally northward from the Carolines to the Marianas, and from there to Japan via the Volcano Islands, and westward from the Marianas via the Carolines and the Palau Islands to the Philippines. The 8.1 square mile Iwo Jima is one of the Volcano Islands.

General (four star) Hideyoshi Obata (1890 Japan – 8/11/1944 Guam, seppuku in lieu of fighting to the death due to superior American forces pressing) commanded the 31st Army. He was charged 3/1944 with garrisoning this inner line.

In 6/1944, Obata assigned Lieutenant General (three star) Tadamichi Kuribayashi (1891 Japan – 3/26/1945 Iwo Jima, probably killed in action on the final day of the battle, not identified as he removed all insignia from his uniform) to command the defense of Iwo Jima.

Both Obata and Kuribayashi were graduates of the Imperial Japanese Army Academy in Tokyo, 1911 and 1914 respectively. Both also graduated from the Japanese Army War College, 1919 and 1923 respectively. To sum up, these two men were elite generals.

Kuribayashi fortified Iwo Jima, including the following:

- Construction of numerous pillboxes; pillboxes are dug-in guard post structures; they have holes, to fire small arms or machine guns through; as hardened (usually made of concrete), they can withstand machine gun bullets as well as small arms fire, and usually even grenades; they are raised above ground, to improve the field of fire
- Current caves were enlarged
- Bunkers were made; the largest bunker (Nanpo Bunker) was located east of Airfield Number 2; it was 90' deep, and had tunnels running off in various directions; it was stocked with a 90-day supply of water, food, fuel, and ammunition
- The extensive tunnel system was 11 miles in length, adding up all the offshoots (although initial goal was 17 miles); the tunnels allowed for troop movement to go undetected to various offensive and defensive positions
- Hundreds of hidden artillery and mortar positions were placed
- Hundreds of land mines were placed

Lucas' unit landed on the first day of the Iwo Jima attack, 2/19/1945. He was 17 years old, plus five days. Again, his superiors thought he was age 21, or near it.

Lucas was part of a four-man fire team from one of C Company's platoons. The foursome creeped though a twisting ravine to a Japanese airstrip near Mount Suribachi on the southwestern tip of the island. The 554' Suribachi is the highest point on Iwo Jima. It was formed by volcanic activity, as was the entire island for that matter. Its peak was the site of Joe Rosenthal's (1911 DC – 2006 CA) iconic photograph of the six marines raising the flag, on day four of the Iwo Jima invasion. This was 2/23/1945.

They approached a pillbox the next day and ducked into a trench for cover. The marines thought that the pillbox was empty. This was the case. The Japanese soldiers had abandoned the pillbox via a tunnel. The Japanese soldiers in this group numbered eleven. They popped up unknown to Lucas' quartet, and entered a parallel trench. A firefight ensued. Lucas' M-1 Garand, eight-round en bloc clip, autoloading .30 caliber rifle jammed.

A Japanese soldier tossed a grenade into the marines' trench. The one pound, Type 97 Japanese fragmentation grenade had 65 grams (0.14 pounds) of trinitrotoluene, to distribute its shrapnel.

Lucas jammed the grenade into the volcanic ash with his rifle butt, and then jumped on it. Another grenade flew in. He grabbed it and pulled it under his body. Only one grenade exploded. The explosion threw Lucas onto his back. His right

arm and wrist and leg and thigh, and his chest took most of the blast. Lucas was conscious, but barely alive. The other three nearby marines were not injured. The marines killed some or all of the eleven
Japanese soldiers.

Lucas' three comrade marines moved on, assuming he was dead. Following marines discovered that he was alive. A Navy corpsman field treated him. This corpsman used his carbine to fend off more Japanese soldiers. Stretcher-bearers carried Lucas to the beach. A landing craft took him to a cargo ship, being used as a hospital.

First day Iwo Jima American Marine casualties were 5,320. Lucas was injured on day two, with many more casualties. The several offshore hospital ships were already full with Iwo Jima wounded. This is why the cargoman was pressed into service, as a hospital ship. Lucas was eventually transferred to the 448' long and 58' beam and 26' draft, 16 miles an hour, USS Samaritan (1921 – 1948 scrapped) hospital ship, which had been converted from a transport.

Lucas received more treatment at land-based hospitals. He arrived San Francisco 3/28/1945. He eventually underwent twenty-two surgeries. For the rest of his life, two hundred pieces of metal remained in his body. Some were the size of .22 caliber bullets. He also carried some slivers of wood from his rifle stock. When Lucas traveled later in life, getting through airport metal detectors was a tedious chore, to say the least.

In 8/1945, the away without leave charge from stowing away aboard USS Deuel was removed from his record. He was a patient at the U.S. Naval Hospital at Charleston, South Carolina, at the time. Lucas was promoted back to Private First Class, 9/1945. Later, all seventeen of his convictions (most for brawling) back at Camp Catlin on Oahu were erased, as well.

The Marines discharged Lucas 9/18/1945, due to his disabilities.

President Harry Truman (1884 MO – 1972 MO) presented the Medal of Honor to Lucas and thirteen others in a 10/5/1945 ceremony, on White House grounds. The other thirteen were another ten marines, and three sailors. One of the marines was Captain Dunlap, to whom Lucas had reported when he was a stowaway on the USS Deuel. Dunlap was rewarded for his heroic actions the second day of the invasion. This was 2/20/1945, which was the same day as Lucas' heroics. Dunlap also received the Purple Heart (shot in the hip).

Lucas' mother and brother attended the ceremony. Dignitaries in attendance at the presentation included U.S. Pacific Fleet Commander in Chief Chester Nimitz (1885 TX – 1966 CA) and Defense Secretary James Forrestal (1892 NY – 1949 MD, suicide jump).

Lucas' Medal of Honor citation reads as follows:

> *For conspicuous gallantry and intrepidity at the risk of his life above and beyond the call of duty while serving with the First Battalion, Twenty-Sixth Marines, Fifth Marine Division, during action against enemy Japanese forces on Iwo Jima, Volcano Islands 2/20/1945. While creeping through a treacherous, twisting ravine which ran in close proximity to a fluid and uncertain front line on D-plus+1 Day, Private First Class Lucas*

and three other men were suddenly ambushed by a hostile patrol which savagely attacked with rifle fire and grenades. Quick to act when the lives of the small group were endangered by two grenades which landed directly in front of them, Private First Class Lucas unhesitatingly hurled himself over his comrades upon one grenade and pulled the other one under him, absorbing the whole blasting force of the explosions in his own body in order to shield his companions, from the concussion and murderous flying fragments. By his inspiring action and valiant spirit of self-sacrifice, he not only protected his comrades from certain injury or possible death, but also enabled them to rout the Japanese patrol and continue the advance. His exceptionally courageous initiative and loyalty reflect the highest credit upon Private First Class Lucas and the United States Naval Service.

The Iwo Jima battle ran five weeks. Twenty-two and five marines and sailors were awarded the Medal of Honor for their actions, over the five weeks. Four of the five Navy men were hospital corpsmen. Of the twenty-seven recipients, fourteen were posthumous. Fleet Admiral Chester Nimitz who was Commander in Chief of the U.S. Pacific Command is recalled for his statement: *Among the Americans who served on Iwo Jima Island, uncommon valor was a common virtue.*

Lucas was seventeen years and six days old at the time of his Medal of Honor actions. He remains the youngest Marine to be awarded the Medal of Honor (another source says the youngest since the Civil War). He was also the youngest of any branch to be awarded the Medal of Honor, for World War II actions. He was also awarded the Presidential Unit Citation, American Campaign Medal, Asiatic-Pacific Campaign Medal, World War II Victory Medal, and of course the Purple Heart.

As a civilian, Lucas worked off and on 1945-1955 for the Veterans Administration at Winston-Salem, North Carolina. During this period, he finished high school (started in the ninth grade). He then earned a college business degree from High Point University, High Point, North Carolina; paid for by the GI Bill.

Lucas joined the Army in 1961, at age 33. He became a paratrooper. He volunteered to be deployed to Vietnam, but was denied because of his previous injuries. He trained troops headed for the Vietnam War. He separated from the Army in 1965 at age 37, as a Captain.

Lucas opened five, retail meat stores in the District of Columbia area. He raised his own beef on a ranch in Maryland. He did not or could not pay all his income taxes, so was in trouble with the Internal Revenue Service. The outcome here included that he was forced to sell or close his meat stores.

When the keel of the Wasp-class, 844' long and 110' beam and 30' draft, 25 miles per hour, 1,082 crew, USS Iwo Jima (2001 – in service) amphibious assault ship was laid down in 1997, Lucas placed his Medal of Honor citation in the ship's hull in a ceremony. This is where it remains to this day.

In a 2006 ceremony, the Medal of Honor flag was presented to Lucas and fifteen other Marine Medal of Honor recipients.

Lucas was diagnosed with leukemia. His kidneys failed. As suffering so, he decided that he had enough, and stopped the dialysis treatments. He was age 80.3 years.

Lucas's first three marriages ended in divorce. Survivors included his fourth wife whom he married in 1998, five children, and thirteen grand and great-grandchildren.

The Navy announced in 2016, that a future Arleigh Burke-class, guided missile destroyer will be named after Lucas. This will be the 75th Arleigh Burke destroyer, and the first of the Flight III variants. The Flight III destroyers have various design improvements. A key one is that the mid-diameter radar antennas have been increased from two feet to four feet. The air and missile defense radars will use digital beam-forming, instead of passive, electronically-scanned array radars. Commissioning is expected in 2023.

Lucas' 2016 autobiography (written with professional assistance) is aptly entitled *Indestructible*.

From the American Revolution to the War of 1812 to the Civil War and World War I which ended in 1918, underage boys (and girls) enlisted in the U.S. Armed Forces. This was frowned upon but tolerated. By the time World War II came around, firm age requirements were in place. These were that the minimum age for men to enlist was eighteen, except for seventeen allowed if a parent gave written permission. The Army though dropped the age seventeen exception 12/1942, which was a year after the U.S. entered World War II.

Enlistees also were not allowed to join more hazardous units such as air services (part of the Army at the time) or paratroopers, until age 21.

Although the age requirements were in place, thousands of boys age 16 or even less enlisted for World War II – and again, also a few underage women (see below for age minimums for women). They forged documents, got somebody to vouch for their false age, stole or borrowed notary stamps, etc. Some got a parent to lie with them. Most though forged documents to state that they were 17, as a solo effort.

One such forged document used by some boys was a modified family Bible, that showed birth dates of family members. The forgers (the underage boys) felt that recruiters would not question something written in the worn, family Bible; and this in fact worked in some cases.

Estimates of the number of underage enlistees for World War II run from 90,000 to 250,000 boys. As enormous as these figures are, they are only 0.6 to 1.6% of the 16.1 Americans in uniform for World War II. This is somewhere between one in every 65 to one in every 179.

Later, studies were done to determine the situations and motivations of these underage enlistees. Commonalties were discovered, including the following:

- A lust for adventure
- Overly patriotic
- Poverty in the household; remember that the U.S. (and much of the world, for that matter) was in the 1929-1941 economic Great Depression; (World War II contributed to ending the Depression in the United States,

and same for most other countries as well); comparatively speaking, the military paid very well; benefits included room, board, clothing, transportation, medical and dental care, etc.; for many of these boys, three square meals a day and hot water and doctor-dental care and etc. were something way out of the ordinary; also, by leaving home, there was one less mouth to feed there

- Familial problems – more often than not, they did not get along with their mother's second husband or current boyfriend
- Trouble with the law, often apprehended for crimes such as vandalism, petty theft, underage drinking, driving violations, etc.; at the time of World War II, some judges in that era gave repeat offenders the option of enlisting in the military in lieu of jail; the offering of this choice was never recorded as a policy, but again did occur from time to time
- Large for their age, which supported their forged documents
- Were athletic
- Generally were not good students

In some cases no doubt, suspecting recruiters went along as well – not requiring proof of age or accepting shaky-looking documents, helping with written tests or fudging scores, etc.; but generally just looking the other way.

The recruiters had quotas to make, you understand; plus their compensation bonuses depended upon the number of men (OK, and boys) enlisted. Perhaps they thought they were doing the boy a favor. This was because as his family was poor, and/or because of some domestic conflict in the family, or because they felt he needed direction and discipline, etc. -- or a combination of these reasons and others.

The recruiters were not the only ones complicit. If anyone can tell a boy's age, these would be examining physicians. They often avoided the issue and passed the boys on through. Perhaps they had unwritten orders to do so – who knows?

Drill instructors at boot camp also realized that some were underage, but kept silent. There was a War going on, you see. Young, healthy males were needed as soldiers, airmen, sailors, marines, and coast guardsmen. The boy was no doubt motivated. The kid's non-military life was not good. The boy did not have a college ambition, or a good job. His family was hard up for the basics of life. Again, these were the rationales for looking the other way.

The boys made up stories for parents and family, as to why they were not at home. In most cases, the parents and other relatives at the time or later became aware that their son had enlisted. In most cases, they chose to not intervene; thinking that this was probably best for their son, brother, nephew, etc.

For World War II, two youths who were only twelve are known to have enlisted, as follows:

- Age 12.1 years at enlistment George Holle (1929 WI – 1993) joined the Marines 10/28/1941, six weeks before Pearl Harbor Day. His stepmother filed for social security benefits when her husband and George's father died. She listed thirteen-year-old George *as a dependent, currently fighting in the Pacific somewhere.* The *somewhere* at the time (12/1942) happened to be Guadalcanal, where young George was fighting the Japanese. The Chicago newspapers got hold of the facts and alerted the Marines. The Marines quickly rounded thirteen-year-old George up, discharged him, and sent him home. He was an instant celebrity. He went on tour with the USO.

He was buried in the same Marine dress-blue uniform he was issued in 1941, fifty-two years later. As far as known, he was the youngest in the U.S. Armed Forces in World War II.

- Age 12.4 years at Navy enlistment Calvin Graham (4/3/1930 TX – 1992 TX) was 3.5 months older than Holle. However, he saw combat at a younger age than Holle.

Graham had an abusive stepfather. When eleven, he and an older brother moved into a cheap rooming house in Crockett, Texas. He supported himself by selling newspapers and delivering telegrams on weekends and after school. Several of his cousins had been killed in the War. He stole a notary stamp from a hotel and forged his mother's signature. He was 5'2" and 125 pounds, when he enlisted 8/15/1942 in the Navy. Graham told his mother he was going off to see relatives.

In a 1977 interview, he stated that the Navy knew that he and others who enlisted at the same time were underage but were desperate for sailors, as losing the war in the Pacific at the time. His statement about the U.S. losing the Pacific Theater naval battle this period was correct. Of note however, American citizens were not fully aware of the great loss of USSs and sailors. Roosevelt kept the results secret or allowed the release of only some information, something that could not be done today.

Graham also said that the drill sergeants at boot camp in San Diego were also aware that he and others were underage, but again chose to remain silent – or maybe they were ordered from above to keep quiet.

Seaman First Class Graham was a gunner on the South Dakota-class, 680' long and 108' beam and 36' draft, 32 miles per hour, 2,364 crew, USS South Dakota (1942 – 1962 scrapped) battleship 11/14/1942, during the Guadalcanal Naval Battle. He was 12.6 years old. South Dakota was walloped, taking forty-two hits. Shrapnel tore through his mouth and jaw. Another blast knocked him off the superstructure. He fell/tumbled 30' to a lower deck. Despite his wounds, he aided other crewmates. He was awarded a Bronze Star for valor, and a Purple Heart of course.

Graham's mother recognized him in a newsreel of the battle and contacted the Navy. He was sentenced to three months imprisonment. He was stripped of his medals and dishonorably discharged. This meant no veteran benefits. When he was in the brig in Corpus Christi, Texas, his sister sprung him by threatening to go to the newspapers – imprisoning a twelve-year-old, Purple Heart sailor who had also been recognized for bravery and awarded a valor medal would not sit well with the public.

Two days after his 13th birthday, he rejoined his Fort Worth, Texas classmates in the seventh grade. He was a star. As a poor student, he dropped out. He wed at age fourteen and became a father at fifteen. He worked in a Houston shipyard as a welder. The marriage failed. He lost his job.

At age seventeen, he was about to be drafted. Instead, he enlisted in the Marine Corps. This was in 1948. He fell from a pier and broke his back. He used a cane the rest of his life. He was discharged in 1951, rank of Corporal. He was granted a 20% service disability, but was denied benefits because of his dishonorable discharge.

He made some money by selling magazine subscriptions.

In 1977, he mounted an aggressive letter-writing campaign when the amnesty program for Vietnam War deserters and draft dodgers was offered. He stated that if they got an honorable discharge for refusing to fight, surely he should as he enlisted voluntarily not once but twice, fought, received a valor medal, and was seriously injured.

In addition, Graham reasoned that 1946 U.S. Naval Academy graduate President Jimmy Carter (1924 GA -) would sympathize with him, as also a Navy veteran. Carter served ten years active duty, and then eight years as a reservist (1943 – 1961 includes his years at the Academy).

Carter was President 1977-1981, so maybe he did influence getting Graham's discharge changed from dishonorable to honorable, in 1978. In addition, Graham's medals were returned, except for the Purple Heart. In 1996 two years after he died, the military relented and sent his Purple Heart medal to his widow.

Legislation was passed in 1988 to grant him VA disability benefits. This was four years before he died.

The movie *Too Young the Hero* about Graham came out in 1988. Ricky Schroder (1970 Brooklyn -) played Graham. Schroder was 17 when the movie was made.

Several other notable cases were as follows:

- Thirteen-year-old Marine William Trero (1928 AL – 2015 TX) was wounded several times, in battle. As a rifleman, he fought at Guadalcanal, Gilbert Islands, and Saipan. He was hospitalized eight months, in one case.
- Clifford Werley enlisted in the Army at age 14.8 years. He was a gunner on a twin engine B-26 Marauder bomber at age fifteen. He flew twenty-two missions in the European and North African Theaters. He shot down one

single engine, Messerschmitt Bf 109 fighter, and was also credited with probable kills or partial kills of fourteen more German fighters. He survived a belly landing. He served 1.4 years, before found out. He separated as a Staff Sergeant and wrangled an honorary discharge. He traveled the U.S. selling war bonds. He got a job in Maryland inspecting machine gun installations at the Martin bomber factory. He enlisted at age seventeen in the Navy. He separated from the Navy, 1.7 years later.

- Philip Schneiderman enlisted the Coast Guard, age fifteen. He was found out, and dishonorably discharged. He eventually got an honorable discharge.
- Dale Schaffer enlisted the Navy, age fifteen. He served through World War II, as a shipboard cook.
- Clifford Warren enlisted the Army, age sixteen. He was on Corregidor (Philippines) when the Americans surrendered. He spent the rest of the war in Japanese POW camps, but survived to be repatriated.
- Bruce Cottington enlisted the Navy, age sixteen. He served throughout out World War II, and also in the Korean War.

Some underage boys died in combat or captivity, including the following:

- Just under 14.5 years, Norman Gibbs (6/21/1927 – 12/28/1942) enlisted in the Marines. He died 12/28/1942 at age 15.5 years when his transport ship exploded near Guadalcanal. It was either hit by a mine or torpedoed. Gibbs is thought to be the youngest American military man (OK, boy) to die in World War II.
- Febert Williams enlisted in the Army at age fourteen. He survived the Bataan Death March. He died at age fifteen of dysentery in a Japanese POW camp.
- Jack Cook enlisted in the Army at age fourteen. He was wounded at age sixteen in Germany and died seven days later.
- James O'Connor enlisted in the Marines at age fifteen. He operated a flamethrower on Iwo Jima. He ran out of fuel. He then fought with his rifle and grenades, until shot to death at age sixteen.
- Robert Fox enlisted in the Marines at age fifteen. He was killed 11/1943 at age sixteen in the Tarawa Battle.
- Carl Reddick enlisted in the Marines at age fourteen. His age was found out, but he was not kicked out. He survived a tropical fever. He fought on Guadalcanal. He was shot in battle and died on Guam, a few weeks before turning seventeen.

Since World War II, the U.S. Armed Forces has greatly increased their scrutiny to ensure that enlistees are age eighteen. If a minor somehow does get in though, his minority time counts toward seniority and benefits, if he is not caught before he/she turns age seventeen. If discovered before age seventeen, the teenager is released with no benefits.

Allen Stover was one exception of not getting screened out, after World War II. He joined the Coast Guard at age fourteen, during the Korean War. He founded Veterans of Underage Military Service (VUMS) in 1991, as a support group for boys (now men) who managed to enlist underage. Its members today span Korea to Vietnam (almost all underage World War II enlistees who were members have since died). VUMS collects the stories on these boys. It assists them in getting Veterans Administration benefits, dishonorable discharges changed, their commendations, etc. Stover's book titled *Underage and Under Fire* book came out in 2014.

Dan Bullock (12/21/1953 NC – 6/7/1969 Vietnam in combat) was one of the (presumably) very, very few underage who enlisted in the military in the Vietnam era. His mother died when he was 12. He and his younger sister moved to Brooklyn to live with their father and his wife. He forged a document and enlisted in the Marines at age 14. He arrived in Vietnam, 5/18/1969. The North Vietnamese attacked his unit at night. He was sent back in a truck to get more ammunition. Private First Class Bullock was killed instantly by small arms fire when driving. This was on day 20 in country. Bullock was not quite 15.5 years old. He was too young to enlist, too young to drive, too young to train, too young to fight, and too young to die. Bullock was the youngest American serviceman (service boy?) killed in action in the Vietnam War.

Some underage females also enlisted during World War II. The age requirements for women to join the Army, Navy, or Marines auxiliaries were three years older than for males. So this was 21, or 20 with parental consent. The women in these auxiliaries were not considered military.

Dorothy Hinson Brandt (1928 - 2???) was one. She joined the Women's Army Corps (WAC) 2/1944, age 16. She got a neighbor to sign a voucher document that she was age 21. Her five older brothers were in the Armed Forces during World War II. She spent 3.5 years in the Army. She served in 1917 U.S. Military Academy graduate General Mark Clark's (1896 NY – 1978 SC) Fifteenth Army in the spring of 1945, as it moved across northern Italy to occupy Vienna, Austria. Brandt edited a book on 25 female teenagers who joined underage during World War II. The 2011 book is titled *America's Youngest Women Warriors*. Most were over the age of 15. The youngest though was only 13. This was Doris Lyles Slatten Gilbert. She lied to enlist, as she later said her family was *dysfunctional*. She trained as a medical corpsman, and then later as a dental technician. She served more than two years before her age was discovered. She was kicked out but got an honorable discharge.

Norma Stuart Bomer is also in Brandt's book. She enlisted when she was 14. As far as known, Lyles Slatten Gilbert and Bomer are the youngest two girls to ever enlist in the U.S military.

An estimate is that up to a quarter million underage men (and a few women) served in World War II, Korea, and Vietnam. Since Vietnam into the computer age, background scrutiny (again, thanks to computer databases, etc.) is such that (in theory), under-aged teenagers are no longer able to enlist.

Today, a man or woman must be age 18 to enlist in any branch of the U.S. military. However, age 17 men and women may enlist, with signed permission from a parent or guardian.

Today, the Air Force enlists up to age 27, the Marines up to age 29, the Army and Navy up to age 34, and the Coast Guard up to age 39. Usually, enlistees may not have more than two dependents.

As noted above, twenty-seven American military men were awarded the Medal of Honor for their Iwo Jima actions; fourteen posthumously. As of 2019, four of the twenty-seven are still living. These four are three soldiers and a marine. Hershel Williams (10/2/1923 WV -) is the Marine. He is also the last surviving World War II Medal of Honor Marine.

Williams was raised on a dairy farm in West Virginia, the last of eleven children. On the day of the 12/7/1941 sneak attacks, he was working for the Civilian Conservation Corps in Montana. This was one of the Great Depression public work relief programs, putting unmarried and unemployed young men to work.

Williams tried to enlist in the Marines in 1942, but he was too short. The Marines reduced their height requirement in 1943, and he enlisted. He fought on Guam, and then Iwo Jima. On 2/23/1945, Corporal Williams charged forward with his 70-pound, dual-tank, M2-2 flamethrower, to reduce the amount of devastating machine gun fire from entrenched, Japanese positions. These were reinforced concrete pillboxes. He was able to place his nozzle in a vent hole, killing enemy in a bunker. His actions allowed tanks to open a lane for infantry. Japanese soldiers charged him, but he burned them before they fired. Four infantrymen covered him

As the equipment was so heavy, flamethrowers had to stand erect. Therefore, small-arms coverage was imperative. Machine gun bullets hit his tanks, but they did not rupture.

The M2-2 used either liquid fuel which was effective up to 20 yards, or a thickened fuel (napalm) with double that range. One tank contained the fuel. The other tank contained the propellant, which was usually nitrogen. The fuel and flames were spent though, in less than ten seconds.

Flamethrowers were used against dug-in Japanese defensive positions, as the flames follow the contour of the hideout which bullets could not do. The capability was added to vehicles (especially tanks) in 1944, reducing the need for the portable version strapped on soldiers.

The flames of course kill. The flames also emit carbon monoxide and consume oxygen – both contributing to asphyxiation.

Williams also received the Purple Heart.

Williams served 1943-1945, 1948-1949, and 1954-1969. He separated as a Chief Warrant Officer 4. After World War II, he worked as a Veterans Affairs counselor for 33 years. He was the chaplain of the Congressional Medal of Honor Society for 35 years.

Williams in 2010 established a Medal of Honor Foundation to erect memorials to honor Gold Star families, and provide scholarships to their surviving children.

Gold Stars signify that a son or daughter died in service to their country. The group also sponsors outreach programs and educational events, etc.

In 2011, Williams appeared on an episode of *Sons of Guns*. On the show, his broken flamethrower was refurbished back to working condition. The episode ended with Williams firing the weapon, at the age of 87.

The *Sons of Guns* reality television series ran 2011-2014 on the Discovery Channel. The episodes all involved weapons of some sort (usually guns), in one way or another.

21- GUNNERY SERGEANT JOHN BASILONE

John Basilone (1916 NY – 2/19/1945 Iwo Jima Island) dropped out of high school. He enlisted in the Army 7/1934, age 17. He served in the Philippines. Of note, he was one of the Army's best amateur boxers, his weight class. He was discharged in 1937. He worked as a truck driver in Maryland. He missed his time and service in the military, and/or did not particularly enjoy driving a truck. He enlisted in the Marines 6/1940. He trained at Marine bases in South Carolina, North Carolina, and Virginia. He was a machine gunner. His unit was deployed to Guantanamo Naval Base, on the southeastern coast of Cuba.

The Empire of Japan sneak attacked thirteen locations in or on the Pacific Ocean 12/7, 8/1941. Japan as usual did not bother to warn the victims, by declaring war. This was in violation of the international rules of war. The 1907 Hague Convention addressed the requirement to declare war in its *Convention Relative to the Opening of Hostilities* statements. These clauses describe the international actions a country should perform, before opening hostilities. Article 1 states: *The Contracting Powers recognize that hostilities between themselves must not commence without previous and explicit warning, in the form either of a reasoned declaration of war or of an ultimatum with conditional declaration of war.* Japan took a pass on giving an advance warning, of maybe attacking. Shame on Japan again (not the first time that Japan attacked other countries without notice).

The attacks were all on the same day, within nine hours of each other. Two days are shown, as the locations were on both sides of the International Date Line. The International Date Line is an imaginary line from the North Pole to the South Pole. It marks the change from one calendar day to the next. It roughly follows the 180° line of longitude, through the middle of the Pacific Ocean. But again, the attacks were all on the same day. The attacked thirteen sites (or ships) were as follows:

- Nine U.S. possessions
  - Storming and capture of a 159' long USS river gunboat and its crew when berthed at Shanghai Harbor; this little Yangtze River gunboat was the only USS that Japan captured in World War II; for good measure, the Japanese also gun-sank a 177' HMS river gunboat in Shanghai Harbor, at about the same time; if counting this British warship, it is fourteen sneak attacks instead of thirteen
  - IJN submarine gun-sank an Army-chartered, 250' long freighter off California
  - Howland and Baker Islands of the Phoenix Islands of the U.S. Minor Outlying Islands were bombed, these two islands are 43 miles apart
  - Five U.S. military installations (harbors, airfields, bases) on five Pacific Ocean islands; these five islands were Oahu (Pearl Harbor), Guam, Midway, Wake, and Philippines
- Three British Crown colonies – Malaya, Hong Kong, and Singapore

- Thailand

Japan ended up occupying the three British crown colonies, Thailand, and Wake Island for the duration of World War II, which ended 8/1945. Japan occupied Guam until the U.S. re-captured 8/1944. Japan occupied the major Philippine islands by the spring of 1942. The U.S. wrested the Philippine islands back beginning 10/ 1944, and into 1945. General Douglas MacArthur (1880 Little Rock – 1964 DC) said he would return and he did, but it took 2.6 years.

Some Japanese soldiers held out though on Mindanao Island (second largest of the Philippines) until the end of the War. Furthermore, 200 more organized and disciplined Japanese soldiers hid out another almost 2.5 years also on Mindanao, before surrendering and returning to Japan (if you can believe it).

In the next few weeks or months after the sneak attacks, Japan also conquered and occupied Borneo, Burma, New Britain, Gilbert Islands, and the resources-rich (oil, rubber, etc.) Dutch East Indies (today, the Republic of Indonesia).

In these thirteen (or fourteen) sneak attacks on the same day, the Japanese Empire was for the most part stupendously successful in terms of devastation and casualties rendered, versus its own loss of equipment and casualties. Japan's planning and executions were brilliant. Said yet a third way, the outcomes were very one-sided in Japan's favor. To quote President Franklin Roosevelt (1882 NY – 4/12/1945 Georgia, cerebral hemorrhage) from his 12/8/1941 speech to Congress, 12/7/1941 was *a date that will live in infamy* for the United States.

Of the five U.S. military targets on the five Pacific Ocean islands, Americans of course most remember Oahu (Pearl Harbor) of the U.S. Territory of Hawaii, again due to the one-sided outcome. Japan launched two air attacks (bombing and strafing) from aircraft carriers, one hour apart on a Sunday morning. The U.S. military had 2,335 and 1,143 men killed and wounded. Another 68 and 35 Hawaiian civilians were killed and injured. In comparison, only 64 Japanese military men died (55 airmen and nine submarine sailors) and one captured (a submariner). This is a ratio of more than 36 American military deaths per one Japanese military death.

The Japanese Navy sank or damaged nineteen USSs, including all eight battleships of the Pacific fleet. Hundreds of aircraft were destroyed, and most of these when on the ground. Japan lost only 29 aircraft, nine and 20 in the first and second wave attacks. These were fifteen, nine, and five dive bombers, fighters, and torpedo bombers. Japan's five mini-submarines were all sunk, which was more or less the (unstated) plan. The other 51 ships and boats of the Japanese Task Force were undetected and unseen, coming and going.

Japan's surprise attacks without declaring war ended the United States' isolationist attitude, left over from losing 116,700 men in uniform (almost 46% in combat) and another 204,000 wounded or made ill (many with permanent disabilities) in World War I. Congress declared war on Japan the next day 12/8/1941, which was a Monday. The peace period for America was a little more than 23 years, from the World War I Armistice Day to the day of the sneak attacks.

Meanwhile, Basilone's unit was transferred to the Pacific Theater, from Cuba.

The Japanese began construction of an airfield early 7/1942 at Lunga Point, on the north central side of Guadalcanal. Guadalcanal is the largest of the 910 Solomon Islands, at 2,047 square miles. For comparison purposes, this is less than 0.8% the size of Texas. Guadalcanal is located off the northeast coast of Australia. An airfield here stocked with Japanese fighters and bombers would greatly threaten the supply routes between the U.S and Australasia. Also, the Allies needed to secure the Solomons as a starting point to capture or isolate the major Japanese base at Rabaul, New Britain, Papua New Guinea, and to support the New Guinea campaign. New Guinea was a mandated territory of Australia, now occupied by the Japanese.

Accordingly, 11,000 marines including Basilone landed on Guadalcanal 8/7/1942 (Operation Watchtower). Another 3,000 marines also waded in the same day on some neighboring Solomon islets, occupied by the Japanese.

Regarding these ocean-to-beach landings on these Solomons Islands, these were the first ever made by U.S. Marines. They did not go well. Information was lacking on weather, terrain, tide, layout (maps were inaccurate); where the enemy was; etc. Luckily, there was no resistance in the case of Guadalcanal, for the following reasons:

- Several days of naval and aerial (these bombers flying off aircraft carriers) pushed the Japanese soldiers and sappers and their forced labor Korean laborers (about 2,800 total) into the jungle; they left behind equipment, supplies, provisions, and thirteen dead
- The landings were made during storms, so cloud cover hid the operation from Japanese scout planes flying off Rabaul, New Britain, Papua New Guinea

There was opposition though on the other islands, and the marines had casualties.

The marines on Guadalcanal advanced to the under-construction airfield, again unopposed. They rushed the completion of the airfield. In so doing, they used some of the machinery that the Japanese had left behind – talk about your feel-good feeling. Navy Seabees arrived 9/1/1942. The sappers made more improvements to the airfield and added infrastructure.

The airfield was named *Henderson Field*, in honor of 1926 U.S. Naval Academy graduate and Marine aviator Major Lofton Henderson (1903 OH – 6/4/1942 off Midway Island). Henderson led sixteen, single engine, Douglas SBD Dauntless dive bombers on a 6/4/1942 glide bombing attack on the 746' IJN Hiryu (1939 – 6/5/1942, scuttled due to aerial bomb damage in Midway Battle, 389 of 1,100 {35%} crew lost) aircraft carrier. An intercepting Mitsubishi A6M Zero or Zeroes shot him down. His gunner Private First Class Lee Reininger (1922 – 6/4/1942 off Midway Island) died as well. This was on the first day of the 6/4-7/1942 Midway Battle.

The Americans' goal now was to clear Guadalcanal of Japanese. Japan's goal was to do likewise, killing or forcing the Americans off Guadalcanal to reclaim the airfield and island. Again, holding the airfield, Guadalcanal, and the Solomons was critical to control the skies and seas leading to Australia and New Zealand; and to have success in other campaigns in the area.

The marines (later joined by soldiers) and Navy won out. However, the ground, ocean, and air war of attrition took six months. Japan finally pulled its remaining troops off Guadalcanal 2/1943. Seven thousand and one hundred and 7,800 American marines and soldiers died and were wounded. The Japanese (and some conscripted South Koreans) had more than four times as many deaths. Three fourths of the enemy deaths were from lack of food and disease.

The 10/23-26/1942 Henderson Field Battle was the last major ground battle of the Guadalcanal campaign. Three thousand Japanese soldiers attacked the Americans in Basilone's area, in an effort to recapture Henderson Field. This area was Lunga Ridge, 1,000 yards south of the airfield. On 10/24/1942, the Japanese attacked in a renewed effort with machine guns, mortars, and grenades; against the Americans' heavy machine guns. Basilone commanded two machine gun sections.

By 10/26/1942, only Basilone and two other marines remained standing in their sector. He positioned another machine gun to keep the fire continuous. Basilone then repaired and manned another machine gun, holding the line until replacements finally arrived. Basilone exposed himself to get more ammunition. The ammunition ran out though. Basilone at this point in time, held off the Japanese using his Colt .45 pistol and even a machete.

Private First Class Nash Phillips of Fayetteville, North Carolina, later recalled as follows:

> Basilone had a machine gun on the go for three days and nights without sleep, rest, or food. He was in a good emplacement, and causing the Japanese lots of trouble, not only firing his machine gun, but also using his pistol.

The marines won the three-plus day battle. Japanese deaths were 2,600, compared to only 72 for the Americans. This is a ratio of more than 36 to one. Oddly, this was the same ratio mentioned for the 12/7/1941 Oahu (Pearl Harbor and bases attack), but in reverse (finally).

Basilone himself killed about 40 enemy soldiers. For his actions, he was awarded the Medal of Honor. The citation reads as follows:

> For extraordinary heroism and conspicuous gallantry in action against enemy Japanese forces above and beyond the call of duty, while serving with the 1st Battalion, 7th Marines, 1st Marine Division in the Lunga Area, Guadalcanal, Solomon Islands, on 10/24-25/1942. While the enemy was hammering at the Marines' defensive positions, Sgt. Basilone, in charge of two sections of heavy machine guns, fought valiantly to check the savage and determined assault. In a fierce frontal attack with the Japanese blasting his guns with grenades and mortar fire, one of Sgt. Basilone's sections with its gun crews was put out of action, leaving only two men able to carry on. Moving an extra gun into position, he placed it in action, then, under continual fire, repaired another and personally manned it, gallantly holding his line until replacements arrived. A little later, with ammunition critically low and the supply lines cut off, Sgt. Basilone at great risk of his life and in the face of continued enemy attack, battled his

way through hostile lines with urgently needed shells for his gunners, thereby contributing in large measure to the virtual annihilation of a Japanese regiment. His great personal valor and courageous initiative were in keeping with the highest traditions of the U.S. Naval Service.

Basilone was one of the eleven recipients of the Medal of Honor from the six months Guadalcanal campaign. The other ten were five marines, three soldiers, one sailor (a Rear Admiral), and one coast guardsman. The latter is the only coast guardsman ever awarded the Medal of Honor. Five of the eleven awardings were posthumous.

Basilone returned to the U.S. in 1943. He participated in war bond tours. His hometown (he was raised in the small town of Raritan, New Jersey) held a parade in his honor 9/19/1943, attended by thousands. He met with politicians and dignitaries. *Life* magazine wrote up and printed the event. Fox Movietone News filmed it. He toured the country to raise money for the War effort. He was a celebrity.

Basilone felt out of place on these tours. He asked to return to the War. The Marine Corps advised him that he was of more benefit helping to sell war bonds and recruiting new marines. The Marines offered him a commission, which he turned down. The Marines offered him a stateside position as an instructor, which he also turned down. Finally, his request to return to combat was approved.

Basilone was sent to Camp Pendleton (San Diego County, California) for more training. There he met 3.7 years older Marine Corps Women's Reserve Sergeant Lena Mae Riggi (1913 OR – 1999 CA). Sergeant Riggi worked at the base as a cook. They wed 7/10/1944.

The Marine Corps Women's Reserve was formed 2/1943. Its purpose as with the other female, military branch auxiliaries was to replace marines with women at shore stations, so the men could go to combat. Nineteen thousand women served in the Marine auxiliary during World War II. It was reduced to 300 women, in 1946.

The 1948 Women's Armed Services Integration Act allowed these 300 women and other women still in World War II female auxiliaries of the other branches to serve in the regular Marine Corps, Army, Navy, Coast Guard, and Air Force (the Air Force became a separate branch in 1947). The law also enabled women to enlist as permanent, regular members of the armed forces – no distinction between male and female.

Prior to this act, women were not allowed to enlist (exception for nurses) except in times of war – and then only in auxiliaries not considered to be full military.

The Army banned women who were mothers with dependent children in 1949, and discharged women who had minor children. These Army regulations for women with dependents remained in place until the 1970s. This point is added, to show that adjustments toward modern thinking took time.

Basilone was shipped out 8/11/1944, one month after the wedding. His unit landed on Iwo Jima the first day of the landings, 2/19/1945. He was a machine gun section leader. Japanese soldiers in a heavily fortified blockhouse pinned his unit down. Basilone sneaked around to the side, and then climbed atop the structure. He destroyed the blockhouse and its defending garrison with demolitions and grenades.

A marine tank was trapped in a minefield, while being bombarded by mortar and artillery. Basilone fought his way under heavy fire over to the tank, to assist. He directed the tank to a safer area. Here, Gunnery Sergeant Basilone was hit and killed by mortar shrapnel and/or small arms fire. He was 29.3 years old. His actions helped the marines penetrate the Japanese defense and move off the landing beach. He was posthumously awarded the Navy Cross. The citation reads as follows:

> *For extraordinary heroism while serving as a Leader of a Machine-Gun Section, Company C, 1st Battalion, 27th Marines, 5th Marine Division, in action against enemy Japanese forces on Iwo Jima in the Volcano Islands, 2/19/1945. Shrewdly gauging the tactical situation shortly after landing when his company's advance was held up by the concentrated fire of a heavily fortified Japanese blockhouse, Gunnery Sergeant Basilone boldly defied the smashing bombardment of heavy caliber fire to work his way around the flank and up to a position directly on top of the blockhouse and then, attacking with grenades and demolitions, single handedly destroyed the entire hostile strong point and its defending garrison. Consistently daring and aggressive as he fought his way over the battle-torn beach and up the sloping, gun-studded terraces toward Airfield Number 1, he repeatedly exposed himself to the blasting fury of exploding shells and later in the day coolly proceeded to the aid of a friendly tank which had been trapped in an enemy mine field under intense mortar and artillery barrages, skillfully guiding the heavy vehicle over the hazardous terrain to safety, despite the overwhelming volume of hostile fire. In the forefront of the assault at all times, he pushed forward with dauntless courage and iron determination until, moving upon the edge of the airfield, he fell, instantly killed by a bursting mortar shell. Stouthearted and indomitable, Gunnery Sergeant Basilone, by his intrepid initiative, outstanding skill, and valiant spirit of self-sacrifice in the face of the fanatic opposition, contributed materially to the advance of his company during the early critical period of the assault, and his unwavering devotion to duty throughout the bitter conflict was an inspiration to his comrades and reflects the highest credit upon Gunnery Sergeant Basilone and the United States Naval Service. He gallantly gave his life in the service of his country.*

Basilone was buried at Arlington National Cemetery.

The Navy named two ships (one under construction) in honor of Basilone, as follows:

- Gearing-class, 391' long and 41' beam and 14' draft, 40 miles per hour, 345 crew, USS Basilone destroyer was commissioned in 1948, decommissioned in 1977, and target practice sank in 1982

- Arleigh Burke-class, 509' and 66' beam and 31' draft, 35 miles per hour 380 crew, USS John Basilone guided missile destroyer under construction is scheduled for commissioning in 2019 or 2020

Sergeant Lena Mae Riggi Basilone sponsored at the 1945 launching of the first destroyer.

Several streets, buildings, etc. were also named after Basilone.

Lena Mae died in 1999, age 86. The marriage ran 7.5 months. Their married time together was only the first month. She never re-married. She worked for an electric company many years. She volunteered countless hours at the Long Beach Veterans Hospital and to veterans' organizations.

The U.S. Post Office featured Basilone and three other marines on its 2005 *Distinguished Marines* stamp series. The other three marines were Daniel Daly (1837 NY – 1937 NY), John Lejeune (1867 LA – 1942 Baltimore), and Lewis Puller (1898 VA – 1971 VA). Daly is noted as one of nineteen men to be awarded the Medal of Honor twice.

Basilone was the first enlisted Marine to receive the Medal of Honor, Navy Cross, and Purple Heart. He was the only enlisted marine who fought in World War II to receive both the Medal of Honor and Navy Cross.

Basilone at the time of receiving his Medal of Honor is shown below. His widow is also shown 12/21/1945 ten months after his death; at the christening of her husband's namesake, Gearing-class destroyer.

22- CORPORAL DESMOND DOSS (CONSCIENTIOUS OBJECTION)

Wars of course have been around, forever. Persons who refuse (forced) military service on the grounds of freedom of thought, conscience, or religion; are known as *conscientious objectors*. They like war itself, have also been around from day one. However, it was not until the early 1900s that conscientious objection was formerly addressed and evaluated; and came to be recognized as a fundamental human right. It is sometimes referred to as *the right to refuse to kill*. Other terms used to categorize conscientious objectors are *pacifists, non-interventionists, non-resistants,* and *anti-militarists.*

The Roman Empire ran 500 years. During this period, the Christian Fabius Victor had been a soldier in the Roman Army. His son, Berber Christian Maximilian (274 in what is now Algeria – 3/12/295 in what is now Algeria), was brought before the Africa Proconsularis Proconsul at Theveste (Theveste today is Tebessa, in northeast Algeria) when he turned age 21, to swear allegiance to the Emperor as a soldier. He refused. He stated that he could not serve in the military due to his Christian beliefs. Proconsul Cassius Dio (the grandson or great-grandson of his namesake, the historian Cassius Dio {155 in what is now Turkey – 235 in what is now Turkey}) ordered his sword beheading, which was done immediately.

Maximilian of Tebessa became a martyr and a saint. His feast day is observed on his execution date. Maximilian is noted as the earliest recorded conscientious objector, although of course others preceded him (notably Christians).

Conscientious objectors over the years have been penalized in some way. These methods included monetary fines, imprisonment, torture, or even execution (dictator-led countries) such as in the case of Maximilian more than 1,700 years ago. These punitive actions were based on the following premises:

- Nobody wants to kill another person; in other words, everybody is a conscientious objector; however, war to defend self, family, community, country, way of life (freedoms), etc., negates the choice to not fight
- Very simply, all citizens have a moral duty to protect their country and its people

These arguments apply to both defensive (defending self in the case of attack), and offensive actions (attacking another country, group, or individual) if necessary when life or way of life is threatened.

Some countries in the past and also still today, take punitive actions. These may be monetary fines and/or imprisonment. In the case of dictator-led countries, penalties have been severe such as long prison terms, torture, and even execution. Even today in a few countries, severe punitive actions are taken against conscientious objectors.

In some countries today and in the past, conscientious objectors may join a military branch and work in a non-combat role, in lieu of fighting. This is a good solution for many conscientious objectors and for the military of that country as well, for the following reasons:

- Many conscientious objectors are willing to serve their country in uniform; but only in a non-combat role
- The number of military personnel required to support those actually fighting is several to many times more, especially in modern times; therefore, the military has many non-combat roles to slot such persons; to sum up, this is an easy accommodation
- As the military is accommodating the conscientious objector, he or she is less likely to denigrate the military, or try to convert fellow military personnel into conscientious objectors as well

In some countries, conscientious objectors may be assigned to an alternative civilian service as a substitute for conscription or military service. The latter solution is the alternative in the case of a person who will not join the military in even a non-combat role, and even again in peacetime. This is based upon the conscientious objector's reasoning that serving in a non-combat role will only free up another soldier, airman, sailor, or marine to fight (or train to fight).

Many countries today offer both options to the conscientious objector – non-combat position in the military, or civilian service. Such programs therefore do allow conscientious objectors to serve their country, in one way or another.

The United Nations General Assembly addressed this conscientious objection issue when it approved a resolution 48-0 (eight abstentions), in 1948. The resolution reads as follows: *Everyone has the right to freedom of thought, conscience and religion; this right includes freedom to change his religion or belief; and freedom, either alone or in community with others and in public or private, to manifest his religion or belief in teaching, practice, worship, and observance.*

Since this 1948 resolution, the United Nations and other international bodies have again addressed conscientious objection. In 1995, a United Nations Commission on Human Rights resolution included the following words: *persons performing military service should not be excluded from the right to have conscientious objections to military service.* This same United Nations Commission in 1998 acknowledged that persons in the military may develop conscientious objections to fighting during their military tenure or career, so accommodations must be made.

To sum up, the United Nations and other international organizations have advised countries that the beliefs of conscientious objection citizens subject to the draft or even in the case of a country with an all-volunteer military, must be accommodated in some non-punitive way. Furthermore per the United Nations, persons currently in the military have the right to change their beliefs – either way.

Well-known pacifists born in the 1800s include the following:

- Novelist Leo Tolstoy, 1828 Russia – 1910 Russia
- Playwright George Bernard Shaw, 1856 Ireland – 1950 England
- Philosopher Bertand Russell, 1872 Wales – 1970 Wales advocated that Great Britain not enter World War I; jailed six months in 1918 for further

advocating that the U.S. also not enter World War to come to the aid of Great Britain

- Novelist Aldous Huxley, 1894 England – 1963 Los Angeles

As notable persons, these men and others influenced tolerance for conscientious objection.

In the case of the United States, some conscientious objection history is as follows:

- The first American war of course was the **Revolution.** This is not counting the innumerable battles with European governments and colonists and later the U.S. government fighting (more like massacring) Native Americans over several hundred years, including after the Revolution. These Indian Wars were intermittent from the early seventeenth century through the Apache Wars in the southwestern part of the United States, which ran until 1924. Mexico was even longer, fighting the Apaches until 1933.

For the Revolution, soldiers were mostly provided from the militias of the various colonies. The colonies required men to enroll in the militia usually at age 16, to receive some military training. They were required to serve, in case of war or emergency. In reality though, the colonial militias were formed to fend off Native Americans. This responsibility to train and respond lasted up to age 60, for some of the colonies.

The Second Continental Congress in 1778 recommended that the *united colonies* that *are, and of right ought to be, free and independent States* provide men from their militias to fight for a one-year period in the Continental Army. These words about independent States that ought to be free came from statesman and Declaration of Independence signer Richard Lee's (1732 VA – 1794 VA) 5/15/1776 Resolution to the Second Continental Congress. The Congress inserted these words into the independence declaration, whose principal author was Thomas Jefferson (1743 VA – 1826 VA). Jefferson wrote the document over 17 days, in the Pennsylvania State House in Philadelphia. That building is where the U.S. Constitution (adopted 1787) as well as the Declaration of Independence were debated and adopted. The Pennsylvania State House today is known as Independence Hall, and is the centerpiece of the Independence National Historical Park.

For the record, the Continental Congress made many changes to Jefferson's document; 86 by one count. The Congress approved the much shortened declaration 7/4/1776.

This first national conscription as recommended by the Second Continental Congress was attempted but irregularly applied; and in too few numbers as well.

In actuality, the Second Continental Congress did not have the authority to draft men, except for naval impressment. Again, Continental Army Commander-in-Chief General George Washington (1732 VA – 1799 VA) had to rely (mostly) on the militias from the various states, to supply soldiers. Of note though, some men enlisted voluntarily, directly in the Continental Army. Conscientious objector exemptions (or lack of) varied, per colony. Some colonies allowed men to pay a fine to duck service (for any reason).

In the case of at least several colonies, those who refused to enlist for conscientious objection reasons were penalized in some way. These included paying penalties or extra taxes, having their property seized, or even jailed – these actions taken or attempted as a deterrent to others. These were mostly members of the Religious Society of Friends (Quakers).

- For the **War of 1812**, President James Madison (1751 VA – 1836 VA) and his War Secretary James Monroe (1758 VA – 1831 NYC) tried to draft 40,000 men with various incentives, but without much luck. They ended up tapping state militias as was the case for the Revolution. Conscientious objection was not addressed.

- The first federal conscription law in the U.S. was for the **Civil War.** Congress passed 3/1863. Exemptions from the draft could be bought for $300, or men drafted could put forth a substitute. In the latter case, the draft dodger compensated the enlistee in some way. The draft law was not used much. Of the 2,100,000 who fought on the Northern side, only two percent were draftees. Another six percent though were paid substitutes.

The estimate is that 12% of those who fought for the South were conscripts. Resistance to the South's draft law was wide-spread and often violent, with some draftees comparing conscription to slavery. To confuse matters in the South even more, the line blurred on those who had religious beliefs against fighting, and those who felt that slavery was wrong, or both.

Some Southern men moved to the northern states or Mexico, or hid out in the mountains for the duration of the war. These men generally were not conscientious objectors. They simply did not believe in slavery (abolitionists) or were neutral on the subject or just did not want to fight.

Some of these Southern men who refused to fight were caught by the Confederate Army or Confederacy-supporting vigilante types. Some were imprisoned. Some were executed, either by authorities or pseudo-authorities. Some of the latter were more like mobs. As an example, a Confederate Army officer set up a citizens' court in Gainesville, Texas, which tried 180 men for being Unionists. Forty-one were hung, and another two shot and killed trying to escape. Texas had several other incidents of this type involving vigilantes. In some cases, those killed were German Texans.

Again though, the line blurred between conscientious objectors and abolitionists, or simply those who just did not want to get involved. The vigilantes in the South did not take time to parse the motivations, of these young men who refused to enlist. Refusing to enlist was evidence enough for their kangaroo courts.

Although neither the North nor South's draft laws addressed conscientious objection, some accommodations were made both sides – allowing non-combat work in the military. Also, both the North and the South's laws allowed men to pay others to substitute, and many (wealthy) men did so. It is likely that at least a few of those who paid for others to serve in their place, may have done so for conscientious objector reasons. However, records for the reasons were not recorded. Conventional wisdom though is that conscientious objection was a very small percentage of the motivation, in the case of these paid substitutes.

- The 1917 Selective Service Act for **World War I** became effective 5/1917, the month after the U.S. entered the War. To avoid the defects in the Civil War draft law, the law allowed an exemption for religious scruples. However, it only applied to members of the peace churches (peace churches are described below). All other objectors were forced to enlist or faced penalties. The law also prohibited paying substitutes.

Almost 65,000 men claimed conscientious objection status. Local draft boards though ruled that 57,000 could serve, which is 88%. Thirty thousand of these passed the physical examination. The 47% failure rate due to physical reasons was very high, for young men. In fact, this has never been publicly explained. Twenty-one thousand were inducted into the Army. Eighty percent of the 21,000 took up arms.

Almost 4,000 draftee objectors refused to serve. Some were imprisoned at military facilities in Washington, California, and Kansas. The thinking at the time was that these men once exposed to military life on these forts, would come around in their thinking. This was rarely the case though. Some were tried, convicted, and sentenced to terms as long as 20 years.

For those incarcerated at the forts, some were abused in a number of ways.

Hutterites are an ethno-religious group, formed in Austria about 1525. The denomination is a branch of the Anabaptists, which include the Amish and Mennonites. The roots of Anabaptists date back to the Radical Reformation of the 16th century. Anabaptists in general are conscientious objectors. The Hutterites are in the category of absolute pacifists.

Due to religious persecution, the Hutterites underwent a number of diasporas in central and eastern Europe. Some moved to Russia. When Russia passed mandatory conscription laws, several groups of Hutterites moved to North America from Russia, beginning in 1874. Today, 45,000 Hutterites live mostly in Canada and the upper Great Plains of the U.S.

The Army drafted four South Dakota Hutterites, to fight in World War I. These included the three brothers David Hofer (1890 – 19??), Joseph Hofer

(1895 – 11/29/1918 Kansas, influenza according to the Army), and Michael Hofer (1896 – 12/2/1918 Kansas, influenza according to the Army). The fourth was Jacob Wipf (1888 – 19??), who was married to the brothers' sister. The four men refused to wear the uniform. They would not take orders.

To set an example specifically for Hutterites and in general for conscientious objectors, the four Hutterite men were court-martialed and sentenced to twenty years of hard labor at the federal military prison at Alcatraz, California. At Alcatraz, they refused to work. They were placed in solitary confinement. They were fed only bread and water for a period. They claimed that they were tortured.

The four men were transferred to the Leavenworth Military Prison in Kansas 11/19/1918. This was eight days after the Armistice ending World War I fighting. According to the Army, Joseph Hofer and Michael Hofer died from influenza. 1918 was the year of an influenza pandemic.

The Army put their bodies in Army uniforms and sent them to their families in South Dakota. The Hutterites did not accept influenza as the cause of death, believing instead that they had died of mistreatment. They engraved the word *martyr* on their grave markers.

The religion's official church history (*Chronicle of the Hutterian Brethren*) states that the brothers *died in prison as a result of cruel mistreatment by the United States military*. The deaths led to the emigration of most Hutterites from the U.S. to Canada. When the U.S. passed laws protecting conscientious objectors, some Hutterites moved back to the Dakotas, beginning in the 1930s.

The National Civil Liberties Bureau (today, the American Civil Liberties Union) cited the Hofer brothers' deaths in accusing the U.S. government of mistreating conscientious objectors during World War I. These deaths played a key role in shaping American future military policy, regarding conscientious objectors.

Eventually, as there was a shortage of men to work on farms, some of these conscientious objecting men were released to do that. Some were sent to France to do relief work. Some worked as firefighters or as attendants in psychiatric hospitals.

World War I started 7/1914. Several activist-pacifist types who lived in a settlement house project on New York City's Lower East Side were outspoken, in keeping the United States out of World War I. From these pacifists, the *Henry Street Peace Committee* was formed. This body changed its name to the *Anti-Militarism Committee*, 1/1915.

At the time, those who favored entering World War I now or later to support the Entente powers (British Empire, France, Russia; later the U.S., Japan, and

Italy allied with) against Germany and the Astro-Hungarian Empire and Bulgaria (called the Central Powers), had adopted the slogan of *Preparedness.* The Anti-Militarism Committee changed its name to the *Anti-Preparedness Committee,* 1/1916. The name was changed later in 1916 to the *American Union Against Militarism* (AUAM).

Roger Baldwin (1884 MA – 1981 NY) earned bachelor's and master's degrees at Harvard University. He was involved in the activities of AUAM's St. Louis chapter. He was named AUAM Executive Director (head official). AUAM was based in New York City. The AUAM lobbied, published, lectured, held meetings, etc. to keep the U.S. out of World War I; to no avail.

The U.S. entered World War I, 4/1917. The fact that German submarines were torpedo sinking American cargo ships in the Atlantic Ocean was a factor. The fact that Germany offered to aid Mexico in wresting a large chunk of America to Mexico if it allied with Germany and attacked the U.S. from the south was another factor (Zimmermann telegram). This large chunk was several western states and parts of western states that the U.S. paid Mexico $18.25 million for. This was per the Hidalgo Treaty peace agreement after the 1846-1848 Mexican-American War. This is $500 million in 2019 money. Mexico had rejected an offer of up to $58 million in 1845, which is $1.583 billion in 2019 dollars.

Baldwin called for the AUAM to create a legal division to protect the rights of conscientious objectors. Accordingly, the AUAM created the *Civil Liberties Bureau* 7/1/1917. Baldwin headed it. The Civil Liberties Bureau broke off from the AUAM 10/1/1917. It became the *National Civil Liberties Bureau* with Baldwin remaining as Director. In 1920, the National Civil Liberties Bureau was renamed the *American Civil Liberties Union* (ACLU). At this time (1920), the ACLU's main focus was freedom of speech, especially for anti-war protestors. Baldwin served as its director until 1950.

The ACLU remains to this day. It is still based in New York City. In the years before the 11/2016 presidential election, the ACLU had a membership of 400,000, and annual donations of about $4 million. In the fifteen months after the 11/2016 election which included the first year of Donald Trump's (1946 NYC -) term, membership shot up to 1.84 million. The ACLU raised $120 million in these 15 months. Much of the new money was used to hire more attorneys for more litigation. Each state now has an ACLU affiliate (California has three), plus Washington D.C. and Puerto Rico have offices. To sum up, the ACLU owes President Trump big time.

Baldwin himself was a conscientious objector. He refused to even register for the draft. He would not take a medical examination. He would not accept alternative civilian service. A federal court sentenced him to a year in prison.

The AUAM opposed peacetime conscription after World War I. It ceased operations in 1920.

The Fellowship of Reconciliation was also formed during World War I, by two European Christians. These were the British physician and Quaker missionary Henry Hodgkin (1877 England-1933 England), and German Lutheran and academic Friedrich Siegmund-Schultze (1885 Germany – 1969 Germany). Hodgkin and Siegmund-Schultze also supported pacifist types and aided conscientious objectors. Today, the organization is known as the International Fellowship of Reconciliation (IFOR). It is based at Utrecht, Netherlands. IFOR today has 72 branches, groups, and affiliates in 48 countries on all continents.

Sixty-eight pacifists formed the U.S. branch of the Fellowship of Reconciliation, in 1915. The U.S. operation also had a conscientious objectors' program, which also played a role in the formation of the already mentioned American Civil Liberties Union. Today, the U.S. IFOR branch is based in Nyack, New York. Nyack is 25 miles north of Manhattan.

To sum up, a number of these pacifist organizations were formed just before or during World War I, in an effort to keep countries out of that War. Some of these organizations much aided conscientious objectors. Some of these groups were women's organizations. Some remain active today. These groups dating back to World War I deserve some to much of the credit, for the acceptance today of persons being conscientious objectors and their assignment to non-combat duties or alternative service.

The Socialist Party of America should be mentioned. It was formed in 1901 with the merger of two other political groups. The Party was staunchly anti-militaristic as one of its platforms. Socialist and pacifist, Presbyterian minister Norman Thomas (1884 OH – 1968 NY) was the Party's candidate for President six consecutive elections, 1928-1948. He got very few votes.

Thomas preached against American participation in World War I. He himself was a conscientious objector. He refused to register for the draft, or to even take a physical examination.

- The draft law (men only) for **World War II** was the first for the U.S., implemented in peacetime. It became effective 9/1940, 15 months before the 12/7/1942 sneak attacks thrust the U.S. into World War II. The Army exploded from 130,000 men in 1939 to 1.4 million in 1941. This was more than ten-fold.

The law exempted those from military service who *by reason of religious training and belief,* opposed war. Such men though were given the option of enlisting, but not fighting.

More than 72,000 men registered as conscientious objectors, for World War II. Almost 52,000 (72%) received conscientious objector status. Of the

52,000, 27,000 (52%) somehow managed to flunk their physical examinations. This is an amazing percentage, for a group of young men (makes you wonder). As with World War I, the reason for this high, medical rejection rate has not been explained (or at least not publicly explained). More than 25,000 entered the military, in noncombatant roles. Many of these men were trained as Army medics. Twelve thousand worked in the Civilian Public Service program (see below for description).

Almost 6,000 men claiming conscientious objector status went to prison. Sixteen hundred of these 6,000 (27%), were referred to as absolute resisters. They refused to enlist, even as a non-combatant. The other 4,400 (73%) imprisoned, claimed to be Jehovah Witness ministers. These maybe yes maybe no Jehovah Witness ministers thought that their treatment (imprisonment) was unfair and harsh.

In Nazi Germany 1933-1945, Jehovah Witnesses suffered religious persecution. This was due to their refusal to perform military service, join Nazi organizations, or pledge allegiance to the Hitler regime. Half of the 20,000 Jehovah Witnesses in Germany at the time were imprisoned. Two thousand of the 10,000 imprisoned were sent to concentration camps, where 250 were executed and another 950 died from other reasons. These reasons included the usual Nazi reasons of worked to death, lack of adequate food and clothing and housing and medical care, and sometimes even outright execution again.

Jehovah Witnesses in Germany could escape persecution and personal harm by renouncing their religious beliefs. This required signing a document indicating renouncement of their faith, submission to state authority, and support of the German military (including enlistment in the case of fighting age men). As harsh as these requirements were, other groups did not have this option. These included Jews, Romani, homosexuals, etc. (referring to the Holocaust). To sum up, being a Jehovah Witness in Germany in World War II was quite a bit different persecution-wise, than for Jehovah Witnesses in other countries.

A very few American conscientious objectors changed their minds after the fourteen, 12/7/1941 Empire of Japan sneak attacks. The statement of one was as follows:

> In the face of this dastardly inhuman attack .... I feel my stand as a conscientious objector is untenable. I feel proud to admit that I have made a mistake in taking the impractical stand of pacifism and repudiate it without the slightest reservation of hesitation. I stand ready to serve.

The newspaper wire story did not include his name.

For the record, the above-mentioned *peace churches* were and are Christian churches, groups, or communities advocating pacifism; to the point where the believers will not even join the military, much less fight for their country. The three historic U.S. peace churches are the Church of the Brethren, Religious Society of Friends (Quakers), and Mennonites. Mennonites includes other Anabaptist groups such as Amish and Hutterites.

These churches then and today took and take the position that Jesus was a pacifist. Some theologians (New Testament Bible scholars) agree with this conclusion, some do not. But again in the case of the peace churches who touted Jesus' pacifism, church members believed (or said they did) accordingly.

However, the beliefs of even the peace churches vary, as to whether their members may use violence in self-defense or to protect others. However again, the tenets of all three denominations was that violence on behalf of a country or a government (and this defines the military) was prohibited by their religious dogma.

These churches had conflicts with the U.S. military during World War I. To strategize to avoid such controversy with another European war looming, representatives from these churches met at Bethel College in North Newton, Kansas, in 1935. North Newton is 30 miles north of Wichita, Kansas. The Mennonite Church USA founded Bethel College in 1887. The college is still affiliated with the denomination. The college today is a four-year, private, Christian liberal arts institution.

Anyway, the *peace churches* term came about, from this initial meeting. Since then, a few other denominations have joined the category of peace churches.

As it turned out, 58% of the World War II conscientious objector men claimed affiliations with one of the peace churches. Thirty-eight per cent claimed affiliation with other church denominations. Four per cent stated no religious affiliation.

The churches' recommended solution was civilian alternative service. There were precedents, worldwide. These included the work done by the American Friends Service Committee (founded in 1917 by the Religious Society of Friends {Quakers}, still active today) in Europe during and after World War I, and forestry service work done by Russian Mennonites in lieu of military service in Tsarist Russia.

The churches lobbied Congress that any draft bills coming before Congress address conscientious objection. They were successful in this regard. The 1940 Selective Training and Service Act (draft law) included exemptions for religious beliefs against fighting. These were for any religious denomination, not just the historical peace churches. The law said that those conscientious objectors who served would do so under civilian control, not military control. Violations if any would be subject to civil law, not military law. The law included appeal procedures. To sum up, the law recognized conscientious objection and provided alternatives to military service. The military was receptive to these clauses in the law, as well:

- The law removed the burden of having to deal with men, who would not fight or serve otherwise
- By segregating conscientious objectors from the military, the military did not have to deal with conscientious objectors trying to convert their fellow soldiers, airmen, sailors, marines and coast guardsmen into non-fighters

The draft law became effective 9/1940. The churches outlined a plan to run the camps with Uncle Sam funding. President Franklin Roosevelt (1882 NY – 4/12/1945 Georgia, cerebral hemorrhage) balked at this, despite the language of the law. He wanted the military to run the program, again despite the wording in the law. The churches agreed to fund the camps. This earnestness convinced Roosevelt to let the churches run the program. The quasi-federal government program was called the Civilian Public Service. Again, the purpose of the program was to provide conscientious objectors with an alternative to military service, for 12,000 approved draftees.

The first camp opened 5/15/1941 near Baltimore. This was almost seven months before the U.S. entered World War II. Over the course of the war into 1947, 152 camps were set up in the U.S. and Puerto Rico. The federal government paid to transport the workers to the camps; and also paid for housing and camp furnishings. The men and/or their families and/or the churches (mostly the churches) paid to run and maintain the camps -- for clothing, food, medical care, wages, etc.

The Association of Catholic Conscientious Objectors and the Methodist World Peace Commission ran four and two of these civilian camps for pacifists.

The young men worked mostly in rural areas – soil conservation, preservation of forests, firefighting (forests), flood control, farming, projects such as dam building and making roads, etc. U.S. agencies such as the Forest Service, Soil Conservation Service, and the National Park Service provided work direction. In many ways, the work was similar in nature to some of the programs created to employ many American men during the financial Great Depression, which ran more or less 1929-1939 in the United States. Gearing up for war and then the U.S. in World War II helped end the Depression in the U.S. (and other countries for that matter), and the need for these government work programs.

The men worked longer than they would have served, if drafted. Some were not released until 3/1947, which was 19 months after V-J Day (8/14/1945).

The men usually worked nine hours a day, six days a week. They were granted two furlough days per month served. They were paid very little (really just an allowance), certainly much less than the prevailing wage for the type of work done. The compensation also of course was much less than what they would have earned as an Army Private or Navy Seaman. And of course these men had no benefits during or after, compared to the prodigious benefits received by military personnel when serving and after discharge. In the case of World War II veterans, these post-discharge benefits were more than enormous (1944 Servicemen's Readjustment Act, also known as the G.I. Bill).

To sum up, the compensation (pay, benefits) received by these men was less than a pittance of that received by either servicemen or average civilian workers. The hours worked were much more.

Some of the men got part-time jobs working on area farms (especially dairies) or nearby communities for normal wages. This did not subtract though from their official, required 54-hour week at the camps. For this part-time work, the wages went to Uncle Sam, not the conscientious objector. Some men objected, reasoning that the money went to the war effort. A compromise was reached, where these wages were put in a fund which remained unused until the end of the war.

As World War II progressed, many mental health care workers at inpatient facilities left their jobs for much better paying jobs with better benefits (and even shorter hours), such as working in defense factories or enlisting in the military. Conscientious objectors were tapped for these psychiatric aide and attendant positions at some of the institutions. By the end of 1945, more than 2,000 Civilian Public Service men had worked at 41 hospitals in 20 states. They sometimes entered where conditions for the patients were appalling and abusive, mainly due to lack of money resulting in inadequate staff – inadequate in number and training received. These pacifist men are credited with being instrumental in making many lasting improvements and reforms in the care and treatment of mental patients in the United States.

Some of the conscientious objectors volunteered to become medical guinea pigs, as their service and contribution. They were infected with infectious diseases such as hepatitis and tropical diseases to test experimental treatment medications. Some were subjected to temperature extremes, to evaluate effects of different types of clothing. Some drank sea water to assess tolerance and effect. Some walked miles a day consuming only 1,500 calories, to determine effects such as on under-nourished and malnourished prisoners of war (POWs) and refugees.

Twelve percent of World War II conscientious objectors transferred to the military service (as non-combatants). The negatives of civilian service as described above (hard work, very low pay, work tenure to exceed that if in the military, no benefits compared to superlative benefits in the military and post-military), obviously contributed to the change of heart.

Some of the camps had educational classes, newsletters, and various types of entertainment. Considering the long work day though six days a week, these were often not well-attended.

Of course, church services were provided. Whether these men were church goers or not in the past, they felt that they now had to attend, as being somewhat observed for their piety. After all, it was their religious beliefs that prevented them from serving in the military and defending their country.

In the case of some men who balked at the living or working conditions or pay pittance, they were sent to a few camps run by the Selective Service. Labor strife (slow-downs, even strikes) was an issue at these camps. Some resistors were tried, convicted, and imprisoned.

In all, some 12,000 young men who were to be drafted worked in the Civilian Public Service program.

One Amish World War II conscientious objector was known for his later statement: *It was not easy being a conscientious objector for World War II.* As aggressors Germany and Japan were doing countless horrible things so heinous that they were beyond understanding and belief and therefore the whole country behind its fighting men, this World War II conscientious objector in his statement was correct.

The program ended 3/1947, 19 months after V-J Day. The program cost the federal government $1.3 million. In return, $6 million of unpaid labor was received. The Civilian Public Service made significant contributions to forest fire prevention, erosion and flood control, medical science, care of inpatients in the mental health system, etc.

The World War II draft law was replaced by the 1948 Selective Service Act. This conscription act served well into the Cold War, including for the hot Korean and Vietnam proxy wars.

The World War II Civilian Public Service program described above served as a precedent for the Alternative Service Program for conscientious objectors, in effect today. The Alternative Service Program is within the Selective Service System. The Alternative Service Program gives conscientious objectors the option of working to improve national well-being, as an alternative to bearing arms. Service periods are established to mirror the duration of a conscription, which is usually two years.

Conscription ended in 1973. The Vietnam War ended in 1975. As the U.S. does not have conscription today, the Alternative Service Program is dormant. If conscription were to resume, presumably the program would be started again as an alternative for conscientious objectors; who refuse even non-combat jobs in the military.

Of course if there is no conscription (again, the U.S. has had an all-voluntary military since 1974), conscientious objection is not an issue. Those who are opposed to the military for whatever reason, simply do not enlist. If they should enlist as a conscientious objector, they would have non-combat options. And some conscientious objectors do enlist in this last category, as they want to serve their country, and as the military pays so well and has golden benefits.

Studies show that since the draft was dropped, that the overwhelming reason why young men and women enlist is economic.

If in the military and viewpoints change from willing to fight to conscientious objection, again accommodation is available and simple.

World War I ended in 1918. After that *War to End All Wars,* many countries moved to a state of isolation and appeasement. These included America, Great Britain, France, Scandinavian countries, etc. These countries had a significant population of pacifists. Some historians state that the actions and effectiveness of these pacifists in convincing others and establishing policy, led these countries to allow Germany and Italy and Japan to arm up without intervention. In turn, many countries including the U.S. and European countries, did not match the build-ups in Germany or Japan. Regarding the military build-up just mentioned, this includes both of the following:

- Quantity   as to number of persons in the military and training for same, amount of weapons and munitions and equipment made and stockpiled, also manufacture and storing of items such as uniforms and food and medical supplies
- Quality   referring to research to develop better weapons and methods and support equipment; in every war, the side with the better technology is at least at a slight advantage; and in many cases, at a major advantage

  World War II American examples would include the Army and Marines' eight round, semi-automatic M1 Garand infantry rifle (using an en bloc clip) compared to the five round Japanese Arisaka bolt-action and the five round German Mauser bolt-action and the six round Italian Carcano bolt-action repeaters, better aircraft and warships (as the War progressed), and of course the atomic bomb

As a result, these countries (including the U.S.) were woefully unprepared for World War II – to the point of being conquered and occupied in the case of some European and Asian countries. Some European countries and the U.S. for that matter lost overseas protectorates.

The militarily weak U.S. (in some ways) had the major advantage of being an ocean distant from Germany and Japan. As a result, the Axis powers were not able to attack the U.S. mainland much after the 12/17/1941 sneak attacks, as follows:

- Germany made plans to do so, but was not able to put any of these plans into action.
- Italy made plans to do so, but again was not able to put any of these plans into action.
- Japan did make attacks, as follows:
  o A submarine shelled a target in California 2/1942, with little damage and no casualties.
  o A submarine shelled a target in Oregon 6/1942, with little damage and no casualties.
  o A seaplane launched from a submarine dropped incendiary bombs on the Oregon forest twice 9/1942, in efforts to start fires.
  o Japan's Aleutians campaign ran more than a year 1942-1943. However, Japan lost 4,350 men and sixteen ships compared to 1,681 men and

three ships for the United States. Japan was not able to hold any of the Islands.

o Japan released 9,300 hydrogen balloons 1944-1945 toting bombs (Operation Fu-Go) from Honshu to be carried by the jet stream at 30,000 to 38,000' over the Pacific Ocean on three-day flights to the U.S. and Canada, where they would drop their bombs. These balloons were the first intercontinental range weapon. Less than five percent are thought to have exploded on the U.S. or Canada. Damages were minor. However, six civilians were killed 5/5/1945 by one in Oregon when they tampered with it in the woods, to see what it was. These were a 26-year-old pregnant lady and five children ages 11-14, on an outing after Sunday school. The fetus died as well.

These Japanese attacks on the Aleutians and U.S. mainland above had little effect on the American Theater of the Pacific War. As far as the American Theater was concerned, the most damage was the sinking of American freighters and tankers off the West Coast, East Coast, and in the Gulf of Mexico by Japanese and German submarines.

Countries that do build-up their military may consider countries that do not do so as not willing to fight, as more willing to negotiate a peace compromise to retain an isolation status and avoid fighting. As a result, these belligerent countries are more likely to attack. Regarding the not willing to fight characteristic, other countries may classify as cowards or weaklings; so again more likely to attack.

Based upon the statements above and to sum up, some historians blame pacifists and their promoted isolation and lack of military build-up in a number of countries including the U.S., for allowing World War II (and other wars for that matter) to happen. If so, the irony of course is great – pacifists (anti-militarists) affecting policy, to the point that wars (and deaths, injuries, illnesses, and capture; and devastation) that could have been avoided, were not.

Of course, the argument from an individual or group that assets and resources be used for peaceful purposes (grow food, make houses and clothes, improve health care, make and improve infrastructure, aid the downtrodden, etc.), in lieu of being used to make weapons and maintain armies and navies and air forces; is most appealing, and certainly not new. This is sometimes referred to as the *swords into ploughshares* concept. Those words come from the *Book of Isaiah,* from the *Old Testament* of the Christian *Bible.* The King James Version reads as follows: *and they shall beat their swords into ploughshares, and their spears into pruning hooks; nation shall not lift up sword against nation, neither shall they learn war any more.* The context in Isaiah (2: 3-4) was just as the words state, that humans should turn to peaceful and humanitarian pursuits in lieu of war (if only it were that simple).

The United Nations' mission is to work on this ploughshares concept, to make a peaceful world. It has had some successes.

But if there are outlier countries (and it seems there always are) headed by tyrants or persons who become tyrants (and it seems that there always are such who manage to get to dictatorial status) who arm up, these dictators seem to be able to find a reason to stomp on their peace-loving neighbor countries, and/or abuse their own citizens. Such countries can be much better negotiated with by countries that have comparable or more firepower. The best offense is a good defense, as they say; and this is very true. Wording of this type is attributed to several. One of these is George Washington who wrote in 1779: ...*make them believe, that offensive operations, often times, is the surest, if not the only (in some cases) means of defence.*

But even then, proxy situations prevent disarming the country run by a rogue leader – witness North Korea, North Vietnam, Syria, Iraq, Pakistan, etc. These small dictator-led (or close to it) countries, considered backwards and uncivilized by most in developed countries can make and accumulate weapons of mass destruction, and therefore bully their citizens and even other countries. Their strength (as proxy states) unfortunately comes from support by (non-democratic) military powerhouses such as Russia and China.

Desmond Doss (2/17/1919 VA – 3/23/2006 AL) was the middle of three children. His carpenter father made little money during the Great Depression. His father had fought in World War I. He suffered from depression and was an alcoholic. These conditions may have been related to war-developed posttraumatic stress disorder.

Doss' mother Bertha was a homemaker. She raised him and his three-year younger brother Harold Doss (1922 – 2007) as devout Seventh Day Adventists, and also vegetarians. Harold enlisted in the Navy. He served on a minelayer in World War II.

Desmond dropped out of school in the ninth grade to work to help support the family. Again, this was during the Great Depression. When the U.S. entered World War II 12/8/1941 after the Japanese sneak attacks, he was working at a shipyard in Newport News, VA. As working in a defense industry, he was exempt from military service. Despite that, he enlisted in the Army 4/1/1942.

Doss advised the Army that because of his personal beliefs, he would not fight. Furthermore, he refused to even carry a weapon. He told the Army though that he was not a *conscientious objector,* as he was willing to serve his country in the military. In fact, he referred to himself as a *conscientious cooperator.* Despite Doss' self-definition, the Army put him in the category of *Conscientious Objector*, as he best fit that category. The Army trained him as a medical corpsman which was acceptable to Doss, and to the Army for that matter. He was assigned to an infantry unit.

Doss was awarded a Bronze Star medal for aiding wounded soldiers under fire, in combat on Guam and Philippines in 1944. The Bronze Star is awarded for either heroism or meritorious service, in a combat zone.

The Okinawa Campaign (Operation Iceberg) was a series of battles fought in the Japanese Ryukyu Islands. The Ryukyus are more than one hundred islands and islets, that stretch southwest from Japan to Taiwan. They comprise together 1,792 square miles, which is less than 0.7% the size of Texas.

The fighting centered on the largest of the Ryukyus, which is the 466 square mile Okinawa Island. Okinawa accounts for more than a fourth of the land area of the Ryukyus. The twelve-week campaign ran 4/1/1945 – 6/22/1945, so late in the Pacific War. The Allies plan was to capture Okinawa and use it as a base for air operations, as only 340 miles distant to the southwest from Japan's main island of Honshu – for the final assault, to end the War.

Okinawa was the Allies' largest amphibious assault in World War II (all the men landed were Americans). It was also one of the bloodiest battles in the Pacific Theater of World War II.

The Japanese military and government and Emperor somehow convinced many civilians on the islands to be prepared to fight as well, or die fighting. In the case of Okinawa, the Japanese Army gave uniforms to civilians, who fought without benefit of any training, or next to no training.

The Emperor is the civilian leader of the government, and also the head of the Shinto state religion. The Japanese were desperate at this stage of the War, and many fought to the death (including civilians) or committed suicide (again, including civilians) in lieu of surrendering. This was from the very effective brainwashing of the ancient bushido samurai code of loyalty, obedience and honor being superior to life. The Japanese military and Emperor much convoluted the code, for World War II.

Of course in regard to suicide, doing so in a manner which took out the enemy or enemy property was even better. These programs included kamikazes, shinyos, kaitens, and fukuryus developed to sink or damage USSs.

These civilians were in no jeopardy from American troops. However, Japan's leaders had also effectively brainwashed them in convincing them that the non-human American monsters would mutilate, torture, rape, execute, etc. Furthermore, Japanese leadership told the civilians that the Americans would then cook up and eat their children.

In the Okinawa campaign, more than 14,000 American (Army, Army Air, Marines, and Navy) military were killed, 55,000 wounded, and another 26,000 fell into the category of psychiatric casualties. Casualties were great, as pre-invasion aerial and ship bombings were not that effective, as the Japanese were dug in so well. Thirty-nine percent of the U.S. dead were sailors, mainly from kamikaze attacks. The Japanese had more than 80,000 soldiers killed, and more than 7,000 captured.

Doss aided and saved the lives of about 75 wounded infantrymen of his battalion over several weeks, fighting on and near a ridge. He himself was wounded four times, at Okinawa. He was evacuated 5/21/1945. For his actions over three weeks at Okinawa, he was awarded the Medal of Honor.

The citation describes his actions, as follows:

The President of the United States of America, in the name of Congress, takes pleasure in presenting the Medal of Honor to Private First Class (PFC) Desmond Thomas Doss, United States Army, for conspicuous gallantry and intrepidity in action above and beyond the call of duty from 4/29/1945 to 5/21/1945, while serving with the Medical Detachment, 307th Infantry Regiment, 77th Infantry Division, in action at Urasoe Mura, Okinawa, Ryukyu Islands. PFC Doss was a company aid man when the 1st Battalion assaulted a jagged escarpment 400' high. As our troops gained the summit, a heavy concentration of artillery, mortar and machine gun fire crashed into them, inflicting approximately 75 casualties and driving the others back. PFC Doss refused to seek cover and remained in the fire-swept area with the many stricken, carrying all 75 casualties one-by-one to the edge of the escarpment and there lowering them on a rope-supported litter down the face of a cliff to friendly hands. On May 2, he exposed himself to heavy rifle and mortar fire in rescuing a wounded man 200 yards forward of the lines on the same escarpment; and two days later he treated four men who had been cut down while assaulting a strongly defended cave, advancing through a shower of grenades to within eight yards of enemy forces in a cave's mouth, where he dressed his comrades' wounds before making four separate trips under fire to evacuate them to safety. On May 5, he unhesitatingly braved enemy shelling and small arms fire to assist an artillery officer. He applied bandages, moved his patient to a spot that offered protection from small arms fire and, while artillery and mortar shells fell close by, painstakingly administered plasma. Later that day, when an American was severely wounded by fire from a cave, PFC Doss crawled to him where he had fallen 25' from the enemy position, rendered aid, and carried him 100 yards to safety while continually exposed to enemy fire. On May 21, in a night attack on high ground near Shuri, he remained in exposed territory while the rest of his company took cover, fearlessly risking the chance that he would be mistaken for an infiltrating Japanese and giving aid to the injured until he was himself seriously wounded in the legs by the explosion of a grenade. Rather than call another aid man from cover, he cared for his own injuries and waited five hours before litter bearers reached him and started carrying him to cover. The trio was caught in an enemy tank attack and PFC Doss, seeing a more critically wounded man nearby, crawled off the litter; and directed the bearers to give their first attention to the other man. Awaiting the litter bearers' return, he was again struck, by a sniper bullet while being carried off the field by a comrade, this time suffering a compound fracture of one arm. With magnificent fortitude he bound a rifle stock to his shattered arm as a splint and then crawled 300 yards over rough terrain to the aid station. Through his outstanding bravery and unflinching determination in the face of desperately dangerous conditions, PFC Doss saved the lives of many soldiers. His name became a symbol throughout the 77th Infantry Division for outstanding gallantry, far above and beyond the call of duty.

Doss is shown below receiving his Medal of Honor from President Truman.

Doss was the first U.S. military person who was a conscientious objector, to be awarded the Medal of Honor. Since then, two other conscientious objector military men have received the medal, both posthumously. Both were Army medics in Vietnam. Both were killed by the enemy (one shot, one by a grenade), when repeatedly put selves in harm's way to shield and render aid to wounded soldiers in 1969 firefights:

- Corporal Thomas Bennett   1947 WV – 2/11/1969 Vietnam
  age 21.8 years
- Specialist 4 Joseph LaPointe   1948 OH – 6/2/1969   Vietnam
  age 20.9 years

LaPointe left a wife, and a son he never saw.

President Richard Nixon (1913 CA – 1994 Manhattan) presented the Medal to Bennett's mother and stepfather 4/7/1970.

Two hundred and fifty-nine Medals of Honor were conferred for actions during the Vietnam War. Twenty went to medical personnel, which is 7.7%.

As noted above, two of the three presenters in the three U.S., Medal of Honor, conscientious objector cases were sitting U.S. Presidents. Again, these were Truman to Doss and Nixon to Bennett. This suggests that the federal government was trying to show support and even welcoming conscientious objectors, serving non-combat roles in the Armed Forces.

Doss by the way contracted tuberculosis when on Leyte (Philippines) in 1944. He was honorably discharged 8/1951 (as a Corporal), with 90% disability. Eventually, surgeons removed a lung and five ribs. A 1976 overdose of antibiotics left him deaf. A cochlear ear transplant helped.

Doss wed 8/1942, several months after entering the Army. They had one son, born in 1946. His wife died in 1991. He remarried in 1993, and his second wife outlived him. He lived most of his post-war life on a small farm in Georgia. He died in 2006 at age 87. He is buried in the National Cemetery, in Chattanooga, TN.

Doss' story is available in both print and film, including the following:

- The Unlikeliest Hero book by Booton Herndon went out of print in 1967; the book was expanded in 2015 to include three times as many pictures, a new Foreword, and an Epilogue; the Epilogue traces Desmond's life after the War, especially his recovery from his wounds and tuberculosis; the expanded book is titled Redemption at Hacksaw Ridge
- Terry Benedict co-produced, co-wrote, and directed the award-winning, 102-minute, 2004 documentary film The Conscientious Objector
- Mel Gibson (1956 NY -) directed a 2016, 139-minute, feature film based upon Doss' life called Hacksaw Ridge; this was the soldiers' nickname for the Maeda Escarpment on Okinawa, where Doss treated soldiers and saved lives; Andrew Garfield (1983 Los Angeles -) played Doss; as is usually the case with movies based on a true story, the movie has many detours from actuality; the movie's box office was $175 million, compared to its $40 million production cost; 40% of the box office take was from the U.S.

The most famous (or infamous in the minds of some) World War II conscientious objector was probably the popular actor Lew Ayres (1908 MN – 1996 CA). He was a big movie star. He was best known for starring in the 1930, anti-war epic movie (no irony here) *All Quiet on the Western Front;* and for playing *Dr. Kildare* in nine successful movies, 1938-1942. In *All Quiet on the Western Front*, he played the lead role of a German soldier – going from a young and naïve man eager to join the army to fight in World War I; to a hardened, tired, and cynical veteran from the fighting. The movie won Best Picture and Best Director Oscars. It was based on German Erich Remarque's (1898 Germany – 1970 Switzerland) 1928 book of the same name.

Remarque by the way enlisted (volunteered) in Germany's army during World War I, when he was 18. He was sent to the Western Front 6/1917. On 7/31/1917, he was wounded when hit by shrapnel in the leg, arm, and neck. He was evacuated to an Army hospital in Germany, where he spent the rest of World War I. This was more than 15 months after his injuries.

Remarque made good money from his books. In 1931, he bought a villa in Switzerland planning to live there and in France as well as Germany, as locations to write more books.

Nazi propaganda minister Joseph Goebbels (1897 Germany – 5/1/1945 Berlin, suicide) banned his books in 1933. They were in fact publicly burned. The Nazis stated that his World War I service was a lie. His German citizenship was revoked. The Nazis stated that he wasn't even German. After all if he was German, his last name would be spelled the German way of *Remark*, instead of the French way *Remarque*.

In 1943, Remarque's younger sister Elfriede Scholz (1903 Germany – 12/16/1943 Germany, guillotine execution) still in Germany was arrested and tried for undermining morale. The Nazis said that she stated that *the War was lost.* She was found guilty. The Nazis removed her head. She left a husband and two children. The costs associated with her arrest, prosecution, and punishment (decapitation) were billed to her sister Erna.

By some reports, Hitler made the decision that death by firing squad was too easy or too dignified or too something for conscientious objectors, so he brought back the guillotine. The guillotine's heyday was in France during the French Revolution (1790s). The usual day and time for guillotine action were Mondays, at 17:00. More than 250 conscientious objectors were known to have been executed in Germany during World War II.

Besides Remarque's sister Elfriede, perhaps the best-known executed war distractor or conscientious objector during World War II was Franz Jagerstatter (1907 Austria – 8/9/1943 Germany, guillotine execution). This was as the Roman Catholic Church declared Jagerstatter a martyr, and beatified him in 2007 sixty-four years after his execution.

German troops moved into Austria 3/12/1938 to annex Austria into Nazi Germany. This grab was called the *Anschluss*. Anschluss translates to *unification*. In this case of course, it was a forced annexation. Jagerstatter (also spelled Jaegerstaetter) voted against the annexation in a referendum the next month, as did others in his village for sure. Despite that, the Nazis declared that the village vote was 100% for the annexation. Jagerstatter remained openly anti-Nazi.

Jagerstatter joined the Third Order of Saint Francis (third order within the Franciscan movement of the Catholic Church). He worked part-time as a sacristan. A sacristan is the person in charge of maintaining, caring for, and storing certain church property (usually this is a Catholic church) -- vestments, furnishings, sacred vessels, parish records, etc.

Jagerstatter was deferred from military service four times, but then drafted. He completed military training. He returned home in 1941. He was exempt from military service, as he was a farmer. However, he was called to active duty 2/23/1943, at the age of 35. He declared conscientious exemption 3/1/1943. He offered to serve in the German Army as a paramedic. This offer was refused. He was imprisoned. He was convicted of undermining military morale. He was sentenced to death 7/6/1943.

A priest from his village visited Jagerstatter in jail and tried to talk him into enlisting, but did not succeed. At this time, Jagerstatter heard of the faith of the Austrian priest Franz Reinisch (1903 Austria – 8/21/1942 Germany, guillotine execution). Reinisch at 39.6 years old was executed for his refusal to take the Hitler oath and refusal to enlist in the Wehrmacht. Reinisch's death inspired Jagerstatter. Like Jagerstatter, Reinisch was also beatified. This was in 2015, seventy-three years after his death.

Jagerstatter was executed 8/9/1943 by guillotine, a year after Reinisch. He was age 36.2 years. He left a wife and three daughters (oldest was six), and a fourth child from a previous relationship.

Terrence Malick (1943 IL -) wrote and directed the 2018 *Radegund* movie about Jagerstatter's life. August Diehl (1976 Berlin -) played Jagerstatter. The movie name comes from Jagerstatter's birthplace, Sankt Radegund, Austria. The town was named after Saint Radegund (520 Germany – 587 France). Radegund was a Thuringian princess and Frankish queen. She founded the Abbey of the Holy Cross at Poitiers, which is in west central France. She is the patron saint of several churches in France and England and of Jesus College, Cambridge (England).

Siblings Hans Scholl (1918 Germany – 2/22/1943 Munich, guillotine execution) and Sophie Scholl (1921 Germany – 2/22/1943 Munich, guillotine execution) co-founded with others the *White Rose.* The *White Rose* was an intellectual, non-violent, resistance movement to Nazi Germany. The two with music and psychology professor Kurt Huber (1893 Switzerland – 7/13/1943 Germany, guillotine execution) and others co-authored six, anti-Nazi, Third Reich political resistance leaflets. They distributed the leaflets in several ways, including by mail. On 2/18/1943, a custodian spotted Hans and Sophie throwing leaflets from the atrium level of one of the buildings at Ludwig-Maximilian University (also known as the University of Munich), where they were students. He reported them. The Gestapo arrested them and co-author Christoph Probst (1919 – 2/22/1943 Munich, guillotine execution). They were tried for treason by the Nazi People's Court in show trials. They were found guilty 2/22/1943.

Several hours later, state-appointed executioner Johann Reichhart (1893 Germany – 1972 Germany) removed the heads of the three. Their ages were 21 to 24. This was only four days after they were arrested.

From 1924 during the Weimar Republic through the Nazi period, Reichhart executed 2,701 men and 250 women, for a total of 2,951. The methods were 2,892 guillotine and 59 hanging. The U.S. Army arrested Reichhart after V-E Day. He was not tried for his executioner duties. The U.S. Office of Military Government hired Reichhart to aid in hanging 156 Nazi war criminals. He retired as an executioner 5/1946, but continued to serve as a consultant. The U.S. again hired him to supervise the construction of the gallows at Nuremberg. Two U.S. Army men hung ten, convicted, former top leaders of the Third Reich 10/16/1946 at Nuremberg.

Reichhart was *incriminated* 12/1948, and imprisoned 1.5 years and fined 30% of his property.

Others involved with White Rose including Professor Huber were caught and beheaded in the next few weeks and later. Others were imprisoned. This pretty much ended the White Rose resistance group. However, there were other such Nazis-resistance groups operating clandestinely in Germany; but with little success.

Lastly, Helmuth Hubener (1925 – 10/27/1942 Germany, guillotine execution) of Hamburg is mentioned. The Nazis controlled radio in Germany, spreading lies of glorious victories and bright prospects. For example, the propaganda stated that Japan had destroyed the United States ability to fight, after the 12/7/1941 sneak attacks. As another example, Third Reich radio reported that German troops were running roughshod over Russia. It was forbidden for Germans to listen to foreign radio stations.

Using his brother's clandestine short-wave radio, Hubener listened to the BBC broadcasting in German. Therefore, he realized that German citizens were being lied to. He and three friends wrote, printed, and distributed pamphlets that described the actual war situation. They tucked these into coat pockets, pinned them on bulletin boards, left them in phone booths, etc.

Hubener got a job working in social administration. A co-worker saw Hubener writing the pamphlets. The co-worker reported same to Nazi officials. He and his friends were arrested and imprisoned. They were tortured ten weeks while awaiting trial. Hubener as leader was found guilty of treason and furthering the enemy's causes. He was sentenced to death. His buddies got lesser punishments, imprisonment at labor camps. Hubener at age 17 was the youngest the Nazis executed for treason, during World War II.

Author Remarque did not know of the fate of his relatives in Germany, until the end of the War. He dedicated his 1952 *Spark of Life* book to his late sister. The book is about a political prisoner in a German concentration camp during the Nazi era. However, the dedication statement to his sister at the front of the book was deleted in the German version. This was because some German decision makers apparently saw him as a traitor, and also considered the execution of his sister as justifiable. This was the case even seven years after the War had ended, and the Nazis atrocities became more well-known.

Actor Ayers requested a draft status, which would allow him to serve as a non-combat medic. However, the military's policy was that servicemen were not allowed to make the decision on where or how they would serve. Ayers then requested and was granted conscientious objector status, opposed to both combatant and noncombatant training and service. This stance greatly diminished his reputation with many Americans.

Ayers was sent to an Army camp for conscientious objectors. He worked as a first aid instructor. He asked for a reduction in rank, which would allow him to serve as a medic and chaplain's assistant in the Pacific Theater. Therefore, he decided he would work in a noncombatant role, but in a combat zone. He was part of a team of 16 medics who arrived under fire during the Leyte (Philippines) invasion, to set up evacuation hospitals. He provided care to soldiers and civilians in both the Philippines and New Guinea. He was awarded three battle stars. He was in the Army 3.5 years, retiring as a Major. He donated his Army income to the American Red Cross.

After the War, Ayers returned to movie acting. However, he was not the star he had been in the past. This may be because some resented his conscientious objector stance, or maybe simply as he had been out of the movie business for more than three years, or a combination of the both.

Ayers was offered the part of Dr. Kildare in 1953 for a TV series, as he had starred in the 1938-1942 movies. He agreed, as long as the network (NBC) would not accept advertising from cigarette companies, as the main character after all was a physician. Ayers was apparently prescient. The Surgeon General's Advisory Committee on Smoking and Health did not issue its report on the negative health effects of smoking until 1/1964, which was 11 years later. In actuality, the health hazards of smoking were already known, or at least somewhat known.

NBC and the show producers would not agree to this though, as not willing to lose advertising dollars from the tobacco companies. The role much later went to Richard Chamberlain (1934 CA -) who played the good doctor in the star series 1961-1966, 191 episodes. Chamberlain was 25 years younger than Ayers, so the character was changed some.

Political activist Lyndon LaRouche (1922 NH -) was also a conscientious objector, for World War II. He was a Quaker. He worked at one of the Civilian Public Service camps. However, he did enlist in the Army in 1944 as a non-combatant. He served in India and Burma with medical units, and then later as an ordnance clerk. After discharge, he attended Northeastern University in Boston, courtesy of the G.I. Bill. LaRouche ran for President eight consecutive elections, 1976-2004; getting next to no votes each time.

Conscientious objectors, or at least as claiming such, were many for the Vietnam War. For one thing, it was an unpopular war on the home front. In assessing whether an applicant is a true conscientious objector though, evaluators must be convinced that the applicant is against fighting or serving in the military for any and all wars. An applicant who picks and chooses his wars to fight or serve in, does not meet the definition of a conscientious objector. Many or most who objected to being drafted during the Vietnam era who claimed conscientious objection, were in actuality protesting the war for other reasons. One of these reasons was fear of dying or injury for a cause they thought lacking, no doubt.

Three well-known Vietnam War conscientious objectors (or as claimed) were as follows:

- Boxer Muhammad Ali (1942 Louisville – 2016 Scottsdale) was classified 1-A when he registered for the draft at age 18, which is fit for service; in 1964, he was reclassified as 1-Y, which is fit for service only in times of national emergency, as he failed the Armed Forces qualifying test because of his sub-standard writing and spelling skills; he quipped at the time, *I said I was the greatest, not the smartest*

Ali beat Sonny Liston (1929 AR – 1970 Las Vegas, heroin overdose) 2/1964 to win the heavyweight championship; he defended his title 5/1965 against Liston, and then beat Floyd Patterson (1935 NC – 2001 NY, dementia and cancer) 11/1965

In 1966, the Army lowered its standards as needed more soldiers for the Vietnam War; Ali was re-classified 1-A; he complained volubly; several of his quotes were as follows:

- *I ain't got no quarrel with them Viet Congs*
- *I pay the salaries of 200,000 men, so I should not have to serve*
- *Why should they ask me to put on a uniform and go 10,000 miles from home and drop bombs and bullets on brown people in Vietnam while so-called brown people in Louisville are treated like dogs and denied simple human rights;* Ali's hometown was Louisville, Kentucky

Regarding this last quote, a prominent American responded as follows: *The tragedy to me is, Ali has made millions of dollars off the American   public, and now he's not willing to show his appreciation to a country that's giving him, in my view, a fantastic opportunity;* this speaker was Jackie Robinson (1919 GA – 1973 CT); Robinson was the first African American to play in Major League Baseball in the modern era (1947 as a Brooklyn Dodger); Robinson served more than two years in the Army during World War II, honorably discharged as a Second Lieutenant

Ali was drafted; he refused to enlist 4/28/1967 in Houston; he was later arrested; he stated at his trial that he was a conscientious objector and a Nation of Islam minister; conscientious objection of course is associated with pacifism which was a major contradiction from his profession, of beating large, healthy, young men to a pulp; he was found guilty 6/20/1967 of draft evasion; he was fined $10,000 and sentenced to five years in prison; his license to box was revoked

This decision was upheld by appellate courts; the U.S. Supreme Court though unanimously overturned his conviction 6/28/1971, 8-0; the Court's decision did not address the merits of his conscientious objector claims; rather, the Court held that since the draft appeal board gave no reason for the denial of a conscientious objector exemption, that it was therefore not possible to determine which of the three basic tests for conscientious objector status the draft appeal board used; therefore, the conviction was reversed; in other words, the reversal was due to a *technicality*

Ali was banished from the ring 3/1967 – 10/1970, when he was ages 25-28; these are certainly prime years for a boxer

African-American, professional heavy weight boxer Jack Johnson (1878 Galveston – 1946 NC, automobile crash) was arrested in 1912 on the grounds that his relationship with a woman violated the Mann Act against *transporting women across state lines for immoral purposes*; the woman in question was a white woman, which is why he was arrested; an all-white jury convicted Johnson 6/1913; he was sentenced to a year and a day imprisonment; Johnson fled to other countries and boxed professionally overseas; he returned to the U.S. seven years later, and served his sentence;   President Donald Trump (1946 NYC -) pardoned Johnson 5/2018

Boxer Johnson is mentioned as President Trump stated 6/2018 that he was considering pardoning Ali posthumously for his draft dodging, as he had pardoned Johnson for having an affair; Ali's estate attorney Ronald Tweel stated such a pardon did not make sense, as the Supreme Court had overturned Ali's conviction

- Author and newspaper columnist Dave Barry's (1947 NY -) father was a Presbyterian minister; Barry graduated Haverford College, Haverford, Pennsylvania, 1969; Quakers founded Haverford, 1833; he cited this, for avoiding military service; he later stated though, that he was an atheist, early on; he did not begin his writing career until 1971, so for the most part his conscientious objection background was not known

- Actor Richard Dreyfuss (1947 Brooklyn -) worked in alternate service for two years, as a Los Angeles hospital clerk; Dreyfuss started acting at age 15, but was a minor name in the movie acting world at the time of his objection; his first big movie was the 1973 *American Graffiti;* he then starred in the 1975 and 1977 blockbusters *Jaws* and *Close Encounters of the Third Kind*

Muhammad Ali of course, was more than enormous. He was celebrated worldwide. He had joined the Nation of Islam in 1964. The Nation of Islam is black supremacist, anti-Semitic, etc. The Montgomery, Alabama based Southern Poverty Law Center (1971 -) classifies it as a hate group. Ali stated that he was for segregation. He said that he would vote for segregationist George Wallace (1919 AL – 1998 AL). He said that women were inferior to men. For his racist and sexist beliefs and as refusing to enlist, he lost many fans.

His statements (again, see the quotes above) also were along the lines of not having to serve as wealthy, of disagreeing with the merits of the Vietnam War, or veering to racism issues in the United States. Again, the definition of conscientious objection includes that the person will not fight in any war, for reasons of anti-violence conscience. Selective rejection or approval of wars related to reasons other than finding violence objectionable, does not make a conscientious objector. For example, Ali's claims that he should not have to enlist as he was a Croesus or because racism existed in America, have no relation to conscientious objection.

To this day, Ali's motivation in refusing military service is still debated. In the Army, he would never have been in harm's way (as he knew), so fear of injury was not the issue. The Army most likely would have him box in demonstration fights, to entertain the troops. The Army also probably would have let Ali fight during his service, professionally.

One would think that Ali's handlers would have advised him to enlist from a public relations standpoint (who knows, maybe some did). This was more or less the case with the seven-year-older Elvis Presley (1935 MS – 1977 Memphis, polypharmacy overdose). With his money and celebrity, Presley probably could have avoided the draft, one way or another. Instead, he enlisted when drafted and served two years, 1958-1960. He could have served in Special Services (the Army's entertainment division), but his manager Colonel Tom Parker (1909 Netherlands – 1997 Las Vegas) convinced him to be a regular soldier. He was in an armored division. He served in Germany part of his two-year tenure. He donated his Army pay to charity, bought televisions for the base, bought more fatigues for the men in his unit, etc. His rank when he separated was Sergeant. Again, his Army service definitely increased his popularity and enhanced his reputation. This translated to more record sales.

Between induction and discharge, Presley had ten top 40 hits, so the Army did not slow his career. RCA also issued four albums of old material during his military tenure, to also keep Presley in the limelight and sales going.

Ali over the years though, did recover his reputation. The fact that the Vietnam War was so unpopular with just about everybody, definitely worked in his favor.

For the record, President Jimmy Carter granted a blanket pardon to Vietnam draft evaders in 1977.

President Thomas Jefferson (1743 VA – 1826 VA) took office 3/1801. Shortly after, he called for and signed legislation establishing a *Corps of Engineers* which *shall be stationed at West Point and constitute a Military Academy,* so as to train young men to be officers in the Army. West Point, New York is 54 miles north of Manhattan. The U.S. Military Academy began training in 1802. Since then, only one student has claimed conscientious objection. This was Cary Donham (1951 IL -) in 1970 in his senior year. The Army gave him an honorable discharge in 1971. This was during the Vietnam War.

The U.S. military over the years has tried to not draft persons, by making efforts to recruit volunteers to meet needs. However, the draft was required to meet said needs 1940-1973, through the Vietnam War. Since 1974, the military has been able to recruit persons in adequate numbers to meet needs, not requiring conscription.

Generally speaking, the military prefers an all-voluntary military; from the standpoint that it can reject those that it does not see as fit for the military for some reason. With conscription, the military gets stuck with some who for some reason or another are a poor match.

Of note however, the Selective Service System remains in place today as a contingency plan. American males are required to register when they turn age 18.

Of course in the case of an all-volunteer army, the conscientious objector issue is moot. Conscientious objectors simply do not enlist, as noted already. Of course, there are exceptions. As already noted, the compensation (wages or salary, benefits) are so great, that some conscientious objectors do enlist. If such a person enlists (or tries to enlist), the militaries of some countries may find a reason to reject him or her. Other militaries will accommodate, even willingly. Most countries are in this category, including the United States.

These conscientious objectors who do enlist of course do not have to fight (directly). In the case of military personnel in imminent danger (actually fighting or other), most nations including the United States increase their compensation. This is called *hostile fire pay/imminent danger pay,* but more commonly called *combat pay.* No one including conscientious objectors have an argument with this policy. All feel that this increased pay is justifiable. The conscientious objector as not fighting would not earn this extra pay.

For the record, most militaries again including the United States pay extra for hazardous duty assignments which may or may not involve combat. These include jobs such as flight deck operations personnel on an aircraft carrier, parachuting, scuba diving, etc. A conscientious objector may work in one of these categories, as not directly involved in fighting.

The table below shows the number of draftees for the four (significant) U.S. wars in the twentieth century:

War	U.S. Time in War		Draftees
World War I	14 months	09/1917 – 11/1918	2,810,296

World War II	72 months	11/1940 – 10/1946	10,110,104
Korea	37 months	06/1950 – 06/1953	1,529,539
Vietnam	126 months	08/1964 – 02/1975	1,857,304
			16,307,243

For World War II, draftees accounted for 63% of those who served in uniform. The table below shows the number of draftees per year, from World War I to the 1974 transition to an all-voluntary U.S. military.

Year	Number of Inductions
1917	516,212
1918	2,294,084
1940	18,633
1941	923,842
1942	3,033,361
1943	3,323,970
1944	1,591,942
1945	945,862
1946	183,383
1947	0
1948	20,348
1949	9,781
1950	219,771
1951	551,806
1952	438,479
1953	471,806
1954	253,230
1955	152,777
1956	137,940
1957	138,504
1958	142,246
1959	96,153
1960	86,602
1961	118,586
1962	82,060
1963	119,265
1964	112,386
1965	230,991
1966	382,010
1967	228,263
1968	296,406
1969	283,586
1970	162,746
1971	94,092

| 1972 | 49,514 |
| 1973 | 646 |

The last man inducted enlisted in the Army 6/30/1973. Age 24 Dwight Stone from California was a pipe fitter for an oil company. The Army trained him to be an electronics technician. He was honorably discharged 11/14/1974. He went back to work for his previous employer in California.

The sum of the draftees comes to 17,710,637. The total from the four wars above of 16,307,243, accounts for 92.1% of the total.

Over the years, many pacifist-type organizations have sprung up. Some are local, some national, and some international. Some have gone by the wayside. Some have combined with others. The lasting international organizations include the following:

- International Fellowship of Reconciliation founded 1914 in Germany, based in Netherlands today (IFOR already mentioned)
- War Resisters' International founded 1921 in Netherlands, based in London today
- Peace Pledge Union founded 1934 in London, still based in London
- Amnesty International founded 1961 in London, still based in London

These organizations are international. They have branch offices in other countries. These other countries include the United States, of course.

Although the last year of conscription in the U.S. was 1973, the draft was still common in European countries in the early 1980s. The tolerance (or lack of) for conscientious objection also varied much, in these countries. Conscientious objectors and pacifist types in 1982 decided to combine their efforts, by hosting simultaneous activities in several countries the same day. The most available date for the transnational event was May 15, so that day was selected.

At the time, annual events were not planned. However as the 1982 event went so well, it was decided to repeat in 1983. The logical date selection was the same date, of May 15. It was decided that the date would be permanent. Over the next few years, May 15 came to be known as *European Conscientious Objectors' Day*. By 1985, the concept of an annual, international celebration and events day had spread to other countries, into what came to be called *International Conscientious Objectors' Day*. They continue each year in a number of countries, to this day.

Lew Ayres was mentioned above, as the most well-known American conscientious objector. Five months younger James Mason (5/15/1908 England – 1984 Switzerland) was Ayres' British counterpart of the same era. Mason made many British movies, followed by many American movies. Mason's refusal to enlist alienated him from some of his family and some friends and some in the industry, plus he lost fans as well. Many criticized him for his stance. The British Army accepted his beliefs though and agreed to enlist him, to do non-combat work in World War II. This he also refused. He was finally exempted, as he was a movie actor -- work in the film industry was deemed to be of national importance (propaganda films, at least) during World War II. Anyway, Mason has a connection with the annual conscientious objectors' celebration date of May 15, as he was born on that date.

Of note, Mason played prominent roles in several war movies. Ayres only starred in the one war movie, *All Quiet on the Western Front*. Of note again, Mason and Ayres were both in 1979 *Salem's Lot;* a television adaptation of the Stephen King (1947 ME -) 1975 horror novel of the same name.

The Women's Co-operative Guild (1883 – 2016) was another of these pacifist groups. The Guild was founded in 1883 in England, to address family issues. In 4/1914 with war clouds forming, the Guild adopted a new objective -- that *civilised nations should never again resort to the terrible and ineffectual method of war for the settlement of international disputes.* No one can argue with this. But of course, it is not that simple.

World War I fighting began four months later. These guildswomen of course were wives, mothers, sisters, cousins, aunts, neighbors, co-workers, etc. of men who fought and died in World War I. The Guild embarked on an active campaign for peace. The Guild and other pacifist groups searched for a symbol which could be worn by members, as a public display against war, and as for non-violence.

The red poppy, also known as the remembrance poppy, came about in 1921 to commemorate military personnel who died in World War I; and later in all wars. Its origin was from the poem *In Flanders Field* that Lieutenant Colonel John McCrae (1872 Ontario, Canada – 1/28/1918 France, pneumonia) wrote on the battlefield, 5/3/1915. College professor and humanitarian Moina Michael (1869 GA – 1944 GA) wrote a response poem, in 1918. Both poems mention the red poppies. Michael conceived and promoted the idea in 1921 of using red poppies, in remembrance of those killed in war. The idea caught on with the Allied countries of World War I.

The white poppy was recommended, as the symbol of conscientious objection. The color white such as in the case of a white flag, symbolizes surrender. Surrender is a form of peace, so this may be one of the reasons why the white poppy was selected. After all, poppies come in many colors.

The Women's Co-operative Guild first sold white poppies in 1933. Other pacifist groups soon also adopted the white poppy, as a symbol of pacifism. The white poppy today is worn as an alternative to the red poppy, or both may be worn at the same time. Neither is meant to contradict the other, or even be controversial to the other.

Proceeds from selling white poppies are used to further the cause of the pacifist organizations, and to aid conscientious objectors.

A cherry tree was planted 8/6/1967 in Tavistock Square, Bloomsbury, London Borough of Camden. This was the 22nd anniversary date of the first atomic bomb, dropped on Hiroshima 8/6/1945. In Japanese culture, the cherry tree and its blossoms symbolize the beauty of life, but also its fragility and shortness. The life of a military person may parallel this premise.

A Mahatma Gandhi (1869 British India – 1948 India, pistol assassinated) statue-memorial was erected in 1968, also in Tavistock Square.

The Conscientious Objectors' Commemorative Stone was unveiled 5/15/1994 on Conscientious Objectors' Day at Tavistock Square. The erection of the massive, volcanic-slate stone was to commemorate the struggle of conscientious objectors, past and present. The inscription includes the following:

To commemorate men and women, conscientious objectors to military service, all over the world and in every age,

To all those who have established and are maintaining to right to refuse to kill, their foresight and courage give us hope,

This stone was dedicated on 5/15/1994, International Conscientious Objectors' Day.

The three features (cherry tree, Gandhi statue, conscientious objectors' stone) have led to Tavistock Square being referred to as a peace park or peace garden. An annual ceremony is conducted here on International Conscientious Objectors Day, May 15. The names of conscientious objectors executed by the Nazis in Germany during World War II are sometimes read off, at these ceremonies. Other names may be stated. A name often stated is Saint Maximilian of Tebessa, mentioned at the beginning of this chapter. Also, white carnations or poppies bearing the names of these objectors are placed on the monument stone as part of the ceremony.

The U.S. is one of about 63 countries, which have an all-volunteer military. Some Americans advocate that the U.S. all-volunteer military be dropped in favor of conscription, as a volunteer military is inappropriate for a democracy. They argue that the military lacks diversity, as those who currently enlist almost all do so for one primary reason – the very, very lucrative income and benefits, including benefits after retirement from the military. This is stated as the often-usual enlistee, has little money and poor job prospects. Also, training for new skills, education, medical care, etc. is free; even after separation. Persons of wealth and status would be required to serve, if selected in a random draft.

Also, being subject to the draft focuses young minds on world events. Being subject as such could even lead to policy changes on a national basis, as to when it is justified to fight.

Today as already stated, American men must register with the Selective Service System, within a month of turning age 18. American women do not, but requiring such is discussed from time to time.

As of 2015, more than 15% of the active personnel in the United States were female. The Marines and the Air Force had the least and the most, at 7.6 and 18.7%.

The countries of Bolivia, Chad, Eritrea, Mozambique, North Korea, Israel, Norway, and Sweden do draft women into military service. The women of some of these countries though can refuse, for one reason or another. For example, Israeli women can get out of their obligation by claiming a religious exemption or other exemption, few questions asked. More than a third of Israeli women, in fact do so. In practice in some of these countries, only women who are motivated to join the military end up enlisting.

Civilians are not in favor of conscription though. For that matter, neither is the military, as their ability to pick and choose would go away. They would be stuck with those who are incompetent; trouble-makers; or for some reason or another, just not a good fit for the military. To sum up, as just about nobody is for re-instating the draft, it is very unlikely that the draft will ever return to the United States.

Some countries today do have conscription. These include about five South American countries, most in Northern Africa, South Korea, and others.

The Korean War ran 6/1950 to the 7/1953 armistice. An armistice is an agreement to cease fighting with neither side surrendering, followed by negotiating a peace settlement. The agreement created the Korean Demilitarized Zone as a buffer to separate North and South Korea and allow the exchange of POWs.

The Korean Peninsula is 85,230 square miles. This is 32% the size of Texas. The 2.5-mile wide, 160-mile long, east-west demilitarized zone location yielded 55% of the Peninsula to North Korea, and 45% to South Korea.

South Korea is a democracy. North Korea is a dictatorship. The populations of South Korea and North Korea are 52 and 25 million. The gross domestic product per capita for South and North Korea is $44,000 and $1,000. The average life span of South Koreans and North Koreans is 82 and 70. To sum up, South Korea is a wonderful place on the planet to live; and North Korea is just the opposite.

No peace treaty was signed though. The leaders of North and South Korea met at the demilitarized zone 4/2018, and agreed to later sign a peace treaty.

South Korea began its military draft in 1949. Its draft since then has been regarded as sacrosanct. The current draft law became effective in 1965. It requires males age 18 to 35 to serve 21 to 24 months, depending upon the military branch. After service, these men are automatically placed on reserve status, and train several days a year, for six more years.

South Korean women are exempt from the law. Korean women may enlist, but allowing such did not start until 2010.

South Korean entry soldiers are not paid much, compared to other countries. The 2016 pay for a Private and a Sergeant were $1,616 and $2,142 a year. This is $135 and $179 a month. Of course as in the case of all or most all militaries, housing and meals and clothing and transportation and medical-dental care is included.

South Koreans though who go on to make the military their career, are paid to compete with the private sector.

If found to be unfit for military service for physical and/or mental reasons, South Korean men must work in civil service. The work tenure here is 24 to 36 months.

An Army stint is considered a rite of passage for young South Korean men. Military influence extends beyond service, to civilian life. For example, schools and companies arrange three-day *boot camps* for students and workers including females, just so to experience or re-experience military life. Therefore, South Korean culture has left little room for conscientious objection.

All able-bodied Korean men are required to serve at least 21 months in the military. Those who refuse are usually sentenced to 18 months of imprisonment, and get a lifetime criminal record. Exceptions have been made for those in poor health, or who have specialized skills needed in the work place.

South Korea created the Constitutional Court in 1988, to review issues under the Constitution of the Republic of Korea (South Korea). In 2004 and 2011, the Constitutional Court ruled that young men who refuse military duty could be imprisoned for compromising national security, given the *unique security situation* on the Korean Peninsula. This of course is in reference to still being in a state of war with the belligerent and dictator-ruled North Korea.

South Korea imprisons more men for refusing service than the rest of the world combined. In numbers though, such imprisonments are rare. For example, South Korea had only 218 young men in prison for refusing enlistment in 2019 -- according to Amnesty International. Most of these men are Jehovah Witnesses (or claim to be).

The Constitutional Court ruled 6/2018 that South Korea's conscription law was unlawful, as the country provided no alternative for those who object on the grounds of their personal, political, or religious beliefs. The Court though did uphold the authority of South Korean courts to imprison young men, if they refused military service and alternative service both. The decision compels South Korea to introduce alternative service programs, by the end of 2019. At the time of the decision as noted above, South Korea was already considering such programs.

The 21 to 24-month, South Korean military service tenure is the fourth longest in the world, behind Israel (28 months), Singapore, and North Korea. Just mentioned Israel also has mandatory military service, since 1948, when the Israel state was founded. The Israeli law applies to Jewish, Druze (esoteric, ethnoreligious group, which originated in Western Asia), and Circassian (Northwest Caucasian ethnic group); but does not include Arabs – the reason for the latter of course is another story.

23- USS INDIANAPOLIS (CA-35)

America's maritime position in the world decreased in the late nineteenth century and into the twentieth century. European shipping companies dominated international trade. American ships had only 10.1% of the international market, by 1915. U.S. shipyards were making ships, but mostly under contract for European countries, or companies based in European countries.

Congress passed the 1916 Merchant Marine Act. The Act established the United States Shipping Board (1916 – 1934, followed though by successor agencies) as an emergency agency. Its goal was to increase the country's percentage in ocean-going transport. The need for ocean-going ships was increased, when the United States entered what much later came to be called World War I, 4/1917.

The U.S. Shipping Board had the 440' long and 60' beam and 28' draft, 13 miles per hour, single screw, 70 crew, War Serpent cargo ship made at a New Jersey shipyard, to start to address the deficiency in international shipping.

World War I started 8/1914. The U.S. entered the War 4/1917, as already noted. While still under construction, the Navy requisitioned War Serpent to support the War effort. Her name was changed to the USS Indianapolis. She was the first naval ship named after the city of Indianapolis. She was launched 7/1918 and delivered 12/1918. This was one month after the fighting of World War I ended with an armistice. For the record, an armistice is an agreement to cease fighting with neither side surrendering, followed by negotiating a peace settlement.

Attached to the Naval Overseas Transportation Service and operating again as the USS Indianapolis, she departed Philadelphia on her maiden voyage 12/28/1918 to carry cargo to England and the Netherlands. She returned to the U.S. at Norfolk, Virginia, 2/23/1919. She departed Norfolk 3/31/1919, carrying cargo to France. She returned to Norfolk 6/22/1919.

As the Navy after World War I had little need for cargo ships, she was decommissioned and returned to the Shipping Board 7/19/1919. As the SS Indianapolis, she transported cargo the rest of her career. She was scrapped in 1933, after a fifteen-year career.

The six, 600' long and 66' beam and 16' draft, four screw, 37 miles per hour, 1,100 crew, Northampton-class heavy cruisers were made at five shipyards. They were commissioned 1928-1931. All six saw much World War II action. The Japanese sank three of the six in fact by 1/1943 – two by torpedoes from warships, and one by air attack. The other three survived World War II. The three survivors were decommissioned in 1946. They were not used for the Korean War. The three were sold for scrap in 1959.

Even before World War II started though, the Navy concluded that the Northamptons were both under-armed and under-armored. The Portland-class of heavy cruisers was the new design. The 1922 Washington Naval Treaty between five countries (U.S., U.K., France, Italy, Japan) limited the construction of battleships, battlecruisers and aircraft carriers. The Treaty did not limit numbers of other categories of warships including cruisers, destroyers, and submarines.

However, these ships were required to have displacements of less than 10,000 tons (per the Treaty).

These five countries had been allies in World War I, and had the largest naval fleets after the War. The purpose of the Treaty was to limit the arms race, so that the money could be used for more peaceful areas – increasing the quality of life of their citizens. They met in Washington D.C., which is why the Treaty was called the Washington Treaty.

The 610' long and 66' beam and 17 to 24' mean and maximum draft Portlands were about the same size as the Northamptons. However, they had more armor and armament, so a little heavier. Their displacement was 9,790 tons so under the Treaty requirement, versus 9,200 tons for the Northamptons. Despite the extra weight and the deeper draft, they could match the Northamptons steaming speed of 37 miles per hour with the same power plants (107,000 shaft horsepower). Eight boilers drove four geared turbines, turning a screw each.

Only two Portlands were made though. The USS Portland (CA-33) was made at Bethlehem Shipbuilding in Quincy, Massachusetts. She was commissioned 2/1933. A Japanese destroyer hit her with a torpedo at the 11/1942 Naval Battle of Guadalcanal. This was either the Fubuki-class IJN Inazuma (1932 – 5/14/1944 USS submarine torpedo sank off Manila, 94 of 219 crew lost {43%}), or the Fubuki-class IJN Ikazuchi (1932 – 4/13/1944 USS submarine torpedo sank off Woleai, all 219 crew lost). Repairs were completed 4/1943. She suffered slight damage from a friendly depth charge off Tarawa, 11/1943. She returned to the War 1/1944 after repairs. She managed to go the rest of the War unscathed. She was sold for scrap in 1959, along with the three remaining Northampton cruisers mentioned above that also survived World War II.

New York Shipbuilding Corporation laid the second (and last) Portland and the second USS Indianapolis (CA-35) down 3/1930 at its Camden, New Jersey yard. She was launched 11/1931, sponsored by Lucy Taggart (1880 Indianapolis – 1960 Indianapolis). Ms. Taggart was the daughter of former Thomas Taggart (1859 Ireland – 1929 Indianapolis), who had been Indianapolis' mayor 1895 - 1901. She was commissioned 11/1932.

The two cruisers were originally designated as light cruisers, as their armor was thin-skinned. As they had 8" guns though, the designation was changed to heavy cruisers. The 1922 Washington Naval Treaty mentioned above, mandated this change in classification labeling.

The two funnels of the Portlands were raked. They had a tripod foremast, and a small tower and pole mast aft. Light tripods were added forward of the rear funnel of each, 1943. Also in 1943, naval directors were installed aft. These electromechanical computers were used to aim the guns, in hitting targets.

Armament included the following:
- 9 × 8" (200 millimeter)/55 caliber guns (3x3)
- 8 × 5" (130 millimeter)/25 caliber anti-aircraft guns
- 6 × quad 40 millimeter (1.6") Bofors anti-aircraft guns
- 19 × single 20 millimeter (0.8") Oerlikon anti-aircraft cannons

- 2 × 3-pounder, 47 millimeter (1.9") saluting guns; saluting guns fire loud and smoky blanks for ceremonial purposes

This large array of guns and cannons were changed (upgraded) over the War years, on both Portlands.

The Portlands did not have torpedoes. Also, they did not have sonar. For surface USSs of World War II, the Navy for the most part limited sonar and torpedoes to destroyers and destroyer escorts. Destroyers in turn escorted cruisers, battleships, and aircraft carriers.

The wartime crew complement for the Portlands was 1,269. The Portland cruisers were also designed to serve as flagships. They had living and office space for an Admiral and his staff. In wartime, this would increase the manifest list by up to 277 more men.

U.S Naval Academy 1906 graduate Admiral Raymond Spruance (1886 Baltimore – 1969 CA) made Indianapolis his flagship in 1943, when he commanded the Fifth Fleet in World War II battles across the Central Pacific. This included landings at Tarawa, the Marshall Islands, Saipan, and the epic battle of the Philippine Sea. Ironically, Spruance was raised in Indianapolis, Indiana.

For the record, the Fifth Fleet was established 4/26/1944, from the Central Pacific Force. By 6/1944, the Fifth Fleet was the largest combat fleet in the world, with 535 warships. The Fifth Fleet was deactivated in 1947. It was reactivated in 1995. Today, it operates naval forces in the Persian Gulf, Red Sea, Arabian Sea, and parts of the Indian Ocean.

The two Portlands had two, aircraft catapults amidships. They could carry four aircraft. The catapults were explosive-powered. The charge was similar to that used for 5" guns. The seaplanes were catapult launched, to avoid buffeting from ocean waves. When landing, they would light on the relatively smooth ocean surface created on the lee side of the vessel as it made a wide starboard turn -- it was a matter of timing and coordination of the warship and aircraft with the ocean. They then taxied up to the awaiting cruiser. A deck crane hoisted the seaplane back aboard. They were then serviced and stowed.

The U.S. seaplanes at the beginning of World War II were usually two crew (pilot and observer/gunner) sitting tandem, single engine, folding-wing, Curtiss SOC Seagull biplanes. The *SOC* stands for *Scout Observation Curtiss*. Seagulls were introduced in 1935.

Seagulls found duty on USS battleships and cruisers. The wings folded back against the fuselage for compact storage ashore or aboard ship. When based ashore, the middle float was replaced by fixed wheeled landing gear. However, the Seagull did not have amphibian capability – it was one or the other. The Seagull's length, wingspan, and height were 31, 36, and 15'.

The Seagull's cruise and maximum speeds were 133 and 165 miles per hour from its air-cooled, nine cylinder radial, 550 horsepower engine. Its range was 675 miles.

For armament, the Seagull had one fixed, forward firing and one flexible-mounted rear-firing Browning M2 AN machine guns; both 7.62 millimeters. The Seagull could also tote a 650-pound bomb.

The Seagull was replaced with the single engine, two crew Vought OS2U Kingfisher midwing later in the War. Its size and speed were about the same as the Seagull, but its range was 805 miles compared to the Seagull's 675 miles. The Kingfisher's armament was the same as the Seagull's. The Kingfisher in turn was replaced with the Curtiss SC Seahawk low wing, toward the end of the War. After World War II, helicopters on warships replaced catapult-launched seaplanes.

Like any aircraft hauling three heavy, bulbous hulls through the air, Seagulls and Kingfishers and Seahawks were slow in speed and maneuverability – easy to shoot down. Therefore, missions were not considered unless there was no risk or little risk of attack – from either fighters, or anti-aircraft fire from land or ship. In practice therefore, the Seagulls were used mostly for limited range scouting and gunfire observation to aid surface warship gun crews in distant aiming; in lieu of offensive bombing or strafing.

Indianapolis' shakedown cruise from New Jersey was down the coast to Guantanamo Bay. She then transited the Panama Canal to train off Chile. She returned to Philadelphia, for an overhaul.

Indianapolis embarked President Franklin Roosevelt (1882 NY – 4/12/1945 GA, cerebral hemorrhage) at Campobello Island, New Brunswick, Canada, 7/1/1933. She arrived Annapolis two days later. Annapolis, Maryland is on Chesapeake Bay, and of course the location of the U.S. Naval Academy. Roosevelt disembarked. She returned to Philadelphia Navy Yard.

On 9/6/1933, she embarked Navy Secretary Claude Swanson (1862 VA – 1959 VA) to inspect the Navy in the Pacific. She toured the Panama Canal Zone, Hawaii, and installations in San Pedro and San Diego (both California). Swanson disembarked 10/27/1933.

On 11/1/1933, she became the flagship of Scouting Force 1. Scouting Force 1 in the early part of World War II, was an umbrella command for Task Forces.

The Indianapolis Task Force maneuvered off Long Beach, California. Indianapolis then departed 4/9/1934, for New York City. She embarked Roosevelt a second time at Charleston, for a naval review. She arrived back at Long Beach 11/9/1934, for more training with Scouting Force 1.

On 11/18/1936, she embarked Roosevelt a third (and last) time at Charleston, and conducted a good will tour to South America. State visit stops were made at Rio de Janeiro in Brazil, Buenos Aires in Argentina, and Montevideo in Uruguay. She then returned Roosevelt to Charleston. U.S. Naval Academy graduate (1906) Admiral Henry Hewitt (1887 NJ – 1972 VT) was Captain for this Presidential transport trip, which was part of the Pan American Conference in Buenos Aires. These conferences have been conducted since 1889, mainly to promote commerce.

Indianapolis was Scouting Force 1's flagship, into 1941.

She was docked at Pearl Harbor 12/5/1941. About two thirds of the crew were ashore. Her Captain issued an order that Indianapolis was sailing in one hour. Fifty Marines in full battle gear and 40 civilian men carrying toolboxes boarded. Sure enough, Indianapolis left within an hour, leaving behind much of her crew. The skeleton crew was not told where they were headed until the ship arrived the morning of 12/7/1941 at Johnston Atoll, 700 miles southwest of Oahu. The Navy had set up a sea base at Johnston in 1935, plus an airfield was made 9/1941. Sailors and marines were based here.

The mission was to conduct a rush mock bombardment, as a training exercise. As the crew unloaded marines and the civilian workers and stores as part of the simulation, word was received that the Empire of Japan was attacking military facilities and ships at Oahu. Captain (Vice Admiral) Edward Hanson (1889 MN – 1959 CA) immediately ordered that Indianapolis prepare for battle. Everything combustible from lumber to small boats to Roosevelt's bedroom suite furnishings was tossed overboard. Of course, it was not lost on the crew what their fate may have been, if still docked at Pearl Harbor.

Indianapolis dashed back to Oahu and was absorbed into Task Force 12, commanded by Vice Admiral Wilson Brown (1882 Philadelphia – 1957 CT). The Task Force searched for the Japanese carriers (and their surface and sub-surface escorts) that launched the fighters and bombers that devastated U.S. military facilities and the USSs at anchor, but did not find them. For that matter, no USS or plane found them – they were long gone by then. Indianapolis returned to Pearl Harbor.

Japan sneak attacked thirteen other sites this day, besides Oahu. They were all in or on the Pacific Ocean. They were all successful. The U.S. declared war on Japan the day after the sneak attacks. This was Monday, 12/8/1941.

Both Portlands saw extensive service in the World War II Pacific War against Japan. USS Portland's career was described above. Indianapolis' World War II actions after 12/7/1941 included the following:

- Indianapolis steamed to the South Pacific with the Task Force escorting the Lexington-class, 888' long, USS Lexington (1927 – 5/8/1942 USS destroyer torpedo sank to prevent capture after severe damage from Japanese aerial torpedoes in Coral Sea Battle, 216 of 2,951 crew {7.3%} lost) aircraft carrier to 350 miles south of Rabaul, New Britain, Papua New Guinea. New Guinea was a mandated territory of Australia. On 2/20/1942, eighteen Japanese aircraft attacked the Task Force. Lexington launched aircraft, which shot down sixteen of the eighteen. Anti-aircraft fire from Task Force ships wasted the other two.

- On 3/10/1942, the Task Force combined with another Task Force centered on the Yorktown-class, 824' USS Yorktown (1937 – 6/7/1942 sank in Midway Battle by Japanese aircraft bombs) aircraft carrier and attacked Lae and Salamaua, New Guinea. The Japanese were marshaling amphibious forces here. Attacking from the south through the Owen Stanley Mountain Range (southeastern part of the central mountain chain in Papua New Guinea), U.S. air forces surprised and inflicted heavy damage on Japanese warships and transports. A few aircraft were lost. These actions were part of the New Guinea campaign.

- Indianapolis returned to the Mare Island shipyard (peninsula at Vallejo, California) for a refit.
- Indianapolis escorted a convoy to Australia. Vice Admiral Morton Deyo (1887 NY – 1973 ME) was now in command.
- Indianapolis then headed for the North Pacific to support American units in the Aleutian Islands Campaign. On 8/7/1942, she and other ships shelled Kiska Island (one of the Rat Islands of the Aleutian Islands of Alaska), where the Japanese were staging men and equipment. Despite foggy conditions, Japanese ships in the harbor were sunk. Japanese shore installations were damaged or destroyed. Escorting destroyers depth-charged approaching Japanese submarines. Japanese seaplanes dropped bombs, but none hit.
- In 1/1943, Indianapolis supported a landing and occupation on Amchitka Island. Amchitka is another of the Rat Islands. This was part of the Aleutian Islands island-hopping strategy.
- On 2/19/1943, Indianapolis led two destroyers on a patrol southwest of Attu Island, searching for Japanese ships trying to reinforce Kiska and Attu (both Aleutian Islands). She intercepted and with other USSs sank the 318' long and 45' beam and 24' draft, Japanese cargo ship Akagane Maru (1940 – 2/20/1943). Akagane was laden with troops, munitions, and supplies. All aboard Akagane were lost; from the shelling, drowned, or exposure (hypothermia).
- Through mid-1943, Indianapolis remained in the Aleutian Islands area escorting American convoys, providing shore bombardments, and supporting amphibious assaults.
- Indianapolis supported the invasion of Kiska Island 8/15/1943, thought to be the final Japanese holdout in the Aleutians. As it turned out, the Japanese had evacuated the 107 square mile Kiska 7/28/1943. Thirty-two Americans and Canadians died in the assault on the abandoned Kiska, and another 250 were injured in some way. This was not the U.S. military's finest moment.
- Indianapolis sortied from Pearl Harbor 11/10/1943 with the main body of the Southern Attack Force for Operations Galvanic and Kourbash, the invasion of the Gilbert Islands. She bombarded Tarawa Atoll 11/19/1943, and then Makin Atoll the next day. She then returned to Tarawa as fire-support for amphibious landings. She shot down a Japanese airplane. She shelled enemy strongpoints, as landing parties fought Japanese defenders in the bloody and costly Tarawa battle. The Gilbert Islands and then the Marshall Islands were captured. These campaigns ran 11/1943 through 2/1944.

- Indianapolis with other ships bombarded Kwajalein Atoll of the Marshall Islands 1/31/1944. She silenced two Japanese shore batteries. On 2/1/1944, she destroyed a blockhouse and other shore installations, and supported advancing troops with a creeping barrage. She sailed into Kwajalein Lagoon 2/4/1944, aiding in mopping up resistance.
- In March and April of 1944, Indianapolis' (still the flagship of the Fifth Fleet) Task Force attacked the Western Carolines. U.S. planes sank three destroyers, seventeen freighters, five oilers, and damaged seventeen other ships off the Palau Islands; the end of March. Airfields were bombed. Waters were mined.

Indianapolis' Task Force struck Yap and Ulithi (both Caroline Islands) 3/31/1944 and 4/1/1944. Japanese aircraft attacked, but were driven off with no damage to USSs. She shot down a torpedo bomber.

- After another refitting at Mare Island, Indianapolis sailed to Hawaii as Vice Admiral Spruance's flagship, commanding the Fifth Fleet. The Fifth Fleet was set up 4/26/1944, from the Central Pacific Force.
- In 6/1944, the Fifth Fleet assaulted the Mariana Islands. Carrier aircraft raided Saipan 6/11/1944, followed by surface bombardment. Indianapolis played a major role.
- On 6/19/1944, Indianapolis' Task Force engaged the Japanese in the Philippine Sea Battle.
- Indianapolis returned to Saipan 6/23/1944 to resume fire support. She moved to Tinian Island (another of the Northern Mariana Islands) 6/29/1944, to attack shore installations. She sailed to Guam, which the U.S. had recently wrested back from Japan. Guam was one of the fourteen targets of the 12/7/1941 sneak attacks. She operated in the Marianas the next few weeks. She then sailed to the Western Carolines. During 9/12-29/1944, she bombarded Peleliu Island of the Palau Group before and after the amphibious landings. She then sailed to Manus Island in the Admiralty Islands where she operated for ten days. She then returned to the Mare Island Naval Shipyard in California for refitting.
- After overhaul, Indianapolis joined a fast carrier Task Force, 2/14/1945. Admiral Marc Mitscher (1887 WI – 1947 VA) commanded. The Task Force launched an attack on Tokyo 2/16/1945, to cover the Iwo Jima landings which began 2/19/1945. This was the first carrier-launched attack on Japan, since the 4/18/1942 Doolittle Raid 2.8 years back. Air facilities (hangars, shops, airfields), factories, and other industrial targets were destroyed or damaged. The Navy lost 49 carrier planes but claimed 499 enemy planes. This was a ten to one kill ratio, U.S. over Japan. The Task Force also sank a carrier, a destroyer, two destroyer escorts, nine coastal ships, and a cargo ship.

- After the Tokyo attack, the Task Force raced to the Bonin Islands (also known as the Ogasawara Islands) to support the Iwo Jima landings, again which began 2/19/1945. She did so through 3/1/1945, protecting the invasion ships and landing boats, and bombarding inland targets on Iwo Jima.
- Indianapolis and other USSs began pre-invasion shelling of Okinawa Island in the Ryukyu Islands 3/24/1945. Indianapolis shot down six planes, and damaged two others.
- On 3/31/1945, a single engine Nakajima Ki-43 Hayabusa fighter emerged from the morning twilight in a vertical dive and dodged much 20 millimeter anti-aircraft fire. The plane was hit, causing it to swerve. The pilot (probably a kamikaze) crashed into the sea, port side of Indianapolis. However, the pilot managed to drop his bomb on Indianapolis' port stern, from only 25' above. The bomb plummeted through the deck armor, mess hall, berthing compartment, the fuel tanks, and then out the ship's bottom. The bomb exploded beneath the cruiser. The concussion blew two more gaping holes in the keel, flooding nearby compartments. The bulkheads prevented progressive flooding. Indianapolis settled slightly by the stern and listed to port.

Nine Indianapolis sailors were killed, and more wounded.

Indianapolis was able to steam though to a salvage ship for emergency repairs. Her propeller shafts were damaged, fuel tanks ruptured, and the water distillation plant was ruined. After partial repairs, she made it to Mare Island in California under her own power for extensive repairs.

Most of the crew assumed that this attack would be the last for Indianapolis, that by the time repairs were done, the War would be over. This did not turn out to be the case.

On 7/16/1945 after these major repairs and an overhaul, the battle-scarred Indianapolis departed Hunters Point Naval Shipyard (San Francisco) carrying key atomic bomb components parts and enriched uranium to Tinian of the Northern Mariana Islands. This was just hours after the proving Trinity Test in New Mexico. The success of this test gave the final go-ahead to drop the atomic bomb, if the U.S. and the U.K. agreed that this was the best strategy.

However, the nature of the cargo was not disclosed to the Indianapolis crew or the marine detachment. The marines were told enough though, to know that they were to provide security for an important, secret cargo. The cargo was two cylindrical containers about the size of five-gallon pails, and a 15' long crate. The crate contained a small Navy cannon in an armored bomb casing. One of the pails was leaded. It contained a nine-ringed uranium bullet. The containers and crate were bolted to eyebolts welded to Indianapolis' deck.

Two Army officers also boarded to bolster security. It was later determined that the Army Major and Captain were not military, but Los Alamos (New Mexico) scientists in disguise. One was an engineer. The other was a radiologist.

These components were assembled into the uranium, gun-type, atomic fission bomb Little Boy, destined for Hiroshima 8/6/1945. The cruiser also carried components for the plutonium implosion, atomic fusion bomb Fat Man dropped on Nagasaki, three days later.

Indianapolis was selected for the transport of the bomb components as she was available for one thing as she had just been repaired and certified as fit, but also because she was one of the Navy's fastest ships. Her 74.1-hour trip from San Francisco to Pearl Harbor set a record for the 2,405 miles, of almost 32.5 miles an hour. She sailed unescorted to not attract attention. Also, it was thought (and hoped) that the Japanese had no warships, along that route.

After a rushed six-hour replenishment, she raced from Oahu unescorted again to the B-29 base on Tinian Island of the Mariana Islands, to deliver the components and radioactive materials of the bombs. She arrived 7/26/1945. Again, Indianapolis set a record. This was San Francisco to Tinian (5,300 miles) via Oahu in only ten days.

The cruiser arrived Tinian 7/26/1945. On this arrival date, five Air Transport Command Douglas C-54 Skymaster cargo planes took off from Kirtland Air Force Base in Albuquerque. They carried the following:

- Six smaller uranium target rings for the fission bomb (Hiroshima); at Tinian, technicians fastened these inside a tungsten steel tamper bolted into the muzzle of the uranium gun; the four bags of cordite were not inserted into the cannon breech until the Enola Gay B-29 was airborne; when the cannon was fired, the bullet rings slipped over and around the target rings, forming a 141-pound critical mass

- The 13-pound, plutonium core of the fusion bomb (Nagasaki); this was two, small nickel-plated hemispheres that technicians assembled into a just-subcritical sphere 3.5" in diameter

For the record, The Army Air Forces created the Air Transport Command (ATC) in 1942 during World War II as the Army's strategic airlift unit. Its three missions were delivering supplies and equipment between the U.S. and overseas combat theaters, ferrying aircraft from U.S. manufacturing plants to training facilities or where needed for combat including overseas, and to transport military personnel. The ATC used many aircraft types. The four engine, four crew, C-54 Skymaster just mentioned was one of its larger cargo planes. It replaced the four engine, Consolidated C-87 Liberator Express for long distance, over water flights. The C-87 was the transport version of the Boeing B-24 Liberator bomber.

The C-54 was the militarized version of the Douglas DC-4. For one thing, additional fuel tanks were added for long distance flights. The Skymaster cruised at 190 miles per hour, and had a maximum speed of 265 miles per hour. Its payload was 23,000 pounds.

The five C-54s from Kirtland arrived Tinian 7/27/1945.

On 7/27/1945, three, four engine Boeing B-29 Superfortress bombers left Kirtland. The B-29 cruised at 290 miles per hour, and had a maximum speed of 357 miles per hour. Each B-29 carried a complete Fat Man pre-assembly (Nagasaki bomb). This was the 10,300-pound ballistic casing and spherical high-explosive assembly that together would squeeze the plutonium core to criticality, setting off the nuclear chain reaction. The second and third units were in case more atomic fusion bombs were needed, if Japan refused to surrender.

After making the delivery to Tinian, Indianapolis sailed to Guam unescorted for a partial crew change and to await orders. She departed Guam 7/28/1945 again unescorted, to join Vice Admiral Jesse Oldendorf's (1887 CA – 1974 VA) Task Force 95. More specifically, she was scheduled for 17 days of training and drills with the New Mexico-class, 624' long and 97' beam and 30' draft, USS Idaho (1919 – 1947 scrapped) battleship at Leyte Gulf in the Philippines. Idaho had been stationed at Iceland 12/7/1941 to reinforce the Neutrality Patrols. As a result, she avoided the fate of the eight Pacific Fleet battleships 12/7/1941 at Oahu's Pearl Harbor – all sunk or greatly damaged when in port. Idaho arrived San Francisco 1/31/1942, taking the Panama Canal of course. She fought the rest of World War II in the Pacific Theater.

The planned training was in preparation for the invasion of the Japanese homeland islands. The training was necessary, as some of the crew were new (switched out at Guam) as was some of the equipment. This was to prepare for the invasion of Japan (Kyushu Island). Kyushu is Japan's third biggest island, and the most southwesterly of Japan's four main islands.

The 1,300-mile voyage started from the relatively safe Mariana Islands area, into the unknown waters of the Philippine Sea.

Steaming at 20 miles per hour midway from Guam to Leyte (Philippines) on 7/30/1945 at 00:14, the Type B3-class, 356' long and 31' beam and 17' draft, 105-crew, seven and 20 miles per hour under and surface, 21,000-mile range, IJN I-58 (1944 – 1966 target practice sank) cruiser submarine launched six Type 95 torpedoes toward Indianapolis. The six were aimed in a fanwise spread to increase the odds of a strike, especially if the cruiser was zigzagging. I-58 had both electronic and acoustic sonar. She had just been fitted with two new kinds of radar equipment – one for detecting surface ships, and the other for detecting aircraft.

Japan's Type 95, 24" torpedo used a kerosene-oxygen wet heater, compared to the compressed air used by most torpedoes. The Type 95 was the fastest submarine torpedo and had the greatest range and the largest warhead, for a World War II torpedo. Its speed was up to 58 miles per hour for 5.5 miles, and a little less fast at 54 miles per hour for 7.4 miles. It left little visible wake. No other country's torpedoes could match Japan's torpedoes, even this late in the War.

Also for the record, I-58 toted six, one-man kaitens (manned suicide torpedoes), for use at the Captain's discretion. The pilots were willing, but Captain (Lieutenant Commander) Mochitsura Hashimoto (1909 Kyoto – 2000 Kyoto) decided to go with multiple (unmanned) torpedoes. He kept the kaitens in reserve. The second team was not needed. Two of the six I-58 torpedoes connected. The first torpedo blew off 40' of bow. The second struck mid-ship (under the bridge) on the starboard side, adjacent to a fuel tank and a powder magazine. The resulting explosion split the ship to the keel, knocking out all electric power. Within twelve minutes, the cruiser went down by the bow, rolling to starboard. She took about 300 men of 1,196 aboard (25%). These men were killed by the explosions or trapped down below (some in sickbay). This was 7/30/1945. The time was 00:26.

Indianapolis was able to send distress calls before sinking. Three U.S. stations received the signals. However, none acted upon the call. Later reports believed to be correct were that one commander was drunk, another had ordered his men not to disturb him, and a third thought it was a Japanese ruse (or at least this is what he later said).

Also, intelligence personnel intercepted I-58's Captain's message to his superiors about sinking a large warship, decrypted, and relayed that message to Admirals at Guam and Pearl Harbor. Still, no action was taken.

The remaining almost 900 men faced exposure, dehydration, and shark attacks as they waited for assistance while floating with very few lifeboats or life jackets, and almost no food or water. Again, Navy command was not monitoring her progress; and her distress calls were ignored or not considered real. Her failure to reach her destination on schedule was not noticed; or if noticed, no alarm was triggered.

On 8/2/1945 at 10:25 (so almost 3.5 days later), pilot Wilbur Gwinn (1919 CA – 1993 CA) of a 51' long and 66' wingspan and 12' tall, twin engine, six crew, midwing, Lockheed PV-1 Ventura patrol and bomber aircraft on routine anti-submarine patrol out of Peleliu Island, left the cockpit to co-pilot Lieutenant Warren Colwell. Gwinn stepped back to assist bombardier Joe Johnson in securing a new type of aerial antenna, which was being tested. Its sock had come off and it had gotten tangled and was banging against the fuselage. The Ventura's altitude was 3,000'. In so doing, he glanced out of the bomb bay window, and thought he spotted something out of the ordinary in the ocean – an oil slick. He assumed the oil slick if there was one was from a Japanese submarine.

Gwinn rushed back to the cockpit to circle back, to attack if a Japanese warship was spotted. He dove to 300'. The crew noticed *bumps* in the water. He made another pass and determined the bumps were men and debris. These were the survivors and remnants of the USS Indianapolis. However, Gwinn and his crew did not know this, nor did they know the nationality of the men floating in the ocean.

The Ventura crew summoned assistance. The Ventura dropped life jackets, a life raft, water canisters (but they broke upon impact), and a radio transmitter. The Ventura crew thought they were aiding Japanese sailors.

The fact that the Ventura flew over the men was very, very unlikely. It is next to impossible to see a human floating in the ocean or even an oil slick at 500', much less 3,000'. Young, military pilots do have superior vision. Still, the sighting and discovery was beyond lucky, almost a miracle. The men below needed a miracle. Gwinn alerted his squadron commander at Peleliu.

The Navy was still in denial that there were men in the water; and if so, that they were Americans. Instead of sending rescue ships, they dispatched a 64' long and 104' wingspan and 21' tall, ten-crew, high wing, Consolidated PBY-5A Catalina flying boat; and this was not until several hours later. En route, the Catalina overflew the Butler-class, 306' long and 37' beam and 9' draft, USS Cecil J.

Doyle (1944 – 1967 target practice sank) destroyer escort. The Catalina alerted Doyle captain Graham Claytor (1912 VA – 1994 FL) of the situation by radio. On his own authority, Claytor diverted to the scene.

Claytor by the way was Navy Secretary under President Jimmy Carter (1924 GA), 1977-1979. He successfully led initiatives to allow women to serve on ships, and for the rights of homosexuals to leave the service without criminal records. By the way again, 1946 U.S. Naval Academy graduate Carter served 18 years active and reserves. He missed fighting in World War II by less than a year.

The Catalina of course with its 125 and 196 miles per hour cruise and maximum speeds, arrived hours before Destroyer Doyle and her 28 miles per hour speed. The floatplane dropped rubber rafts, water, food, etc. Observing sailors attacked by sharks, pilot Lieutenant Adrian Marks quickly polled his crew on whether to land, to assist. They all agreed to do so; even though landing on the open sea due to the size of even calm ocean swells was against standing orders. The landing was so rough in fact, that some hull rivets popped out. This was Marks' first open sea landing, and his last as well. During the night, he and his crew taxied around, pulling 56 sailors from the water. Marks thought that these were the ones at the most risk of shark attack. When the fuselage was full, Marks cut his engines; so that survivors could be hauled onto the high wings. The Catalina crew tied the exhausted sailors onto the PBY floats and wings with parachute cord. The Catalina's wings were damaged, as was the hull from the rough landing. In fact, some bailing was required.

Doyle homed in on the Catalina, arriving at night. She halted though in fear of striking survivors in the water. She took aboard the 56 sailors collected by the Catalina, and the Catalina crew. Doyle shot the Catalina to the bottom, with one of her deck guns.

At great risk, Doyle pointed its largest searchlight into the night sky, to serve as a beacon for other rescue vessels, as well as let the floating survivors know that rescue was imminent.

Three destroyers were ordered to respond from Ulithi (an atoll of the Caroline Islands), as follows:

- Bagley-class, USS Helm, 1937 - 1947 scrapped
- Bagley-class, USS Ralph Talbot, 1937 - 1948 target sunk in atomic tests
- Benson-class, USS Madison, 1940 - 1969 target sunk

Four destroyer escorts (but see notes on conversions) were dispatched from the Philippine Sea Frontier to assist, as follows:

- Rudderow-class, USS Register (converted to a high-speed transport), 1943 - 1966 transferred to China
- John C. Butler-class, USS Dufilho, 1944 - 1973 scrapped
- Rudderow-class, USS Ringness   (converted to a high-speed transport), 1944 - 1975 scrapped
- Buckley-class, USS Bassett (converted to a high-speed transport), 1945 - 1968 transferred to Columbia

These seven rescue ships arrived 8/3/1945, from 00:15 to 10:25. Note that the Little Boy atomic fission bomb was detonated over Hiroshima three days later. The search continued until 8/8/1945.

Again, the USS Doyle was the first to arrive. Doyle rescued 93 men. Basset rescued the most, 154 men. In all, 321 sailors and marines were scooped up. Four died shortly thereafter. Death was due to injuries, lack of food and water, exposure (hypothermia, hypernatremia, photophobia, etc.), dehydration, saltwater poisoning, severe desquamation, drowning, and shark attacks. Some killed themselves or others, as in various states of delirium and hallucinations, or just terrorized by the sharks and other conditions.

One thousand and one hundred and ninety-six men were aboard. These were 1,157 Navy crew, and a 39-man marine detachment. Eight hundred and seventy-nine men died – 849 Navy and 30 marines. Three hundred and seventeen men survived – 308 Navy and nine marines. The fatality rate was 73.4%. The estimate is that 35% died at the time of the torpedo strikes, and the other 65% in the ocean before rescue. The 879 deaths are still the record for the U.S. Navy, of a warship lost at sea.

The Pennsylvania-class, 608' long and 97' beam and 29' draft, USS Arizona (1915 – 12/7/1941 Pearl Harbor) battleship at anchor at Pearl Harbor at 1,177 dead was more, but she was in port. Arizona still holds the record for the most deaths on a USS.

Indianapolis was the last significant warship, the Allies lost in World War II.

A 2007 episode of the Discovery Channel TV documentary series *Shark Week* entitled *Ocean of Fear* stated that the Indianapolis sinking resulted in the most shark attacks on humans in history. The documentary stated also that oceanic whitetip sharks were probably the main killers, but that tiger sharks may have also dined. These are both requiem migratory sharks. Most marine biologists agree, with these conclusions.

Bigger oceanic whitetips are up to 10' long. Larger tigers are up to 16' long. As to how many men were killed and eaten alive or consumed when already dead; will never be known. The survivors though made statements that sharks did not eat many live men, that they were successful in kicking them away.

The pictures below show the oceanic whitetip and tiger sharks.

In regard to the pelagic, oceanic whitetip, their numbers have decreased 93% 1995-2019. Pelagic means the ocean zone of neither near the shore nor near the sea bottom. They are caught for their fins to make shark fin soup, consumed in Asia. Despite the fact that the fins have no taste or nutritional value, they sell for up to $1,300 a pound in Japan. The whitetip's fins are much larger than those of other shark species, which is why they are hunted. Cat Island in the Bahamas, the Red Sea, Cayman Islands, and Hawaii are some of the few places left where whitetips are seen.

U.S. Naval Academy graduate (1920) Charles Butler McVay III (7/30/1898 PA – 11/6/1968 CT) served with distinction as Executive Officer (second in command) of the Cleveland-class, USS Cleveland (1942 – 1960 scrapped) light cruiser during the 11/1942 North Africa landings. Cleveland arrived in the Pacific Theater 1/1942. She fought in the Solomons the next two months – Rennell Island, Kolombangara, Blackett Strait, etc. McVay earned a Silver Star for conspicuous gallantry and intrepidity on Cleveland in these Solomon Islands campaigns. The Silver Star is the Navy's third-highest personal decoration for valor in combat. He also was injured in one battle, earning the Purple Heart.

McVay chaired the Joint Intelligence Staff in Washington D.C. 5/1943 – 10/1944. McVay returned to sea 11/1944, taking command of Indianapolis. As already mentioned, a Nakajima Ki-43 fighter (thought to be a kamikaze) dropped its bomb from only 25' on Indianapolis's port stern. This was 3/31/1945, when Indianapolis was pre-invasion shelling Okinawa. The strike killed nine sailors and injured many more. American soldiers and marines landed the next day (4/1/1945). McVay earned a Bronze Star with combat V for his leadership and effectiveness in that campaign.

The Japanese submarine sank the Indianapolis 7/30/1945. This was Captain McVay's birthday (47 years old). He was among those rescued. A Navy Court of Inquiry recommended that he be court-martialed for the loss of Indianapolis and crew and marines. Fleet Admiral (five star) Chester Nimitz (1885 TX – 1966 CA) disagreed. Nimitz was Commander in Chief of the U.S. Pacific Fleet for U.S. naval forces, and also Pacific Ocean Areas Commander in Chief for U.S. and Allied air, land, and sea forces. Nimitz instead issued a letter of reprimand. Nimitz served from 1905 to his 1966 death.

Fleet Admiral (five star) Ernest King (1878 OH – 1956 ME) overturned Nimitz's decision, and recommended a court-martial. King was U.S. Commander in Chief, and Chief of Naval Operations. He served from 1901 to his 1956 death.

Navy Secretary James Forrestal (1892 NY – 1949 MD, suicide jump) ordered the trial. The Navy Secretary is a civilian position. Forrestal though was a Navy veteran, an aviator. He served during World War I, separating as a Lieutenant.

McVay was charged with failing to zigzag and failure to order abandon ship in a timely manner. He was convicted on the former, 12/1945 – especially as unescorted, and especially again as a moonlit night (three quarters moon). The court-martial decision was controversial, as follows:

- As Navy knowledge that Japanese submarines were in the area was not relayed to McVay; of note, this fact was withheld at the time of the trial, as well
- Zigzagging
  - There was evidence that the Navy itself had placed the ship in harm's way, in that McVay's orders were to zigzag at his discretion, weather

permitting; zigzagging in conditions of poor visibility (night time, inclement weather) was uncommon for USSs, especially this late in the War; zigzagging increases travel time thereby increasing time exposed to attack between safe harbors, and consumes more fuel

- o American naval experts testified that zigzagging was of dubious benefit, in evading torpedoes from Japanese or German submarines; 1927 U.S. Naval Academy graduate Commander Glynn Donaho (1905 TX – 1986 AZ) commanded submarines in World War II; he was awarded four Navy Crosses, two Silver Stars, and a Bronze Star; he was one of the experts like Hashimoto below who testified that zigzagging would not have saved the Indianapolis

- o IJN I-58 submarine Captain Hashimoto testified that zigzagging would not have prevented him from successfully torpedoing Indianapolis; decades later, he sent a letter to that effect to Navy Secretary John Warner (1927 DC -), as part of an effort to exonerate McVay

  Hashimoto by the way had been at sea four years, with no luck; he was desperate for a kill, and he got a big one

- Indianapolis was not equipped with submarine detection equipment (sonar or hydrophones); for World War II, such equipment was installed on destroyers and destroyer escorts, but usually not on larger warships (cruisers, battleships, aircraft carriers); as already stated, this is one of the reasons why destroyers accompanied aircraft carriers, cruisers, and battleships

- McVay's request for a destroyer escort was denied due to the priority for destroyer escorts and destroyers to protect transports steaming to Okinawa, and rescue downed B-29 airmen from bombing raids over Japan

- Six days before, a kaiten manned torpedo (one suicide operator) launched from a submarine sank the Buckley-class, 306' long and 37' beam and 14' draft, USS Underhill (1943 – 7/24/1945 northeast of Cape Engano, 112 of 234 crew lost {48%}) destroyer escort in the same area where Indianapolis was hit; McVay was not informed of this and several other attacks in the area as well

Kaitens were 48' long and weighed 16,000 pounds (the warhead itself was 3,420 pounds, which is 21% of the total); their range was 27 miles at low speed; their top speed was 23 miles an hour; when they ran out of propulsion, they sank until the ocean crushed machine and man

The U.S. had developed an ingenious code-breaking program called *ULTRA*, so was able to decipher encrypted Japanese command messages. However, the Navy withheld some information from USS captains, as always knowing the Japanese plans and avoiding or attacking (whichever was the case), would tip off the

Japanese that their messages were being read. If so, the Japanese would change their codes, and the enormous advantage lost.

In the case of Indianapolis, Navy Pacific Command as already noted knew that the Japanese Tamon submarine group was patrolling in the area where Indianapolis was sailing. The Tamon submarine group was six submarines. The six in fact were the last operating submarines that Japan had. But again, Command chose to not advise the Indianapolis of this fact; or even advise Captain McVay to take precautions, such as zigzagging or waiting until sonar-equipped destroyers or destroyer escorts could be arranged to escort.

McVay asked repeatedly why it took the Navy so long to rescue him and other survivors. He was never given a definitive answer. The Navy obviously goofed up here, in more ways than one. It is impossible to estimate, but the delays probably more than doubled the death count. Four Navy officers were admonished or reprimanded for not recognizing the cruiser's delay, or for being aware of the delay but not acting, and/or for not responding to SOS calls. However, the reprimands were later rescinded.

The court sentenced McVay to lose 200 numbers in both his temporary rank of Captain and his permanent rank of Commander. This meant that 200 men of McVay's rank would move ahead of him, for promotion.

Later in 1946, Navy Secretary Forrestal remitted McVay's sentence, and restored him to duty. Forrestal did so mainly upon the recommendation of Admiral Nimitz, who was now Naval Operations Chief.

McVay worked in the New Orleans Naval District. He retired in 1949 at the age of 51, rank of Rear Admiral.

Seven hundred Navy ships were sunk in World War II. Three hundred and eighty were warships, which is 54%. Indianapolis was among the largest sunk. Indianapolis was also the only USS sunk in World War II, which left the enemy unscathed in that event or battle.

McVay was the only World War II Navy Captain court-martialed. In fact, he is the only warship commanding officer in the history of the U.S. Navy, to be court-martialed for negligence resulting in the loss of his ship during wartime. It was recognized quickly that the court-martial was unfair, and that McVay had been made a scapegoat for the Navy's failings. As noted above, Admiral Nimitz remitted his sentence, and restored him to active duty.

Others made efforts to defend McKay, including the following:

- Associated Press editor and former Pacific Theater wartime correspondent Richard Newcomb wrote the first book (1958) detailing the sinking and the aftermath, entitled *Abandon Ship*. His research vindicated McVay, concluding that he had made no errors in judgement.

- Giles McCoy (1926 – 2009 FL, prostate cancer) was one of the nine marine survivors. He wrote letters and made phone calls to track down other survivors to organize a reunion, and to collect opinions from others as to whether they thought McVay was culpable. From his Herculean effort (this was way before computers and the Internet), he located 220 of the 317 survivors (69%). Most of these with wives and children along attended the first reunion the last weekend of 7/1960 weekend in Indianapolis. This date corresponds to the sinking date, fifteen years back. Captain McVay attended and spoke. At the reunion, the survivors strategized on defending and even exonerating McVay.

These reunions have been conducted since, but not every year.

- McVay's son Kilo McVay (1928 DC – 2001 HA) lobbied much of his adult life, on his father's innocence.
- Sixth grader Hunter Scott (1983 -) from Pensacola, Florida, saw the 1975 *Jaws* movie in 1995 with his dad. He was transfixed by the Quint character's account of the USS Indianapolis sinking (see below), not even knowing if it was true or made up for the movie. It was made up. The shark hunter Quint character in the movie was a survivor of the Indianapolis sinking (as part of the plot).

When Scott got older, he interviewed more than 150 survivors. He collected and reviewed more than 800 documents. He concluded that Captain McVay was not derelict in his duty, and that the Navy just needed a scapegoat. This was Scott's project for a high school class. However, he ended up writing an article which appeared in *Naval History* magazine.

Fifteen naval officers met at the U.S. Naval Academy in 1873 to discuss the implications of a smaller, post-Civil War Navy and other issues of concern or professional interest. This was the establishment of the United States Naval Institute as a forum for the exchange of ideas, to disseminate and advance the knowledge of sea power, and to preserve American naval and maritime heritage.

Today, the Naval Institute is a private, non-profit, professional military association that develops and offers nonpartisan and independent forums for debate of national defense and security issues. Most of its 50,000 members are active or retired Navy, Marine Corps, and Coast Guard persons. Members though live in more than 90 countries. Its home office is on the grounds of the U.S. Naval Academy. However, the Naval Institute is private, and not part of the Academy. It receives no government funding.

In 1874, the Naval Institute began to accept papers and publish a summary of its discussions, in a publication titled *Proceedings.* That publication continues to this day, monthly. Since then, other publications have been released. These include naval guides, historical articles, biographies, current affairs, etc. The Naval Institute began a new publication entitled *Naval History* in 1987. This is the publication that printed Hunter Scott's article. Today, *Naval History* is a 72-page bimonthly. Again, this was the publication that Scott's article appeared in.

Hunter Scott studied economics and physics at the University of North Carolina at Chapel Hill, on a Naval ROTC scholarship. He graduated 5/2007. He became a naval aviator. He piloted the Sikorsky, twin engine Sea Hawk helicopter.

- In 1999, Captain Hashimoto assisted, as he had at the court-martial trial decades back. His letter to the Senate Armed Services Committee stated again that zigzagging would not have not prevented him from hitting the Indianapolis. His to the point words were as follows: *I would have been able to launch a successful torpedo attack against his ship whether it had been zigzagging or not.* In the same letter regarding McVay's conviction, Hashimoto wrote: *I have met many of your brave men who survived the sinking of Indianapolis. I would like to join them in urging that your national legislature clear their Captain's name. Our peoples have forgiven each other for that terrible war and its consequences. Perhaps it is time your peoples forgave Captain McVay, for the humiliation of his unjust conviction*

Congress did review the information again, especially that from schoolboy Hunter Scott and the opinions from Hashimoto; and passed a resolution exonerating McVay in 2000. All mention of the court-martial and conviction was eliminated. President Bill Clinton (1946 AR -) signed the resolution. This was 56 years after the sinking, 32 years after McVay's death, and five days after Hashimoto's death. Navy Secretary Gordon England (1937 Baltimore -) ordered McVay's record cleared of all wrongdoing.

The families of some of the men who died hounded McVay – hate mail, threatening telephone calls, etc. Indianapolis sailor Tom Brophy's father Thomas Brophy was one of these. Brophy Senior had political influence, and lobbied Forrestal and Truman both to do all they could do to destroy McVay.

McVay's wife Louise learned to intercept the mailman and discard the hate mail, and answer the telephone to hang up on death threats. This worked, until she died of cancer in 1961. A beloved grandson died in 1965. This hounding, coupled with loneliness after his wife died and sadness on his grandson's death and as the Navy had made him a scapegoat for its failings, led to his 1968 suicide. He stepped out of his house, sat on a stone step, and used his Navy-issue .38 revolver. In this way, the Indianapolis claimed her last victim. This was 23 years after the sinking. He was age 70.

A toy sailor given to him by his father Charles Butler McVay, Jr. (7/30/1898 PA – 1949) when he was a child, was found in his non-pistol hand.

McVay's father was also an Annapolis graduate (1890). He commanded several vessels during the 1898 Spanish-American War and 1914-1918 World War I. Later, he served as Commander-in-Chief of the Asiatic Fleet, which mainly patrolled the Philippines. He retired as a four star admiral in 1932. Father and son served 40 and 33 years respectively.

Another dozen Indianapolis survivors also committed suicide later in life, related to posttraumatic stress disorder and survivor's guilt.

Efforts to locate the wreck in the Philippine Sea were not successful, until 2017. This seems odd, considering that two aircraft and eight USSs were involved in the rescue.

Paul Allen (1953 Seattle – 2018 Seattle, non-Hodgkin's lymphoma complications) and Bill Gates (1955 Seattle -) formed Microsoft Corporation in 1975. Allen was diagnosed with Hodgkin's lymphoma in 1981. He left Microsoft in 1982, due to his illness. He retained partial ownership of Microsoft. His net worth in 2018 was more than $20 billion.

Allen was treated successfully with radiation therapy and a bone marrow transplant in 1981 and 1982. In 2009, he was diagnosed with non-Hodgkin's lymphoma. He was again treated successfully. However, the cancer returned in 2018 with a vengeance. His billions could not save him.

Allen's 414' long and 69' beam and 19' draft, Octopus mega-yacht was completed in 2003. Besides pleasure use, he made it available for humanitarian work, research, etc. He has also used it to search for shipwrecks.

In 2016, Allen bought a 13-year-old, 251' long and 49' beam and 24' draft, offshore platform service vessel. He had the ship modified and refitted to be a dedicated deep submergence search, research, and equipment test vessel. RV Petrel's autonomous underwater vehicle and remote operated underwater vehicle are able to explore more than 3.7 miles deep. The RV Petrel crew is twenty-one. The project staff is ten.

Petrel has since discovered many World War II shipwrecks in the Pacific Ocean, Atlantic Ocean, and Mediterranean Sea. Archival documents (ship logs, battle reports, etc.) are studied to estimate where the wrecks lie, as a starting point to begin searches.

Allen and Petrel found the Indianapolis wreck 9/8/2017. This was more than 72 years after she sank. She was 18,044' (3.4 miles) down.

Allen reported his findings and sent pictures to the Navy. The Indianapolis still belongs to the Navy. Allen did not reveal its location publicly.

Captain McVay and the USS Indianapolis are shown below:

Books and memoirs on the Indianapolis sinking and survival have been written. References to the sinking and aftermath have been included in film, stage, television, etc. These include the following:

- Commander Hashimoto wrote the 1954 book *The Story of the Japanese Submarine Fleet, 1941-1945*, in which he detailed World War II Japanese submarine operations. The book included an account of his sinking of Indianapolis.

Hashimoto by the way met with some of the Indianapolis survivors at Pearl Harbor, 12/1990. This was at an anniversary meeting of the 12/7/1941 sneak attacks (49 years). He stated *I came here to pray with you for your shipmates, whose deaths I caused.* Indianapolis marine survivor Giles McCoy responded: *I forgive you.*

- As already mentioned, Associated Press editor and former wartime correspondent Richard Newcomb wrote the first book on the sinking and its aftermath, the 1958 *Abandon Ship*. His research vindicated McVay, concluding that he had made no errors in judgement.
- Stacy Keach (1941 GA -) portrayed Captain McVay in the 1991 made for TV movie, *Mission of the Shark: The Saga of the USS Indianapolis*.
- Doug Stanton's *In Harm's Way: The Sinking of the U.S.S. Indianapolis and the Extraordinary Story of Its Survivors* book came out in 2001.
- Documentary filmmaker Sara Vladic and Navy veteran Lynn Vincent (1962 MA -) made the 2005 *USS Indianapolis: The Legacy* documentary film which tells the fate of Indianapolis from survivors' accounts.

These two women came out with the *Indianapolis: The True Story of the Worst Sea Disaster in U.S. Naval History and the Fifty-Year Fight to Exonerate an Innocent Man* book in 2018. It was a bestseller. They interviewed more than a hundred survivors and rescuers over 20 years.

One of these stories was that of Lieutenant Commander Earl Henry (1912 – 1945). Dr. Henry was the ship's dentist. In his spare time over several months on Indianapolis, he made a six-foot long scale model of the cruiser to give to his newborn son. His son never saw it. Dr. Henry never saw his son.

- Author and screenwriter Peter Benchley (1940 NYC – 2006 Princeton) fished as a child with his father off Nantucket. Later in life, he went on shark fishing and hunting expeditions with sport fisherman and fishing charter boat operator Frank Mundus (1925 NJ – 2008 HA). Mundus is known for catching a 3,427-pound, great white shark 28 miles off Montauk, New Jersey. This is the record for a fish caught by rod and reel.

The pair were filmed on a fishing trip in a 1974 episode of *American Sportsman*. This ABC television show about fishing, hunting, and other outdoor activities ran 1965-1986.

Doubleday commissioned Benchley to write a novel, about sharks. The 1974 *Jaws* turned out to be a bestseller. The novel is about a rogue, great white shark killing and dining on swimmers off the beach of a Long Island, New York, summer resort town. The town's leaders and merchants downplay the deaths, so that tourist income is not decreased. As if this was not enough, another plotline is that the mafia is involved as it owns land in the area, which would go way down in value if the water unsafe.

A marine biologist from the Woods Hole Oceanographic Institution (Woods Hole, Massachusetts), the town's sheriff, and a professional shark hunter try to kill the shark.

- The most well-known such reference (already mentioned above) as the movie was a blockbuster, was in the 1975, Stephen Spielberg (1946 Cincinnati -) directed thriller film *Jaws*. The movie was based on Benchley's novel (many deviations though).

Robert Shaw (1927 England – 1978 Ireland) played Quint, the professional shark hunter. In a monologue in the movie, he explains his shark-hater obsession, by describing the fate of the Indianapolis sinking survivors. In his story in the movie, he was a sailor on the Indianapolis. He was one of the few survivors witnessing his fellow sailors eaten alive, one by one. This part about the USS Indianapolis was not in Benchley's *Jaws* book.

Benchley co-wrote the original movie script with Carl Gottlieb (1938 NYC -), which also did not include the Indianapolis. The idea of adding the Indianapolis disaster was conceived by playwright Howard Sackler (1929 NYC – 1982 Spain), and lengthened by screenwriter John Milius (1944 St. Louis -). Benchley and Gottlieb then had a disagreement on the wording. Actor Shaw rewrote the passage. Benchley and Gottlieb agreed with Shaw's revisions.

The movie plot suggests that the Quint character likely suffered from mental health issues (posttraumatic stress disorder, survivors' guilt), from the Indianapolis sinking. Richard Dreyfuss' (1947 Brooklyn -) character is Matt Hooper, a concerned scientist (oceanographer). Roy Scheider (1932 NJ -) plays Martin Brody, the harried police chief of the little, Long Island beach town losing swimmers and tourists and their money to sharks in the surf. Shaw again plays Quint, the expert at finding great white sharks. The three men are offshore in a small boat loaded with chum, looking for the rogue killer shark. Quint owned the boat, named *Orca* (of course). The monologue is as follows:

- Hooper: *You were on the Indianapolis?*
- Brody: *What happened?*
- Quint: *Japanese submarine slammed two torpedoes into our side, chief. It was comin' back, from the island of Tinian to Laytee, just delivered the bomb. The Hiroshima bomb. Eleven hundred men went into the water. Vessel went down in twelve minutes. Didn't see the first shark for about a half an hour. Tiger. Thirteen footer. You know how you know that when you're in the water, chief? You tell by lookin' from the dorsal to the tail. What we didn't know... was our bomb mission had been so secret, no*

distress signal had been sent. Huh. They didn't even list us overdue for a week. Very first light, chief. The sharks come cruisin'. So we formed ourselves into tight groups. You know it's... kinda like ol' squares in battle like a, you see on a calendar, like the battle of Waterloo. And the idea was, the shark comes to the nearest man and that man, he'd start poundin' and hollerin' and screamin' and sometimes the shark would go away. Sometimes he wouldn't go away. Sometimes that shark, he looks right into you. Right into your eyes. You know the thing about a shark, he's got...lifeless eyes, black eyes, like a doll's eye. When he comes at ya, doesn't seem to be livin'. Until he bites ya and those black eyes roll over white. And then, ah then you hear that terrible high pitch screamin' and the ocean turns red and spite of all the poundin' and the hollerin' they all come in and rip you to pieces.

Y'know by the end of that first dawn, lost a hundred men! I don't know how many sharks, maybe a thousand! I don't know how many men, they averaged six an hour. On Thursday mornin' chief, I bumped into a friend of mine, Herbie Robinson from Cleveland. Baseball player, boson's mate. I thought he was asleep, reached over to wake him up. Bobbed up and down in the water, just like a kinda top. Up ended. Well... he'd been bitten in half below the waist. Noon the fifth day, Mr. Hooper, a Lockheed Ventura saw us, he swung in low and he saw us. He's a young pilot, a lot younger than Mr. Hooper, anyway he saw us and come in low. And three hours later a big fat PBY comes down and start to pick us up. You know that was the time I was most frightened? Waitin' for my turn. I'll never put on a lifejacket again. So, 1,100 men went in the water, 316 men come out, the sharks took the rest, June the 29, 1945. Anyway, we delivered the bomb.

For the record, although Quint stated the date of 6/29/1945 for the sinking, this was in error. The actual date was 7/30/1945. June 29 was the date that the boy in the movie was eaten by the shark, which is seen on the hand-written reward notice put up on the beach in the movie. This is apparently where Shaw got the wrong date, and nobody else caught it. Also, he says they were spotted on the fifth day, when it was the fourth (3.5 days after the sinking). Also, his casualty figures are off. No matter – the monologue was a dramatic statement and based on historical fact. Kudos to Shaw's creativity in writing the inserted script, and also for his masterful delivery of same in the movie.

Also, Shaw in his monologue mentioned crewmate Cleveland Indians baseball player Herbie Robinson, bit into two by a shark. There was no such person. Shaw made him up.

For the record, 95% of 1941 season major leaguers did serve in the military during World War II. These numbered 473 players. Most served in the Navy. Very few saw combat. Big name exceptions who saw combat were Yogi Berra Navy, Gil Hodges Marines, Bob Feller Navy, and Phil Rizzuto Navy. These four were ages 16, 17, 23, and 24 when the U.S. declared war on Japan. They enlisted voluntarily. These four players had long successful baseball careers after World War II. They all lived very long lives.

Ted Williams was in the Navy during World War II. He became a Marine aviator. He did not fly in combat. He was called up at the age of 33 for the Korean War, as a Marine pilot. This was the case despite not having flown a plane in more than six years. He flew the Grumman, single engine, folding midwing, F9F Panther jet fighter 39 combat missions. The F9F was one of the Navy's first successful carrier jet fighters.

Williams was hit by enemy gunfire on three of these missions. In one case 2/16/1953, he had to make a crash landing and was bruised up. For some missions, the future astronaut and long-term Ohio Senator John Glenn (1921 OH – 2016 OH) was his wingman.

For the record, Williams fought bitterly about being drafted for World War II, and then the same for his call-up for the Korean War.

None of the 473 major leaguers died in World War II. They promoted the sale of war bonds, recruited, boosted spirit, and yes – played exhibition baseball. Many worked in the military as physical fitness trainers. Very few saw combat.

Minor leaguers were not so well protected. Many found themselves in combat. One hundred and twenty-seven minor leaguers died in World War II. As already noted, *Jaws* was a blockbuster. Its box office was $471 million, versus its only $9 million production costs.

- The Indianapolis story was repeated in the 2016 *USS Indianapolis: Men of Courage* movie. Nicholas Cage (1964 Long Beach -) played Captain McVay. It was filmed in Mobile and the Mobile, Alabama area. During the filming, Cage and others connected with the movie met Richard Stephens, who was one of the few survivors still living.

The South Dakota-class, 680' long and 102' beam and 36' draft, USS Alabama battleship (1942 – 1969 museum ship) and Gato-class, 312' long and 27' beam and 17' draft, USS Drum (1941 – 1969 museum ship) submarine on display at the Battleship Museum Park in Mobile, subbed for the Indianapolis and the Japanese submarine in some of the scenes.

A flying restored Ventura and a flying restored Catalina were hired for the filming as well. The Catalina took on water. The pilot and the co-pilot beached it. They were not injured, but the Catalina was damaged beyond repair.

In the movie, Matt Lanter (1983 OH -) plays a fictional role of a signalman aboard Indianapolis. Matt's grandfather Kenley Lanter (1925 – 2013) was a signalman on Indianapolis and one of the survivors. Furthermore, his father Joe Lanter was the chairman of Second Watch, an organization of Indianapolis survivors, family members, friends, etc. The group promotes citizenship and patriotism, as well as honors the memory of those who did not survive.

The predecessor name of Second Watch was the USS Indianapolis Survivors Organization. As only a few survivors are still living, the new name was adopted as most members are relatives of those who died when the Indianapolis was sunk or survivors who have since died.

The movie was made for $40 million. For some reason, it was a major flop. Its box office was only $1.6 million. This is only 4% of the production costs. Seventy-nine percent of the meager attendance was in the U.S.

The movie *Hacksaw Ridge* about a World War II, conscientious objector Army medic who was awarded the Medal of Honor was released two weeks before the *Indianapolis* movie, so maybe moviegoers had enough of World War II movies. *Hacksaw Ridge* was a moneymaker. Its box office was $175.3 million, versus its also $40 million production costs. And then another World War II movie came out nine months later. *Dunkirk* was also even more of a big hit, with a box office of $527 million versus its $125 million production costs. It is about the air, sea, and land evacuation of Allied soldiers from the beaches and harbor of Dunkirk, France May and June, 1940; during World War II.

The Second Watch group mentioned above designed, erected, and paid for the USS Indianapolis National Memorial, which was dedicated in 1995 in Indianapolis. The names of the marines and sailors aboard when torpedoed are part of the display (plus the name of one civilian passenger).

A museum also in Indianapolis opened in 2007.

Survivors, family members, and others meet annually in Indianapolis, on or near the date of the sinking. The first reunion was in 1960, on the 15th anniversary of the sinking. At the 70-year, 8/2015 anniversary meeting, fourteen of the thirty-two remaining survivors attended. The reunions are now annual or every other year. Younger relatives of the survivors now run the organization. As noted above, this group is called the *Second Watch*.

Commander Hashimoto lost his family in the Hiroshima atomic bombing – instantly incinerated. He re-wed. He attended some of the reunions in Indianapolis before his 2000 death. His descendants attend the reunions as well.

Indianapolis and the next three Navy ships on this list with the most military lost to enemy submarine torpedoes were all during World War II, as follows:

Dead Saved Death %	Name Type Date	Comments	Sinking Submarine's Fate
879 317 73.5%	Indian apolis Cruiser 7/30/1945	Japanese submarine, Philippine Sea; most deaths due to rescue delay; Captain survived but court-martialed, later exonerated	Type B3, 357' long, 31' beam, 17' draft; I-58 commissioned 1944; toted kaitens in career, which did some damage; surrendered 9/1945; Navy scuttled off Japan 4/1/1946
683 10 98.6%	Juneau Cruiser 11/13/1942	Japanese submarine, Guadalcanal; many died due to rescue delay; dead included Captain and the five Sullivan brothers	Type B1, 357' long, 31' beam, 17' draft; I-26 commissioned 1941; sank Army-chartered cargoman off CA 12/7/1941; USS destroyers sunk 10/26/1944 off Leyte, all 94 crew lost
675 230 74.6%	Dorche ster troops hip 3/3/1943	German submarine, Greenland; remembered for four Army chaplains, who gave their life jackets to soldiers, and drowned	Type VIIC, 220' long, 20' beam, 16' draft; U-223 commissioned 1942; British warships depth charges and gunfire sunk 3/30/1944, 27 of 50 crew lost
644 172 78.9%	Liscom e Bay carrier 1943	Japanese submarine, Butaritari Island; Messman Doris Miller, Captain I.D. Wiltsie, and Admiral Henri Mullinnix among lost	Type Kadai 346' long, 27' beam, 15' draft; I-175 commissioned 1938; USS destroyer escort hedgehog sank off Wotje Atoll 2/4/1944; all 100 crew lost
2,881 729 79.8%			

For these four largest above, this is an average of 720 men lost per torpedoed ship. Of the crew and military men on board the four ships, almost 80% died.

As already noted above, Indianapolis holds the USS record for most men lost at sea in combat, at 879. The 1,177 lost men on the Pennsylvania-class, 608' long and 97' beam and 29' draft, USS Arizona (1915 – 12/7/1941 Pearl Harbor, Oahu) battleship killed by a Japanese dive bomber bomb which exploded Arizona's forward ammunition magazine, is the record for deaths on a USS. This of course was 12/7/1941, Pearl Harbor Day. Arizona was not at sea, but in port. One thousand and five hundred and twelve crewmen were aboard, yielding a death rate of 77.8%. Seven hundred more crew were on weekend shore leave, so there was some luck here – the strike was at 7:30 on a Sunday morning.

For a USS aircraft carrier, the most killed was 807 sailors and 487 wounded on the Essex-class, 872' long, USS Franklin (1944 – 1966 scrapped). This was

3/19/1945. This was out of a crew complement of 2,600 (31% dead). Captain Leslie Gehres (1898 NY – 1975 San Diego) was one of the survivors.

Franklin was 50 miles from the Japanese mainland 3/19/1945, the closest of any U.S. carrier thus far in World War II. A Japanese dive bomber favored by a low ceiling just before dawn, dropped two, 550-pound, semi-armor-piercing bombs. Both connected. One bomb struck the flight deck centerline penetrating to the hangar deck, igniting fires through the second and third decks. The second bomb struck further aft and tore through two decks. At the time of the strike, Franklin had 31 armed and fueled aircraft warming up on her flight deck. Sixteen more were fueled on the hangar deck, and five of these were armed. Planes exploded. Munitions went off. The 1,294 casualties are a large number, considering that Franklin did not sink. Accounts vary as to whether or not the bomber escaped or was shot down. It appears that the pilot was not a kamikaze.

Temporary repairs on Franklin were made at Ulithi Atoll of the Caroline Islands, and then Pearl Harbor. She made it back to Brooklyn 4/1945, for extensive repairs. However, she never went to sea again. She was scrapped in 1966.

The Essex-class, 872' long, USS Bunker Hill (1943 – 1973 scrapped) was third to Franklin (bombs) and Liscome Bay (submarine torpedo, included on chart) in lives lost on an aircraft carrier, but way back. She was hit by two kamikazes over just 30 seconds apart 5/11/1945, when covering the invasion of Okinawa. She had 433 crew and airmen dead. She was under repair, when Japan surrendered.

These American warship fatality figures though may not impress the Royal Navy and its World War II experience, as follows:

- The Admiral-class, 862' long and 104' beam and 32' draft, HMS Hood (1920 - 5/24/1941 gun-sank in the Denmark Strait Battle) battlecruiser was the largest and most powerful warship in the world from its 1920 commissioning to 1940. Her nickname was *The Mighty Hood.* Hood and the new King George V-class, 745' long and 103' beam and 34' draft, HMS Prince of Wales (1941 - 12/10/1941 Japanese aircraft sank off Kuantan of the South China Sea, 327 of 1,521 crew lost {21%}) battleship were ordered to intercept the new, German Bismarck-class, 773' long and 118' beam and 31' draft, Bismarck (1940 – 5/27/1941 sank in North Atlantic, 2,091 of 2,205 crew lost {95%}) battleship, and the also new German Admiral Hipper-class, 697' and 71' beam and 24' draft, Prinz Eugen (1940 - 12/22/1946 capsized and sank due to damage from earlier nuclear tests) heavy cruiser. The Bismarck and Prinz Eugen were en route to the Atlantic Ocean, to attack convoys.

  The intercept was made. Bismarck and Prinz Eugen shelled Hood. It is thought that a 15" shell penetrated Hood's aft magazine which exploded. Hood sank in three minutes. One thousand and four hundred and fifteen men of a crew of 1,418 died. This is 99.79%. Unbelievably, the three survivors found each other in the ocean. The E-class HMS Electra (1934 – 2/27/1942 Japanese warships gun-sank in the Java Sea Battle, 121 of 173 crew lost {70%}) destroyer picked the three up two hours later.

Ordinary Signalman Ted Briggs (1923 England – 2008 England) was the last of these three Hood sailor survivors to die. Briggs first saw the HMS Hood at anchor off the River Tees when he was 12 years old. The River Tees is in northern England and flows into the North Sea. Briggs was enamored, to say the least. He volunteered the join the Royal Navy the next day. He was told he would have to wait until he was 15. He enlisted a week after turning 15. After training, he was assigned to Hood, 7/1939. Briggs served in the Royal Navy 35 years. He retired in 1973 as a Lieutenant.

Bismarck fled. Forty-two British ships chased. British ships and torpedo bombers sank Bismarck three days later as a cumulative effort, with more than 2,000 German sailors dying.

Hood's wreck was discovered in 2001, 9,200' down. One of her bells was recovered in 2012. That bell is on display at the National Museum of the Royal Navy, Portsmouth, England. This bell was first used on an earlier HMS Hood (1891 – 1914 sunk as a block ship in Portland Harbor), which was a pre-dreadnought battleship.

As noted above, Hood was considered the best for a twenty-year period. Its loss and of almost all its crew were a major psychological blow to Britons. The British were already much demoralized, as just coming off eight months of the Blitz (Germany's offensive bombing).

- German battleships gun-sank the Courageous-class, 735' long and 91' beam and 28' draft, HMS Glorious (1917 – 6/8/1940) battlecruiser, which had been converted to an aircraft carrier 1924-1930. Glorious was evacuating aircraft from Norway when sunk. One thousand, two hundred and seven British sailors died.

The 1,415 and 1,207 dead in the case of these two Royal Navy warships are way ahead of the American record of 879 for a warship at sea (USS Indianapolis cruiser in 1945) or 1,177 for a warship in port (USS Arizona battleship in 1941). As noted above though, the Germans lost 2,091 men on the Bismarck.

However for World War II warships, the 839' long and 128' beam and 36' draft, 31 miles per hour, Yamato-class IJN Yamato (1941 – 4/7/1945 off of Kyushu) battleship holds the record. USS carrier aircraft sank Yamato. Deaths were 2,498 of 2,778 crew, which is almost 90%. Another source though says that Yamato's deaths were 3,055 of 3,332 crew (almost 92%). Some were killed in the water when American planes strafed. Whichever, Yamato's death total is not just the record for a warship in World War II, but for all time. Bismarck at 2,091 is runner-up, again for a warship all time.

Fleet Commander Admiral Seiichi Ito (1890 Japan – 4/7/1945 off Okinawa) chose to go down with Yamato.

Yamato and sister ship IJN Musashi (1942 – 10/24/1944 USS carrier aircraft sank in Leyte Gulf Battle, 1,023 crew lost) were the heaviest and most powerfully armed battleships ever constructed. They displaced 72,800 tons at full load. Their armament included nine, forty-six centimeter (18.1") main guns. Japan made these two monsters to counter the numerically superior U.S. Navy battleship fleet. As it turned out, Japan took out all eight battleships anyway 12/7/1941 at Pearl Harbor, so that was not an issue. On top of that, naval warfare at this time was centered on aircraft carriers, not battleships.

These enormous death figures though pale compared to deaths of refugees when non-military ships were sunk in World War II. For example, Soviet Union submarines torpedo sank ships evacuating Germans in the Baltic Sea in 1945, killing 9,300 and 6,500 in two cases.

The U.S. Navy had 104,270 World War II casualties, compared to 66,241 for the Royal Navy. This is 57% more.

The Los Angeles-class, nuclear-powered, 362' long and 33' beam and 31' draft, USS Indianapolis (1980 – 1998 decommissioned) submarine, was named in honor of the World War II Indianapolis. Many survivors of the sunk World War II Cruiser Indianapolis attended the commissioning ceremony. A much smaller group (these men now in their 70s and 80s) attended the submarine's deactivation ceremony in 1998.

As of 2019, construction is underway on the Freedom-class, 378' long and 57' beam and 13' draft, USS Indianapolis littoral combat ship. This will be the fourth USS Indianapolis. It is scheduled to be commissioned in 2020.

These littoral ships are very fast at 54 miles per hour, and agile. They are made to function close to shore including for mine, surface ship, and submarine warfare.

24- REAR ADMIRAL RICHARD NOTT ANTRIM

Richard Antrim (1907 IN – 1969 AR) was a football star on his Peru, Indiana, high school team. He played football three years at the U.S. Naval Academy in Annapolis, graduating in 1931. He got married. He and Mary Jean had daughters, born 1933 and 1935.

His duties and training up to the start of World War II included the following:

- Served briefly in the 11th Naval District
- Served on the New York-class, 573' long and 95' beam and 30' draft, USS New York (1915 – 1945 target sunk) battleship, as fire control officer
- Began flight instruction 4/1932 at the Naval Air Station, Pensacola, Florida
- Served on the Patoka-class, 478' long and 60' beam and 26' draft, USS Salinas (1921 – 1946 sold) replenishment oiler
- Served on the Pyro-class, 483' long and 61' beam and 21' draft, USS Nitro (1921 – 1949 scrapped) ammunition supply ship
- Served on the Omaha-class, 556' long and 55' beam and 14' draft, USS Trenton (1924 – 1946 scrapped) light cruiser
- Assisted in fitting out the Portland-class, 610' long and 66' beam and 24' draft, USS Portland (1933 – 1959 scrapped) heavy cruiser; served as a division officer on Portland until the spring of 1936
- Served on the Wickes-class, 314' and 32' beam and 9' draft, USS Crowninshield (1919 – 1940 transferred to U.K.) destroyer, as First Lieutenant
- Took instruction in lighter-than-air flight at Naval Air Station, Lakehurst, New Jersey; received naval aviator designation as qualified for duty as an airship, kite, or free-balloon pilot
  Was on the mast to anchor the alighting Hindenburg-class, 804' long and 135' diameter, rigid-frame, LZ 129 Hindenburg (1936 – 5/6/1937) hydrogen airship at Lakehurst Naval Station in New Jersey 5/1937; the airship caught fire; 35 of the 97 (36%) aboard died; these were 13 passengers and 22 crew; most burned to death, some from jumping to death, some from smoke inhalation; a civilian lineman on the ground also died
- In 1938, served as Executive Officer of the Lapwing-class, 188' long and 36' beam and 10' draft, USS Bittern (1919 – 12/10/1941 Japanese aircraft bombed and damaged Manila Bay, scuttled to prevent capture) minesweeper
- In 1939, served as Executive Officer of the Clemson-class, 314' long and 32' beam and 9' draft, USS Pope (1920 – 3/1/1942 Japanese aircraft sunk in Java Sea Battle) destroyer

As noted above, Antrim was Executive Officer on two ships in 1938 and 1939. In the U.S. Navy, the Executive Officer is second in command of the ship. The

Executive Officer of course is always a commissioned officer. His or her rank varies.

The Empire of Japan conducted sneak attacks at fourteen Pacific Ocean locations 12/7/1941, which was a Sunday. Nine of the fourteen belonged to the U.S. The U.S. declared war on Japan the next day which was a Monday, and Germany and Italy a few days later.

Although only ages eight and ten at the time of the sneak attacks, daughters Judy and Nancy knew that it would be a long time before they saw Daddy again. They and their mother did not realize just how long it would be though. It turned out to be 3.75 years.

The USS Pope was in the Philippines at the time of the sneak attacks, which was one of the nine U.S. locations attacked. Pope was on neutrality duty near Manila, but distant from the Japanese attack that day. Again, Antrim was Executive Officer.

Pope got underway 12/11/1941 for Balikpapan, Borneo, Dutch East Indies (today, the Republic of Indonesia). Balikpapan is a seaport city on the east coast of Borneo. At the time of World War II, the area around Balikpapan was a major petroleum-producing area. The oil was shipped out on ocean-going tankers from Balikpapan Port.

On 1/9/1942, Pope and four other destroyers and two cruisers escorted the 488' long, Dutch MV Bloemfontein (1934 – 19??) transport from Darwin to the seaport city of Surabaya (Java, Dutch East Indies). This voyage was uneventful.

However, Pope's World War II career ran less than three months. During this time, she engaged in three major battles, as follows:

- 1/23-24/1942   Balikpapan Battle; the Japanese landed and seized the oil facilities, and held Balikpapan until the end of the War; however, the Allies sunk six Japanese transports and a patrol boat, suffering only damages to a destroyer and a submarine

  Pope delivered close-range attacks which helped delay the Japanese landings at Balikpapan; Antrim selected targets for guns and torpedoes, placing his shots accurately in striking Japanese ships

- 2/19-20/1942   Badung Strait Battle (off Bali Island, Dutch East Indies); the Allies had a destroyer sunk, and a destroyer and cruiser damaged; the Allies damaged three destroyers and a transport; this was yet another naval battle where the Imperial Japanese Navy demonstrated its superiority in night fighting; the Allies did delay the Japanese invasion of Bali; after this engagement, Pope's Commander reported that his Executive Officer (Antrim) was *highly deserving of commendation for the meritorious performance of his several duties before and throughout the action...* and cited Antrim as a *ready assistant in navigation fire control, and torpedo fire*; he recommended Antrim for an appropriate decoration, and furthermore for a destroyer command

- 3/1/1942   Second Java Sea Battle; Pope and two British ships slipped out of Surabaya at night in a desperate effort to escape the noose that the Japanese had tightened around the Dutch East Indies island of Java; Surabaya is the capital of Eastern Java; Japanese spotter aircraft off carriers though sighted them in the morning; the Japanese Task Force of four heavy cruisers and four destroyers was much larger, plus included distant aircraft carriers; the fate of the three Allied ships was as follows:
    - Japanese surface warships sank the York-class, 575' long and 58' beam and 17' draft, HMS Exeter (1931 – 3/1/1942) heavy cruiser with guns and torpedoes; Japanese rescued 652 of Exeter's crew (some died in the attack and sinking) including her captain; 152 of the 652 died in captivity (23%)
    - Japanese surface warships damaged the E-class, 329' long and 33' beam and 13' draft, HMS Encounter (1934 – 3/1/1942) destroyer; eight sailors died in the attack; her captain scuttled her; Japanese rescued 149; one fourth of these died in captivity
    - Japanese surface warships much damaged Antrim's USS Pope destroyer; she limped away and hid in a passing rain squall for an hour after the two British warships above were sunk; 12 dive bombers from Japanese aircraft carriers found Pope though and attacked; Pope was hit many times, and sank a few hours later

All the Pope crew except for one made it to lifeboats, and Pope's only motor whaleboat. The one dead sailor had been hit in the head by shrapnel. He died instantly. The wounded Antrim aided in collecting the lifeboats around the whaleboat, to facilitate distribution of food and water; and elude Japanese warships. He rallied the men, as of course fearing capture. That (capture) is what happened.

Imperial Japanese Naval Academy 1923 graduate Commander Shunsaku Kudo (1901 Japan – 1979 Japan) ordered the Fubuki-class, 389' long and 34' beam and 11' draft, IJN Ikazuchi (1932 – 4/13/1944 USS submarine torpedo sank off Guam, all 219 crew lost) destroyer and the also Fubuki-class IJN Inazuma (1932 – 5/14/1944 USS submarine torpedo sank Celebes Sea, 85 of 210 crew lost {40%}) destroyer to recover survivors from HMS Exeter, HMS Encounter, and USS Pope. Ikazuchi and Inazuma did so, collecting 442 American and British sailors, 20 hours to four days after their ships sank.

In ordering the rescue, Commander Kudo probably put his destroyers at risk, as USS submarines may have been in the area. Commander Kudo's humanitarian act so atypical of the Japanese even this early in the War was recognized much later, in books and a 2007 television documentary.

The Japanese destroyers delivered the prisoners of war (POWs) to the Japanese Army at Makassar, Celebes Islands, Dutch East Indies. To say the least, Commander Kudo's humanity was not followed on land. Many of these Brits and Americans died in captivity.

Antrim was later awarded the Navy Cross for his actions at Badung, Balikpapan, and the Java Sea. The citation reads as follows:

The President of the United States of America takes pleasure in presenting the Navy Cross to Commander [then Lieutenant] Richard Nott Antrim, United States Navy, for extraordinary heroism and distinguished service in the line of this profession as Executive Officer of the Destroyer USS Pope (DD-225), in combat with the enemy in the Java Sea on 3/1/1942, when his ship engaged an overwhelming number of Japanese surface and aircraft. An experienced destroyer officer, tried in two previous battles, Commander Antrim for a period of over five hours, under intense hostile fire and bombings, coolly, calmly, efficiently, with contempt for danger and with remarkable judgment carried out his vital battle tasks of navigation, fire direction, and damage control with a preciseness that left nothing to be desired, and in such a manner as to be highly instrumental in causing the enemy extensive damage. He was exact and sound in his advising his Commanding Officer regarding maneuvering, target selection, and the use of smoke. Finally, with his ship sinking as a result of enemy bombing, although bruised and shaken and painfully injured by an explosion within the ship, he continued with extraordinary heroism and perseverance in his immediate task of supervising the abandoning of the ship. Courageously exposing himself to low-flying enemy bombers, he directed the men over the side in such a manner that group targets would not be offered the enemy from the air, at the same time supervising the removal of the wounded from the ship and the launching of the one available boat. Later events indicated the soundness of his judgment and showed him to be a prime factor in the ultimate survival of not only the wounded men in the boat, but also the entire ship's complement still alive after the actual sinking. No deaths resulted from repeated enemy strafing attacks on the crew in the water. The boat, directed by Commander Antrim, after his being picked from the water, rounded up three life rafts and 151 survivors into a controllable group, and for a period of almost three days until their capture by a Japanese destroyer, this boat served to supply personnel in the sea with the necessary minimum life-sustaining requirements of water, food, and rest. There was no loss of life in the water. Commander Antrim's performance of duty in battle contributed immeasurably to the damage inflicted on the Japanese force and to his sound judgment are owed the lives of many who might otherwise have perished. His meritorious performance of duty and heroic conduct were at all times in keeping with the highest traditions of the United States Naval Service.

The POWs faced cruel, sadistic guards. This stemmed from the brainwashing on a convoluted interpretation of the samurai warrior bushido code. The code as revised by the Emperor and Japanese military generals and admirals was that death in battle was sublime, and wonderful things happened to the military man's spirit. Conversely, surrender and capture was shameful to self, family, community, country, and the Emperor. With this philosophy, those enemy that Japan captured were considered inhuman; simply as they did not fight to the death. The Japanese did not provide adequate food or clothing or housing or medical care, beat and tortured daily, and sometimes executed. Furthermore, the guards and their superiors did so, without remorse. Again, the Japanese propaganda program that capture was so shameful so this abuse appropriate, was unbelievably that effective.

In 4/1942 when imprisoned at Makassar, Antrim and hundreds of other POWs observed a Japanese guard brutally beating American Lieutenant Junior Grade Allan Fisher for some supposed transgression, with his swagger stick. Lieutenant Antrim stepped forward and asked the guard for mercy with words and gestures. Antrim's request was denied. The guards quickly created a kangaroo court, and sentenced Fisher to 50 lashes from a thick, raw hawser. The already severely beaten Fisher was unconscious by the fifteenth lash, and bleeding. The guards also kicked Fisher during this abuse.

Antrim stepped in again and stated that he would take the rest of Fisher's punishment, this to save Fisher's life. This action and offer stunned the guards. They stopped beating Fisher, who survived. As to why Antrim's intervention did not result in him being treated the same or even executed (along with Fisher) -- who knows, as such was often the way of the Japanese military with POWs. Antrim was later awarded the Medal of Honor, for this action. The citation reads as follows:

> *For conspicuous gallantry and intrepidity at the risk of his life above and beyond the call of duty while interned as a prisoner of war of the enemy Japanese in the city of Makassar, Celebes, Dutch East Indies, in 4/1942. Acting instantly on behalf of a naval officer who was subjected to a vicious clubbing by a frenzied Japanese guard venting his insane wrath upon the helpless prisoner, Commander (then Lieutenant) Antrim boldly intervened, attempting to quiet the guard and finally persuading him to discuss the charges against the officer. With the entire Japanese force assembled and making extraordinary preparations for the threatened beating, and with the tension heightened by 2,700 Allied prisoners rapidly closing in, Commander Antrim courageously appealed to the fanatic enemy, risking his own life in a desperate effort to mitigate the punishment. When the other had been beaten unconscious by 15 blows of a hawser and was repeatedly kicked by three soldiers to a point beyond which he could not survive, Commander Antrim gallantly stepped forward and indicated to the perplexed guards that he would take the remainder of the punishment, throwing the Japanese completely off balance in their amazement and eliciting a roar of acclaim from the suddenly inspired Allied prisoners. By his fearless leadership and valiant concern for the welfare of another, he not only saved the life of a fellow officer and stunned the Japanese into sparing his own life but also brought about a new respect for American officers and men and a great improvement in*

camp living conditions. His heroic conduct throughout reflects the highest credit upon Commander Antrim and the U.S. Naval Service.

In the years that followed until the end of the War, torture and abuse and executions continued.

Antrim was forced to lead a labor detail assigned to construct slip trenches, for protection during air raids. He made suggestions for *improvements* to the design and construction, which the Japanese accepted. Under close guarding, the POWs dug the trenches, in the shape of the letters *US*. The initials though were so large, that not readily recognized except at altitude. U.S. bomber pilots saw the initials and knew to not bomb there, as American POWs present. Of course if the Japanese had recognized the letters, Antrim would most likely have been tortured, before executed. For his cleverness and leadership, Antrim was awarded the Bronze Star. That citation reads as follows:

> *For heroic service, while a Japanese Prisoner of War. He was forced to take charge of a labor party, and assigned the task of constructing slit trenches for bomb protection. Through self-effacing courage and sheer audacity of purpose, he caused to be constructed under the very eyes and alert surveillance of Japanese guards, a huge sign "U.S." This was done by rearranging the construction work of the slit trenches from the Japanese approved plan to one of his own devising, after causing the Japanese to concur in the changes suggested. The sign, if recognized by the Japanese, would have resulted in Antrim's immediate beheading, but Antrim's well-thought plan would result in Allied photographs indicating the occupants of the trenches and thus save hundreds of prisoners' lives.*

Antrim survived imprisonment. He and his fellow prisoners were repatriated 9/1945. He was placed on recovery leave. As for all POWs, he attended the Repatriated POW Refresher Course, 5/1946. The purpose of this training and counseling course was to assist former POWs in dealing with posttraumatic stress disorder, developed due to such harsh conditions as a POW in the Pacific Theater.

For the record, the below statement is from Japanese Army Regulations, in place at the time of World War II:

> *Prisoners of war shall be treated with a spirit of good will, and shall never be subjected to cruelties or humiliation.*

President Harry Truman (1884 MO – 1972 MO) presented the Medal of Honor and Bronze Star to Antrim at a White House ceremony, 1/30/1947.

Antrim took more pilot training at Naval Air Station, Lakehurst, New Jersey. He completed a course at the Naval War College, Newport, Rhode Island. He served at the Fleet Sonar School in San Diego in the summer of 1947.

Antrim returned to sea, commanding the Gearing-class, 391' long and 41' beam and 12' draft, USS Turner (1945 – 1970 scrapped) destroyer. As noted above, his Captain on the USS Pope had recommended Antrim for a destroyer command, after the 2/1942 Badung Strait Battle.

He took more training at Naval Air Station Lakehurst, preparatory to assuming duties of Assistant for the Lighter-than-Air Planning and Programs Office of the Chief of Naval Operations, Washington, D.C., 12/1948. He next transferred to the

Policy Advisory Staff, Department of State, and then the Psychological Strategy Board. The latter was formed 4/4/1951 to research methods and recommend covert actions for the Korean War.

Antrim returned to sea yet again, commanding the Haskell-class, 455' long and 62' beam and 24' draft, USS Montrose (1944 – 1970 scrapped) attack transport. From there, it was back to Washington, for a brief tour of duty as Head, Amphibious Warfare Matters Section, Office of the Chief of Naval Operations. He retired 4/1/1954. He served 23 years (1926-1954), including for the Korean War as well as World War II. He was advanced to Rear Admiral on the retired list, on the basis of his combat awards.

Antrim and his wife moved to the small town of Mountain Home, Arkansas; where he ran a small tour boat business. Mountain Home is in northern Arkansas, near the Missouri border. Army Air Forces veteran and friend Tom Dearmore (1927 AR – 2004) asked Antrim about his medals. Dearmore was editor of the local newspaper. Antrim did explain his medals, and why they were awarded. However, he asked Antrim not to publish anything in the newspaper. Thirty years after Antrim's death though in 1999, Dearmore finally did write the story up.

Antrim's daughter Judy Antrim Laylon later made this statement:

> My father was a very modest man and probably would not have contributed the information about his heroism, but I feel this generation who has not really experienced war, needs to know about the people who came before them, and what they did to preserve our freedom.

Antrim was buried at Arlington National Cemetery.

The Oliver Hazard Perry-class, 445' long and 45' beam and 22' draft, USS Antrim (1981 – 1997 transferred to Turkey) guided missile frigate was named in his posthumous honor. Family members including his wife attended the launching and commissioning ceremonies.

25- COLONEL WENDELL W. FERTIG

Most historians recognize that Norse-Icelandic explorer and merchant Bjarni Herjolfsson was the first European to sail to the Americas. Herjolfsson sailed to Canada when blown off course by a storm in 986. He chose not to land though.

Herjolfsson was followed by Norse explorer Leif Eriksson (970 Iceland – 1020 Greenland) in 1000. Eriksson landed and wintered over. Other Viking/Scandinavian types sailed to Canada in the next 11 years.

Explorer Christopher Columbus (1451 Genoa – 1506 Spain) made the voyage after a 483-year gap. He sailed west under the Spanish flag from southwestern Spain to find a new trade route to the East Indies. This was 1492. Spain wanted to enter the spice trade with Asia. One of his sailor lookouts spotted land. This was one of the Bahama Islands – maybe the 63 square mile San Salvador Island. San Salvador is 376 miles east-southeast of Miami.

Of note, Columbus later claimed that he with his own 41-year-old eyes had spotted a light on land several hours before his own lookout, thereby claiming for himself the lifetime pension promised by the Spanish royalty to the first person to sight land. Whatever.

Anyway, Columbus landed an exploration party.

On this voyage and later ones, Columbus landed on several islands. He claimed these islands as belonging now to the Kingdom of Spain. The locals were Tainos. The Tainos were not given the option of remaining independent. The natives were told that their new highnesses were a King Ferdinand V (1452 Spain – 1516 Spain) and a Queen Isabella I (1451 Spain – 1504 Spain), who lived in a 117-room castle in a place called Madrid of the country of Spain on the peninsula of Iberia on a continent called Europe. This did not confuse them necessarily, as they did not understand Spanish. When some learned Spanish, such information was hard to grasp, to say the least.

Spain and other countries began more colonies later, in the New World. The early settlers were mostly farmers, ranchers, soldiers, and priests.

Ferdinand Magellan (1480 Portugal – 1521 Philippines, killed in battle) sailed to the Philippines in 1521, also under the Spanish flag. He claimed the islands for Spain. The Filipinos were told that their new highnesses were a King Charles V (1500 Netherlands – 1558 Spain) and a Queen Joanna (1479 Spain - 1555 Spain) – but mostly Charles in reality, as Joanna was mentally insane. They were told (as others before) that their new rulers lived in a castle in a city called Madrid of the country of Spain on the Iberian Peninsula on a continent called Europe. As in the case above with the Tainos, the Filipinos were probably just as confused by such statements.

Spain colonized some of the largest of the 7,641 Philippine Islands, beginning in 1565.

The U.S. won the ten-week, 1898 Spanish-American War. The main issue had to do with Cuban independence from Spain. Per the negotiated treaty, Cuba became a protectorate of the U.S. The U.S. set Cuba on the path to independence, which happened in 1902.

Also per the treaty, Spain ceded ownership of Puerto Rico, Guam, and the Philippines to the U.S., as well as Cuba. For the Philippines, the U.S. paid Spain $20 million ($599 million in 2019 money) for made infrastructure.

This resulted in increased trade and business between the U.S. and Philippines. Some Americans moved to the Philippines, connected with their employment. A number of international companies had operations in the Philippines. These were mostly American, British, and Australian companies. Some foreigners worked for Filipino companies, in the Philippines.

The U.S. replaced its military government of the Philippines territory with a civilian government in 1901. It was called the Philippine Islands Insular Government, or the Second Philippine Government. The U.S. gave the Philippines Commonwealth status in 1935; as a step to transitioning to independence and self-rule, ten years later.

Wendell Fertig (1900 CO – 1975 CO) graduated from the Colorado School of Mines (Golden, Colorado), as a civil engineer. He took military classes in college. From this program, he held a Reserves commission in the U.S. Army Corps of Engineers; rank of Captain.

After college, Fertig wed. They had two daughters. The family moved to the Philippines in 1936, where he worked for a company as a civil engineer. He was based on Samar, the third largest Philippine Island. At 5,184 square miles, Samar is a little less than 2% the size of Texas.

U.S. War and State Department analysts (and most others, for that matter) had anticipated war with the Empire of Japan; based mainly upon Japan's imperialism, extreme belligerence, and unfathomable and countless abuses of Chinese military men and civilians in the 1930s and into the 1940s. Furthermore, the U.S. also reasoned that the Philippines or Thailand would be one of the first places that Japan would attack. As it turned out the experts were right. Both the Philippines and Thailand were sneak attacked 12/7/1941. The experts though missed another dozen locations and targets (see below) that day.

Per this thinking, the Army called Captain Fertig up 6/1/1941, to be based in the Philippines. This was more than six months before the sneak attacks. Engineers were needed to prepare the U.S. for war in the Pacific Theater. The fact that Fertig was already in the Philippines, an engineer, and knew the country (geography, language, culture, etc.); most likely hastened his call-up.

Captain Fertig's first Army assignment was as Assistant Engineer, Bataan Field Area. Bataan is a coastal province on Luzon, which is the largest and most populous Philippine island. At 42,458 square miles, Luzon is 16% the size of Texas. The country's capital city of Manila and its most populous city of Quezon City are on Luzon.

Luzon Force Commander Major General Edward King (1884 Atlanta – 1958 GA) next sent Fertig, to the North Luzon Area.

By 11/1941, Fertig was General Headquarters Construction Section Chief. He spent most of his time overseeing construction and improvement of airfields on

Luzon and other Philippine Islands. Again, this was in anticipation of defending the Philippines if Japan should invade.

The Empire of Japan invaded and occupied the key and larger islands of the Philippines, beginning 12/1941 and into the spring of 1942. During the occupation, Japan forcefully established the Philippines as a collaborator state, deposing the Second Philippine government. The provisional Philippine government was established in exile in the United States, until the War ended in 1945.

Filipino independence and self-rule did happen though, the year after World War II ended. This was the Third Philippine Republic, as a sovereign state. The country later changed its name to the Republic of the Philippines. As mentioned above, the plan in 1935 was for the Philippines to assume self-rule in 1945. The 45-month Pacific War delayed independence, but only by a year.

In late 1941 including after the 12/7/1941 sneak attacks and also into 1/1942, the wives and children of military men based in the Philippines were evacuated back to America. These included Fertig's wife and daughters. This was done for the obvious reason of relieving the concerns of these military men, about the safety and welfare of their families.

The families of American civilian workers were not evacuated (some returned to the U.S. on their own though), as it was thought that doing so would greatly decrease the morale of Filipinos. Also, the U.S. assumed that if Japan should occupy the Philippines, that civilians who had no connections to military personnel would be allowed to go home, or at least not harmed. Neither turned out to be the case.

As already noted, the U.S. assumptions about War with Japan, and Japan attacking U.S. military fortifications and harbors in the Philippines early on were correct. The Empire of Japan sneak attacked thirteen locations in or on the Pacific Ocean 12/7, 8/1941. Nine of these thirteen locations (two of the nine were isolated ships) belonged to the United States. Japan as usual did not bother to warn the victims (declare war), in violation of the international rules of war. The 1907 Hague Convention addressed the requirement to declare war in its *Convention Relative to the Opening of Hostilities* statements. These clauses describe the international actions a country should perform, before opening hostilities. Article 1 states: *The Contracting Powers recognize that hostilities between themselves must not commence without previous and explicit warning, in the form either of a reasoned declaration of war or of an ultimatum with conditional declaration of war.* Japan took a pass on issuing a warning, as it had done in the past.

The attacks were all on the same day, within nine hours of each other. The last attacked was the Philippines. Two days are shown, as the locations were on both sides of the International Date Line. The International Date Line is an imaginary line from the North Pole to the South Pole, which marks the change from one calendar day to the next. It roughly follows the 180° line of longitude, through the middle of the Pacific Ocean. But again, the attacks were all on the same day. The attacked thirteen sites (or ships) were as follows:

- Nine U.S. possessions
  - Storming and capture of a 159' long USS river gunboat and its crew when berthed at Shanghai Harbor; this little Yangtze River gunboat was the only USS that Japan captured in World War II; for good measure, the Japanese also gun-sank a 177' HMS river gunboat in Shanghai Harbor, at about the same time; if counting this British warship, it is fourteen sneak attacks instead of thirteen
  - IJN submarine gun-sank an Army-chartered, 250' long freighter off California
  - Howland and Baker Islands of the Phoenix Islands of the U.S. Minor Outlying Islands were bombed, these two islands are 43 miles apart
  - Five U.S. military installations (harbors, airfields, bases) on five Pacific Ocean islands; these five islands were Oahu (Pearl Harbor), Guam, Midway, Wake, and Philippines
- Three British Crown colonies – Malaya, Hong Kong, and Singapore
- Thailand

Japan's surprise attacks without declaring war ended the United States' isolationist attitude, left over from losing 116,700 men in uniform (almost 46% in combat) and another 204,000 wounded or made ill (many with permanent disabilities) in World War I. Congress declared war on Japan the next day, which was a Monday. The peace period for America was a little more than 23 years, from the World War I Armistice Day to the day of the sneak attacks.

To repeat again, the American government's assumption that American civilians in the Philippines would be allowed to leave and/or not harmed if Japan attacked and occupied the Philippines, was definitely not correct. This was the case for all foreign civilians (excepting Japanese) living in the Philippines, caught up in the War. Besides Americans, these were mostly British and Australian civilians. This harm to Western citizens caught in the Philippines although great, was miniscule to the harm done to Filipinos. Five percent of the civilian population died due to the actions of the Japanese, during the more than three years occupation. This was 900,000 Filipinos. Atrocities were innumerable, and beyond heinous. Many Filipinos were pressed into forced labor. Filipina children and women were forced to be sex slaves.

As noted above, Japan air attacked the Philippines 12/8/1941, plus landed some troops that day. This was nine hours after the attack on Oahu (Pearl Harbor). The U.S. at the time controlled the Philippines, and had many military installations there. These included forts, air bases, harbors, shipyards, fuel tank farms, etc.

General Douglas MacArthur (1880 AR – 1964 DC) was the Commander of U.S. and Filipino forces in the Philippines. However, these combined forces and armaments were not adequate to defend the Philippines in the case of a large, well-equipped assault.

On top of that, appropriate Allied defensive actions (much less offensive actions) after learning of the Oahu attack (Pearl Harbor) were faulty, allowing Japan easy success. For example, American bombers and fighters at airfields on Luzon were on the ground when Japanese bombers and fighters arrived. Many were destroyed, as sitting ducks.

MacArthur was a brilliant General. But all brilliant generals goof up once or twice. MacArthur's poor response even after being advised of the Oahu (Pearl Harbor) attack resulted in disaster for the Philippines. This was the case, even though MacArthur had a nine-hour warning.

Japan landed more troops 12/20/1941, taking Davao City on Mindanao Island. Mindanao Island is the second largest and southernmost major island in the Philippines. At 40,360 miles, it is 15% the size of Texas.

Allied forces were overwhelmed. These were mostly Filipinos led by U.S. Army officers, but also some American military. They lacked food, medicine, clothing, ammunition, weapons, vehicles, fuel, etc. Reinforcements of any amount and type were not on the way. The Japanese had blocked Allied forces' communication and travel between the Philippine Islands, so the troops on each island were forced to operate independently, unable to support the other. As a result of the above, the Allies were more in defense than offense, and mostly in retreat.

President Franklin Roosevelt (1882 NY – 4/12/1945 GA, cerebral hemorrhage) ordered General MacArthur to escape to Australia. On the night of 3/12, 13/1942, several wooden hull, 17 crew, triple engine, fast-attack, 80' long patrol torpedo boats (PT boats) ferried him and his family and his staff from Corregidor to Mindanao. From Mindanao, four-engine Boeing B-17 bombers flew the group on to Australia. The remaining hapless generals in order to prevent a massacre, surrendered their troops over seven weeks as follows:

4/9/1942	The above-mentioned Luzon Force Commander Major General Edward King surrendered on the Bataan Peninsula; again, the Bataan Peninsula is part of the largest and most populous island of Luzon
5/6/1942	Philippine Department Commander Major General Jonathan Wainwright (1883 WA – 1953 TX) surrendered on Corregidor Island; the twelve square mile Corregidor Island is located at the entrance of Manila Bay; due to its location, fortifications (coastal artillery and ammunition magazines) had been installed to defend the entrance to Manila Bay and the capital city of Manila, which is 30 miles inland; these fortifications included ground to ship guns, anti-aircraft guns, mortars, etc.; installations on Corregidor and neighboring smaller islands included Fort Mills, Fort Drum, Fort Hughes, and Fort Frank
	Corregidor also was the location of the 831' long and 24' wide and 18' high Malinta Tunnel (with 24 lateral tunnels) made by the Army Corps of Engineers 1922-1934; it was used as MacArthur's headquarters, the base for the Filipino government, for bomb-resistant shelter and storage, and as a hospital; the Japanese also used the Tunnel, after capturing Corregidor
5/10/1942	Major General William Sharp (1885 SD – 1947 GA) surrendered on Mindanao Island

5/27/1942   Brigadier General Guy Fort (1879 MI – 11/11/1942 Mindanao, firing squad) surrendered on Mindanao Island

To sum up, the Japanese overran the Philippines within the first six months after the 12/7/1941 sneak attacks, as a much more organized and superior force compared to the combined American and Filipino troops.

From the above, General Fort was the last General to surrender. He commanded the 81st Division of the Philippine Army, which was under the control of the U.S. Army. Fort withdrew the 81st to the Lanao province, on the west coast of Mindanao. He added to the 81st by organizing and outfitting several battalions of Moro soldiers. The Moros were and are today the Muslim population of the Philippines. Fort strategized a defense. However he foresaw defeat, so also trained his division in guerrilla warfare. The 81st began fighting 4/29/1942, against the better-organized and equipped Japanese army. Fort closed a main road on Mindanao with demolitions, which delayed the Japanese Army's advance.

Fort's superior General Sharp ordered him to surrender his troops, to avoid annihilation. Fort protested this order, but did comply 5/27/1942 as noted above. The 81st was the last U.S./Filipino Army group to surrender. Some of Fort's soldiers though, probably with his encouragement, chose to escape into the jungle and hills instead of surrendering. These were mostly soldiers from the Maranao tribe, who were Moros (Muslims). The Maranaos lived in the southern part of Mindanao. General Fort arranged for them to sneak off with rifles and equipment. The Maranaos put this equipment to good use, in guerrilla warfare.

In 11/1942, the Japanese ordered the now imprisoned Brigadier General Fort to communicate with the Maranao Moros, who had started a new guerilla rebellion against the occupying forces. Specifically, Japanese military commanders told Fort to tell the Moro that since the U.S. Army had surrendered, they also must surrender. Fort refused to do so, despite torture. Lieutenant Colonel Yoshinari Tanaka (???? – 4/9/1949 Tokyo, executed by hanging) ordered Fort's execution, by firing squad. This was less than six months after his capture. General Fort is the only American-born General officer to be executed by enemy forces.

After the War, Tanaka was captured, tried, convicted, and sentenced to death for the execution of Fort and three other Americans, and other war crimes. He was hung 3.7 years after V-J Day.

During this time, Fertig's duties had segued to the destruction of American supplies left behind by the retreating Americans, and destruction of roads and bridges. This was to prevent use, by the soon to be occupying Japanese Army. As an extension, this included pushing his new Dodge sedan off a pier into Manila Bay, received in better times. The essence of civil engineering of course is building infrastructure, so this destruction work was different for him.

General King had sent Fertig to assist Mindanao Force Commander General William Sharp. As noted above, Mindanao is the second largest Philippine Island, and the southernmost of the major islands of the archipelago. It is about one-seventh the size of Texas, in area. By the end of 4/1942, Fertig was stranded on Mindanao. This was by apparently a mix of bad luck such as aircraft failures when shuttled between islands, or aircraft getting lost so landing at the wrong place, or as higher-ranking officers or even civilians taking all the aircraft seats, or maybe by his own choosing to some degree. By this time, he had been promoted twice, to Major and then Lieutenant Colonel.

Fertig knew that General Sharp who commanded Allied troops on Mindanao was likely to retreat and then surrender, as no support was coming. He considered surrendering as well, and hoping for humane treatment as a hopefully short-time prisoner of war (POW) of the Japanese. This would be until either the U.S. liberated the Philippines, or the U.S. negotiated a prisoner exchange or release agreement. Knowing well the proclivity of the Japanese in abusing massive numbers of civilians as well as military men (mainly from their innumerable crimes in China, not to mention the reports of more of the same since the 12/7/1941 sneak attacks) in other countries including the Philippines, Fertig second thought. He chose to flee to the hills and jungle. He searched several weeks for General Sharp, but never found him. He then finally heard that General Sharp had surrendered with his Mindanao forces, 5/10/1942.

As the highest-ranking officer hiding out (in Mindanao at least as far as he knew, Fertig decided his mandate was to fight with whatever resources he could develop. He wrote the following in his diary:

> I am called on to lead a resistance movement against an implacable enemy under conditions that make victory barely possible, even under the best circumstances. But I feel that I am indeed a Man of Destiny, that my course is charted and that only success lies at the end of the trail. I do not envision failure. It is obvious that the odds are against us and we will not consistently win, but if we are to win only part of the time and gain a little each time, in the end we will be successful.

So as a 41-year-old civil engineer and Army reservist who had never had the benefit of even boot camp and whose active service had been as an engineer, Fertig became a guerrilla, and then quickly a guerrilla leader – on Mindanao.

Fertig grew a goatee, thinking that would make him look older and wiser – important attributes to Filipinos. To the Filipinos in fact, he became known as Tatay (Father in Filipino).

Fertig also reasoned that he needed a higher rank. Such would be necessary to recruit individuals, and also to have some sway with other guerrilla groups. He self-promoted to Brigadier General (one star). By the way, this later got out to MacArthur and his staff in Australia, which did not sit well with Command.

Many of the emerging guerrilla forces at that time were simply bandit groups. They pretended to fight the Japanese. In reality though, they used the collapse of the Filipino government to set themselves up as rulers of small areas. Their hope was that by displaying a show of unity and force, that the Japanese would ignore them for the duration of the War in favor of bigger and/or easier targets. These fiefdoms competed for territory and authority.

On 9/12/1942, the leader of one such group contacted Fertig, in an effort to gain control over the entire island of Mindanao. Fertig consented, but then used his knowledge of the Filipino people and the current situation in Mindanao to eventually take over the command of that group. He did likewise with other guerrilla groups, as well.

Fertig was not power hungry. He just knew that island-wide leadership and order would be necessary, to have an effect. Also, he realized that cooperation with the dominant Allied military power (this of course was the United States, with Australia a much distant second) would go better, American to American (the language barrier, for one major factor). In fact, the U.S. was the only Allied country with any strength in the area, and this did not change for the duration of the Pacific War. In fact again, no country was of much ongoing aid to the U.S. in the Pacific Theater during World War II.

The occupying Japanese confiscated food, clothing, vehicles, etc., from the Filipinos. This along with the Japanese bombings, destruction by retreating American troops, deprivations by bandit bands, inability to communicate, inability to move in own area (and this varied much island to island) much less travel between islands, and hoarding by civilians -- greatly reduced available war supplies. Fertig used his engineering skills, plus borrowed skills from other escaped Americans and resisting Filipinos, and his knowledge of the Filipino people; to improvise in many ways. Examples included the following:

- Brewing tuba (this is palm alcohol) from coconut palms to provide alcohol, to fuel gasoline vehicles
- Recharging batteries by soaking them in tuba
- Using fence wire (conductors) and soda bottles (insulators) to make a telegraph
- Making ammunition out of curtain rods, for .30 caliber rifles
- Shaving steel from automobile springs, and curling the steel to make recoiling springs for rifles
- Printing money in both English and the local language, using wooden blocks
- Making soap from coconut oil and wood ashes; the soap was traded for sugar, used to make alcohol for fuel
- Had fishermen tow Japanese mines ashore, made gunpowder from the explosive amatol in the mines
- Made radios from parts scrounged from old radio receivers (vacuum tubes) and movie projectors (speakers); this allowed communication with guerrillas on other islands; on 1/31/1943, the Navy radio monitoring station in San Francisco answered their call sign

These radios were a critical accomplishment, as U.S. military commands at first in the Pacific did not know the level of guerrilla activities (even if any), on the major Philippine Islands.

Early on, the Japanese announced that they had killed Fertig in a bombing raid. This was MacArthur's first awareness of Fertig and his guerrilla activities on Mindanao. However, Command thought that Japan had made up the story on Fertig and his led resistance and killing him; as propaganda. MacArthur assumed that Fertig had surrendered with the others or that he had been dead for months. More intelligence in the next few weeks though, revealed the efforts of Fertig and his guerilla fighters.

With this tenuous confirmation, MacArthur appointed Fertig as Commanding Officer of the Tenth Military District, on Mindanao. During the initial exchange of messages, MacArthur disallowed any promotion of American armed forces personnel in the Philippines to General rank. As a result, Lieutenant Colonel (in actuality) Fertig self-breveted to Brigadier General, compromised. He demoted himself in rank, to Colonel. However, he continued to wear the one star of a Brigadier General. He had a Filipino metalsmith fashion these stars.

As already noted, Fertig had little in the way of supplies – food, fuel, medical supplies, clothing including shoes, weapons, ammunition, etc. The Filipino guerrillas' rifles were mostly World War I surplus and needed replacement parts, not to mention ammunition.

These were major problems, but paled compared to the rawness of the guerrillas he recruited. The guerrillas were more irregular than most irregulars. They needed much training, and discipline.

The common approach when the Japanese attacked or even approached was to flee. This was understandable, as the Japanese were a regular army. The Japanese had vehicles, fuel, weapons (rifles, tanks, artillery, gunboats, etc.), food, clothing, medicine and medical equipment, etc. Most of the guerrillas had little to fight with. In some cases, their only clothing was what they were wearing. Many were barefoot.

Another reason to flee the Japanese, was that all Filipinos were aware (many personally) of the atrocities rendered by Japanese soldiers on Filipino citizens. All Filipinos whether they had been victimized or not, were aware of the atrocities – enslaving thousands, beatings, torturing, executions, children and women raped, etc. These were good reasons to run, unless the odds were evened up somehow.

Fertig's first approach was to recruit other Americans who had avoided surrender by taking to the hills or jungle, or the very few that had escaped from POW camps. These he used to train the Filipinos. Some of these Americans though refused to join up preferring to escape to Australia (by submarine), and re-join the regular Army, Army Air Forces, Navy, or Marines (whichever was the case). Fertig did assist in returning these Americans to Australia, if possible.

American airmen sometimes had to bail out of both carrier and land-based planes or crash-landed when Japanese fighters or anti-aircraft guns on ships or land shot them down, or they developed mechanical problems, or if they ran out of fuel. Often, they were rescued by guerrillas, either on land or water. These Fertig generally did not give the opportunity to sign on as guerrillas, even though some volunteered to do so. He sent them back as he knew airmen were much needed.

Fighter pilot William Dyess (1916 TX – 12/22/1943 CA; twin engine, single crew, Lockheed P-38 Lightning crashed on a training flight) was one of these airmen. Dyess was a Squadron Commander of a fighter pursuit group, based on Bataan. As Squadron Commander, he gave his single engine, Curtiss P-40E Warhawk to another pilot, who escaped.

Dyess transitioned to an infantry officer as his only choice. He was captured 4/9/1942 on Bataan when Major General King surrendered his forces. He survived the 65 mile Bataan Death March which began the next day. The death estimates for this march are up to 18,000.

Dyess was imprisoned at Camp O'Donnell (central Luzon region), and then transferred to Cabanatuan 10/26/1942 (also in the central Luzon region). He and other POWs were transported by ship to the Davao Penal Colony on Mindanao, arriving 11/7/1942. Dyess, nine other Americans, and two Filipinos escaped 4/4/1943, after a year in captivity. The ten Americans were three Army, three Army Air Forces, three Marines, and one Navy.

The twelve evaded recapture for several weeks, and then linked up with Fertig's guerrillas. Seven of the ten Americans were transported out by submarine over the next seven months to Australia, and then back to the United States for rehabilitation. Of the three who stayed behind to continue guerrilla fighting, the enemy killed one. This was Army Air Forces Engineering Officer Leo Boelens (1914 – 1/22/1944 Mindanao).

Back at the Davao Penal Colony, the Japanese beheaded 12 POWs in retaliation for the escape. This definitely put a damper on POW future thoughts of escape.

Dyess was transferred out on the Tambor-class, 307' long and 27' beam and 15' draft, USS Trout (1940 - 2/29/1944 lost northwest of Philippines, either sank by depth charges or struck by own torpedo on a circular route, all 81 crew lost) submarine to Australia 7/1943.

Lieutenant Colonel Dyess died when training on a new twin engine fighter, in preparation for returning to the Pacific War. It crash-landed just after takeoff, when an engine caught fire. Dyess Air Force Base, seven miles southwest of Abilene, Texas, is named in his honor.

Jack McLaren (1902 Scotland – 1956 New Guinea, accident when a rotten tree fell on him) should be mentioned as well. He fought for the British Army in World War I. After that *War to End all Wars*, he moved to Australia. He joined the Australian Army 3/1941. He was captured with all other Australian troops in Singapore 2/1942, age 39. He escaped, was captured, and escaped again. During this time on marches, he observed thousands and thousands of mutilated, murdered, and raped Chinese of all ages; by the Japanese.

McLaren eventually made it to Mindanao, and joined Fertig's guerrilla forces. Fertig offered McLaren submarine transport to Australia. McLaren refused, as he knew the Australian Army would not let him fight due to his age (now forty years old). He so hated the inhumane Japanese that he chose to join Fertig's guerillas, and fight the Japanese. He spent most of the rest of World War II as a coastwatcher and guerrilla leader. He participated in numerous raids on Japanese posts. He sometimes commanded small, heavily armed (machine guns and mortars) hit and run boats – shooting at Japanese supply ships and shore installations at great risk.

As a coastwatcher, McLaren radioed location information on a Japanese troops transport. American submarines sank the transport, killing most of the 3,000 soldiers and crew aboard. The Filipinos finished off those who survived, as they floated ashore.

By this time, the Japanese were well aware of Fertig's leadership role. They put an award up for his capture or death.

Fertig field promoted some Filipinos. So some Filipino Navy and Army men and even a few civilians, now found themselves as (sort of) U.S. Army enlisted men or officers. MacArthur eventually approved all Fertig's enlistments and promotions. He did so, even though Lieutenant Colonel Courtney Whitney (1897 DC – 1969) advised against it. Whitney was MacArthur's staff officer for Filipino civilian affairs.

The same was the case, in regard to American military men who had chosen to not surrender or escaped. Fertig sometimes promoted them in the Army, even though some had been Navy or Marines. Even some American civilians now found themselves enlisted in the Army, courtesy of Lieutenant Colonel Fertig.

Age 13, 14, and 15 Larry, Frank, and Charles Smith's father had a thriving business in Dansalan on the northern part of Mindanao, until the Japanese showed up. The Japanese were taking civilians including Americans to concentration camps, so the family fled to the hills. They hid out for eight months. Charles now age 16, heard about Colonel Fertig, commanding guerrilla forces. He sought Fertig out and joined up. His two younger brothers followed shortly after. As they knew the terrain and were fluent in Filipino, they were major assets. They scavenged for weapons; helped unload supplies from submarines; harassed the enemy in surprise attacks; scouted perimeter zones; and spied on Japanese ship movements from the vantage point of Mount Malindang, an extinct volcano. At 7,887', Mount Malindang is the highest point on Mindanao.

Middle brother Frank Smith was killed in 1944, on a mission on the Liangan River in the Lanao province of Mindanao. He was hit by fire from a Japanese gunboat.

After World War II, oldest brother Charles Smith (1927 – 2013) enlisted (re-enlisted more or less) in the Army in 1946 and made it his career. He served in Greece during the 1946-1949 Greek Civil War, and then in the Korean War. He retired from the military as a Master Sergeant in 1968, age 41.

From 6/1942 to 5/1944, Fertig created and commanded the Mindanao segment of the *United States Forces in the Philippines* (USFIP). Again, the members were those very few of the U.S. Armed Forces who did not surrender by escaping into the jungle or who later escaped POW camps, airmen who bailed out or crash-landed, and Filipinos. The Filipinos mostly had been in the military, but a few were civilians. Fertig also coordinated the work of other guerrilla groups.

USFIP's main strength came from thousands of country-loving Filipinos. These men were outraged and sickened from the Japanese atrocities against themselves, their family members, and countrymen; and the fact that the Japanese had forced so many to work as pretty much slaves (including sex slaves). They joined up with Fertig or other guerrilla units that Fertig created, or other guerrilla units operating independently of Fertig (but these groups still somewhat coordinated by Fertig).

USFIP harassed the Japanese Army (and this they did, very well). The guerrillas mostly conducted hit-and-run raids. The purpose again was to harass (and kill when possible) the Japanese, capture or damage supplies, and otherwise stymie Japanese operations. These goals were met, and then some.

MacArthur's Intelligence Chief Major General Charles Willoughby (1892 Germany – 1972 FL) was convinced that providing Fertig's guerrillas was an unnecessary risk and a waste of resources. He felt that Fertig's guerrillas were few and not effective. He reasoned that if the regular army had been defeated and surrendered, how could irregulars do better. He advised MacArthur accordingly to use resources elsewhere, and to order Fertig to limit his activities to intelligence gathering, especially on shipping (coastwatching).

MacArthur adhered somewhat to Willoughby's advice. He told Fertig to collect intelligence including coastwatching and to defend self, but not engage in offense. However, Fertig knew that he could not maintain loyalty from his Filipino guerrillas or recruit more guerrillas in the wake of Japanese atrocities, unless he allowed them to strike the Japanese and their collaborators; and otherwise try to prevent future atrocities. The war crimes were so many and horrible that the Filipinos could only be vengeful, when they felt that had at least half a chance. Therefore against MacArthur's orders, he allowed (and presumably even encouraged) the guerrillas to strike the Japanese.

After such attacks though, the Japanese often initiated terrible reprisals against Filipino civilians. Fertig issued orders that the guerrillas avoid situations, which would lead to such reprisals. But the Japanese often retaliated this way, no matter what the situation.

Fertig also warned MacArthur that other (Filipino) guerrilla leaders would not cooperate with MacArthur, and comply with his non-aggressive directives. These arguments finally swayed MacArthur to give Fertig full rein, despite Willoughby's recommendations. MacArthur provided medical supplies, medicine, clothing, food, weapons, ammunition, radios, etc. This was done by a few airdrops, but mostly by arranging for the Navy to send loaded submarines. The submarines surfaced just offshore at night, to meet up with the guerillas.

These submarine runs numbered 41, from 1/1943 to 1/1945. The Narwhal-class, 371' long and 33' beam and 12' draft, USS Narwhal (1930 – 1945 scrapped) submarine made nine of these runs, from 10/1943 through 11/1944. Narwhal was much welcomed, due to her size. The beam of other World War II era USS submarines was about 27'. These were the Gato, Balao, and Tench classes. Narwhal was 19% longer than the Gato, Balao, and Tench submarines, and 22% wider at its widest point. Therefore, she could tote more supplies and equipment.

Submarines by design are not cargo ships. Their innards are chock full of machinery, equipment, weapons, etc., leaving little space for the men, much less storage. In fact, diminutive sailors work best. Besides taking up less space, small men eat and drink less, inhale less air, generate less waste, etc.

Even Narwhal though could not stock Fertig, to the point of being able to mount a major attack.

On the return trips to Australia, the submarines evacuated Americans and Filipinos both, especially if they required advanced medical care. These were guerrillas and civilians (often families) both.

A total of 1,325 tons of supplies and equipment were delivered over these two years. Three hundred and thirty men were landed to assist Fertig in a number of ways, and 472 people evacuated.

Fertig thought of everything. He created a military band, in uniform no less. Arriving sailors on submarines sometimes were entertained with *Stars and Stripes Forever* or *Anchors Aweigh*, when they opened the hatches.

Fertig even set up a printing press. He printed script for money. He paid the guerrillas with this script, which the U.S. Army honored when Mindanao was finally liberated 6/1945.

On a 3/5/1943 submarine arrival at Mindanao on the Tambor-class, 307' long and 27' beam and 15' draft, USS Tambor (1940 – 1959 scrapped), two men were aboard who had been living and working in the Philippines, who had known or at least knew of Fertig. These two men were as follows:

- Charles Smith (19?? – 1981) (not the teenager Charles Smith mentioned above) was a civilian mining engineer on the Philippine island of Masbate (central Philippines). He fled to Panay, then Mindanao. He put himself at the service of the U.S. Army Forces Far East defending the islands, before the 5/1942 capitulation. Like Fertig, he chose to evade capture instead of surrendering. Therefore, he fled into the jungle. He found and hooked up with Fertig.

Smith, some other mining engineers, and a few Moros (again, Moros were Muslim Filipinos) outfitted a sailboat. They departed from Minda, Samar (Samar Island is the third largest Philippine Island and the easternmost) 12/4/1942 with only a few charts, and Smith's Brunton compass. The Brunton Pocket Transit is a precision compass, which utilizes magnetic induction damping instead of fluid to dampen needle oscillation. It was invented in 1894.

They sailed 2,000 miles to Darwin, arriving 1/4/1943. This voyage by the way was the longest such small boat, ocean sail since Captain William Bligh's (1754 England – 1817 London) 47-day, 4,164-mile voyage in 1789. Mutineers of the HMS Bounty merchantman (1784 – 1790 sunk by deliberate burning) set Bligh and some of his crew adrift in a 23' launch.

Smith and the others were whisked off to MacArthur's Headquarters in Brisbane for debriefing. Much of this debriefing was on Fertig's fledgling guerrilla efforts.

MacArthur made civilian Smith a U.S. Army Captain, just like that. His assignments along with Charles Parsons (see below) was to assess the efficacy of Fertig's guerrilla organization, check out guerrilla organizations on other islands, and set up a system of coastwatchers.

Smith was sent to Samar (Eastern Philippines) on the USS Narwhal 12/1943 to set up a radio station and organize guerrillas. He remained there until the Americans returned to Leyte 10/1944. He was present for the liberation of

Manila 1/1945, and the Los Banos and Santo Tomas Internment Camps 2/1945. The Japanese Army interned enemy civilians at these camps. These were almost all Americans, British, and Australians. Santo Tomas housed 3,000 enemy civilians, mostly Americans. Three hundred and ninety (13%) died there, mostly from lack of food. Los Banos had deaths also.

Smith worked at MacArthur's Headquarters, until the War ended.

- Charles Parsons (1902 TN – 1988 Manila) moved to the Philippines in 1927, to work. In 1930, he enlisted in the U.S. Navy Reserves, commissioned as a Junior Grade Lieutenant.

Since 1940, some Danish ships had been interned in the Philippines, as Germany had conquered Denmark. When the U.S. entered World War II, these ships were seized and registered under the Panamanian flag, as the Philippines were a U.S. territory. Parsons agreed to serve as the temporary Panamanian consul, until a Panamanian from Panama arrived. Panama selected Parsons for several reasons. One was because he spoke Spanish, as did all his family. Parsons now had identification papers with corresponding documents in Manila's government house, identifying him as a Panamanian. He and his family purposely spoke only Spanish. The ruse worked. The Japanese designated his home as the Panamanian Consulate.

It was apparently a matter of diplomatic honor that no one from other legations (including Axis allies Germany and Italy) told the Japanese that Parsons was American not Panamanian, and in the United States Navy Reserves. After all, these legations knew his status (American citizenship, in the Navy). Some Japanese businessmen that he also had worked with, also chose to not uncover him to the occupying Japanese Generals.

Another factor of course, was that the word *Panama* was magic in World War II. Physician, writer, and politician Arnulfo Arias Madrid (1901 Panama – 1988 Miami) was elected President of Panama in 1940. Dr. Madrid declared in his inaugural address: *As Panama has ceded its territory to the United States to construct the Canal, Panama also can cede territory to the Germany of Adolf Hitler so they can construct here what they wish and can help us against Imperialism.* Madrid was an iron-fisted Axis sympathizer. He jailed dissidents, suppressed Panamanians who did not speak Spanish, and enacted legislation barring citizenship to West Indian and Asian Panamanians. The Allies were concerned that he would try to take over the Canal Zone, and limit Canal passage to the Axis powers only.

President Madrid was ousted in 10/1941, in a bloodless coup supported by the United States. Ricardo Adolfo de la Guardia Arango (1899 Panama – 1969 Panama) succeeded Madrid and served through 6/15/1945, which was almost to the end of World War II. Panama under Arango declared war on Japan on 12/7/1941, the same day of the sneak attacks. In so doing, Panama beat the U.S. by one day. Panama then declared war on Germany and Italy

12/13/1941. Panama was the first Latin American country to declare war on the Axis Powers.

President Arango allowed the U.S. to make military fortifications on Panama, to protect the Canal. The agreement was not made though until 5/1942, as Panama demanded so much money to allow the U.S. to make infrastructure and facilities. The U.S. paid Panama $50 per hectare a year for the bases, except paid $10,000 a year for the Rio Hato base on the Pacific Ocean side. A hectare is 2.47 acres. Also, the U.S. agreed to make or complete a number of public works projects for Panama. These included the Rio Hato Road, the bridge over the canal, and a third set of locks for the canal itself. These projects did much to modernize Panama and boost its economy.

The United States had completed the Atlantic Ocean to Pacific Ocean and Pacific Ocean to Atlantic Ocean massive short-cut Canal across the Panama Isthmus in 1914. The first ship passage was only a few weeks after the start of World War I. Considering the strategic importance of the Canal in the War, no country wanted to irritate Panama. This was the case, even though the U.S. controlled the Canal Zone. Of course, Axis countries were denied use of the Canal.

To sum up, Panama did cooperate with the U.S. in World War II, but greedily demanded much in compensation. Panama's military never fought in World War II.

Of note, both Japan and Germany hatched plots to bomb the Canal, to put it out of commission. These plans involved seaplane bombers toted in waterproof deck hangers by submarines. Neither Japan nor Germany though were able to get their plans into action.

Parsons was called up 12/8/1941 when Japan attacked the Philippines. He was promoted to Lieutenant. He worked resupplying American submarines which came into Manila Bay, or relocating supplies to Bataan and Corregidor. As the Japanese army approached Manila at the end of 1941, he destroyed what was left of the Navy's supplies. He burned his Navy uniforms, as he decided he was not retreating with the rest of the American-Filipino forces. He continued to present himself as Panama's consul to the Philippines.

After the 4/18/1942 Doolittle Raid, the attitude of the Japanese occupying forces changed toward all Caucasians, even those from non-belligerent nations. Parsons was arrested, interrogated, and tortured. However, he was released because of his Panamanian diplomatic status. He and his family were allowed to leave 6/1942. They made it back to the U.S. Parsons as now on active duty then traveled to Australia, and reported to General MacArthur for orders.

Parsons' had an established network of trusted, Filipino contacts. This with his great knowledge of the Islands and its people made it possible for him to travel Philippine Island to Philippine Island, and communicate well with

Filipino and American guerrillas. He made eight submarine missions, and also some air trips. His first such mission was to Mindanao to supply and evaluate Fertig's guerrilla organization, along with Charles Smith.

Parsons also organized and maintained extensive intelligence networks and coastwatcher radio stations in the Philippines. Like Smith, he participated in the liberation of Manila and internment camps. He retired as a Lieutenant Commander.

Fertig's radios were makeshift. He was supplied with quality military radios. However, even these were marginal due to his isolated locations in the jungle. Therefore, most of his communications with MacArthur's Command were face to face with Army or Navy officers on the submarines. Again, the main role of Smith and Parsons was to verify that Fertig was leading an effective and ongoing resistance movement; and if so, MacArthur would continue to supply him.

In 8/1943, based mainly upon favorable reports from Parsons and Smith, MacArthur promoted Fertig to Colonel. Also, he was awarded the Distinguished Service Cross. The citation reads as follows:

> *The President of the United States of America, authorized by Act of Congress 7/9/1918, takes pleasure in presenting the Distinguished Service Cross to Colonel (Corps of Engineers) Wendell W. Fertig, U.S. Army, for extraordinary heroism in connection with military operations against an armed enemy while Commanding the Mindanao-Visayan Force (Philippine Guerrillas), in action against enemy forces 5/8/1943 to 8/6/1943, in the Philippine Islands. Refusing to surrender when the major defense forces were overcome, Colonel Fertig assumed command of scattered forces, continuing resistance on the island of Mindanao. He effectively organized many dispersed elements throughout the island, held much stronger enemy forces continuously at bay, and denied them some of the country's resources. He improvised tactics for effective warfare with limited means, and ingenious methods for supplying his men and their families. He persisted in this enterprise, although a large price was set on his head, and he was of necessity in constant proximity to the enemy. His courage and resourcefulness enabled him to avoid capture, to inspire in the people of Mindanao a will to resist, and to furnish the United States Command with information of great military value. The exemplary heroism displayed by Colonel Fertig in the face of enemy fire and his constant, fearless leadership under adverse conditions reflect great credit upon himself and were in keeping with the highest traditions of the military service.*
>
> *In recognition of your meritorious services as District Commander and extraordinary heroism in action during the period of 5/8/1942 – 8/6/1943, I have awarded you the Distinguished Service Cross. Announcement of your award is published in GO Headquarters, USAFFE, dated 8/18/1943. I congratulate you on the distinguished service to your country and to the Filipino people that has so well earned for you such recognition, and hope*

that in it you will find inspiration for even greater future
service. Quezón congratulates you on promotion.

Manuel Quezón (1878 Philippines – 8/1/1944 NY, tuberculosis) was the President of the Philippines, in exile in the U.S.

At first, Fertig's forces were able to repel Japanese attempts to recapture territory on Mindanao held by the guerrillas. For one thing, the Japanese had sent many troops elsewhere. For another, there were several guerrilla groups that the Japanese had to contend with. Fed up though with the constant harassment and loss of men; and equipment, supplies, munitions, and fuel sabotage; the Japanese greatly increased their efforts in the spring of 1943. As they had superior equipment, weapons and numbers, the guerrillas were forced to retreat into the jungle and hills. They lost some camps and some infrastructure to the Japanese.

Fertig's resulting strategy was to allow the Japanese to advance, with little or no resistance. In so doing, the Japanese divided into smaller groups. These Fertig then had his guerrillas attack. The Japanese suffered heavy casualties, in hundreds of firefights. The Japanese moved in more men. To supply that many soldiers, they had to stay near the coast. The Japanese did control the towns on the coast. The USFIP guerillas were kings of the other 90% of Mindanao though.

The guerrillas were so effective in some areas, that local Japanese commanders made separate truces with them. In exchange for not attacking Japanese troops, the Japanese agreed to stay out of those areas.

American air and naval forces sank many Japanese ships, killing thousands of Japanese sailors and troops. When exhausted survivors of the sinking ships floated to shore, Filipino guerrillas and civilians would wade out and finish them off. This they often did with bolo knives (Filipino machetes), to save bullets. They did so to avenge for the myriad atrocities the Japanese had doled out and were still doling out, during the occupation.

The Japanese released an official communique stating that the U.S. had developed an aerial bomb, which somehow sought out concentrations of ammunition and fuel. Of course, this was not the case. The bombs landed on ammunition and fuel sites, from the information collected and provided by the guerrillas.

Fertig set up a navy, of sorts. He armed several small merchant vessels to protect convoys of small boats used to aid in the distribution of supplies, delivered by submarine. Some of these armed vessels also attacked Japanese shipping. These were mostly small cargomen, plus some patrol boats. Fertig armed the USFIP vessels with various machine guns salvaged off downed bombers, homemade cannons, and even mortars. Later, he installed 20 millimeter cannons which had been delivered by a submarine. He *armored* one vessel, by attaching large, circular forestry saw blades to the hull, collected from abandoned plantations. The vessel crews were fearless, engaging in battle with much large Japanese steamers.

The vessels also shot at Japanese aircraft. One and this was a sailboat no less downed a twin engine, Mitsubishi bomber. Guerrillas salvaged the bombsight from that bomber and sent it to Australia on the next submarine, for analysis.

To help prepare for the eventual invasion of American forces, Fertig made airstrips. The strips were covered with topsoil, and crops planted atop for concealment. Once a bulldozer scraped off this top layer, the airstrip was ready. One of these strips was 7,000' long. It took a year to build. The marines ended up using some of these airstrips during the return invasion, to provide close-air support.

The USFIP provided intelligence which contributed to victories in the 6/19, 20/1944 Philippine Sea Battle, and the 10/23-26/1944 Leyte Gulf Battle. Fertig's gathered intelligence was so accurate in some cases, that aerial reconnaissance flights before attacks were often canceled. This had the added advantage of not tipping the Japanese off, that U.S. surveillance had detected the locations and types of their ships in the area.

Japan was forced to send more troops to the Philippines in an effort to throttle the guerrillas. These of course were troops that Japan needed elsewhere.

By late 1944, Fertig commanded 35,000 men, with 16,500 armed (47%).

Japan stationed 288,000 troops in the Philippines throughout World War II. The number on Mindanao varied from 43,000 to 60,000. These numbers were large, due to the efforts of the guerrillas.

Early in 1945, the Japanese Army once again launched a major effort, to destroy the guerrillas on Mindanao. In this case, they concentrated not on seeking them out and killing them, but on cutting off their supply sources. This effort had some effect.

To show USFIP strength on Mindanao in January and February 1945 in preparation for the return of regular American forces, the guerrillas seized the Dipolog airstrip. Dipolog is the capital of the province of Zamboanga, Mindanao. Zamboanga is the westernmost province of Mindanao. The guerillas held the airstrip, even though surrounded by the Japanese.

As the date for landings approached, Fertig sent word that the guerrillas controlled Malabang (town in eastern Mindanao) and its airstrip. Beginning 4/5/1945, marine aviators from Dipolog moved to the Malabang airstrip. Using targeting information from the guerrillas, the pilots proceeded to bomb the Japanese positions. By 4/11/1945, the remaining Japanese forces fled toward Parang (also eastern Mindanao). Friendly forces were in complete control of Malabang. The 24th Division came ashore at Parang, much closer to Highway 1. To sum up, the information from the guerrillas and the fact that they had secured airstrips, greatly speeded up the successful American invasion.

The U.S. Army and Navy finally returned, landing on Leyte (island just north of Mindanao) 10/20/1944, and then Mindanao six months later. Guerillas were on other of the Philippine Islands as well, although not as many or effective as those on Mindanao.

During this time of the American Army returning to the Philippine Islands, the guerrillas got bolder, striking openly against the Japanese. They of course took their places in battle as well, as the American troops landed and advanced.

Mindanao was the last of the Philippine Islands taken back. This delay may have been because of the effectiveness of Fertig's guerilla the past few years. Presumably, MacArthur made his decision to delay Mindanao's invasion to last, again due to the guerillas' success.

The Japanese army pulled its troops out of Mindanao, to defend other parts of the Philippines. MacArthur though quickly invaded and occupied Panay, Cebu, Negros, and several islands in the Sulu Archipelago; routing the Japanese there.

After the War, a review of Japanese records showed that the Japanese high command felt that 24 battalions of troops would be needed to guard rear areas against guerrillas, once the American invasion of the Philippines began. This meant that one fourth of its force would be required to hold off guerrillas, from the interior. Japanese high command concluded that *It is impossible to fight the enemy* (referring to the expected, landing American Army), *and at the same time suppress the activities of the guerrillas.* To sum up, the invasion from the sea along with the guerillas in the jungle, put the Japanese in a pincher. The Japanese knew this, but still did not surrender.

As already noted, the Mindanao guerrillas participated in the invasion attack and push back, as well. They kept necessary roads free of congestion, provided intelligence on the whereabouts of the Japanese, etc.

The Filipino guerrillas also over this period, maintained public order – advising civilians of what progress was being made, and also what civilians could do to support their efforts.

The USFIP killed 7,700 Japanese soldiers and wounded others. Its own casualties were only a fraction of this amount. By keeping pressure on the Japanese, the Japanese were forced to divert resources. The efforts kept Japan from using some of the natural resources, in the Philippines. These gains shortened the delay until the U.S. Army returned, and overall probably shortened the War some as well.

Fertig disbanded the guerrillas. The War was pretty much over on Mindanao, by 6/1945. Many Japanese soldiers and even Japanese civilians (collaborators) living in the Philippines did what American soldiers and many Filipinos had done in 1942 – fled to the jungle and mountains. They were compressed into isolated pockets including on Mindanao and Luzon, until Japan surrendered 8/15/1945. These numbered 22,250 troops and 11,900 civilians.

Even then, many Japanese soldiers refused to surrender. They considered reports of Japan surrendering to be lies, or maybe they just could not accept defeat. Top Japanese military leaders and officials including members of the Imperial family, had to visit in person to convince these holdout soldiers to surrender.

The last holdouts on Mindanao were 200 well-organized and disciplined soldiers, who surrendered 1/1948. This was almost 2.5 years after the War ended (hard to believe).

Second Lieutenant Hiroo Onoda (1922 Japan – 2014 Tokyo) was the last Japanese holdout of World War II, on another Philippine Island (Lubang). In 1974 twenty-nine years after the War ended, his former commanding officer traveled from Japan to personally issue orders relieving him from duty (again, hard to believe). He became a major celebrity back in Japan. He married in 1976, at age 54.

When the Philippines re-organized its Army 9/1945 after World War II, its ranks were heavily seeded with USFIP Filipino veteran guerrillas, from enlisted men to high levels of command.

In 5/1946, Colonel Fertig was awarded the U.S. Army Distinguished Service Medal. The citation is as follows:

The President of the United States of America, authorized by Act of Congress, 7/9/1918, takes pleasure in presenting the Army Distinguished Service Medal to Colonel (Corps of Engineers) Wendell W. Fertig, U.S. Army, for exceptionally meritorious and distinguished services to the Government of the U.S., in a duty of great responsibility as commander of the Mindanao-Visayan Force (Philippine Guerrillas) at Mindanao, Philippine Islands, from 9/16/1942 to 3/25/1945. When the surrender of U.S. Forces in the Philippines left the civilian population, U.S. and Philippine Army personnel in a state of chaos, Colonel Fertig accepted the tremendous responsibility of organizing both civil and military resistance in Mindanao. Although confronted with almost insurmountable difficulties, he organized a well-disciplined and highly effective fighting force of 25,000 men which confined the foe, vastly superior numerically, to certain heavily fortified areas. He developed an espionage system, coastal watching stations, and vast radio communications of 58 stations scattered throughout the island, many of which were in heavily garrisoned areas. Gaining contact with General Headquarters in Australia, he transmitted vital intelligence on enemy ground, sea, and air activities. One of his reports made possible the decisive Japanese defeat in the Naval Battle of the Eastern Philippines. Colonel Fertig was responsible for the construction of havens for distressed American planes, pilots and crew. Denying the enemy access to the greater part of the island and its resources, his military activities paved the way for the virtually unopposed landing of U.S. Forces, with a minimum of casualties. Constantly engaged with vastly superior enemy forces, he engendered Filipino faith and confidence in their ultimate deliverance, instilled in them the will to resist, and united them in the cause of freedom. By his outstanding courage, tireless determination, and brilliant leadership, Colonel Fertig made an inestimable contribution to the liberation of the Philippine Islands.

Constantly engaged with vastly superior enemy forces, he engendered Filipino faith and confidence in their ultimate deliverance, instilled in them the will to resist, and united them in the cause of freedom. By his outstanding courage, tireless determination, and brilliant leadership, Colonel Fertig made an inestimable contribution to the liberation of the Philippine Islands.

Fertig returned to his civilian engineering career after World War II, but retained his reserve commission.

He spent four years as the officer-in-charge of the Reserve Officers' Training Corps, at his alma mater Colorado School of Mines.

During the Korean War, Fertig spent two years at the Pentagon with a psychological warfare unit. From 7/1951 to 6/1952, he was the Special Forces Plans Officer in the Office of the Chief of Psychological Warfare. From then until 8/1953, he was Deputy Chief of Psychological Warfare. During this time, he assisted in establishing the Army's Psychological Warfare Center at Fort Bragg, North Carolina (now the John F. Kennedy Special Warfare Center and School). To sum up, Fertig was one of three Army men most credited with formulating the doctrine of unconventional warfare, that became the cornerstone of U.S. Special Forces (Green Berets). The other two men were as follows:

- 1934 U.S. Military Academy graduate Russell Volckmann (1911 IA – 1982 IA); like Fertig, avoided surrender to the Japanese in the Philippines by escaping into the jungles and mountains; played a similar role to Fertig on Mindanao, but on Luzon; had 22,000 guerrillas under his command toward the end; retired in 1957 as a Brigadier General
- Aaron Bank (1902 NYC – 2004 CA) assisted the French Resistance as an Office of Strategic Services officer; retired in 1958 as a Colonel

Colonel Fertig retired from the Army, 1955. He had been direct-commissioned into the Army as a Captain, as the Army in the Philippines was in dire need of engineering talent. He had no formal military training, not even boot camp. His accomplishments were therefore even more impressive. Some military historians question why Fertig did not receive the Medal of Honor; because of the risks he took, his leadership, his guile, and his great achievements.

Others question why Fertig who commanded so large an army of irregular guerrillas was not promoted to Brigadier General (one star). After all, other men who were never in combat in World War II received that rank, as the U.S. Army grew in World War II.

In 6/1958, Fertig and his wife went to Mindanao on a business trip. Many Filipinos knew of his leadership, of guerrilla forces. Thousands met them at dockside, to cheer him.

The popular television game show *To Tell the Truth* has appeared off and on since 1952. The host introduces three guest contestants, and describes the unusual actual occupation or experience of one of the three to the four celebrity panelists. Two of the three contestants are liars. The third is the actual person as described by the host. The panelists quiz the contestants, to try and determine who is the Real McCoy. Anyway, Fertig appeared on a 1961 episode.

Over the years, there has been talk on making a movie about Fertig.

In 2015, the Filipino Veterans of World War II Congressional Gold Medal Act became public law. The honor recognizes both Filipino regular and irregular Filipino Army units, between 7/26/1941 and 12/31/1946. The presentation ceremony was in 2017. The Medal is on display at the Smithsonian.

26- ONLY USS, ENTIRE CREW ARRESTED

David Porter (1780 Boston – 1843 Constantinople {now Istanbul, Turkey} when an ambassador) commanded several USSs. These included the 304' long and 44' beam and 22' draft, wood hull, three mast, 44-gun, USS Constitution (1798 – 1907 Boston Harbor museum ship) heavy frigate.

The Constitution was one of three ships launched in 1797, as the first warships of the new country's second Navy. Today, she is the oldest, operating, naval ship in the world, still in commission. This is 221 years. George Washington (1732 VA – 1799 VA) named her.

Porter saw action in the War of 1812, 1815 First Barbary War, and in the West Indies campaign theater of the 1898 Spanish-American War. He served 27 years 1798-1825, retiring as a Commodore. Commodore is not an official Navy rank. The designation was used in Porter's time as a courtesy title, for a Captain in command of a fleet or squadron. This is what is called a flag officer today, and would be an Admiral heading a Task Force.

Porter had ten children, including six sons. Two of his sons served in the Navy including during the Civil War. These two sons were as follows:

- William David Porter (1808 New Orleans – 1864 DC) served 1823-1855 and 1859-1864 for a total of 38 years
- David Dixon Porter (1813 PA – 1891 DC) served 1829-1891 for a total of 62 years

Both were Admirals. Both served until death.

Five USSs were named after the father and his son David Dixon. These were a torpedo boat and four destroyers. One of the destroyers was the Fletcher-class USS Porter (1944 – 1974 scrapped). The last of the four destroyers is an Arleigh Burke-class guided missile destroyer commissioned in 1999, and now in service. Although the five were named for both the father and his son David Dixon, all five went by the name of USS Porter.

One warship was named after the older son William David Porter. This was the also Fletcher-class, 377' long and 40' beam and 18' draft, 40 miles per hour, 273 crew, USS William D. Porter (1943 – 6/10/1945 kamikaze sunk off Okinawa) destroyer.

The new USS William D. Porter and three other destroyers were assigned to escort the also new Iowa-class, 887' long and 108' beam and 37' draft, 38 miles per hour, USS Iowa (1943 – 2012 San Pedro {Los Angeles}, California museum ship) battleship, taking President Franklin Roosevelt (1882 NY – 4/12/1945 GA, cerebral hemorrhage) to the 11/1943 Cairo and Tehran Conferences during World War II. State Secretary Cordell Hull (1871 TN – 1955 DC), Chief of Naval Operations Fleet Admiral Ernest King (1878 OH – 1956 ME), the Chiefs of Staff of the military branches, and other staff were aboard for the voyage. The Presidential team numbered 80. As noted above, both Iowa and William D. Porter were newly commissioned.

This mission of course was top secret. The 80-person, presidential party slipped out of Washington as quietly as possible on the 165' long and 24' beam and 8' draft, 15 miles per hour, Potomac (1934 – 1982, a museum ship at Oakland, CA) presidential yacht. They cruised down the Potomac River to rendezvous with Iowa at the river's mouth in Chesapeake Bay.

The 45,000-ton Iowa battleship sailing up Chesapeake Bay from its Norfolk, Virginia berth had to discharge most of its fuel to reduce its draft, to not drag bottom in the Bay. The yacht pulled up to the battleship and off-loaded the 80 persons and their luggage onto Iowa. Iowa headed for the open sea. She underway fueled from an oiler. Her escorts joined her. These were two aircraft carriers to provide scouts and combat air patrol, and as mentioned three other destroyers besides William D. Porter.

William D. Porter mishaps on this escort mission included the following:

- 11/12/1943   when departing the naval base at Norfolk, Virginia, to join the convoy and maneuvering astern, her anchor was not fully raised; it dragged over a docked sister destroyer, damaging railings and lifeboat mounts and life boats
- 11/13/1943   armed depth charge fell into ocean and exploded, causing Iowa and other escort ships to go into anti-submarine mode and take evasive maneuvers, under assumption that the Task Force had come under torpedo attack by a German submarine; this was supposed to be a drill, with disarmed depth charges
- 11/13/1943   freakish wave swept over her tearing loose life rafts and railings; water poured down the intakes into the firerooms, leaving her without power; one sailor was washed overboard and never seen again
- 11/13/1943   boiler tube failed so boiler lost, fell out of formation, repaired and caught up
- 11/14/1943   demonstrated with the other escort ships a torpedo drill, by simulating a launch at Iowa; by mistake, sent a live torpedo in the direction of Iowa, with Roosevelt and entourage aboard; William D. Porter tried to signal Iowa about the incoming torpedo using a signal lamp, as the convoy was in radio silence; however, William D. Porter first misidentified the direction of the torpedo and then relayed the wrong message, informing Iowa that William D. Porter was backing up, rather than that a fish had been launched; in desperation, William D. Porter finally broke radio silence; Iowa's Captain called general quarters; Iowa gunners fired on the torpedo; Iowa turned hard to avoid the torpedo; which detonated in Iowa's wake 3,000 yards (1.7 miles) back

Iowa trained her guns on William D. Porter. This was under the assumption that commandos had hijacked her and fired the torpedo in an effort to assassinate Roosevelt and kill others of his support staff, and sink Iowa.

William D. Porter was ordered to drop out of the convoy, and to sail to the Naval Air Station in Bermuda. A squadron of marines met her and removed and arrested the entire crew. This is the only time in U.S. naval history that an entire USS crew has been arrested. The inquiry confirmed that the torpedo was launched in error.

Some were court-martialed, and some reprimanded. Contrary to Internet legend, Captain Wilfred Walter (1908 – 1996) was not removed and assigned to obscure shore assignments. He remained in command of William D. Porter until 5/1944. He retired after World War II as a Rear Admiral.

The torpedoman was sentenced to 14 years hard labor at Portsmouth Naval Prison (1908 – 1974) in Maine, for failing to remove the torpedo's primer.

President Roosevelt reviewed the inquiry proceedings and vacated all punishments.

USS Iowa by the way is the only USS that had a bathtub, installed for the polio-stricken Roosevelt. Also, an elevator was installed between decks for the President, as well.

William D. Porter was sent to the Aleutians. Just to show that she had not lost her touch, a drunk William D. Porter sailor returning from shore leave fired an inert, 5" shell into the front yard of the Commander of the naval operating base. This was during a party at his house for officers and their wives.

Later, she sailed to the Pacific. She had some success here, shooting down several Japanese aircraft. However, she was also implicated in shooting down (probably with assistance from other USSs) three American patrol aircraft.

The Battle of Okinawa ran 4/1/1945 – 6/22/1945. In the first month, William D. Porter riddled the also Fletcher-class, USS Luce (1943 – 5/4/1945 two kamikazes hit and sank, 126 of 312 crew lost {40%}) destroyer off Okinawa, with anti-aircraft fire. The bullets were intended for attacking, wave-skimming Japanese aircraft.

Due to the constant air raids including kamikazes launched from Kyushu (southwestern-most of Japan's four largest islands) and Formosa (today Taiwan), the U.S. placed radar picket ships around Okinawa. William D. Porter was part of the picket team, warning the fleet of the approach of enemy aircraft – so that other ships could be alerted, and to launch interceptors from the aircraft carriers.

On 6/10/1945, a kamikaze pilot flying an obsolete, single engine, very heavy bomb-laden, Aichi D3A dive bomber aimed for William D. Porter. She managed to evade and divert with anti-aircraft fire. The bomber splashed nearby, ended up under Porter and exploded. The explosion damaged Porter's keel and ruptured her hull. Her steam lines were broken. She lost power. Multiple fires broke out. For three hours, Porter's crew fought the fire struggling to keep the destroyer afloat.

1932 U.S. Naval Academy graduate Captain (Commander) Charles Keyes (1910 – 19??) ordered William D. Porter abandoned. Twelve minutes later, the destroyer heeled over to starboard and sank by the stern. Miraculously, her crew suffered no fatal injuries; although 61 were injured. The USS William D. Porter was one of the very few USSs sunk in World War II destroyer-size or larger, that had no deaths.

William D. Porter received four battle stars for her service in World War II.

As the Pacific War progressed and Japan's successes waned, Japan moved to suicide methods of sinking Allied ships, such as the kamikaze sinking of the William D. Porter just mentioned. Although just stated as Allied ships, these were all or almost all USSs. These methods included diving bomb-laden aircraft into

USSs; crashing small and fast, bomb-laden motorboats into USSs; ramming hulls with manned torpedoes; and even weighted and air-supplied men (or women for that matter) carrying bombs and walking out on the sea bottom to where Allied ships were anchored, while breathing tank air. These four methods were called kamikazes, shinyos, kaitens, and fukuryus. These methods and attempts were all or near all suicidal missions. Of these methods, only the kamikazes were effective.

The kamikazes were laden to the max with a combination of explosives, bombs, torpedoes, and full fuel tanks. The Empire of Japan considered the sacrifice of a young aviator and a patched together aircraft to cripple or sink Allied ships, particularly larger ships and even more particularly aircraft carriers, a bargain.

The kamikaze attacks began 10/1944. By this time, Japan's aircraft were outdated. Resources to make new and better aircraft were absent. Pilots, especially experienced pilots, were in short supply. The pipeline to train new pilots was long. These factors in combination along with Japan's unwillingness to surrender, led to the use of these suicide methods.

The kamikaze aircraft were converted from fighters or bombers, or were purpose-built. The estimate is that 3,862 Japanese Navy and Army kamikaze pilots died in these suicide efforts. Another estimate is that 19% of efforts were successful, in hitting an Allied ship. The U.S. Navy stated that 34 and 368 Allied ships were sunk and damaged, killing and injuring 4,900 and 4,800 sailors. Another source though states that 7,000 American sailors were killed by kamikazes. This was the case despite radar detection and cueing, airborne interception, and bullet-laden anti-aircraft barrages from multiple USSs.

The kamikaze attacks peak came during the above-mentioned Okinawa Battle, when William D. Porter was sunk. Thirty USSs were sunk or put out of action. Most lost were destroyers or smaller warships, serving as picket and protector ships.

Kamikazes did not sink any aircraft carriers, battleships, or cruisers (as further back from the picket ship sentries) at Okinawa. However, several were much damaged. The Essex-class, 820' long, USS Bunker Hill (1943 – 1973 scrapped) aircraft carrier was one of these. She was Vice Admiral Marc Mitscher's (1887 WI – 1974 VA) Task Force 58 flagship. Two Mitsubishi A6M Zeroes piloted by Ensign Kiyoshi Ogawa and Sub-Lieutenant Seizo Yasunori dived in tandem to hit Bunker Hill, 30 seconds apart. This was 5/11/1945. Four hundred and thirty-three sailors, airmen, and members of Mitscher's flag staff were killed; and 264 wounded. Bunker Hill was much damaged. Repairs were completed, the month after the War ended.

Admiral Mitscher relinquished command by visual signal. A breeches buoy (rope-based rescue device) was set up to transfer him and his remaining staff to the Sumner-class, 377' long and 40' beam and 16' draft, USS English (1944 – 1970 transferred to Taiwan, 2003 target sunk) destroyer. From English, Mitscher and staff transferred to the Yorktown-class, 770' long, USS Enterprise (1938 – 1960 scrapped) aircraft carrier. Enterprise became Mitscher's flagship.

Kamikazes also sank or damaged three U.S. freighters at Okinawa.

As noted above, the kamikaze program was a success. In Japanese reasoning, sacrificing the following for putting a ship out of action or even sinking it and killing sailors, was a very, very lopsided victory. After all, losses were limited to the following:

- One young, unskilled pilot (and hey, he got to achieve martyrdom); most were ages 18 to 20; they were (supposedly) volunteers
- An antiquated and/or cheap, poorly maintained rickety assembly of bomb-laden aluminum; this may be misleading, as Japan had a shortage of aluminum at this point in World War II; some were patched up with wood, canvas, and tape

In actuality, only one in seven kamikazes connected. No matter. The Japanese still considered this a major victory, in their desperation. Again, one spindly, derelict plane and an amateur, nobody pilot was lost, compared to a disabled or even sunk USS and multiple American casualties. At this stage in the War, Japan considered this quite a one-sided victory, and it was.

On the other hand by this time in World War II, U.S. shipbuilders were turning out more ships than were needed. The damaged or sunken ships were quickly replaced or repaired. On top of that, the replacement ships were state of the art, so better in just about all ways. The improvements included better anti-aircraft guns.

To sum up, the success of the Japanese kamikaze program did not extend the war much. In fact, it probably hastened President Harry Truman's (1884 MO – 1972 MO) decision to use atomic weapons, which of course ended the Pacific War. Unbelievably though, it took a second atomic bomb three days after the first for Japan to surrender – and the surrender did not come until five days after the second atomic bomb. On top of that, the U.S. also heavily bombed two Japanese cities with conventional bombs, between the two atomic bombs.

27- HIROSHIMA AND NAGASAKI ATOMIC BOMBS

Some nuclear physics technical terms are defined below for explanation and reference, as follows:

- An ion is an atom or molecule that has a net electric positive or negative charge, due to the loss or gain of one or more electrons.
- Ionization is the process by which an atom or a molecule acquires a negative or positive charge by gaining or losing electrons to form ions, often in conjunction with other chemical changes. On the electromagnetic spectrum, gamma rays, X-rays, and the high end of ultraviolet are ionizing. Ionization is harmful to living things (causes cancer, for one), including human beings.
- Radioactive decay or radioactivity is the process by which an unstable atomic nucleus loses energy by emitting electromagnetic waves or subatomic particles.
- An isotope is a variant of an element that has the same number of protons as the element in the nucleus of its atoms, but a different number of neutrons. Accordingly, the isotope's atomic weight is the same as the element, but its atomic mass is different. Therefore, it has excess nuclear energy so is unstable, to the point where powerful enough to liberate an electron from another atom. Some isotopes are radioactive. These isotopes are called radioisotopes or radionuclides. This liberation of atoms is ionizing radiation.
- Fission is either a nuclear reaction or a radioactive decay process in which the nucleus of an atom splits into smaller parts. The fission process releases a very large amount of energy.
- Fissile means able to undergo nuclear fission.
- Critical mass is the minimum amount of fissile material, needed to sustain a nuclear reaction.
- Fusion is a reaction in which two or more atomic nuclei come close enough to form one or more different atomic nuclei and subatomic particles (neutrons or protons). Although therefore the opposite of fission, fusion like fission results in a release of enormous energy.
- A linear particle accelerator accelerates charged subatomic particles or ions to a high speed by subjecting them to a series of oscillating electric potentials along a linear beamline. They have a number of practical applications as well as for nuclear research.
- A cyclotron is another type of particle accelerator, in which charged particles accelerate outwards from the center along a spiral path. The particles are held to a spiral trajectory by a static magnetic field and

accelerated by a rapidly varying, radio frequency electric field. Cyclotrons are used to produce radioisotopes (radionuclides).

- A gas centrifuge uses centripetal force to accelerate molecules so that particles of different masses are physically separated in a gradient, along the radius of a rotating container. The process is used to separate gases into isotopes. A common use is to separate uranium-235 from uranium-238.

High degrees of separation and concentration require multiple centrifuges, arranged in a cascade.

In 1898, physicists and chemical scientists (also spouses) Marie Sklodowska Curie (1867 Warsaw – 1934 France, aplastic anemia) and Pierre Curie (1859 Paris – 1906 Paris, run over by a horse-drawn cart) discovered the alkaline earth metal radium in the form of radium chloride. They did so by extracting the radium compound from uraninite. Uraninite is a radioactive, uranium-rich mineral and ore. It is mostly uranium dioxide. The word used for uraninite at the time was *pitchblende.*

Marie Curie and Andre-Louis Debierne (1874 Paris – 1949 Paris) later (1911) isolated the discovered radium in its metallic state, through electrolysis of radium chloride.

All isotopes of radium are highly radioactive. Madame Curie in fact is usually credited with coining the word *radioactivity,* as the emission of particles from an unstable atomic nucleus.

Marie Curie and her physicist husband Pierre and physicist Antoine Becquerel (1952 Paris – 1908 France) received the 1903 Nobel Prize in Physics, for their pioneering work studying radioactivity. Marie also won the 1911 Nobel in chemistry. She was the first person to be awarded two Nobels (three men have since joined her with a double). She remains the only woman to win two Nobels. She is the only person to win a Nobel in two different sciences.

Marie Curie died from aplastic anemia. This is a rare disease in which the bone marrow and hematopoietic stem cells in the bone marrow are damaged. This results in a deficiency of all three blood cell types, as the stem cells are unable to generate mature blood cells. The disease is triggered in a number of ways, including exposure to ionizing radiation. She contracted the disease from her long-term, unprotected exposure to radiation from her research; and also from her exposure to X-rays from unshielded equipment while serving as a radiologist in field hospitals during World War I.

Marie's husband Pierre most likely would have died of some radiation sickness as well, if he had not been killed in a road accident as a pedestrian at age 46. He was crossing a busy street in the rain. He slipped and fell under a heavy horse-drawn cart. One of the wheels rolled over his head.

Marie and Pierre's daughter and son in law were also physicists, and did research on radiation. Daughter Irene Joliot-Curie (1897 Paris – 1956 Paris, leukemia) died at age 58 of leukemia, caused by radiation exposure from her research. Leukemia is a group of cancers that form from bone marrow.

Irene's husband Jean Frederic Joliot-Curie (1900 Paris – 1958 Paris, after surgery to treat internal hemorrhaging) died at also 58, from post-surgery complications. His ailment which triggered the surgery attempt was also caused by exposure to radiation.

Treatment for aplastic anemia which killed Marie Curie, today is by suppressing the immune system with medications. In severe cases, bone marrow transplants are done. Today, five-year survival rates exceed 85%. Of course in Curie's time, there was no treatment.

Likewise, there was no treatment then for leukemia, which killed Marie's daughter. Today, the five-year survival rate for leukemia is more than 50%.

In Marie Curie's time and also one generation later in the case of her daughter Irene and her husband Jean, the damaging effects of ionizing radiation were not understood. If they had known of these risks, they obviously would have taken precautions.

To this day, Marie and Pierre's papers from the 1890s and even Marie's cookbooks are too dangerous to touch without protective equipment. They remain radioactive from her handling them with contaminated hands from her research work.

Ten years after the senior Curies isolated radium chloride in 1909, radio-chemist and 1921 Nobel Prize chemistry winner Frederick Soddy (1877 England – 1956 England) stated at a prominent lecture that the energy released in radioactivity, could be *employed as an explosive, incomparably more powerful in its activities than dynamite.* Soddy with Ernest Rutherford (1871 New Zealand – 1937 England), determined that radioactivity is due to the transmutation (change from one substance to another) of elements. Rutherford won the 1908 Nobel Prize in chemistry.

Soddy's ideas inspired author H.G. Wells (1866 England – 1946 London) to write the 1914 *The World Set Free* novel. In his book, Wells made several predictions, which included the following:

- That biplanes would drop atomic bombs on the enemy in a nuclear war; this was the first use of the words *atomic bombs;* two atomic bombs (one fission, one fusion) were dropped 8/1945 on Japanese cities to end World War II, and none since (in anger); for the record, the bombers that dropped the nuclear weapons were not biplanes; they were four-engine, midwing monoplanes (Boeing B-29 Superfortress {Silverplate modifications})

- That energy released in radioactivity would be used to generate electricity, in 1953; Wells was off a year here; the first nuclear energy plant adding to the grid went on-line 6/27/1954 and generated for five years; this was the five-megawatt net, co-generation pilot plant at Obninsk, Russia; the isotope used was 5% enriched uranium, moderated with graphite; the coolant was water; Obninsk is 68 miles southwest of Moscow; Russia's next nuclear plant used to generate electricity was not until 1964

Wells is best known for his 1895 science fiction novel, *The Time Machine*.

Research in this area lagged during World War I, but revived in the 1920s and even more so in the 1930s.

Jewish physicist Leo Szilard (1898 Budapest – 1964 CA, heart attack) attended university in Budapest. He was drafted and joined the Austro-Hungarian Army in 1917, for World War I. He contracted influenza 5/1918, which kept him out of combat. He was honorably discharged 11/1918, shortly after Armistice Day. Universities in Hungary changed their policies, banning Jews from enrollment. Szilard moved to Germany 12/1919 to continue his studies and do research. He submitted patent applications for a linear accelerator and a cyclotron, 1928 and 1929.

Ernest Rutherford mentioned above directed the Cavendish Laboratory at the University of Cambridge, Cambridge, England. The laboratory was named in honor of theoretical chemist and physicist Henry Cavendish (1731 in what is now Italy – 1810 London), known for discovering hydrogen.

Under Rutherford's direction in 1932, students John Cockcroft (1897 England – 1967 Cambridge) and Ernest Walton (1903 Ireland – 1995 Belfast) conducted the first experiment which split a nucleus, in a fully controlled matter.

Szilard conceived the concept of a nuclear chain reaction in 1933. He fled Germany to England that year, when Adolf Hitler (1889 Austria – 4/30/1945 Berlin, pistol suicide) took power. He and Enrico Fermi (1901 Rome – 1954 Chicago, stomach cancer) co-patented the idea of a nuclear reactor in 1934. The patent introduced the term *critical mass*, as the minimum amount of fissile material needed to sustain a nuclear reaction.

Szilard moved to the U.S. from England in 1938, to continue his research with Fermi and Walter Zinn (1906 Canada – 2000 FL).

Ernest Lawrence (1901 SD – 1958 CA) conceived the concept of a nuclear chain reaction via neutrons, in 1933. He is credited with inventing a working cyclotron, in 1934. He received the 1939 Nobel Prize in Physics for the invention. He worked on uranium isotope separation for the Manhattan Project (see below).

Fermi received the Nobel Prize in Physics, in 1938. After receiving the prize in Stockholm, he traveled to the United States with his family, for good. He did so to escape from Fascism in Italy. Also, new Italian Racial Laws affected his Jewish wife Laura Capon (1907 Rome – 1977). Like in Germany, these were anti-Semitic laws. These same laws put many of his research assistants out of work. This defection to the U.S. after receiving the Nobel Prize in Sweden was a clever move on the part of Fermi, as Italian leaders probably would not have allowed such a renowned and brilliant scientist to otherwise leave the country in the late 1930s.

Many scientists worked on the atomic bomb. Fermi is often considered the most knowledgeable in all phases of nuclear physics – quantum, particle, condensed matter, and astro. He is considered as one of the few physicists in history who excelled both experimentally and practically. Put yet a third way, Fermi has been judged as the first and last nuclear physicist who understood all aspects of nuclear physics, as an integrated whole. A number of biographies have been written. In fact, the most recent one (2017) is titled *The Last Man Who Knew Everything:*

The Life and Times of Enrico Fermi, Father of the Nuclear Age. David Schwartz is the author. Schwartz's father Melvin Schwartz (1932 NYC – 2006 ID) shared the 1988 Nobel Prize in Physics for the demonstration of the doublet structure of the leptons through the discovery of the muon neutrino, and the development of the neutrino beam method.

Fermi died of stomach cancer in 1954 at age 53. It does not appear that he developed cancer though from his radioactive research. He left a wife and two children.

Ida Tacke Noddack (1896 Germany – 1978 West Germany) along with Szilard is credited with being the first or at least among the first to mention the concept of nuclear fission.

The above-mentioned scientists (also spouses) Irene Joliet-Curie and Frederic Joliet-Curie declared 4/1939 in the British multidisciplinary scientific journal *Nature* (1869 England – still published weekly) that atomic fission was possible and could produce immense amounts of power. They stated in that article that this energy could be used as a source to generate power, or to create extremely powerful weapons.

Again, Irene Curie was the daughter of Marie and Pierre Curie, introduced at the start of this article. Irene's husband Frederic Joliet was their son-in-law. When they married, both changed their surnames to *Joliet-Curie*, combining their two pre-marriage surnames. The couple were awarded the Nobel Prize in chemistry in 1935.

To continue this trend, Irene and Frederic's daughter Helene Langevin-Joliot (1927 Paris -) is a nuclear physicist and a professor of nuclear physics at the Institute of Nuclear Physics at the University of Paris – this at age 92. Her brother Pierre Joliot-Curie (1932 Paris -) is a noted biologist and researcher. Her son Yves (1951 -) is an astrophysicist.

These Curies (and the mates they select) obviously excel at passing their scientific aptitude and intelligence genes down, generation after generation.

In regard to Japan and more on Germany, note the following:

- Japan
  - Yoshio Nishina (1890 Japan – 1951 Tokyo) established his own Nuclear Research Laboratory to study high-energy physics in 1931 at the Riken Institute. The *Riken* name is a contraction of *Rikagaku Kenkyushol* which translates to the Institute of Physical and Chemical Research. Riken was established in 1917 at Tokyo, Honshu Island. It is still in Tokyo and employs 3,000 scientists in several fields today.

    Dr. Nishina made a 26" cyclotron in 1936; and a 60", 220-ton cyclotron the next year.

    In 1938, Riken bought a cyclotron from the University of California, Berkeley. One has to question the wisdom of that sale, so late in the 1930s.

In 1939, Dr. Nishina recognized the military potential of nuclear fission. He headed Japan's nuclear weapons research program, during World War II.

In 4/1945, the U.S. bombed Riken's laboratories. In 11/1945, Allied soldiers destroyed Riken's two cyclotrons. This was three months after Japan surrendered.

o Tohoku University at Sendai (Sendai is also on Honshu Island, 219 miles north-northeast of Tokyo) Professor Hikosaka Tadayoshi released his atomic physics theory, 1934. He noted the huge energy contained by nuclei, and the potential that such energy could be harnessed for both nuclear power generation of electricity and mass destruction weapons.

▪ Germany – note that Hitler became Chancellor in 1933, and Leader and Chancellor (dictator) in 1934; the scientists below were Jewish, or the Nazis considered them assimilated Jewish

o Arnold Berliner (1862 Poland – 3/22/1942 Berlin, suicide) graduated from a Polish university in 1886, with a degree in physics. He went to work in the research and development laboratories of Allgemeine Elektrizitats-Gesellschatt (AEG), based in Berlin. *AEG* translates to *General Electricity Company*. AEG designed, engineered, made, marketed, and sold electrical equipment.

The Berlin-based scientific papers publisher Springer-Verlag was formed in 1842. It is still in the same business. In 1912, Springer-Verlag appointed Berliner as editor of the new scientific journal *Naturwissenschaften.* Berliner in fact is considered a co-founder of the journal, with the publisher.

The first edition came out in 1913. It is still published today. The new journal was inspired by the prestigious British scientific journal *Nature* first published in 1869 (and still also published). Today, *Nature* is a weekly, and *Naturwissenschaften* is a monthly.

German chemists Otto Hahn (1879 Germany – 1968 West Germany) and Fritz Strassmann (1902 Germany – 1980 West Germany) sent a manuscript to Springer-Verlag 12/1938 to consider for publishing in *Naturwissenschaften,* which was then a weekly. It was published. The article described the detection of the element barium, after bombarding uranium with neutrons. In other words, they had discovered nuclear fission from their radio-chemical experiment -- splitting the atomic nucleus of uranium into two smaller nuclei. Hahn won the Nobel Prize in chemistry in 1944.

Berliner was Jewish. For this reason, the Nazis removed him as editor. *Nature* journal reported his dismissal the next month in its 9/28/1935 issue, in an editorial:

> *We much regret to learn that on 8/13/1935, Dr. Arnold Berliner was removed from the editorship of "Die Naturwissenschaften," obviously in consequence of non-Aryan policy. This well-known scientific weekly, which in its aims and features has much in common with "Nature", was founded twenty-three years ago by Dr. Berliner, who has been the editor ever since and has devoted his whole activities to the journal, which has a high standard and under his guidance has become the recognised organ for expounding to German scientific readers, subjects of interest and importance.*

Berliner had made several efforts to flee Germany which were not successful. He committed suicide the day before an evacuation order (meaning deportation to an extermination camp) became effective. He was age 79.2 years. He thought this was the best approach. He thought right.

- Hahn and Strassman communicated their experiment results to Lise Meitner (1878 Vienna – 1968 England) and her nephew Otto Frisch (1902 Germany – 1980 West Germany). They provided theoretical explanations on nuclear fission as soon as 1/1939, including the recognition that fission is accompanied by an enormous release of energy. Frisch confirmed this experimentally, also 1/1939. Frisch is credited with coining the term *fission*. Maybe he came up with the term, as it sort of resembles his surname, or maybe not.

  Frisch researched in Hamburg with Otto Stern (1888 Prussia – 1969 Berkeley). He fled to London in 1933. He later researched in Copenhagen with Niels Bohr. Frisch was Jewish.

  Theoretical physicist Stern was nominated for 82 Nobel Prizes, the second most to Arnold Sommerfeld (1868 Prussia – 1959 Munich who had 84 nominations. Sommerfeld never won a Nobel though. But Stern did in 1943. He like Frisch fled Germany in 1933, moving to the Carnegie Institute of Technology in Pittsburgh.

  Meitner spent most of her scientific career in Berlin. She was the first woman to become a full professor of physics in Germany. She was removed from these positions in the 1930s as Jewish. She fled to Sweden in 1938.

- Rudolf Peierls (1907 Berlin – 1995 England) also explained and confirmed nuclear fission, in 1939. He went to university in Switzerland, in 1929. He moved to England to do research

(Rockefeller scholarship at Cambridge). He was born Jewish. He chose to remain in England.

Columbia University (Manhattan) scientists replicated the experiment of Meitner and Frisch 1/25/1939, as the first nuclear fission experiment in the U.S. In 1940, Columbia scientists identified the active component of uranium, as the rare uranium-235 isotope. Uranium-238 is the most common isotope of uranium found in nature, accounting for 99%. However, uranium-238 is non-fissile, which means that it cannot sustain a chain reaction. Uranium-235 is fissile, but comprises only 0.72% of natural uranium isotopes.

To sum up from the above, Germany was the mecca of atomic energy research after World War I into the 1930s. Most of the leading scientists studying, teaching, and researching nuclear physics in Germany were either Germans, or German émigrés. Other countries such as the U.S., Great Britain, France, Australia, Canada, and Japan were researching, but certainly lagging the progress being made in Germany.

As just noted, Hitler came into power 1/1933. He quickly began persecuting Jews, in one way or another. The anti-Semitic Jewish Restoration of the Professional Civil Service Law was enacted 4/1933. This law and its subsequent related ordinances politicized the education system in Germany. This had immediate negative effects on the physics research and capabilities of Germany.

Furthermore, combined with the *Deutsche Physik* movement, the deleterious effects were intensified and prolonged. The *Deutsche Physik* movement was the Nazi-formed nationalist movement in the German physics community in the early 1930s. It was opposed to the work of Jewish physicist Albert Einstein and other modern theoretically based physics, labeled *Jewish Physics* – with no scientific reasons given as to why the opposition. As a result, the negative consequences to physics research and development in Germany and its subfield of nuclear physics were multifaceted and many.

As persecution of Jews began and increased, many Jewish intellectuals fled Germany in the 1930s. Some of these have already been mentioned above. Others who were not Jewish but sympathized with the Jews and other persecuted groups or fearful of war coming, or feared that they would be persecuted themselves, left Germany as well. Some others not in the intellectual class but predicting a dark future under Hitler and the Nazis, also fled. Their destinations were usually other European countries, but sometimes Canada or the United States.

Jewish scientists (chemists and biologists, as well as physicists; also mathematicians and engineers) who stayed in Germany were ostracized, demoted, dismissed, etc. If they distanced themselves from the Nazis or spoke out, they were blacklisted or much worse.

Some scientists were conscripted into the military, ending their academic careers (teaching and research). On top of that, they probably did not make good soldiers or sailors.

As just stated, many fled to other countries. To emphasize again the outflow of these important scientists, note the following two declarations:

- At least 19 of the scientists who fled Germany were Nobel laureates.

- In the field of nuclear physics, 13 of 26 fleeing were cited in the literature before 1933.

As a result of these internal actions against Jewish scientists and the migration of same (again, also mathematicians and engineers) to other countries, Germany's research into nuclear weapons was enormously stunted. By demoting, shuffling aside, drafting into the military, withdrawing funding for research, and the more severe persecutions; Hitler and the Nazis transformed Germany from being the world leader in nuclear research, to something less than a second banana.

Quantum theory is the subset of physics explaining physical behaviors at the molecular, atomic and sub-atomic levels. 1918 Nobel Prize winner in physics Max Planck (1858 Germany – 1947 Germany) is known as the *Father of Quantum Physics*. Planck was president of the prestigious Kaiser Wilhelm Society for the Advancement of Science. This society was formed in 1911. It was named in honor of Wilhelm II (1859 Prussia – 6/4/1941 Nazi-occupied Netherlands). Wilhelm was the last German Emperor (Kaiser) and King of Prussia. He ruled the German Empire and the Kingdom of Prussia 30.4 years, 1888-1918. He abdicated and moved to Netherlands in exile, at the end of World War I.

The Society is still in operation today. Its name was changed to the Max Planck Society for the Advancement of Science in 1948, to honor Planck. This was a year after his death.

The 75-year-old Planck met with Hitler, 1933. This meeting was per Hitler's request. During the meeting, Planck told Hitler that forcing Jewish scientists to emigrate or removing their roles as academic and research leaders would slow Germany's progress, and benefit foreign countries. The negative to Nazi Germany was obviously two-fold – Germany was losing intellectuals, and foreign countries were gaining these intellectuals. Predictably, Hitler responded to Planck's assertions with a rant against Jews. Planck could only take his leave. In retrospect, it is likely that Planck preferred that Germany under Hitler not be a leader in nuclear research.

In 1933, the American Rockefeller Foundation (1913 – still in operation) created a fund to financially support refugee academics. 1922 Nobel Prize physicist Neils Bohr (1885 Copenhagen – 1962 Copenhagen) traveled to the U.S. 5/1933 and discussed this program with Foundation President, mathematician Max Mason (1877 WI – 1963 CA). Bohr played a key role here for the Foundation, serving as a go-between. The outcome was that the Foundation financially supported some refugee scientists with jobs and work at Bohr's Institute of Theoretical Physics, at the University of Copenhagen.

Besides these fellowships at Bohr's Institute, other scientists were placed at other institutions around the world – again, with Rockefeller Foundation money. Those assisted included Guido Beck, Felix Bloch, James Franck, George de Hevesy, Otto Frisch, Hilde Levi, Lise Meitner, George Placzek, Eugene Rabinowitch, Stefan Rozental, Erich Ernst Schneider, Edward Teller, Arthur von Hippel, and Victor Weisskopf.

In 9/1941, 1932 Nobel Prize physicist Werner Heisenberg (1901 Germany – 1976 Munich, kidney and gall bladder cancer) visited Bohr in Copenhagen. Heisenberg headed Germany's nuclear energy research program. During this visit, the two scientists had private discussions. Bohr was left with the impression from Heisenberg's comments, that Hitler was headstrong for the development of nuclear weapons. After the meeting, Bohr passed his opinions and concerns on to the Danish underground, who in turn relayed Bohr's concerns to British intelligence.

Non-Jew Heisenberg was about the only leading physicist left in Germany. After Hitler rose to power in 1933, elements of the Deutsche Physik attacked him as a *White Jew* in the press, as his teachings described the progress made by Jewish scientists. The definition of a *White Jew* has varied per country, and also over time. During the Nazi regime though in Germany, a White Jew was a non-Jew who aided or supported or recognized in some way or even just sympathized with, one or more Jewish people. Per the Nazis viewpoint, this put non-Jew Heisenberg somewhat in the same category as a Jew, or subhuman per the Nazis' definition.

The Schutzstaffel (1925 – 1945) investigated Heisenberg. The Schutzstaffel was Hitler's paramilitary organization most responsible for the genocidal killing of six million European Jews, and hundreds of thousands of others in the Holocaust.

Heisenberg was libeled viciously a number of times in newspapers, controlled by the Nazis. One such attack was published in *Das Schwarze Korps*, which was the Schutzstaffel's newspaper. That article called Heisenberg a *White Jew*, who should *be made to disappear*. He was denied a leadership role at the University of Munich. Heisenberg died in 1976 at age 74 of cancer of the kidneys and gall bladder, so he was not arrested and executed. This was presumably as Hitler knew that he had to hang on to at least some scientists.

Heisenberg was about Hitler's last chance for progress in nuclear physics research. Instead, Hitler and the Nazis suppressed him, snuffing out his opportunity to contribute and lead. Again, the Nazis did so simply as Heisenberg recognized the contributions of scientists who happened to be Jewish.

Germany invaded and occupied Denmark 4/1940. Denmark was not able to put up much resistance. Instead of suffering an inevitable and painful defeat with many casualties, the Danish government negotiated with the Nazis that Germany would be lenient with the country, respecting its rule and neutrality. The occupation lasted until World War II in Europe ended, 5/1945.

Starting soon though after the occupation, some Danes resisted the Nazis in various ways. In response, the Nazis in 1943 ordered the Danish government to set a curfew, forbid public assemblies, and apprehend and execute saboteurs. The Danish government refused. The Nazis removed the Danish government and implemented martial law. The Nazis especially targeted Jews. By this time, the Holocaust was in full swing across occupied Europe.

The word was out 9/1943 that the Nazis planned to capture Danish Jews, and send them to concentration camps in other countries. The already mentioned Neils Bohr of the University of Copenhagen learned that the Nazis considered him to be Jewish, as his mother was Jewish. These actions occurred in the next few days:

- 9/29/1943   The Danish resistance spirited Bohr and his wife by sea, to Sweden.
- 9/30/1943   The Swedish actress Greta Garbo (1905 Stockholm – 1990 NYC) contacted Sweden's King Gustav V (1858 Sweden – 1950 Sweden), asking him to grant an audience to Bohr. The 85-year-old monarch agreed. Bohr at that meeting requested that Sweden provide asylum to Danish Jews. Gustav did not hesitate and approved the plan.
- 10/1/1943   Hitler ordered that Danish Jews (remember, the Nazis now occupied Denmark) be arrested and deported to Germany. This met death for the Danish Jews – worked to death, die of starvation or lack of medical care or exposure to the elements, or exterminated outright. Hitler had avoided persecution of Danish Jews up to this point, for several reasons:
  - As there were not many Jews in Denmark
  - As Denmark was a major supplier of food to Germany (mainly meat and butter)
  - As resistance at first was minimal
- 10/2/1943   King Gustav invited Danish Jews to move to Sweden, as a refuge state. Sweden had done the same several years before, for some Norwegian Jews. Sweden broadcast its asylum stance by radio.

Despite great personal risk, the Danish resistance movement with the assistance of many Danish citizens managed to evacuate 7,220 of Denmark's 7,800 Jews (this is 92.6%) plus 686 non-Jewish spouses by sea to nearby neutral Sweden. Most Danish Jews lived in Copenhagen or the Copenhagen area. The distance across the Strait of Oresund to Sweden was only 2.5 to 6 miles, depending upon the departure and arrival points. The Strait of Oresund connects the Baltic Sea to the Atlantic Ocean, and separates Denmark from Sweden.

Passage time was usually less than an hour. Transports ranged from kayaks to 20-ton fishing boats. Young, old, and sick Jews were smuggled across in rail cars, shuttled onto ferry boats.

Some 580 Danish Jews failed to escape, for one reason or another. Some remained hidden to the end of the War. A few committed suicide. The Nazis did capture 464 of these 580 though (80%). They were sent by rail to the Theresienstadt concentration camp in Germany-occupied Czechoslovakia. Danish civil servants convinced the Nazis to accept donated food and medicine for these Danish Jews at Theresienstadt. Denmark also got the Nazis to not send these Jews on to extermination camps. The Danish Red Cross monitored conditions at Theresienstadt. Four hundred and twenty of these 580 survived captivity (72%) until repatriation at the end of World War II.

The Theresienstadt camp is also known for the actions taken by the Nazis prior to a 6/1944 International Red Cross inspection tour. Gardens were planted, barracks renovated, streets cleaned, etc. Thousands of prisoners were sent to other camps, so that Theresienstadt was not overcrowded. The tour included an evening performance by the camp's choir. This was Giuseppe Verdi's (1813 Italy – 1901) *Requiem,* which is a Christian piece. The musicians were Jews. Czech composer, pianist, and conductor Rafael Schachter (1905 – 1/1945 on a death march when Auschwitz was evacuated) changed the ending notes to communicate a subtle resistance signal. Holocaust organizer and operator Lieutenant Colonel Adolf Eichmann (1906 Prussia – 1962 Israel execution hanging for war crimes and crimes against humanity) was in attendance. However, Eichmann did not recognize the resistance signal in the music. Schachter in so doing was placing his life in danger, especially as he was Jewish.

One hundred and fifty thousand Jews were sent to the Theresienstadt camp during World War II. Only seventeen thousand (13%) survived.

But Danish Jews fared much better. More than 99% of Danish Jews survived the Holocaust; thanks to King Gustav and Sweden, and other efforts. This less than 1% Jewish extermination rate was the lowest for any Germany occupied country or area during World War II.

To sum up again from the above described research, physicists worldwide realized that nuclear chain reactions could be produced with enormous release of energy, which could be used productively (such as to heat water to steam to generate electricity), or to make weapons of mass destruction. Governments were aware. The two main Axis powers of Germany and Japan as noted above, were leaders in the field of nuclear fission research. Their war-thinking governments supported this research money-wise, recognizing the potential for super weapons of mass destruction.

Into the 1930s, much of this research was public – the findings and conclusions were published. When War looked imminent and in fact started, the research went secret. As a result, the Allies were in the dark as to the research developments being made, in what became the Axis countries. The Allied countries quickly reciprocated, and kept their research and findings confidential, as well.

The above-mentioned key researcher Leo Szilard in consultation with fellow Hungarian physicists Edward Teller (1908 Budapest – 2003 CA) and Eugene Wigner (1902 Budapest – 1995 NJ), wrote a letter to U.S. President Franklin Roosevelt (1882 NY – 4/12/1945 GA, cerebral hemorrhage), warning that Germany might develop atomic bombs. Szilard, Teller, and Wigner were all Jewish, and fled Germany to the United States in 1933 or 1934. Wigner much later in life was awarded the Nobel Prize in physics, 1963.

Their letter was dated 8/2/1939. The letter suggested that the U.S. accelerate its own nuclear research program.

The three physicists got the renowned, now age 60, 1921 Nobel Prize winner physicist Albert Einstein (1879 Germany – 1955 NJ) to sign the ghost-written letter, for impact. The letter had the desired effect (the letter is attached to the end of this chapter). Roosevelt responded by starting a U.S. nuclear fission research program. It was low funded. The funds though were increased after 12/7/1941, when the Empire of Japan sneak attacked fourteen sites in or on the Pacific Ocean. Nine of the fourteen targets were U.S. owned or operated. In fact, the acceleration in spending has never been equaled – not even by the space program which began less than half a generation later. This increase came at the same time that military spending was increased exponentially. For the record, most of the money was borrowed.

But even so for 18 months after Pearl Harbor Day, research in Great Britain outpaced U.S. research. The reason was obvious. The U.S. was full-bore gearing up for war, in both the European and Pacific theaters (and already fighting in the China-Burma-India Theater). Also, the U.S. was supplying its Allies with massive amounts of war goods, at great costs.

Research by German refugee scientists Rudolf Peierls and Otto Frisch (both Jewish) mentioned earlier at the University of Birmingham (England) determined 3/1940, that as little as one to ten kilograms of uranium was all that was needed to make a bomb with the power of thousands of tons of dynamite. The British program code named *Tube Alloys,* was established to further research and build such a weapon.

In 7/1940, Great Britain offered its research findings to the U.S. The U.S. was behind Great Britain some, in this area. The British and Americans exchanged nuclear research information, but did not combine their efforts. The U.S. suggested a combined project 8/1941, but the British did not respond. The U.S. suggested the same again 11/1941 but the Brits demurred, ostensibly as concerned about American security.

Great Britain should have been more concerned about its own security. Soviet spies had penetrated the British program. As it turned out, the Soviets became an ally though -- at least for World War II. This occurred as the Nazis invaded the Soviet Union 6/22/1941. This was despite the fact that Germany and Russia had negotiated a non-aggression agreement in Moscow 8/1939 (Molotov–Ribbentrop Pact). Hitler wanted to move Soviets out of the western part of the Soviet Union and populate that area with Germans. His plan then was to use Slavs (especially Poles) as slave labor for the Axis war effort, to seize the oil reserves of the Caucasus, and to grab agricultural crop harvests. The Caucasus Mountains lie between the Black Sea to the west and the Caspian Sea to the East. They today occupy Russia, Georgia, Azerbaijan, and Armenia.

All in all though, Germany's invasion of Russia was an extraordinarily stupid move on the part of the overly ambitious and confident megalomaniac Hitler.

At first, the U.S. did not put much money into research. As noted already, the U.S. at the time was putting much money into supplying Great Britain, France, Russia, China, and other countries with war goods. The U.S. was also fighting the Japanese in China, which was very expensive.

Great Britain lacked resources for the program, and the U.S. pulled ahead in progress made. As the U.S. was doing 90% of the work to make a nuclear bomb, Roosevelt decided 12/1942 to restrict the scientific information being sent to Britain. The British retaliated likewise, by withholding its information and access to its scientists. The U.S. stopped sending any information.

Great Britain finally realized that due to their desperate situation in trying to defend itself much less make offensive attacks, that development of such a weapon was much beyond its capability. Only the U.S. had the broad science and technology base, vast military and civilian human resources of skilled and semi-skilled manpower, industrial infrastructure, and money to undertake the burden of developing and producing nuclear weapons, while fighting worldwide. In regard to that last commodity of money, it should again be noted that this money was mostly borrowed.

Also, U.S. land was in little danger of being attacked and had defenses, so a secure site.

Accordingly, Prime Minister Winston Churchill's (1874 England – 1965 London) scientific and war mobilization advisors advised him to ask the U.S. to take the lead, on developing nuclear weapons. He and Roosevelt discussed the situation at the 5/1943 The Third Washington Conference (code-named Trident).

By 7/1943, Roosevelt decided to pull the British back in. The two countries formalized the agreement 8/19/1943, at a meeting in Quebec (Canada). The *Quebec Agreement* outlined the terms of coordinated development of the basic science and advanced engineering developments as related to nuclear energy; and, specifically weapons that employ nuclear energy. The agreement included these three main clauses:

- That the U.S. and the U.K. would never use atomic weapons against each other
- That the U.S. and the U.K. would never use atomic weapons against another country, unless both nations approved
- That the U.S. and the U.K. would not give information and data on the bomb to third parties, unless both in agreement to do so

The U.K. transferred its research and development to the U.S. subsuming Tube Alloys, to what came to be called the *Manhattan Project*. Much of the early research was conducted at ten locations in Manhattan, which led to the project's name.

A large team of British and Canadian scientists moved to the U.S. Also as noted above, many of the scientists who moved to the United States to work on the project were Germans; or scientists from other European countries who had studied and researched in Germany.

Major General Leslie Groves (1896 NY – 1970 DC) of the U.S. Army Corps of Engineers directed the Manhattan Project. Groves was a 1918 graduate of the U.S. Military Academy. His time at West Point was shortened, as the Army needed officers for World War I.

Groves is also known for overseeing the construction of the Pentagon, as well as coordinating the Manhattan Project. The Pentagon is the headquarters of the U.S. Department of Defense. The five story (plus two basement levels) Pentagon was completed 1/1943 over only 16 months, during World War II. To this day, it remains the largest office building in the world.

The Manhattan project grew to employ 130,000 people, and cost almost $2 billion ($28.6 billion in 2019 money). Research and development took place at more than 30 sites across the U.S., plus also at a few sites in Great Britain and Canada.

Groves' handling of the Manhattan Project was considered masterful, except for one major failing. This was that Groves' efforts in maintaining secrecy and security did not prevent the Soviet Union from conducting a successful espionage program. The Soviets stole some of the program's most sensitive data and specifications. This was not an issue during World War II, as the U.S. and the Soviet Union were allies. However, the secrets the spies stole gave the Soviet Union a head start in developing its own nuclear weapons after the War. This triggered the Cold War, which ran 1947-1991. This was 44 years. The Cold War was easily avoidable, by dethroning tyrant Joseph Stalin (1878 Russia – 1953 Moscow, cerebral hemorrhage) after World War II. This would have been easy to do, considering that the Soviet Union was devastated in all ways as a result of the War. However, that is another story.

Groves served in the Army 1918-1948, retiring as a Lieutenant General (three stars).

The world's first nuclear reactor was assembled in Chicago as a major breakthrough in the research. Enrico Fermi of the University of Chicago mentioned above led the first self-sustaining nuclear chain reaction. This was 12/2/1942. The location was under the bleachers at the university's football stadium, called Stagg Field (1893 – 1957). Fermi described the apparatus as *a crude pile of black bricks and wooden timbers*. In fact, this first nuclear reactor came to be called the *Chicago Pile-1*. This experiment validated the theories of the scientists, that chain reactions could be triggered which released energy from uranium atoms in a sustained way. As already mentioned several times, it was realized that such energy could be used to make weapons more potent than ever, or could be used as an energy source for peaceful purposes. Again, the Chicago Pile-1 experiment confirmed this.

The experiment also cleared the way for production of plutonium.

Fermi had moved to the U.S. in 1938, as noted above. In 8/1939, the already mentioned German physicist (still in Germany) Werner Heisenberg visited Fermi in Chicago. Fermi was blunt with Heisenberg. He advised him to defect to avoid working on atomic weapons for the Nazis, especially as the Nazis had reduced his leadership role and effectiveness. Heisenberg refused, stated that he must be loyal to his country. He stated such, despite the abusive way that the Nazis were treating him.

Heisenberg and his wife had seven children, born 1938-1950. He knew that getting them out of the country was probably not possible, as the Nazis would block such a move. This was especially the case, after Germany invaded Poland 9/1/1939. Heisenberg's loyalty lay with his family, not with Nazi Germany. He was stuck.

This discussion with Heisenberg further motivated Fermi to hasten his research, to beat Germany in developing atomic weapons – and save the world maybe. As just noted, Nazi Germany invaded Poland 9/1/1939, just after Heisenberg's visit to the U.S. This date is given as the usual start of what came to be called World War II.

Engineer and industrialist Samuel Eyde (1866 Norway – 1940 Norway) bought the rights to several waterfalls in Telemark Province, Norway. Telemark is in southern Norway on the Skagerrak Strait between Norway and Sweden. Eyde founded Norsk Hydro-Elektrisk Kvælstofaktieselskab (Norwegian Hydro-Electric

Nitrogen Limited) in Notodden in Southern Norway, in 1905. This was the predecessor company of Norsk Hydro, still in business today.

The company made two hydroelectric plants in Norway. One was at Svelgfossen Waterfalls near Notodden. The other was near the town of Vemork which is near Rjukan Falls, Tinn municipality. The two falls are 49 miles apart. The 60-megawatt plant near Vemork established the company town of Rjukan. The plant came on-line in 1911, as the largest hydroelectric generation plant in the world. Both plants though were somewhat seasonal, as the falling water came from snowmelt.

The Rjukan hydroelectric generation plant was made mainly to power a factory, manufacturing artificial fertilizer for crops. The plant used the novel Birkeland-Eyde process, of fixing atmospheric nitrogen from the air (air is 79% nitrogen) to make ammonia, which in turn was used to make the fertilizer. Scientist Kristian Birkeland (1867 Norway – 1917 Norway) developed this electric-arc process in 1903. The process required great amounts of energy, available from the hydroelectric generation plant. It started production as soon as the hydroelectric generation facility was up and running in 1911. Birkeland and Eyde partnered, to make fertilizer as a commercial business.

The residues from the Birkeland-Eyde artificial fertilizer plant were analyzed. The findings showed a concentration of one part deuterium oxide (D_2O) to 2,300 parts of water (H_2O). Deuterium is a form of hydrogen which contains a neutron and a proton in its nucleus, whereas the element of hydrogen has a proton only. Deuterium oxide is therefore a different form of water than regular water consisting of the protium hydrogen. Deuterium oxide occurs naturally, at a concentration of one part per 41 million parts of regular water. This meant that the concentration of deuterium oxide as discharged residue from the Vemork fertilizer plant was 17,826 times denser, than existed naturally. The common name for deuterium oxide is heavy water.

At the time, heavy water was nothing more than a scientific curiosity. However, scientists worldwide heralded the Vemork plant's heavy water by-product as a break-through -- eager to use the oddity in chemical and biomedical research.

Two Norwegian scientists enter the picture, as follows:

- Leif Tronstad (1903 Norway – 3/11/1945 Norway; shot in a skirmish) graduated from the Norwegian Institute of Technology (1910 – 1968 merged with the University of Trondheim) in Trondheim in 1927, studying chemistry. Trondheim is in south central Norway.

Tronstad studied atomic physics at stints at Cambridge University (1209 – still in operation) in England under Ernest Rutherford (1871 New Zealand – 1931 Cambridge), who is sometimes known as the *father of nuclear physics*. Dr. Tronstad was a prolific researcher and writer of academic publications. He became a chemistry professor at his alma mater in 1936. He was a pioneer in heavy water research.

- Chemical engineer Jomar Brun (1904 Norway – 1993 Norway) graduated from the Norwegian Institute of Technology same as Tronstad, in 1926. He went to work for Norsk Hydro in 1929.

The two men knew each other well from their overlapping student and teaching days at the Institute.

Norsk Hydro decided to make a commercial plant with an output of highly concentrated heavy water, again as a chemical substance byproduct from the plant. The plan was to make money, selling heavy water for research and maybe other purposes later. Brun and Norsk Hydro hired Tronstad to design, engineer, oversee construction, and then monitor production of the plant.

The initial step in the process was distillation, using the strong base potassium hydroxide (caustic potash). Distillation is the process of separating the components or substances from a liquid by selective boiling and condensation. It is a physical separation process, not a chemical reaction.

The distillation was followed by a series of cascading electrolysis towers. Electrolysis is the technique of using a direct electric current to perform a chemical reaction. At the bottom, the finished product was 99.5% heavy water. The new plant was adjacent to the artificial fertilizer plant, again whose deuterium-enriched residue was the raw ingredient. The heavy water plant's capacity was 26,000 pounds a year.

This was the world's first heavy water plant. Previously, heavy water was only made in laboratories and in only very small quantities, and at great cost.

The first heavy water shipment to a research laboratory was 1/1935.

Fairly soon, scientists came to realize that heavy water was an excellent substance in slowing neutrons to moderate fission in producing isotopes. These isotopes in turn could be used to make powerful weapons. Heavy water also has the advantage of a moderator that works well with unenriched natural uranium. Again, such moderators are necessary to slow neutrons to sustain a nuclear chain reaction.

At the time, the Norwegian plant was the only worldwide efficient producer of heavy water. To say the least, the Third Reich (one of Hitler's names for his Nazi Germany) and other countries doing research on nuclear physics quickly developed an unquenchable thirst for heavy water. Researchers in Germany had first tried using graphite as a moderator, but concluded that graphite did not work from flawed experiments.

After several forced annexations of neighboring lands, Hitler as already noted started the European War 9/1/1939, invading Poland without warning. Norway was then neutral in the War, but it was thought that Germany was likely to attack and occupy Norway. Also by this time, German company IG Farben (formed 1925) owned part of Norsk Hydro.

Norsk Hydro partnered with IG Farben and Nordische Aluminum Aktiengesellschaft (Nordag) in making new aluminum and magnesium plants, to support the German war effort. Allied bombers dropped more than 1,600 bombs on the aluminum plant under construction at Heroya 7/24/1943. Heroya is located on a peninsula on Norway's west coast, on the North Sea. Norsk Hydro has a large facility there today.

The bombs destroyed the construction to date, and also killed 55 construction workers. Other plants under construction were bombed. To sum up, Herman Goring's (1893 Germany – 10/15/1946 Germany, potassium cyanide suicide after conviction of war crimes and crimes against humanity) plan to greatly increase production of metals to make more military aircraft, did not happen. Goring was a World War I ace. He was the Reich Minister of Aviation, along with other duties. Goring was also addicted to morphine.

As Germany's defeat and surrender seemed likely, Norsk Hydro reduced its collaborative relations with IG Farben during the War. No Norsk Hydro directors, officers, or employees were convicted of collaboration, after the War ended.

The *Deuxieme Bureau de l'Etat-major general* (translates to *the Second Bureau of the General Staff*) was France's external military intelligence agency, 1871-1940. It was dissolved when Germany invaded and occupied France 6/1940 and set up the Vichy government. However, the use of the *Deuxieme Bureau* name persisted in France, used by several resistance and intelligence groups during the occupation.

Deuxieme Bureau offered to store the Norway plant's current supply of heavy water, or buy and store. Germany made the same offer. Norsk Hydro Director Axel Aubert (1873 Norway – 1943 Norway) selected the French. Deuxieme Bureau sneaked out 408 pounds in 26 cans in early 1940. The timing was fortuitous, as Germany invaded and occupied Norway 4/1940.

When Germany invaded and occupied France 5/1940, the above-mentioned nuclear scientist Frederic Joliot-Curie took charge. He hid the heavy water in a bank vault, then a prison, and then in the Bordeaux region of France.

Joliot-Curie of course realized that the heavy water was not secure in Germany-occupied France. He shipped it across the English Channel to England on the British, 446' long and 56' beam and 26' draft, SS Broompark (1939 – 7/25/1942 German submarine torpedoed when en route to NYC with ballast only, four of 49 crew lost including Captain John Sinclair, sank three days later when under tow) tramp steamer, 6/19-21/1940. The voyage was from the Gironde Estuary (southwest France) to Falmouth (south coast of England), and uneventful. In England, the heavy water was to be used in the British Tube Alloys nuclear research program.

Broompark on that short voyage carried 100 refugees, fleeing France. These included 33 eminent French scientists and technicians with their families.

Antwerp Diamond Bank Managing Director Paul Timbal (1901 – 1971 Brussels) was one of those fleeing. Timbal was also a Belgian Army Lieutenant. He brought aboard Broompark diamonds worth millions. Other cargo included 610 tons of machine tools. The diamonds and the heavy water were strapped to the deck on wooden pallets, so that if the ship was sunk they could be loosened and float free. Hopefully then, the Allies could recover, not Germany.

Again, the heavy water transfer out of Norway to France and then England was done out of fear that Nazi Germany would invade Norway. That very thing did happen as noted above, 4/1940. Norway was occupied through V-E Day, 5/1945. The Nazis took over the Vemork plant a month later, 5/1940. German scientists replaced the Vemork process equipment with improved methodology. This increased production of heavy water.

Scientist Tronstad conducted domestic resistance. With the Gestapo hot on his tail, he fled to England 10/1941. In England, he gathered valuable intelligence from Norwegian sources (spies); both on the development of the liquid-propellant, long-range, guided V-2 ballistic missile at the Peenemunde Army Research Center, and the growing German interest in heavy water. The Peenemunde Army Research Center was located near the village of Peenemunde on the 172 square mile Usedom Island in the Baltic Sea. This is on Germany's northeastern coast. The island belonged to Germany. After the war, Usedom Island was divided between Germany and Poland (still the case today).

From his sources, Tronstad learned that the Germans had greatly increased the production of heavy water at Vemork. With Germany in control of the plant and increasing production, Tronstad decided that the plant (again realize that the plant was his baby) must be destroyed. He decided to lead a commando raid, as no one knew and understood the plant layout and process more than he.

However, the Norwegian military and intelligence sources now based in exile in England, and this supported by the British and Americans as well, would not risk Tronstad; because of his heavy water and other scientific knowledge and expertise, and his many intelligence sources. In fact, the information that he collected from his Norwegian spies on Germany's plan to use the Vemork heavy water to make atomic weapons contributed to kicking off the Manhattan project in the United States. Tronstad instead was consigned to devising a demolition plan, to be executed by commandos.

The already mentioned Jomar Brun of Norsk Hydro also somehow made it to London. He worked with Tronstad on the sabotage plan.

Elinar Skinnarland (1918 Norway – 2002) was a native of the Vemork area. He had worked at the hydroelectric plant. He escaped Norway to Scotland in 1942. He enrolled as a member of the Norwegian underground. He was parachute dropped into the plant area at night, 3/28/1942. He made contact with the plant's chief engineer and confirmed that Germany had increased production of heavy water. He was able to accomplish this as a local and former employee. Also, his brother and several of his friends worked at the factory. They became sources for information.

The reinforced concrete heavy water plant was snug against a cliff, 600' above the river. The rock cliffs were steep. The critical processing equipment was located in the basement. Its isolated location and fortress-like nature made it seem impregnable, from either ground or air attack. The only access was by a 246', single-lane suspension bridge. The bridge was 660' above the Mane River.

Despite the above, the Germans were not taking any chances. They installed floodlights and barbed wire fences. They planted mines in the surrounding hills. They installed machine gun nests. Soldiers were on duty around the clock. They conducted frequent area patrols. The bridge was guarded 24/7, of course. Luftwaffe fighters in the area were on alert.

By early 1942, the Allies knew the Nazis were racing to harness nuclear energy. British intelligence surmised that the Nazis planned to make a self-sustaining reactor to produce plutonium, a highly fissile element ideal for making atomic bombs. Plutonium is best prepared in systems using heavy water as a moderator.

Great Britain and the U.S. and also per Tronstad's recommendation above pushed to destroy the plant in an air or ground attack, as a joint effort of the Combined Operations Headquarters (1940 – 1947). The London-based Command Operations Headquarters was a unit of the British War Office department. It was tasked with conducting commando raids against German forces on the Continent.

Aerial bombing was first considered. However, British bombers would most likely not be able to hit the target precisely. The Nazis had plentiful anti-aircraft guns in the area. Also, German fighter aircraft were nearby and on call. On top of that, the structure was reinforced concrete and the critical equipment was way down in the basement. Nearby ammonia tanks would likely explode killing many civilians (ammonia is a very toxic gas). Bombing was ruled out.

The next steps, actions, and outcomes follow below:

- 10/18/1942   Norway had set up its interim government in exile in England.

Norwegian Army reservist Martin Linge (1894 Norway – 12/27/1941 Maloy, South Vagsoy, Norway) was a stage and screen (movies) actor. He joined his unit, shortly after Germany invaded Norway 4/9/1940. He was wounded by bombs and evacuated by boat to Britain. He recovered. He with other exiled or escaped Norwegians proposed formal resistance activities against the German occupation.

Linge was appointed 6/1940 as liaison to the British War Office to set up such a unit. He recruited Norwegian men. The unit was named the Norwegian Independent Company 1 (NIC1).

Captain Linge at age 47 was killed in the 12/27/1941 Operation Archery, a combined British and Norwegian commando raid at Maloy which happened to be his home town, against German military positions on Norway's Vagsoy Island. Maloy is on the southeast side of Vagsoy Island. Vagsoy Island is in the North Sea off the west coast of Norway. It is less than a mile from the mainland. The Germans operated a plant on Vagsoy which made explosives.

Subsequently, NIC1 was commonly called *Kompani Linge* in Linge's posthumous honor.

These commandos had escaped Norway to England, when Germany occupied the country. These young Norwegian men had watched the Nazis invade and occupy their country 4/1940, curtail their rights, humiliate them, press their women into sex, starve them, torture them, and execute them.

Norway had few Jewish citizens, about 2,200. During the occupation, the Nazis arrested, detained, and deported 772 Jews (35% of the total); most to Auschwitz. 742 of these 772 (96%) were murdered. This genocide was another reason why these young Norwegian men took the never anticipated leap, of becoming trained commandos. Most of the remaining Norwegian Jews escaped to Sweden or Great Britain.

The British Special Operations Executive was formed 7/1940 from three previous British organizations. Its purpose was to conduct reconnaissance, espionage, and sabotage in occupied Europe against the Axis powers, and to aid local resistance movements. NIC1 was a sub-unit of the British Special Operations Executive, tasked with conducting commando missions in Norway.

NIC1 or Kompani Linge was under the control of the Norwegian Army High Command and the British Special Operations Executive. The NIC1 was one of the most decorated World War II commando or military units. Five hundred and thirty Norwegian men served. Fifty-seven (11%) lost their lives.

Four NIC1 Norwegian commandos as an advance team, parachuted into Norway this date. They cross-country skied to the Hardanger Plateau, above the plant. They then hid. Tronstad had trained the four on the plant layout and operation. This phase was called Operation *Grouse.*

- 11/19/1942   As the second phase (*Operation Freshman*), two, four-engine, RAF Handley Page Halifax heavy bombers towed British commandos in wooden British Airspeed AS.51 Horsa gliders. The two crew (pilot and co-pilot) Horsa troop transport glider was 67' long and 20' tall, with an 88' wingspan. Its empty and loaded weights were 8,400 and 15,500 pounds. It could carry 30 troops. Its glide ratio was five to one, at speeds up to 100 miles an hour. Its landing speeds were 60 miles an hour empty and 75 miles an hour loaded, with flaps down. Horsas could be towed at up to 150 miles per hour.

The gliders had two pilots and carried fifteen Royal Engineers. The plan was for the gliders to land on a frozen lake only 3.1 miles from the Vemork plant, rendezvous with the four advance men, hike to the plant, blow it up, and then escape to Sweden.

The tow rope on one of the gliders snapped, probably due to ice formation on the two aircraft and the tow rope. The glider crash-landed, killing some and wounding others.

The second tug released its glider at high altitude. The Halifax then crashed into a mountain in high winds and rain and hail, killing the seven crew. The detached glider also crashed, killing several and wounding the rest.

The Gestapo captured the survivors, interrogated them, tortured them including the wounded, and then executed them by either gunfire or injection of air into their bloodstreams. This was per Hitler's 10/1942 order that captured commandos were to be executed. Of course, this was a flagrant breach of the Geneva Convention which bans summary execution of prisoners of war (POWs).

Forty-one airmen and sappers on the mission died. Two gliders and a heavy bomber were lost. Also, the Nazis now knew that the Allies were bent on destroying the heavy water plant. Already tight security was increased.

In the British Army's airborne operations, this was the first use of gliders in an airborne military mission as opposed to parachutes (helicopters are considered airborne, their military use came more than five years after World War II). As both gliders and one tug bomber and all men lost except the crew of one of the bombers from crashes or captured and then tortured and executed, it did not go well.

- 02/16/1943   The four advance men who had parachuted in 10/1942 had a long and arduous and cold winter wait, in their mountain hideaway. They survived on moss and lichen. They got lucky though the end of 12/1942, killing a reindeer for food (protein). Of course, they were on edge the whole time, fearing that the Germans would discover them.

A RAF Handley Page Halifax bomber dropped six Norwegian Special Operatives Executive agents onto the plateau above the plant, this date. These were men also from the NIC1 Linge unit. This area is now Telemark National Park. Besides all their gear (skis, explosives, weapons, clothing, food, etc.), they carried a cyanide pill. After several days of cross-country skiing and searching they united with the first four, isolated for almost four months. Blizzards further delayed the raid.

Joachim Ronneberg (1919 Norway – 2018 Norway) was one of those who parachuted in. He escaped Norway in 1940 after Germany occupied, to Scotland by boat. The British trained him on military skills and guerilla war tactics. He led the raid as a First Lieutenant. Joachim's brother Erling Ronneberg (1923 – 2008) was also a commando, trained by the British.

- 2/27, 28/1943   Milorg was the main internal Norwegian resistance group during World War II. Resistance work included intelligence gathering, sabotage, supporting long-term missions, spying, clandestine transport of weapons and explosives, aiding the escape of

Norwegian prisoners, assisting and escorting citizens to safety (neutral Sweden in this case), etc. Milorg assisted the ten commandos in several ways.

The ten commandos descended into the ravine, forded the icy river, and then climbed the steep gorge cliffs. They followed a single railway track into the plant area without encountering any guards. The British Special Operations Executive had by this time recruited a Norwegian plant worker. Gunnar Syverstad (1910 – 3/11/1945 shot and killed along with Dr. Tronstad, in a skirmish in a cabin at Rauland, Norway) worked in the plant laboratory. He supplied detailed plans and schedule information, which the commandos used to advantage.

A door that a Norwegian collaborator was supposed to leave unlocked, was locked. Two commandos crawled through a cable shaft for entry. Two more broke a window, and climbed in. Inside the plant, the four came upon only one worker as after hours. This was a Norwegian caretaker. As it turned out, Mr. Johansen was cooperative; terrified, but cooperative. The saboteurs later referred to him as a *good Norwegian*.

The saboteurs placed explosive charges on the heavy water electrolysis chambers. They attached a fuse, allowing only a half minute of time for escape. They purposely left behind a Thompson submachine gun to indicate that this was the work of British or American forces, and not of caretaker Johansen and/or the local resistance.

1882 U.S. Military Academy graduate John Thompson (1860 KY – 1940 NY) served in the Army 1882-1914 and 1917-1918 (called back for World War I), retiring as a Brigadier General. He was in the Ordinance Department most of that time. He began developing the machine gun during World War I. He completed the design in 1918. The weapon was introduced in 1921. The Thompson machine gun was called the *tommy gun* for short. It became famous during the 1920s-1930s Volstead Act (prohibition of alcohol products) period. Criminals and police both used it during Prohibition.

The Germans would presumably know that the local Norwegian resistance would not have access to this type of gun. This was done to hopefully avoid reprisals from the Germans, against employees that the Germans may suspect were insiders.

A bizarre episode ensued when the fuses were about to be lit. Plant caretaker Mr. Johansen had misplaced his spectacles in all the excitement. During the German occupation of Norway, replacement eyeglasses were nearly impossible to acquire. A frantic search for the caretaker's spectacles was successful. Johansen was very grateful for the delay. He exited.

The fuses were lit. The commandos dashed out. The explosive charges detonated, destroying the electrolysis chambers. Eleven hundred pounds of heavy water which was five months production were dumped down the drains. Twenty-eight hundred German soldiers pursued the saboteurs, but all escaped – thanks to a little head start, knowledge of the terrain, and some luck. Four laid low in the mountains to conduct later missions. Two escaped to Oslo, again for later resistance work as part of the Milorg effort. Five cross country skied 280 miles in 18 days (a feat in of itself) to reach Sweden and safety. They told the Swedes they were refugees. These five were led by Joachim Ronneberg, mentioned above.

This last phase known was known as *Operation Gunnerside*. Many rank this commando raid as the most daring and successful act of sabotage of World War II. Many deserve credit, such as Dr. Tronstad. He designed and oversaw construction of the plant, which allowed him to plan and prepare the raid so well.

The next events were as follows:

- 4/1943   German scientists repaired the plant, and production resumed.
- 8/1943   Production was at full capacity. Another ground raid was planned. However, the Germans increased security even more. The British and the Norwegians decided that another commando raid would be too risky and not successful.

- 11/16 and 18/1943   The USAAF conducted two daytime bombing raids, from U.K. bases. In all, 176 B-17s and B-24s dropped 900 bombs. Most missed the targets. The errant bombs killed 22 civilians including some in a bomb shelter – bad luck, direct hit. The Norsk Hydro buildings were wrecked. However, the heavy water plant deep inside the plant walls and at the lowest levels sustained only minor damage.

    The nitrogen plant was also hit. This had not been cleared with the Norwegian government in exile. This led to a diplomatic crisis, as the nitrogen plant was used to make fertilizer only for Norwegian agriculture.

    These air raids were out of RAF Wendling Station. Wendling is on England's east coast, but towards the south. The two missions were the longest for this bomber group to date, at 9.5 and 10.5 hours respectively.

At this time in the War, the Germans did not have much in the way of defensive air cover in the area. Realizing that the USAAF could and probably would conduct more raids and could do so in the daytime which greatly increased accuracy, the Nazis decided to move the just produced heavy water stocks and production equipment to Germany. The deuterium-enriched wastewater from the plant would be shipped in rail tanker cars by ferry and then rail to Germany, to make more concentrated heavy water.

Spies reported the plan and planned ferry date. The British War Cabinet assessed and ordered Norwegian saboteur Knut Haukelid (1911 Brooklyn of Norwegian parents – 1994 Oslo) to sink the Norwegian ferry SF Hydro (1914 – 2/20/1944 bomb sunk) during transport. Haukelid had been part of the commando team that blew up the plant. He had stayed undercover in the area.

The ferry shuttled back and forth to connect the two railways Rjukanbanen and Tinnosbanen, at the Mael and Tinnoset terminals on opposite sides of the 19-mile wide Lake Tinn. Ferry service began in 1914. The combined track and ferry service was primarily used to transport raw materials and finished product (fertilizer in this case) from Norsk Hydro's factory at Rjukan, to the port in Skien (also in Telemark Province).

The 174' long and 31' beam, nine miles per hour, SF Hydro steam-powered railway ferry had two parallel tracks on its deck, totaling 260'. Capacity was 12 railcars, six per track section. The heavy water was packed into steel barrels and loaded onto the rail cars. The rail cars were rolled onto SF Hydro and secured.

Haukelid was the only trained commando in the area. He recruited three other men, probably from Milorg. They broke into the ferry quay at night, by cutting through a fence. They boarded the ferry. One of two civilian guards discovered them. The saboteurs convinced the guard that they were civilian ferry employees and just wanted to sleep aboard. They carried 18 pounds of Nobel 808 plastic explosive and two fuses fashioned from alarm clocks on board in an old sack. Two of the four commandos sneaked into the hull and placed in the ferry's bow. The saboteurs left the ferry unseen.

The timer was set to detonate the explosive to sink the ferry at the deepest part of the lake, but close enough to shore to allow any survivors a chance of rescue. On

2/20/1944, the bomb exploded out on the lake as scheduled. The ferry sank quickly.

Farmers heard the explosion and rushed out onto the lake in small boats to investigate and rescue survivors, if any. In all, 18 and 29 aboard died and survived. The dead included eight German soldiers, the crew of seven, and three passengers (Norwegian civilians). Some of the Norwegian rescuers reasoned that the live German soldiers floating in the water should not be rescued, or even just shot in the water. However, this attitude did not prevail. The four German soldier survivors in the water were fished out and saved.

Most of the heavy water was lost. A few of the storage barrels were less than full, so floated. The Germans may have recovered some or all of these barrels. To sum up, this sinking greatly delayed or maybe even halted, Germany's atomic bomb development program during World War II. The Allies did not have intelligence of this though, and continued to bomb in an effort to damage or destroy research laboratories in Germany. This they would have done anyway.

A mini-submarine found the SF Hydro wreck 1,410' down in 1993, forty-nine years after the sinking. One thousand, three hundred and twenty pounds of heavy water were found in the wreck. One of the barrels was salvaged and is on display at the Norsk Industriarbeidermuseum (Norwegian Industrial Workers Museum) at Vemork, Rjukan.

Norsk Hydro closed the heavy water plant in 1971. Today, the original power plant is an industrial museum, just mentioned. The museum is mostly on the Norwegian labor movement. An exhibit though addresses the heavy water manufacture, its take-over by the Germans, and sabotage operations.

Norsk Hydro Company today is still in operation as an aluminum manufacturer and renewable energy (hydro and solar power) company. Today, it is 34% owned by the Norwegian government. It is based in Oslo and has 35,000 employees. 2017 revenues were $16.8 billion.

Tronstad pestered the Norwegian military authorities in Britain to be allowed to sneak back into Norway, to defend Norwegian infrastructure. The Germans as they were retreating in Norway were using a scorched earth policy. The authorities finally gave in. He along with six other commandos parachuted in 10/4/1944. One of these six was Gunnar Syverstad mentioned above who had worked at the plant, but fled to Great Britain when it was blown up by the saboteurs. He feared that the Nazis would suspect him.

In his sixth month in Norway undercover, Tronstad and his commandos took the sheriff of the area around Vemork prisoner as he was a Nazi sympathizer. The sheriff's brother followed their tracks to a cabin. The brother burst into the cabin firing his rifle. In the melee, Tronstad and Syverstad were shot and killed. They were ages 41 and 35. This was less than two months from V-E Day.

Dr. Tronstad was in the Norwegian Army 1924-1927 and 1940-1945. His rank at the time of his death was Major.

The Sheriff and his brother survived. After the War ended, they were tried and convicted for Tronstad's and Syverstad's deaths. The sheriff was sentenced to five years, and his brother ten.

Tronstad's wife and their two young children survived the Nazis and the War. The Gestapo questioned her frequently. She could not tell them much, because she did not know much. She was not in communication with her husband.

A number of articles, books, and films have been made about the destruction of the plant, and the sinking of the ferry. One was the 1948 Franco-Norwegian docudrama film *The Battle for Heavy Water*. It is an accurate description of the raid. Eight of the actual Norwegian commandos played themselves in the film.

Raid member Knut Haukelid wrote a 1954 memoir of the attack, *Skis against the Atom*. John Drummond wrote a novel on the raid, *But for These Men*. From these two resources, Ben Barzman (1910 Toronto – 1989 Santa Monica) and Ivan Moffat (1918 Havana {but British} – 2002 Los Angeles) wrote the screenplay for the 1965, British Eastman Color *The Heroes of Telemark* film. Benjamin Fisz (1922 Poland – 1989) produced. Anthony Mann (1906 San Diego – 1967 Germany) directed. Fisz by the way flew in the RAF Polish unit during World War II.

The film covered the unsuccessful attempts, the successful raid, the escape, the sinking of the ferry, etc. Age 46 Kirk Douglas (1919 NY -) played the Norwegian scientist (Tronstad). Age 35 Richard Harris (1930 Ireland – 2002 London) played the raid leader (Haukelid). Like most *historical* films, deviations from the actual are many.

In 2015, the Norwegian Broadcasting Corporation (state broadcaster) aired a well-watched, six-part TV mini-series based on the events (*The Heavy Water War*). The series emphasized Tronstad's role.

Progress reports in lay language on the development of the atomic bomb were sent to President Roosevelt, and then President Harry Truman (1884 MO – 1972 MO). These same reports were also sent to the British government. The atomic weapons were tested and near ready, by 6/1945.

Truman decided that bombing Japan with nuclear weapons was the best way to end the war, and that doing such would save hundreds of thousands of lives, especially Japanese lives.

Per the Quebec Agreement with the U.K. that mutual consent was required, Truman's proposal was relayed 6/1945 to the head of the British Joint Staff Mission. Field Marshal Henry Wilson (1881 London – 1964 England) concurred that the use of nuclear weapons against Japan would be officially recorded as a mutual decision of the Combined Policy Committee. The Combined Policy Committee was created as a result of the above-mentioned Quebec Agreement between the U.S. and the U.K. Churchill's statement was *There was unanimous, automatic, unquestioning, agreement.*

At the Potsdam Conference in Potsdam, Germany which ran 7/17/1945 to 8/2/1945 (8/2/1945 was four days before the first atomic bomb was dropped), Truman agreed to Churchill's request that Great Britain be represented when the atomic bomb was dropped. Potsdam by the way is a suburb of Berlin, located 15 miles southwest of Berlin's city center.

Great Britain selected William Penney (1909 Gibraltar – 1991 England) and RAF Group Captain Leonard Cheshire (1917 England – 1992 England) to observe.

Mathematical physicist Penney was the head of the British delegation working on the Manhattan Project. Cheshire was a highly decorated RAF pilot and commander.

The two Brits flew to Tinian of the Marinara Islands. This was the launch base for B-29 bombers. Major General Curtis LeMay (1906 OH – 1990 CA) however decided that they would not go on the Hiroshima mission, so they did not.

LeMay did allow the pair to go on the Nagasaki mission three days later, on one of the accompanying B-29s. Major James Hopkins (1918 TX – 1951 crashed in the North Atlantic Ocean for unknown reasons, 52 dead) as commander though took this B-29 up to 39,000' instead of 30,000' plus was 100 miles distant; when the bomb went off. Hopkins later said that he did this to protect his VIP observers. However, a buffer of that distance was not necessary, which Hopkins knew. Hopkins may have other reasons, as to why he was so afar at the time of detonation (maybe following orders from LeMay, for one). Hopkins later did fly over after detonation, for a closer look.

Cheshire had medical issues, and retired from the Royal Air Force 1/1946, at the age of 28. Nagasaki was his 103rd and last air mission.

Penney by the way was a member of the team of scientists and military analysts who entered Hiroshima and Nagasaki 8/15/1945 after Japan surrendered, to assess the effects of nuclear weapons on humans, foliage, structures, etc.

Due to the size and weight of the atomic bombs, extensive modifications to B-29s were required. The code name for the modifications was *Silverplate*. The four bomb bay doors and the fuselage section between the bays was removed, to form one 33' bomb bay. This required new suspensions and bracing. Pneumatic actuators for rapid opening and closing the bomb bay doors were installed and tested. New, bomb twin-release mechanisms were installed and tested.

To reduce aircraft weight, the rear anti-aircraft guns and the armor plating were removed. The reduction was 7,000 pounds. The result was an agile aircraft for a four engine heavy bomber. Much of this agility though was lost, from toting the five-ton bombs.

Other Silverplate modifications included converting to fuel-injected engines and reversible-pitch propellers.

The modified U.S. Boeing B-29 Superfortress bombers took off from the 39 square mile Tinian of the Northern Mariana Islands. The 2,000-mile flight distance took six hours. The Hiroshima and Nagasaki nuclear bombs were dropped August 6 and 9, 1945, from 30,000'. The high altitude was to avoid anti-aircraft fire from the ground and Japanese fighters, and to be distant from the shock wave.

Both bombs immediately destroyed more than three square miles.

Information on the bombs and the outcome is shown in the table:

City	Bomb	Casualties
Hiroshima	16 kilotons: 120" and 28" long and wide, 9,700-pound *Little Boy* triggered 1,968' above ground 8/6/1945 Monday at 08:15; 2.1 pounds of 140 pounds (1.5%) of enriched U-235 underwent gun-type fission, as sub-critical U-235 mass forced solid target cylinder into a super-critical mass, initiating a chain reaction	75,000 immediate deaths included 20,000 Japanese soldiers, 20,000 Korean forced laborers, 8 American POWs; 2 and 2 American POWs executed by guards and stoned to death by civilians; 128,000 more deaths in next 4 months; 270,000 deaths total as of 2013; 4.7 square miles of buildings destroyed
Nagasaki	21 kilotons: 128" and 60" long and wide, 10,300-pound *Fat Man* triggered 1,539' above ground 8/9/1945 Thursday at 11:02; fission of 2.2 pounds of the 13.6 pounds (16.2%) of imploding plutonium fusion in the pit; one gram of matter converted into active energy of heat and radiation	58,000 immediate deaths included 26,000 Mitsubishi munitions plant workers, 150 Japanese soldiers, 2,000 Korean forced laborers, 10 Allied POWs from the bomb or executed; 70,000 more deaths in next 4 months; 150,000 deaths as of 2013; 1.5 square miles of buildings destroyed
Total	1 gun-type uranium fission bomb 1 implosion-type plutonium fusion bomb	133,000, 331,000, and 420,000 immediate deaths, in first 4 months, and as of 2013

The U.S. dropped conventional bombs two days after Hiroshima, 8/8/1945. The targets were Yawata (Kyoto Prefecture) and Fukuyama (Hiroshima Prefecture). Twenty-one and 73% of these cities' urban areas were destroyed, respectively. Japan's air corps scrambled and shot down a B-29 and five fighter escorts.

The U.S., its Allies, and the whole world for that matter were sure that Japan would surrender after the atomic bomb was dropped on Hiroshima. This did not happen. The U.S., its Allies, and the whole world for that matter were sure that Japan would surrender after the two major conventional bombings two days after the Hiroshima atomic bomb. This did not happen.

Inexplicably despite this carnage and threats of more to come, Japan and the Emperor did not respond. Therefore, the U.K. and U.S agreed to drop a second atomic bomb, 8/9/1945 on Nagasaki. This was done. The U.S., its Allies, and the whole world for that matter were sure that Japan would now surrender. The Emperor did so but he took his time about it -- five days.

To sum up, the Manhattan Project culminated in the bombing of two Japanese cities with nuclear bombs (one uranium fission, one plutonium fusion) three days apart, 8/1945. The bombs were effective in ending the World War II Pacific War with Japan – although the fact that the Emperor required a second bomb showed that he and other Japanese leaders apparently could not stomach defeat, in favor of saving Japanese lives and stopping destruction. This was the case even though Japan had been operating in a stratum of obvious defeat, for more than a year and a half. To add to the disbelief, the U.S. did away with large portions of two Japanese cities with conventional bombs, in between the two atomic bombs.

The U.S. never bombed the Emperor's castle, so the Emperor assumed (correctly) they never would. This may have been some type of factor as well in the Emperor putting off surrender, that he and his family and staff were never endangered.

Lieutenant General Ian Jacob (1899 Pakistan {British Army father stationed in Pakistan} – 1993) was the Military Assistant Secretary to Winston Churchill's war cabinet. In regard to German scientists being demoted or otherwise curtailed, sent to concentration camps, forced into the German Army, or fleeing; he famously remarked after World War II *that the Allies won World War II, because our German scientists were better than their German scientists.*

Before the atomic bombs, 241,000 to 900,000 Japanese civilians had been killed by American (conventional) bombs. The most commonly accepted numbers are around 333,000 and 473,000 killed and injured. But again, another source states that deaths and injured were as high as 900,000 and 1.3 million. Whichever, the sum was much greater than the immediate number killed by the atomic bombs – 133,000. Even the sum of those killed by conventional bombs in the deadly year of 1944, was more than the atomic bombs killed immediately. Most of these killed were from fire-bombing raids on Japanese cities.

The U.S. lost more than 400 B-29s on these bombing raids. Twenty-six hundred Army airmen died in combat or during captivity.

The most damaging of these conventional bomb raids was 3/9-10/1945 (*Operation Meetinghouse*). Three hundred and forty-six B-29s took off from the Marianas (Saipan, Tinian) for Tokyo. Two hundred and seventy-nine of the 346 B-29s (81%) dropped 1,665 tons of fire-bombs. Sixteen square miles of the city were destroyed, representing 7% of the city's urban area. Ninety-two thousand and 41,000 people were killed and injured. More than a million Japanese were made homeless. Schoolchildren in grades three to six in larger cities were sent to live in the country. War factory damage was substantial.

Japanese opposition was weak at this time in the War, but not that weak. Anti-aircraft gunners shot down and damaged twelve and forty-two B-29s on this raid. Ninety-six airmen were killed. Japan scrambled fighters, but they had no luck. Meetinghouse remains as the most destructive, conventional, air bombing raid in history.

U.S. World War II bombing cost $33 billion. This was 91 and 9% in the European Theater and the Pacific Theater. The entire war cost the U.S. $330 billion, so the bombing accounted for 10% of the total costs.

Another source says that the War cost the U.S. $350 billion. This was twice what the federal government had spent since the country was formed in the 1770s. Forty percent came from taxes, and 60% came from borrowed money. For the record, $350 billion spent in the first half of the 1940s is equivalent to $5.3 trillion dollars in 2019 money.

In March, 1945, B-29s began dropping leaflets calling on Japanese civilians to demand that its leaders surrender or face destruction. The U.S. did this in an effort to save many, many, many Japanese civilian and military lives; and many Allied military lives.

B-29s dropped ten, twenty, and thirty million leaflets over Japanese cities May, June, and July 1945. Japan's leaders told its civilians that they would face harsh penalties if they picked up and read these leaflets. The penalties were increased if they kept them.

Also, the U.S. broadcast similar messages to Japan, from a radio station it controlled in Saipan. Saipan is the largest island of the Northern Mariana Islands.

Two days before the Hiroshima atomic bomb, the U.S. showered thirty-four Japanese cities (not Hiroshima though) with more than five million leaflets, warning civilians of the impending attack. The leaflet had a picture of a B-29 dropping bombs on one side. On the other side, the message was as follows:

> *Read this carefully as it may save your life or the life of a relative or friend. In the next few days, some or all of the cities named on the reverse side will be destroyed by American bombs. These cities contain military installations and workshops or factories which produce military goods. We are determined to destroy all of the tools of the military clique which they are using, to prolong this useless war. But, unfortunately, bombs have no eyes. So, in accordance with America's humanitarian policies, the American Air Force, which does not wish to injure innocent people, now gives you warning to evacuate the cities named and save your lives. America is not fighting the Japanese people, but is fighting the military clique, which has enslaved the Japanese people. The peace which America will bring will free the people from the oppression of the military clique, and mean the emergence of a new and better Japan. You can restore peace, by demanding new and good leaders, who will end the war. We cannot promise that only these cities will be among those attacked, but some or all of them will be, so heed this warning and evacuate these cities immediately.*

The above-mentioned Saipan radio station broadcasted a similar message to the Japanese people, every 15 minutes.

After Hiroshima and before Nagasaki, another 16 million leaflets were dropped. This leaflet stated as follows:

> *America asks that you take immediate heed, of what we say on this leaflet. We are in possession of the most destructive explosive, ever devised by*

man. A single one of our newly developed atomic bombs is actually the equivalent in explosive power, to what 2000 of our giant B-29s can carry on a single mission. This awful fact is one for you to ponder, and we solemnly assure you it is grimly accurate.

We have just begun to use this weapon against your homeland. If you still have any doubt, make inquiry as to what happened to Hiroshima when just one atomic bomb fell on that city.

Before using this bomb to destroy every resource of the military by which they are prolonging this useless war, we ask that you now petition the Emperor to end the war. Our President has outlined for you the thirteen consequences, of an honorable surrender. We urge that you accept these consequences and begin the work of building a new, better, and peace-loving Japan.

You should take steps now to cease military resistance. Otherwise, we shall resolutely employ this bomb and all our other superior weapons, to promptly and forcefully end the war.

Truman also broadcast a statement that an atomic bomb had been dropped on Hiroshima and more were to follow unless Japan surrendered, per the terms of the 7/26/1945 Potsdam Declaration issued by the U.S. and the U.K. and China. These terms included the following:

- Military demobilization
- Allied occupation
- Purging those who deceived the Japanese people
- Submitting to war crime trials administered by Allied jurists

Truman's statement included wording *that Japan would be subject to a rain of ruin from the air, the like of which has never been seen on earth.* Of course, Japan already knew this as its scientists immediately evaluated the damage at Hiroshima to determine the type of weapon used.

As to why Emperor Michinomiya Hirohito (1901 Tokyo – 1989 Tokyo) did not surrender after Hiroshima, this is not known. As to why he waited five days after Nagasaki to announce that Japan was surrendering – again he did not address. In fact for the rest of his long life, Hirohito never addressed any aspect of the War verbally or in writing.

Michinomiya Hirohito died in 1989, at age 87. He reigned 62 years (1926 – 1989). He never abdicated. Fifty-five year old Akihito Hirohito (1933 Tokyo -) succeeded his father. Akihito announced in 2017 that he will abdicate the Chrysanthemum Throne 4/30/2019, in favor of his son Naruhito Hirohito (1960 Tokyo -).

The purpose of the nuclear bombs was to save lives and end the war. U.S. estimates of the number of American military who would die invading Japan were up to 800,000; and up to 10 million Japanese. This does not include the 27,000 American POWs held by Japan. Japan had made it known that these men would be executed if the U.S. invaded Japan. As it turned out anyway, some were executed after the atomic bombs were dropped. In regard to this goal of saving lives, the atomic bombs were very effective in doing so.

In anticipation of the casualties from invading Japan, the U.S. made almost a half million Purple Heart medals. To this date, the Purple Hearts awarded to U.S. military personnel, are from these made during World War II. As of 2019, 118,000 remain in storage. Unfortunately, these are occasionally awarded to U.S. military personnel injured or killed, in the seemingly endless War on Terror.

The U.S. hoped to destroy military facilities and factories with the atomic bombs including the Toyo Kogyo Co. Ltd. (1920 – still in operation) factory, based in Hiroshima. Toyo Kogyo made three-wheel trucks and military hardware. The latter most notably included the Arisaka-design, five round internal magazine, Series 30 through 35, bolt-action, Type 99 repeater rifle, chambered for the 7.7×58 millimeter cartridge. This was comparable in power to a modern .308" round. This rifle was used by both the Imperial Japanese Army and Navy.

Lieutenant General Baron Arisaka Nariakira (1852 Japan – 1915 Tokyo) designed the rifle, in 1897. The Arisaka was a good rifle, matching the muzzle velocity and kill range of other World War II rifles. It was made at nine arsenals during World War II – seven in Japan, one in China, and one in Korea. Variants included a long rifle (Toyo Kogyo made most of these), a carbine such as for use by paratroopers, a sniper, etc. A wire monopod and an anti-aircraft sighting device were standard.

The Type 99 was the first mass-produced infantry rifle to have a chrome lined bore, to ease cleaning. The rifling was polygonal. However, some of these features were dropped by 1943. Also, quality greatly lagged in the rifles made in 1943 and on.

Japanese infantry (and sailors) were at a disadvantage using a repeater rifle, compared to autoloaders used by the Americans. This was the .30 caliber, eight round, M1 Garand rifle; which used an en bloc clip. The five round German Mauser and the six round Italian Carcano were also both repeaters. Like the Arisaka, the Mauser and Carcano were bolt-action.

As a side note, Lee Oswald (1939 New Orleans - 11/24/1963 Dallas, shot as a prisoner) used a World War II Italian war surplus Carcano to shoot President John Kennedy (1917 MA - 11/22/1963 Dallas, rifle assassinated) and Texas Governor John Connally (1917 TX – 1993 Houston, idiopathic pulmonary fibrosis) 11/22/1963 in Dallas. Oswald bought the 6.5×52 millimeter Model 91/38 infantry carbine under a made-up name by mail order, for $26.95 ($19.95 for the rifle, and another $7 for a 4x18 Japanese-made telescopic sight). The rifle was made at the Turin Army Arsenal in Italy in 1940.

Allied Russian soldiers mostly used the five round Mosin-Nagant, bolt-action repeater. However, some Russian soldiers in World War II used the 10 round detachable box magazine, SVT-40 autoloading rifle. German soldiers sent SVT-40s from killed Russians back to Germany for examination. In 1943, Walther combined the SVT-40's gas system with its current rifle, ending up with an autoload rifle. This rifle was called the Gewehr 43. It was comparable in quality to the M1 Garand. In fact, it carried ten rounds compared to eight for the Garand. Walther made more than 400,000 1943-1945.

U.S. soldiers and marines brought thousands of these Arisakas home as War trophies, during and after World War II. In most cases, the imperial, sixteen petals, chrysanthemum atop the receiver had been scratched off. The emblem indicated that the rifle was the Emperor's personal property. The few that still have the emblem are worth a lot.

U.S. soldiers also brought many Walther Gewehr 43s home, as souvenirs.

The Toyo Kogyo plant in Hiroshima mentioned above was 3.3 miles from the explosion point. That distance and as the blast was deflected much by a sizable hill between the epicenter and the plant, meant that plant damage was only minor. The plant was back to full production by the end of 1945.

Toyo Kogyo's headquarters building though was much damaged. Repairs were made. The offices of the Hiroshima bureau of Japan's public radio broadcaster were demolished. Toyo Kogyo founder Jujiro Matsuda (1875 Hiroshima – 1952 Hiroshima) offered building space to the radio operation, which accepted.

The company changed its name to the Mazda Motor Corporation in 1984. It is still based in Hiroshima. Today, it is an automobile manufacturer. Its largest market is North America. 2018 gross revenues were $820 billion.

Both bombs were set to explode high off the ground -- .37 and .29 miles for Hiroshima and Nagasaki. As a result, most of the radiation debris was carried aloft and dispersed by the mushroom cloud. The amount of fissionable material was only a few pounds. Compare to the 1986 Chernobyl Nuclear Power Plant meltdown in Ukraine, then part of the Soviet Union. Two tons of material were released at ground level, with no mechanism for rapid dispersal.

An earthquake triggered a tsunami which caused the 3/11/2011 Fukushima Daiichi nuclear disaster. The radiation fallout was mammoth, compared to the World War II atomic bombs.

Today, Hiroshima and Nagasaki have background radiation levels well below allowable minimums.

The Japanese refer to the survivors of the two bombings as *hibakusha*, which translates to *explosion-affected people*. Japan recognized 650,000 persons as hibakusha. Japan provided no assistance to hibakusha, until 1952. Japan's Atomic Bomb Survivors Relief Law defines hibakusha as people who fall into one of the following categories:
- within a few kilometers of the hypocenters of the bombs
- within two kilometers of hypocenters, within two weeks of bombings
- exposed to radiation from fallout
- in utero of a pregnant woman in one of the above categories

Fourteen percent of the Hiroshima victims were Korean forced laborers. These mostly men were denied payments. They sued Japan for money, successfully.

Hibakusha and their children are discriminated against (socially, economically, employment, etc.) in Japan, due to ongoing public ignorance about the consequences of radiation sickness. Much of the public to this day still believes that hibakusha are somehow contagious, and/or that their offspring are mutagenic. This is despite the fact that no statistically demonstrable increase of birth defects/congenital malformations has occurred. Again, Hiroshima and Nagasaki exposed women went on and had children, with no higher incidence of abnormalities/birth defects than the Japanese average rate.

Hibakusha formed the Japan Confederation of Atomic and Hydrogen Bomb Sufferers Organization in 1956. Its goals are to pressure the Japanese government to improve support of the victims, and to lobby for the worldwide abolition of nuclear weapons.

Of the about 650,000 hibakusha, about 485,000 (64 and 36% Hiroshima and Nagasaki) have died as of 2018; most from old age. This leaves 165,000 surviving (as of 2018), which is about one fourth. Almost all these survivors were minors at the time of the bombings. Most live in Japan. They are entitled to government support and receive a pension. The 1% that have radiation sickness receive more, for medical costs.

The country that has the most hibakusha besides Japan today is the U.S., for the following reasons:

- A plurality of the Japanese immigrants to the U.S. (and also Hawaii) before World War II came from the Hiroshima prefecture. Many came from Nagasaki as well. Common mainland U.S. and Hawaiian Issei practice was to send their children on extended trips to Japan to live with relatives, study, etc. They did so, so that their children would get to know their relatives back in Japan, learn Japanese culture, master the language, and also as they thought that the schools back in Japan were better.

The term the Japanese used for these children born in Hawaii or the United States who were educated in Japan but then moved back to Hawaii or the U.S. was *Kibei*. They comprised a sizable group, as about 12% of school age children were sent to Japan to live with relatives and attend school.

When World War II started, Issei efforts to get their Nisei and Kibei children and young adults out of Japan back to Hawaii or the United States were not successful. These numbered about 15,000. Many lived in their parents' hometowns of Hiroshima and Nagasaki with relatives at the time of the atomic bombings. Three thousand of such children survived the bombings but were exposed, and moved back to the U.S. after the War.

- American military men met exposed Japanese women during the occupation at the end of World War II. Weddings occurred, in Japan or later in the U.S. These women moved to the U.S. with their new American husbands. After all, devastated Japan was in shambles in many ways. Therefore, neither the American soldier nor his new bride even considered living in Japan.
- Some hibakusha moved to the U.S. in the 1950s and 1960s immigration wave, seeking educational and economic opportunities that were scarce in Japan, as Japan still in recovery from World War II.

People who had the misfortune to be at Hiroshima 8/6/1945 and then traveled 257 miles southwest to Nagasaki for number two, are called *niju hibakusha*. Hiroshima is on Japan's largest island of Honshu. Nagasaki is on Kyushu, Japan's third largest island. At least three trains departed Hiroshima for Nagasaki between bombs, each packed with refugees. The estimate is that about 140 niju hibakusha are still living as of 2019.

In 2009, Japan officially recognized Tsutomu Yamaguchi (1916 – 2010 stomach cancer) as its first recognized niju hibakusha, who survived both atomic explosions. Japan though for some reason has only recognized Yamaguchi as a niju hibakusha.

Yamaguchi was from Nagasaki He worked as a draftsman for Mitsubishi Heavy Industries, designing seagoing tankers. He was on a three-month assignment for Mitsubishi in Hiroshima. He was 1.9 miles from ground zero. He suffered burns on the upper half of his left side. His eardrums were ruptured. He spent the night in Hiroshima in an air raid shelter. He traveled to Nagasaki 8/8/1945 by train. Despite his burns, he showed up for work 8/9/1945. He was not affected by the Nagasaki bomb that morning. His wife was burned though. Their two daughters were not affected.

In 1964, Richard Nixon (1913 CA – 1994 Manhattan) spoke at a gathering of Japanese leaders in Hiroshima. As had many foreign dignitaries, he laid a wreath at the Memorial and offered a silent prayer. He stated that *Hiroshima has made the world promise to strive for peace.* Nixon had been Vice President 1953-1961 under Dwight Eisenhower (1890 TX – 1969 DC, congestive heart failure). He was elected President four years later. At the time of his visit, Nixon was associated with a law firm, but also campaigning for some Republicans.

Jimmy Carter (1924 GA -) toured the Hiroshima Memorial in 1984, 3.3 years after leaving Presidential office. However, official visits to the Hiroshima or Nagasaki Memorials or memorial events by U.S. officials or diplomats, did not occur until much later, as follows:

- 9/2008   52nd House Speaker Nancy Pelosi (1940 Baltimore -) visited the Hiroshima Peace Memorial Park at the time of a G8 meeting of lower legislative body leaders; she placed flowers; as House Speaker then (and again assumed this position in 2018), she holds the title of highest rank for an elected American female politician
- 8/2010   U.S. ambassador to Japan John Roos (1955 San Francisco -) attended a commemoration event in Hiroshima; he was the first American ambassador to Japan to attend an event at either Hiroshima or Nagasaki
- 8/2014   Roos' ambassador successor to Japan Carolyn Kennedy (1957 Manhattan -) attended a similar memorial service, as did Roos
- 4/2016   State Secretary John Kerry (1943 CO -) visited Hiroshima during a diplomatic conclave to set the stage for the 42nd G7 meeting; he wrote in the guest book: *It is a stark, harsh, compelling reminder not only of our obligation to end the threat of nuclear weapons, but to re-dedicate all our efforts to avoid war itself.*
- 5/2016   President Barack Obama (1961 Honolulu -) visited Hiroshima Peace Memorial Park with Prime Minister Shinzo Abe (1954 Tokyo -); they both laid wreaths; Obama's speech addressed the elimination of nuclear weapons worldwide; Obama made clear that Japan

despite its highly advanced culture at the time was to blame for the War, which *grew out of the same base instinct for domination or conquest, that had caused conflicts among the simplest tribes;* his visit was during the 42nd G7 summit in Japan; Obama was the first sitting U.S. President to visit the Hiroshima or Nagasaki memorials

Hiroshima and Nagasaki bombing survivors attended the 2016 event with Abe and Obama. Obama in fact met, embraced, and shook hands with some of these survivors. These included the following:

- Sunao Tsuboi (1925 Hiroshima -) was the fourth of five brothers. His two older brothers went to war in China and did not return. He was walking to school when the bomb exploded. He was badly burned. At the time, Japan was evacuating only young men for treatment, as they were needed for the war effort – at this stage, more or less for cannon fodder, but that is another story. As Tsuboi was 20 years old, he was evacuated and treated. He developed aplastic anemia, same as Marie Curie from the first page of this chapter He almost died. Today, he still suffers from illnesses, including cancer. He was a teacher and school principal. He married. He retired in 1986.

After retirement, Tsuboi got more involved in anti-nuclear and anti-war activism. He participated in sit-ins, demonstrations, and rallies. He was the Nihon Hidankyo (Japan Confederation of Atomic and Hydrogen Bomb Sufferers Organizations) co-chair, a member organization of atomic bomb victims. The Confederation lobbies for better treatment of hibakusha including paying for medical costs, financial support as not able to work, and even compensation from Japan for launching and pursuing the war which led to the bombings. It also lobbies for the abolition of nuclear weapons.

- Shigeaki Mori (1937 Japan -) was also walking to school in Hiroshima, when the bomb went off. He was not injured severely though. He has spent more than 30 years researching and obtaining official recognition for U.S. airmen, who were killed while being held as POWs at the Chugoku Military Police Headquarters. They died from the bomb, or were executed by either the police or civilians because of use of the atomic bomb. The Headquarters were located only a quarter mile from ground zero in Hiroshima. His book is titled *A Secret History of U.S. Service Members Who Died in Atomic Bomb.*

Since 2008, Mori has tried to locate relatives of airmen from one of the aircraft shot down during a 7/27/1945 bombing raid on Kure. Farmers who had hidden the wreckage turned it over to Mori, hoping that the pieces could be given to surviving family members for purposes of closure.

Japanese citizens sued the Japanese government twice for damages from the bombings (conventional including incendiary bombs, and the atomic bombs); arguing that the government was culpable for waging a reckless war that provoked the bombings, and for requiring citizens to remain in targeted areas (not warning to move to safer places). Japanese district courts in 2009 and 2011 handed down rulings, dismissing the lawsuits.

The below shows the atomic bomb memorials in Hiroshima and Nagasaki, and mock-ups of Little Boy and Fat Man.

The inscription on the arch at the Hiroshima memorial reads in part: *We shall not repeat the evil*. Which evil, the bombing or the conflict itself, and who is to blame, are left unsaid.

Einstein's Letter to President Roosevelt - 1939

Albert Einstein
Old Grove Road
Peconic, Long Island
August 2nd, 1939
F.D. Roosevelt
President of the United States
White House
Washington, D.C.

Sir:

Some recent work by E. Fermi and L. Szilard, which has been communicated to me in manuscript, leads me to expect that the element uranium may be turned into a new and important source of energy in the immediate future. Certain aspects of the situation which has arisen seem to call for watchfulness and if necessary, quick action on the part of the Administration. I believe therefore that it is my duty to bring to your attention the following facts and recommendations.

In the course of the last four months it has been made probable through the work of Joliot in France as well as Fermi and Szilard in America--that it may be possible to set up a nuclear chain reaction in a large mass of uranium, by which vast amounts of power and large quantities of new radium-like elements would be generated. Now it appears almost certain that this could be achieved in the immediate future.

This new phenomenon would also lead to the construction of bombs, and it is conceivable -- though much less certain -- that extremely powerful bombs of this type may thus be constructed. A single bomb of this type, carried by boat and exploded in a port, might very well destroy the whole port together with some of the surrounding territory. However, such bombs might very well prove too heavy for transportation by air.

The United States has only very poor ores of uranium in moderate quantities. There is some good ore in Canada and former Czechoslovakia, while the most important source of uranium is in the Belgian Congo.

In view of this situation you may think it desirable to have some permanent contact maintained between the Administration and the group of physicists working on chain reactions in America. One possible way of achieving this might be for you to entrust the task with a person who has your confidence and who could perhaps serve in an unofficial capacity. His task might comprise the following:

a) to approach Government Departments, keep them informed of the further development, and put forward recommendations for Government action, giving particular attention to the problem of securing a supply of uranium ore for the United States.

b) to speed up the experimental work, which is at present being carried on within the limits of the budgets of University laboratories, by providing funds, if such funds be required, through his contacts with private persons who are willing to make contributions for this cause, and perhaps also by obtaining co-operation of industrial laboratories which have necessary equipment.

I understand that Germany has actually stopped the sale of uranium from the Czechoslovakian mines which she has taken over. That she should have taken such early action might perhaps be understood on the ground that the son of the German Under-Secretary of State, von Weizsacker, is attached to the Kaiser-Wilhelm Institute in Berlin, where some of the American work on uranium is now being repeated.

Yours very truly,

A. Einstein

Albert Einstein

28- LAST AMERICAN DEATH - WWII

Great Britain and France set up the *Anglo-French Purchasing Board* in the late 1930s to arrange the production and purchase of armaments from North American manufacturers. It was based in New York City. A few military equipment manufacturers were in Canada, but most were in the United States. Britain and France did so as the two countries had little capacity in this area, and as alarmed at the imperialism and belligerence of Germany and Italy.

U.S. neutrality laws passed earlier in the 1930s blocked some purchases. However, some war-related products made in the U.S. were shipped over the border to Canada, and then put on a ship to Great Britain. As a dominion of the United Kingdom, Canada had no such restrictions on trading with Great Britain.

Germany sneak attacked Poland 9/1/1939, and conquered that country within two months. This was the start of what later came to be called World War II.

Purchase and transport were made easier with the implementation of the U.S. Cash and Carry program, 10/1939. This allowed the sale of non-war materials to countries as long as they paid up front in cash, and used their own ships to transport the goods. Most Congress members were not in favor of this program. However, the Nazis sneak attacking and invading Poland 9/1/1939 as stated above, gave the impetus for it to be approved. The Cash and Carry program much supported Great Britain and France to a lesser extent. President Roosevelt (1882 NY - 1945 GA, cerebral aneurysm) publicly promoted the program from the standpoint that bolstering Great Britain and France would help these countries tamp down the Fascists (Italy) and Nazis (Germany), so that the U.S. would not have to come to their rescue by entering a War.

Germany invaded Norway, Denmark, France, Belgium, and Luxembourg in the spring of 1940. These countries soon capitulated. The Anglo-French Purchasing Board became the *British Purchasing Commission,* as now Germany controlled France. The Commission now handled requests from these occupied countries as well (their governments in exile), as much as these countries were able to buy and use.

The Lend-Lease program began 3/1941. The U.S. supplied the U.K., Free France, Republic of China, and later the Soviet Union and other countries with food, oil, and materiel through the end of the War. The supplies and equipment included war goods such as ships, planes, munitions, etc. All was free. In return, the U.S. got free leases on some of the possessions in Allied territory of the countries being supported, for military bases and ports.

The Cash and Carry and Lend-Lease programs in actuality were set up to much aid countries fighting Axis countries, by getting around the Neutrality Laws. For the record, these programs much favored the recipient countries price-wise and benefit-wise, over what the U.S. received in money or other.

As it turned out, the British Purchasing Commission mostly focused on buying military aircraft. The Commission asked North American Aviation (NAA) 4/1940 to make single engine, single crew, low wing Curtiss P-40D Warhawk fighters under license, for use by the Royal Air Force to supplement its single engine, single crew, low wing Supermarine Spitfires and Hawker Hurricanes monoplane fighters. This was because the Curtiss Warhawk plant was running at capacity.

The P-40 was introduced in 1939, a year after the Curtiss P-36 Hawk. It was a much larger and faster fighter than the Hawk. However, it was already outdated performance-wise, compared to German and Japanese fighters.

NAA instead proposed the design and production of a state-of-the-art fighter. NAA contended that it could design and make a better fighter, and have it in the air faster than setting up a production line to make obsolescent if not obsolete Warhawks. The British Purchasing Commission gave the go ahead. NAA officers knew what they were talking about. The first prototype was ready 102 days after the agreement was made. This was 9/9/1940. It was labeled the P-51.

The single crew, single engine, conventional landing gear, low wing, long range, P-51 fighter-bomber first flew 10/26/1940. The square-cut, laminar-flow airfoil was thickest well aft. The result was a very low drag airfoil; in fact, the lowest drag of any fighter to date. As a result, its miles per pound of fuel was great. After testing and tweaks, the first batch was shipped to England.

The fighter with its Allison engine was called the P-51 Mustang Mk I. It was a winner, especially when the original Allison engine was replaced with a supercharged Rolls Royce powerplant. This greatly improved high altitude performance, to be able to compete with Luftwaffe fighters. Both the Allison and Rolls Royce power plants were 60° V-12s. The plane's name was changed to just the P-51 Mustang, with the engine switch.

The Royal Air Force first used 1/1942, for tactical reconnaissance and ground-attacks (strafing). Later, the British and the U.S. (and other Allied countries) when it entered the War used the P-51 for bomber escort. However, the first use by the U.S. Army Air Forces in Europe was not until the winter of 1943-1944.

The Allies used the P-51 in the Mediterranean and Northern Africa campaigns, as well as Europe.

With an extra, 85-gallon internal tank and external drop tanks, the fighter could escort four engine heavy bombers from England to Germany, and back. The range was 1,650 miles (P-51D variant). The additional internal tank when full of 511 pounds of fuel hampered longitudinal stability and performance. Therefore, the 500 pounds of fuel in this extra tank were used first.

By the last half of 1944, the German Luftwaffe was not much. Therefore, the need for escort fighters to protect plodding bombers flying off England was not much either. Therefore, these fighters were available for use in the Pacific Theater. They first flew there in late 1944. Again due to their range, they were used for reconnaissance. Into 1945, they were also used to escort bombers.

The Mustang was a winner. During World War II, Mustang pilots claimed 4,950 enemy aircraft kills.

More than 15,000 Mustangs were made. The 1945 price was only $50,985, which is $721,000 in 2019 money.

Five years later when the Korean War started, the Mustang (re-designated as the F-51) was the United Nations' main fighter. However, it was quickly replaced by the also NAA, single jet engine, single crew, low swept-wing, tricycle landing gear, F-86 Sabre fighter. Its maximum speed was 687 miles per hour, much more than the Mustang's 440 miles per hour. The Sabre jet aircraft was definitely necessary, to compete with the Soviet MiG-15 jet plane in high-speed dogfights.

Back to World War II. The U.S. dropped the first atomic bomb used in war ever. The date was 8/6/1945, a Monday. It exploded a little more than one third of a mile above Hiroshima. Immediate deaths were 75,000.

Lieutenant Marcus McDilda (1922 FL – 2008 FL) was one of the pilots flying Mustangs in the Pacific Theater. His engine seized up two days after the Hiroshima bombing when only five hundred feet up (another source says he was shot down), when on a bomber escort mission over Japan. He bailed out over water near one of the Japanese home islands. He survived the jump and salt water. The Japanese captured him quickly. The U.S. lost seven Mustangs that day which was a Wednesday, August 8.

The Japanese blindfolded McDilda. They dragged him through the streets of Osaka (on the main island of Honshu), allowing civilians to taunt and strike him.

Kempeitai interrogators asked him about the P-51 Mustang, not used in the Pacific Theatre until late 1944. The Kempeitai was Japan's Army and Navy secret police force, akin to Nazi Germany's Gestapo in some of its ruthless and grisly methods. McDilda provided some information, already known to the Japanese. He provided some data which were in fact fiction.

The next day which was August 9 and a Thursday, the U.S. dropped the second atomic bomb on Nagasaki. Immediate deaths were 58,000.

Of course, the interrogators very much wanted information about the new American weapon. McDilda as was the case with almost all American soldiers and sailors and airmen and marines knew next to nothing about the weapon, or even if there was a new weapon for that matter. It was all just rumors. Even after the first bomb was dropped, the technology behind it of course was not known by fighting men. In fact, only a few scientists of the many who worked on the Manhattan Project, had an understanding of the entire technology of the atomic weapons.

For yet another thing, the two bombs were different types. Hiroshima was a gun-type, uranium fission bomb; while Nagasaki was an implosion-type, plutonium fusion bomb.

McDilda's interrogators realized he knew nothing, which is what they expected anyway. That did not stop them from beating him.

A Japanese General entered McDilda's cell, drew a samurai sword, and pressed the blade against McDilda's face hard enough to draw blood. He told the American that if he didn't come clean, he was going to cut his head off then and there.

At this point, McDilda had an epiphany, saying, *Oh! THAAAAAAT atomic bomb!* He focused on remembering what he had learned in high school chemistry, six years back. In desperation he improvised, informing his fascinated captors that the Americans had figured out a way to split atoms. As he patiently explained it, the positive and negative charges were then forced into separate containers using a special process. The separated particles were then placed in the bomb shell, with a lead sheet in the middle. When the trigger was activated, the lead sheet was heated to the point where it melted, allowing the pluses and minuses to re-combine into a large atom creating an enormous lightning bolt, which shoved the surrounding atmosphere out of the area.

This combining relates to the concept of fusion (well, not really) a little, but of course fusion was not a word in McDilda's vocabulary.

Upon additional threatening questioning, McDilda reluctantly told his captors that the U.S. had more than one hundred atomic bombs, each 24' wide and 36' long, cushioned on metal racks on aircraft carriers. He explained that these aircraft carriers were steaming toward Japan, and in fact some were already offshore Japan. The carrier Captains were awaiting orders for transfer, to be loaded onto specially-modified B-29s.

Getting specific, McDilda added that he had heard through the grapevine that the next targeted cities would be Tokyo and Kyoto. And furthermore this was the case; if not tomorrow, pretty darn quick. Tokyo is Japan's capital of course, as well as its largest city. Kyoto was considered Japan's intellectual capital. Both Tokyo and Kyoto are located on Japan's largest island of Honshu.

The interrogators of course were not nuclear scientists, so they like McDilda had zero understanding of the atomic bombs. Despite all common sense though but ample desperation, they concluded that some of what the 23-year-old pilot was saying was accurate. They sent him to the Japanese Army administered Omori prisoner of war (POW) camp near Tokyo, for further questioning.

In Tokyo, an American-educated (New York City College) Japanese civilian physicist asked him again for the technical explanation of how the bomb worked. McDilda warily re-told his lies. The Japanese scientist could not stop laughing. McDilda was taken back to Omori Camp.

Despite his ignorance and the obviousness of his lies, these stories saved McDilda's life. In the days after Emperor Michinomiya Hirohito (1901 Tokyo – 1989 Tokyo) broadcast surrender, angry and vengeful Japanese Army officers murdered (beheaded) the other 50 airmen imprisoned at the secret police headquarters in Osaka, where McDilda was first incarcerated.

These 50 were all or almost all four-engine, Boeing B-29 Superfortress heavy bomber airmen. B-29s have a crew of eleven. B-29s were used to bomb Japan with conventional bombs. Modified B-29s (called Silverplate) dropped the atomic bombs on Hiroshima and Nagasaki.

In reality, the U.S. would not have a third atomic bomb ready until two weeks after Nagasaki, and a fourth not until mid-September. These would have been fusion atomic bombs.

Some historians credit McDilda with hastening the end of the war -- the hundred bombs ready to go, Tokyo and Kyoto on the short list, etc. This terrorized Japanese leaders, even after McDilda was exposed. The effects of the Hiroshima and Nagasaki bombings spoke for themselves.

Only 71% of American POWs hosted by the Japanese survived captivity. McDilda was one. He was repatriated 8/30/1945, and returned to his small Florida home town, Dunnelloon. Dunnelloon is 76 miles north of Tampa. He worked in road construction until retirement. He spoke little about his War and POW experiences. He spoke often though of his buddies who did not come home. He died in a nursing home in 2008.

Philip Schlamberg (1926 – 8/14/1945) was another P-51 Mustang pilot. He flew off Iwo Jima 8/14/1945 with three other P-51s to strafe airfields near Tokyo, to damage Japanese aircraft. The pilots before and after takeoff hoped that their mission would be called off, as this was after all five days after the second atomic bomb was dropped over Nagasaki. The Mustangs dropped their long-range fuel tanks, and strafed. As it turned out, Japan did surrender unconditionally to the Allied Powers per the terms of the 7/26/1945 Potsdam Declaration; while the pilots were on their strafing runs. Emperor Hirohito announced the surrender the next day, in a recorded 8/15/1945 radio broadcast to the people of Japan.

Returning to Iwo Jima, Flight Leader Captain Jerry Yellin (1924 NJ – 2017 FL, lung cancer) led the group through some clouds. Yellin's wingman Schlamberg and his Mustang were never seen again. The cause of his disappearance and death is not known, and will never be known.

By the Emperor's official, surrender announcement date of 8/15/1945, Second Lieutenant Schlamberg was the last American military to die in World War II. This was the last air combat mission of World War II, five days after the second nuclear bomb was dropped.

Yellin was working at a steel mill 12/7/1941. Two months later on his 18th birth anniversary, he enlisted in the Army Air Corps. He trained as a fighter pilot, graduating 8/1943. He flew the Curtiss P-40 Thunderbolt, the Republic P- 47 Warhawk, and the NAA P-51 Mustang in combat missions in the Pacific, with the 78th Fighter Squadron. He was on the first land-based fighter mission over Japan 4/7/1945. He served 1942-1945. Sixteen of his fellow aviators did not survive the War.

As noted above, the NAA P-51 Mustang was introduced in 1940. The version flown by Yellin and Schlamberg was the fourth variation, capable of speeds well over 400 miles an hour. It was the world's superior fighter. The U.S. Air Force introduced jet fighters in 1949. However, Mustangs played a significant role in the 1950-1953 Korean War, even including after the above-mentioned NAA F-86 Sabre jet entered the Korean War.

The movie actress Scarlett Johansson (1984 NYC -) is Schlamberg's grandniece. She and Yellin made a public service announcement video in 2015 to honor her great uncle's memory and the others who died in World War II, encourage patriotism, and promote understanding of World War II. This was part of the not for profit *Keep the Spirit of '45 Alive* campaign, on the 70th anniversary of the end of the Pacific War.

Yellin worked with the actor Ernest Borgnine (1917 CT – 2012 Los Angeles), and U.S. Senators Daniel Inouye (1924 Honolulu – 2012 MD) and Frank Lautenberg (1924 NJ – 2013 NYC) to lobby Congress to approve Spirit of '45 Day, to honor the men and women of the World War II generation. Congress did so unanimously, in 2010. The day is the second Sunday of August each year. This day was selected to coincide with 8/14/1945, which was the day that President Harry Truman (1884 MO – 1972 MO) announced that World War II was over.

Yellin traveled the country, speaking in support of Spirit of '45 Day and veterans.

Borgnine served in the Navy 1935-1941. He was discharged two months before the 12/1941 sneak attacks. He re-enlisted 1/1942. He served on an anti-submarine warfare ship, which was also used to train sailors on the operation of sonar. This ship patrolled the U.S. Atlantic Coast. McHale was discharged 9/1945, as a First-Class Gunner's Mate.

McHale after the War had no job or career. He decided to try acting. His first play was in 1947. He moved to movies in 1951. He won Best Actor for his portrayal of the warm-hearted butcher in the 1955 romantic drama *Marty*. *Marty* also won best picture, best direction, and best screenplay.

However, McHale is best remembered for starring in the screwball, television, situation comedy *McHale's Navy* 1962-1966 (138 half hour episodes). He played a stranded PT boat Lieutenant Commander with his zany sailors on an isolated Pacific Ocean Island, during World War II.

Senator Inouye of course was a Medal of Honor and Purple Heart recipient (lost his right when struck by a rifle grenade that did not explode), for his actions in Italy in World War II. He served four years in the Army (1943 – 1947), retiring as a Captain. He was a U.S. Senator from Hawaii from 1963 to his 2012 death, and President pro tempore of that body the last 1.5 years.

Senator Lautenberg served four years also (1943 – 1947) in the Army Signal Corps, including overseas. He retired as a Technician Fifth Grade in the Army Signal Corps. He was a U.S. Senator from New Jersey 1982-2001 and 2003 to his 2013 death.

Yellin, Inouye, and Lautenberg were all contemporaries, born within eight months of each other. Borgnine, Inouye, and Lautenberg all died within 11 months of each other.

Yellin said after the War that he did not think of his contemporaries who died in the War as getting killed. Instead, he convinced himself that they had simply been transferred to another squadron. This got him through the War. The demons came though, after the War. He suffered from posttraumatic stress disorder and survivors' guilt. He had difficulty keeping a steady job. He moved his family a dozen times in the United States, and once to Israel (Yellin was Jewish).

Yellin's wife suggested transcendental meditation. The twice a day mantra meditation worked for Yellin, allowing him to approach normalcy.

In 2010, Yellin co-founded *Operation Warrior Wellness*, as a division of the David Lynch Foundation. The program teaches military veterans with posttraumatic stress disorder the transcendental meditation technique, that saved Yellin. Lynch (1946 MT -) is a big-name movie and television show producer and director. He became a transcendental meditation adherent in 1973, and promotes the technique worldwide.

Yellin by the way flew back seat in a Mustang in 2014, after a 69-year hiatus. Some tandem seat Mustangs were made for training purposes.

Yellin and his wife had four sons. One married the daughter of a kamikaze pilot, so three of their grandchildren are half Japanese.

Yellin even into his 90s addressed veterans' groups. He worked with veterans, suffering from posttraumatic stress disorder.

Yellin came out with his memoir in 2017, written by bestselling author Don Brown (1960 NC -). It is titled *The Last Fighter Pilot: The True Story of the Final Combat Mission of World War II*. It was released 4.4 months before his death. Besides providing the information for the book, Yellin wrote the Foreword. When U.S. soldiers on the island of Okinawa got word that the Japanese surrendered 8/15/1945, they fired their weapons in the air. Sixty were wounded, and seven killed; from falling bullets. These are sometimes considered the last World War II American casualties – killed by self-stupidity, created from ecstasy though.

However again, the last World War II death (as judged by some) was 19-year-old Army Sergeant gunner and aerial photography assistant Anthony Marchione of PA. This situation is described below:

- 8/13/1945   A squadron of 82' long and 135' wingspan and 32' tall, four-engine, tricycle landing gear, Consolidated B-32 Dominator heavy bombers flew to Okinawa, four days after the Nagasaki atomic bombing. Japan surrendered two days later on 8/15/1945. However, the U.S. feared that its occupation forces would be attacked. The B-32s were used to fly photographic reconnaissance flights, to monitor Japan's compliance with the cease fire.
- 8/17/1945   Three B-32s on a similar mission, were attacked by both Japanese ground fire and fighters over Tokyo. During the two-hour engagement, the B-32s were damaged some but the airmen were not injured. The B-32s shot back but missed. Based upon these attacks, U.S. commanders decided to continue the reconnaissance missions over Tokyo. The purpose was to determine if the attacks would continue, as follows:
  - o   Either Japan rejecting its cease fire order
  - o   Or, Japan not taking action, to stop its fanatic diehards from fighting
- 8/18/1945   Two B-32s took off on another reconnaissance mission. Their assignment was to photograph seven crucial airfields, in the Kanto region. The Kanto region includes the Greater Tokyo Area. As they flew over Tokyo, seventeen Japanese fighters appeared and attacked the B-32s. Fourteen of these were single engine Mitsubishi A6M Zeros. The other three were single engine Kawanishi Shiden-Kai N1K-Js.

The Zero was introduced in 1940. At the start of the Pacific War, it was superior to American fighters in performance. The U.S. in the next few years came out with better fighters though, that out-performed the Zero. These were the Grumman F6F Hellcat, the Vought F4U Corsair, and the NAA P-51 Mustang already mentioned. Japan responded, and came out with the

Shiden-Kai. It was introduced in 1943, again as Japan's effort to match the newer American fighters. The Shiden-Kai met that test.

The Shiden-Kai was the land-based version of a single-pontoon floatplane fighter. It had heavy armament. It was very maneuverable, due to a mercury switch that automatically extended the flaps during turns. The flaps angle was adjusted in response to acceleration, to reduce the chance of stalling in a dogfight. The additional lift from the flaps allowed tighter turns. Its top speed was 408 miles per hour, compared to 332 miles per hour for the Zero. It climbed at almost a thousand feet per minute more than the Zero. The Shiden-Kai was put into service early 1944.

One thousand, five hundred and thirty-two Shiden-Kais were made, compared to almost 11,000 Mitsubishi Zeros. If the Shiden-Kai had been flying in 1941 and ten thousand made, U.S. losses would have been much greater for sure.

One B-32 was flying high at 20,000' and absorbed only minor damage. This B-32 shot down one of the fighters. The other B-32 was flying at 10,000' and heavily damaged by the Japanese fighters. Two crew members were hit, as follows:

o   Photographer Staff Sergeant Joseph Lacharite (19?? – 2000) was machine gun wounded in the legs; his assistant Sergeant Anthony Marchione (8/12/1925 – 8/18/1945) provided first aid, including applying two tourniquets; Lacharite recovered, but it took several years

o   As Marchione was tending to Lacharite, a bullet hit him just below the sternum; first aid was provided, but he died a half hour later midair, age 20 years and six days

Marchione had been in the hospital earlier for some reason; he wrote a 7/13/1945 letter to a friend back home, in which he said that he *wished to hell that he would heal up so that he could put in some combat time*; his motivation here was to get more points, so that he could return home to Pottstown, Pennsylvania (40 miles northwest of Philadelphia)

This was the first B-32 flight for both Lacharite and Marchione. Despite the damage, the B-32 made it back to Okinawa. Some consider Marchione the last American to die in air combat in World War II, even though this was three days after Japan's surrender.

So the Pacific War for the U.S. began at Oahu, Territory of Hawaii (and to be correct, at eight other Pacific Ocean sites the same day) and ended over Tokyo, both with sneak air attacks. These sneak attacks both ends of the War were technically during peacetime. The span was 3.75 years.

The last B-32 photography reconnaissance missions were completed 8/28/1945. Two B-32s were destroyed in separate accidents, with 15 of the 26 crewmen killed. So again, some consider these airmen to be the last Americans to die in World War II, thirteen days after the surrender announcement.

On the other hand yet again, some count Marine Private First Class Patrick Bates (10/7/1925 AL – 12/14/1945 rifle-shot on Guam) as the last American killed in World War II. A Japanese sniper holdout shot and killed Bates, when he was part of a team mopping up Guam 12/14/1945, flushing out Japanese holdouts. This was four months after Japan's surrender. Bates had fought and survived the campaigns at Bougainville 1943-1944, Guam 1944, and Iwo Jima 1945. He was scheduled to return home in two weeks. He was 20.2 years old.

Almost 417,000 Americans in uniform died in World War II. 297,136 of these, or 71.3% died in combat. The remaining 28.7% died in captivity, from disease, or in accidents. The chart below shows the number of deaths per military branch and percentages:

Service Branch	Number Died	% of the 416,816	Combat Non-Combat	% Combat % Non-Combat
Army	230,155	55.2	182,701 47,454	79.4 20.6
Army Air	88,119	21.1	52,173 35,946	59.2 40.8
Navy	62,614	15.0	36,950 25,664	59.0 41.0
Marines	24,511	05.9	19,733 4,778	80.5 19.5
Merchant Marine	9,500	02.3	5,005 4,495	52.7 47.3
Coast Guard	1,917	00.5	574 1,343	29.9 70.1
	416,816	100.0%	297,136 119,680	71.3% 28.7%

Of the Army deaths, these include 5,337 Filipinos serving in the Philippine Scouts. Five thousand, one hundred and thirty-five (96.2%) of these Filipinos died in combat. This is an extraordinarily high percentage of casualties being deaths, in the World War II era. One of the reasons was because the Filipinos were fighting at home, so were immune to diseases which Americans caught and died from.

Of the 297,136 Americans killed in combat, more data include the following:

- 63% died in the European Theater. These was 77, 20, and 3% Army, Army Air, and Navy/Coast Guard.
- 37% died in the Pacific Theater. These were 38, 29, 18, and 14% Army, Navy/Coast Guard, Marines, and Army Air.

Of course, there were some deaths and wounded as well in the CBI Theater.

Of the 416,816 American military killed in World War II, 543 were women. This is 0.130%, or one in every 768. Five hundred and twenty-seven of the 543 (97.1%) died in accidents or from illness or during captivity. Sixteen died from enemy fire (usually aerial bombs).

The survival rates of American prisoners of war in the European (this though not counting the Eastern Front) and Pacific Theaters, were about 96 and 71%. The 29% death rate at the hands of the Japanese was due to lack of food, clothing, housing, hygiene, and medical care; and executions. Many deaths occurred during forced marches and when being transported on hell ships. Many POWs were murdered.

For the record, the Japanese Army Regulations manual in place at the time of World War II, included this statement:

> *Prisoners of war shall be treated with a spirit of good will, and shall never be subjected to cruelties or humiliation.*

29- JAPANESE HOLDOUTS

Military officers in ancient Japan were known as *samurai*. Samurai were elite warriors, master of several martial arts. They were at the beck and call of the Shogun rulers (see below). They date back to at least the seventh century.

The Tokugawa Shogunate was the last, feudal Japanese military government. It ran 265 years, 1603-1868. Shoguns were hereditary military governors from the Tokugawa clan. Again, they ruled Japan. They governed from Edo Castle which was in Edo, the previous name for Tokyo (name changed in 1868).

Edo (Tokyo) is on Honshu, Japan's largest and most populous island. Honshu at 87,200 square miles in size is 32% the size of Texas. For the record, all of Japan amounts to 54% of the size of Texas.

The era therefore was called the Edo period. Fifteen Shoguns ruled during this period. Japan's Emperor during this period was just a figurehead with little power. Again, the shoguns were in charge, including appointing successors over this time. The Shoguns continued the tradition of training selected boys, to be samurai.

Even though the Shoguns were essentially dictators, this 265-year Edo period of the 15 Tokugawa Shogunates is Japan's longest run of peace and stability. Fortunately, most of the Shoguns were in the category of benevolent dictators. No wars or even civil disturbances of note occurred. It was rare that a Shogun felt that he had to order a samurai to discipline someone, to act as an enforcer, etc. As a result, samurai gradually lost their military function. They remained, but transitioned to being administrators, managers of civic programs, scholars, and courtiers. A courtier is a person in attendance at the court of a monarch or other leader. The samurai were upper class – sort of a junior nobility.

The samurai kept their swords, but mostly as just symbolic of their heritage.

Young samurai over the centuries were trained by their seniors, on how to live and act morally. This way of life was called *bushido*. The five basic tenets of classical bushido were courage, propriety, righteousness, humanity, and shame of surrender. Other preached bushido traits included honesty, honor, duty, loyalty, benevolence, compassion, respect, self-control, self-sacrifice, austerity, frugality, cleanliness, maintenance of physical health, etc. It was an honor to be selected to be trained as a samurai. Samurais because of their traditions and exemplary code were well respected, and even revered.

This codified samurai way of life was similar to the tenets of chivalry, in Europe. The chivalric code in Europe (this was mainly Great Britain and France) came later than the samurais, developed between 1170 and 1220. Chivalry was associated with the medieval institution of knighthood. To sum up here, bushido and chivalry were similar, with their members called samurais and knights respectively.

Japan's 59th Emperor Uda (867 Japan – 932 Japan) ruled 887-897. He conceived the idea of a national poetry anthology. Uda's son and 60th Emperor Daigo (885 Japan – 930 Japan) ruled 897 – 930. Daigo hired four court poets to write the anthology that his father recommended. It was published in 905. The anthology was called the *Kokin Wakashu, or Kokinshu* for short. The first known written mention of the word *samurai* appears in the just described *Kokinshu* anthology. This was in reference to civilian public servants, dating back to about 670. To sum up, samurais pre-date chivalry and knights by at least 500 years.

Over the years, the Japanese government and military and Emperor used the bushido code as a propaganda tool, but modifying it to fit their needs. For World War II, the revised samurai bushido code was used to indoctrinate the armed forces in obedience and extreme militarism. War was presented as purifying. Surrender and capture were presented as a disgrace to self, family, community, country, and Emperor.

Emperor Michinomiya Hirohito (1901 Tokyo – 1989 Tokyo) reigned 1926 to his 1989 death (62 years) which of course included World War II. The Emperor was the head of the Shinto state religion and considered divine. Hirohito played a key role in promoting the modified bushido code.

The propaganda and brainwashing worked. As a result, Japanese sailors, soldiers, marines, and airmen of World War II rarely surrendered. They fought to the death.

Again, this was per the bushido code as explained and preached by the Emperor and military leaders. If defeat was imminent, Japanese military men usually fought either when victory was out of the question to get killed, or even committed suicide.

In the days of the ancient samurai, this suicide was by the ritualized, prolonged, disembowelment method of *seppuku*. For the record per the bushido code, seppuku was not *committing* suicide but *performing* suicide, usually to avoid capture by one's enemies. Seppuku allowed the warrior to replace failure and disgrace with honor, and even martyrdom.

Some Japanese military men did perform seppuku during or at the end of World War II, although many of these selected a more efficient suicide method. For example, some had a relative or military underling simply shoot them in the head; or just pulled the trigger themselves. These were all or mostly all high-ranking officers.

Towards the end of the Pacific War or after surrender in the case of some high-ranking officers, their suicide decision did not relate so much to honor and obedience; but to avoid trial, conviction, and punishment for war crimes. The latter may have been imprisonment or execution in the case of commission of war crimes.

Suicide by enlisted men (and even civilians) was a departure or a convolution from traditional samurai traditions. The samurai creed was that only the highest-ranking officers should fight to the death or perform suicide, if that. Again, the bushido code in the past never required or even recommended that common soldiers and sailors (enlisted men) or non-commissioned officers or junior commissioned officers take their lives (fight to the death even when futile, or suicide).

However, the Emperor and the Japanese military were astonishingly successful in brainwashing all Japanese military men regardless of rank or tenure that they were modern samurai, that death in battle was honorable, that capture was abhorrent, and that suicide was exemplary when unsuccessful in battle. Incentive-wise, suicide and especially suicide to avoid capture led to great things in the afterlife.

Of course in regard to suicide later in the War, doing so in a matter which took out the enemy or enemy property was even better. The Japanese military developed several suicide methods of sinking or damaging USSs. The best known was the kamikazes. Other methods to attack USSs were shinyos, kaitens, and fukuryus. These methods are further discussed below.

A corresponding and virulent racist component of the propaganda was that Japanese were superior physically and mentally to other races or nationalities. A sub-component of this facet of the brainwashing was that the Japanese were especially superior to other Asians. Furthermore for some reason per the propaganda, the Japanese were especially, especially superior to Koreans and Chinese.

The teachings were that Japanese were semi-divine (the Emperor was divine), with maybe total divineness waiting in the wings, dependent upon beliefs and actions taken during life.

This brainwashing led to the Japanese's horrible abuses of Allied prisoners of war (POWs). The previous samurai quality of humanity as one of the five key tenets somehow got dropped. To the Japanese military, Allied POWs were obviously inhuman:

- For one important thing, they were not Japanese so inferior in all ways
- As evidence of being inhuman, they allowed themselves to be captured; instead of dying in battle, or taking their own lives to avoid capture

There was yet another extension of the propaganda. This was that Americans were inhumane, as well as inhuman. If given the opportunity, Americans would mutilate, rape, and torture Japanese civilians as well as military men; and then execute. They would then cook up their children, for supper. This facet of the propaganda took with Japanese military men, and Japanese civilians as well.

In World War II, the death rate of Allied POWs was about 4% in the European Theater (not counting Eastern Front POWs). The rate was 29% in the Pacific Theater. Germany's 4% rate was considered normal for the time. Japan's 29% rate reflects the executions, slave labor, and lack of nutrition and clothing and housing and medical care which resulted in death.

To contradict the above and for the record, note the below statement from the Japanese Army Regulations in place at the time of World War II:

> *Prisoners of war shall be treated with a spirit of good will, and shall never be subjected to cruelties or humiliation.*

Ensign Kazuo Sakamaki (1918 Japan – 1999) was the first Japanese prisoner of war. He was one of the ten mini-submarine crewmen which were part of the 12/7/1941 sneak attack on Oahu (Pearl Harbor), Territory of Hawaii. He ended up abandoning his sinking mini-submarine and swam to shore, almost drowning. He made it to the beach, and lost consciousness. Two U.S. Army men out on patrol just after the attack stumbled on him.

The other nine midget submarine crew died in the attack (killed from gunfire or depth charges, drowned, or suicide). These included Sakamaki's crewman Chief Warrant Officer Kiyoshi Inagaki (1915 Japan – 12/8/1941 drowned Pearl Harbor). His body washed ashore the next day and was picked up.

By the way, all five Japanese mini-submarines sank, which was the (unstated) expectation. These ten sailors were on a mission most likely to end in death, and they and everybody else involved knew it.

When Sakamaki came to and realized he was a POW, he asked for a weapon to kill himself. His American captors of course refused to oblige. By the time he was repatriated 8/1945, he had become a pacifist.

As already stated, very few Japanese military though were captured, per the bushido samurai code. For every 120 Japanese killed in battle, one Japanese surrendered. The figure for the Allies was one man surrendering, for every three killed in battle.

The (relatively) few Japanese who were captured were imprisoned in the U.S. or Australia, until the War ended. These POWs were shocked at the humane treatment they received, as they had been told repeatedly that the inhuman Americans (and Australians for that matter) were therefore inhumane – who would mutilate, torture, beat, and execute them. Also, they knew how their side treated Allied POWs. So from a reciprocity standpoint, they could only assume torture and execution. Again, they were shocked at how well they were treated and cared for.

In war or battle, military casualties are killed in action, wounded in action, missing in action (these almost always turn out to have been killed in action), not physically wounded but unable to function mentally, desertions, and captured. For World War II, Japan's military deaths as a percentage of casualties was extremely high. This was because as already noted, Japanese military men were brainwashed to fight to the death (or suicide), even when there was no hope of victory.

Another reason was that Japan's military field medical corps for combat areas and to the rear were not much. This was a reflection of the following:

- As Japanese were superior, they were immune to injury; this one component of the propaganda obviously did not take or did not last long if accepted at first, when Japanese observed deaths and injuries to their fellow soldiers and sailors
- That medical care was not needed, as Japanese military were to fight to the death or commit suicide

An occasional common method for the latter (suicide) in the case of Japanese infantry was the banzai charge, usually at night. In these cases, the infantry ran openly toward enemy lines (Americans in this case), screaming and shooting in the dark. As in large numbers and densely concentrated, the intention was to overrun the defenders by surprising and shocking with this human sea attack, engaging in melee combat.

The *banzai term* comes from *Tennoheika Banzai,* which translates to *Long Live His Majesty the Emperor.* The Japanese military considered banzai charges to be one form of *gyokusai. Gyokusai* translates to *shattered jewel,* a euphemism for *honorable suicide.*

Such charges may have some success when charging an enemy of not too many, armed with repeating rifles. If the enemy is armed with automatic weapons and especially machine guns such as was the case for American soldiers and marines on Pacific Ocean islands, the banzai runners become cannon fodder. Many Japanese soldiers were killed on Pacific Ocean Islands, with little injury to the Americans. Again, the Japanese in these cases were cannon fodder. To be more specific, they were deliberate cannon fodder.

American soldiers were usually able to mow these human wave attacks down with automatic rifle and machine gun fire. Afterwards, it was determined that sometimes the Japanese soldiers were out of ammunition. They planned to use their rifles as bludgeons and their bayonets or knives, if they were able to get close enough for hand-to-hand combat.

For such a human wave attack to happen, courage or coercion or esprit de corps was required. In the case of the Japanese, it was esprit de corps per the very successful brainwashing of obedience to the emperor and that death in battle would lead to martyrdom, and that failure or surrender was somewhere beyond shameful.

General Tadamichi Kuribayashi (1891 Japan – 3/26/1945 Iwo Jima, cause of death not known, body never identified) graduated from the Imperial Japanese Army Academy (Tokyo) in 1914 and the Army War College in 1923. He commanded the Japanese garrison for the 2/19/1945 – 3/26/1945 Iwo Jima stand. Kuribayashi banned banzai attacks, as knowing that such attacks resulted in so many soldiers killed, with so little injury to the Americans. The outcome was that the Japanese did kill and wound more Americans, before being wiped out.

Captain Samaji Inouye though bucked General Kuribayashi. On the evening of 3/8/1945, Inouye ordered a banzai charge, in an effort to capture the 554' Mount Suribachi, on the southwest tip of the island. Suribachi is the highest point on Iwo Jima. The charge killed 90 Americans. The Japanese had 784 dead. Other banzai charges on Pacific Ocean islands were much less successful.

The U.S. lost 6,821 men on Iwo Jima. Only two Americans were captured. Neither survived captivity.

The Japanese lost 18,000 men. Only 216 Japanese were captured, again as many fought to the death even though victory was futile. Another 3,000 Japanese remained in hiding though. Japanese soldiers Yamakage Kufuku and Matsudo Linsoki went the longest. They managed to hide out for another 3.8 years on the only eight square mile Iwo Jima. They surrendered 1/6/1949.

The American military had predicted it would take five days to take Iwo Jima. The Japanese held out 36 days though, based on Kuribayashi's preparations and fighting methods. The U.S. had more than 26,000 casualties, compared to 18,000 for the Japanese. The Japanese had many more deaths though, as noted above.

Captured Japanese military men had to deal with the shame of being a POW. The tradeoff was a long life after the War as opposed to death in one's teens or twenties. The shame problem tended to dissipate to zero in POW camps over time.

Japanese captives and also German and Italian captives quickly learned that an American or Australian POW camp was a wonderful place to be. In reality, they could not believe their good fortune in getting captured. Prison life in the United States was sometimes better than their pre-War lives in Japan (or Germany or Italy) as civilians, excepting lack of freedom. The worldwide, economic Great Depression ran 1929-1941. Adequate housing, three meals a day, suitable clothing, medical and dental care, recreation, etc. was something new to many Japanese POWs (and many German and Italian POWs as well).

These captives of course though knew enough to keep their mouths shut about their good fortune – during the War, and after.

As it turned out, the Japanese POWs' main concern when imprisoned was how their countrymen would treat them for not dying in battle or by their own hand, when repatriated when the War concluded. When imprisoned though, this concern diminished over time as already noted, as the War went poorly for Japan. Also, the POWs, Germans as well as Japanese for that matter, learned of the unjustness and abuses and atrocities by their country's military; as did Japanese and German civilians. This certainly changed their thinking, while prisoners.

As noted above, Japanese propaganda described Americans as inhuman brutes. To be fair, American propaganda during World War II also described Japanese as such. To be fair again, the latter was often an accurate description.

As already noted, Japan treated its killed, World War II military men as godlike. This started with the few Japanese soldiers killed in the Second Sino-Japanese War, which Japan began 7/1937 by attacking China without provocation.

The U.S. declared War on Japan, when the Empire of Japan sneak attacked five U.S. military installations (harbors, airfields, bases) on five Pacific Ocean islands on the same day of 12/7, 8/1942. This was in violation of the international rules of war. The 1907 Hague Convention addressed the requirement to declare war in its Convention Relative to the Opening of Hostilities statements. These clauses describe the international actions a country should perform, before opening hostilities. Article 1 states: *The Contracting Powers recognize that hostilities between themselves must not commence without previous and explicit warning, in the form either of a reasoned declaration of war or of an ultimatum with conditional declaration of war.* Japan took a pass on giving an advance warning, of maybe attacking. Shame on Japan again, as Japan had a history of attacking without declaring war.

The two dates are shown, as the attacked locations were on both sides of the International Date Line. The International Date Line is an imaginary line from the North Pole to the South Pole. It marks the change from one calendar day to the next. It roughly follows the 180° line of longitude, through the middle of the Pacific Ocean.

These five attacked islands were Oahu (Pearl Harbor), Philippines, Guam, Wake, and Midway. Japan lost 64 military men (55 airmen and nine midget submarine sailors), compared to 2,335 American military men dead at Oahu. The ratio of American deaths to Japanese deaths at Oahu was more than 36. Another 1,143 American military men were wounded. Japan had only a handful wounded.

The few men that Japan lost on the Oahu attack (compared to the U.S.), were described in the Japanese press as martyrs, or cherry tree blossoms. To be correct, Japan conducted sneak attacks at fourteen locations this day. The U.S. was the target in nine cases. Five were the islands mentioned in the paragraph above. Two were Howland Island and Baker Island (were air bombed) of the U.S. Minor Outlying Islands, which in turn are part of the Phoenix Islands. Japanese marines stormed and captured a USS river gunboat and its crew when in port at Shanghai Harbor (this was the only USS the Japanese captured in World War II). A submarine gun-sank an Army chartered freighter off California. There were more American military deaths and injuries and captives at some of these locations. American civilians were also killed at some of the locations.

Cherry trees and blossoms play a role in Japanese culture. The attraction dates back to the eight century, when Japanese aristocrats had the trees planted. The aristocrats would stroll among them when they blossomed.

The eighth Tokugawa shogun Yoshimune (1684 Japan – 1751 Japan) ruled 1716-1745. He had cherry trees planted in public places, for all to enjoy. Japanese to this day gather under cherry trees when they flower.

The buds usually all bloom at the same time, and then quickly wither. In Japan, they symbolize beauty and growth, but also that these qualities are fleeting and fragile – such as may be the case for a military man.

The Japanese military starting in the late 1800s made cherry blossoms a symbol, that life is beautiful but can be cut short. Military men were told that their deaths if death happened or if they self-made death happen, were like falling cherry blossoms.

Many cherry trees were planted from the late 1800s through World War II in Japan. Cherry blossom images appeared on army and navy insignias. The cherry blossom symbol was used to foster nationalism and militarism with citizens, as well as military men.

Kamikaze pilots (and other suicide method operators) painted cherry blossoms on their planes. Some even took cherry blossoms with them in their cockpits. Cherry blossoms and petals came to represent the sacrifice of youth in suicide missions, to honor the Emperor. The government preached that the souls of downed warriors were reincarnated in cherry blossoms.

Pioneering feminist, pacifist, social reformer, author, and poet Akiko Yosano (1878 Osaka – 5/29/1942 Tokyo, stroke) referred to this cherry blossoms concept in her poetry. Despite just noted as a pacifist, Yosano in her writings supported the war in China and later the war against the Allies. She urged and encouraged Japanese military men to endure sufferings in the Chinese invasion and occupation, and later World War II. So despite her reputation of being a pacifist, she was at least a chauvinist if not a militant. Excuse the contradiction.

Yosano died in 1942. As Japan's war crimes continued and became more known, maybe Yosano's sentiments would have changed.

Yosano was a popular poet, even more so in some circles due to her extreme nationalistic views. Again, she compared dead Japanese soldiers to cherry blossoms, in one or more of her poems.

Protests and sorrows from Japanese families on military deaths of their sons, brothers, fathers, etc. were countered with pleas to allow military men to *bloom as flowers of death.*

Cherry trees remain popular in Japanese gardens (if space allows).

Tokyo Mayor Yukio Ozaki (1859 Japan – 1954 Tokyo) led a program to donate cherry trees to be planted in the District of Columbia. Two thousand trees were received 1/1910. These trees though were infested with insects and nematodes, so were destroyed (burned). Another 3,020 trees of twelve cultivars were shipped in 1912 and planted. This was two years before World War I began.

For the record, Japan for World War I was one of the Allied Powers (same side as the U.S.). Of note though, Japan took the opportunity during World War I to grab Germany controlled islands in the Pacific Ocean and increase its sphere of influence over China. This increased Japan's imperialism efforts leading up to the 12/7/1941 sneak attacks.

Most of the saplings were planted in West Potomac Park, which is adjacent to the National Mall. This is in the Tidal Basin area. The Tidal Basin is a partially manmade reservoir between the Potomac River and the Washington Channel, and again part of West Potomac Park.

The purpose of the donated trees was to enhance the growing friendship between the two countries.

The annual National Cherry Blossom Festival has been conducted each spring since 1934, although the World War II years and 1946 were skipped. The Festival is to celebrate the coming of spring, but also commemorates the donation of the trees from Japan. Other U.S. cities and states by the way also conduct cherry tree bloom festivals of this type.

The Japanese military was shockingly successful in spreading the bushido message described earlier to non-military Japanese, at least by the June-July, 1944 Saipan Battle. The estimate is that 1,000 Japanese civilians on Saipan committed suicide in the last days of the battle, most by jumping off cliffs onto rocks below or the ocean. Some killed themselves with grenades they got from the Japanese Army. Some even killed their children. They did so for the following reasons:

- To avoid torture and rape followed by execution to be delivered by the Americans; and this to be followed by mutilation of their bodies, and then cooking and consumption of their children; yes, the brainwashing was that effective

- Emperor Hirohito knew that Americans would treat civilians humanely as they did Japanese POWs, providing food and clothing and shelter and medical care; he personally found the threat of defection by Japanese civilians disturbing, knowing that word would get out about the humane treatment, decreasing the will of soldiers as well as civilians to resist; he issued orders for military commanders to promise civilians who died fighting or by suicide a spiritual status in the afterlife, equal to that of military men who perished in battle

These suppositions just stated about Emperor Hirohito are from the 1971 historical *Japan's Imperial Conspiracy* by David Bergamini (1928 – 1983, Tokyo); the book is about the role of Japanese elites in promoting Japanese imperialism and the Greater East Asia Co-Prosperity Sphere, which was Japan's name for its planned enormous empire and dictatorship; Bergamini examines in his book the role of Emperor Hirohito as leader of Japan's Imperial conquest, and his role also in Japanese society after the War; some historians doubt the depth of the correctness of some of Bergamini's opinions

The Japanese imprisoned Bergamini when he was age thirteen, his younger sister, and his parents in the Philippines during World War II; his father was an architect, working for the American Episcopal Mission in the Philippines when Japan sneak attacked the Philippines 12/8/1941

As already noted, an estimate for Saipan is that a thousand civilians committed suicide, as did 7,000 military men. USSs though rescued some, who landed in the water. The two main cliffs that people jumped off on Saipan were later named *Suicide Cliff* and *Banzai Cliff.* Today, both sites are memorials. Japanese civilians visit to honor those who jumped and died.

The case was similar in the Ryukyus (Okinawa) campaign in the spring of 1945. Civilians believed that dying for their country in either fighting the enemy or by suicide would transform them into something like a lesser deity (the Emperor being a full deity) – cherry blossoms up in the heavens. Accordingly, civilians armed themselves, and were prepared to die in battle (or suicide if more convenient) if the U.S. invaded the homelands. If they did not have a gun, they improvised -- a knife, a knife tied to a stick, a bamboo spear, a broken bottle, a baseball bat, a pitchfork, a big rock, etc. Again, many Okinawans (meaning civilians) committed suicide and some even killed their children, after the Americans landed 4/1945.

The Japanese Army provided uniforms for Okinawan citizens (but no or next to no training), so that they could die as soldiers of the Emperor.

This brainwashing led to the ease of recruitment of operators of suicide machines and methods in 1944 and 1945, to damage or sink USSs. These methods included the following:

- Kamikazes   these were essentially pilot-flown, bomb-laden aircraft as precision guided missiles; the aircraft were converted from fighters or bombers, or purpose made; the pilot flew or tried to fly into USSs
- Shinyos   these small, bomb-laden power speedboats crashed or tried to crash into USSs
- Kaitens   these manned torpedoes crashed or tried to crash into USSs

- Fukuryus — these persons walked on the sea bottom using breathing apparatus with a bomb in a back pack to a USS, and then detonated it against the hull

For all these methods, the toted bomb load was enormous. Kamikazes were dispatched with full fuel tanks, to add to the damage upon impact.

Kamikazes killed 7,000 naval personnel and sank or damaged hundreds of ships. Shinyos and kaitens sank and crippled less than 20 American ships and boats. It appears that the Fukuryus program was never implemented. However, several suicide swimmers conducted attacks with at least one USS damaged.

The Japanese military's manual on defending the homeland called for the execution of any Japanese, who had a defeatism attitude. Therefore, none spoke out. Naysayers whether civilian or military knew to keep their dangerous opinions to themselves, or only others of like mind.

If they spoke out on the futility of the war and sacrifices and were reported, the Kempeitai would arrest them, torture them, and lock them up if not execute them. The Kempeitai were the military police arm of the Imperial Japanese Army, 1881-1945. They were known for acting as prosecutor and judge and jury without the accused having benefit of a defense, and swiftness and ruthlessness of punishment. The German counterpart of the Kempeitai was the Gestapo.

Japan was defeated by 1945, if not before. Any country with half-logical leaders would have surrendered. The Emperor appeared to prefer noble extermination of his nation.

The U.S. chose to not bomb the Emperor's palace. Therefore, the Emperor knew that he and his family and staff were safe. Maybe this was a mistake. Bombing the Emperor (his castle) and his family and staff would certainly have changed his thinking.

The Emperor though of course had taken precautions. The grounds had several bomb shelters (bunkers). Anti-aircraft guns were installed, with expert gunners on duty 24/7. Fighter aircraft patrolled.

The Allies were forced to use the atomic bomb to change thinking, in an effort to save countless thousands of lives – especially Japanese lives. Even then, it took two atomic bombs. The second was three days after the first – with conventional bombing in between that did major damage to two cities. Even then again, Japan did not surrender until 8/14/1945, five days after the second atomic blast.

The Emperor recorded the surrender speech 8/13 or 14/1945 on a phonograph. The 644-word radio announcement was broadcast 8/15/1945. The speech was titled the *Imperial Rescript on the Termination of War,* but came to be called the *Jewel Voice Broadcast.* This was the first time that almost all Japanese had heard their Emperor's voice. However, note the following:

- The audio quality was so poor, that most could not understand what the Emperor was saying
- It was delivered in formal, classical Japanese; few Japanese understood this courtly language
- The Emperor stated that the Japanese Government had accepted the 7/26/1945 Potsdam Declaration which demanded the unconditional

surrender of the Japanese military; the Emperor never stated that Japan had surrendered; the Emperor apparently could not be that straight-forward; most Japanese citizens did not know what the Potsdam Declaration was anyway, as Japan censored all news

Confusion was anticipated. Therefore, the radio announcer at the end of the speech clarified the Emperor's message -- that Japan had surrendered.

The phonograph disappeared. However, a radio technician had secretly made a copy. This was turned over to the Occupation authorities. It is the source of all recordings today. A digitally remastered version of the broadcast was released in 2015.

The original was later found, but never played again.

From the above and to sum up, the phenomenon of the many Japanese holdouts after Japan surrendered was because of the following:

- The contorted bushido philosophy for World War II, its promotion, and its mass acceptance; these soldiers could accept defeat; however, they could not accept defeat with surrender, or defeat without death (in battle, or by own hand)

- The success of the brainwashing fostering the Japanese superiority complex dogma, that Japan and Japanese were so great, that surely there was no way they could be defeated; therefore, these soldiers assumed that reports of surrender were obvious lies

   The U.S. air-dropped thousands of leaflets that the War was over; these holdouts again assumed that the leaflets were lies, as again Japanese were so superior that could not be beat

   Much later Japan also air-dropped leaflets that the War was over where it knew or suspected that soldiers were holding out; the words came from the Emperor, previous Army Commanders, and even family members (letters and pictures of family); again, some holdouts thought these were fakes dropped by Americans, to trap them into death or surrender

- As an incentive to fight to the death or die by one's own hand; this would avoid the mutilation, torture, rape, and execution that the Americans would render (again, the brainwashing took to this effect)

- As an incentive to fight to the death, to attain divineness

The successful propaganda brainwashing, despite these notions being impossible for most human beings to grasp, again led hundreds if not thousands of Japanese military men to hold out.

As already noted, the brainwashing was extended to civilians as well. Thousands killed themselves when American soldiers and marines landed, especially on Saipan (June and July, 1944) and Okinawa (April-June, 1945).

Another factor though was that many of the holdouts simply had not gotten the word of the surrender, as Allied advances had cut off communications.

The Japanese Army holdouts were almost all isolated on Pacific Ocean islands, when Japan surrendered. Some data on these is provided below (names provided when available):

Name Life	Date	Island	Comments
Sakae Oba 1914-1992	12/1945	Saipan Northern Marianas	Led 46 soldiers and 200 Japanese civilians into jungle; conducted guerrilla warfare against U.S. Marines; finally surrendered; he reunited with wife and met his 8-year-old son first time; became a successful businessman; elected to city council
	12/1945	Guam American territory	Sniper soldier shot and killed Marine Private First Class Patrick Bates (1925 AL – 12/14/1945), as Bates was mopping up Guam; Bates considered by some as the last American killed in World War II, four months after Japan surrendered
	1/1946	Corregidor Philippines	20 soldiers who had been hiding in a tunnel surrendered to a U.S. soldier
	1/1946	Luzon Philippines	120 soldiers routed in a battle in the mountains, 150 miles south of Manila
	2/1946	Lubang Philippines	A Filipino and American Task Force took 7 weeks to remove 30 hiding Japanese; 6 and 2 Americans and Filipinos killed
	3/1946	Guam American territory	Japanese soldiers kill a six-man patrol; these eventually caught
	4/1947	Lubang, Philippines	41 Japanese solders emerge from the jungle, stating that unaware War had ended
Ei Yamaguchi	4/1947	Peleliu Palau	He and his 33 soldiers emerged from jungle 3/1947, attacked U.S. Marine detachment with hand grenades; American patrols along with a Japanese admiral convinced Yamaguchi that the War was over, and he surrendered his troops
	4/1947	Palawan, Philippines	7 soldiers armed with a mortar launcher emerge from jungle, and surrender
	10/1947	Guadalcanal Solomons	Last soldier surrenders; only belongings a water bottle, a broken Australian bayonet, and a Japanese entrenching tool
	1/1948	Mindanao Philippines	200 well-organized and disciplined troops surrender
	5/1948	Guam American territory	2 soldiers surrendered to civilian policemen
	12/1948	Manchuria China	15,000 well-equipped troops in mountains, caught up in civil war between Communist and Nationalist forces; in this case, perhaps not easy

			to surrender
Yamakage Kufuku Matsudo Linsoki	1/1949	Iwo Jima Japanese possession	Battle ended 3/1945, with 3,000 soldiers holed up in tunnels-caves; some died, some committed suicide, some surrendered; these two machine gunners last to surrender
Yuichi Akatsu	3/1950	Lubang Philippines	Surrendered at the Philippine village of Looc
	6/1951	Anatahan Northern Marianas	USSs sank 3 Japanese ships 6/1944, survivors swim here; discovered 2/1945 when recovering bodies of a U.S. B-29 bomber that crashed on Anatahan; survivors salvaged the B-29 to make items and to arm selves; did not believe dropped pamphlets; family members wrote letters which were dropped advising that war over; finally surrendered
Murata Susumu	1953	Tinian Northern Marianas	Soldier living in a small shack near a swamp
Simada Kakuo Simokubo Kumal Odima Mamoru Jaegasi Sanzo	1955	Hollandia Dutch New Guinea	Survivors of originally a much larger group surrendered
Noboru Kinoshita	11/1955	Luzon Philippines	Seaman made it to shore when troopship sank; captured in jungle; killed self (hanging), rather than return to Japan in defeat, more than 10 years after War ended
9 soldiers	1956	Morotai Philippines	Discovered, and sent back to Japan
Sigheichi Yamamoto Unitaro Ishii Masaji Izumida Juhie Nakano	1956	Mindoro Philippines	All airmen, surrendered
Masashi Ito Bunzo Minagawa	5/1960	Guam American territory	Woodsmen captured Ito; Minagawa surrendered soon after
	9/1960	Vella Lavella Solomons	Japanese ambassador to the Solomon Islands flew to Vella Lavella to convince soldier, that it was time to go home

Shoichi Yokoi 1915-1997	1/1972	Guam American territory	U.S. wrested Guam back 8/1944; War ended 8/1945; 7 of 10 holdouts returned to Japan; remaining 3 hit out, but re-joined on occasion to discuss their situations; 2 drowned in 1964 flood; 2 locals captured Yokio; sent home; wrote book about experiences; whirlwind media tour of Japan; wed; became popular TV personality; advocated austere living; 1977 TV documentary on life made; made following 3 known statements: 1) *It is with much embarrassment that I return alive,* when he returned. The remark quickly became a popular saying in Japan. 2) *We Japanese soldiers were told to prefer death, to the disgrace of getting captured alive.* 3) *Your Majesties, I have returned home ... I deeply regret that I could not serve you well. The world has certainly changed, but my determination to serve you will never change.* He stated this on the grounds of the Imperial palace.
Yuichi Akatsu Shoichi Shimada Kinshichi Kozuka 1922-1972 Hiroo Onoda 1922-2014	3/1950 5/1954 10/1972 3/1974	Lubang Philippines	Japanese withdrew, as Americans returning soon; left some soldiers though, telling that would come back for them later; Americans landed 2/28/1945; they hid out; they harassed Filipinos, burning crops, raiding farms, etc.; they killed and wounded 30 and 100 Filipinos; they did not believe dropped leaflets from Japan including messages from the Royal Family, personal family members, General Tomoyuki Yamashita (1885 Japan – 2/23/1946 execution hung Philippines) who was military governor of the Philippines; eventually all Japanese killed or surrendered except for these 4 1) Akatsu walked away, 9/1949; lived solo 6 months; surrendered; led Filipino soldiers to search for the other 3, unsuccessfully 2) Fishermen shot Shimada in the leg 6/1953, but Onoda nursed him back to health; Filipino search party shot and killed Shimada 3) Kozuka and Onoda set fire to rice piles gathered by farmers; local police responded, and shot and killed Kozuka, but Onoda escaped; Kozuka is sometimes called the last military person to die in World War II

			4) A Japanese civilian tracked Onoda down 2/1974 in the jungle, who again told him War was over; still refused to surrender; civilian returned to Japan, to report; Japan sent Onoda's previous commanding officer to Philippines who released him from duty; Philippines President pardoned; became a celebrity in Japan; wrote memoir
Teruo Nakamura 1919-1979	12/1974	Morotai Indonesia	Japan ruled Formosa (Taiwan), drafted Taiwanese to fight; Allies overran Morotai 9/1944; hid out, lived with other holdouts or solo; made a hut on a 66' X 98' fenced in area 1956; pilot spotted the hut from the air 1974; Indonesian soldiers arrested; repatriated to Taiwan; last Japanese military holdout; as not ethnic Japanese (was Taiwanese), no hoopla in Japan in his case

Hiroo Onoda listed above enlisted in the Army Infantry when he was age 18. He was trained as a commando intelligence officer. Onoda was sent to Lubang Island in the Philippines 12/26/1944. He was told to destroy the airstrip and harbor pier. His orders included that under no circumstances was he to surrender or commit suicide until he accomplished these goals.

Onoda found other Japanese soldiers on the island and joined up. The officers in this group outranked him and prevented from attempting his assigned missions, for which he did not have the resources to accomplish anyway. American and Filipino forces landed Lubang 2/28/1945. Within a few weeks, all Japanese soldiers on Lubang except for a few had either died or surrendered. Onoda was now a Second Lieutenant, and senior in rank. He ordered three other soldiers to take to the hills with him.

Norio Suzuki of Japan is often described as a *hippie*. He traveled around the world. He said he was looking for Lieutenant Onoda, a wild panda, and the Abominable Snowman, in that order. He went to Lubang Island of the Philippines. He found Onoda 2/20/1974 after four days of searching. They became buddies. Suzuki urged Onoda to surrender. Onoda refused, unless he had orders from a superior officer.

Suzuki returned to Japan with photographs of himself and Onoda as proof of their encounter. The Japanese government located Onoda's commanding officer. This was the now elderly Yoshimi Taniguchi, working as a bookseller. Major Taniguchi flew to Lubang. He met with Onoda 3/9/1974 and issued him the following orders, which were in writing:

- *In accordance with the Imperial command, the Fourteenth Area Army has ceased all combat activity.*
- *In accordance with military Headquarters Command No. A-2003, the Special Squadron of Staff's Headquarters is relieved of all military duties.*
- *Units and individuals under the command of Special Squadron are to cease military activities and operations immediately and place themselves under the command of the nearest superior officer. When no officer can be found, they are to communicate with the American or Philippine forces and follow their directives.*

In his mind, Onoda was thus properly relieved of duty. He surrendered. He turned over his sword, his still functioning Arisaka Type 99 repeating rifle, 500 rounds of ammunition, three hand grenades, and the dagger his mother had given him in 1944 to kill himself with if he was captured. Onoda was 23 years old when World War II ended, and almost 52 when he surrendered. His holdout period was more than 28 years.

Even though Onoda had shot and killed Filipinos and engaged in shootouts with the police, Philippines President Ferdinand Marcos (1917 Philippines – 1989 Honolulu) pardoned him, based upon the circumstances of Onoda believing that the War was still on.

Onoda wrote an autobiography shortly after his return to Japan. *No Surrender: My Thirty-Year War* detailed his life as a soldier and then a soldier guerilla. He omitted the fact that he shot and killed several Filipinos post-War.

The Japanese government offered him a large sum of money in back pay, which he refused. Japanese people donated money to him, which he gave to the Yasukuni Shrine. This is a Shinto shrine located in Chiyoda, Tokyo, Japan. It was founded in 1869. It commemorates Japan military men who died in military service.

Onoda felt that traditional Japanese values had deteriorated. He followed his older brother to Brazil in 1975 to raise cattle. He wed in 1976 at age 54.

A Japanese teenager murdered his parents in 1980, which made big news in Japan. This upset Onoda and worried him on the future of Japan. His response was to return to Japan in 1984 and establish educational camps for young Japanese, teaching traditional values.

Onoda affiliated with the openly revisionist organization *Nippon Kaigi,* which advocates a restoration of the administrative power of the monarchy and militarism in Japan. Onoda's wife Machie Onoda was of like mind. She became the head of the conservative *Japan Women's Association* in 2006.

Onoda returned to Lubang Island (Philippines) in 1996. He donated $10,000 ($16,043 in 2019 money) to a local school.

Onoda died in 2014 of pneumonia and heart failure, age 91.

Onoda was the last, ethnic Japanese holdout – he came home 28.5 years after the War ended to much fanfare. He is shown below during the war and in 1974.

Since Onoda and Nakamura (last holdout in chart above) in 1974, rumors of more holdouts occurred; but these were never confirmed. Some later labeled these rumors as marketing efforts of some sort – to create buzz to attract tourists.

Most of these holdouts were enlisted men. Some though were officers, either non-commissioned or commissioned. These officers continued to command, if escaped with enlisted men.

Most of the holdouts were Army men. However, some were sailors who had made it to shore when their ships sank from combat, a mine, etc. A few were airmen, who survived being shot down or when their engine failed or if they ran out of fuel.

The holdouts when finally surrendered or captured were sent home to Japan, to resume their lives as civilians

A few Japanese military men decided to not return home at all, maybe to *avoid the shame*. Instead, they joined local independence movements or other conflicts. Six were as follows:

- Sei Igawa volunteered as a Viet Minh staff officer and commander in the First Indochina War. French troops killed him in battle, 1946. The Viet Minh was an organized anti-French and anti-Japanese resistance group, formed to seek independence for Vietnam from the French Empire after World War II. The war ended 12/1954. French Indochina was divided into the three countries of Vietnam, Cambodia, and Laos.

- Hideo Horiuchi volunteered for the Indonesia Army in its war for independence from Netherlands, as a Lieutenant Colonel. Dutch troops arrested him 1946, when incapacitated due to wounds from battle. He was eventually sent home to Japan.

- Takuo Ishii volunteered as a Viet Minh adviser, staff officer, and commander in the First Indochina War. French troops killed him in battle, 1950.

- Kikuo Tanimoto volunteered as a Viet Minh adviser and commander in the First Indochina War. He returned to Japan in 1954.

- Shigeyuki Hashimoto and Kiyoaki Tanaka joined the Malayan Communist Party's guerrilla forces to continue fighting against the British. The Malayan Communist Party signed a peace treaty and laid down their arms in 1989. The two returned to Japan, 1990. This was 45 years after World War II ended.

At the end of the war, one thousand Japanese soldiers in the Dutch East Indies deserted as fearing captivity for failure (not the case), or being sent home to Japan in shame and disgrace. They lived with Indonesians, mostly in small towns. Many of these soldiers later joined the Indonesian National Armed Forces or other Indonesian military organizations. Some died in the Indonesian National Revolution (against the Netherlands), which ran from the end of World War II to 12/1949. Indonesia by the way won this war and became an independent country (today, the Republic of Indonesia).

Army Ishinosuke Uwano (1922 Japan -) was stationed in the Japanese half of Sakhalin Island when World War II ended. The island wholly went to Russia then. He married a Ukrainian woman and settled in Kiev (capital and largest city in Ukraine). The couple had three children. He returned to Japan to visit +family in 2006. He was age 84. This was 61 years after the War ended.

30- U.S. PRESIDENTS, WWII MILITARY INVOLVEMENT

The first Europeans to sail to the Americas (North, Central, or South) were as follows (hang on, we will get there, to World War II):

- 986 Norse-Icelandic explorer and merchant captain Bjarni Herjolfsson was based in Norway. However, he visited his parents every summer in Iceland. This summer he sailed to Iceland to visit his parents as usual. However, his father had sailed off with Erik the Red Thorvaldsson (950 Norway – 1003 Greenland) to Greenland. Herjolfsson left Iceland headed for Greenland to find his father. He had no map or reliable navigation tools. A storm blew him off course, way off course, to what is today Canada. He sighted the mainland and islands. He decided not to land, again as he was intent on finding his father in Greenland. He turned around and sailed back.

  His crew begged him to anchor, land, and explore, but again he chose not to. He was much chided later by many including leaders, for this decision to not land and explore. But again, Herjolfsson was the first known European to sail to the Americas.

- 1000 Norse explorer Leif Eriksson (970 Iceland – 1020 Greenland) was Erik the Red Thorvaldsson's son. Intrigued by Herjolfsson's account of his voyage fourteen years back, Eriksson bought Herjolfsson's ship, hired a crew of 35 men, and sailed to Canada. The party landed on the northernmost tip of Newfoundland Island. Wild grapes grew in the area, so they christened the land *Vinland.* They wintered over here and explored the area. They encountered natives. They then sailed back to Greenland.

  Locals thought that mounds in that area were made by Native Canadians. However, an archeological dig in the 1960s confirmed that it was Eriksson's settlement. The site is called *L'Anse aux Meadows.* L'Anse aux Meadows is a French-English name, which translates to *the bay by the meadows.* The origin of the name for the area is not known.

- 1004 Thorvald Eriksson who was Erik the Red Thorvaldsson's son and Leif Eriksson's brother made the voyage to Canada with 30 men. They wintered over at Leif's camp from four years back. They attacked nine natives, who were sleeping under three skin-covered canoes. One of these nine escaped and returned with a larger force. They shot and killed Thorvald with an arrow. Thorvald was the first known European and white person to die in the Americas. Thorvald was married to Gudrid Thorbjarnardottir (mentioned below), but she was not on this voyage.

- 1009 Icelandic merchant and explorer Thorfinn Karlsefni (known as Thorfinn the Valiant) wed Thorvald Eriksson's widow and Leif Eriksson's sister-in-law Gudrid Thorbjarnardottir (980 Iceland - ????). The couple led an expedition of 65 settlers (60 men and five women) from Greenland to Vinland. Their son

Snorri Thorfinnsson (1009 Vinland – 1090) was born in Vinland, the first known European and white child born in the Americas.

They brought cattle to raise. They cut timber, harvested grapes, and caught fish and game. They bartered with the natives. The colony was not successful, mainly due to conflict with the natives. They returned to Greenland.

- 1492 More than five centuries after number one Herjolfsson and after a 483-year gap, Christopher Columbus (1451 Genoa – 1506 Spain) departed Spain sailing west under the Spanish flag. The goal was to find a new trade route to the East Indies. The East Indies are the Indonesian Archipelago of 18,306 islands (largest archipelago on the planet, in number of islands) and the Philippines Archipelago of 7,641 islands. An archipelago is a group of islands. Spain wanted to enter the spice trade with Asian territories.

  Seventy days later, a lookout spotted land. This was one of the Bahama Islands – maybe the 63 square mile San Salvador Island. San Salvador Island is 376 miles east-southeast of today's Miami.

  Of note, Columbus later claimed that he had spotted a light on land several hours before his lookout with his own 41-year-old eyes, thereby claiming for himself the lifetime pension promised by the Spanish royalty to the first person to sight land. Whatever.

  Columbus landed an exploration party.

The first four voyages described above by Viking-Scandinavian types to Canada and their landings and settlements are addressed in several chronicles. These include the work of German Adam of Bremen written about 1075, the *Book of Icelanders* written about 1122 by Ari Thorgilsson known as Ari the Wise (1067 Iceland – 1148 Iceland), the *Saga of the Greenlanders* written in the 1200s, and the *Erik the Red Saga* also written in the 1200s. As the accounts vary (including on some of the dates mentioned above) and as some of the writing is fanciful, some historians doubt some of the claims made in the sagas. On the other hand, the accounts are generally interpreted as factual. And as already mentioned, archeological evidence in Canada from at least one of the wintering over periods was noted and confirmed.

Columbus made four voyages to the New World from Spain, the last in 1502.

To his dying day at age 54, Columbus believed that the islands and mainland he saw and landed on were on the back side of Asia. He never realized or accepted that he had re-discovered continents, reached more than 500 years earlier by other Europeans. Columbus called the inhabitants Indios, as he thought he landed on an island of the East Indies. This is why Native Americans are often called Indians, to this day.

On his second voyage over (1493), Columbus landed on what is today Cuba. He claimed the 42,426 square mile island (16% the size of Texas) for Spain. The locals were not given the option of remaining independent. The natives were told that their new highnesses were a King Ferdinand II (1452 Spain – 1516 Spain) and a Queen Isabella I (1451 Spain – 1504 Spain), living and ruling from a palace in a city called Madrid in a country called Spain on the Iberian Peninsula of a continent called Europe. As they were told in Spanish and as they did not understand Spanish well if at all, this may not have been an issue at the time. Even when they learned Spanish or the Spaniards learned the native language, such astounding statements were a bit much, probably beyond the understanding of these primitive people.

Issues began soon enough though.

The Spaniards started a settlement on Cuba in 1511. The Spanish settlers forced the native Taino to work to support the settlement. The Tainos were one of the indigenous peoples of the Caribbean. At the time of Columbus' arrival, they were the principal inhabitants of most of Cuba, Trinidad, Jamaica, Hispaniola (Hispaniola is Haiti and the Dominican Republic today), and Puerto Rico. The Tainos of course resisted this slave labor.

Due to the harsh living conditions and hard work coupled with lack of resistance to Eurasian infectious diseases (measles and smallpox mainly) that they were not immune to, almost all the Taino in the area died off. The Spaniards decided to import Western Africans as considered hardier and also thought to be more tractable, for cheap labor.

Tainos on other islands also succumbed to European diseases. Today, there are no or very few full-blooded Tainos left.

Portugal and France moved quickly to establish a presence in the New World, as did Spain. Other European countries lagged. Most of these efforts though were not successful. The Cuban settlement mentioned above which again was the first, was the first successful colony in the New World, by Europeans. To accomplish this though, the Spaniards had to capture and execute the Taino leaders (burned them alive), and also use slave labor.

The joint stock, Virginia London Company of London financed the James Fort settlement in the Colony of Virginia. The settlement was named in honor of sitting monarch James VI and I (1566 Scotland – 1625 England). James was King of Scotland 1567-1603. He was then King of Scotland, England, and Ireland when the Scottish and English crowns merged in 1603, to his 1625 death. This is how he ended up with two numbers. Anyway, the venture's goal was to make a fortune, finding and selling gold.

The settlement was located on the east bank of the Powhatan River. This intrastate Virginia river today is called the James River. The 444-mile with its longer source tributary (this is the Jackson River) James River drains into the large natural harbor of Hampton Roads, Virginia. Hampton Roads is on Chesapeake Bay, Atlantic Ocean.

The settlement was located 51 miles southeast of present-day Richmond, which is Virginia's capital today. This is seven miles southwest of present-day Williamsburg, Virginia. Historical Williamsburg was founded in 1632.

The first wave of British settlers arrived 5/4/1607. Only sixty of the initial 214 (28%) were alive a few years later. Besides this bad news, the gold thing did not work out either. The Virginia London Company sent more settlers over, in several waves.

The Europeans encountered people, as already mentioned. These were the Paleoamericans. Other common terms used are Native Americans, Paleoindians, or just Indians as already mentioned. Paleoamericans migrated to the Americas fifteen to thirty thousand years ago from Eurasia. They walked across Beringia. Beringia was the land bridge which connected Siberia to Alaska. The migrations continued until about ten thousand years ago when the land bridge became submerged by rising sea level, due to melting glaciers.

The Paleoamericans spread southward to sparsely occupy much of the Americas. They diversified into many hundreds of culturally distinct nations and tribes. These persons are referred to below as Native Americans.

The skin of the Native Americans that the British encountered in Virginia was darker than their own. Their clothing, food, abodes, language, social mores, spiritual beliefs, etc. were also different. European colonists considered the Native Americans to be pagans, defining a pagan as a person whose religious beliefs were different from their own. Somehow, the European colonists decided that the Native Americans were inferior, pagan savages. Accordingly, the colonists generally decided that genocide, enslavement, and forced removal were the best approaches in the case of these *godless hostiles,* in the name of civilization and Christianity -- so much for British birthright equal rights and religious tolerance premises. Such conclusions and actions are even more startling, considering that the British were the interlopers.

Most Native Americans died as a result of European settlers moving to the Americas, from the following:

- European diseases – the Native Americans had never been exposed to certain pathogens, and therefore were not immune; these diseases were many, and included smallpox and measles which were the most lethal for the Native Americans; pathogens of other infectious diseases that the Europeans brought over as endemic to European countries that the Native Americans had not been exposed to so again not immune to were chickenpox, bubonic plague, cholera, the common cold, diphtheria, influenza, malaria, scarlet fever, sexually transmitted diseases, typhoid, typhus, tuberculosis, and pertussis; in some cases, entire communities and tribes of Native Americans were wiped out or almost wiped out

- Slavery – slavery was not new to some Native Americans; some tribes enslaved members of other tribes; these were usually war captives; some tribes sold or traded these slaves to other tribes, and later to the Europeans; some Native American slaves died from hard work or as not cared for

- Warfare – killed in innumerable battles and massacres; these ran into the 1920s in the southwest United States against the Apaches; the Europeans had superior weapons (muskets compared to bows and arrows and spears) and horses, so the fights were one-sided, at least in the early days; the Native Americans later got horses, firearms, etc., from the Europeans; but the ships kept coming; the droves from Europe were too many, and the Native Americans were overwhelmed

- Forced removals – often to land where difficult to make a living, with poverty and sometimes death resulting; many Native Americans fled though to these undesirable areas, in an effort to avoid an earlier, violent death thought more likely

The estimates of the number of Native Americans living in what is today the United States at the time Columbus sailed at the end of the 15th century, range from 2.1 to 18 million. Their numbers in what is today the United States were only 600,000 and 250,000 in 1800 and 1890. Epidemic diseases accounted for most of the precipitous decline. Today, there are 5.2 million Native Americans living in what is the United States. This is 1.6% of the population.

If some European colonists were remorseful on this treatment and outcomes, this was never documented or at least not documented much.

At the time, Spain had a near monopoly on selling tobacco to smokers in European countries. The Spanish colonies were located in southern climates favorable to the growing of tobacco, compared to Virginia. As Spain dominated the market, the balance of trade between Great Britain and Spain was one-sided. To maintain its dominance, Spain declared the death penalty to anybody selling tobacco seeds to a non-Spaniard.

A tobacco variety though grew naturally around Virginia. It was harvested and processed. However, European smokers (and Virginians as well) considered its taste to be too harsh.

John Rolfe (1585 England – 1622 VA) married Sarah Hacker (1590 England – 1612 Bermuda). They had a daughter. They sailed for Jamestown, as part of the third supply to the settlement. A storm blew their ship off course, and they ended up in Bermuda. Their daughter Bermuda Rolfe was born on Bermuda. Sarah and the baby died on Bermuda, in 1612.

Widower Rolfe arrived Jamestown in 1612. He somehow got tobacco seeds from a currently popular strain (*nicotiana tobacum*), then being grown in Trinidad. This was a sweeter tasting tobacco, which Rolfe called *Orinoco* tobacco. Orinoco tobacco grew well in Virginia. Its taste was pleasing to most, and it sold well. It quickly became a cash crop. This was the settlement's first cash crop. This was in the settlement's third year, 1610. Tobacco in fact probably saved the colony from failure.

Rolfe is known for being the first European to marry a Native American. This was in 1614. His second wife Pocahontas (1596 VA – 1617 England) was the daughter of a local Powhatan tribal chief. The marriage was key to creating a climate of peace between the English settlers and the Powhatan Indians in the area, for at least several years.

Rolfe and Pocahontas had a son. Thomas (1615 Virginia – 1680 Virginia) accompanied his parents to England when six months old. The family were celebrities in England. Rolfe presented Pocahontas to England as an example of a *civilized savage*, in an effort to raise more investment money for James Fort and future settlements in Virginia colony.

The name of the community was changed to James Towne in 1610, later written as Jamestowne, and finally as Jamestown. By that year, the settlement was considered permanent. It was the first successful European colony in North America. Almost all the settlers were British.

The first Africans arrived in 1619. They were 20 to 50 men, women, and children brought by either English or Dutch privateers (sources vary on this) who had captured the Africans in the West Indies from either a Spanish or Portuguese slave transport ship (again, sources vary). Records are sketchy, but it is thought that these blacks were considered free persons upon arrival. Free or not, it is believed that there was some compensation to the privateers for the human delivery. That speaks for itself.

As the African Americans had no assets and therefore were not able to support themselves, the British settlers transitioned them to being indentured servants. They were released as free persons, seven years later.

An indentured servant is a person bound to a master employer by a contract which in fact is called an indenture, to work for that employer for a specified period of time. Typically, the servant makes the arrangement to pay for living costs, or to pay off a debt of some type. In the case of indentured servants in the British colonies, paying off the cost of transatlantic transport to the ship's owner or captain was very common. The servant's master paid this amount and provided room and board and clothing for the length of the indenture. The term length was a function of a number of factors, the size of the debt being the primary one. Contracts ran three to seven years.

The servant was required to work for no compensation as reimbursement to the master employer. The servant usually often learned new skills though, from the work. This may have been farming, a trade, working as a store clerk, etc.

At the end of the contract period, indentured servants could do what they wanted. They could continue to work for their former employer but now for wages, work for somebody else, start their own business, try farming or fishing or hunting, go back to the old country, etc. Sometimes they were given money or land at the end of their tenure, as part of the deal.

The estimate is that half to two thirds of white European immigrants to the American colonies from the 1630s to the start of the American Revolution in 1775, arrived as indentured servants. Almost all were under the age of 25. Some were underage. Most ended up in Virginia, Maryland, Delaware, Pennsylvania, and New Jersey. To sum up, indentured servitude accounted for a majority of newcomers to the British North American colonies for more than 140 years.

These were poor Europeans, with also poor economic prospects. Moving to the New World from overpopulated European countries as indentured servants was a good solution out of poverty. The colonies were considered the land of opportunity and they were, once the indenture was worked off. As noted above though, the European economic diaspora was disastrous for Native Americans.

As already stated, the first Africans who arrived in Virginia in 1619 were released from their indentures seven years later, so were free persons. More Africans were brought over later. However, it appears that the indentured servant program in their case was then or soon after skipped. They somehow evolved to be chattel slaves, for life.

The Colony of Virginia codified chattel slavery in 1656. In 1662, Virginia also approved the principle of *partus sequiter ventrem*. This translated from the Latin as *that which is brought forth follows the womb*. This meant that children of slave mothers were also slaves for life, regardless of paternity.

The U.S. (also Great Britain) in 1808 barred the importation of slaves to the country. Slave owner President Thomas Jefferson (1743 VA – 1826 VA) promoted the ban. An estimate though is that another 50,000 slaves were illegally imported into the U.S. after 1808, mostly through Spanish Florida and Texas, before Florida and Texas were admitted to the Union.

In all, about 550,000 Africans were brought to what is now the United States as slaves. All U.S. slaves were freed by 1865. However, this took a civil war. It is estimated that about 690,000 military men (North and South) died in the American Civil War, as did many civilians. This is the most by far who have died in an American war. Runner up World War II was 417,000 military men lost. The Revolution is number six on the list, with 25,000 men dying.

Today, such indenture arrangements are considered a form of slavery. The 1948 Universal Human Rights Declaration adopted by the then two-year-old United Nations General Assembly, stated as much.

The success of tobacco as a cash crop was the result of cheap white (some indentured servants worked with tobacco) and black (these persons now slaves) labor. As already noted, this success and income is much credited with saving the settlement.

More settlements in the area followed. For example, Rolfe's tobacco plantation was on the James River 45 miles upstream (north) of the original James Fort settlement. Rolfe called his plantation Varina Farms, named after a mild tobacco variety. This land is still farmed. The land was listed on the National Register of Historic Places in 1977.

Today, Jamestown is a historic site called Historic Jamestowne. Preservation Virginia operates the 22.5 acres of land where the archaeological remains are. It was founded in 1889, and is based in Richmond today. The U.S. National Park Service holds the surrounding 1,500 acres, as part of the Colonial National Historical Park.

Virginia grew to become a successful colony. It was followed by twelve more British colonies founded later that century and the next. Virginia was the first, with the first settlers arriving 1607 as already noted. The Province of Georgia was the last of the thirteen, established 125 years later in 1732.

All thirteen colonies were on the Atlantic Ocean coast, except for one. The Province of Pennsylvania was the outlier. Pennsylvania though has eventual access to the Atlantic Ocean via the Delaware River, which flows through adjacent Delaware to the ocean. Pennsylvania also borders one of the five, interconnected, fresh water Great Lakes. This is Lake Erie.

The Province of New York colony bordered two Great Lakes. These were Erie and Ontario.

The Great Lakes did not have access to the Atlantic Ocean, until 1829 (canals and locks completed).

During British colonial America, all able-bodied men were eligible to serve in that colony's militia, and train to fight. The colonies generally defined able-bodied, as age 16 to 60. The main purpose was defense from Native Americans.

As already mentioned above and for whatever reason, the settlers considered themselves superior to the Native Americans. With that convenient philosophy, the settlers generally did not have an issue with murdering or enslaving or pushing (often violently and brutally) Native Americans to the side. The fact that these indigenous people were living there when the colonists arrived, was not an issue with the colonists. Again, the colonies established militias to eliminate Native Americans (kill or force away). This thinking was inexplicable and inexcusable, but it happened.

The organization of these militias was written up as *public safety*. This euphemism was used to obscure the murder of Native Americans, and forcible displacement of those not killed.

If no threats were present, militia training was often just quarterly. If conflict seemed likely, training frequency was increased.

From a command standpoint, these militia units differed from the traditional European model. The European practice was that officers made decisions unilaterally, which enlisted men and draftees and mercenaries were to obey without question. In the case of the colonial militias though, officers if time allowed consulted with their men, seeking a consensus. Of course, militiamen were expected to obey, even if disagreeing with their officers. This collaborative, joint decision-making approach was carried over to the new nation to come and its government type – a self-ruling, representative democracy.

As early as 1651, the British Parliament tried to regulate trade in the American colonies. The 1651-1673 Navigation Acts limited the colonies' trading countries, to Great Britain only.

British governments later enacted taxes or controls on wool, hats, molasses, etc. Molasses is the viscous product generated from refining sugar plants (cane or beets) into sugar. The 1733 Molasses Act taxes much affected the economy of the New England states, as molasses was a major trade product. Molasses was used to make rum, among other uses. Smuggling, bribery, and intimidation of British customs officials resulted.

Many military historians consider the 1914-1918 World War I and the 1939-1945 World War II to be World War II and World War III. The First World War per these historians was the 1756-1763 Seven Years' War. This War involved every European great power at the time. It spanned five continents. Europe, the Americas, West Africa, India, and the Philippines were most affected.

The prelude to the Seven Years' War was the 1754-1763 French and Indian War, as the North American theater of the Seven Years' War. This war pitted the British American colonies against those of New France, over settlement rights in the Great Lakes and Ohio River Valley areas. Throughout the 1740s into the

1750s, British and French-Canadian settlers and traders had increasingly come into contact and conflict in this area.

New France authorities became more aggressive in their efforts to expel British traders and settlers. In 1753, New France began construction of a series of fortifications in the area. At the time, the thirteen British North American colonies had two million settlers, compared to only 60,000 in the French North American colonies. This was 97% to 3%.

The dispute over territory erupted into violence. The 5/1754 Jumonville Glen Battle in southwestern Pennsylvania (Fayette County) was the first fighting, again of what came to be called the French and Indian War. Major George Washington (1732 VA – 1799 VA) commanding Virginia militiamen allied with a band of Native Americans ambushed a French-Canadian patrol. Washington lost one man, and another wounded. Some Canadiens were killed and captured. French Commander Joseph Coulon de Villiers, Sieur de Jumonville (1718 New France – 1754 PA) was killed.

Mother countries Great Britain and France supported their New World settlers in the French and Indian War. The thirteen British colonies financially supported the British Army, in the fight. Some of the colonies' militias fought against the French along with British regulars. French settlers in the New World were too few and scattered, to assist mother country France (or very little) in the fighting.

Native American tribes also allied and fought for one side or the other, much more though for France than Great Britain.

Great Britain and France declared war on each other in 1756. This escalated the French and Indian War into an intercontinental conflict. Again, this war came to involve much of the world, and was called the Seven Years' War. Most of the North American fighting though ended by 1760.

Great Britain and its colonies won the French and Indian War. Great Britain gained all the French territory east of the Mississippi River. This included Quebec, the Great Lakes area, and the Ohio River Valley area. Spain ceded Florida to Britain, in exchange for Britain returning Havana (Cuba) to Spain.

Great Britain also with others won the Seven Years' War -- or World War I if you will. The main losers were France, the Austrian-led Holy Roman Empire, Russia, Spain, and Sweden. The enormous Prussia which then included parts of today's Germany, Poland, Russia, Lithuania, Denmark, Belgium, and the Czech Republic; came out on the winning side with Great Britain.

A key reason as to why Great Britain emerged triumphant in this world war was its superior control of the seas – *Rule Britannia, Rule the Waves.* Today, this is a British patriotic song. It originated from the poet, playwright, and lyricist James Thomson's (1700 Scotland – 1748 London), 1740 *Rule, Britannia* poem. Composer Thomas Arne (1710 London – 1778 London) set Thomson's lyrics to music, also in 1740. The song is strongly associated with the Royal Navy to this day. The British Army also uses it.

The United Kingdom in the 18th century did dominate worldwide merchant shipping and was also a naval powerhouse. The reasons include the following:

- Had more ships than other countries, even more than expected for an island kingdom; included both merchant ships and naval warships
- These sailing ships were more modern, so superior in methods and performance (faster, for one) and efficiency (smaller crew size)
- Ship crews (merchant marines and sailors) were better trained
- Had many colonies/protectorates/territories worldwide, all in or on an ocean; this came about due to Great Britain's just mentioned large ocean-going fleet, being able to trade with so many countries; these were (generally) friendly ports to trade with (commerce), for replenishment, etc.

War is not cheap. In winning the Seven Years' War, Great Britain's debt went way up. The national debt increased 79%, 1755 to 1764. Great Britain needed money, a lot of money.

After the Seven Years' War, the British government decided to base 10,000 British regular soldiers in the colonies. One reason was to keep 1,500 military officers employed. Many of these officers were well connected with Parliament. Of course, these officers had to have enlisted men to command, which helps explain the 10,000 troops. Maintaining this standing army of course was very expensive. Great Britain told the North American colony assemblies that they would have to pay, to partially support this standing force.

However, British North America Army Commander-in-Chief and Massachusetts Bay Colony Governor (appointed Governor in 1774) Thomas Gage (1718 England – 1787 London) and other British colony governors, found it difficult to get the Colonial Assemblies to pay for housing and provisioning of troops. As already noted, the colonies had supplied provisions and money during the French and Indian War. However, most colonists did not see any reason to pay for such during peacetime and said so.

Great Britain had not kept a standing army of regulars in the colonies before the French and Indian War. Again, the colonies saw no reason to have one now, with no conflicts on the horizon. After all, the colonies still had their own militias to protect from Native Americans. After all again with Great Britain winning the Seven Years' World War, the threat of French or immigrants from other European countries moving to North America east of the Mississippi River no longer existed.

Governor Gage asked Parliament to address these payment deficiencies. The result was the Quartering Act, passed by the British Parliament. King George III (1738 London – 1820 England) gave his royal assent 4/15/1765. The Act now by British law required the thirteen American colonies to provide provisions and housing for the British soldiers, stationed in the colonies.

The 1765 Quartering Act in turn was part of the Mutiny Acts. The Mutiny Acts were a 190-year series of annual laws (1689 – 1879) passed by the Parliaments of England, Great Britain, and the United Kingdom; for governing, regulating, provisioning, and funding the English Army, and later the British Army.

The first Mutiny Act was passed in 1689, in response to the mutiny of a large portion of the army. These soldiers stayed loyal to James II (1633 London – 1701 France), upon William III (1650 The Hague – 1702 London, pneumonia as a complication from a broken collarbone from falling off his horse) taking the crown of England. It was a mess. William III (also known as William of Orange) though did assume the throne in 1689. He ruled thirteen years until his 1702 death.

The 1765 and 1774 versions of the British Mutiny Acts were the North American colonies 1765 Quartering Act just mentioned, and a 1774 revision to the Quartering Act nine years later (see below).

This was two years after the Seven Years' War ended. Again, Great Britain was strapped for cash. Requiring the colonies to pay these room and board costs would save much money. As noted a third time, the settlers saw no reason to fund a standing British Army in the colonies as was peacetime, and no war was looming. Colonial militiamen of course had their own quarters (their homes). They provided their own food and clothing and transportation (they ran on foot, but some had horses). They were not paid. The colony assemblies though provided weapons, ammunition, and some other military supplies. To sum up, the militia forces were a bargain moneywise. Other advantages were that there were many militiamen, that they were trained, and that they were everywhere.

The colonists also felt then and now (correctly, as it turned out) that Britain was sending troops and sailors not to protect the colonists, but for the following reasons:

- To collect taxes and duties (see below)
- To enforce laws suppressing the colonists
- To ensure that they did not revolt

Conflict with Great Britain was never anticipated, related to the settlers' formation of militia groups in the 1600s. As already noted, the colonies formed militias for one primary purpose – to fend off Native Americans. As described, a secondary later impetus though was to keep out settlers from other European countries. The French and Indian War ended the encroachment threat from France. To sum up again, incursion attempts by foreigners from non-British countries seemed very unlikely.

King George III and Parliament also decided to tap the thirteen, thriving American colonies to supplement Great Britain's coffers by enacting taxes on products sold to the colonists. These included the 1764 tax on sugar, followed by the 1765 Stamp Act. The Stamp Act was passed just before the already mentioned 1765 Quartering Act. The Stamp Act required that printed materials in the colonies be done on paper produced in London. This approved paper had an embossed revenue stamp, hence the name. These printed materials included legal documents, magazines, newspapers, even playing cards, etc. The paper was expensive.

The purpose of the tax was to pay some of the costs for stationing troops in North America, not covered by the Quartering Act. As already noted, the colonists were balking anyway with complying with the Quartering Act, of paying to house and feed British regulars.

Colonists from all thirteen colonies met for the first time to protest the Stamp Act. They stated that Parliament had no right to tax them per the 1689 English Bill of

Rights, as they had no elected or appointed representation in Parliament. The English Bill of Rights was an act of Parliament approved by Royal Assent. It was passed the same year as the first Mutiny Act (1689).

The English Bill of Rights laid down limits on the powers of the monarch and set out the rights and limitations of Parliament. The latter included the requirement for regular Parliament sessions, free elections, freedom of speech, prohibition of cruel and unusual punishment, right for citizens to arm themselves, etc.

The slogan *no taxation without representation* arose, meaning that the thirteen colonial governments should be represented in Parliament.

Great Britain had other colonies besides the North American colonies. None had representation in Parliament. Parliament considered colonies to be possessions to be managed. To sum up, Parliament did not consider allowing the North American colonies representation (until too late).

The colonists pretty much refused to pay the tax on paper. They acquired paper, from other sources. The Stamp Act was repealed 3/1766.

At the same time though of the repeal in 1766, Parliament passed the very broad Declaratory Act, which stated Parliament had full authority over the colonies.

The five Townshend Acts were passed in 1767. Charles Townshend (1725 England - 1767) was the Chancellor of the Exchequer. This is the British official in charge of the Treasury. Today, this is a British Cabinet-level position.

The Townshend Acts placed import duties on glass, lead, paints, paper, and tea. These products were not grown or made in the colonies, so were imported from Britain. The purposes of the Townshend Acts included the following:

- Raise revenue to pay the salaries of governors and judges; besides saving British money, this was to also sway those paid with tax money collected by Great Britain to stay loyal to Great Britain
- Create a more effective method of enforcing compliance with trade regulations
- Punish the New York colony for refusing to put up money to quarter British soldiers
- Re-establish that the British Parliament had the right to tax the colonies, after the 1764 Sugar Act and the 1765 Stamp Act were repealed in 1766

One of the Townshend Acts also authorized British authorities to search houses and businesses for smuggled goods. This aggravated the colonists no end, as there were no legal steps (warrants approved by elected judges) taken for what they considered to be home invasions.

Again, the colonists protested in a number of ways. These included refusing to pay the new taxes (black market smuggling), or finding other sources or substitutes for these products, or simply not buying these products. Due to this resistance, Great Britain sent more troops over in 1768 to occupy Boston where resistance was great. The main purpose was to support Crown-appointed colonial officials trying to enforce the Quartering Act and the Townshend Acts.

Great Britain also sent several schooners to suppress smuggling and enforce the collection of duties, especially on molasses. Molasses was much used in Rhode Island, to make rum. Rhode Islanders fired shore cannon at one of these schooners in 1764, when berthed in Newport. This was the HMS St. John. The cannonballs missed.

In 1768, the British Navy seized Patriots leader and merchant John Hancock's cargo sloop Liberty for alleged smuggling. The British converted Liberty into a customs enforcement ship. Patriots set HMS Liberty afire in 1769 when berthed in Newport (Rhode Island) Harbor. She sank.

The use of the word *Patriots* in the paragraph above is the first such use in this chapter. Patriots were simply the colonists who felt that Great Britain was abusing the colonies, to the point where separation and independence was necessary. They were also sometimes called *Whigs*.

Loyalists had issues with Great Britain but felt that they could be worked out, and the American colonies remain part of the United Kingdom. Loyalists also went by the term *Tories*.

Besides the above, several events in the next few years continued to change Loyalists to Patriots. These included the following:

- 3/5/1770   Boston Massacre A group of Bostonians formed around a uniformed and armed British sentry on station in the vicinity of the Boston Custom House (money was stored here) and the Old State House in downtown Boston. British soldiers of course were a symbol of British authority. Citizens were frustrated with the presence of British soldiers on their streets. The citizens became unruly. Eight more British soldiers came to sentry Private Hugh White's aid. The mob insulted the nine soldiers verbally, threw snowballs and other objects at them, and even hit them with clubs. One soldier was knocked to the ground. The soldiers fired their guns into the crowd, killing five and wounding others. Nine British troops including an officer and four civilians were arrested and charged with murder. Two soldiers were convicted of manslaughter. They were sentenced to branding on their thumbs. This was the case, despite the fact that the British soldiers were defending themselves from physical attack by a frenzied mob.

  Stevedore Crispus Attucks (1723 MA – 3/5/1770, shot in Boston) was believed to be the first killed. Some also consider him the first killed in the American Revolution, although most historians consider the start date of the Revolution to be 4/1775, which was more than five years later. Attucks' body lay in state three days at Faneuil Hall. Then he and the other victims were buried together in the same gravesite in Boston's Granary Burying Ground. This is notable as Attucks was a man of color – part Native American and part African American.

The three buildings and the cemetery mentioned above are as follows:

- Boston Custom House The first one was made in the late 1600s, near the waterfront. It was located on King Street, near the Old State House. Several other buildings for handling the collection of customs followed. The federal government made the current, neoclassical building in 1849, at a cost of a little more than a million dollars in 2019 money. A tower was added in 1915. The building was added to the National Register of Historic Places in 1973. The Boston Landmarks Commission designated it as a Boston Landmark in 1986.

The U.S. Customs Service moved to another building in 1986. The federal government sold the 1849 building to the City of Boston in 1987. The city left it unoccupied. The City sold it to Marriott Vacation Club International, which converted it into an 84-room time share resort. Time-share operations began in 1997.

- The Old State House in downtown Boston was completed in 1713. It is at the intersection of Washington and State Streets. The Declaration of Independence was proclaimed here. It was used by the Massachusetts Bay Colony for British and then American government offices, and later same by the City of Boston. At various times, some or all was rented out for commercial use. In 1880, it faced demolition as its real estate (the land it sat on) was valuable.

The Bostonian Society was formed in 1881 to preserve and steward the building. Renovations were completed in 1882, to operate as a museum. The City of Boston owns the building. Since 1904, subways have operated out of the building. It was added to the National Register of Historic Places in 1960. Today, at more than 300 years old, it continues as a museum. A research library is in a building across the street.

- Faneuil Hall was made as a market house in 1743 near the Boston waterfront. Patriots such as Samuel Adams and James Otis gave speeches here, favoring independence from Great Britain. Today, it is part of the Boston National Historical Park.
- The Granary Burying Ground on Tremont Street is Boston's third-oldest cemetery, founded in 1660. Besides the five Boston Massacre dead, Paul Revere, Samuel Adams, John Hancock, Robert Paine, and others notable in American Revolutionary history are buried here.

The shootings came to be known as the *Boston Massacre*. Again considering that the armed British soldiers were being attacked not just verbally but physically, *self-defense* instead of *massacre* may be a more appropriate term. This occurrence is considered one of the most important events, that turned colonial sentiment against King George and British Parliamentary authority. Many Loyalists converted to being Patriots.

- 6/9/1772   Gaspee Affair   As already noted, Great Britain sent customs enforcement schooners to catch smugglers to enforce the collection of taxes and duties. This was especially the case for trade in Rhode Island, as the British thought much smuggling occurred in this area (which was the case). The colony of Rhode Island was south of the Massachusetts Bay Colony.

The coastal-packet sloop Hannah was sailing from Newport, Rhode Island, this afternoon on her customary way up Narragansett Bay to Providence, Rhode Island. Packet boats of that time were medium-sized boats that carried mail, freight, and passengers; usually at scheduled times on the same routes. They were large enough to ocean sail along the coast, but also small enough (shallow draft) to sail up rivers and canals.

Captain Lieutenant William Dudingston (1740 – 1817) commanded the HMS Gaspee armed schooner. When patrolling, he and other HMS Captains stopped American vessels to search for merchandise to ensure that British taxes had been paid. Dudingston fired a shot to signal Hannah to stop to be searched. Hannah's Captain Thomas Lindsay kept sailing. Gaspee pursued several miles.

Gaspee ran aground at low tide on Namquid Point. Lindsay knew about that sandbar. He tricked the unaware Dudingston into hitting it. Namquid Point is on the northeast side of Narragansett Bay off Pawtuxet, Rhode Island. Namquid Point is now called Gaspee Point. Gaspee was stuck for a half day before she would float off. High tide was at 03:00.

When Captain Lindsay docked at Providence, he reported to Bristol County Sheriff John Brown (1736 RI – 1803 RI) that Gaspee would be stuck for a few more hours. Brown owned and operated merchant ships. He was also a slave trader. Brown notified Continental Navy Commander Abraham Whipple (1733 – 1819 OH).

Whipple quickly took charge of leading an expedition of eight large longboats (these were rowboats) with 50 to 100 armed Patriots to Gaspee that night, before high tide. Sheriff Brown was on Whipple's longboat. The oars were muffled. Gaspee's watch woke Dudingston when he saw the longboats approaching. The Patriots asked for permission to board, which was denied. The Patriots fired their muzzles. Patriot Joseph Bucklin shot Dudingston in the abdomen. Dudingston survived. The Patriots boarded.

As the Patriots outnumbered the Gaspee crew of 20 sailors and as Captain Dudingston thought he was dying, he surrendered. The Patriots rowed the Gaspee crew ashore, where they were imprisoned. The Patriots torched Gaspee.

These men led by Sheriff Brown who rowed out were members of the Sons of Liberty. The Sons of Liberty was a secret society formed to protect the rights of the colonists and to fight taxation by the British government. The group played a major role in protesting the 1765 Stamp Act. After the Stamp Act was repealed in 1766, the Sons of Liberty disbanded. However, the same name was used later for other local, separatist groups of Patriots. Such groups functioned up until the time the Revolution began, 4/1775.

- 12/16/1773   Boston Tea Party   Due to the great resistance, most of the Townshend duties were repealed in the next few years. However, the import duty on tea remained as Parliament wanted to show its sovereign authority to tax the colonies per the already noted 1766 Declaratory Act; and to keep at least a little money flowing to Great Britain.

  The duty act on tea was revised 5/1773 in an effort to save the British East India Company from bankruptcy. The company's London warehouses were overflowing with tea as the colonists were buying tea on the black market (this was mostly tea bought from Dutch merchants), or otherwise just not drinking tea or drinking something else (coffee).

  This new tea tax was minimal. In fact, the cost of the tea including the tax was less than smuggled tea from the Netherlands. However, still in resentment of a tax with no say on the levying of that tax, 80 Patriots boarded three British East India Company cargo ships in Boston Harbor at night. They dumped all 342 wooden chests containing tea overboard. These men were members of a successive Sons of Liberty group.

  Some of the boarding colonists disguised themselves as Mohawk Indians. The Mohawks lived mainly in upstate New York west of the Hudson River at the time the settlers arrived. However, their territory ranged into Pennsylvania, New Jersey, Vermont, and into Canada. The Mohawk population was reduced 63% in 1635 by smallpox. The Native Americans were not immune to smallpox, brought over by the Europeans.

  One purpose of the Indian costume was to ensure that they were not recognized, and later arrested. Also though, dressing as Mohawk warriors was to show symbolically that the rebels identified with the American continent, as opposed to being official subjects of Great Britain.

  The history of the European settlers abusing Native Americans horribly began soon after the formation of the James Fort (Jamestown) settlement 166 years back, and since. Despite that, wearing Native American disguises did not raise a hypocrisy issue of any sort.

  Anyway, this destruction later came to be called the *Boston Tea Party*. Of note, colonists later similarly boarded other British merchantmen transporting tea in other colonial ports, including New York City. Again, British East India Company tea was dumped.

Most of the colonists were British. As everyone knows, the British then and now love their tea, served warm. Many colonists though after the Boston Tea Party now considered drinking tea unpatriotic. In fact, many who had not switched to coffee now did so, as the preferred hot drink.

These events and especially the tea dumping sparked Parliament to pass the 1774 reprisal *Intolerable Acts* (but take your pick, other terms were the *Coercive Acts* or the *Repressive Acts* or the *Punitive Acts)*. The Intolerable Acts included the following:

- The Second Quartering Act was part of the successive Mutiny Acts, and also considered one of the Intolerable Acts. It modified the 1765 original American colonies Quartering Act, by authorizing the Royal Governor to house soldiers in vacant buildings if the colonies would not make housing arrangements. It also gave the Royal Governor authority to enforce payments from the colonies for quartering expenses.

- The Massachusetts Government Act effectively abrogated the 1691 Massachusetts Charter, which included self-governance rights. The Act gave the Royal Governor dictatorial type powers. Citizens were no longer allowed to elect members of its executive council and other officials. Citizens were not even allowed to conduct town meetings unless the Royal Governor approved.

- The Administration of Justice Act granted Massachusetts' Royal Governor the authority to prevent prosecution of British officials, if the Governor felt that local juries would be prejudiced against the defendant, for simply being in the King's employ.

- The Boston Port Act closed the port until the colonists paid custom duties to Great Britain and provided restitution to the British East India Company for the dumped tea.

- The Prohibitory Act (came in 1775) blockaded American ports. The goal was to destroy the American economy by prohibiting trade with any country, other than Great Britain.

These drastic reprisal laws removed Massachusetts' self-governance and historic rights. The restrictions also rallied the other colonies to support Massachusetts. The thirteen colonies set up bodies of elected representatives. These were called Provincial Congresses. They replaced the previous Colonial Assemblies. The Provincial Congresses were Patriots-oriented, compared to the now disbanded colonial governments. The Provincial Congresses acted to suppress the Loyalists, within the colonies.

Great Britain also responded by sending more military over (Navy, Marines, and Army) to enforce collection of taxes. The British put Boston under martial law and closed the port. Outrage resulted. Resistance increased. More Loyalists (Tories) shifted over to the pro-revolt side. Some of these lived in colonies other than Massachusetts. As already stated, the other colonies sympathized with the Massachusetts colonists. They also were aware of course that Great Britain was trying to quell patriotic ardor in all the colonies.

The colonies through their Provincial Congresses decided that a joint meeting was in order. The First Continental Congress met 9/5/1774 in Philadelphia to address the colonies' grievances, especially the Intolerable Acts, and coordinate a protest. All thirteen colonies sent representatives, except the newest and most distant colony of Georgia.

Georgia as already noted was founded in 1732, the last of the thirteen colonies. Georgia was named for King George II (1683 Germany – 1760 London). He ruled

Great Britain 1727 to his 1760 death. His already referred to several times son George III was now King, leading up to and through the American Revolution. George III ruled more than 59 years, from 1760 to his death in 1820 at age 81.

For the record, six of the thirteen colonies were named for British royalty. The other five were Virginia, Maryland, North Carolina, South Carolina, and Delaware.

The First Continental Congress adjourned seven weeks later, 10/26/1774. It did not go so far as to demand independence. However, it did denounce taxation without representation. The Congress also denounced the placing of a British Army in the colonies without consent. The Congress issued a declaration of the rights due every citizen – including life, liberty, property, assembly, and trial by jury. The Congress petitioned King George III for redress of these grievances. George did not respond.

The First Continental Congress recommended a trade boycott of British products. This was formalized by the Continental Association, which became effective 12/1/1774. The goals here were to force Great Britain to drop all or almost all taxes and tariffs and rescind the Intolerable Acts, by not trading with Great Britain. This would allow the colonies to continue as part of the United Kingdom. The boycott was very effective. Imports from Britain dropped 97%. However, King George and Parliament did not rescind the Intolerable Acts.

Hardheaded and slow-learning Parliament passed the 1775 Restraining Acts, which limited the North American colonies' export and import of goods to Great Britain and its other colonies only. The Restraining Acts also prohibited the colonists from fishing in the Atlantic Ocean, unless they got permission from British governors in advance. King George gave royal assent. Of course, these Acts only increased the rebellious resolve of the colonists.

Massachusetts Patriot leaders set up their own government. This substitute government controlled Massachusetts, excepting Boston where the British had troops.

By this time, Boston area militias increased the frequency of training, up to four times a week. This was especially the case for the younger men.

Massachusetts British Governor General Gage knew that violent confrontations with the colonists were likely. He requested reinforcements from Great Britain. The British government though was not willing to spend the money to support a larger standing Army; especially again as the colonists were balking at shouldering some of the costs. Instead, British officials told Gage to seize Patriot arsenals.

British commanders by now had through spies (Loyalists) determined that Massachusetts Bay Colony militia forces had weapons, ammunition, and other military equipment caches in Boston suburban towns, for use if necessary. Of course, this was not new. Militias had always stored such supplies, to defend against pushed out Native Americans. But these were in greater amounts and more types (cannons, for example) than in the past, as thought required to fend off Native Americans.

From their own spies and scouts, the colonists were aware that the British might try to confiscate or destroy their supplies.

On 4/8/1775, Patriot and Bostonian Paul Revere rode from Boston to Concord twenty miles to the west-northwest, to warn the inhabitants that the British Army may be planning an incursion. Upon this warning, the militia moved and hid their stored military supplies (at least most of them) to other towns in the area. This included the largest cache at Concord, which was moved.

Revere obviously was a Patriot. By trade, he was a silversmith and engraver. He was a military officer during part of the American Revolution. After the Revolution, he became an industrialist.

On 4/14/1775, General Gage received a letter from William Legge (1731 England – 1801 England) advising him *to arrest the principal actors and abettors in the Provincial Congress whose proceedings appear in every light to be acts of treason and rebellion.* These included Patriot leaders Samuel Adams (1722 Boston – 1803 MA) and John Hancock (1737 MA – 1793 Boston). Adams and Hancock knew they could be arrested, tried, convicted, and executed (hung) for treason.

Legge was also known as the *Second Earl of Dartmouth.* He was the State Secretary for the Colonies. This was the British Cabinet minister in charge of managing the United Kingdom's various colonial dependencies. In the case of the North American colonies at this time, the Patriots did not feel they needed Great Britain's aid in any way. They considered Great Britain just another trading partner.

The colonists were aware of Great Britain's attitude and intention on arresting and trying Patriot leaders, as London newspapers had reached Boston with these reports. These newspaper articles specifically mentioned Adams and Hancock.

On the night of 4/18, 19/1775, General Gage ordered Lieutenant Colonel Francis Smith (1723 - 1791) to lead 700 British Army regulars out of Boston to Concord. The troops crossed the Charles River in naval barges to Cambridge, and then marched. The objective of the mission was to capture and confiscate or destroy the military supplies reportedly stored at Concord.

Per many historical accounts, General Gage instructed his men to capture and arrest Adams and Hancock, so they could be tried for treason. However, Gage's written orders to Smith made no mention of arresting the Patriot leaders. Some historians believe that Gage backed off the ambitious plan of capturing Adams and Hancock, reasoning the following:

- That such would make them martyrs if captured, and especially so if tried and convicted and hung for treason
- That such would transform many current Tories (Loyalists) to Patriots
- That other Patriot leaders would step forward anyway
- That more men would be motivated to join and train with the local militias

Patriots leader, physician, and Major General Joseph Warren (1741 MA – 6/17/1775 MA, killed in Breed's Hill Battle, Charleston, MA) dispatched the already mentioned silversmith Paul Revere (1735 Boston – 1818 Boston) and tanner William Dawes (1745 Boston – 1799 MA) to spread the alarm that the

British garrison in Boston was setting out to raid Concord, and arrest Hancock and Adams.

General Warren sent Revere on a northern route. Revere crossed the mouth of the Charles River to Charlestown by rowboat, slipping past the 160' long and 45' beam, 70-gun, HMS Somerset (1748 – 1778 ran aground and wrecked off Provincetown, Cape Cod) third-rate ship of the line, at anchor. Dawes took the southern route, across Boston Neck and over the Great Bridge. General Warren dispatched the two riders on the different routes, to ensure that at least one messenger would get through. Also, other messengers when notified by Revere and Dawes took off to notify others, who in turn notified others. It was a relay system.

Dawes and Revere galloped off at 22:00. Dawes rode seventeen miles in three hours. He and Revere warned the residents of almost every house on the route to Lexington. Dawes and Revere met just before 1:00 at the Hancock-Clarke House (made in 1738) in Lexington. Hancock's family had lived in the house several years when he was a child. The current residents were Hancock relatives. Lexington is two thirds of the way to Concord from Boston Harbor. The 281-year-old House today is a National Historic Landmark. Lexington and Concord were in Middlesex Shire, called Middlesex County today.

Messengers Revere, Dawes, and physician Samuel Prescott (1751 Concord – between 11/23/1776 and 12/26/1777 at Halifax, Nova Scotia; maybe died when imprisoned) were detained by a British Army patrol in Lincoln at a roadblock on the way to Concord. Dawes and Prescott managed to escape. Dr. Prescott was the only rider in fact, who made it to Concord to give the warning. However as already noted, the system was a network with one messenger informing others, who took off in different directions informing residents and militia in other areas.

The British questioned Revere at gunpoint. He told them that the militia had been warned and was on the way, and that it would be best for the British soldiers to turn back. The British officers let Revere go but took his horse. Revere walked to the house in Lexington where Hancock and Adams were staying. Revere in fact assisted Adams and Hancock (and Hancock's relatives) in fleeing the advancing regulars.

Hancock and Adams had attended a meeting of the Massachusetts Provincial Congress that day in Concord. They stayed in Lexington, fearing capture and arrest if they returned to Boston. Upon the warning from Revere and Dawes, they made their way to what is now Burlington for safety, seven miles to the north-northeast. They later moved from Burlington to Billerica, six miles more to the northwest.

Earlier in April, Revere had charged Boston patriots Robert Newman and John Pulling to hang one or two lanterns in the steeple of the Old North Church in Boston, when the British regulars were on the move. The Church was the highest point around. Today, the church is a mission of the Episcopal Diocese of Massachusetts. Its official name today is Christ Church in the City of Boston. It is the oldest standing church building in Boston, made in 1723, so almost 300 years old. It is a National Historic Landmark.

The purpose of the lantern signals was to advise the riders and also warn the Charlestown patriots across the Charles River of the regulars' movements, as follows:

- One lantern was to signify that the British regulars were advancing by land over Boston Neck and the Great Bridge. The Boston Neck was a narrow strip of land or isthmus, created by the combined delta of the Charles, Mystic, and Chelsea Rivers. Boston Neck connected the then peninsular city of Boston to the mainland city of Roxbury. Roxbury today is a Boston neighborhood.

  This was the only land route into Boston. It was 120' wide at high tide. Over the years, this tidal marsh area was filled in (and widened), so it is no longer swampy.

- Two lanterns signified that the British regulars were crossing the Charles River in boats (naval barges were used).

Two lanterns were hung to inform the Patriots that the regulars were rowing across the river. The lanterns were placed for only a minute, so that the British troops would not likely notice.

The first shots were fired en route to Concord, at Lexington at sunrise. This was 4/19/1775. Eight and ten militiamen were killed and wounded. The militia's third highest-ranking officer was one of the eight killed. This was Ensign Robert Munroe (1712 – 4/19/1775). No British were killed. Only one regular was injured. Of note, it is not known which side fired first at Lexington. Accounts of the fighting were confused and contradictory. Some historians characterize it as a massacre, rather than a battle. It is usually described as a skirmish. Whichever, the town of Lexington claims that the American Revolution started there.

The Patriots had a force of 400 militiamen at Lexington, versus a hundred British regulars.

The British soldiers marched on. The next gunfire was at the Old North Bridge over the Concord River in Concord at about 11:00. This was a pedestrian bridge made in the 1760s. These were the first shots fired by organized militiamen acting under orders. The first British casualties (including deaths) occurred here. The British retreated. Per these actions and results whether justified or not, Concord claims that it was the origin of the Revolution, not Lexington. Whatever.

The above-mentioned General Warren participated in the Lexington and Concord Battles. Warren and another 114 Patriots were killed two months later 6/17/1775 at the Breed's Hill and Bunker Hill Battle, in Charlestown. The British had 226 dead, in this battle. Warren was a physician. He was a widower, leaving four children without a parent.

The Concord River is formed by the confluence of the Assabet and Sudbury Rivers. The Concord River itself is a tributary of the Merrimack River, which flows into the Atlantic Ocean at Newburyport, 38 miles north of Boston. The Old North Bridge over the Concord River is a half mile northeast (so downstream) of the merge point of the Assabet and Sudbury Rivers.

The bridge was dismantled in 1793. A replacement was made several hundred yards away from the original. It was rebuilt several times. The current replica bridge is based upon drawings of the 1760s bridge. It was made in 1956 and restored in 2005. Its current site is thought to be very near the original site.

The regulars did look for military supplies. They found some and destroyed. As more militiamen were arriving, they retreated. Other skirmishes occurred as the regulars marched back to Boston at Lincoln, Menotomy (today, Arlington), and Cambridge. The retreating regulars only made it back to Charlestown though, which is less than two miles north of Boston. The British sent out an additional 900 troops, to aid the regulars in retreating back to Boston. The British regulars now numbered about 1,700.

Over the course of the day, the colony militia had 49, 39, and 5 men killed, wounded, and missing. The figures for the British regulars were 73, 174, and 53 killed, wounded, and missing. The main reasons why the *Rebels* (per King George III and Parliament) or the *Patriots* (their name for themselves) came out ahead were several, as follows:

- Although the militia were civilians so irregulars, they had much self-trained in weaponry, tactics, and strategy
  Furthermore, a sub-unit of the militia of about one fourth of the members consisted of younger men in their twenties who trained much more frequently and intensely, including in the very key area of being able to respond quickly when alerted; the members of this well-trained, rapid deployment group were in fact called *minutemen;* their weapons were at the ready, they had horses, etc.
- Militiamen and non-militiamen and women were appointed as spies/scouts/sentinels to report any British Army movements or activities that suggested planned actions; an elaborate intelligence and signaling system was set up, and fresh horses kept available; this system worked very well
- Not at Lexington but at Concord, militiamen collected in small groups placed on different sides of the regulars, which mostly stayed in one group; therefore per this battle strategy, the militia attacked the clustered Redcoats from several directions

As already noted, Paul Revere was one of the couriers. He was honored by an 1860, Henry Longfellow (1807 MN – 1882 MA) poem, titled *Paul Revere's Ride*. The poem has inaccuracies but became popular. The first two lines were as follows:

Tis all very well for the children to hear, Of the midnight ride of Paul Revere.

This poem also includes the line *One if by land, and two if by sea.* This is in reference to the one or two lanterns hung in the Old North Church steeple, advising the Patriots of the route that the British regulars were taking.

Unlucky for Dawes and other messengers, Longfellow did not include them in his poem. The (probably apocryphal) story is that he could not find words to rhyme, with the last names of the others – but could rhyme with Revere. Therefore to this day due to the popularity of the poem, many believe that Revere was the sole rider and messenger, warning that the British regulars were marching. Again, this was not the case. Revere was part of a team.

Again, the poem is credited with creating the national legend of Revere and his horse ride as a Sons of Liberty courier on the night of 4/18-19/1775, to alert the militia that the British regulars were marching.

Longfellow had climbed the Old North Church's tower 4/5/1860, where the two lanterns were hung. This reportedly inspired him to write the poem.

Longfellow was an ardent abolitionist. He wrote the poem in 1860 eighty-five years after the Boston courier and skirmishes. The U.S then was on the brink of the Civil War. Longfellow hoped to inspire men to join the Union army, by telling the story of how one man could make a difference. The poem was published in the 1/1861 *Atlantic Monthly*. Only a few read it at the time. The Civil War began 4/1861.

This legend creation came more than ten years after the poem came out, in the 1870s. This was during the Colonial Revival Movement. The Movement was a national expression of early North American culture. This was mainly a celebration of the made and artistic environments of the east coast colonies. To sum up, Revere's recognition and celebrity from the poem came a hundred years after the event.

Gage later issued a proclamation granting a general pardon to all who would *lay down their arms, and return to the duties of peaceable subjects*. However, he excepted Hancock and Adams in the proclamation.

So the Revolution started 4/19/1775. At the time, Great Britain had eight million residents. The population of the thirteen colonies was 2.5 million, 80 and 20% free and enslaved.

Revere served in the Massachusetts Militia or Continental Army 4/1776 to 9/1779 in an artillery unit during the Revolution. He was dismissed from the Army when a Lieutenant Colonel, due to his perceived failings in the July-August, 1779 Penobscot Expedition debacle in Maine. Maine at the time was part of Massachusetts. The Patriots lost almost all 19 warships and 25 support vessels. Revere was charged with incompetence, disobedience, and cowardice. He was asked to resign his post, which he did do 9/1779. He repeatedly requested a court-martial to clear his name. Revere was exonerated finally by a 2/1782 court-martial, or similar review.

The Second Continental Congress met 5/1775 in Philadelphia (also convened some in Baltimore). This was 6.5 months after the First Continental Congress adjourned. Twelve colonies sent delegates. The thirteenth colony or Georgia finally did as well, but the Georgia delegation arrived ten weeks later. This was three weeks after the Revolution started. The Second Continental Congress organized the defense of the colonies, urging the colonies to set up large militias and train the civilian soldiers.

Members of the Second Continental Congress had many disagreements over the ways to run the Revolution. However, the decision to select George Washington as Commander of the Continental Army was not one. The decision was rapid and unanimous, made 6/15/1775. This appointment was made eight weeks after the skirmishes in the Boston suburbs.

Virginia's Royal Governor Robert Dinwiddie (1692 Scotland – 1770 England) had appointed Washington a major in the provincial militia 2/1753. As noted above, Washington when a major led militia forces in the first battle of the French and Indian War, in southwestern Pennsylvania. This was the 5/28/1754 Jumonville Glen Battle. Major Washington had been an able commander in that War.

Governor Dinwiddie rewarded Washington in 1755 with a commission as *Colonel of the Virginia Regiment and Commander in Chief of all forces now raised in the defense of His Majesty's Colony*. Washington's assignment was to defend Virginia's frontier. The Virginia Regiment of a thousand soldiers was the first full-time American military unit in the colonies. Washington exceeded in killing and pushing Native Americans back, compared to the other colonies.

Washington greatly yearned for a commission in the British Army, to be a career soldier. This never came, for some reason. Maybe the British governors or generals sensed that his loyalty to Great Britain could falter, even though this was more than sixteen years before the Revolution started. Therefore, Washington resigned his Virginia Colony commission 12/1758. He married wealthy widow Martha Dandridge Custis (1731 VA – 1802 VA) the next month.

Martha's twenty-year-older first husband planter and politician Daniel Custis (1711 VA – 1757 VA) died a year and a half back, probably of a heart attack. Their four children were born 1751-1756. Two died in childhood. Martha and George raised the other two, a girl and a boy. These two died fairly young though, at ages 17 the daughter and 26 the son in 1773 and 1781.

The son John Custis (1754 VA – 11/5/1781 VA) was age 20 when the Revolution started. Per one account, he served on his stepfather's staff during the 1775-1776 Boston Siege, as a civilian emissary to the British forces. He also served as a civilian aide-de-camp to Washington during the September-October, 1781 Yorktown Siege. During the siege, he became sick (probably typhus or dysentery) and later died.

John Custis and his wife had seven children, born 1775-1781. Four were still living when he died. His widow sent the two youngest to George and Martha to raise. She remarried and had 16 more children.

George and Martha were ages 27 and 28 when they wed. They did not have children together. Again though, they raised two of Martha's children and two of Martha's grandchildren.

The Washington newlyweds moved to Mount Vernon near Alexandria, Virginia This was a plantation estate passed down in Washington's family. Alexandria is eight miles south of the District of Columbia. Washington became a planter and a political figure. He was Commander of the Continental Army 1775-1783, so was mostly away from his wife and children and grandchildren and home more than eight years.

Mount Vernon today is 500 acres. It is a historical site, owned and maintained and operated by the Mount Vernon Ladies' Association, which bought the property in

1860. The Mount Vernon Ladies' Association was the nation's first national historic preservation organization, formed in 1853. It is the oldest women's patriotic society in the United States.

Washington insisted on serving without compensation. This he in fact did 1775-1783, the remaining 8.25 years of the Revolution.

Washington even put his own money into the Revolution. For example, he rented the young nation's first naval warship. This was the Hannah fishing schooner (different ship than the already mentioned coastal-packet sloop pursued by the HMS Gaspee). The fee was one dollar per displacement ton per month. She was converted to a gunboat with the mounting of 4 × 4 pounder guns, and commissioned 9/1775.

The USS Hannah captured the HMS Unity hoy merchantman 9/7/1775, the first foreign vessel captured by what later became the United States. A hoy is a small, sloop-rigged, coastal ship. The Royal Navy had recently captured Unity from a private owner. Washington returned Unity to its owner. This was Founding Father John Langdon (1741 New Hampshire – 1791 New Hampshire). Langdon served as a delegate to the Constitutional Convention, signed the United States Constitution, and was one of the first two United States senators from New Hampshire.

Hannah's fighting career was short though. On 10/10/1775, the British HMS Nautilus sloop ran Hannah aground after a four-hour engagement with Continental militias on shore. Hannah was not much damaged though. It is believed that General Washington decommissioned Hannah then, in favor of larger ships for his cruisers.

The Second Continental Congress decided that King George's rule was tyrannical and infringing upon the rights of North American Englishmen. The Congress established a five-man committee to draft an independence declaration. Thomas Jefferson (1743 VA – 1826 VA) was one on the team, and the primary author of the document, declaring the colonies to be free and independent states. The declaration, after the Congress much revised and shortened it, was approved 7/4/1776. This was fifteen months after the Lexington and Concord battles, and 12.5 months after Washington was named Commander in Chief of the Continental Army.

From the above-mentioned 4/19/1775 skirmishes in the Boston suburbs of Lexington and Concord, the British Army casualties were more than thrice that of the Patriots. This was an eye opener for King George III and the British Parliament – that the colonist rebels were serious and earnest about this independence quest, and had worthy military capabilities even as citizen soldiers (the militias).

As already noted, Parliament passed the Prohibitory Act 12/1775 as one of the Intolerable Acts. This act blockaded colony ports, and limited trade only to Great Britain. Great Britain now enforced the ban with an even tighter blockade, plus penalties in the case of caught violators were increased.

Parliament repealed the 1774 Massachusetts Government Act, in 1778. This was the Intolerable Act that blocked self-governance, giving all power to the Royal Governor.

Also in 1778, Parliament passed the Colonies Taxation Act, which stated that Parliament would not impose any duty or tax on the British American colonies or the British West Indies. The conciliatory goal here was Parliament's effort to end the Revolution, in a compromise of sort. This did not happen.

The Second Continental Congress oversaw the war effort. It disbanded 3/1/1781, leading the new country 5.8 years. It was replaced with the Confederation Congress, which governed 3/1/1781 to 3/4/1789. The First United States Congress began proceedings 3/4/1789. First U.S. President George Washington was inaugurated 4/30/1789.

Essayist, lecturer, and poet Ralph Emerson (1803 Boston – 1882 Concord) much later described the initial skirmishes of the Revolution in his 1836 *Hymn: Sung at the Completion of the Concord Monument, April 19, 1836*, as the *shot heard round the world*. Emerson wrote the poem now just referred to in short as the *Concord Hymn* on commission for the 7/4/1837 (this Independence Day of course, the 61st anniversary) dedication of the Obelisk. This is a monument in Concord, commemorating the start of hostilities of the American Revolution.

Emerson then lived with his clergyman, step-grandfather Ezra Ripley (1751 CT – 1841 Concord). Ripley's house in Concord was only several hundred feet distant from the fighting at the Old North Bridge. In fact, Ripley and his five-year-old son William Emerson (1769 Concord – 1811 Concord) saw the battle from Ripley's house. William Emerson was Ralph's father.

Ripley later gave the land to the city, for the memorial monument.

By the way, this house is known as the *Old Manse* and is still there. It is open to the public as a nonprofit museum. As just noted, it is near the Old North Bridge which in turn is part of Minute Man National Historical Park. The 970-acre park is in the towns of Concord, Lexington, and Lincoln. The linear park covers much of the route of the British Regulars coming out of Boston, back in 1775.

The Revolutionary War of course was the first American war, not counting the innumerable battles with Native Americans. For the record, these conflicts with Native Americans lasted all the way into the 1920s (in the southwest United States). This was 141 years after the end of the American Revolution.

The Revolution ran 8.4 years, from the first fighting 4/1775 to the signing of the Paris Peace Treaty 9/1783. As we all know, these new *united colonies* that *are, and of right ought to be, free and independent States* (6/7/1776 Lee Resolution) won their independence; with assistance from France, Spain, and Netherlands. France had secretly aided the colonies since 1775, sending free supplies (mostly gunpowder at first). France officially declared war on Great Britain 6/1778.

As already noted, Great Britain had defeated France in the Seven Years' War that ended in 1763. France lost its vast holdings in North America. France was extremely bitter at this and sought revenge. France wanted Great Britain strategically weakened. Declaring war against Great Britain and aiding the colonies in ejecting Great Britain was a no-brainer.

Spain lost much also in the Seven Years' War to Great Britain, and had an ongoing dispute with Great Britain over colonial supremacy. Therefore, Spain was similarly motivated to aid the Patriots as was France. Spain allied with France; and provided supplies and munitions beginning in 1776. Later, Spain provided money. Spain declared war on Great Britain 6/1779.

The Netherlands traded with the colonies, providing needed supplies.

Of note, France and Spain did more than provision. They fought as well, on land and sea. This was especially the case for France, which fought in the colonies beginning in 1779. Some historians state that the British Army may have been able to subdue the North American rebellion to the point where a compromise would have been reached; if not for France's fighting aid. If so, the United States today would maybe be something like Canada – an independent country, but also a constitutional monarchy of Great Britain. How does *God Save the Queen* sound, compared to the *Star-Spangled Banner?* Think about it!

A Spanish general commanded troops composed of Spaniards, Puerto Ricans, Venezuelans, Dominicans, Salvadorians, Nicaraguans, and Mexicans during the Revolution. They distracted the British by capturing the cities of Mobile (Alabama), Pensacola (Florida), and St. Louis (Missouri).

Besides Washington, three other future presidents served in the Revolution, as follows:

- Fourth President James Madison (1751 VA – 1836 VA) served as a Colonel in the Orange County (Virginia) Militia 10/1775 for five months, not involved in the fighting; Madison was President 1809-1817
- Fifth President James Monroe (1758 VA – 1831 NYC) dropped out of the College of William and Mary in Virginia (1693 -) to enlist as a Lieutenant in the Third Virginia Regiment; sustained severe injury (severed artery) in a surprise attack on a Hessian encampment, and almost died; fought off and on through 1780; discharged as a Colonel; Monroe was President 1817-1825
- Seventh President Andrew Jackson (1767 Carolinas – 1845 Nashville) was a courier for a Carolina militia unit, at age 13; captured 1780, almost died in prison; fought in War of 1812, and then later against the Seminoles; discharged as a Major General; Jackson was President 1829-1837

Second President John Adams (1735 MA – 7/4/1826 MA) was age 39 when the Revolution started. He was never in a militia or the military. He was President 1797-1801.

Third President Thomas Jefferson (1743 VA – 7/4/1826 VA) was a Colonel in the militia when the Revolution started 4/1775. He was age 32. He was named commander of the Albemarle County Militia 9/1775. The county seat of Albemarle County is Charlottesville.

A year later, Jefferson was elected to the Virginia House of Delegates for Albemarle County. He was elected Virginia's second governor serving two one-year terms, 1779-1781. The British tried to capture him and other officials in 1781 but he escaped Richmond, just barely. Richmond was Virginia's capital city. The British burned Richmond to the ground, 1/1781.

Later in 1781, the British again tried to capture Jefferson and members of the Virginia Assembly at Monticello; but the Virginia militia successfully intervened. Monticello was Jefferson's estate, just outside Charlottesville, Virginia. Charlottesville is 115 miles southwest of the District of Columbia. Jefferson fled to Poplar Forest, his plantation to the west of Monticello.

Virginia's General Assembly in 1781 conducted an inquiry into Jefferson's actions. The body eventually concluded that Jefferson had acted with honor. However, his bid to be re-elected Virginia Governor for a third one-year term was not successful. To sum up, Jefferson did not fight in the Revolution. He was President 1801-1809.

Sixth President John Quincy Adams (1767 MA – 1848 DC) was too young to fight in the Revolution, and too old to fight in the War of 1812. He was President 1825-1829.

The Mohawks were mentioned earlier. For the record, the Mohawks mostly aligned with the British during the Revolution. They had a long trading relationship with the British. Their hope was that the British if they won, would allow the Mohawks to continue to live in the Hudson Valley. Of course, the Patriots won. The new Americans forced some of the Mohawks to move to Canada.

This is the 30th and last chapter of this book which is all in one way or another on the Pacific Theater of the Second World War, so so much for the American Revolution.

Germany in 1938 and 1939 seized Austria, parts of Czechoslovakia (Sudetenland, Bohemia, Moravia, Czech Silesia), the Slovak Republic, and Lithuania. Germany invaded without warning and occupied Poland, 9/1/1939. This is usually the date stated as the start of what later came to be called World War II.

The U.S. formally entered the War 12/8/1941, which was 2.3 years later. This of course was as the Empire of Japan sneak attacked five U.S. military locations (bases, airfields, and harbors) on five Pacific Ocean islands (Oahu, Guam, Wake, Midway, and Philippines) on one day. Japan also this same day boarded and captured a USS river gunboat and its crew in Shanghai Harbor. This was the only USS that Japan captured in World War II. Also, a Japanese submarine gun-sank a U.S. Army chartered cargo ship carrying lumber to Hawaii, 300 miles off California with all aboard lost. This sinking was at the same time as the attack on Pearl Harbor, Oahu. And yet again on this day, Japanese aircraft off Kwajalein Island (Kwajalein is one of the Marshall Islands) bombed two Phoenix Islands (Howland and Baker) which belonged to the U.S.

For the U.S., World War II ran almost three years and nine months – from Pearl Harbor Day 12/7/1941 to V-J Day 9/2/1945.

Of all U.S. conflicts, more Presidents and future Presidents were directly involved in World War II than any other American war or conflict. These number nine. The first two were Presidents during World War II. The second seven were in uniform during World War II and later became President. The first two who were Presidents during the World War II years, were as follows:

- Franklin Roosevelt (1882 NY – 4/12/1945 GA, cerebral hemorrhage) was inaugurated 4/4/1933. He served until his death at age 63, 82 days into his fourth term. This was 12.1 years. So Roosevelt was President in the 1930s, when the U.S. had an isolationist attitude. This attitude was left over from losing more than 116,000 men in uniform (almost 46% in combat) and another 204,000 wounded or made ill (many with permanent disabilities) in World War I. World War I fighting ended in 1918. World War II for the U.S. started a little more than 23 years later.

  Roosevelt himself presented an isolationist front as his political stance. This was necessary to get re-elected 11/1936. This was the case despite the fact that it was known that both Germany and Japan were making modern, deadly war machines; had dictatorial-type leaders; were very belligerent; and were imperialistic.

  Roosevelt also had to maintain an isolationism front four years later, to get re-elected 11/1940. This was the case again despite the fact that Germany had started the European Theater war fourteen months back; and reliable (but unbelievable) reports of Germany's and Japan's innumerable, heinous abuses to civilians much less enemy military men were known.

  For the record, Roosevelt was elected four times. He carried 42, 46, 38, and 36 states 1932, 1936, 1940, and 1944. This was when the United States was 48 states. His popular vote majorities were 57, 61, 55, and 53% for the four elections.

  By the late 1930s if not before, Roosevelt along with many others knew that it was probably inevitable that the U.S. would have to go to War in Europe or the Pacific, or both.

  On top of these factors, Germany and Japan's neighbors were all militarily weak. The latter was inexcusable in the case of Europe, as if European countries learned nothing from World War I, allowing Germany to re-arm – instead of nipping the build-up in the bud. Germany's arming up was in violation of the disarmament terms of the 6/1919 Versailles Treaty, which ended World War I. Again, other European nations should have quashed this effort, early on. As Germany was an economic and devastated shamble after World War I, this would have been easy to do.

  For what it is worth, these same countries also again after World War II, seemingly still had their heads in the sand. The Allies including the United States allowed despot and mass murderer Premier Joseph Stalin (1878 Russia - 1953 Soviet Union, cerebral hemorrhage) to remain in power. Removal would have been easy, as the Soviet Union was devastated from World War II. Dictator Stalin became even more of a tyrant. He grabbed other territory that he said the Soviet Union required as buffers. He was allowed to get away with this. As a result, the very easily avoidable and costly and terrifying (nuclear armament) Cold War ran 1946-1991, which is 45 years.

Roosevelt of course was President when the U.S. entered World War II. He was President for the first 40.4 months of the 45-month War for the U.S., which is 90%.

As far as known, Roosevelt never considered enlisting in one of the military branches. He was certainly physically capable, playing several sports as a youth. He was 32 years old when World War I started in Europe in 1914, 35 when the U.S. entered that War in 1917, and 36 at the time of the 11/11/1918 Armistice. Some men in their mid-thirties enlisted for World War I, but not many.

Roosevelt's 1913-1919 tenure as Assistant Navy Secretary (this is a civilian position) under President Woodrow Wilson (1856 VA – 1924 DC) of course included World War I. Wilson was President 1913-1921.

Roosevelt contracted crippling poliomyelitis in 1921, at age 39.

Roosevelt and his wife Eleanor Roosevelt Roosevelt (1884 NYC – 1962 NYC) had six children, born 1906-1916. The *Roosevelt Roosevelt* is not a typo. Eleanor's maiden name was Roosevelt. Her father was her husband Franklin's fifth cousin, and Theodore Roosevelt's fifteen months younger brother. Her uncle Theodore Roosevelt (1858 NYC – 1919 NY, blood clot in lungs) was President 1901-1908.

The couple had five sons and one daughter. One son died soon after birth. The other four sons were born 1907-1916. All four served in the military as commissioned officers during World War II. Two were in the Navy, one in the Marines, and one in the Army Air Corps. The two Navy men separated as Lieutenant Commanders. The other two separated as Brigadier Generals (one star).

Oldest son James Roosevelt (1907 NYC – 1991 CA) was the Marine. In full dress uniform, James assisted his father up a ramp to address Congress in the Capitol Building Monday 12/8/1941, asking Congress to declare war on Japan.

James served 23 years, 1936-1959. He served for the Midway Atoll and Makin Island invasions in the Pacific Theater during the War. He was awarded the Navy Cross and the Silver Star.

- Vice President Harry Truman (1884 MO – 1972 MO) held that position only 82 days, until becoming President upon Roosevelt's death. He was elected to a second term. His tenure as President during World War II was a little more than four months, which was the last 10% of the War for the U.S. He made the decision to use the atomic bomb against Japan. To be correct, this was a combined decision with Great Britain, per an earlier agreement requiring consensus.

Truman was an Army veteran. As a Captain, he fought in the Vosges Mountains, St. Mihiel, and Meuse-Argonne offenses (these all in France); of World War I. His time in France was a year, 4/1918 - 4/1919. The Armistice went into effect 11/11/1918.

Truman served in the National Guard and Army 41 years, active and reserves – 1905-1911 in the Missouri National Guard, 1917-1919 active duty in the Army for World War I, and 1920-1953 in the Army reserves. He separated as a Colonel. Truman was President 1945-1953. It is not common for a President to retain his commission in the reserves when serving as President, but Truman did. Lyndon Johnson was in the Navy Reserves when Vice President, but separated shortly after becoming President. Eisenhower separated from the Army when he became President, but returned to the Army Reserves after his presidential tenure (Ike served two terms).

Truman volunteered for active duty for World War II at the age of 57. He was denied due to his age. Also, Roosevelt 7/9/1942 asked all Congressmen (Truman was a Senator from Missouri, at the time) to continue their legislative duties in lieu of enlisting.

The Trumans had one child. Daughter Margaret (1924 MO – 2008 Chicago) was a classical soprano, actress, journalist, radio and television personality, writer (some claim though that most of her 35 books were ghost-written), and New York socialite. She had no involvement with World War II.

The next eight presidents after Truman were Dwight Eisenhower, John Kennedy, Lyndon Johnson, Richard Nixon, Gerald Ford, Jimmy Carter, Ronald Reagan, and George H. W. Bush. All served active duty as commissioned officers during World War II, except for Carter. Carter though served. He graduated from the U.S. Naval Academy in Annapolis (60th of a class of 820, which is 93 percentile) in 1946. This was the year after World War II ended. Carter served on surface ships and submarines. He served on the Balao-class, 313' long and 27' beam and 17' draft, USS Pomfret (1944 – 1971 transferred to Turkey, 1987 scrapped) submarine 14 months, 1948-1951.

Carter applied for and was selected to be an officer on a nuclear-powered submarine, in 1953. This was the unique USS Seawolf (1957 – 1997) submarine. It was the Navy's second, nuclear-powered vessel. The first was also a submarine. This was the USS Nautilus (1954 – 1986 museum ship in Connecticut) which set many endurance records. The most notable of these was the first submerged transit of the North Pole (1958).

Carter's father died in 1953 at age 59 of pancreatic cancer. Carter retired from active duty to return to Georgia and run the family peanut farming business.

The Seawolf-class, nuclear powered, 453' long and 40' beam and 36' draft, USS Jimmy Carter (2005 – active) fast-attack submarine was named in his honor. His wife Rosalynn Smith Carter (1927 GA -) sponsored 6/5/2004 at the christening. Seawolf is one of the few USSs named for a living person; and the only USS named for a living, former President.

Carter was the only President to graduate from the U.S. Naval Academy. He is the only President who was in the Navy who was a submariner. He served in the Navy 18 years (1943 – 1961), active and reserves. He separated as a Lieutenant. Two U.S. Presidents graduated from the U.S. Military Academy. These were Grant and Eisenhower.

No Presidents attended the Coast Guard, Marines, or Air Force academies.

Information on the seven later Presidents who served in the military during World War II is shown below, in the order of their terms as President:

President Term Military Branch Military Tenure Discharge Rank Life	Comments
Dwight Eisenhower 1953 - 1961 Army 1915 - 1953, 1961 - 1968 General of the Army 1890 TX - 1969 DC	Graduated U.S. Military Academy West Point 1915; his tank unit was due to go overseas but World War I ended first; worked on special projects and as an aide to Generals between World Wars; for World War II, commanded forces in North Africa, Sicily, Italy; Roosevelt named Supreme Commander of Allied Forces in Europe 12/1943; planned and executed the invasion of the Continent beginning 6/6/1944 from Normandy, France beaches; Military Governor of U.S. Occupation Zone in Germany when War ended; anticipated that some would later re-characterize Nazi crimes as propaganda (Holocaust denial mainly), so had many and extensive photographs and videos made
John Kennedy 1961 - 1963 Navy 1941 - 1945 Lieutenant 1917 MA - 1963 TX	Joined Naval Reserves 9/1940; commanded an 80' long and 20' beam and 3.5' draft, wooden PT boat, sank off Solomon Islands while idling and obviously no lookout 8/2/1943 night when run down by a Japanese destroyer; 2 crew killed; 11 survivors clung to hull timbers, kicked to deserted island; later swam to larger islands looking for food and water; Australian coastwatcher sent natives who found and rescued; received medals, whereas some thought should be court-martialed; remarked himself that did not deserve medals; took command of another PT boat 9/1/1943; rescued 87 marines 11/2/1943 stranded on two rescue craft; relieved of command 11/18/1943, due to a bad back
Lyndon Johnson 1963 - 1969 Navy 1940 - 1964 Commander 1908 TX-1973 TX	Requested active duty 12/10/1941; at his request, inspected shipyard facilities in TX and on West Coast; Roosevelt assigned to survey Navy operations in Southwest Pacific; volunteered as observer for a twin engine Martin B-26 Marauder bombing mission on Lae, Papua New Guinea; Japanese Zeroes hit the B-26 disabling an engine; it returned to base; another account though was that it turned back due to a defective generator, not encountering any enemy fire; whichever, Johnson awarded Silver Star; reported to Roosevelt and Navy that conditions in Navy in the Pacific deplorable; made chairman of a high-powered Naval Affairs Committee subcommittee to address these deficiencies

Richard Nixon 1969 - 1974 Navy 1942 - 1966 Commander 1913 CA - 2003 NY	Aide to Naval Air Station Commander at Ottumwa, IA; assigned as naval passenger control officer for South Pacific Combat Air Transport Command supporting logistics operations in Southwest Pacific Theater; Officer in Charge of Combat Air Transport Command at Guadalcanal in Solomons and then Green Island off Queensland, Australia; his unit prepared manifests and flight plans for C-47 Skytrain operations and supervised loading and unloading of cargo aircraft; administrative officer of the Alameda Naval Air Station, CA; transferred 1/1945 to Aeronautics Bureau office in Philadelphia to help negotiate the termination of war contracts
Gerald Ford 1974 - 1977 Navy 1942 - 1966 Lieutenant Commander 1913 NE - 2006 CA	Enlisted after Pearl Harbor; taught elementary navigation skills, ordnance, gunnery, first aid, military drill; coached 9 sports, mostly swimming, boxing, football; served 18 months as assistant navigator, athletic officer, anti-aircraft battery officer on new USS Monterey (1943 – 1971 scrapped) light aircraft carrier, operating Pacific Theater; Monterrey saw much action, but not hit; left Monterrey when in for repairs due to a typhoon-caused, 12/1944 shipboard fire; assigned to Athletic Department at Navy Pre-Flight School at Saint Mary's College, California; on staff of Naval Reserve Training Command, Naval Air Station, IL, as Staff Physical and Military Training Officer
Ronald Reagan 1981 - 1989 Army Air Forces 1937 - 1945 Captain 1911 IL - 2004 CA	Completed 14 home-study Army extension courses to be commissioned as Army Reserves Second Lieutenant (Calvary) 5/25/1937; assigned as liaison officer of Port and Transportation Office at San Francisco Embarkation Port at Fort Mason; transferred to Army Air Forces 5/1942; did public relations work; then to Army Air Forces First Motion Picture Unit, Culver City, California; then to Provisional Task Force Show Unit of *This Is the Army*, Burbank, California; then returned to First Motion Picture Unit; participated in Sixth War Loan Drive in NYC; returned again to First Motion Picture Unit 11/1944; discharged 12/1945; his units produced 400 training films for the USAAF
George H. W. Bush 1989 - 1993 Navy 1942 - 1955 Lieutenant 1924 MA -	Enlisted on 18th birthday, despite Yale acceptance; youngest Navy aviator ever at 18.99 years old; his single engine, Grumman TBM Avenger torpedo dive bomber shot down by anti-aircraft fire at age 20.2 years on bombing run on Japanese communication installations on Chichijima Island; bailed out; crewmen William White and John Delaney died; in ocean 3.5 hours before rescue; flew more missions in Philippines; trained carrier torpedo plane pilots back in U.S.; flew 58 combat missions in career; made 127 and 125 carrier takeoffs and landings in career (ditched 6/1944 after takeoff but he and crew rescued, besides being shot down); received Distinguished Flying Cross, three Air Medals

The seven future Presidents when in the military for World War II are shown below in the order listed above – Eisenhower, Kennedy, Johnson, Nixon, Ford, Reagan, and Bush:

As already noted, the Empire of Japan conducted sneak attacks at thirteen locations 12/7/1941. Nine of the 13 targets belonged to the United States. The ages of the seven at the time of the surprise attacks were as follows (listed in the order they were President):

- 51.1 years   Eisenhower
- 24.5 years   Kennedy
- 33.3 years   Johnson
- 27.9 years   Nixon
- 27.4 years   Ford
- 29.8 years   Reagan
- 17.5 years   Bush

The average age of the seven was 30.2 years. Eisenhower was the only career military man. The other six were discharged after the War ended, if not before. The average age of the six not counting Eisenhower on Pearl Harbor Day, was 26.7 years. This is in line with the average age of 26, for U.S. military men in World War II. In fact, the average age of these six (omitting Eisenhower) was several years younger, for World War II junior officers.

Only Eisenhower and Reagan served two full terms. All were elected to office at least once, except for Ford who succeeded Nixon when Nixon resigned.

To sum up, five of these seven World War II future Presidents served in the Navy, one in the Army, and one in the Army Air Forces. All were commissioned officers. All served overseas or on ocean-going ships, except for Reagan. Reagan was barred from overseas assignment due to poor vision. Five served in the Pacific Theater, and the other (Eisenhower) in the European Theater.

Only several future World War II Presidents saw combat. Three of these though came close to death in combat, in World War II. These three were all Navy men. Two of these three found themselves floating in the Pacific Ocean. Details are included in the table above.

All seven Presidents who served in the military during World War II had new naval ships named after them (two are under construction, as of 2019), except for Nixon – and that probably only because of that 6/1972 break-in of the Democratic National Committee's headquarters in the Watergate office building thing, and Nixon's subsequent cover-up attempt.

Two ships were named after Kennedy. Kennedy served as President only 2.8 years. However, his assassination resulted in thousands of streets, buildings, etc. named in his honor; as well as these two warships.

These ships were and are as follows:

- 1,052' long, John F. Kennedy-class USS John F. Kennedy aircraft carrier, commissioned 1968, decommissioned 2007
- 1,092' long, Nimitz-class USS Dwight D. Eisenhower aircraft carrier, commissioned 1977
- 1,092' long, Nimitz-class USS Ronald Reagan aircraft carrier, commissioned 2003
- 1,092' long, Nimitz-class USS George H. W. Bush aircraft carrier, commissioned 2009
- 1,106' long, Gerald R. Ford-class USS Gerald R. Ford aircraft carrier, commissioned 2017
- 1,106' long, Gerald R. Ford-class USS John F. Kennedy aircraft carrier, scheduled for 2020 commissioning
- 600' long, Zumwalt-class USS Lyndon B. Johnson guided missile destroyer, scheduled for 2022 commissioning

Six of the seven above were or are aircraft carriers. The carriers were or are all nuclear-powered except for the first USS John F. Kennedy. It was the last conventionally powered (petroleum fueled) USS carrier.

Of note, naming Navy ships after Presidents is common. Of the 44 men who were President through Donald Trump, twenty-five had USSs named in their honor. These number 53 warships total.

George Washington had the most, with five. The last of these five was a 191' long and 55' beam and 24' draft, ship of the line man o' war commissioned in 1815 and decommissioned in 1820 and scrapped in 1843. Another four USSs were named in honor of the state of Washington, which of course was named in honor of George Washington. This then in a way makes nine USSs named for George Washington, directly or indirectly.

Of course, Washington was an Army man. He was much behind though creating the Continental Navy. In fact, Washington rented the new Navy's first ship with his own money, 8/1775. As already noted, this was the fishing schooner Hannah, converted to a gunboat.

Of these nine Washington ships, one is in commission today. This is the Virginia-class, 377' long and 34' beam, nuclear-powered, USS Washington submarine, which was commissioned in 2017. It is named for the state of Washington.

Most likely, future warships will be named after some of the 19 not yet honored Presidents, after their terms and deaths.

As already mentioned, the Seawolf-class USS Jimmy Carter nuclear submarine is the only USS named after a living ex-President; and also one of the few USSs named after any living person. It was commissioned in 2005.

Historians generally credit these seven, future Presidents with serving honorably and dutifully. To contradict though, many historians consider Johnson an exception here. Johnson was elected as a Representative from Texas. His term began 4/1937. He served as a Representative for 12 years. He was immediately appointed to the House's Naval Affairs Committee.

Johnson somehow got himself appointed as a Lieutenant Commander in the Navy Reserves 6/1940 despite no training (even skipped boot camp). This somehow of course had to do with his membership on the House Naval Affairs Committee. Lieutenant Commander is the fourth commissioned officer up. Even graduates of the four-year U.S. Naval Academy in Annapolis (much training and education, but not much experience) are only Ensigns. Ensign is the lowest Navy commissioned officer rating. Ensigns reach Lieutenant Commander rank three promotions later.

On 12/10/1941 which was three days after the sneak attacks, Johnson and also Democrat Representative Warren Magnuson (1905 MN – 1989 Seattle) representing the state of Washington called on Rear Admiral Chester Nimitz (1885 TX – 1966 CA). Nimitz placed them on active duty. Magnuson was also on the Naval Affairs Committee with Johnson, and also a Lieutenant Commander in the Navy Reserves. They asked for combat. Nimitz told them that they were not trained for combat.

Johnson accepted the no combat status. He was sent for some training, probably of short duration and dubious value.

Magnuson on the other hand did not accept being denied combat. He appealed to Naval Affairs Committee Chairman Carl Vinson (1883 GA – 1981 GA). Democrat Vinson told the Navy that it would be invaluable to the workings of his Committee, if one of its members had combat experience. Magnuson was assigned to the Yorktown-class, 825' long, USS Enterprise (1938 – 1969 scrapped) aircraft carrier for five months. He was age 36, 3.4 years older than Johnson. The Enterprise during these five months was the target of bombs, shells, and torpedoes in battles off the Solomon Islands and Wake Island.

Republican Melvin Maas (1898 MN – 1964 MD) was a third member of the Naval Affairs Committee. He represented Minnesota. Maas enlisted in the Marines at age 18.9 years. He trained as a pilot, got his wings, and flew toward the end of World War I. He was 20.5 years old when World War I ended.

The Marines called the 42-year-old Maas up for World War II. He earned a Silver Star and Purple Heart in World War II. His reelection bid in 1944 was not successful, so he stayed in the Marines. He served active duty 1917-1925 and 1941-1952. He separated as a Major General. He later went blind from damage to his optic nerve, when hit by shrapnel from a Japanese bomb or shell on Okinawa in 1945.

In all, twenty-seven Representatives served in the military in World War II. President Roosevelt ordered them back to their legislative duties in 1942. However, some chose to resign from the House and remain in the military. These men either reasoned they were of more benefit to the nation in the military than as a legislator, or felt that their re-election odds were slim, or maybe they just preferred the military life to that of a legislator. Some were not re-elected including Maas, so stayed in the military. All twenty-seven survived the War.

For the record, no U.S. Senators left office to enlist (or if had been in the Reserves) for World War II. Senators on average are at least five years older than Representatives.

Johnson asked Navy Undersecretary James Forrestal (1892 NY – 1949 MD, suicide jump) for an assignment evaluating training programs at shipyards, making naval warships under contract. Forrestal granted the request, with Johnson practically writing the orders up to his liking. This assignment was odd, as Johnson knew next to nothing about the subject he was evaluating.

Johnson took his assistant John Connally (1917 TX – 1993 Houston) along. Connally was also in the Naval Reserves. Per reports, the two men did much carousing; despite both being married. Connally like Johnson was a Democrat. However, he switched to the Republican Party in 1973.

Connally by the way served in the Navy with distinction. He was part of Eisenhower's planning staff for the invasion of North Africa. He transferred to the South Pacific Theater. He was a fighter-plane director aboard the Essex-class, 872' long, USS Essex (1942 – 1975 scrapped) carrier, and then the also Essex-class, USS Bennington (1944 – 1994 scrapped) aircraft carrier. He was involved in the Gilbert, Marshall, Ryukyus, and Philippine Islands campaigns. He was awarded the Bronze Star for bravery, and the Legion of Merit. He was discharged in 1946, rank of Lieutenant Commander. He was Navy Secretary eleven months in 1961 in the Kennedy administration.

The almost six-foot-tall Alice Glass (1911 TX – 1976) was Johnson's mistress, since probably 1937. Noted New York society photographer Arnold Genthe (1869 Berlin – 1942 NYC) called her *the most beautiful woman I have ever seen*. Glass was also the mistress of wealthy newspaper publisher Charles Marsh (1887 OH – 1964). Marsh and Glass had two children. Glass later married Marsh (1941), but Johnson was her first choice (this per Johnson biographer Robert Caro, see below). Anyway, Glass was on some of these shipyard inspection trips. The Glass affair probably ended in 1942. It does not appear that Marsh ever learned of Glass' relationship with Johnson.

Johnson wed Claudia Taylor (1912 TX – 2007 TX) in 1934. He would not divorce Lady Bird (this her nickname) though, as divorce in those times effectively ended the careers of politicians. Lady Bird was aware of this affair and others, but put up with it. Their two daughters were born in 1944 and 1947.

Johnson decided that he wanted to be promoted to Admiral and placed in charge of all production of naval equipment. All other Admirals would have to report to him, related to new ships and equipment. Johnson knew next to nothing about ships or other naval equipment. He had never managed manufacturing. Therefore, this effort failed. Thank goodness.

By the spring of 1942, President Roosevelt felt that he needed independent opinions on the progress of the War in the Southwest Pacific, to verify or contradict reports that flowed up the military chain of command. Roosevelt wanted reports on the state of preparedness and ability to take the offense. For the record, Generals and Admirals planning and executing combat do not necessarily welcome these assessments as the investigators may not have had combat experience, may know little coming in, and their recommendations may not be logical.

The three men selected to evaluate air operations, ground operations, and naval operations were as follows:

- Lieutenant Colonel Samuel Anderson (1906 NC – 1982) for the Army Air Forces; career military man Anderson served 35 years 1928-1963, retiring as a four star general
- Lieutenant Colonel Francis Stevens (1903 AL – 6/9/1942 as an observer on a B-26 Marauder, Zero shot down over Port Moresby; seven crew also lost) for the Army; graduated from the U.S. Military Academy in 1924, so his intention was to have a long Army career
- Lieutenant Commander Lyndon Johnson (1908 TX – 1973 TX) for the Navy, this per Forrestal's suggestion

General Douglas MacArthur (1880 Little Rock – 1964 DC) was Commander of U.S. Army Forces in the Far East. His headquarters were in Melbourne, Victoria, Australia at the time (moved to Brisbane, Queensland, Australia 7/21/1942). Melbourne is on the southeast coast of Australia.

The three investigating Lieutenant Colonels/Commander met with MacArthur. MacArthur sent the three men to the Royal Australian Air Force (RAAF), 22nd Bomb Group base at Garbutt Field, Queensland. Garbutt is located on the northeast coast of Australia. Garbutt Field (1939 – still in operation, known today as RAAF Townsville) was (and is) a RAAF base. The USAAF operated from here. The USAAF took over operation of the base 6/1943.

The 22nd was assigned the high-risk mission of bombing the Japanese airbase at Lae, on the northeast coast of Papua New Guinea. When situated at Garbutt Field, Johnson asked to go on a bombing mission as an observer. His request was accepted. There are two accounts of the 6/9/1942, twin engine, seven crew, 216 and 287 miles an hour cruise and maximum speeds, Martin B-26 Marauder bomber mission, as follows:

- The Marauder developed a mechanical problem (generator failed) soon after takeoff. As a result, it jettisoned its bombs and returned to base safely.

- En route, the Marauder was attacked by Mitsubishi A6M Zero fighters, and hit numerous times. The bombs were jettisoned to improve maneuverability and speed. The Marauder lost an engine when hit by bullets, or the engine was lost due to a generator problem.

The Marauder was equipped with 12 × .50 inch (12.7 millimeter) Browning machine guns. Three of the seven crew were gunners. Tail gunner Corporal Harry Baren shot down a Zero. The Japanese fighters had enough and departed. Pilot Lieutenant Walter Greer's brilliant, evasive flying along with the gunners' hustle and skill saved the aircraft and crew. Greer and his co-pilot were able to return the crippled bomber safely to base.

Lieutenant Colonel Stevens' Marauder was on the same mission as Johnson's Marauder. Stevens' Marauder was shot down. He and the seven crew died. In fact, Johnson was supposed to be on the aircraft that Stevens was on, but they switched at the last moment when Johnson took one last bathroom break at the edge of the field just before takeoff.

Back in Melbourne, MacArthur chastised Johnson for getting on an Army Air Forces bomber without higher-up permission. After all, Johnson's assignment was to study the fighting status of the Navy – not the Army Air Forces. Of note though, the Navy did later use a variant of the B-26 Marauder for target tugs and gunnery trainers. This was the JM-1 model.

Stevens' assignment was to assess Army operations, not Army Air Force. MacArthur did not chastise Stevens though, as he was dead. MacArthur awarded the Distinguished Service Cross posthumously to Stevens. This is the Army's second highest valor medal. He awarded the Silver Star to Anderson and Johnson, which is the third highest.

Awarded may not be the proper word. MacArthur per one report just reached into his desk drawer which had many Silver Stars at the ready and tossed two across the desk to Anderson and Johnson.

Per another report, MacArthur was out of Silver Stars but had (Silver Star) ribbons. Per this report, Johnson never received his Silver Star medal through the military. He ended up buying one at an Army-Navy store in Washington (per Robert Caro again, see below). This makes one wonder how official the Silver Star medal was, in Johnson's case.

By the way, the seven Marauder crewmen on this mission with Johnson received no medals. It goes without saying that observers on military missions do not receive valor medals unless they somehow choose or are pressed into the fight, putting themselves at risk and accomplishing something.

Johnson biographer Robert Caro (1935 NYC -) includes the second account above in his 1990 *The Years of Lyndon Johnson: Means of Ascent*. This is the second of four Caro volumes out on Johnson. Caro as of 2019 is working on the fifth and last volume. As he is age 84, the fifth volume may not be completed.

Caro did extensive research. Therefore, it appears to be the correct version. Johnson certainly put himself at risk. As to why though he was awarded a valor medal as again only an observer, this remains a mystery. Again, none of the crew despite their bravery and risk and exceptional merit in flying and shooting received any commendation of any type on this mission – it was just all in a day's work. Many airmen who flew more than 20 missions never received valor medals. Again, it appears that the awarding of the Silver Star to Johnson was a trumped up, political deal. Presumably, MacArthur's superior told him to make the presentation. Whatever.

During and after the War, Johnson was known for exaggerating his military accomplishments. Furthermore, these exaggerations expanded greatly over time. The number of Zeroes shot down went from one to fourteen. The number of missions he flew on went from one to many. The pneumonia he contracted overseas became dengue fever. The 25 pounds he lost when sick overseas became 35 pounds, and then 45 pounds. He told these mis-truths, even when in the White House as President.

Johnson also arranged for the Silver Star medal to be awarded to him publicly on several occasions – as if each occasion was the first.

Johnson wore the lapel insignia of the Silver Star, the rest of his life. As it was small, he pointed it out during speeches.

As mentioned above, President Roosevelt on 7/9/1942 ordered all Representatives in the armed forces to return to the House. At the time, eight Representatives were in the military. Four chose to resign from the House. As noted above, these four reasoned that they were of more benefit to the nation in the military, or maybe they preferred the military to legislating, or maybe they thought that their reelection chances were slim. The other four including Johnson left active military duty and returned to their legislative duties.

Of the 44 men who have been President of the United States from George Washington through Donald Trump, 33 were in the military (counting enlistments in national and state guards). This is 75%. Of the 33, 24 (73%) served during a war or more than one war or conflict. However, most did not see combat.

Of the 33 Presidents who were in the military, six were considered professional, career soldiers. These six were as follows:

- George Washington, 1732 VA – 1799 VA, President 1789 -- 1797
- Andrew Jackson, 1767 NC – 1845 TN, President 1829 -- 1937
- William Harrison, 1773 VA – 1841 DC, President 1841 -- 1841
- Zachary Taylor, 1784 VA – 1850 DC, President 1849 -- 1850
- Ulysses Grant, 1822 OH – 1885 NY, President 1869 -- 1877
- Dwight Eisenhower, 1890 TX – 1969 DC, President 1953 -- 1961

All six were career Army Generals. Their military responsibilities and accomplishments were great. In fact, their actions formed the United States and the world that is today. They were in the category of being military heroes, and immensely popular as a result. These factors all contributed to their being elected to high office, including the Presidency.

All six served two terms except for Harrison and Taylor. Harrison and Taylor both died in office of some ailment. Harrison died at the age of 68, after only one month in office. This is the shortest presidential term ever. Taylor died at the age of 65, serving 16 months. This was the third shortest presidential term. For the record, the pistol-shot assassinated James Garfield (1831 OH – 1881 NJ) served the second shortest term at 6.7 months. Garfield was only 49 years old. He served two years in the Army during the Civil War, retiring as a Major General (two star).

The Presidency was the first position ever elected to, for four of these six Generals. These were Washington, Taylor, Grant, and Eisenhower. Again, their military records were key to winning their presidential elections. The other two or Jackson and Harrison had both been Representatives and then Senators before elected President.

Washington as first President established many precedents. He did this purposely. One was on how the President should be addressed. He decided on *Mr. President*, used to this day. Washington presented the annual State of the Union report as required by the Constitution, as a speech to Congress. Third President Jefferson dropped this practice though in 1801, but Wilson resumed it in 1913. Washington established a Cabinet of key advisors, still the case today.

Washington also established the precedent of serving only two terms. He was in good health at the end of his second term, at age 65. If he had run for a third term, he most likely would have been re-elected. This two terms rule lasted until Democrat President Franklin Roosevelt, who was elected a third time in 1940 and a fourth time in 1944. The Republican backlash here though for electing the same Democrat in four consecutive elections, was the 1951 twenty-second amendment to the Constitution. This amendment limits Presidential tenure to ten years.

Washington died 33 months after leaving office, from a sudden disease. He was 67.8 years old. As part of his treatment, half of his blood was drained out. For sure, more modern medicine would have diagnosed and treated him successfully.

Republican Eisenhower was also likely to win a third term if he was so inclined even though he was age 70 at the end of his second term and had a heart condition. However, he was term-limited by the new 22nd amendment.

Military service for Presidents (for all national, state, and local politicians; for that matter) over time though has become less common. For the last 18 presidents of Taft (Taft was President 1909-1913), Wilson, Coolidge, Hoover, Franklin Roosevelt, Truman, Eisenhower, Kennedy, Johnson, Nixon, Ford, Carter, Reagan, Bush Senior, Clinton, Bush Junior, Obama, and Trump; nine served in the military (50%). These were Truman, Eisenhower, Kennedy, Johnson, Nixon, Ford, Carter, Bush Senior, and Bush Junior. Furthermore, seven of these nine served in World War II as described above. A very high percentage of military age men served in World War II. This was the case pretty much regardless of social standing, wealth, education, etc.

Before World War II, most future Presidents who were in the military were in the Army. During and after World War II, more were in the Navy. No President was in the Marines, Coast Guard, or Air Force after it was established as a separate military branch in 1947.

All the 33 Presidents with a military history reached officer rank, except for the fifteenth President. James Buchanan (1791 PA – 1868 PA) served one term, 1857-1861. When the British invaded neighboring Maryland in 1814 in the War of

1812, he joined the Pennsylvania militia at age 23. His light dragoons unit was sent to Baltimore to defend the city. He enlisted in 1814 as a Private and was discharged the same year as a Private.

The future President with the highest military rank was George Washington. Congress promoted Washington posthumously to the rank of General of the Armies of the United States, in 1978. The Congressional resolution was worded to explain that no general past or present or future, would ever outrank Washington. This is the highest possible rank in the United States Armed Forces. This rank is also described as being a six star general.

Only two men have held this rank. John Pershing (1860 MO – 1948 DC) who led Army forces in World War I was the first. Pershing was promoted to this rank in 1919 when on active duty. However again per the 1978 legislation, Washington is considered to outrank Pershing as he attained the rank (from the Congressional retroactive appointment) before Pershing, albeit posthumously promoted. Once again per the legislation, Washington is the highest ranked United States military person ever; and furthermore, will never be out-ranked.

The next two Presidents with the highest rank were Grant and Eisenhower. Their rank was General of the Army. This is a five star general. Grant was appointed to this rank 7/1866, more than a year after the Civil War ended. In fact, Congress created this rank specifically for Grant. Grant served in the Army 1839-1854 and 1861-1869. He was elected President 11/1868 and took office 3/1869. He served two terms.

Eisenhower was promoted to this rank 12/1944, five months before World War II ended in Europe. He also served two terms. Ike served in the Army 1915-1953, and then 1961 to his 1969 death.

Four other Army Generals were promoted to General of the Army or five star, in U.S. history. These four others were all World War II Generals. The four were as follows:

- George Marshall   1880 PA – 1959 DC
- Douglas MacArthur   1880 AR – 1964 DC
- Henry Arnold   1886 PA – 1950 CA
- Omar Bradley   1893 MO – 1981 NY

Marshall, MacArthur, and Arnold were promoted to this rank 12/1944, when on active duty during World War II. Bradley was appointed to this rank in 1950, when still on active duty.

No President retired from service as a Lieutenant General (three star) or General (four star).

Another nine Presidents attained one (brigadier general) or two (major general) star General rank. To sum up, 12 U.S. Presidents attained general officer rank, all in the U.S. Army. Again, nine were one or two star generals, two were General of the Army (five star), and one was General of the Armies of the United States (six star). These are summarized in the chart below:

Rank	President
Brigadier General ★	Franklin Pierce, A. Johnson, Rutherford Hayes, Chester Arthur, B. Harrison

Major General ⭐⭐	Andrew Jackson, William Harrison, Zachary Taylor, James Garfield
Lieutenant General ⭐⭐⭐	
General ⭐⭐⭐⭐	
General of the Army ⭐⭐⭐⭐⭐	Ulysses Grant, Dwight Eisenhower
General of the Armies of the United States ⭐⭐⭐⭐⭐	George Washington

Six Presidents reached Colonel Rank in the Army. Theodore Roosevelt (1858 NYC – 1919 NY, blood clot in lungs) was one of these. He is the only future President to be awarded the Medal of Honor. The award was made for his actions and valor in the 1898 Spanish American War. This was mainly the 7/1/1898 charge up San Juan Hill, Cuba, on a horse; leading his men who were on foot. The U.S. and Cuba had 144 and 1,024 killed and wounded. The Spanish had 114 and 366 killed and wounded. Despite the U.S. and Cuba having many more casualties, they held the territory.

Roosevelt was nominated for the award at the time. However, it was not approved. It was thought that he was denied as he complained often about the delay in returning his men to the U.S. extending the time that they were exposed to the risk of contracting tropical diseases (malaria, yellow fever, typhoid fever) in Cuba. Roosevelt himself contracted *Cuban fever* (malaria).

Also, Roosevelt's superiors thought he grandstanded too much, making headlines with public statements while in the military.

Finally, Roosevelt was awarded the medal posthumously, in 2001. This was 103 years after his actions, and 82 years after his death.

For the record, Roosevelt's son also Theodore (1887 NY – 7/21/1944 France, heart attack) was awarded the Medal of Honor for his World War II service. This included the directing of troops at Utah Beach during the Normandy landings. Junior is remembered for his quote when he and his men landed one mile south of where they were supposed to land on a Normandy beach (code-named *Utah Beach*) on D-Day, 6/6/1944: *We'll start the war from right here!*

Roosevelt Junior served in the Army 1917-1919 and 1940-1944, during the World Wars. He was a Brigadier General (one star) at the time of his death from a heart attack in France 6.5 weeks after the D-Day landings. He had heart problems but kept them secret. He was age 56. He was in the process of being promoted to Major General (two star), when he died of a heart attack.

Between World Wars, Roosevelt Junior was a state Assemblyman for New York, Assistant Secretary of the Navy, Puerto Rico Governor, Philippines Governor General, and also a businessman.

Father and son Medal of Honor awarding have happened only one other time. These were also Army men Douglas MacArthur (1880 AR – 1964 DC) and his father Arthur MacArthur (1845 MA – 1912 WI). The father when a nineteen-year-old First Lieutenant earned the Medal of Honor for seizing the regimental colors at a critical moment and planting them on the crest of Missionary Ridge. This was the 11/25/1863 Missionary Ridge Battle of the Civil War near Chattanooga, Tennessee. One thousand and twenty-five men died at Missionary Ridge. These were 65 and 35% Union and Confederacy.

Douglas the son was awarded the Medal of Honor 5/1942. The citation read as follows: *For conspicuous leadership in preparing the Philippine Islands to resist conquest, for gallantry and intrepidity above and beyond the call of duty in action against invading Japanese forces, and for the heroic conduct of defensive and offensive operations on the Bataan Peninsula. He mobilized, trained, and led an army which has received world acclaim for its gallant defense against a tremendous superiority of enemy forces in men and arms. His utter disregard of personal danger under heavy fire and aerial bombardment, his calm judgment in each crisis, inspired his troops, galvanized the spirit of resistance of the Filipino people, and confirmed the faith of the American people in their Armed Forces.*

Douglas had been nominated for the Medal of Honor twice before, for his actions in 1914 in the Veracruz Expedition and 1918 in France in World War II. These were denied, but he did receive the Army Distinguished Service Cross in both cases (plus he received a third Cross for his actions in World War II).

In receiving the Medal of Honor, Douglas had not performed any acts of valor. George Marshall (1880 PA – 1959 DC) decided to award MacArthur the decoration *to offset any propaganda by the enemy directed at his leaving his command.* This was in reference to fleeing from Corregidor (Philippines) 3/12/1942 to Melbourne (Australia) in an 80' long and 21' beam and 4' draft, wooden hull, patrol torpedo boat to avoid capture.

President Roosevelt ordered this retreat. MacArthur chose to accept the Medal of Honor on the basis that *this award was intended not so much for me personally as it is a recognition of the indomitable courage of the gallant army which it was my honor to command.*

Arthur the father served 1861-1909 which was 48 years. He retired as a Lieutenant General (three star). Douglas the son served 1903 to his 1964 death at age 84. This was 61 years. He was a General of the Army (five stars).

The highest rank reached by a future President in the Navy was Commander. These two were Lyndon Johnson and Richard Nixon both in the Naval Reserves, and both placed on active duty during World War II. Commander is one rank (Captain) away from Rear Admiral. A Rear Admiral is a one or two star Admiral (Rear Admiral lower half, Rear Admiral upper half).

The President of the United States of course is Commander-in-Chief of the armed forces. Some feel strongly that a President who has served in the military makes for a better Commander-in-Chief – not just in overseeing the military, but in other ways as well. Others disagree, stating that the plethora of military advisors (Joint Chiefs of Staff, etc.) suffices. Military experience, especially in the case of a career soldier or sailor or airman or marine, probably at least somewhat forms the way such Presidents governed or will govern.

The 2012 Presidential election was the first one in which both the major party nominees for president and vice president had never been in the military (Obama, Biden, Romney, Ryan) since the 1932 election (F. Roosevelt, Garner, Hoover, Curtis). This was repeated for the 2016 election. Trump, Pence, Clinton, and Kaine were never in the military. These statements apply to state military enlistment as well as federal.

In the past, serving in the military was considered a plus in getting votes, when running for high office. Active, reserves, and military retirees tend to favor a candidate with past military experience, so often vote that way. Few voters today though are in the military or retired military, so this appears to not be an issue with these voters. For that matter, few politicians these days are retired from the military either, compared to the last two generations. This includes persons running for national, state, and local offices.

Several of these military men who went on to be President were lauded in song about their military actions and leadership. The best known as a big hit is folk music songwriter and musician Jimmy Driftwood's (1907 AR – 1960 AR, heart attack) *The Battle of New Orleans*. The song describes lightheartedly the last engagement of the 12/1814-1/1815 New Orleans Battle of the War of 1812, from the perspective of an American soldier. Andrew Jackson was mentioned twice in the song – once by his name, and the second time by his nickname of *Old Hickory*. Many recorded this song, but Johnny Horton's (1925 CA – 1960 TX, automobile accident) 1959 version was the biggest version. It was number one on the *Billboard Hot 100* that year, plus *Billboard* ranked it as number one for the year.

Johnny Horton had a big World War II hit song also. This was the 1960 *Sink the Bismarck* march song, which he co-wrote with bassist, songwriter, and band manager Tillman Franks (1920 AR – 2006 LA). The song reached number three on the charts.

Jimmy Dean's (1928 TX – 2010 VA) 1962 *PT-109* song was about Jack Kennedy's combat service in World War II, and his patrol boat crew. Dean's biggest career song was *Big Bad John*, the year before. Actually, it was a talk song, no singing. Dean and country music singer and fiddler legend Roy Acuff (1903 TN – 1992 Nashville) wrote and composed *Big Bad John*. John in the song was a coal miner, who sacrificed his life in an underground collapse to save the lives of his fellow miners. *Big Bad John* hit number one on both the country and pop charts. The song is still played today on golden oldie radio stations (these in the sub-category of classic country stations).

Dean included a reference to *Big Bad John* on his one-year later *PT-109* song, perhaps to boost sales. Kennedy was in the White House at the time of the release, and popular. *PT-109* made the top ten.

The biographical, 1963 *PT-109* war film depicts Kennedy's actions in World War II. Cliff Robertson (1923 CA – 2011 NY) played Kennedy. This was the first commercial film ever released about a sitting U.S. President. It came out five months before his assassination. The film did poorly. Its $3.5 million box office did not cover its $4 million production costs. As in the case of most all historical movies, deviations from the actual were many.

Of course, actors have played future Presidents and Presidents in many television shows and television movies and feature movies. The most common such portrayals by far are those who had served in the military during hot and big wars such as the American Revolution, Civil War, and World War II. These include Presidents George Washington, Ulysses Grant, and Dwight Eisenhower in minor to major roles. Abraham Lincoln is also in many movies, as President during the Civil War, the war in which the most Americans died. Lincoln served in the Illinois militia three months in 1832.

To sum up, nine Presidents had involvement in World War II. Two were President during the War. One of these two was a military veteran. The other seven were in uniform during World War II, and President later. They were all commissioned officers. The seven were five Navy, one Army, and one Army Air Force. The last of these seven was George Bush, who died 11/2018 at age 94.5 years. In so doing, he set a record for the longest living ex-president (Gerald Ford is runner-up, at 93.5 years). Bush was the youngest of the seven, almost ten years younger than the second youngest (Gerald Ford again).

Bush enlisted on his 18th birthday. He became one of the Navy's youngest pilots. He flew 58 combat missions. He had to ditch once, and was shot down once. In the latter case, he was almost captured. Bush earned the Distinguished Flying Cross and three Air Medals. He served 39 months, separating as a Lieutenant.

ABOUT THE AUTHOR

Bennett Fisher's father was Chief Quartermaster on the Mahan-class USS Preston DD-379 destroyer at the Second Naval Battle of Guadalcanal, 11/13 and 14/1942. This destroyer was the fifth Navy ship of six named after 1861 U.S. Naval Academy graduate (first in his class) Lieutenant Samuel Preston (1840 Canada – 1/15/1865 Fort Fisher, North Carolina). Preston was killed in a ground assault on the Confederate Fort Fisher, which protected the South's trade routes from Europe and the Caribbean to Wilmington, North Carolina, during the Civil War.

Preston was part of a six warship Task Force (four destroyers and two cruisers) in the 11/13-14/1942 Naval Battle of Guadalcanal. The Task Force intercepted a much larger Japanese Task Force delivering troops and supplies to Japanese strongholds on Guadalcanal Island. The Japanese Navy sank or heavily damaged all six American ships except for one cruiser. The Preston sank with more than half its crew lost, including 1924 U.S. Naval Academy graduate Captain (Commander) Max Stormes.

Bennett's father survived, after 14.5 hours in the ocean sharing a life jacket with a crewmate. Most of his shipmates did not.

After World War II, his father married and moved to the Rio Grande Valley of Texas to farm dryland he inherited from his mother. Bennett was the first of four children born.

Bennett's father would not talk of his Navy and War experiences. After his father died, Bennett researched his father's six-year military career. This led to his interest in military history, especially the Pacific Theater of World War II. Bennett took a continuing education course at Rice University on WWII, Pacific Theater. He has given talks on World War II history. He has assisted senior veterans in preparing presentations on their time in the military. He currently coordinates a Veterans group for seniors at a YMCA in Houston.

The USS Preston, and Bennett's father and uniform insignia are shown here:

36746131R10307

Made in the USA
Middletown, DE
18 February 2019